INSIDE 3D STUDIO MAX 3
MODELING, MATERIALS, AND RENDERING

By Ted Boardman
and Jeremy Hubbell

Cover Art by Frank DeLise
Cover Art Design by Ellen Atkins

201 West 103rd Street, Indianapolis, Indiana 46290

COLOR GALLERY

Inside 3D Studio MAX 3 Modeling, Materials, and Rendering takes you deep into the complexities of 3D Studio MAX. The authors provide dozens of hands-on examples for you to practice with and use as you go through the book. Renderings of these examples, as well as other necessary images, are provided on the following pages in color.

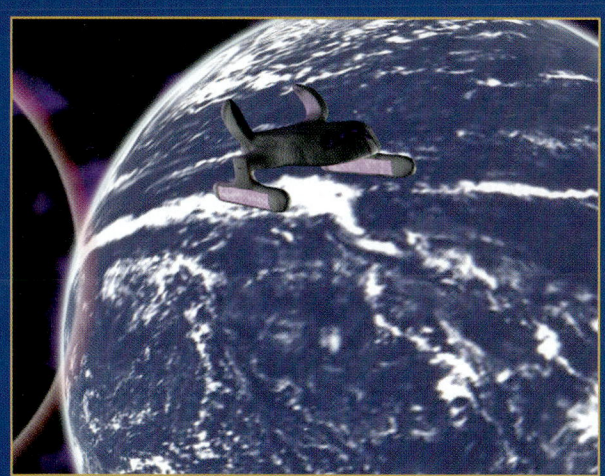

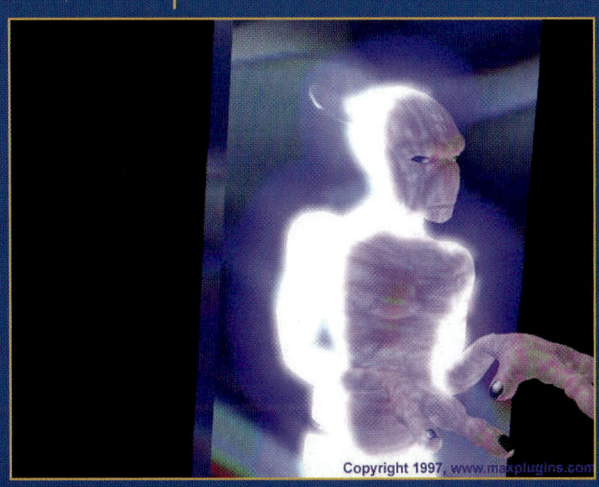

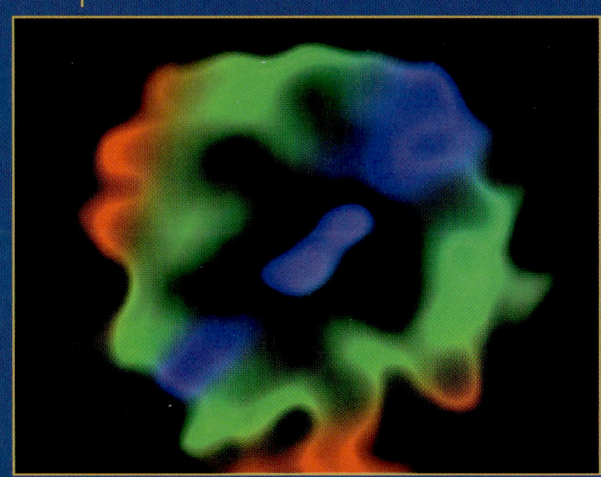

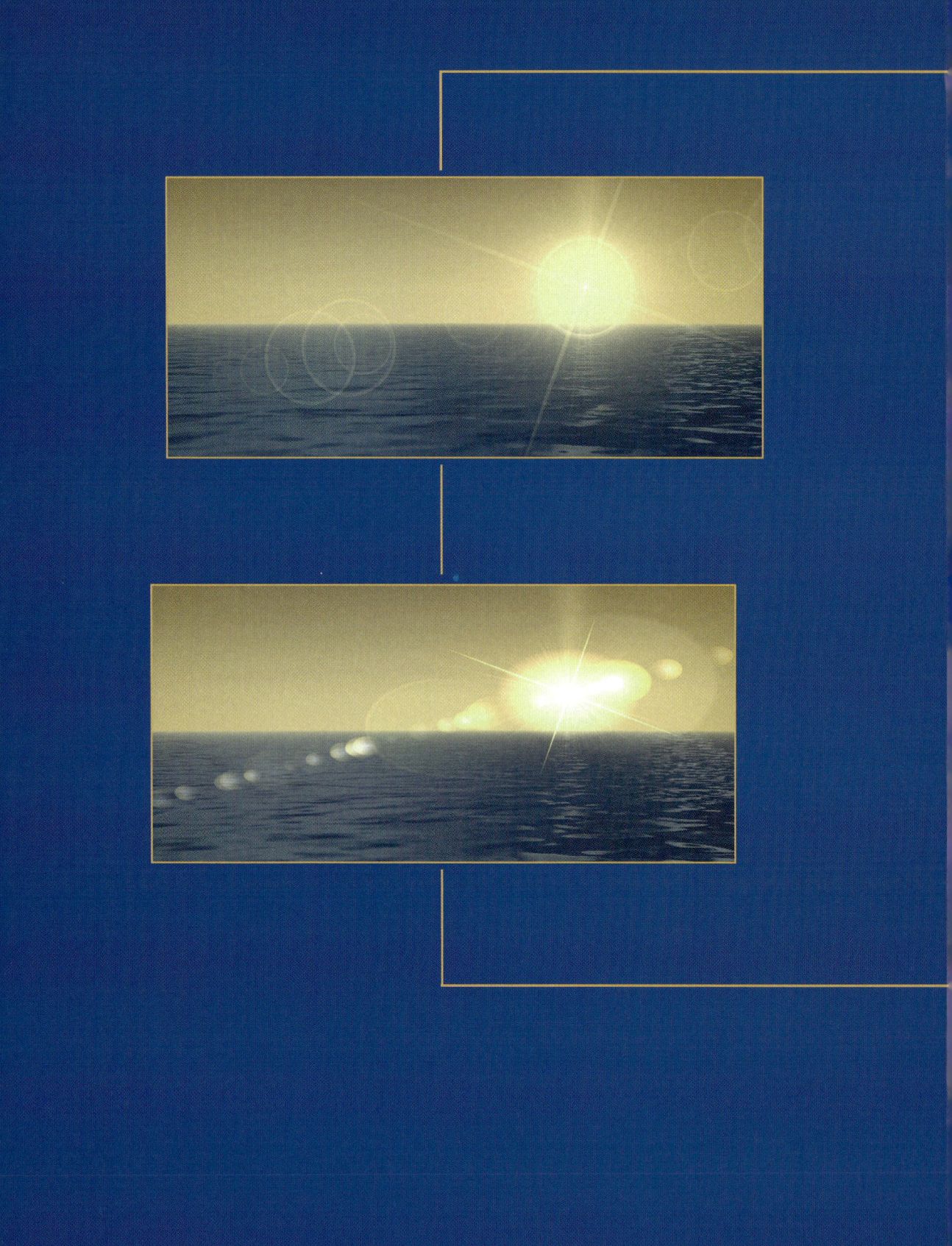

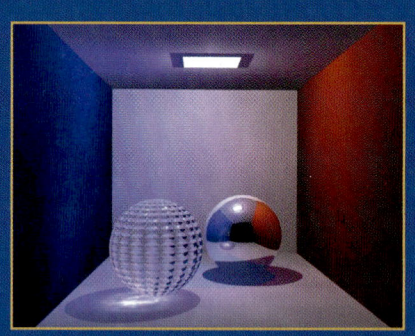

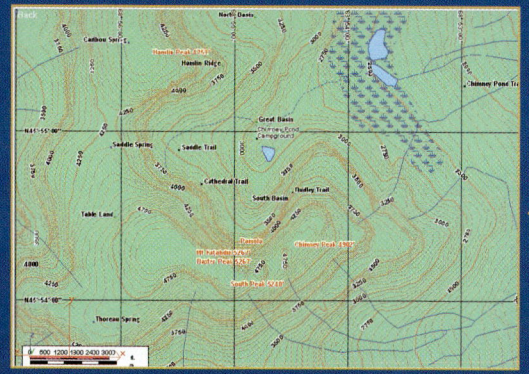
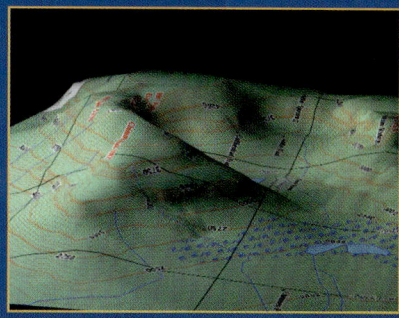

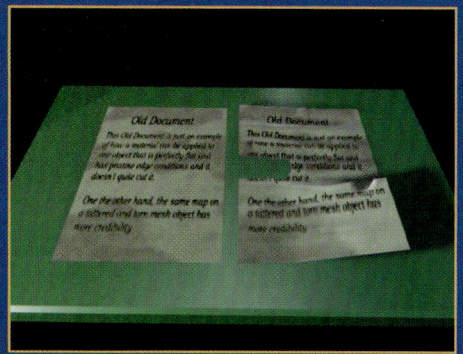

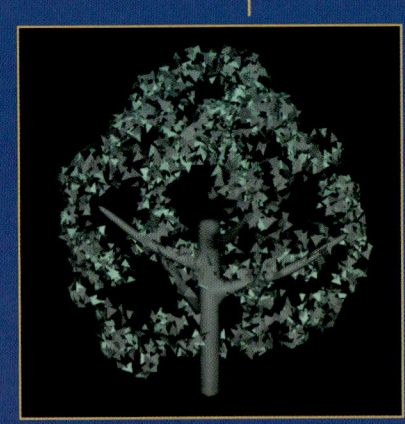

INSIDE 3D STUDIO MAX® 3

MODELING, MATERIALS, AND RENDERING

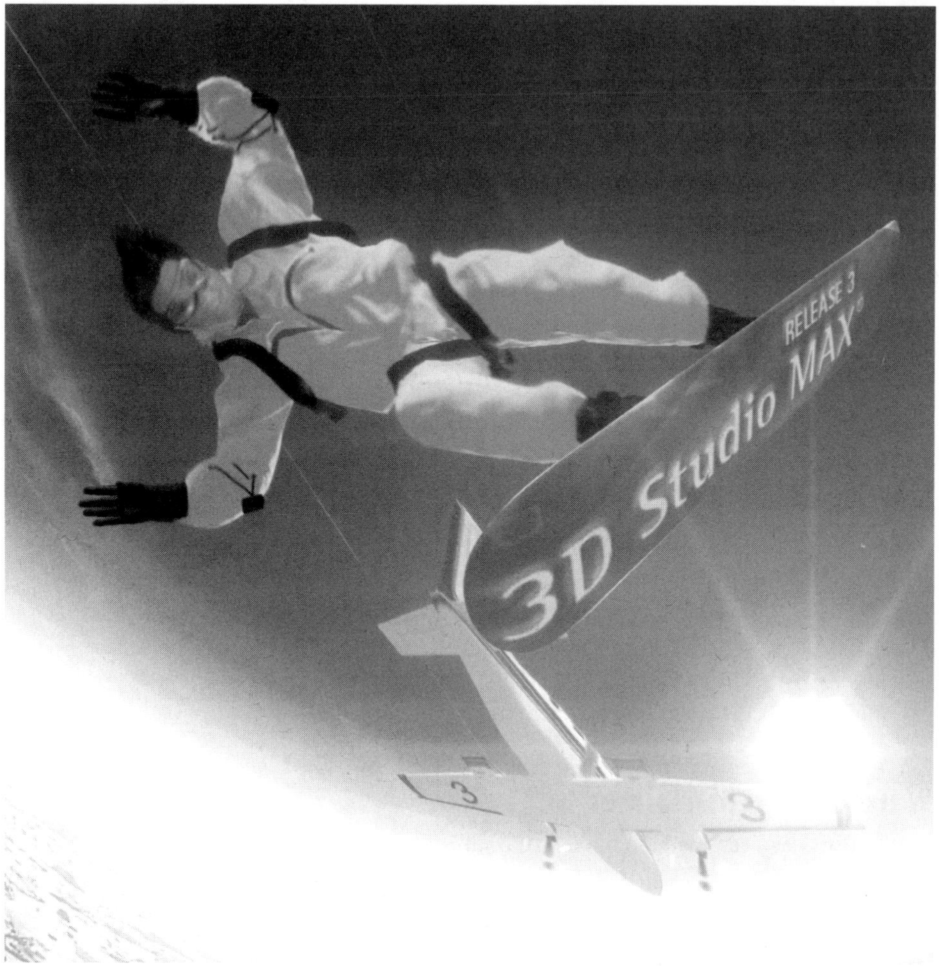

New Riders

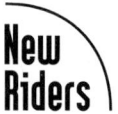

TED BOARDMAN AND JEREMY HUBBELL

Inside 3D Studio MAX 3
Modeling, Materials, and Rendering

Copyright © 1999 by New Riders Publishing

All rights reserved. No part of this book shall be reproduced, stored in a retrieval system, or transmitted by any means—electronic, mechanical, photocopying, recording, or otherwise—without written permission from the publisher. No patent liability is assumed with respect to the use of the information contained herein. Although every precaution has been taken in the preparation of this book, the publisher and author(s) assume no responsibility for errors or omissions. Neither is any liability assumed for damages resulting from the use of the information contained herein.

International Standard Book Number: 0-7357-0085-0

Library of Congress Catalog Card Number: 99-64953

Printed in the United States of America

First Printing: September, 1999

03 02 01 00 99   7 6 5 4 3 2 1

Interpretation of the printing code: The rightmost double-digit number is the year of the book's printing; the rightmost single-digit number is the number of the book's printing. For example, the printing code 99-1 shows that the first printing of the book occurred in 1999.

Trademarks

All terms mentioned in this book that are known to be trademarks or service marks have been appropriately capitalized. New Riders Publishing cannot attest to the accuracy of this information. Use of a term in this book should not be regarded as affecting the validity of any trademark or service mark.

3D Studio MAX 3 is a registered trademark of Autodesk, Inc.

Warning and Disclaimer

Every effort has been made to make this book as complete and as accurate as possible, but no warranty or fitness is implied. The information provided is on an "as is" basis. The authors and the publisher shall have neither liability nor responsibility to any person or entity with respect to any loss or damages arising from the information contained in this book or from the use of the CD or programs accompanying it.

Publisher
David Dwyer

Executive Editor
Steve Weiss

Acquisitions Editor
Laura Frey

Development Editor
Linda Laflamme

Managing Editor
Sarah Kearns

Project Editor
Alissa Cayton

Copy Editor
Jacqui Franklin

Indexer
Lisa Stumpf

Technical Editors
David Marks
Mark Gerhard

Software Development Specialist
Jason Haines

Proofreader
Debra Neel

Compositor
Gina Rexrode

Contents at a Glance

Introduction

Part I Modeling

1 Modeling Concepts 4
2 Architectural Modeling 44
3 Landscapes and Building Enhancements 118
4 Industrial and Mechanical Design Modeling ... 152
5 Modeling for Real-Time 3D Games 188
6 Cinematics and High-Detail Modeling 232
7 Character Modeling 274

Part II Materials

8 Material Concepts 322
9 Designing Naturally Occurring Materials 380
10 Designing Man-Made Materials 426
11 Designing Fictional and Special Effects Materials ... 454
12 Animated Materials 482
13 Using MAX 3 as a 2D Paint Tool 504

Part III Rendering Effects

14 Cameras, Camera Effects, and Lighting 534
15 Glows and Lens Flares 582
16 Highlights 616
17 Focal Effects 630

Part IV Appendixes

A AutoCAD and 3D Studio MAX: Sharing Files 646

B Designing with Plug-Ins 668

Index 680

Table of Contents

Introduction

Part I   Modeling

1   Modeling Concepts 5

Polygonal Modeling 6

   Faces, Edges, and Vertices 7

   Polygonal Modeling Uses 9

   Editable Mesh 10

   Polygonal Modeling Shortcomings 15

Patch Modeling 20

   Patches, Edges, and Vertices 21

   Patch Modeling Uses 25

   Patch Modeling Shortcomings 30

NURBS Modeling 30

   Surfaces, Curves, Points, and CVs 31

   NURBS Modeling Uses 32

   NURBS Modeling Shortcomings 36

Scripted Modeling 36

   Using the Command Line 37

Determining a Starting Point 38

   The Right Modeling Method for the Job 39

   Where to Start 40

In Practice: Modeling Concepts 42

2   Architectural Modeling 45

Think Before You Work 46

   Developing a MAX R3/AutoCAD Strategy 46

   Starting Off 48

Level of Detail 53
    Plan Ahead 54
    Model Size and Complexity 55
    Walkthroughs: Avoiding Trouble (and Walls) 56
Wall Systems 57
    2D Floor Plan Extruded for Height 58
    2D Wall Elevation Extruded for Thickness 69
    Creating a Curtain Wall System 79
Roof Systems 89
    Gable Roofs I 89
    Gable Roof II 92
    Gable Roof III 95
Windows and Doors 100
    Extruded Doors and Windows 100
    Bevel Doors and Windows 102
    Bevel Profile Doors and Windows 104
Space Frames 107
    Wire Baskets 107
    Architectural Framework or Expansion Joints 111
In Practice: Architectural Modeling 117

3 Landscapes and Building Enhancements 119
Landscape 120
    Importing Survey Data from AutoCAD 120
    Using the Terrain Compound Object 121
    Landscape Using NURBS Surface or Patch Grid 130
Trees and Bushes 138
    Modeled Generic Hardwood Tree 139
In Practice: Landscapes and Building Enhancements 150

4 Industrial and Mechanical Design Modeling 153

Mechanical Modeling Issues 154
    Presentation Focus 155
    Modeling Tools 156
    Output Process 157
    Workflow 157

Simulating Surface Geometry 158
    Bump Mapping 159
    Opacity Mapping 161
    Displacement Mapping 162

Cross-Sectional Modeling 164
    Creating a Threaded Bolt 164
    Creating a Patch Surface from Cross-Sections 169
    Generating Cross-Sections from Free-Form Mesh Objects 174
    Sectional Views 179

Modeling with XRefs 181

In Practice: Industrial and Mechanical Design Modeling 186

5 Modeling for Real-Time 3D Games 189

2D Versus Real-Time 3D Graphics 191

Real-Time 3D Basics 193
    The Transform Matrix 195
    Surface Properties 198

Differences Between Real-Time and Prerendered 3D 198
    Z-Buffering 199
    Levels of Detail 199
    Shadows 203
    Map Size and Color Depth 205
    Shading Modes 206

Modeling for Real Time 206
    Put the Detail in the Map, Not in the Mesh 206
    Don't Build What You Don't Need 208
    Model Convex (Whenever Possible) 208
    High-Res for Low-Res Modeling 210
Real-Time Modeling Techniques 211
    Modifying Primitives for Low-Resolution Models 211
Dealing with Texture Limitations 214
    Dealing with Limited Colors 214
    Limited Map Size 215
    Adding "Impossible" Detail 216
    Other Tricks 221
Simplifying Things with Scripting 223
    Using the Macro Recorder 224
Final Thoughts 230
In Practice: Modeling for Real-Time 3D Games 231

6 Cinematics and High-Detail Modeling 233
High-Resolution Modeling Pitfalls 234
    Hardware Limitations 235
    RAM 236
    CPU 237
    3D Acceleration 237
Editing Issues 238
    Hide Geometry 239
    Using Object Xrefs 243
    Streamline Texture Mapping 244
    Level of Detail Utility 246
    Inactive in Viewport Toggle 246

Contents IX

    Building the Basic Model 248
        Starting with Primitives 249
    MeshSmooth 251
        Applying MeshSmooth to Your Model 253
    Using MAX's Animation Tools to Create Models 258
    Using the Clone System 261
    Lofting for Detail 262
    Creating and Working with Xrefs 264
        Scene Xrefs 264
        Object Xrefs 265
    NURBS U-Lofts and UV-Lofts 269
    Optimizing the Model for Animation 270
        Determining Animated Entities 271
        Camera Angle Optimization 272
        Texture Map Considerations 272
    In Practice: Cinematics and High-Detail Modeling 273

7 Character Modeling **275**
    Character Modeling Basics 276
        Types of Characters 277
        Common Starting Points 279
        Modeling Various Forms 282
    Character Modeling with NURBS 284
        U/UV-Lofts and Ruled Surfaces 285
        Ruled Surfaces 288
        Blend Surfaces 290
    Character Modeling with Patches 293
        Quad Versus Tri 294
        Building in Sections 296
        Using Surface Tools to Build Characters 298

Polygonal Character Modeling 303
    Using Editable Mesh and MeshSmooth 304
    NURMS in MeshSmooth 307
    Using FFDs on Polygonal Objects 310
    Skinning a Model 314
In Practice: Character Modeling 317

Part II Materials

8 Material Concepts 323
Shaders 324
    Types of Materials 325
    The Standard Material 329
    The Raytrace Material 347
    Other Material Types 355
Reflection and Refraction Concepts 355
    Light Rays and Illumination 356
    Reflection and Reflective Surfaces 356
    Transparency and Refractive Surfaces 356
What Is Raytracing? 359
    Recursive Raytracing 359
    Lighting and Raytracing 360
    Scanline Rendering Versus Raytraced Rendering 361
    Antialiasing 362
Raytracing Optimizations 365
    Voxel Trees 365
    Single Versus Dual-Pipe Acceleration 366
    Global Exclude 368
    Local Exclude 368
    Global Ray Antialiaser 368
    Using Blurs and Attenuation 371

	Rendering Limitations and Problem Areas	373
	Antialiasing Speed Hits	*373*
	SuperSampling	*373*
	Organizing Your Materials	374
	Building Libraries	*374*
	Naming Materials	*376*
	Creating a Macroscript to Launch Your Libraries	*378*
	In Practice: Material Concepts	379
9	**Designing Naturally Occurring Materials**	**381**
	General Tips for Mimicking Nature	382
	Creating Ground Cover	383
	Rough Ground	*383*
	Wildflowers	*387*
	Striped Lawn	*392*
	Creating Sky Materials	395
	Cloud Map Skies	*396*
	Gradient Map Skies	*399*
	Blend Material with a Mask	*401*
	Simulate Cloud Shadows	*404*
	Creating Water Materials	406
	Pond Water	*406*
	Rough Water	*409*
	Beachfront Surf	*413*
	Trees	415
	Mapped Trees on Plane	*416*
	Vegetation	418
	Blowing Grass	*418*
	Leaves	*421*
	In Practice: Designing Naturally Occurring Materials	424

10 Designing Man-Made Materials 427

New Shaders for Specular Highlights 429

Creating Material Imperfections 430

Mesh Distortions *430*

Material Corruption *432*

Creating Man-Made Materials 432

Paper and Cardboard *433*

Paint *439*

Glass *441*

Metal *446*

Black Plastic *451*

In Practice: Designing Man-Made Materials 452

11 Designing Fictional and Special Effects Materials 455

Building a Fictional Material 456

Use the Real World as a Starting Point *456*

Start from a Concept *457*

Use Procedural Maps *457*

Procedural Map Tutorials *471*

Illumination Effects 476

Clear and Soft Light Bulbs *477*

Candles and Other Light Sources *478*

In Practice: Designing Fictional and Special Effects Materials ... 480

12 Animated Materials 483

Natural Animated Materials 484

Maps to Use with Natural Materials *485*

Animated Water *489*

		Man-Made Animated Materials 491
		Maps to Use with Man-Made Materials 491
		The Ballpark Sign 494
		Dropping a Bomb 498
		Fictional Animated Materials 500
		"Plasma Engine" Exercise 500
		In Practice: Animated Materials 502
	13	**Using MAX 3 as a 2D Paint Tool** **505**
		Still Image Maps and Masks 506
		Exterior Night Lighting 506
		Valley Landscape 515
		Animated Maps and Masks 520
		Burning Fuse 520
		Digging a Trench 526
		In Practice: Using MAX 3 as a 2D Paint Tool 531

Part III Rendering Effects

	14	**Cameras, Camera Effects, and Lighting** **535**
		Real-World Cameras 536
		Film-Based Cameras 537
		Video-Based Cameras 538
		Film Versus Video-Playback Speeds 539
		Lens Types 540
		F-Stops 543
		Film Speed 545
		Lens Attachments 546
		Composition 547

MAX Cameras 550
    Using the Right Camera 551
    Matching a Real-World Camera 553
    Simulating Real-World Effects 553
    Framing 555
    Shot Angles 558
Real-World Scene Lighting 559
    Studio Lights 560
    Flashes 563
    Subject Lighting 564
    Natural Lighting 566
MAX Lights 568
    Using the Right Light 568
    Simulating Real-World Lighting Effects 572
Lighting Techniques 573
    Building Up Your Light 573
    Lighting Options 575
    Interior Lighting Simulations 577
In Practice: Cameras, Camera Effects, and Lighting 579

15 Glows and Lens Flares 583

Natural Glow and Flare Causes 585
Glow-Keying Elements: Sources 587
    Glowing Objects 588
    Glowing Material Effects Channels 591
    Glowing Unclamped Colors 592
    Additional Glowing Source Options 593
Glow Effect Restrictions and Controls 595
    Glowing the Whole Source: The All Filter 595
    Glowing the Perimeter 596

Using Maps and Gradients in Glow 602
    Radial Color and Falloff 602
    Circular Color and Falloff 604
Using Gradient in the Glow Module of Video Post 605
    Radial Versus Circular Uses in Glow 606
    Gradient Composition Techniques 607
Building a Glow 608
    Determining the Source 608
    Determining the Color 609
    Determining the Intensity 609
Building a Flare 609
    Determine the Source 612
    Account for the Environment 613
    Account for the Camera Type 613
In Practice: Glows and Lens Flares 614

16   Highlights 617

Working with Highlight 619
    Using Highlight's Effect Section 620
    Using Highlight's Vary Section 620
    Color Usage with Highlight 621
Using Flare Versus Highlight 621
Combining Highlight with Glow 622
    Shiny Surfaces 622
Candlelight Highlights with Flare 624
    Using Highlight on an Entire Object 626
In Practice: Highlights 627

17 Focal Effects ... 631

- Depth of Field Terminology ... 633
  - Focal Loss ... 633
  - Focal Range ... 634
  - Focal Limit ... 635
- General Focal Effects ... 636
  - Scene Blur ... 637
  - Radial Blur ... 638
- Determining the Focal Point ... 638
- Depth of Field Shift ... 640
  - A Cityscape in Depth of Field ... 640
- In Practice: Focal Effects ... 643

Part IV Appendixes

A AutoCAD and 3D Studio MAX: Sharing Files ... 647

- Why Doesn't 3D Studio MAX R3 Do...? ... 648
- The File Import Options ... 649
  - AutoCAD DWG Import Dialog Box ... 649
  - Import AutoCAD DWG File Dialog Box ... 650
- AutoCAD DWG and 3D Studio MAX R3 Entities Translation ... 654
- Other Import/Export Format Options ... 656
  - 3D Studio 3DS, PRJ ... 656
  - Adobe Illustrator AI ... 656
  - AutoCAD DXF ... 656
  - 3D Studio SHP ... 660
  - 3DSIN and 3DSOUT ... 660
  - Stereolithography STL ... 662

    IGES Files *663*

    VRML Files *665*

    In Practice: AutoCAD and 3D Studio MAX: Sharing Files 665

B Designing with Plug-Ins **669**

    Plug-In Names 670

    Plug-In Sources 671

    To Pay or Not to Pay? 671

        Pay *671*

        Don't Pay *672*

    Objects and Modifier Plug-Ins 672

    Material Editor Plug-Ins 674

    Rendering and Special Effects Plug-Ins 674

    Other Plug-Ins 675

    Unplugging Plug-Ins 676

    In Practice: Designing with Plug-Ins 678

Index **680**

About the Authors

Ted Boardman skipped college. After completing a two-year Voc-Tech drafting program, he spent a short stint in the Infantry in Korea. Then he went to Europe to travel before settling down to work. That European trip lasted three years and included jobs ranging from Architectural Drafter for Daimler-Benz in Stuttgart, Germany to all-around-man at the Adambreau Brewery in Innsbruck, Austria. Work and travel time were divided equally during those years.

On returning to the United States in the mid-1970s, he traveled and skied a while before starting a nationwide architectural service, specializing in hand-cut, post-and-beam structures. That business was suspended for another European visit and a six-month trip around India and Sri Lanka, overland across Afghanistan and Iran, then back to Germany.

Back in the United States, the business returned to post-and-beam design and construction, and full-service architectural design. It was only interrupted to deliver sailing yachts to and from the Caribbean and New England in the spring and fall.

Ted introduced AutoCAD into his practice in 1983 with Version 1.4. He eventually converted his business to presentation and animation services with the release of 3D Studio. He started training in AutoCAD in the mid-1980s.

His business is now primarily training users of 3D Studio MAX around the world, and writing books and training guides on 3D Studio MAX and VIZ. Ted is a Discreet Authorized Training Specialist.

Jeremy Hubbell is the Design Products Marketing Manager at Discreet. Within the Design Visualization group, Jeremy is responsible for the development and implementation of various marketing components of 3D Studio VIZ and its associated family of products. Prior to his current role, Jeremy was the Senior 3D Studio MAX instructor. He served on the 3D Studio MAX and VIZ development teams as the worldwide training liaison. He also implemented the Kinetix Training Specialist program. It was designed for 3D Studio experts who wanted to instruct others on the intricacies of the 3D Studio family of products. Prior to joining the former Autodesk Multimedia Division in 1994, Jeremy was an Autodesk reseller in his hometown of New Orleans. He currently resides in San Francisco.

Dedications

Ted Boardman

I'd like to dedicate this book to Sally Turner. Thanks for creating an atmosphere that allows me the freedom to work.

Jeremy Hubbell

I'd like to dedicate this book to my fiancée, Akiko, for her courage and desire to take my hand and join me in this rat race we call software development.

Acknowledgments

Ted Boardman

Writing and self-employment are two very time-consuming endeavors. If it were not for the support and encouragement I have received from Laura Frey, as lead editor at New Riders; Linda Laflamme, as development editor; and Dave Marks and Mark Gerhard at Discreet, as tech editors, it would be an impossible task. I'd like to thank them and the support staff at New Riders for a job well done. Although the author's names appear on the cover, the book would never happen without a dedicated and professional team behind the scenes. I'd also like to thank Jeremy Hubbell for his portion of the book and for filling in some gaps for me. Thank you all.

Jeremy Hubbell

This book, more so than the previous edition, was a real accomplishment for all involved. The whole team at NRP, including Laura Frey, kept this book's schedule moving along, keeping in line with MAX R3's ever-changing ship date. The editing team—consisting of Linda, Dave, and Mark—made sure that Ted and I were always in line. Most importantly, this release of MAX is a significant achievement for Discreet—something that shouldn't go unrecognized. Not only has the MAX development team undergone a merger with one of the most well-known software companies in the world; they've also seen new talent, like Frank DeLise and Peter Watje, join them. Even with all the office chaos, the MAX R3 development team has produced yet another great release. Hats off to everyone involved.

Tell Us What You Think!

As the reader of this book, *you* are our most important critic and commentator. We value your opinion and want to know what we're doing right, what we could do better, in what areas you'd like to see us publish, and any other words of wisdom you're willing to pass our way.

As the Executive Editor for the Graphics team at New Riders Publishing, I welcome your comments. You can fax, email, or write me directly to let me know what you did or didn't like about this book—as well as what we can do to make our books stronger.

Please note that I cannot help you with technical problems related to the topic of this book, and that due to the high volume of mail I receive, I might not be able to reply to every message.

When you write, please be sure to include this book's title and authors, as well as your name and phone or fax number. I will carefully review your comments and share them with the authors and editors who worked on the book.

Fax: 317-581-4663

Email: graphics@mcp.com

Mail: Steve Weiss
Executive Editor
Graphics
New Riders Publishing
201 West 103rd Street
Indianapolis, IN 46290 USA

Introduction

Welcome...

...to *Inside 3D Studio MAX 3, Modeling, Materials, and Rendering*! This edition of the Modeling, Materials, and Rendering reference focuses on exactly what the new release of

MAX focuses on: productivity. Once again, Ted and I saw the need for more information than you get just from the documentation. How-to's, tips, and tricks are always great. They're even better when you know how they make your life easier and more productive while using MAX. We've done our best to give you what you need.

In our experiences as instructors, our students regularly begged for information that would make them power users So we said, "Why not put it in a book?" What you hold in your hands right now contains the fruits of our labor. If you want to learn more about the intricacies of modeling, working with materials, or achieving the best rendering effects, this book is for you. Furthermore, if you purchased this book's last edition on MAX R2, in this one you find a host of updated content—designed specifically to address the new R3 release. For instance, many of the new modeling features (such as the right-click menu) are addressed in the first chapter. Also note that with the new rendering effects in MAX R3, there are new ways—discussed in this book—to achieve effects not possible before.

Out of the Box, into the Book

While writing this book, we purposely avoided using third-party plug-in routines within the exercises. Our intention allows you to execute the exercises with 3D Studio MAX R3 just as they are programmed in the software. We feel it is important to be familiar with the enhanced capabilities of MAX R3 and to understand what you can accomplish with the built-in tools. Understanding the functionality of the program makes you more productive and makes it easier to write useful, custom routines using MAXScript.

Real-World, Real-Work Examples

We try to use everyday, real-world examples in the exercises. We understand that it is fun to create flashy, deep-space scenes crawling with slimy aliens in full battle mode, but most of us need to create more immediate, practical renderings and animations. That doesn't mean to forego creativity. We emphasize adding that extra edge of realism to your scenes—that thin patina of reality that we see and take for granted in our everyday world. Train yourself to see the world around you as it really exists; use the principles in these chapters and exercises to simulate the details most people overlook.

Productivity Is the Key

It is important to us that these exercises assist you, the MAX R3 user, to be more productive. Precise realism and beauty are noble goals in creating renderings and animations. However (except for those few true artists), if it can't be accomplished on time and on budget, then you won't win many friends in the workplace. We try, where appropriate, to use the most efficient method of creating any given effect. Keep in mind that the quickest and easiest method may not ultimately be the most productive. Anticipate future editing needs and adapt your work habits accordingly.

Get the Most from the Exercises

Execute this book's exercises with careful thought. The intention is not to teach you how to read or follow instructions, but to make you think about how MAX's tools work and how to use the demonstrated techniques in your own projects. An exercise is valuable only if you learn something from it. These exercises are tested and work if you follow the steps carefully. However, take the time to think and take notes on the introduced process or concept, so that you can apply it to your own work. Simply performing the steps, getting the desired results, and moving on to the next exercise is not particularly helpful in the learning process.

The Book's Organization

When browsing through this book, notice that it is divided into three distinct sections. The first is a comprehensive discussion on modeling techniques in various industries. Even though the subject material addresses using MAX in different industries, don't limit yourself to just your profession. There are many helpful techniques to assist you. The second section covers materials. Here we focus not only on the Material Editor's features, but also on making the most of them. Some discussions are straightforward and practical. Others require a more "out there" way of thinking (often required when using the Material Editor). The third section is on rendering. While rendering is a bit nebulous, the chapters cover many aspects of rendering—from cameras and lighting techniques to using the new rendering effects in R3.

Building Up: One Chapter at a Time

The chapters within the three major sections are arranged to build each upon the other. This is especially true for the three Concepts chapters at the beginning of each section. These chapters set the tone for the rest of the section and provide a good foundation for the preceding material. This doesn't mean that you must read the chapters consecutively. Of course, feel free to jump around!

A Note about Knowing MAX

We set out to write a book that took users beyond what's covered in the MAX documentation. While there is some overlap, there are many discussions and exercises that talk far above what the MAX reference material covers. That said, we strongly recommend that you take the time to do the MAX tutorials before tackling this book. You get much more out of the book this way.

Let the Fun Begin!

We hope that you enjoy and value the material presented in this book. As authors and instructors, we know the importance of having good reference material. It's our desire to provide the MAX-user community with the best possible information about using this product to its fullest. Enjoy the ride!

Sincerely,

Ted Boardman & Jeremy Hubbell

Part I

Modeling

1 **Modeling Concepts**

2 **Architectural Modeling**

3 **Landscapes and Building Enhancements**

4 **Industrial and Mechanical Design Modeling**

5 **Modeling for Real-Time 3D Games**

6 **Cinematics and High-Detail Modeling**

7 **Character Modeling**

Chapter 1

Modeling Concepts

When modeling in 3D, the most important thing to remember is that no matter what technology you have at your fingertips, the final model can be produced only through the creative design process. That is, without that gray matter called your brain, the flashiest software is nothing. While MAX can provide you with a multitude of tools to create your model, your creativity is the fuel that drives them.

The tools that an animator uses can vary a great deal, but the end result is the same—a quality 3D model that fits the particular job. 3D Studio MAX offers several different modeling technologies. Much like the workbench in your basement, MAX puts several tools at your disposal. In the base package, you can choose between three different modeling methods: Polygonal, Patch, and NURBS. However, the good old saying, "The right tool for the right job" still holds true in this digital 3D world. So how do you go about selecting that right tool? More importantly, what *are* the tools and what is good or bad about them?

This chapter seeks to explain anything and everything about the modeling technologies in MAX, how to use them, and how to eventually master them. The several exercises scattered through the chapter were designed to hone your skills. More specifically, this chapter covers:

- Modeling technologies and methods
- Strengths and weaknesses of each modeling type
- Choosing the right modeling type
- Picking a place to start your model

Polygonal Modeling

While perhaps not the oldest form of modeling, *polygonal modeling* has been around for quite some time. As a matter of fact, it has even withstood the tests of newer modeling technologies such as patch, NURBS, and hybrids such as metaballs. Why? It makes sense to novices and experts alike. The geometry you see on your screen is made up of little interconnecting triangles, called *faces*, of various sizes and orientations. By arranging the faces, you can build from a very simple 3D model to a very complex one. Polygonal models are also easily animated. By altering the size and orientation of the faces you can produce simple animations, such as bends or twists, to more complex animations such as morphing.

What makes polygonal modeling useful (and popular) is the fact that you have explicit control over the features that shape the model. The most basic of these features are the points, called *vertices*, which define exactly how a model will look. Usually polygonal models begin with low-detail objects called *primitives*. Primitives, as their name implies, are the most basic types of shapes that can be created with polygons. Almost every software package available has a set of primitives with which to begin modeling. MAX R3 comes with a collection of 22 primitives, contained within the Standard Primitives and Extended Primitives category of the Create panel or the Tab panel's Objects tabs. There is a special 23rd primitive described just below.

Most people who use polygonal modeling actually don't even bother with most primitives; they just start from a box. A box? "What's so great about a box?" you may ask. A box is perhaps the most simple 3D form of all. Much like a house's foundation, a box can serve as the foundation for any number of models, ranging from spaceships to characters' bodies. (Getting from a box to your desired model is a story for later chapters, however.)

It's safe to say that MAX has some of the best polygonal modeling tools in the industry. Some tools are better than others, but on the whole, you've got a multitude of ways to shape your simple primitives into beautiful models. Choosing the tools, and even base primitives, requires a certain amount of experience and skill. Not to worry. This chapter will take you through a few exercises to get you going with polygons. Before you dive into modeling, however, take a look at a few key concepts when talking about modeling in MAX.

Faces, Edges, and Vertices

As mentioned in the previous section, polygonal objects are comprised of control points called *vertices*. Two vertices in 3D space connected by a straight-line segment form an *edge*. Connect three vertices together to form a triangle and you now have a *face*—or polygon. The construction of polygonal models essentially involves the connecting of vertices. If all of the faces of a model share an edge with at least three other faces, the model is said to be *closed*. If a model contains faces that do not share edges, the model can be considered *open*. Most polygonal models that you'll deal with will be closed. In most cases, the only time that you'll desire to have an open model is if you plan to fill the open area with another object.

A polygon has no thickness. It's a flat object. When you interconnect several polygons together, however, you can form all sorts of 3D objects. Interestingly enough, the object formed is 3D, but the components that make them up are truly 2D in a 3D world.

Parametric Objects Versus Editable Objects

There are 22 parametric objects whose attributes are controlled by variables, such as a sphere defined by *Radius*. A special 23rd object is the *Editable Mesh*. This object is created by choosing a special command that shuts down the parametric controls for the object and reduces the object to a simple collection of faces, edges, and vertices. Editable Mesh contains a series of powerful tools for polygonal modeling. Later you will learn about a special modifier, *Edit Mesh*, that offers many of same benefits, while still retaining the parametric base object.

Sub-Object Mode

Before we get too deep into the concepts of modeling in MAX, it's important to talk about one crucial element—something called *Sub-Object mode*. To specify which component you wish to work with on a model, you must select a Sub-Object mode. Sub-Object modes expose the vertices, edges, and faces that comprise the Editable Mesh, and reveal tools that act on those elements. Sub-Object modes are accessible in the Modify command panel, used to review and alter an object's base parameters. In the Modify panel, you can also add *modifiers* to further manipulate your objects. Later, you will see that modifiers also contain Sub-Object modes to affect how they alter the primitives.

For many new users of MAX, using Editable Mesh is one of the first times that they're exposed to the whole idea of the Sub-Object mode. Actually, this is the case where Sub-Object, as a name, makes sense. In the case of polygonal objects, you're truly tapping into the foundation of an object when you're in Sub-Object mode with Editable Mesh. As mentioned earlier, Editable Mesh is really a special-case primitive. However, unlike the other 22 standard primitives, Editable Mesh objects are defined by parameters such as a radius, edges, and so on. In fact, Editable Mesh has no concept of special parameters such as these. Instead, Editable Mesh stores only the vertex locations of a polygonal object and how those vertices are connected. This is a big deal, even though it may not sound like it. Primitives condition you to dimension objects based on their parameters. Editable Mesh allows you to push, pull, add, or delete any of the Sub-Object elements since you're working with the building block elements rather than the object as a whole.

So, as a golden rule, you'll always need to be in Sub-Object mode whenever editing the building blocks of an object or the modifiers applied to it. MAX reinforces the idea of being in the mode, by turning the Sub-Object button yellow and by not allowing you to select another object. To select another object, you must first turn off Sub-Object mode by either pressing the Sub-Object button or Ctrl-B on your keyboard. The latter shortcut is much more efficient, so take some time to learn it if you haven't already. Figure 1.1 is a simple diagram that illustrates how MAX thinks about objects and how to navigate them.

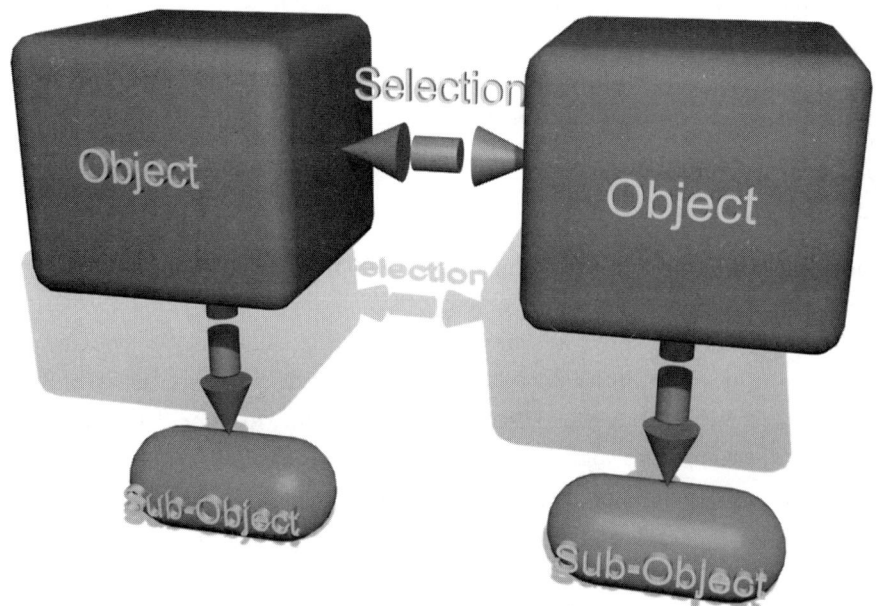

Figure 1.1 The four main components of an object that are accessible in Sub-Object mode. From top-to-bottom and left-to-right, they are: Object, Face, Edge, and Vertex selection modes.

The moral to this particular section is to get friendly with Sub-Object mode. If you're serious about modeling, you're going to use it frequently, whether as polygons, patches, or NURBS.

Polygonal Modeling Uses

The good thing about polygonal models is that they can be just about anything. Very little is impossible. Many of the limitations imposed by NURBS, patches, and other modeling techniques don't apply to polygons. This means that as long as you can build, twist, bend, push, pull, and whatever else to a polygon, you probably can create anything.

To model effectively in MAX using polygons, work with the Editable Mesh object or the Edit Mesh modifier. Understanding how these features operate will make your life much easier. Fortunately, they're nearly identical in functionality. Learn one and you've practically learned the other. The next section takes a closer look at Editable Mesh and the best way to use it.

Editable Mesh

The Editable Mesh object and Edit Mesh modifier are your keys into editing polygonal objects in MAX. While most of the modifiers in MAX are deformation-based, Editable Mesh is really the only feature that allows you to really get in and explicitly shift vertices around, create faces, or just about anything else.

We'll focus on Editable Mesh for this section, but the commands for Editable Mesh and Edit Mesh are nearly the same.

Editable Mesh has two main editing modes, Object and Sub-Object. As their names imply, you're selecting and editing different parts of the object based on what mode you're using. This can sometimes be confusing because the panel has so many commands on it. It's often difficult to know what commands work on what part of your object. Fortunately, in MAX R3, Discreet took great strides to simplify the interface by activating the commands you could use and deactivating the ones you couldn't. Similar commands are grouped together. Inappropriate commands are deactivated, but they remain visible as grayed-out buttons. Where previously you had to learn the location of tools in three separate Sub-Object panels, you can now learn the layout of one panel that functions equally in the five modes. Let's explore some of the features of Editable Mesh by building a small model.

NEW TO R3

> **Note**
> For R3, Kinetix has added two new Sub-Object modes to Editable Mesh: Polygon and Element. These modes have always been available as special cases of Face mode, but have now been combined into the consolidated interface.

EXERCISE 1.1   Using Editable Mesh to Build A Polygonal Cannon

1. Click the Objects tab in the Tab bar. Choose the Box button. Create a long, rectangular box in the Perspective viewport. Use the default settings. After creating the box, for more accurate dimensions, enter Length:110, Width:25, and Height:25.

> **Note**
> To better see the results of the following steps, it's a good idea to turn on Edged Faces from the Perspective viewport or to work in Wireframe mode. Simply right-click the Perspective viewport label and choose Edged Faces.

2. Right-click the box, and choose Convert to Editable Mesh. Notice that you are automatically switched to the Modify panel and are now ready to edit the model.

3. Click the Edge button in the Selection rollout in the Modify panel. Observe that the Sub-Object and Edge buttons turn yellow to indicate your current mode.

4. Click the Slice Plane button in the Edit Geometry rollout. (You may need to scroll down the Modify panel a bit to see the Slice Plane button.) Once clicked, the button turns green to indicate the active mode.

5. Use the Rotate command to rotate the Slice Plane 90 degrees on the X-axis. This is easily accomplished by right-clicking the Slice Plane, choosing Rotate, and then click-dragging the Transform Gizmo's X-axis handle in the viewport. Observe the rotation angle in the status line as you drag the mouse. Release the button when X equals 90 degrees.

NEW TO R3

> **Note**
> The Transform Gizmo and enhanced right-click menus were introduced in MAX R3 as productivity enhancements. The right-click menu now places several commonly used tools at your cursor. The Transform Gizmo provides a mechanism to constrain movement, rotation, and scaling to specific axes without typing a command or moving the mouse to the toolbar. In any of the transformation modes, simply click one of the arrows and drag the mouse to transform on that axis.

6. Use the Move command to move the Slice Plane along the Y-axis so that you're about ¾ of the distance from either end. Once again, the Transform Gizmo provides the easiest way to do this. In the Top view, right-click the Slice Plane and choose Move. Click the Transform Gizmo's Y-axis handle and drag the plane to the desired location.

7. Click the Slice button. This adds edges where the Slice Plane intersects the box.

8. Repeat this process at a similar distance from the other end. Refer to Figure 1.2.

9. Turn off the Slice Plane by clicking the Slice Plane button. Switch to Face mode by clicking the Face button or choosing Face from the Sub-Object drop-down list.

10. Select the interior faces as indicated in Figure 1.2. This is easiest to do if you select by dragging a window around the interior faces. Make sure to be in the Window mode.

11. Choose Select and Non-uniform Scale (which I'll call Non-uniform Scale from now on) from the Scale flyout button in the Main Toolbar tab.

12. At the same time, interactively scale the interior faces on the Z- and X-axes to about 40 percent. This is most easily accomplished by using the Transform Gizmo's ZX-plane constraint in the Perspective viewport. The plane constraints are the 90-degree V-marks in the gizmo perpendicular to the XY, YZ, and ZX handle pairs. Click the ZX constraint and drag until the status line shows 40 percent and release the mouse.

13. Click the Bevel button in the Modify panel, and select the end faces of the box (either end will do at this point). Because the square end contains two triangular

faces separated by an invisible edge, it is easier to select them both by switching Sub-Object modes again. Choose the Polygon button to enter Polygon mode. This Sub-Object mode is a special case of Face that ignores hidden edges.

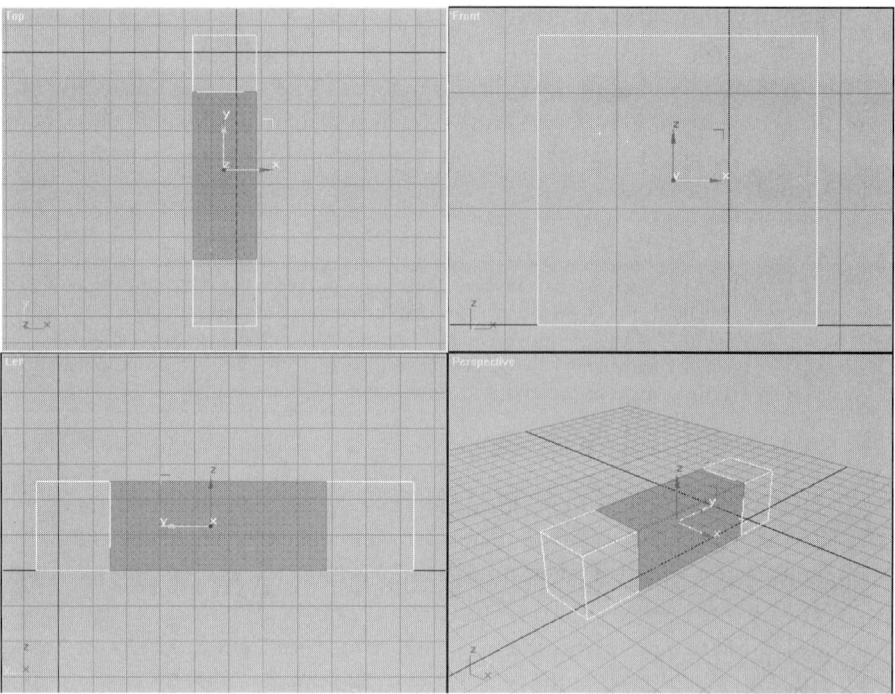

Figure 1.2 The sliced box produced by Steps 1-8, with the faces to select for Step 10 highlighted in red.

14. Interactively drag out the selection about 10 units. When you release the mouse, you can bevel the new extrusion. Bevel inward about 7 units. The end faces remain selected.
15. Use the Extrusion amount spinner to extrude the selection inward. (A value of about −16.0 works well.) Refer to Figure 1.3 as an example.
16. Use the Perspective viewport's Arc-Rotate command to spin around to the other end of the cannon. If you have a three-button mouse, press the Alt key and middle mouse button together. This is a shortcut new to MAX R3 to activate Arc-Rotate.
17. Click the Extrude button in the Modify panel, then select and interactively extrude the butt-end of the cannon about 40 units.
18. Select Edge Sub-Object mode, and click the Chamfer button.

19. Select and interactively chamfer the top-end edge of the butt-end of the cannon about 20 units.
20. Turn off Sub-Object by clicking the Sub-Object button or by pressing Ctrl-B on the keyboard, then click the More button in the Modify panel.

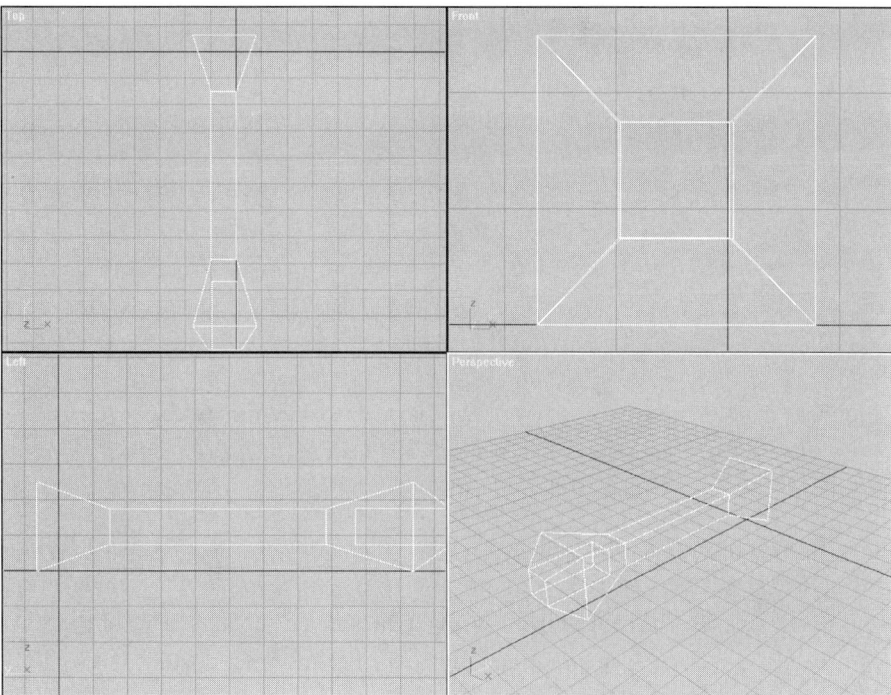

Figure 1.3 The barrel of the cannon built in Steps 11 through 15.

21. Choose MeshSmooth. When the model is smoothed, alter the settings so that the cannon is less round. Try setting MeshSmooth Type to Classic. In the Smoothing Parameters area, set Strength to 0.4. In the Subdivision Amount area, set Iterations to 3. In the Display/Weighting area, turn on Display Control Mesh. The end result should be similar to Figure 1.4.
22. Save your work.

You can also go back in the Modifier stack and add the scope (as in Figure 1.4) using the same techniques of beveling and extruding faces that you used to make the cannon.

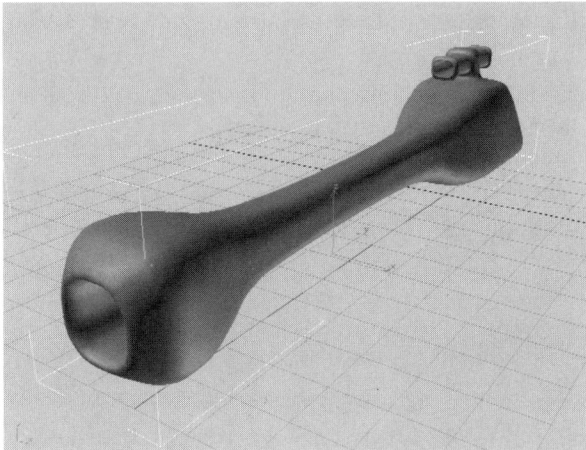

Figure 1.4 The completed cannon with the optional scope attachment, using the same face extrusion and bevel techniques that created the cannon.

If you take a moment to notice a few things that occurred in this exercise that may have been different from MAX R2, you'll realize some features have been added and some steps saved:

NEW TO R3

- You can now right-click on any primitive and convert it to a polygon, patch, or NURBS editable object. This feature also saves you the hassle of switching to the Modify panel. The context-sensitive right-click menu contains many of the tools available in Sub-Object mode and can be further customized with MAXScript.

- The Sub-Object selection modes are now accessible via buttons at the top of Editable Mesh. Note that this also exists for Editable Patch and Editable Spline.

- Editable Mesh contains a new interactive Chamfer tool that works at the Edge and Vertex levels.

- MeshSmooth uses a number of new options, including the ability to output the smoothed polygon as a NURBS object.

 Note

MeshSmooth is based on a technology sometimes known as "subdivision surface" that was first made famous by the Academy Award winning *Geri's Game* from Pixar. When applied to a relatively low-detail model and deactivated in the interactive viewports, MeshSmooth can be a strong contender to the patch and NURBS technologies described below. You get a simple cage to work with and high-detail mesh at render time.

- The absolutely easiest way to transform objects is to use the new Transform Gizmos.

Polygonal Modeling Shortcomings

While polygonal modeling is the most widely used modeling technology, it has a few shortcomings. First and foremost, it's not ideally suited for modeling organic shapes. Things like bodies, faces, liquid, or any other model that moves organically is a real challenge for polygons. For a polygonal model to look nice and smooth, it needs to have a great amount of detail—that means more faces. As demonstrated in the previous exercise, you see how many more faces a smooth surface requires than an angular, faceted object. The more faces you have, the longer it takes to render and the more memory MAX needs to operate properly.

Complex polygonal models also make editing quite difficult. Due to the large number of faces in detailed areas of a polygonal model, making small changes often creates a significant challenge, as Figure 1.5 illustrates. Even with all of MAX's selection tools and editing capabilities, you'll find that getting into the nooks and crannies of a detailed mesh can be tough.

Figure 1.5 This polygonal model of the *Titanic*, available from REM Infografica, represents a serious challenge for any modeler. Attempting to edit this model poses the rather ominous question, "Where do I start?"

As face count increases, MAX's interactive performance will begin to decrease. Don't worry! On a decent workstation, it takes tens of thousands of faces to notice *any* degradation in performance. It just means that you must be careful when building geometry.

The shortcomings of polygonal modeling are not just restricted to organic shapes. Essentially anything that requires a smooth, flowing surface with many complex curves is going to cause problems if it exists as a polygonal model. For instance, many car manufacturers prefer to construct prototypes using NURBS, a tool more ideally suited for curvaceous shapes. Many industrial product designers also prefer using NURBS.

By the same token, all the previous examples accept polygon modeling. You can use polygons to model just about anything. With enough detail, you can create any surface. However, there are particular models that lend themselves to polygon creations more than others. For instance, squared-off models can be most effectively worked through polygons. Traditional architectural models are ideal for polygons. The reason is that many angles are right angles on objects like walls, windows, doors, and even most interior furniture. It just goes back to the example of choosing the right tool for the right job.

Sometimes the best approach is to model one component of an object with one method and another component with a different method. To illustrate this, we'll create a model of the grim reaper—a model citizen and personal fan of 3D Studio MAX—in three exercises over the course of the next few sections. Exercises 1.2–1.4 demonstrate not only the various modeling technologies, but also the fact that you can use them together to create the right look.

Naturally, we start with the polygonal exercise and create the sickle that our angel of death likes to brandish when visiting friends—or clients. You notice that there's no need to actually start with a standard primitive, but you can also use shapes to build 3D objects. Exercise 1.2 is not an in-depth look at polygonal modeling, but it does give you an idea of how to quickly use the default MAX tools to whip up a nice blade. Enjoy.

Exercise 1.2   Creating a Sickle

1. Start 3D Studio MAX R3, and choose Reset from the File pull-down menu.
2. Click the Shapes button in the Create command panel or select the Shapes tab from the Tab panel, and choose Arc.
3. Starting at any point in the Front view, click and drag out a line segment. This determines the beginning and end points of the arc. Release the mouse to define the radius of the arc. It should be enough of a curve to look like the leading edge of the sickle. Your measurements for Radius, From, and To values should be about 90, 2, and 110, respectively.

4. Create another arc that begins near the endpoint of the first arc but with a shallower curvature, as in Figure 1.6. The measurements for Radius, From, and To should be about 130, 33.5, and 95, respectively.

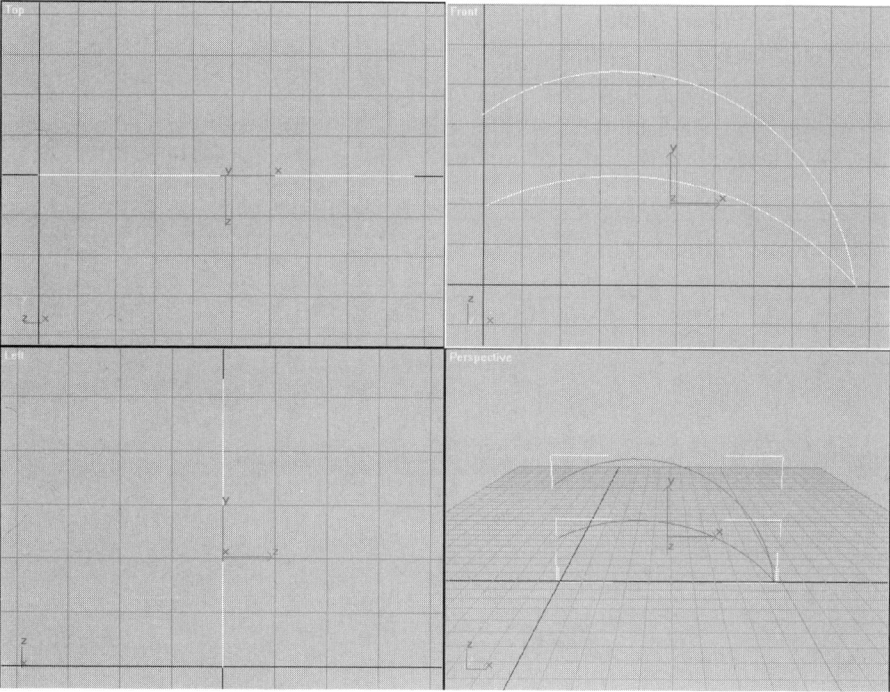

Figure 1.6 The two arcs created in Steps 3 and 4 form the shape of the blade.

5. Go to the Modify panel (make sure that just one of the arcs is selected), and click the Edit Spline button.
6. From Edit Spline's Geometry rollout, click Attach. The button turns green to indicate Attach mode. Select the other arc in the viewport.

Tip
Once again, you could easily accomplish the same task using the context-sensitive right-click menu. Right-click over the arc and observe that most of Edit Spline's tools, including Attach, are available there.

7. Switch to Vertex Sub-Object selection mode by clicking the Vertex button.
8. Select the two vertices at the point of the sickle, then right-click and select the Weld command to join the two. If, for some reason, they don't weld, try increasing the Weld threshold (the value next to the Weld button in the Command panel) until they do.

9. Switch to the Spline selection level, and then click the Close button to close the shape.
10. Click the More button in the Modify panel, and choose Bevel.
11. In the Bevel Values section, turn on Level 2 and set the Height of both Level 1 and 2 to the same value. It should be enough to have a noticeable thickness to the blade, but not too thick!
12. Increase the Outline value of Level 1 to about 1 unit. Set the Outline value of Level 2 to the exact inverse, (−1) for example. Your sickle blade should now look like Figure 1.7.

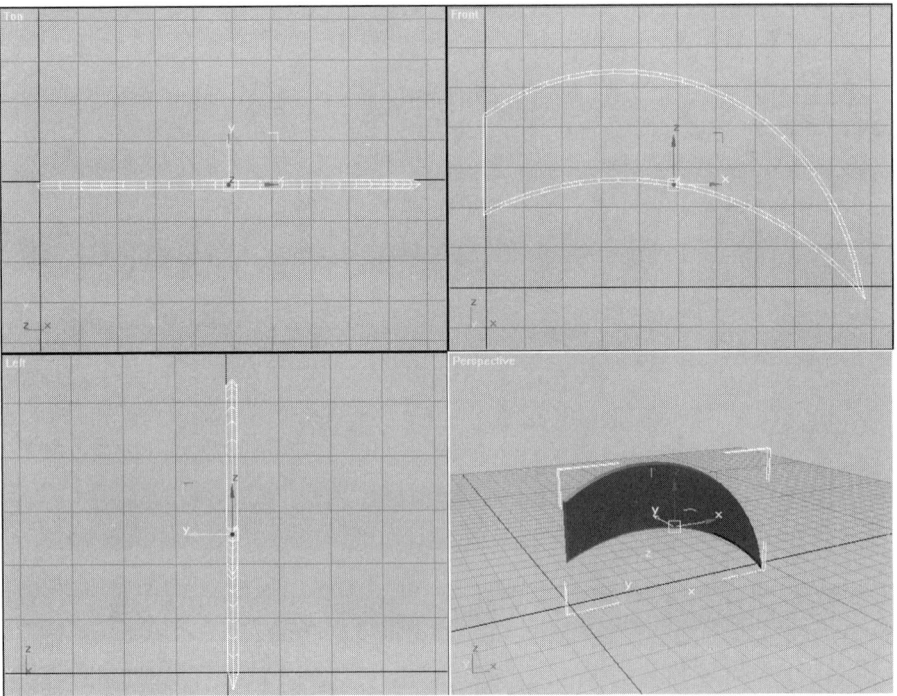

Figure 1.7 The sickle blade after completing Steps 5 through 12.

13. To create the staff that connects to the blade, use a Chamfer Cylinder. Go to the Create panel, and then choose Extended Primitives from the Geometry category or click the Objects tab in the Tab panel. Then, interactively create a chamfer cylinder anywhere in the Perspective or Top viewport. (You'll probably want to create it near the blade for reference.) Adjust the cylinder's height, radius, and fillet radius/segments to give it a nice, rounded-pole look. Use the Transform Gizmo to finally put the pole into place.

14. To create the attachment piece, use a simple shape with the Bevel Profile modifier attached to it. Start by creating a circle shape: Click the Shapes button in the Create panel, and then choose Circle. In the Top viewport, interactively click-drag out a circle shape that's slightly bigger than the pole you just created.

15. Click the Line button in the Create command panel. In the front viewport, draw a "squiggly" vertically oriented line that looks like a series of about four full waves. This will become the profile. Refer to Figure 1.8 if you need a reference. (You may need to go to the Modify panel to make slight edits to the shape.)

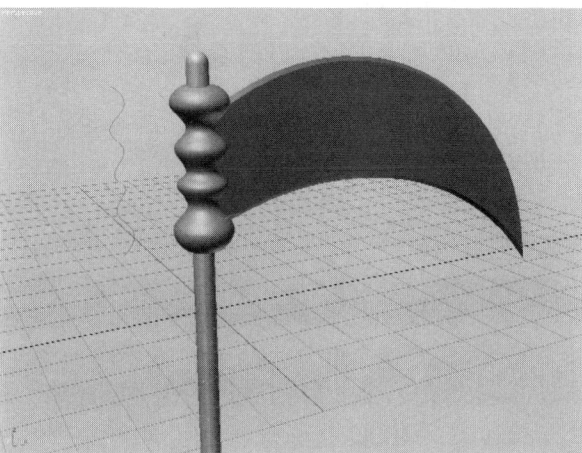

Figure 1.8 The completed attachment in place, holding the blade to the pole.

16. Select the circle shape, and go to the Modify panel, if you're not there already.
17. Click the More button, and choose Bevel Profile.
18. When the Profile parameters appear, click the Pick Profile button and choose the squiggly line you just drew. This may create an object slightly larger than you anticipated. Don't worry; edit the original line until the new holder looks more like Figure 1.8.

 Tip
You can also enter Sub-Object mode and move the Profile Gizmo toward and away from the circle to affect the finished diameter of the object.

19. If necessary, move the holder into place so that it intersects the pole and covers the width of the blade.
20. Apply your favorite materials such as wood, cloth, and metal. Then save the file.

Although this exercise didn't focus on features specific to MAX R3, you probably did notice some new things about the Edit Spline modifier:

NEW TO R3

- The Edit Spline modifier now has convenient selection level buttons at the top. Its interface has been simplified. Rather than the whole panel changing with each selection level, the buttons remain constant and activate only if valid for that level.
- You can also right-click on spline shapes to perform many Edit Spline operations, such as welding and outlining.

Patch Modeling

The second modeling technology native to MAX is *patch modeling*. While patch modeling and patches are newer to the scene than polygons, they still have quite an encampment of dedicated users. As a matter of fact, most character modelers prefer patches to anything else. Patches are lighter, computationally speaking, when compared to polygons and don't suffer from some of the extra overhead that you might find with NURBS. A huge benefit of patch models is their ability to represent smooth surfaces easily, as Figure 1.9 illustrates. Unlike polygonal models, patch models require less detail to represent smoother, more contoured shapes.

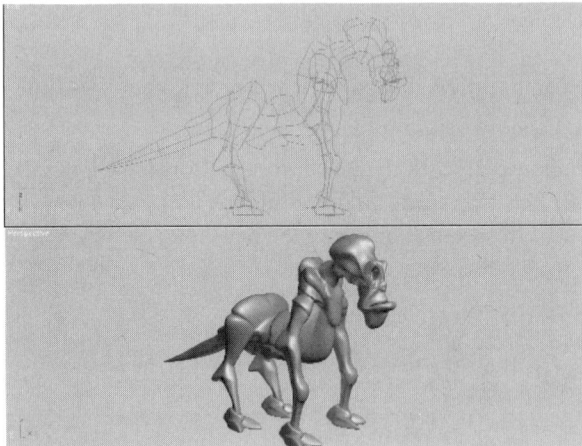

Figure 1.9 An ominous-looking creature created in MAX using patch modeling methods. This particular creature was built using a feature now included in MAX R3 called Surface Tools.

Chapter 1: Modeling Concepts   21

When thinking about patches, the easiest relationship that you might think of is to a patchwork quilt. The quilt is made up of several patches, usually of varying colors and sizes, to form a much larger surface. However, rather than being constructed from polygonal faces, patches are defined by their boundaries. This means that where the boundaries exist and how they're oriented control the interior of the patch. The interior of the patch is governed by the *Bézier technology*. Bézier technology allows for smooth areas within the interior of the patch. Wrapped around the patch is a series of interconnecting points called a *lattice*. While the lattice itself is not editable, it does allow you to see the way a patch is constructed rather easily.

Note
B-Spline curves were the result of mathematician Pierre Bézier. Surface patches are an extension of his work with spline curves.

Patches, Edges, and Vertices

Patches are made up of components similarly named as a polygonal model's components. As mentioned before, a patch model is actually composed of several smaller patches. Patch surfaces in MAX are defined as four-sided surfaces. Each side is referred to as an *edge*. Where two or more edges intersect is a point called a *vertex*. Lastly, there is a noneditable lattice that defines the overall shape of the patch itself. Figure 1.10 shows the components of a patch model.

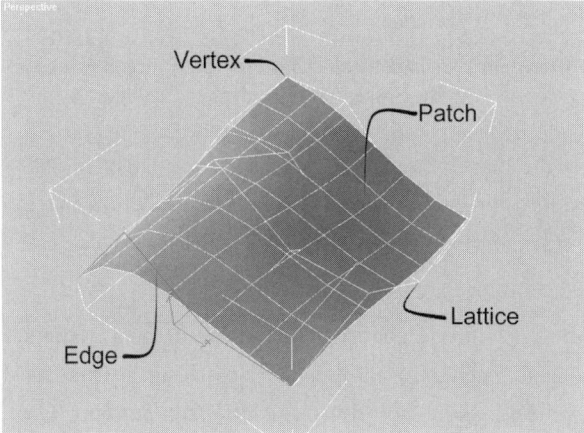

Figure 1.10 The breakdown of a patch model. Notice that the concepts of vertices and edges are similar, but the resulting geometry is much more smooth when compared to polygons. This "smoothness" is directly related to the Bézier technology built into patches.

The vertices of a patch have *Bézier tangent handles*, very similar to the Bézier splines that you can create within MAX. The handles control the overall curvature of the patch around the area of the vertex. By manipulating the vertex's handles, you can alter the shape of the patch from that corner. An important note about Bézier handle control, though: By default, MAX will lock the handles on either side of the vertex to provide consistent tangency. This behavior is very similar to NURBS. The main difference is that you can break the tangency in patches—creating a sharp edge at the vertex. Figures 1.11 and 1.12, respectively, show a patch model before and after breaking tangency. Notice the obvious seam where the vertex point is broken. To break tangency, just hold down the Shift key while moving a handle.

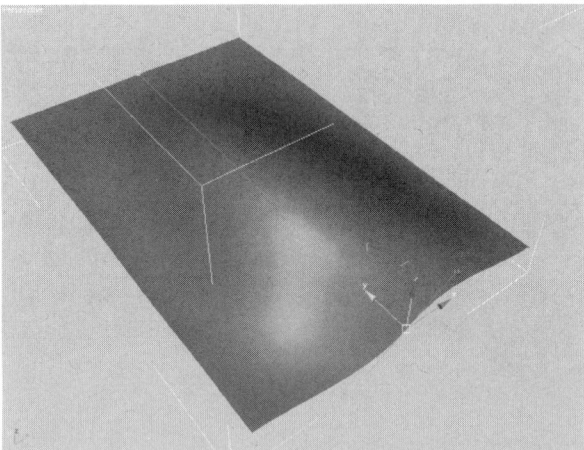

Figure 1.11 A patch where the vertex tangents remain constant. This provides a nice, flowing surface through the vertex point. Contrast this with the broken tangents depicted in Figure 1.12.

You use edges of patches to alter the shape of a patch along a specific edge or to define where you want to add patches onto the existing patch. This is primarily how patches work—by propagation. By adding adjoining patches to existing patches, you can easily build complex surfaces.

Patches themselves can be defined by either a quadrilateral surface or by a triangular patch. *Triangular patches* work best for corners or places where a patch surface may need to come to a peak. For general-purpose usage, however, a *Quadrilateral patch*, or *Quad Patch*, works best.

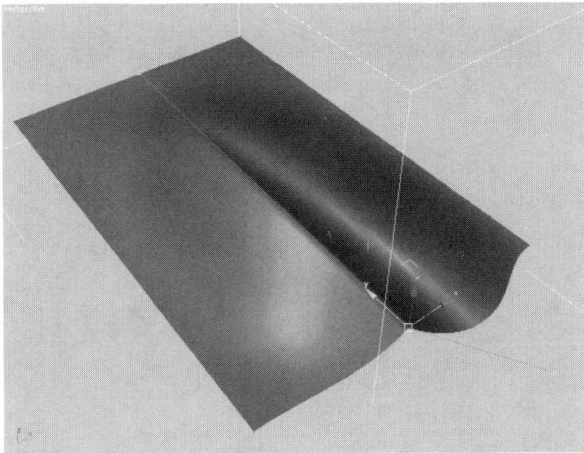

Figure 1.12 The same patch object as in Figure 1.11 with the tangencies broken on one vertex. The end result is a seam or crease at the vertex extending outward into the patch.

Tessellation and Surface Approximation

A feature that both Patches and NURBS surfaces share is their ability to have relatively low-detail models in the viewports and then render high-detail versions. This feature, called *Tessellation* for patches and *Surface Approximation* for NURBS surfaces, allows you to specify both the viewport quality and rendering quality of a model independently. This makes building and editing both patch and NURBS surfaces very easy—yet detailed enough for rendering.

Note
Tessellation is a technology whereby polygons are subdivided into smaller polygons where the end result usually is a smoother surface due to a higher polygon count.

You may be asking, "Tessellation—on patches and NURBS?" You've been told that patches and NURBS don't use polygons in modeling, so why is there a tessellation setting to control the number of faces? The answer is actually quite simple. Patches and NURBS both use their respective technologies for creating and representing your 3D model in a wireframe view. However, when the model needs to be represented in a shaded mode, either in the viewport or rendered window, the patch or NURBS surface needs to be "converted" into faces for it to render properly. Your model is still a patch or

NURBS surface, it's just converted at rendering time so that the renderer can shade it properly. The Tessellation or Surface Approximation setting in MAX allows you to control the amount of complexity for the conversion from patch or NURBS to polygons when MAX renders. The whole reason for this process happening is that the default MAX scanline renderer is only capable of rendering polygonal objects. Therefore everything needs to be converted prior to the rendering.

Figure 1.13 shows the settings for Tessellation for patch objects. By default, patches use the Step Settings value, called Fixed, to control the detail level. This is the easiest setting to change, but it suffers from the drawback that the detail level must be reflected in the viewport and the renderer. In complex patch models, this can degrade interactive performance quite significantly.

You can refer to the MAX documentation for the exact meaning of each of the settings, but here's a basic breakdown of how the different options work:

- **Fixed:** Uses the Steps setting (in the Topology area of the Geometry rollout) to control the detail level. This is best for quick and easy detail settings. The lower the number of steps, the less detail is needed. Each increase of the Steps setting creates an extra row and column of quad faces in the patch.
- **Regular:** Tessellates a patch just like the Tessellate Modifier does to meshes. Increasing the numbers in the U and V fields will result in higher detail patches. This option, while less controllable than the remaining options, does afford you independent U and V (length and width) tessellation, something that Fixed does not do.
- **Parametric:** Gives you U and V control just like Regular, but actually tessellates nearly twice as much, resulting in a higher detailed model. For more information about UV coordinates, refer to "Part II: Materials" later in this book.
- **Spatial:** Tessellates the model based on edge length set in the Edge field. The lower the number, the more faces are

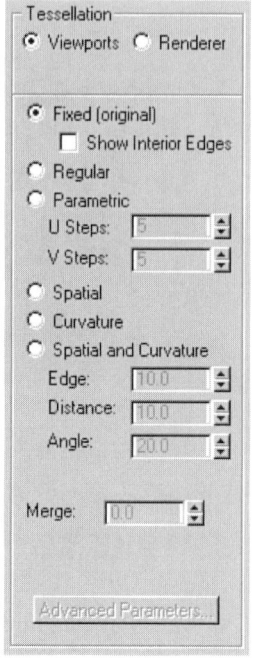

Figure 1.13 The default settings for the Rendering tessellation of a patch model. Depending on the final model, you may want to tweak these settings to use the Spatial or Curvature settings to produce a smoother patch at render time.

added. Note that this setting will alter the number of faces over time if the patch is animated. If your model is stretching, twisting, or just moving in general, then this setting may have adverse effects on your model because faces "pop" on and off depending on the edge distance on a given frame. This is really only a problem if the face counts are low and adding more detail is easy. On higher face counts, this is less of an issue and you usually can't tell.

- **Curvature:** Tessellates the model based on the angle of adjacent faces to each other. More curvature means more faces. While subject to the face-popping issue like Spatial, it usually produces better results because it adds detail only where needed—in the curvaceous places. However, it doesn't allow you to control the amount of detail given a specific distance from edge to edge.

- **Spatial & Curvature:** This combines the features of both the spatial and curvature tessellation methods, giving you the most control. With this option, you not only have the ability to tessellate based on curvature, but also to add tessellation based on edge length. Like both of the previous methods, Spatial & Curvature can change face count based on the animation. The combination does greatly reduce the problem of face popping, though, while still providing you the best tessellation. The only hitch: slightly longer rendering times.

Note

Fixed or Regular form a basic grid pattern and may or may not put the detail where needed to represent the curves. Spatial and Curvature put the detail where needed, giving the benefits of a smooth approximation of the curve, without the burden of extra faces where not needed.

Patch Modeling Uses

Patches can be used to model mostly smooth surfaces. While patch modeling can handle edges very easily, edge- and angle-heavy modeling is best suited for polygons. Creating organic shapes is very easy. For the most part, you need to think about building patch-based objects from a center point outward. Through patch propagation, simply add more and more patches as you build outward. Eventually, you end up with a smooth-flowing surface with no seams.

NEW TO R3 New additions to MAX R3 are the Cross Section and Surface modifiers. These two modifiers, originally part of a plug-in called Surface Tools, give you an incredible amount of new modeling flexibility with patches. As a matter of fact, they actually make patches useable.

Surface Tools

Surface Tools, now a part of MAX R3, takes patch modeling to new levels. If you have never worked with the plug-in, then you haven't seen the complete capabilities of patches. Using Surface Tools is a three-step operation:

1. Create shapes representing the cross sections.
2. Apply the Cross Section modifier to connect the cross sections.
3. Apply the Surface modifier to wrap a patch surface on the cross sections.

Once you have these basics down, patch modeling with Surface Tools will be the only way you'll want to model. Figure 1.14 demonstrates how complex a model can be with patches and the Surface Tools modifiers.

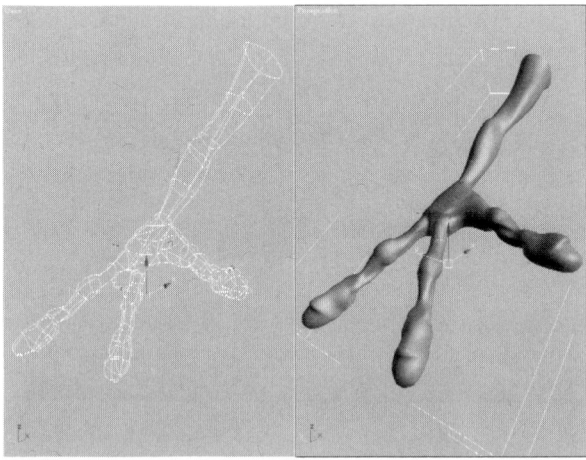

Figure 1.14 This figure represents a hand from a creature that was modeled using patches via the Surface Tools features of MAX R3.

Editable Patch

NEW TO R3 Editable Patch, depicted in Figure 1.15, is new for MAX R3. While you could collapse a patch in MAX R2 after applying the Edit Patch modifier, you couldn't directly collapse a patch to an Editable Patch object. Much like Editable Mesh, Editable Patch allows you to easily get at the building blocks of a patch object. Also like Editable Mesh, it enables you to reduce memory overhead by collapsing a patch down to an Editable Patch.

Discreet made a smart move with Editable Patch in that it now functions like Editable Mesh. The user interface is familiar and doesn't change when you switch Sub-Object modes. All you have to do now is pick the type of element you want to edit—patch, edge, or vertex—and you're off and running. Like with Editable Mesh, MAX grays out the commands that aren't valid for a particular Editable Patch mode.

You typically use Editable Patch on a model assembled with the Surface Tools modifier, and then collapsed. So once you have the basic shape of the model using Surface Tools, you can further tweak the model using Editable Patch. Exercise 1.3 walks you through a sample of how you might model using patches.

Exercise 1.3   Creating the Bony Hand for the Grim Reaper

1. Start 3D Studio MAX, and open the file 01max03.max from the CD-ROM.
2. Select the circle nearest the viewpoint, and go to the Modify panel.
3. Click the Edit Spline button to apply the Edit Spline modifier.
4. Click the Attach button in the Geometry section of the Edit Spline parameters, and click each circle in order from front to back. Make sure not to skip a circle; they must be attached in sequential order.
5. When the circles are all attached, click the More button in the Modify panel and select the Cross Section modifier. This will connect your circles through the vertex points using four separate splines.
6. Set the type of cross section to Bézier.
7. Click the More button again and scroll down to the Surface modifier. Select Surface to apply a patch surface to your spline objects.
8. Turn on the Remove Interior Patches feature.
9. Click the Edit Patch button in the Modify panel to apply the modifier. Click the Vertex button to change to Vertex Sub-Object mode.
10. Using the Move and Scale commands, shape the cylinder into a bone segment, as depicted in Figure 1.16.

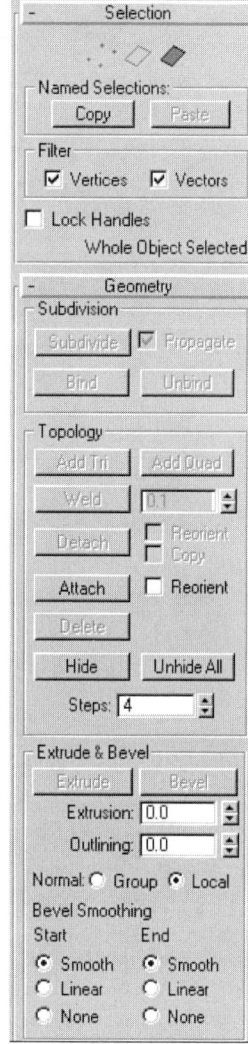

Figure 1.15 The geometry editing section of the Editable Patch object. Editable Patch works in a similar manner to the Edit Patch modifier, except for the fact that it exists at the base level instead of somewhere in the stack.

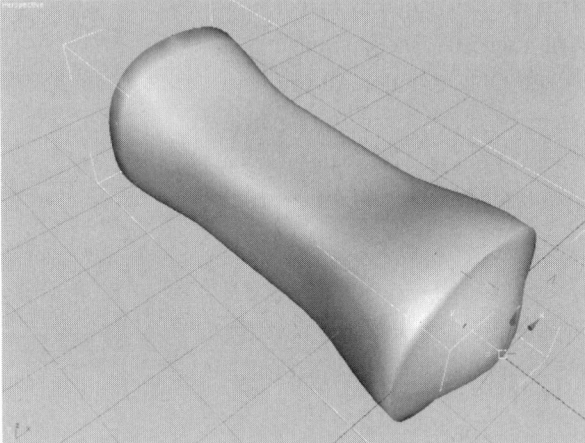

Figure 1.16 The finger bone segment created in Steps 1–10. The rounded ends are created through subdividing the end patches one time and pulling out the middle vertex slightly.

 Tip
To get the rounded ends, you need to switch to Patch editing mode and subdivide the end patch one time. That will create a vertex in the center, which you can pull out to create the rounded edge on both ends.

11. Click the Sub-Object button to exit Sub-Object editing mode.
12. Clone the bone two times on the Y-axis, by holding down the Shift key and using the Move command. Make sure to make the copies so that they don't overlap each other and that they're made going away from your viewpoint.
13. Select the bone segment farthest from you, and switch to Vertex editing mode.
14. In the Top viewport, select half the vertices and move them in Y toward the center to shorten the fingertip length. If you'd like, you can even make it a bit fatter to look more like a tip. The final result should look something like Figure 1.17.
15. Click the Select and Link button in the Main Toolbar tab of the Tab Panel.
16. Click and drag from the fingertip bone to the middle bone to link the two. Repeat the process, this time going from the middle bone to the base bone. You now have a simple hierarchy from which to build.
17. With a little more work, you could clone four more fingers and adjust them to make a bony hand. Instead, from the Display panel, choose Unhide All to reveal the rest of the hand provided for you. Adjust your middle finger to match the rest. Figure 1.18 shows the complete bony hand.
18. From the Edit menu, choose Select All. Then choose Group from the Group pull-down menu. Name the group "Bony Hand."
19. Save the completed file. You'll need the completed file for later in this chapter.

Chapter 1: Modeling Concepts   29

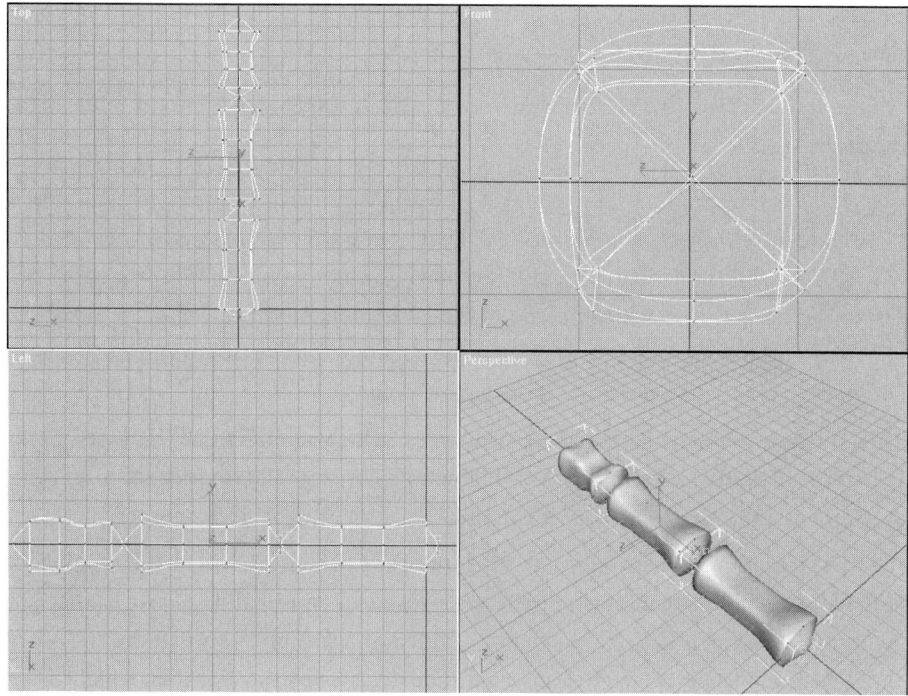

Figure 1.17 The bony middle finger completed, using three independent patch objects.

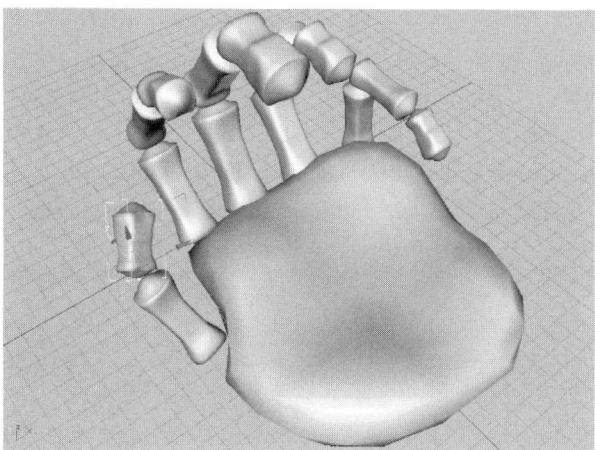

Figure 1.18 The completed bony hand which will be used later in this chapter to complete the Grim Reaper model.

For a twist to the exercise, try curling the hand as in Figure 1.18. This will help you later when you have the Grim Reaper grasp the sickle.

NEW TO R3   This exercise was intended to show you a few new features that have been introduced for patches in MAX R3. More specifically:

- The Cross Section modifier connects the spline elements in a spline-based object. The process is fairly straightforward. First, create a series of closed or open splines with similar vertex counts. Second, attach them together in sequential order using the Attach command of the Edit Spline modifier. Third, apply the Cross Section modifier. Be careful of the alignment of the first vertex, as this is how Cross Section determines its starting point.

  The four spline types available in the Cross Section modifier determine what types of vertices are created at each juncture. For smoother models, choose Smooth or Bézier. For sharper corners, choose Corner or Bézier corner.

- The Surface modifier wraps a patch surface across a properly sectioned spline object. Note that you don't have to use Cross Section to build the proper shape, but it does help. The only catch for Surface to work properly is that the enclosure where you want a patch to appear must be divisible by three or four, which means you need at minimum three vertices to define a closed surface. Numbers such as five vertices will produce uncapped holes—basically nonexistent patches.

Patch Modeling Shortcomings

With the addition of Surface Tools, the shortcomings of patch modeling have been significantly reduced. The whole process of patch modeling just requires a different way of thinking. Rather than dealing with faces and vertices, you're really working with edges and their tangent relationships. In that sense, many traditional polygonal modelers have a difficult time giving up their explicit control of faces. This limitation is, however, pretty insignificant given what you get in return.

NURBS Modeling

Perhaps the most popular modeling technology to come around has been *NURBS modeling*. NURBS is an acronym for Non-Uniform Rational B-Spline. Simply put, NURBS excels at smooth surfaces, but can also do sharp edges very well. These days, everyone seems to be using NURBS to build their 3D models—from characters to cars. Like patches, NURBS allows you to create complex detail that is rendered but not necessarily displayed in the viewports. This means that both the construction and editing of NURBS surfaces is fairly straightforward. Figure 1.19 shows a model built with NURBS surfaces.

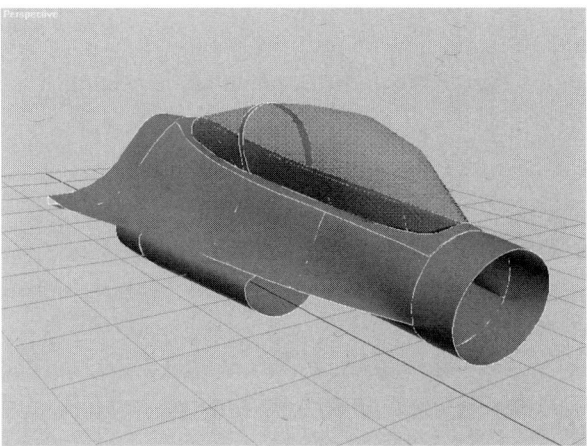

Figure 1.19 The cockpit area of an F-16 modeled with NURBS surfaces. Special thanks to Yoi Hibino of Discreet Japan for the model.

Surfaces, Curves, Points, and CVs

NURBS surfaces are defined by a series of curves and control points. Depending on the type of surface or curve you use, your editing capabilities differ somewhat. Let's first start by talking about the different curves and their control points.

NURBS curves can be defined by either *points* or *CVs* (control vertices). The closest comparison for points is vertices. Points lie on the curve itself and directly control the shape of the curve. CVs are a bit different. Instead of lying directly on a curve, CVs are part of a lattice that acts more like a magnet. As you move the CVs on the lattice around on a NURBS curve, they push and pull on the curve, itself. CVs also have weights that control the influence of the CV on the curve. All CVs have independent weights that can be edited both in a static nature and over time. Figure 1.20 shows the difference between a Point curve and a CV curve.

Curves can act as the building blocks of a NURBS surface. However, you can also build straight NURBS surfaces much like patches. You can create either a point surface or a CV surface, and determining which one you use depends on how you like to model. CVs act more like pressing on a lump of clay to shape it. Points act more like applying pinpoint pressure on a gel-filled object. Manipulating a point will affect both that point as well as the immediate surrounding areas. As you can see from Figure 1.20, moving a point on a point surface directly affects the surrounding areas of the surface. A CV surface behaves a bit differently. Not only does the CV need to be pulled much higher, it also doesn't have the same affect on the surrounding areas as the point does. The CV surface tends to "gravitate" to the CV. The point surface seems to push and pull from the point that was moved.

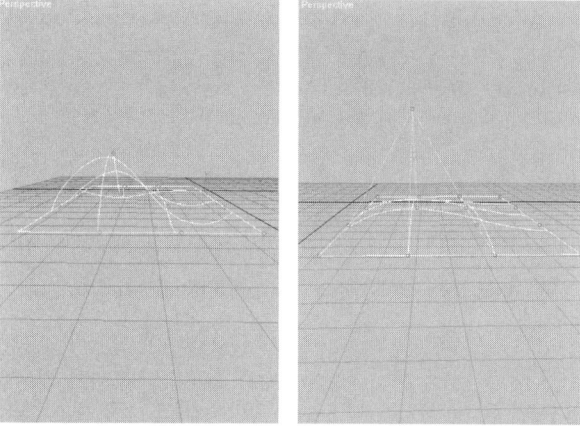

Figure 1.20 A PointSurf primitive on the left versus a CVSurf primitive on the right. Notice how the control points on the point surface act more like vertices where the points on the CV surface act more like magnetic attractors that pull or push on the surface depending on their distance from the surface.

NURBS Modeling Uses

If you can dream it, you can build it using NURBS, although it takes a little time to get used to NURBS concepts. The primary benefit of NURBS is that it has the modeling and editing flexibility of a polygonal model, but doesn't rely on complex meshes for detailed surfaces. In this respect, it's much like patch modeling. You model by simply using curves to define surfaces. Those surfaces look rather low detail in the viewports, but can render at a much higher level of complexity. Simply put, there are fewer points to deal with during modeling than in a polygon model.

Many animators use NURBS to build characters, primarily because NURBS gives you both smooth, contoured surfaces and keeps mesh detail relatively low. Characters tend to be very complex, so using NURBS can significantly increase performance versus the same model in polygonal form.

Chapter 1: Modeling Concepts 33

Note

As recently as two years ago, many animators would argue that realistic characters could only be created with NURBS. However, with MAX offering powerful tools in each of the three schools of modeling—polygons, patches, and NURBS—you need not feel pressured to use one technique over another. If you are most confident with polygonal modeling, you can build a relatively low-detail character and add detail at the end with MeshSmooth, as you did in Exercise 1.1. As you saw in Exercise 1.3, MAX's new patch tools (Surface Tools) provide an easy way to build a smooth-skinned model with a spline frame and patch control points. As explained in the next exercise, NURBS provides a powerful method of creating smooth models, by giving you high-powered tools (such as Sweeps and UV-Lofts). If you find yourself frustrated with one method, by all means, stay with the one you prefer.

Car manufacturers seem to be in love with aerodynamic shapes. Have you noticed how many smooth-looking cars are on the road these days? Much of this stems from the manufacturers adopting CAD design packages that model with NURBS technology. With NURBS, you can model in a free-form like method, but also have accuracy and flexibility. Because of its flexibility with NURBS, MAX is a great front-end conceptual tool and even better back-end tool for post-production renderings.

Exercise 1.4 Creating the Cape and Hood of the Grim Reaper

1. Start or reset 3D Studio MAX and load 01max04.max from the CD-ROM.
2. This file contains two NURBS curve objects, one curve for the hood, and a series of three curves for the robe. Let's start by making the body. Select the Robe object, and go to the Modify panel.
3. Click the NURBS Creation Toolbox button in the General section of the NURBS Surface object. Select the Create U-Loft Surface button.
4. Move the cursor over the bottom curve until it turns blue, then click it. Move the cursor to the middle curve, which will turn blue, then click it. A surface will connect the curves. Repeat the process from the middle curve to the top curve.
5. Click the Create Cap Surface button in the NURBS Creation Toolbox, then select the top curve in the viewport to cap off the robe.
6. Select the Hood object next. While holding down the Shift key, use the Move command to copy the hood object back slightly on the Y-axis, about 15 to 20 units. Make five copies when the Clone Options dialog appears.
7. Click the Attach Multiple button in the Modify panel. In the Attach Multiple dialog, select all the curves listed, and then click Attach.
8. Click the Sub-Object button and select Curve selection level.
9. Using Move and Scale, transform the curves so they create a drooping hood effect. Refer to Figure 1.21 for reference.
10. Switch to Point selection and move the points (as in Figure 1.21) to create an irregular shape.

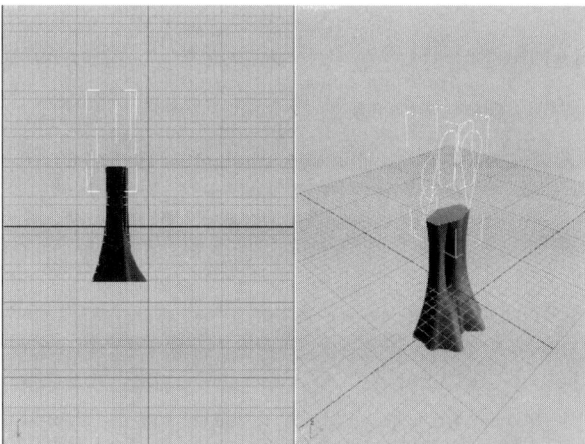

Figure 1.21 The robe is completed with the proper shapes and alignments for the curves that will soon become the hood of the grim reaper.

11. If the NURBS Creation Toolbox is closed, reopen it by leaving Sub-Object mode and clicking the NURBS Creation Toolbox button in the Modify panel.

12. Click the U-Loft button in the toolbox. Starting from the front of the hood, click each curve, in succession, from the front to the back. If you make a mistake, either undo and start over or rearrange the curve order in the Modify panel.

 Note

When working or building at the Curve level of a NURBS object, name the curves to make it easier to distinguish each one.

13. After completing the hood, all that's left for the illusion of a figure is to create a cape. This is easily done with a PointSurf primitive. Start by clicking the Create panel.

14. Select NURBS surfaces from the Geometry category in the Create panel or select the Objects tab in the Tab panel, then click the PointSurf button. If you decide to skip the creation of the cape, simply go to the Display panel and Select Unhide All to unhide the cape object.

15. Click and drag out a surface about 180 units long and 180 units wide with both Length and Width at 5 points.

16. Go to the Modify panel, and select Sub-Object mode. Switch to Point editing level. Now you're on your own to create the cape just as you want it. Refer to Figure 1.22 for a completed version. Take note of the locations of the points and the shape of the cape in the wireframe views. When you like your cape, move on to Step 17.

17. You still have a few final steps to make the reaper look complete. You need to add in the objects you created in the earlier exercises and also apply materials. Select Merge from the File pulldown menu. Choose the file you saved as the hand in Exercise 1.3. (You can also load bony_hand.max from the CD-ROM.)
18. When the Merge dialog box appears, choose All of the Geometry and then click Merge.
19. Use the Move, Rotate, and Scale commands to position the hand into place. If you created the hand similar to the example, you first need to move the hand object to the left hand position.
20. Next, use the Mirror command in the Main Toolbar to mirror the hand on the X-axis. If you prefer, make a copy so that you can edit it independently.
21. Use the Merge command again to merge in the sickle you created at the beginning of this chapter, or just merge the sickle.max file from the CD-ROM.
22. Again, use Move, Rotate, and Scale to position the sickle in the left or right hand.
23. Save the file.

You're done! Pat yourself on the back because you managed to use all three main modeling technologies to create a single character. Your finished model should look like something similar to Figure 1.22. You can also load the final model, called "grim reaper.max" from the CD-ROM.

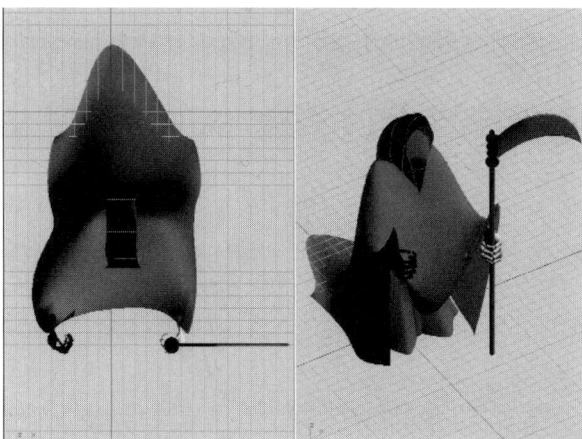

Figure 1.22 The completed Grim Reaper model that uses patches, polygons, and NURBS to produce the entire model.

NURBS Modeling Shortcomings

When speaking of shortcomings of NURBS models, it's difficult to point out serious problems. NURBS models, for all intents and purposes, work in almost every situation. However, there is one area where NURBS just can't compete with polygons—simplicity.

NURBS models are designed to eventually be complex. If you build a foundation based on complexity, you've already set the stage to rule out any type of simple modeling. For instance, if you model a box, copy it, and then convert one to a polygonal mesh and the other to a NURBS surface, you might be surprised. The polygonal mesh is 8 faces. The NURBS box is 34. That means that a simple NURBS model, such as a box, already has over four times as many faces as the polygon version.

> **Note**
> MAX R2.5 introduced a feature called Transform Degrade that forces the currently edited NURBS object to shut off all surfaces, so you can manipulate CVs, points, or curves. This will help when editing complex models, but you may want to disable it when editing more simple objects. The checkbox for Transform Degrade is located at the object level of any NURBS object under Display in the General rollout.

NEW TO R3 MAX R3 introduces NURBS Tessellation presets easily accessible via keyboard shortcuts as another way to simplify your NURBS work. Also, there is an option for Shaded Lattice under Surface Display in the NURBS General rollout.

Aside from the complexity issue, it's very difficult to extrude sections of a model at right angles with NURBS. For the most part, NURBS models want to have curvature. That means that even if a model looks like it has right angles, close inspection shows that it does, in fact, have some smoothness around the edges.

For most MAX users, the biggest issue they have with NURBS is its interface. Put simply, it isn't pretty. It also isn't streamlined, whereas the Editable Patch and the Editable Mesh interfaces are more simplified. This can increase your learning curve, but some find it well worth the extra effort.

Scripted Modeling

While not a technology in itself, *scripted modeling* is a powerful way to build and edit models in MAX. All the commands necessary to create, modify, and execute scripts are accessed through a feature called MAXScript. You can access MAXScript through the MAXScript pulldown menu (see Figure 1.23) in the top toolbar.

Scripting has come a long way since Release 2. As a matter of fact, if you haven't learned scripting yet, you're really missing a powerful and fun component of MAX. We'll talk about modeling using scripts here, but look for tips on using scripting for both materials and rendering later in the book. Let's take a look at some of the myths about scripting:

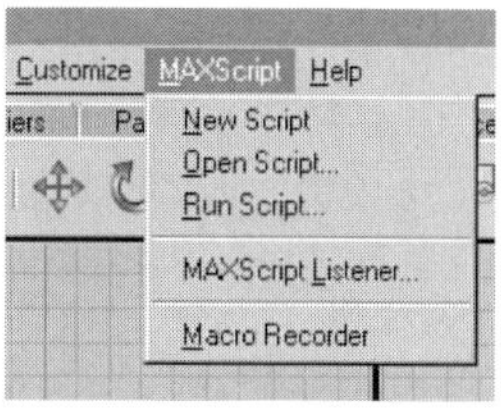

Figure 1.23 The new MAXScript pull-down menu. You no longer have to go to the Utility panel to access, run, and edit your scripts.

- **Myth 1—Scripting is a macro language.** This is both true and false. It's true because you can record nearly every operation in MAX and turn it into a script, a button, or embed it within another script. It's also false, because scripting is not in any way limited to just macro recording.

- **Myth 2—Scripting is not for the mathematically challenged.** Not true. Scripting works more from logic than math. Knowing what happens if you click A versus B is more important than $(A\div B)\times C^2$. Granted, math is nice to know, but it is not a requirement for using MAXScript.

- **Myth 3—You need to be a programmer.** Absolutely not true. What you need to be is a visionary artist, a person who looks at the tools in front of you and determines how to get maximum use from each one. MAXScript is a way to combine your favorite tools into a single powerful feature that suits your needs and makes you more productive. This kind of thinking isn't just for the programming types—anyone can do it.

With those myths dispelled, it's no secret that learning anything new takes a little time. MAXScript does require some amount of ramp-up time, but once you've learned a little, learning the rest is easy. Let's put those three myths to the test, though.

Using the Command Line

NEW TO R3

You may have noticed that there's now a command line in MAX R3. If you don't see it, grab the vertical bar aligned with the left side of the prompt area in the lower part of the interface and drag it right. You should see two color-coded regions, as shown in Figure 1.24. The pink area is MAXScript's feedback area where the program displays events it "sees" happening within MAX and MAXScript. It's also the area where you look when you record a macro. The white area is the user input area where you enter in your own commands.

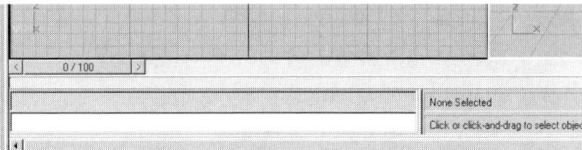

Figure 1.24 The new command line interface in the lower part of the MAX interface. You can choose to use this interface instead of the main MAXScript Listener window (see Figure 1.25) to minimize screen real estate usage.

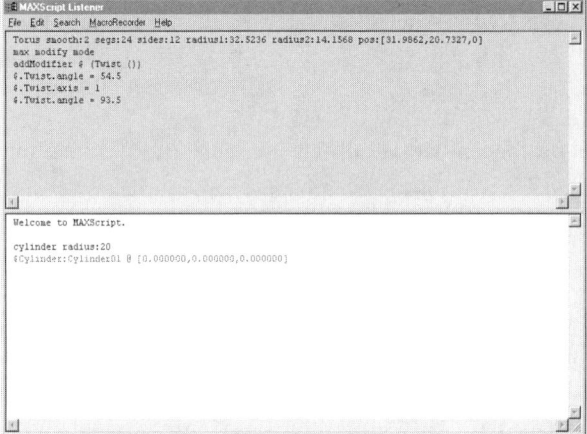

Figure 1.25 The new MAXScript Listener window. Notice the window is now divided into two parts. The upper part records Macro data that you use to create custom scripts. The lower part mimics the old style MAXScript Listener where you type in commands and get feedback from MAXScript as well.

Determining a Starting Point

Now that you're more familiar with the modeling technologies within MAX R3, it's time to start modeling! Wait a minute, though. Where do you start? There are a few things to consider when you're building a model.

- **What's the easiest way to build this model?** There are so many ways to model in MAX that you can usually approach a modeling problem from many different angles. Determining which one is based mainly on your knowledge of the software. For instance, do you feel comfortable modeling with NURBS, or perhaps MAXScript?

- **Which modeling technology will work the best?** Depending on the situation, you need to evaluate which modeling type works best. Polygonal modeling works best for low detail or more rigid-looking models, but with MeshSmooth, improvements can now be used for more organic shapes. Patches and NURBS work well for more complex and organic models. Scripted modeling can go beyond simple object creation and editing.

- **What's the final output supposed to be?** If your model is going to be examined either in a still frame or very closely during the course of an animation, you either want to take the complex modeling approach or use high-resolution bitmaps for textures. For models that are either moving quickly through a frame of animation or are in the distance, lower detail should be your thinking.

After you've considered these things, you can begin to figure out how to model your design. At this point, you've also probably given some thought to which modeling process you want to use. It may be polygonal, NURBS, or some combination. Whatever the case, you need to figure out which place on your model is the right place to start.

To determine a good starting point, ask yourself, "Where is my foundation?" For an architectural design, it's often the actual foundation, or at least a floorplan. Rarely would you start to build a house by constructing the roof—unless you're designing a country house in Japan. For a character, you usually start at the center of gravity and work outward. For a mechanical design, you often start with the smaller, essential components and build outward. Whatever your situation calls for, starting from some foundation point for modeling is the most sure-fire way to begin the process.

The Right Modeling Method for the Job

So far, this chapter has discussed quite a bit about the four different modeling methods available in MAX. You have all these choices. So how do you choose the right modeling technology for your object?

Choosing Polygons

These are the key points to remember about using polygons:

- Great for low detail.
- Great for architectural models.
- High-detail meshes equal more computer resource usage.
- Not good for low-detail organic meshes.
- Apply MeshSmooth to add detail and soften the edges of your polygonal model.

Choosing Patches

When working with patches, the following are several points of interest about them:

- Great for smooth or organic surfaces modeling.
- Works well for most complex models.
- Requires a "building-out" mentality.
- Variable level detail through surface approximation feature.

Choosing NURBS

The following are highlights of this choice:

- Nearly a catch-all for modeling.
- Works great for high-detail smooth models.
- Building-block mentality. Start with simple shapes and construct more complex surfaces from them.
- Does not work well for more rigid-looking surfaces.

Choosing Scripted Modeling

The key points when considering scripting are as follows:

- Has incredible extensibility.
- Best for repetitive tasks.
- Offers the ability to combine polygons, patches, and NURBS in one interface.
- Has significant learning curve for new users.
- The Macro Recorder automatically creates scripts and simplifies repetitive tasks. Simply execute the macro.

Where to Start

There are several ways to approach a modeling task. What you feel the most comfortable with is almost always the answer. That, of course, just comes from experience. If you have limited experience modeling, it's a good bet that there are better ways to create them than what you are currently using.

So what are those better ways? Well, it depends largely on what you're building. For simple, low-detail objects, your obvious choice should be a primitive as your start shape. That way, you're already starting out with a low face count.

In reality, you always start from some sort of simple shape. (Although it would be nice to have a "make-a-really-complex-model" button!) Choosing primitives or choosing shapes are your choices. If you work with primitives, you already have a 3D object. If you start with 2D shapes, you have a little more work to do, but it's actually easier to create very complex objects in the end. In the next section, choosing shapes or primitives becomes more obvious when you know what the foundation of your model is.

Base Points

A *base point* is really the starting point of your model. Knowing (or at least guessing) your start point helps determine the shape or object with which to begin. For instance, it's much easier to create an eyeball using a sphere primitive as your base than to use a shape. In contrast, to create a soda pop bottle, you'd use a profile shape of a bottle and lathe it to create the 3D model. Some people might attack the bottle problem by shaping a cylinder object. While both work, it's much easier to lathe a profile and then manipulate the resulting 3D shape rather than twisting and scaling a cylinder.

Throughout this book, the term "building out" is used. Essentially, this means that you build from your base point rather than from some arbitrary point. Almost all modelers have their favorite base point, depending on the model. For a character, it might be the torso; for a spaceship, it might be the hull. Building out is easy for several reasons:

- **Building out gives your model a sense of scale from the very beginning.** By defining the base point size, you set the stage for sizing the rest of the model.

- **Building out forces you to think a little about the model and how it will be built rather than "shooting from the hip"—only to discover that you're going in the wrong direction.** By giving a little thought to how the model will be built, you'll save yourself a great deal of time down the road. While this may sound a bit restrictive, it actually becomes second nature the more you create things in MAX.

- **Building out keeps detail in check.** Because you build from a base point of relatively low detail, you find yourself automatically adding detail only where and when you need it. This helps keep the face count down, as well as disproportional detail levels.

Material Application Considerations

When you are constructing your model, an important item to keep in mind is how the materials will be applied to the model. There are really four approaches to applying materials to a model:

- **Model the faces or seams so they match material boundaries.** For instance, you might create a visible neckline in the model because that's where you want the clothing to stop and the skin to begin.
- **Create separate objects for each of the respective materials.** That way, you can precisely and individually control the material and mapping.
- **Create a single bitmap for each material that contains the various elements needed to map to the entire piece of a model.** A wing of a jet, for instance, could have a single map applied to it that consists of the flaps, ailerons, and weathering marks without having to break the material down piece by piece, especially if you're never going to see the components up close or moving.
- **Use MAX's Material Editor to combine multiple decals into a single material that gets applied to the entire model.** Using the eyeball example before, you could have a separate map for the eyeball and the iris, which could be composited using a composite-map type in the map channel.

The first two options are used by almost all modelers, but more frequently by novice modelers because they are more tangible. Working in the Material Editor to control how the material will be applied can often be too difficult a concept to grasp.

The latter two usually result in lower detail objects, but require more up-front work with the Material Editor and some sort of paint and image editing tool. In the end, you'll need to choose which method is more comfortable for you. Just remember that almost all modelers live by the creed that "less is more."

In Practice: Modeling Concepts

- **Polygonal modeling excels at low detail or architectural models.** Because polygonal models are made up of faces, they're very easy to edit and animate when you're working on a relatively low-detail model.
- **Patch modeling is for smooth models that are built from the foundation outward.** Patch modeling works by attaching small grids, called patches, which are based on Bézier-spline technology. This provides for smooth surfaces with relatively low-detail geometry in the viewports.

- **NURBS modeling works best for complex, smooth, or organic surfaces.** Because NURBS models are just as smooth as patches, they work well for complex models. Unlike patches, NURBS surfaces can be built from defining curves that allow construction of your surfaces based on simple objects instead of small patches.

- **Scripted modeling can help automate tedious tasks.** Use scripting when you need to do a repetitive task or something that would normally take a long time through traditional modeling methods. This could be a completely new modeling technique, like your own metaballs script!

- **Use combinations of all three for best results.** While using each modeling technology separately works well, using a combination of all three can often produce the best results. Since patch and NURBS surfaces are close in their behavior, there's no need to use both at the same time. More than likely, once you get comfortable with NURBS, you'll leave patch modeling behind.

Chapter 2

Architectural Modeling

Offering only the parametric door and window Extended primitives and the Terrain Compound object, 3D Studio MAX R3 is lean on specific architectural features.

Note

You should be aware that Discreet produces another software package called 3D Studio VIZ, which is specifically intended for the architectural and mechanical industry. MAX R3 is a broad general-purpose system, but leans on tools specific to architectural renderings. VIZ is a lower-priced little brother to MAX, specifically designed for architectural renderings. The exercises in the chapter teach modeling techniques that apply to both programs, but VIZ offers some improved tools to get the job done more quickly.

With a little ingenuity you can use MAX R3 to create complex, easily edited building components. In this chapter, you learn actual modeling techniques for constructing buildings and other architectural elements, as well as learn some modeling concepts that make you more productive at render time. The following are some of the areas we cover in Chapter 2:

- Conceptual architectural modeling
- Level of detail
- Wall systems
- Roofs
- Doors and windows
- Space frames

Think Before You Work

Modeling in MAX R3 is only part of the equation. You must model efficiently to be productive in a working environment. Efficient modeling refers to models with a minimum of faces and vertices for a given detail level.

Another issue addressed in most architectural offices is how MAX R3 integrates with AutoCAD. While the functionality of AutoCAD and MAX R3 are converging, the programs are designed for completely different purposes and there are potential problems with sharing data. Knowing when to use each program is as important as knowing its features.

Developing a MAX R3/AutoCAD Strategy

One of the most important steps in integrating 3D Studio MAX R3 into an architectural office is analyzing the way your office works. Look at the talent available, the quality of AutoCAD work that is produced, and your visualization needs. Perhaps your office benefits most from a staff that models quickly and accurately in 3D with AutoCAD and exports the models to Max R3. That, however, makes them difficult to edit. Maybe a better approach is to export accurate 2D data from AutoCAD, which in turn allows 3D creation in Max R3 with flexible editing capabilities.

When to Model in MAX R3

There are a few rules of thumb to determine what objects are best created in MAX R3. These are general rules; you make the final decision by your company's workflow needs.

- **Soft objects.** Soft objects are not necessarily soft to the touch, but have softer, non-rectilinear edges and include furniture, rocks, trees, and hilly landscapes.
- **Bézier objects.** Objects with complex, compound curves or helical shapes, such as walks and paths, parking ramps, and retaining walls. MAX is especially important for objects that need materials aligned with their curvature. For example, a curving brick walkway created in MAX R3 can have mapping coordinates assigned during the lofting process to allow the bricks to follow the path. A walkway imported from AutoCAD does not have this capability.

When to Create in AutoCAD

It is often best to create models in AutoCAD, either 2D or 3D, when the following are present:

- **High accuracy is of prime importance.** MAX R3 creates to the nearest 1/100 of an inch, but the tools in AutoCAD create accurate architectural elements more quickly.
- **You have complex 3D-Boolean operations.** AutoCAD solid objects are efficient in Boolean operations. However, AutoCAD-Boolean operations also generate models with long thin faces, which present a problem in MAX R3.
- **You have access to third-party AutoCAD tools for accurate survey and highway design.** Autodesk Land Development Desktop and other third-party civil applications create 3D landscape and highways more efficiently.

Smoothing MAX/AutoCAD Transfers

Some of the problems encountered in the AutoCAD-to-MAX R3 data transfer are due to poor AutoCAD techniques, layer management, and lack of an understanding of the basics of how each program handles data. Some areas to concentrate on are shown on the following page.

- **Set up an AutoCAD layer system to integrate with MAX R3.** Freeze all text, dimension, symbols, and layers.
- **AutoCAD drawing techniques.** Draw with polylines, use Osnaps, avoid coincident lines, and avoid construction lines on working layers.
- **Elevation and Thickness settings on AutoCAD 2D drawings.** Avoid drawings with layers at one thickness and/or elevation and other layers at a different thickness/elevation, as they generate unwanted results.

Note
Appendix A details the nuts and bolts of importing AutoCAD files into MAX R3.

Starting Off

Before you model, make sure your scene is set up for your required degree of accuracy. MAX R3 contains a flexible grid system that allows you to change settings on the fly while retaining the required accuracy at all zoom levels. Always start a new scene with the following set to your requirements:

- Display Units
- Home Grid Spacing
- Snap settings

In the following exercises, you set up a scene with Units Setup, Home Grid Spacing, and Snap Settings. Adjust the settings in your work environment according to your needs.

Tip
This may appear to be a basic topic, but it is important enough for review.
If you are familiar with unit and grid settings and prototype scenes, you can skip these sections. Do not ignore the process, though, as it adds to productivity.

Display Units

Display Units in MAX R3 set the appearance of numeric values in display fields and is accessed through Units Setup in the Customize pull-down menu. Just as there are many equivalent ways in the real world to measure a distance, this setting in MAX determines the system you use to measure your virtual world. For example, a common wooden measuring stick is considered a length of 100 centimeters, 1 meter, 39.37 inches, 3.28 feet, or 3 feet 3-3/8 inches, to name a few. The numeric value represented by these numbers is the same—only the method of display is changed. Display Units are set before the Home Grid Spacing parameter. The steps are as follows:

1. From the Customize pull-down menu, click Units Setup. (See Figure 2.1.)
2. In the Units Setup dialog box (see Figure 2.2), pick US Standard, and choose Feet w/Fractional Inches from the list. Leave the other settings at default values, and click OK.

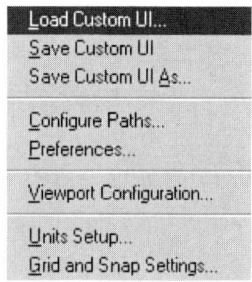

Figure 2.1 The Customize pull-down menu.

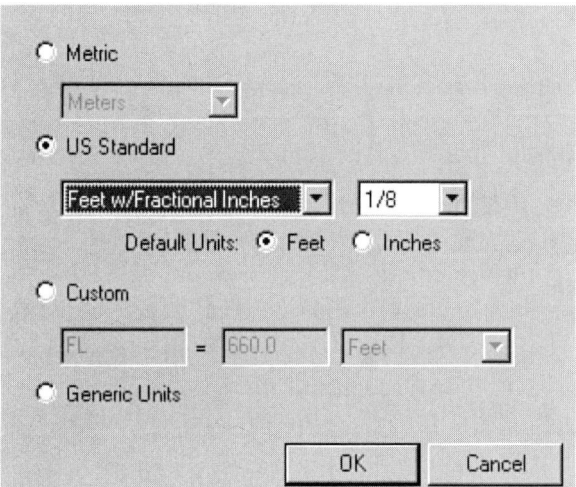

Figure 2.2 The Units Setup dialog box.

Home Grid Spacing

Once you have completed your Units Setup, you can set up the grid. From the Customize menu, choose Grid and Snap Settings. The setting you choose for the Grid Spacing parameter depends on the required accuracy and the necessary zoom level. The grid is dynamic so if you zoom in or out, the grid spacing adjusts by a factor set in the Major Lines Every Nth field. Start with a grid spacing that makes sense for the way you

50   Part I   Modeling

typically start a new scene. For example, residential work may start out at 1'0" spacing to rough out the wall outline, but it can be more flexible if you set the grid spacing to 0'1" and the Major Lines field to 12. This lets you zoom in to a one-inch grid spacing and zoom out to a one-foot spacing (1"×12), then out farther to a 12-foot spacing (1'×12). To set these, see the following:

1. In the Customize pull-down menu, click Grid and Snap Settings.
2. Click the Home Grid tab.
3. Enter 0'1" in the Grid Spacing field.
4. Enter 12 in the Major Lines Every Nth field.
5. Close the Grid and Snap Settings dialog. (See Figure 2.3.)

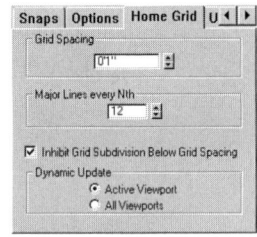

Figure 2.3 Grid and Snap Settings dialog box, Home Grid tab.

Notice that the Home Grid tab has a check box for Inhibit Grid Subdivision Below Grid Spacing. This works in conjunction with the Grid Spacing and the Major Lines Every Nth settings. If you zoom out of the Top viewport, for instance, note that the grid lines become denser until they jump to a new spacing. If you look at the bottom of the display, left of the Animate button, you see a current grid spacing field. Each time the grid spacing jumps, it is by the factor set by the Major Lines field. Using the above settings, the grid changes to 1', 12', 144', and so on.

The Inhibit Grid Subdivision Below Grid Spacing check box keeps the grid from jumping to less than 0'1".

Tip
You also access the Grid and Snap Settings dialog by right-clicking on the Snap, Angle Snap, or Percent Snap button at the bottom of the display.

Display Units Versus System Units

Setting the display units in MAX R3 converts the internal math to a format of your choice. There is also a setting in MAX R3 for the internal system unit scale. As Figure 2.4 shows, the setting is found in the General tab (choose Preferences from the Customize pull-down menu).

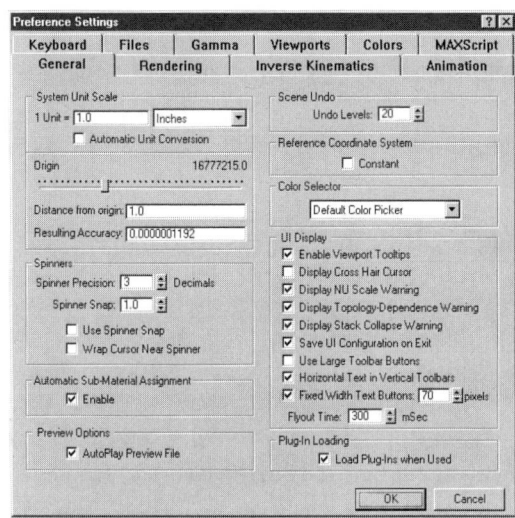

Figure 2.4 Preferences menu, General tab, and System Unit Scale.

The System Unit Scale setting is usually changed only if you are working in native metric units. However, if you work on scenes of very large or very small size, it's sometimes necessary to set the System Unit Scale for the viewports to handle the large or small numbers. For example, if you are working on a civil site of several miles by several miles, MAX R3 has problems creating objects or zooming in or out of the scene. In such a case, you want to try a System Unit Scale of 1 unit = 1 foot instead of the default of 1 unit = 1 inch. Conversely, if you are working on small mechanical parts, you want to set the System Unit Scale to 1 unit = 0.1 inch.

NEW TO R3

Note

MAX internally uses a type of computer mathematics known as single-precision, which provides a good balance between numeric precision and computer RAM usage. There is a resulting dependency between the size of your scene and the amount of precision you can achieve. For example, when placing a building in a 3D scene, you are possibly using state-plane coordinates provided on a surveyor's map. These numbers are notoriously large, sometimes showing distances in the millions of feet. If you construct your building model at about 10 miles from the origin, MAX is unable to accurately handle details smaller than a dime. A simple utility, the Accuracy Explorer, is provided in MAX to demonstrate this relationship and alert you to problems. Right below the System Unit setting in the Preferences General tab is a slider that moves through the range of MAX coordinate sizes. You see a distance from the origin and the corresponding accuracy as measured in the current units. If you find that you can't get the accuracy you need, move everything in the scene closer to the origin or cut the scene into smaller pieces.

Warning

Only change System Unit Scale when you know exactly why you are doing so. Notify everyone who handles the file that System Unit Scale has been changed to avoid any confusion. Objects merged into a scene with a different system-scale setting cause the merged objects to be too large or too small.

Prototype Scenes

You do not want to go through the process of entering the display units and Grid/Snap Settings each time you reset a file or start a new scene. Once you adjust the settings to your liking, use Save As in the File pull-down menu to save the empty file, with the name MAXSTART.MAX in the \3DSMAX R3\Scenes sub-directory. Subsequently, each time MAX R3 starts, it sees MAXSTART.MAX and pre-loads all the settings saved in that file.

Tip

If you have several prototype files you want to use, create WinNT desktop shortcuts to start MAX R3, with C:\3dsMAX R3\3dsmax.exe –o C:\path\filename.max to use any file with .max ending as a prototype. Be sure to include the spaces after '.exe' and 'o' or the shortcut won't work.

Object Naming

One of the most important aspects of setting up a production system is a well thought-out and documented object-naming scheme. All objects in MAX R3 are assigned default names upon creation, but you quickly get lost if you accept these default names. Following are several helpful aids:

- Important objects are all caps.
- Secondary objects start with a capital letter.
- 2D objects and helper objects are lowercase.

- Material names are all caps.
- Map-level names are lowercase.

By using caps and lowercase, you choose the Case Sensitive check box in the Name dialog box to place the more important objects at the top of the Select By Name lists. (See Figure 2.5.)

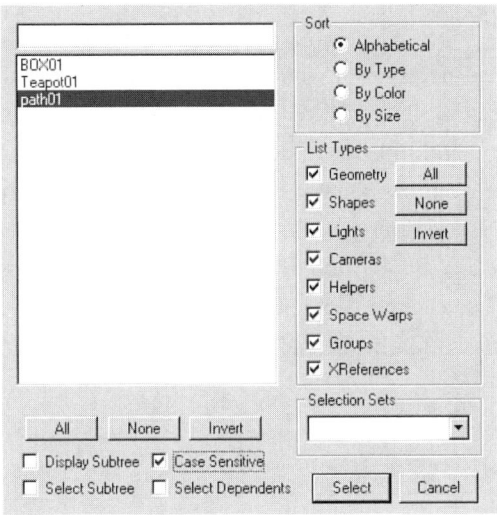

Figure 2.5 The Select By Name dialog box.

Tip
If you have several objects that you frequently select for an editing session and they are spread throughout the list, change the name of each by adding a numeral to the beginning of the name. This sorts them at the top of the list for easy access. When the edit session is finished, delete the number.

Level of Detail

Most architects believe that the entire building must be modeled to the nearest 1/16 inch and even the smallest objects must be included in the scene. This makes as much sense as hiring a traditional model builder to work to the same specifications. Working efficiently is of prime importance. If your office can afford the cost and time of unlimited detail, great, but not many have that luxury. When planning a project, look at three areas that help to streamline the process. This minimizes client changes, leads to efficient models, and cuts render problems significantly. Those three areas are:

- Planning and storyboarding
- Model size and complexity
- Animated walkthroughs

Plan Ahead

Careful planning of the scope and detail necessary to convey the information to the client is essential. This planning process is ideally completed and signed off by the client *before* any work is started on the computer. Most offices deal with works in progress, however, so do the best you can in pre-planning. One of the best methods to convey information to the client is through the use of a *storyboard*. Storyboards are traditionally used in the film and animation industry as a graphic outline of the project. Storyboards can be incredibly detailed works of art, but a simple series of sketches is often sufficient. Figure 2.6 shows a simple storyboard sketch that is the end result of some exercises in this book. Included in the storyboard are

- Object placement in the scene
- Atmospheric information, such as clouds, landscapes, and lighting
- Color information
- Camera motion

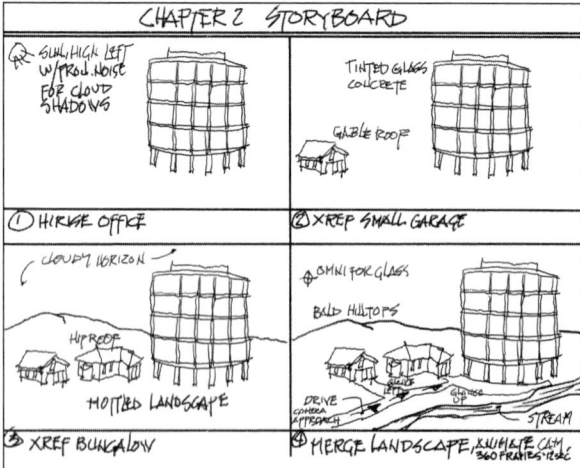

Figure 2.6 A simple storyboard.

A storyboard serves the same purpose for an animator as a set of floor plans does for a builder or an outline does for the author of a technical paper. It documents expectations and responsibilities, so that you and the client are talking about the same objectives.

Tip
For interior scenes or other scenes where color information is important, use Pantone color charts to pick specific colors and include the Pantone numbers on the storyboard. This reduces the confusion associated with calling a color light blue, for example, then making twenty changes until you arrive at the light green the client wanted all along.

Model Size and Complexity

Efficient modeling is not just the ability to quickly create a model. The trick is to do so while setting up the scene for flexible editing and optimizing models with a minimum number of vertices and faces. Architectural models tend to contain the highest face/vertex counts in the computer-modeling industry. Because each face and each vertex use somewhere in the neighborhood of 100 bytes of memory, dense models use system resources that are better applied to lighting, materials, or rendering. It is imperative that you create models with minimum face/vertex counts, but still retain enough detail to render properly.

It usually doesn't make sense to create models with infinite accuracy in all details. The long render times required by high-density models are counterproductive. Following are some considerations when planning the model:

- **Viewing distance.** Fit the level of detail to the situation. For example, you're modeling an office building for massing studies that shows the proposed structure in context with its neighborhood. The building will be viewed from a distance of several hundred or thousands of feet. You need not add small details and certainly not interior walls or fixtures.

- **Render resolution.** A common render resolution for viewing animation on videotape is 720 pixels × 486 pixels. At that resolution it is difficult to distinguish details smaller than two inches or even one foot, based on the viewing distance. Rendering for still-image prints contains more detail at the higher resolutions.

Warning
Small, high-contrast details in animated scenes cause rolling edges to appear when the animation is played back. This is distracting to the viewer. While it is mitigated with antialiasing methods, it is best to avoid the detail altogether when appropriate.

- **Presentations focus.** Limit the detail in portions of the model and add detail to more important objects to capture the viewer's attention. Also use lighting to direct the viewer's focus away from low-detail objects.

Tip
Take a trip to an art museum or the local library. Study how traditional artists convey powerful messages with very little detail, and how they use light to draw the viewer's attention. The technology is different, but you can transfer some of the techniques for focusing attention to modeling, materials, and lighting in MAX.

Instead of creating one very large model with high detail throughout, consider several models at varying amounts of detail. If you already have a large model, try breaking it into separate smaller models. Then, for your next office building project, for example, try using the following models:

- **Full exterior, low detail.** Used for distant shots and site massing. The detail can include some trim and perhaps window and door openings. Stay away from details smaller than six inches.
- **Front entry, moderate detail.** Uses trim details and window and door mullions. No detail smaller than two inches are seen at this distance and render resolution. Nor is the rest of the building in this model.
- **Reception area, high detail.** Contains details as small as 1/2 inch. None of the rest of the building is in this model.

Tip
Using the Slice modifier to lop off entire portions of a model and saving the results as a new file is a good approach to cutting down the working file's size. This works well with models from AutoCAD with little MAX R3 editing capability to reduce mesh density.

Tip
If an object will not be seen, do not model it!

Walkthroughs: Avoiding Trouble (and Walls)

Avoid architectural *walkthroughs* as often as possible! What? That's sacrilege; that's why you bought MAX R3 in the first place, right?

Most architectural walkthroughs are rough on both the animator and the client. They are often too fast, cover areas that are not important to the presentation, and take too long to produce. They make the customer feel as if they are pushed rapidly through the building in a shopping cart that is steered by their ears.

Tip
Create walkthroughs by animating a camera along a Spline path. Use the Measure Utility in the Utilities panel to determine the length of the camera path and use *one frame of animation per one inch of camera path* as a starting point for walkthrough speed. That works out to 30 inches per second or one adult stride per second.

An architectural presentation must be informative, entertaining, and to the point. Short, snappy animated video clips of small models, edited together for a seamless presentation, convey a lot of information. Using film techniques (like cuts and fades between short scenes) and editing the scenes into a seamless presentation is much more efficient and easier to manage.

Tip
Watch feature films and count the seconds that any one scene is on screen before a cut and you will be amazed to find that most last less than ten seconds. Television ads also use the technique to convey a lot of information in a short time.

The important information is often conveyed to the client through a series of still images stitched together in MAX R3 Video Post or other editing software, without using an animated sequence.

Note
A good architectural animated walkthrough is worth its weight in gold, but a bad animation can do irreparable damage to a presentation. Clients have a tendency to focus on problem areas of an animation (flashing shadows or rolling edges) and miss the intended point.

Wall Systems

With all the advance planning and setup out of the way, you're ready to think about some actual architectural modeling. As they are a major part of most architectural scenes, wall systems are a good place to start. There is no one correct or appropriate method of creating walls for all situations. This section illustrates the following three approaches:

- 2D-floor plan extruded for height
- 2D-wall elevation extruded for thickness
- 2D-curtain wall cross-section lofted on a path

Try each, weigh its benefits and match it to your needs for each job. Do not limit yourself by getting stuck on one creation method.

A fourth creation method, not used in this chapter, is to import 3D models from AutoCAD. This is valid in some cases, but severely limits the editing ability of the model. The biggest advantages of the methods presented here are flexibility and ease of editing.

However, importing 2D information from AutoCAD for the three methods listed above offers the best of both worlds—the accuracy and the keyboard input of AutoCAD, coupled with the flexibility and the efficiency of MAX R3.

Save the buildings you create in Chapter 2 to use throughout this chapter and in Chapters 9 and 10 (designing materials).

2D Floor Plan Extruded for Height

Extruding 2D-plan information to a specific height for creating wall systems is the logical approach for many architects. Everyone is familiar with the plan view, and it clearly represents the wall position and thickness throughout the building. Each floor of a multi-story building is created as a separate object. As with each method in this chapter, there are pros and cons to the technique. A few of the advantages are

- Good for wall systems that contain many small jogs.
- Good for wall systems with curved wall sections.
- Works well for interior partitions.
- Initial extruded mesh objects are efficient with low face and vertex count.

The method's disadvantages are:

- All walls are the same height throughout the mesh object.
- Window and door openings are created using 3D-Boolean subtraction, greatly increasing computer system overhead and creating long, thin faces during the process.

Tip
Long, thin triangular faces that are sometimes created by 3D-Boolean operations lead to flashing surfaces during animation and problematic shadows.

Avoid long, thin triangular faces during 3D-Boolean operations by increasing the density of the mesh objects before using Boolean operations. This is done by adding vertices on the 2D-Spline floor plan and adding Height Segments in the Extrude modifier. However, after the Boolean, the new mesh object needs an Optimize modifier to reduce the extra faces and vertices. The Optimize modifier contains its own computer resource overhead.

- You must use complex combinations of MeshSelect, Material, and UVW Map modifiers with complex Multi/Sub-Object materials to apply color and texture to the individual walls' surfaces.

Extruding the Floor Plan

In this exercise (Exercise 2.1.1), use the Extrude modifier to give height to a 2D-floor plan. This is best done on a floor plan without window and door openings, thus creating a contiguous set of walls at a given height.

Exercise 2.1.1   2D-Floor Plan Extruded for Height

1. Open the file called 02max01.max. It is a scene with a 2D-floor plan showing a half-round bay, an ell, and several interior partitions. The scene is set to Architectural display units, and the Grid is set to one inch. See Figure 2.7.

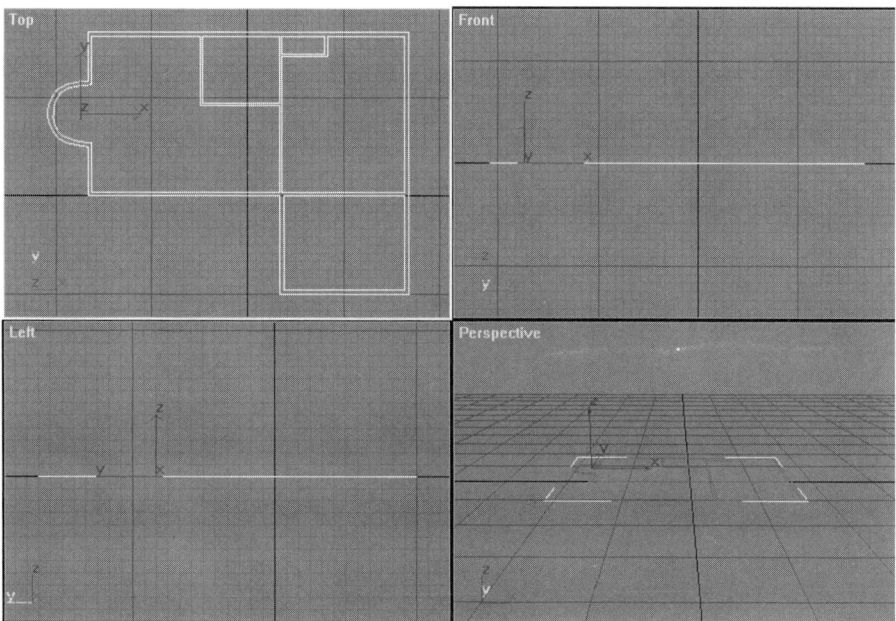

Figure 2.7   2D-floor plan.

2. Right-click the Top viewport to activate it.

 Tip
Right-clicking is the preferred method for activating viewports. Left-clicking is actually a selection tool and potentially picks or transforms objects by accident.

3. Click the Select by Name button in the Main Toolbar (or type H), and double-click floor_plan in the list to select it.
4. Right-click anywhere in the Top viewport, and choose Move in the pop-up menu. See Figure 2.8.

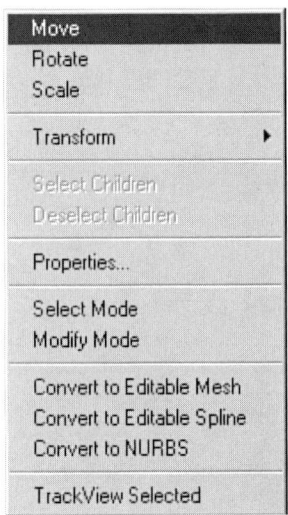

Figure 2.8 Right-click pop-up menu.

Tip

You can now right-click anywhere in a viewport to open the pop-up menu. Previously you right-clicked only on a selected object.

NEW TO R3

You can return to the old method of right-clicking by opening Customize/Preferences. In the Viewports tab, clear Right Click Menu Over Selected Only in the Mouse Control area.

NEW TO R3

5. Hold the Shift key down, click and drag the X-axis of the new Transform Gizmo tripod, and move the clone to the original floor_plan's right side. In the Clone Options dialog box, choose Reference Object, rename it FLOOR_PLAN, and click OK. See Figure 2.9 and Figure 2.10.

Tip

Clicking on an axis of the new Transform Gizmo tripod restricts the transformation to that axis. This eliminates the need for clicking the X button in the Main Toolbar or accessing the Transform X restriction from the right-click menu.

Chapter 2: Architectural Modeling   61

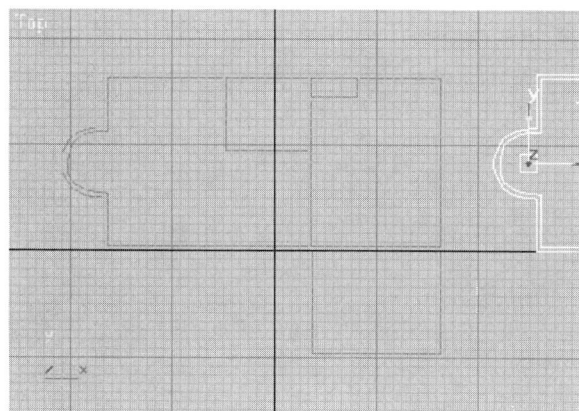

Figure 2.9 Reference clone with Transform Gizmo tripod.

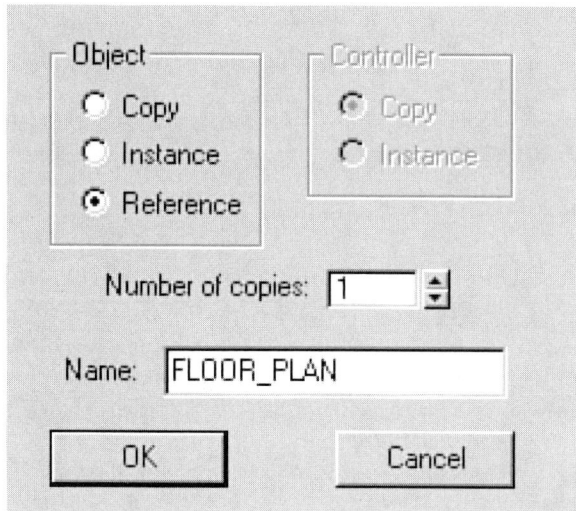

Figure 2.10 Clone Options dialog box.

6. Click the Zoom Extents All button to zoom out and view the floor_plan and the FLOOR_PLAN objects. See Figure 2.11.

Part I Modeling

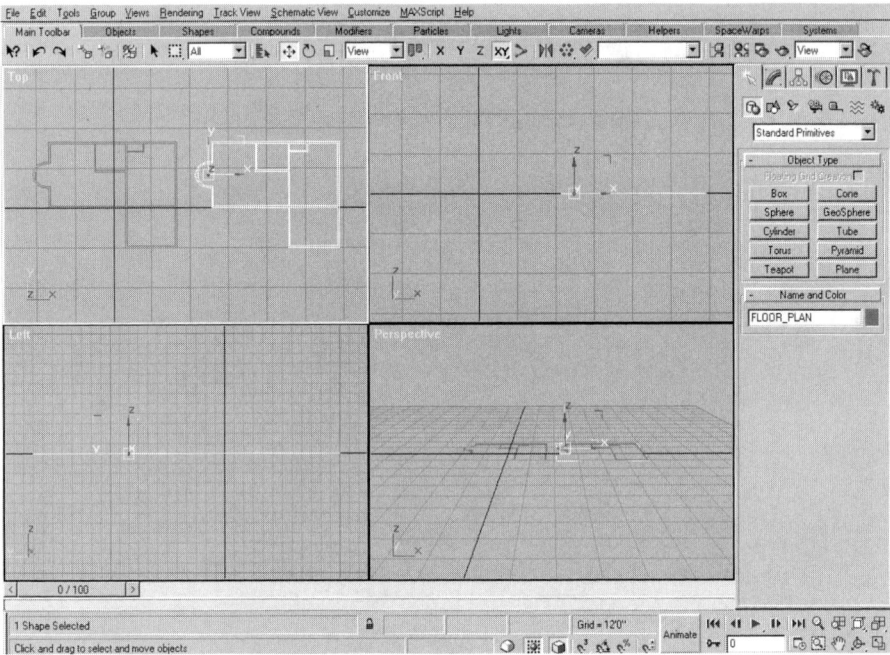

Figure 2.11 The Reference clone renamed FLOOR_PLAN.

 Tip

It's often a good idea to work with a Reference clone of the original 2D shape. In this case, the floor_plan is duplicated to a Reference clone called FLOOR_PLAN, which in turn, is extruded into a 3D mesh object.

A Reference clone allows modifications to pass from the original to the Reference clone, but no modifications are passed from the clone back to the original.

This is a fundamental concept in the three methods of creating walls demonstrated in this chapter. It allows flexible editing of simple 2D shapes to effect 3D mesh objects, regardless of position or orientation in the scene.

The original 2D-control shapes do not render and require few computer resources.

7. In the Top viewport, select FLOOR_PLAN (if it is not already selected).
8. In Modify panel, click the Extrude button and enter 9'0" in the Amount field of the Parameters rollout (see Figure 2.12). FLOOR_PLAN now consists of nine-feet-tall walls, but the original shape is still in 2D.
9. Save the file with the name 02_extwall_01.max.

Creating Rough Opening Boxes for Windows

In this exercise (Exercise 2.1.2), you create 3D-box primitives and position them as window rough openings. Then you use the Boolean subtractions to cut the rough openings from the extruded walls.

Exercise 2.1.2   Create and Position 3D Boxes for Window Boolean Operations

1. Open your file from Exercise 2.1.1 (if it is not already open), or open 02_extwall_01.max from the CD-ROM.
2. Right-click the Front viewport to activate it, and in the Create panel, click the Geometry button. Choose Standard Primitives, and click the Box button. Click and drag a box with any dimensions in the Front viewport—within the wall—just to the right of the curved wall section. This looks like dense vertical lines in the mesh. This box is the window rough opening.
3. In the Modify Panel, enter 5'0" in the Length field, 2'8" in the Width field, and 2'0" in the Height field. Rename the window rough-opening box ro01. See Figure 2.13.
4. Right-click the Perspective viewport, and type U to change to a User viewport. This makes it easier to zoom in on portions of the mesh.
5. In the User viewport, right-click the User label, and choose Wireframe from the list. The display switches from a Shaded to a Wireframe view. Select FLOOR_PLAN.
6. In the Display panel's Display Properties rollout, clear Backface Cull to display the mesh's hidden edges. This makes it easier to select hidden edges.
7. Click the Zoom Region button and zoom in on the front wall's upper left, near the half-round ell. Use ArcRotate, and Pan to adjust the User viewport for a birds-eye view of the walls and ro01.
8. Click, then right-click the 3D Snap button. In the Grid and Snap Settings dialog box, uncheck Grid Points, and check only Vertex and Midpoint. This helps position the ro01 in the wall. See Figure 2.14. Click the Options tab, and make sure Use Axis Constraints is cleared.

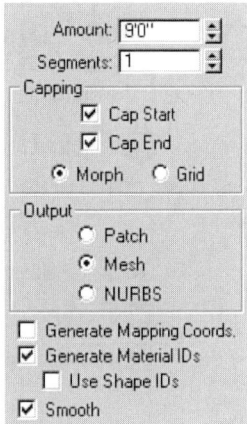

Figure 2.12   Extrude Modifier Parameters rollout.

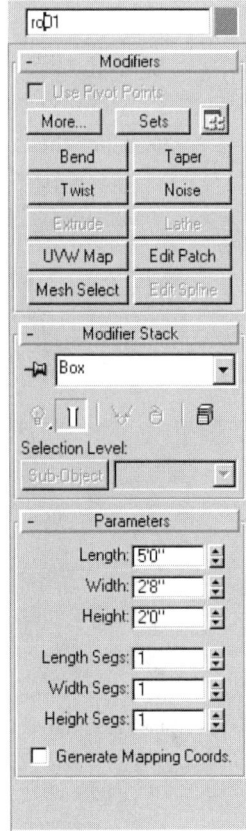

Figure 2.13   Modify panel for ro01.

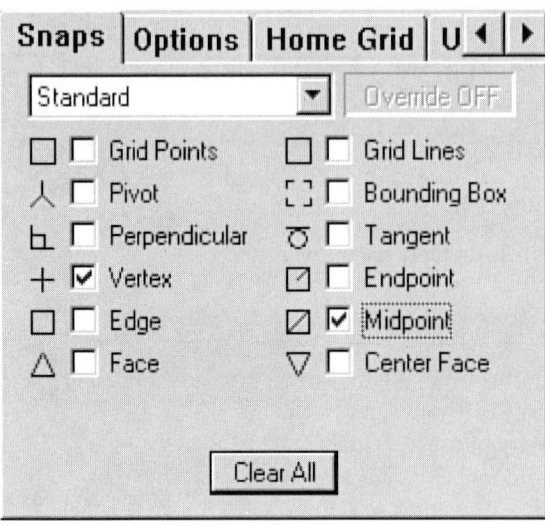

Figure 2.14 Vertex and Midpoint Snap options.

9. Type W or click the Min/Max Toggle button to fill the display with the User viewport. Select ro01 and right-click. Choose Move in the pop-up menu.

10. Click the upper-left edge midpoint of ro01, and drag ro01 to the upper-left vertex of FLOOR_PLAN's front wall. See Figure 2.15. This provides a known starting point to accurately position the rough-opening object.

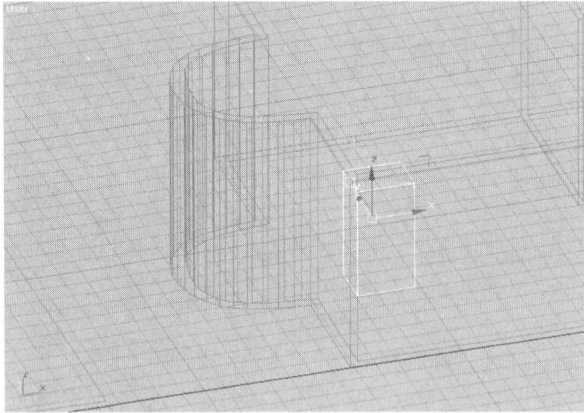

Figure 2.15 Snap ro01 to the upper left of the front wall.

11. Right-click the Select and Move button to open the Transform Type-In dialog box. Enter 4'0" in the Offset: World X-axis field, then enter –2'0" in the Offset: World Z-axis field. This moves ro01 into place on the wall.

12. In the Edit menu, choose Clone, check Instance, and click OK. This creates an Instance clone, and names it ro02.
13. In the Transform Type-In dialog box, enter 12'0" in the Offset: World X-axis field. This moves ro02 into place: twelve feet to the right. Close the dialog box.
14. Type W to switch to four-display viewports, and right-click the Top viewport to activate it. Type H, and select ro01 and ro02 in the list.
15. Click the 3D Snap button to turn it off.
16. Verify that you are still in Move mode. Hold the Shift key, then click and drag the Y-axis of the Transform Gizmo. Drag the windows into position on the back wall. In the Clone Options dialog box, check the Instance option, and click OK. The Top viewport looks similar to Figure 2.16.

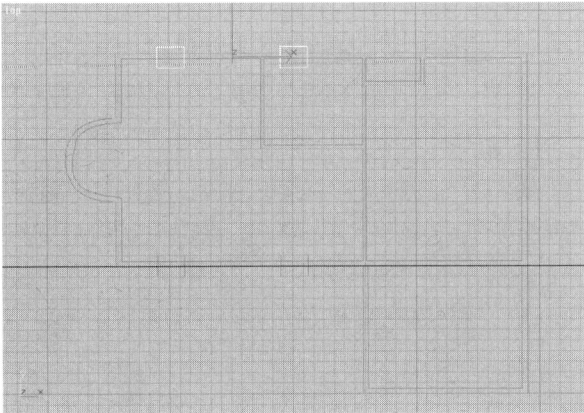

Figure 2.16 Window rough-opening boxes in front and back walls.

17. Create one more Instance clone, and position it in the middle of the front ell wall. It looks similar to Figure 2.17.

Tip
Center the new clone by activating the Top viewport, setting 3D Snap to Midpoint only, and moving it into place.

18. Save the file as 02_extwall_02.max.

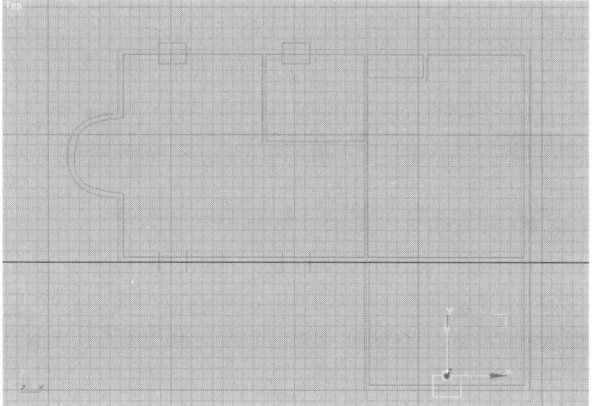

Figure 2.17 Move rough-opening box ro05 into front ell wall.

3D-Boolean Operations

3D-Boolean operations work fairly well in MAX R3. However, each Boolean operation should be distinct from the others to ensure predictable results. Always click the Boolean button at the start of a new Boolean process, thus creating a distinct operation. Just clicking the Pick Operand B button again causes the operation to fail. If you experience problems, there are several other Boolean rules-of-thumb to consider:

- Operands must overlap.
- Faces of both operands are roughly the same size.
- Moving an operand even slightly affects results.
- The STL-Check modifier is used to identify problems caused by multiple Boolean operations.

With these tips in mind, Exercise 2.1.3 will help you give Booleans a try on your extruded wall.

Exercise 2.1.3   Boolean Subtract of Rough Openings

1. Open your file from Exercise 2.1.2, or open 02_extwall_02.max from the CD-ROM.
2. In the User viewport, zoom and pan to fill the viewport with a bird's-eye view of FLOOR_PLAN.
3. Right-click the User label to set the viewport to Smooth+Highlights.
4. Type W to fill the display with the User viewport. The display looks like Figure 2.18.

Chapter 2: Architectural Modeling   67

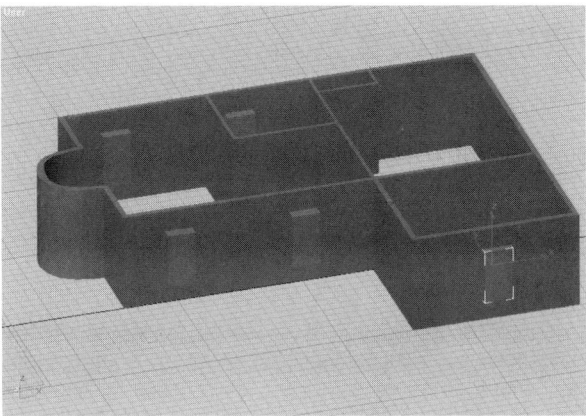

Figure 2.18   User viewport with Smooth+Highlights.

5. Type H, and double-click FLOOR_PLAN in the list, or click the viewport to select it.
6. In the Create panel, choose Compound Objects, and click the Boolean button. Click the Pick Operand B button, and pick one of the 'ro' boxes in the User viewport. The rough opening for the window is cut out of the wall. See Figure 2.19.

Figure 2.19   Rough-opening Boolean subtracted from wall (Subtraction A-B).

7. Even though the Boolean button is still highlighted after you complete one operation, you *must* choose the Boolean button again to start a new process. Click the highlighted Boolean button, click the Pick Operand B button, and pick another 'ro' box in the User viewport.
8. Repeat Step 7 until you subtract the remaining 'ro' boxes from the walls.

Tip
If you have trouble picking a rough-opening box in the scene, click Pick Operand B, and type H to select the next box from the list.

9. Save the file as 02_extwall_03.max. It looks similar to Figure 2.20.

Figure 2.20 Window rough openings subtracted from walls.

Tip

NEW TO R3

To move or resize a window rough opening, use the new Schematic View. Click the Schematic View menu, choose Open Schematic View, and click the FLOOR_PLAN box to select it. It turns yellow when selected. Click the Toggle Visibility Downstream to expand the booleaned walls. Double-click any of the Box boxes, and the Modify panel opens so you can make adjustments to that box's base parameters.

Tip
If you don't intend to move or resize the openings, select the wall, and in the File menu, choose Save Selected, and give the new file a name. This saves the object to disk—in case you need to edit it at a later date. Then merge or replace it back into the scene. In the Modify panel, click Edit Stack. In the Edit Modifier stack dialog box, click Collapse All. This reduces the overhead associated with multiple Boolean operations and frees up computer resources.

Creating walls from extruded 2D-floor plans is fine for small, simple projects or perhaps projects with many curved walls. However, the process requires contiguous and closed compound shapes, which take extensive editing to create. Also, 3D-Boolean operations are more prone to problems in a surface modeler (such as Max R3) than in solid modelers (such as AutoCAD). The problems are: high computer resource requirements; Boolean failure; and long, thin faces.

2D Wall Elevation Extruded for Thickness

Extruding a wall elevation to give the wall thickness is also a valid method for building wall systems with editing flexibility. Exterior wall elevations are often developed early in the design process. The 2D information is imported from AutoCAD.

The advantages of this method are as follows:

- Allows flexible, easy editing
- Window/door openings are added or subtracted
- Odd-shaped wall elevations are accommodated
- High-rise facades are created
- Very low overhead on system resources

Following are the disadvantages:

- This method does not work well with curved walls.
- Causes problems with material assignments at intersecting corners.
- Management issues with shapes for Reference objects. For example, if 2D objects are converted to Editable Splines after the Reference clone is made, the Reference is broken and editing capability is reduced.

In the next exercise series (Exercises 2.2.1, 2.2.2, and 2.2.3), let's create a small garage, using the extruded elevation method.

Extruding and Aligning the Walls

The first phase of the project is to extrude and align the four walls of a garage. The Align tool is one of the most productive features of MAX R3. Just be aware that the alignment axes depend on the active viewport and reference coordinate system.

Exercise 2.2.1   Extruding and Positioning Reference Clones

1. Open 02max02.max. It's a file with three 2D Shapes. Two are compound shapes with multiple splines for window rough openings. See Figure 2.21.

70   Part I   Modeling

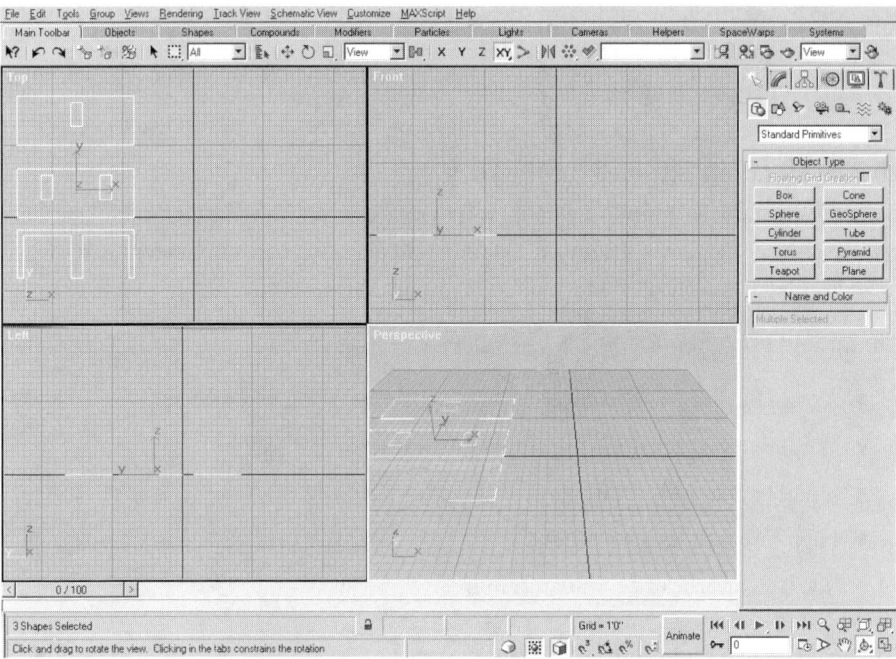

Figure 2.21   Compound 2D-shape wall elevations.

2. In the Top viewport, select the three wall elevations, right-click the viewport, and choose Move in the pop-up menu. Hold the shift key, and click the Transformation Gizmo's X-axis. Drag the three objects to the right of the originals. Check Reference in the Clone Options dialog box, and click OK. The Top viewport looks similar to Figure 2.22.

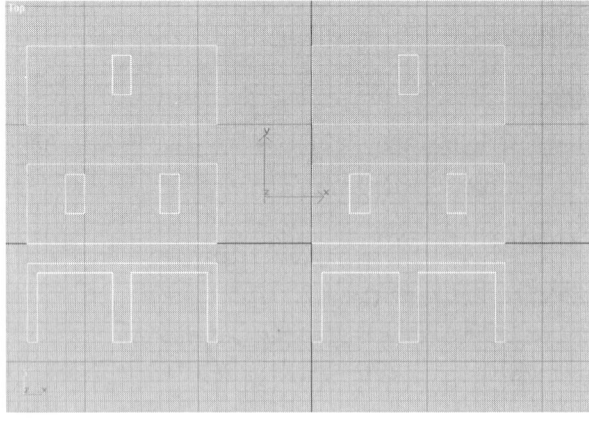

Figure 2.22   Reference clones of three 2D wall elevations.

3. With the three Reference clones still selected, in the Modify panel, click Extrude, and enter 6' in the Amount field.

Note
By making the clones References, you extrude the Reference without affecting the original. You can also edit the original to affect the Extruded Reference—allowing easy and powerful editing.

Tip
Applying an Extrude modifier to all walls at once creates an Instanced modifier. This allows you to select any wall and change the thickness of all. If you want different wall thickness, apply separate Extrude modifiers to each wall.

4. Right-click the Top viewport if it is not already active. Click, then right-click the Select and Rotate button in the Main Toolbar. Type 90 in the Offset: Screen X-axis field of the Transform Type-in dialog box. Click Enter to complete the rotation. This rotates all three walls for correct vertical orientation. Close the dialog box.

5. Select each object individually, and rename them as follows: from gar_frnt01 to GAR_FRNT, gar_side01 to GAR_SIDE , and gar_back01 to GAR_BACK. The Perspective viewport looks similar to Figure 2.23.

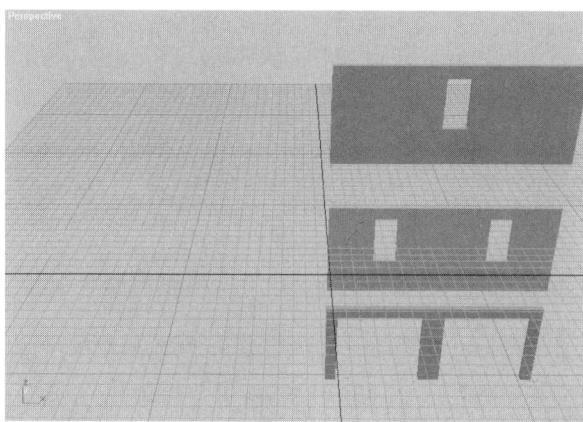

Figure 2.23 The rotated 3D walls.

6. In the Perspective viewport, select GAR_SIDE, and click. Then right-click the Rotate button, and type 90 in Offset: World Z-axis. Click Enter to complete the rotation. Close the dialog box.

7. In the Perspective viewport, right-click anywhere, and choose Move from the pop-up menu. Hold the Shift key, click the Transform Gizmo X-axis, and drag GAR_SIDE to the left. Check Instance in the Clone Options dialog box, and

accept GAR_SIDE01 as a name. Click OK. The Perspective viewport appears similar to Figure 2.24.

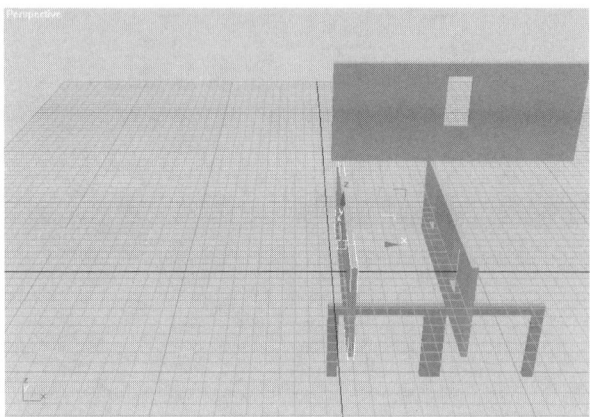

Figure 2.24 New instance of GAR_SIDE.

8. In the Perspective viewport, select the four extruded walls, click the Align button on the Main Toolbar, and select any one of the original 2D Shapes.

9. In the Align dialog box, check Z Position, and check Minimum and Minimum in the Current Object and Target Object columns. This aligns the bottom of all three walls with the shapes on the World Grid. Click OK to close the dialog box.

Tip

When using Align, Transform Type-in, and Array, always check what coordinate system is used for the transform. It varies for each viewport and/or active Reference Coordinate System (View, Screen, Local, Grid, and so on).

10. GAR_FRNT stays in position. You now align the others to it. In the Top viewport, select GAR_SIDE.

11. Click the Align button, type H, and double-click GAR_FRNT in the list. In the Align Selection dialog box, check X Position and Maximum for both Current and Target Object. Click the Apply button to reset the check boxes. Check Y Position, and Minimum and Maximum, respectively, in the Current Object and Target Object areas. Click OK. GAR_SIDE aligns with GAR_FRNT, as shown in Figure 2.25.

Chapter 2: Architectural Modeling 73

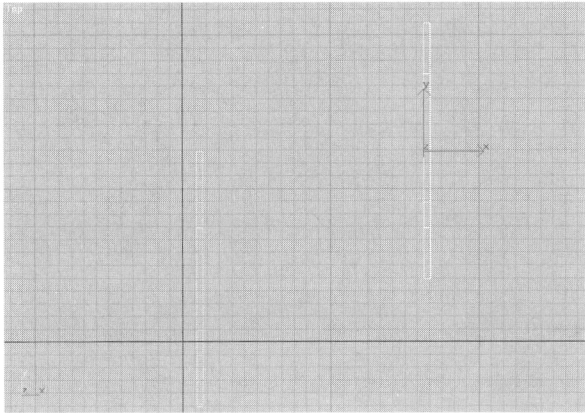

Figure 2.25 GAR_SIDE aligned to GAR_FRNT.

12. In the Top viewport, select GAR_SIDE01, and use Align to position on the other side of GAR_FRNT. Then select GAR_BACK, and align it to GAR_SIDE. For aligning GAR_SIDE 01 to GAR_FRONT: Choose Y, Minimum and Maximum, and apply. Choose X, Minimum and Maximum, and OK. To align GAR_BACK to GAR_SIDE: choose X, Minimum and Maximum, and apply. Choose Y, Minimum and Maximum, and OK. The walls look like Figure 2.26.

Figure 2.26 The walls, aligned to form a garage.

13. Save the file as 02_extelv_01.max.

Adding Gable Ends

In this next portion of the exercise, put to use the fact that the 3D walls are Reference clones of the original 2D Shapes. Various editing tasks finish the walls. This is tedious if you create a new work plane for each wall and edit the 3D mesh objects at the Sub-Object Level.

Don't worry about position and orientation of the 3D walls. All edits pass via the Reference, and the 2D Shapes remain in the original work plane.

Exercise 2.2.2   Editing at 2D Sub-Object Level

1. Open 02_extelv_01.max (if it not already the current scene).
2. In the Top viewport, pan and zoom so the three 2D shapes fill the display. It looks similar to Figure 2.27.

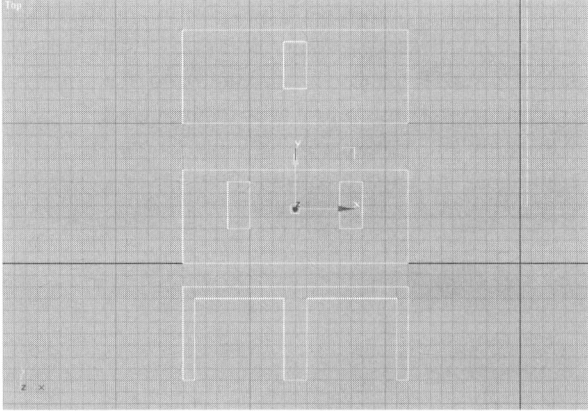

Figure 2.27   The three original 2D shapes.

3. Now create gable ends for gar_frnt and gar_back. In the Top viewport, select gar_frnt.

 Note
You are modifying the 2D-shape gar_frnt, not the 3D extrude-mesh GAR_FRNT.

NEW TO R3

4. In the Modify panel, click the Segment button in the Selection rollout to immediately jump to Sub-Object mode. See Figure 2.28.
5. Choose the top edge of gar_frnt to select the segment. It turns red when selected.
6. In the Modify panel's Geometry rollout, click the Divide button. Its default is 1. This adds a vertex in the middle of the selected straight segment at the top edge of gar_frnt.

Chapter 2: Architectural Modeling 75

 Note
If the segment isn't a straight segment, the vertex isn't placed in the middle. Rather it's weighted toward one end or the other—depending on the tangency at either end.

7. In the Modify panel's Selection rollout, click the Vertex button and select the new vertex in the middle of the top-wall segment.

8. Click, then right-click, the Select and Move button in the Toolbar. Enter 10'0" in the Offset: Screen Y-axis field of the Transform Type-in dialog. This moves the new vertex up 10'—to a 12/12 pitch gable. However, the vertices have Bézier tangency and create a curved profile. Close the dialog box.

9. In the Top viewport, click the Select button. Drag a selection window around all vertices for gar_frnt. Right-click any selected vertex, and choose Corner from the center of the pop-up menu to set the tangent type for each vertex. Click the Sub-Object button to exit Sub-Object mode. Gar_frnt appears similar to Figure 2.29. Note that modifying the original shape changes the Reference 3D mesh accordingly. This is a powerful editing method, especially with a complex project. This editing process also adds little overhead.

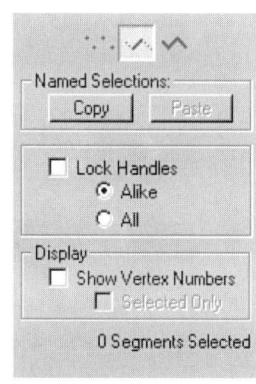

Figure 2.28 The new Vertex, Segment, Spline buttons, respectively, in the Selection rollout.

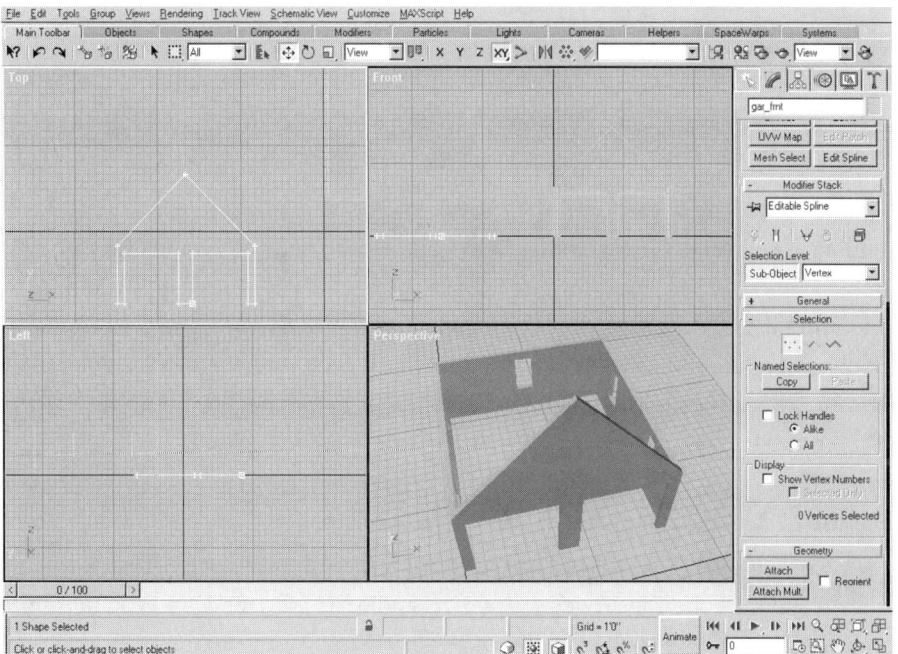

Figure 2.29 GAR_FRNT, with a 12/12 pitch gable.

10. Repeat Steps 3–9 on the gar_back 2D shape. The Perspective viewport looks similar to Figure 2.30.

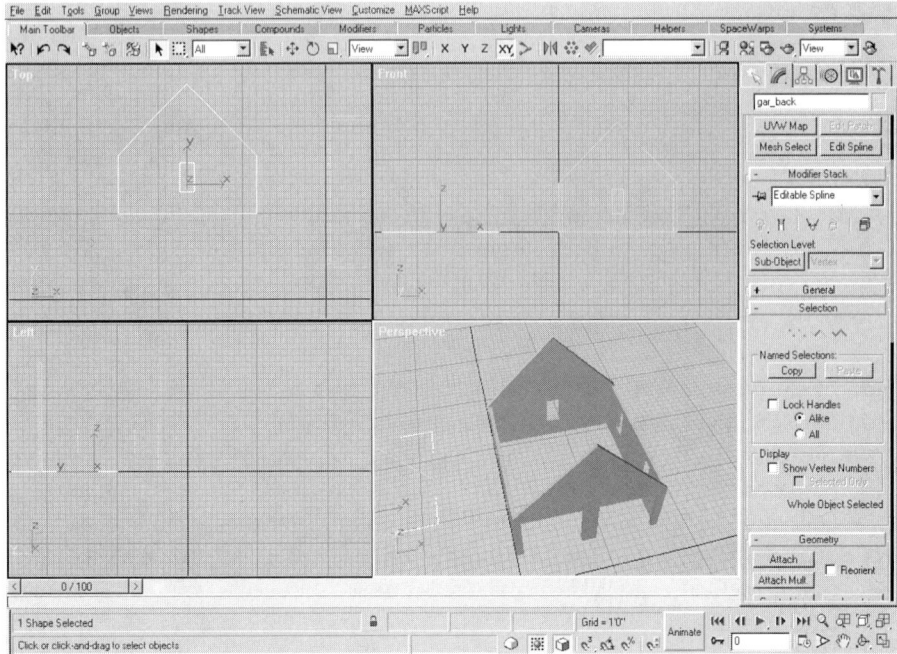

Figure 2.30 12/12 pitch gables at front and back.

11. Save the file as 02_extelv_02.max.

Adding a Gable Window

Adding a gable-end window to the front end of the garage is accomplished by a 3D-Boolean operation, as performed in Exercise 2.1.3. This method requires you to create and position a 3D box, find the 3D wall, align the box to the wall, and perform the 3D Boolean. The Boolean *may* create unwanted long faces and use considerable system resources. In this exercise, you create a new 2D rectangle and attach it to the 2D wall. This creates the opening in the wall with very little system overhead.

Exercise 2.2.3   Attaching Shapes to Create New Openings

1. Open 02_extelv_02.max (if it is not already the current scene).
2. Right-click the Top viewport. Zoom in, and select gar_frnt. Type W to maximize the Front viewport. It looks similar to Figure 2.31.

Chapter 2: Architectural Modeling 77

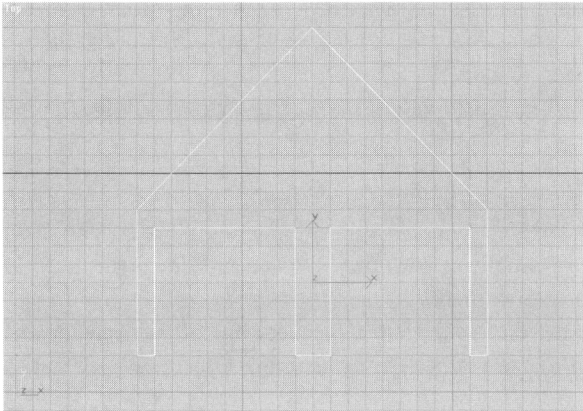

Figure 2.31 The Top viewport, with gar_frnt.

3. Click the 3D Snap button to toggle it on, and right-click the button to make sure the Snap is set only to Grid Points.
4. In the Create panel, click the Shapes button, and select Rectangle. Then click and drag a 4'0" x 4'0" square that is centered in the gable, as shown in Figure 2.32. Turn off Snap.

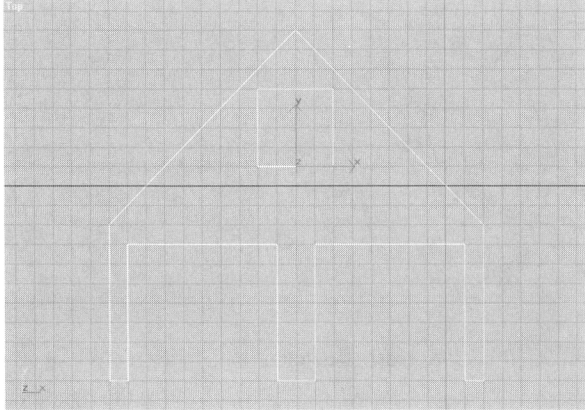

Figure 2.32 The rectangle, centered in the gable of gar_frnt.

 Warning

It is *very* important that you select the original 2D shape, and attach the new rectangle to it. The reference is based upon the object's node. Attaching rectangle01 to gar_frnt does not disturb the original node. Attaching gar_frnt to the rectangle deletes the original node and breaks the reference.

5. Select gar_frnt. In the Modify panel's Geometry rollout, click the Attach button, then move the cursor over the new rectangle. When the cursor changes to the attach cursor, select the new rectangle.

6. Type W to display four viewports. Notice that the new window is cut from the front-gable wall.

7. In the Modify panel, click the Spline button in the Selection rollout.

8. In the Top viewport, click the New Window Spline to highlight it red; right-click, and choose Move in the pop-up menu. Pick the rectangle and drag it around a bit. While still pressing the mouse's left button, right-click to cancel the move operation. This demonstrates that Spline Sub-Object editing interactively moves openings around. You can also use Vertex or Segment Sub-Object Level editing to resize objects.

Tip
To move, rotate, or scale splines with accurate numeric entry: Click, then right-click the Transform buttons, and use Transform Type-in.

Warning
Take care not to move the 2D splines out of plane, for example, in the viewport Z-axis. You can try it to see what happens, but moving anything out of plane causes unexpected results in your extrusions. Before you experiment, save your work first, or click Edit/Hold.

9. Save the file as 02_extelv_03.max.

Tip
You can open several alternate window layouts. Create the splines for a new layout, select the splines, and apply a DeleteSpline modifier. Create another window layout, add a SplineSelect modifier, and apply a DeleteSpline modifier to those splines. Now in the Modifier Stack, use the Active/Inactive Modifier toggle (or the Show End Result on/off toggle) to display the desired window layout. Again, 3D objects reflect the state of the 2D shapes.

Extruding 2D-elevation views is a method for creating efficient walls that require ongoing edits. The original 2D information is easily accessed and edited to affect the reference 3D object anywhere in space. Because window and door openings are not 3D-Boolean operations, the resulting mesh is far more efficient. The next exercise uses a similar process to simulate curtain wall systems, a type of building system that hangs the façade and windows from a steel or concrete support frame.

Creating a Curtain Wall System

The third common wall-creation method is lofting a 2D curtain wall cross-section on a path. The example here is a fairly complex curtain wall system for a curved-wall building. In this case, the cross-section includes an upper- and lower-concrete section, horizontal glass, and horizontal window trim or mullions. The cross-section lofting approach is used successfully for high-rise curtain-wall buildings, large sports stadiums, interior walls with complex molding, kitchen cabinets, and mechanical parts.

When lofting in this example, take advantage of the Instance option with the cross-section shape. This allows you to modify the original 2D shape to affect the curtain walls throughout the building.

NEW TO R3 Enjoy a new MAX R3 feature that allows you to assign Material IDs to segments of a spline. This enables you to apply materials to any surface defined by a segment of the 2D shape.

The following are advantages to lofting cross-sections on a path:

- Easy 2D edits to change complex 3D objects
- Flexible material assignments and editing
- Complex curved walls are possible
- Easy to adjust mesh density for efficient models

The method's main disadvantage is that it's difficult creating multiple-wall elevations on a single path.

Lofting a Curtain Wall Level

In the first exercise, you use existing 2D shapes to loft the first level of a multistory high-rise building. You learn how to adjust a shape's pivot point so the cross-section attaches correctly to the path. You also learn how to flip cross-sections on the path for the desired orientation. The building has an elliptical plan and the levels start twelve feet off-grade.

You create and use clones of the ellipse, instead of the original ellipse. The original is cloned again and extruded as an elliptical building core or a 2D path along which vertical columns are positioned. For an example of what the building looks like, refer to Figure 2.41. Open the file 02_cwall_finished.max to see how clones of the ellipse were extruded as a core and used to position columns.

The 2D shapes were created in MAX R3, but could have come from AutoCAD.

Exercise 2.3.1 Create the First Level

1. Open 02max03.max. Notice the 2D ellipse in the Top viewport and a 2D-compound cross-section in the Front viewport. It looks like Figure 2.33.

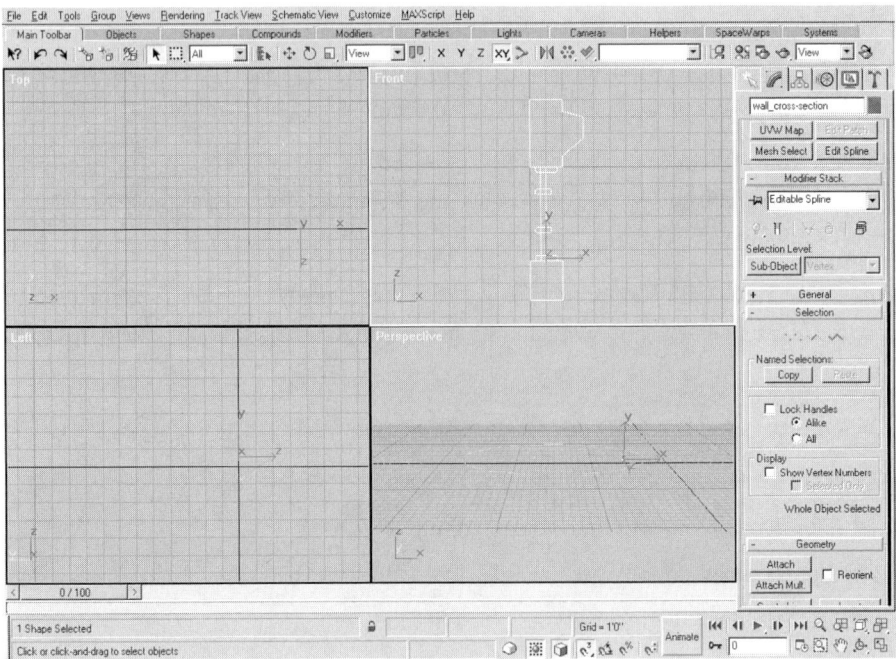

Figure 2.33 2D ellipse path and 2D cross-section compound shape.

2. In the Top viewport, select the ellipse called inside_ext_wall_path. In the Edit pull-down menu, choose Clone. Then in the Clone Options dialog, check Instance, and name the new shape wall_master. See Figure 2.34. This creates a master wall ellipse that controls all aspects of the wall.

3. Right-click the Perspective viewport to activate it, type W to fill the display, and use Zoom and Arc Rotate to position the view—like Figure 2.35.

4. In the Perspective viewport, type H, and select the 2D shape called inside_ext_wall_path.

5. In the Create panel, click the Geometry button, choose Compound Objects, and click the Loft button.

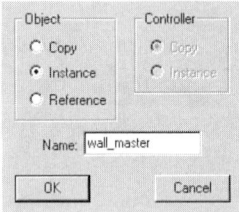

Figure 2.34 Clone Options dialog box.

Chapter 2: Architectural Modeling   81

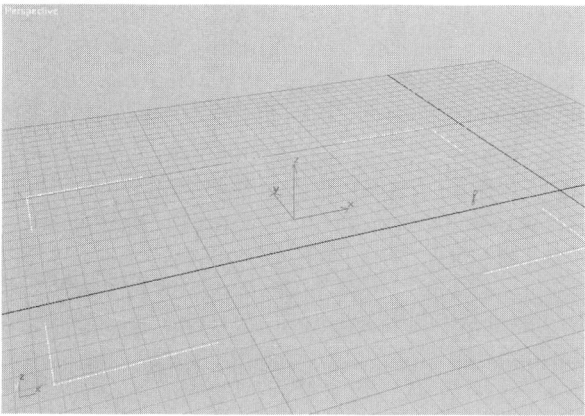

Figure 2.35 Use Zoom and Arc Rotate in the Perspective viewport.

6. In the Creation Method rollout, click the Get Shape button, and select the 2D shape called wall_cross-section. Name the new object CWALL01. The 2D shape is lofted along the path to create an elliptical curtain wall. However, notice the bullnose on the top spandrel is on the inside of the ellipse, whereas it should be on the outside. Also, notice that the new object is partially below the World Grid. You must make two changes in order to flip the cross-section on the path and place it 12'0" above the World Grid. These two steps illustrate how to control the position and orientation of a shape on a path. See Figure 2.41, which is a finished example.

7. Type W, activate the Front viewport, and zoom and pan. Then type W again for a view like Figure 2.36.

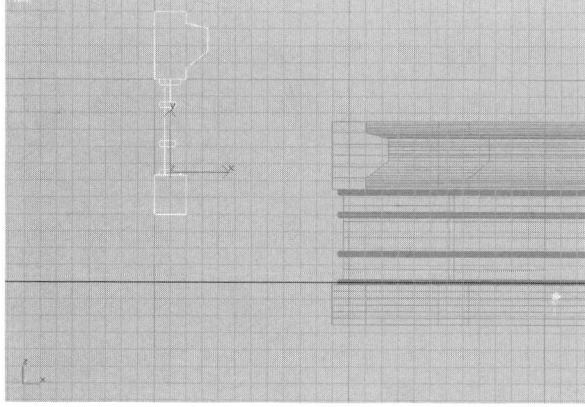

Figure 2.36 Front viewport, with cross-section and loft object.

82   Part I Modeling

8. Select CWALL01. In the Modify panel, click the Get Shape button, hold the Ctrl key, and choose wall_cross-section again. This replaces the Instance of wall_cross-section with one that is flipped 180 degrees on the elliptical path. Now the bullnose is on the outside of the wall.

9. Click the Select button to cancel Get Shape. In the Front viewport, select wall_cross-section. Note the pivot point is centered near the bottom spandrel shape's top. The loft process positions the pivot point on the path. Now move the pivot to a point aligned to the left edge of wall_cross-section and twelve feet below. This simulates a building with the curtain wall system starting twelve feet off the ground plane, with the ellipse describing the inside radius. See Figure 2.41 to see the finished building.

10. In the Hierarchy panel, click the Affect Pivot Only button. This gives you access to the pivot point.

11. Click the Align button on the Toolbar, and select anywhere on wall_cross-section. You align the pivot to the shape itself.

12. In the Align Selection dialog, check X Position and Y Position at the top, Pivot Point in the Current Object column, and Minimum in the Target Object column. This aligns the pivot to the lower-left corner of the shape. See Figure 2.37. Click OK.

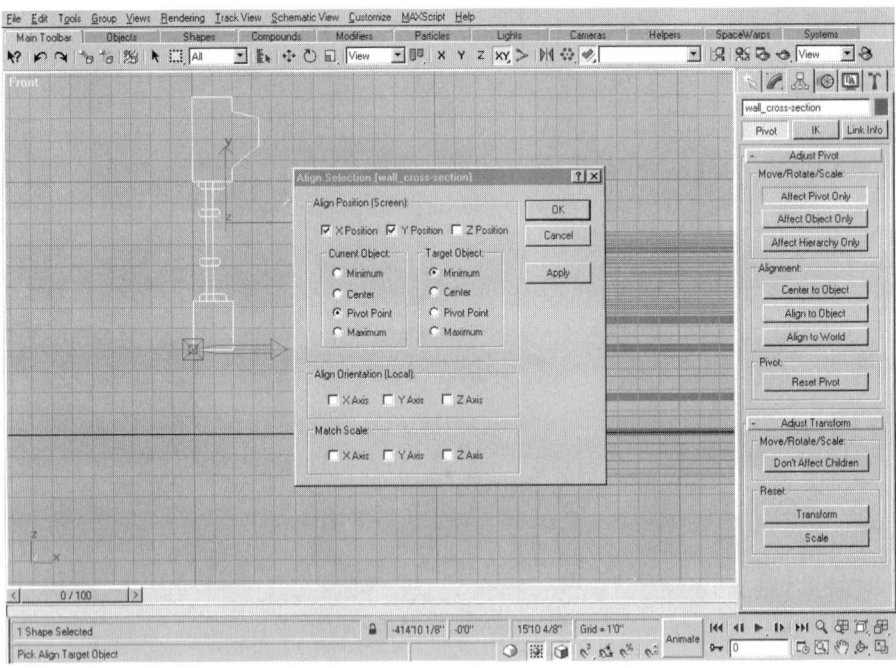

Figure 2.37 Pivot point, aligned with lower-left corner of shape.

13. Click, then right-click the Select and Move button in the Main Toolbar, and type –12'0" in the Offset: Screen Y-axis. Press Enter and the scene looks similar to Figure 2.38. In the Hierarchy panel, click the Affect Pivot Only button to turn off that mode. Close the Transform Type-in dialog box.

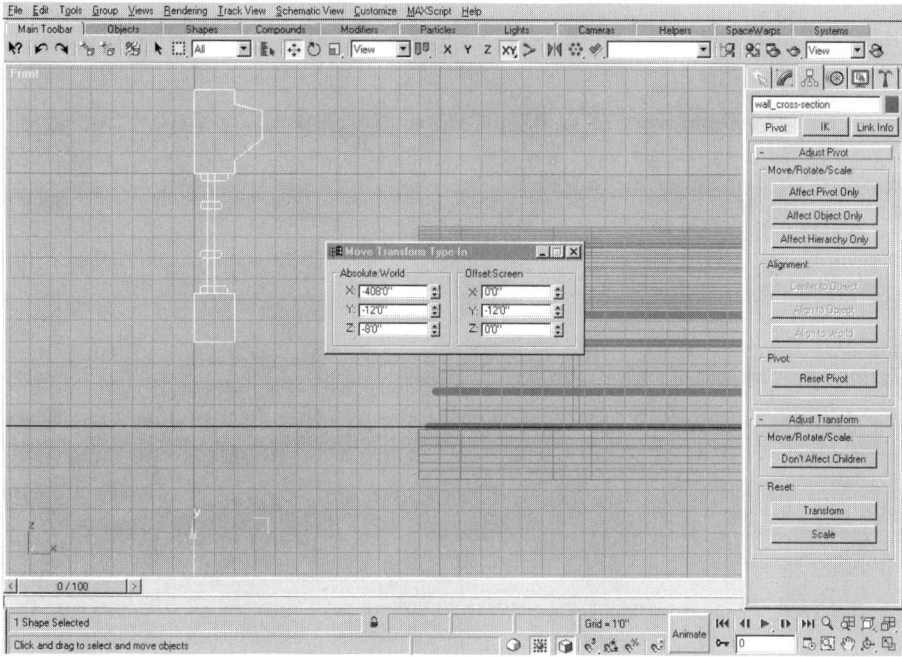

Figure 2.38 Pivot point, 12'0" below the bottom of the shape's left edge.

14. Type W, activate the Perspective viewport, and type W again. Select the CWALL01 mesh object.
15. In the Modify panel, click the Get Shape button, hold the Ctrl key, and select the wall_cross-section in the viewport. Click the Zoom Extents Selected button. The scene looks similar to Figure 2.39. The lofted curtain wall is now twelve feet above the World Grid, and the bullnose is on the outside. The wall may look a bit segmented where it rounds the tight ends of the ellipse, but you adjust that in the next exercise.
16. Click the Get Shape button to exit that mode.
17. Save the file as 02_cwall_01.max.

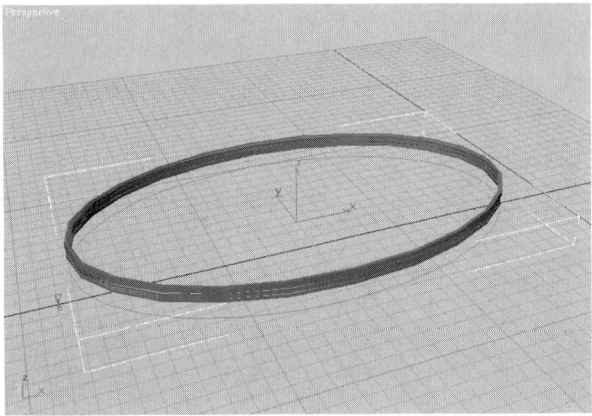

Figure 2.39 Lofted curtain wall, twelve feet above World Grid.

Optimizing the Lofted CWALL Objects

In Exercise 2.3.2, you use the Optimize Shapes option to reduce the number of faces and vertices in the curtain wall. The optimization has no effect on the look of the mesh object but noticeably decreases rendering time. You also smooth the segmentation at the tight curves of the ellipse without adding significantly to rendering time.

Exercise 2.3.2 *Optimizing the Lofted CWALL Objects*

1. Open 02_cwall_01.max (if it is not already open). Select the CWALL01 object.
2. In the File pull-down menu, choose Summary Info. Note that the CWALL01 object has 6,336 vertices and 12,672 faces. Close Summary Info dialog box.
3. In the Modify panel, expand Skin Parameters rollout, and check Optimize Shapes.
4. Move the cursor over CWALL01, right-click, and choose Properties from the pop-up menu. This is an alternative method for finding the properties of a selected object. Note that the CWALL01 object now has only 1,056 vertices and 2,112 faces. You have made a significant increase in efficiency with no degradation of the mesh.

 Note

Optimize Shapes is an "intelligent" process that retains any curved segments and reduces steps only on straight segments of a shape.

Shape steps are intermediate steps between each vertex on the 2D wall_cross-section. These intermediate steps control the segment curvature. All segments in this shape are straight, so reducing the intermediate steps doesn't affect the flat surfaces. In this case, setting the Shape Steps to 0 in Skin Parameters accomplishes the same reductions. If the cross-section has rounded segments, reducing the Shape Steps to 0 turns them to flat segments.

Chapter 2: Architectural Modeling   85

5. In the Skin Parameters rollout's Options area, enter 8 in the Path Steps field. Notice the mesh becoming smoother on the tight turns of the ellipse.

6. Check Summary Info again. The CWALL01 object now has 1,584 vertices and 3,168 faces—an acceptable increase for the extra smoothness in the curtain wall.

> **Note**
> Increasing the Path steps adds intermediate steps between the vertices on the ellipse. Because the ellipse is curved, the extra steps increase the smoothness of the mesh. For a smoother curve section, add more Path steps, but only as many as you need to get visually acceptable results.

7. Save the file as 02_cwall_02.max.

Setting Up for Material Assignments

NEW TO R3 At this stage in the creation process, it is wise to add material assignments to the lofted curtain wall. MAX R3 boasts a new feature that simplifies the process: You change the Material IDs for each segment of a shape. These Material IDs are now part of the lofted object's faces. Then use the Material IDs in the faces to assign sub-materials (that are part of a Multi/Sub-Object material type) to those particular faces. Material ID #1 is assigned by default.

Exercise 2.3.3   Assigning Material IDs

1. Open 02_cwall_02 (if it is not already open).

2. In the Perspective viewport, type U to change from Perspective to User. Use Zoom Region to zoom in on the left end of the CWALL01 in order to view it and the wall_cross-section shape. See Figure 2.40.

3. Click the Material Editor button. Then drag and drop the multicolored sample sphere onto CWALL01. This assigns the CWALL Multi/Sub-Object material to the lofted wall. All faces turn gray in the display because they default to Material ID #1, thus using the first material in the Multi/Sub-Object material. That changes in this exercise.

4. Type W to return to four viewports. In the Front viewport, select wall_cross-section. In the Modify panel, click the Edit Spline modifier button. Click the Segment button. This gives you access to each Segment on the Shape.

5. In the Front viewport, select the three projecting segments that make up the top spandrel bullnose. See Figure 2.41. Hold down the Ctrl key while adding to the selection set. The segments turn red when selected.

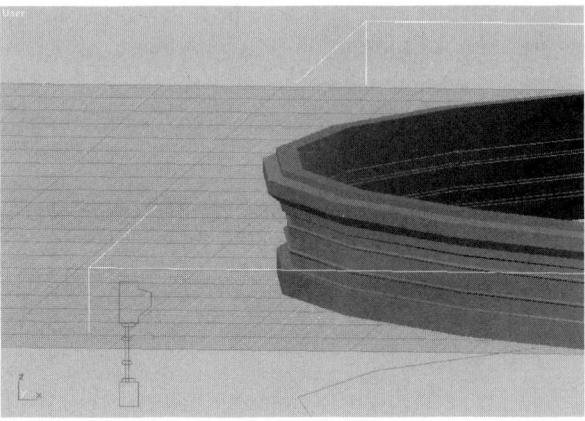

Figure 2.40 Close up of CWALL01 and wall_cross-section.

6. In the Surface Properties rollout at the very bottom of the Modify panel, change Material ID from the default 1 to 2. The corresponding surfaces on the CWALL01 object receive Material #2 of the Multi/Sub-Object material. In the User viewport, the bullnose turns red.

 Note

Note the Material ID assignments on a sketch of the cross section so you know what they refer to as you create the materials. See Figure 2.41.

Figure 2.41 Sketch of Material ID assignments.

7. In the Modify panel, click the Edit Stack button. In the Edit Modifier stack, click Edit Spline. In the Name field at the bottom of the dialog box, change the name to read Edit Spline-top spandrel. This added notation helps the Modifier Stack follow what you are doing. Click OK to close the dialog box.

8. In the Modify panel, click the Edit Spline button. Now click the Segment button again. Click anywhere in an empty area of the Front viewport to clear the selection set. Select the two vertical segments of the glass and change the Material ID to 3. See Figure 2.41. Open the Edit Modifier Stack dialog box, and rename this modifier to Edit Spline-glass, then click OK.

9. In the Modify panel, click the Edit Spline button, and click the Segment button again. Click anywhere in an empty area of the Front viewport to clear the selection set. Select all segments for the horizontal mullions. The easiest way to do this is to drag a window around them and the glass. Finish selecting by holding the Alt key and selecting the two glass segments to deselect them. Change the Material ID to 4. See Figure 2.41. Open the Edit Modifier stack dialog box, and rename this modifier to read Edit Spline-mullions. Click OK.

10. In the Modify panel, click the Edit Spline button, and click the Segment button again. Click anywhere in an empty area of the Front viewport to clear the selection set. Select the right vertical segment of the bottom lintel. Change the Material ID to 5. See Figure 2.41. Open the Edit Modifier stack dialog box. Rename this modifier to read Edit Spline-bottom spandrel, and click OK. The remaining segments are assigned the default Material ID #1.

11. In the Modify panel, click the More button, double-click the Spline Select button, and click the Sub-Object button to exit that mode. This adds a Spline Select that is not a Sub-Object mode, giving you control of the whole shape again. The User viewport shows a multicolored curtain wall with the colors corresponding to the Multi/Sub-Object material. See Figure 2.41 for an example of realistic materials.

Note

Each Edit Spline stores a copy of the entire shape in memory using valuable resources. However, adding separate Edit Spline modifiers to select segments and assign new Material IDs gives you the flexibility to later delete the Edit Spline modifier. Another big advantage to multiple Edit Spline modifiers is the ability to add notations to each modifier in the Edit Modifier Stack dialog box to make its use more obvious to other members of the design team.

12. Save the file as 02_cwall_03.max.

Creating Multiple Curtain Wall Levels

Next you use the Array tool and make instanced clones. With an Instance clone you can edit only one, and all the instances are edited. Because the original 2D cross-section was lofted as an instance, any changes to 2D shape affects the 3D mesh. Also, because the 3D mesh is instanced, your change appears at all levels. Thus the result from careful planning and use of instances is a simple change to the shape that changes all levels of the building. You also applied materials before arraying the curtain wall. The material assignments are now part of the instance definition, and any changes to the material affect all levels of the curtain wall.

Exercise 2.3.4 Creating Multiple Levels

1. Open 02_cwall_03.max (if it is not already open).
2. In the User viewport, select CWALL01, and click on the Array button in the Toolbar. Notice the top left of the Array dialog box indicates that you are using the world-coordinate system. This specifies that the X-, Y-, and Z-axis are related to the world-coordinate system.
3. Enter 12'0" in the Incremental Z Move field at the top of the Array dialog box. Check Instance in the Type of Object area, and enter 10 in the ID Count field. Figure 2.42 shows the entries in the Array dialog box. Click OK. You now have a ten-story curtain wall.

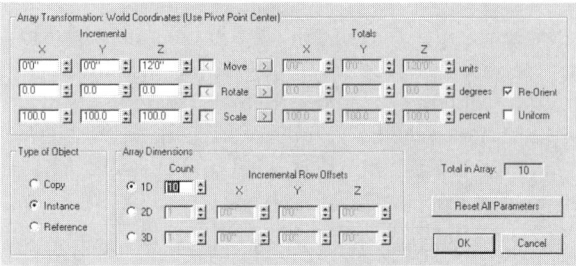

Figure 2.42 The Array dialog box in world-coordinate system.

4. Click the Zoom Extents button to view the complete array. It looks like Figure 2.43.

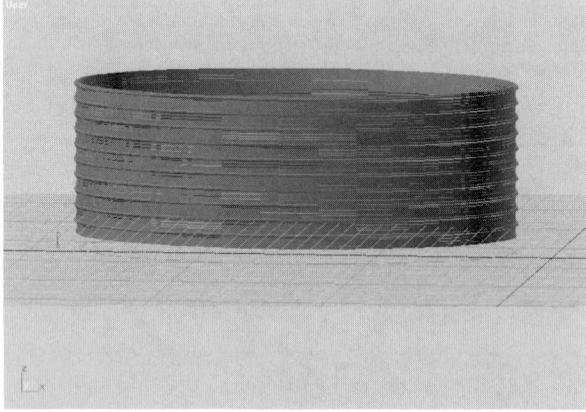

Figure 2.43 Ten-story curtain-wall façade.

5. Save the file as 02_cwall_04.max. For a more complete scene using this curtain-wall method, open 02_cwall_finished.max, and look at Figure 2.41.

Roof Systems

As with walls, you can use several methods to create roof systems in MAX R3. The following are the three common roof styles you investigate here:

- Gable
- Hip
- Conical

Roof systems can be complex and variable, so in this section you focus on the fundamental steps for starting different styles of roofs. Use the new MAX R3 AutoGrid system for alignment and the Grid Helper for accuracy. Also, use existing geometry to make 2D path and shapes to help in the roof creation. The purpose of these exercises is not so much to create a roof, but more to illustrate creative problem-solving techniques.

Gable Roofs I

Gable roofs are relatively simple, yet if the creation process is approached without an understanding of the tools and options, a lot of production time is wasted. The first roof you work on is an equal leg width, L-shaped gable.

Exercise 2.4.1   Creating an L-Shaped Gable Roof

1. Open the file 02max04.max. It contains a simple extruded wall system, two 2D-gable elevations, and a 2D-centerline path on top of the walls. Loft the larger elevation along the path to create the roof.

2. In the Top viewport, select large_gable_shape. Notice the position of the pivot point, and remember, the pivot point determines the attachment of the shape to the path during lofting. The loft path is on the top of the walls, so the pivot point of the shape needs to be centered in the shape and at the same elevation as the seat of the rafter cuts. Use a construction line to accomplish proper alignment.

3. In the Top viewport, click Zoom Extents Selected to fill the display with large_gable_shape, and press W to maximize the viewport.

4. Click, then right-click the 3D Snap Toggle button, and set the snap settings to Only Vertex. Close the dialog box.

5. In the Create panel, click the Shapes button, click the Line button, and create a line from rafter seat to rafter seat. This is only a construction line. It appears similar to Figure 2.44.

90   Part I   Modeling

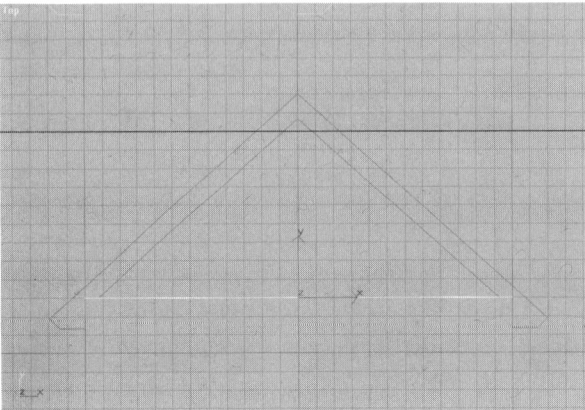

Figure 2.44   Gable shape, with construction line.

6. Select large_gable_shape, and in the Hierarchy panel, click the Affect Pivot Only button.

7. Right-click 3D Snap Toggle, and set Snaps to Pivot and Midpoint. Close the dialog box.

8. Right-click the viewport, and choose Move in the pop-up menu. Move the pivot point from its present location to the midpoint of the construction line. The cursor changes shape and position to indicate your snap locations. Click Affect Pivot Only to exit that mode. Select the construction line, and press Delete to delete it from the scene.

 Warning

Using Pivot Point Snap settings can be disconcerting, at first. The Snap indicator appears to jump all over the screen as the cursor passes over objects. Practice a little and you quickly get the hang of it.

9. Right-click 3D Snap Toggle, and click Clear All to turn off snap settings. Close the dialog box.

10. Press W to return to multiple viewport display, right-click in the User viewport, and press W again to maximize the User viewport.

11. Select roof_path.

12. Choose Compound Objects, and click the Loft button.

13. In Creation Method rollout, click Get Shape, and choose the large_gable_shape in the User viewport. Name the new object LARGE_ROOF. Your roof is similar to Figure 2.45. You correct the dark area near the valley in the next step.

Chapter 2: Architectural Modeling   91

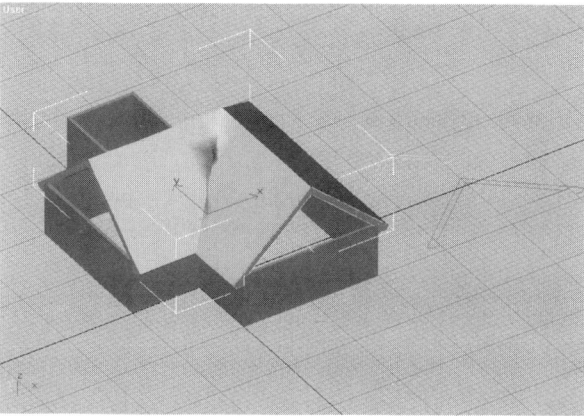

Figure 2.45 Initial lofted gable ell roof.

14. In the User viewport, right-click on the User label, and choose Wireframe from the pop-up menu. Notice how the roof geometry turns in on itself inside the 90 degree bend. This is because the default loft settings are for objects that contain sweeping bends rather than sharp angles; consequently, the number of intermediate Path Steps is set to 5. This creates enough segments for lofts to bend smoothly, but has a negative impact in this case. See Figure 2.46.

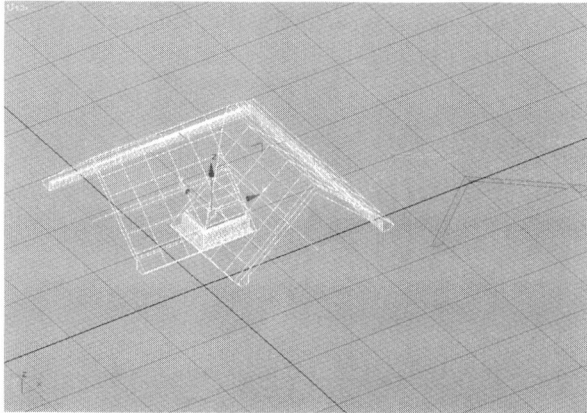

Figure 2.46 Lofted roof, with default path steps.

15. In the Modify panel's Skin Parameters rollout, change the number of Path Steps to 0. This creates a clean 90 degree bend and eliminates the dark, overlapping faces.

16. In the the User viewport, right-click the User label, and choose Smooth+Highlights. The roof still shows odd shading in the valley area. This is

due to the Smoothing Groups (assigned during the loft process) trying to smooth the bend.

17. In the Modify panel's Surface Parameters rollout, uncheck Smooth Length and Smooth Width. The roof/trim surfaces now appear flat.

18. In the Modify panel's Skin Parameters, check Optimize Shapes. This reduces the number of intermediate steps along each segment of the loft shape. Along with lowering the Path Steps, it reduces the number of faces and vertices.

Note

The effects of Path Steps = 0 and Optimize Shapes on this lofted roof reduces the number of faces/vertices from 1,868/936 to 68/36. This is a very significant reduction! Paying particular attention to the face/vertex count results in lower RAM usage, quicker render times, and faster viewport navigation speed.

19. Save the file as 02_gable_01.max.

Gable Roof II

The next gable roof is a straight gable that ties into the main one. First, align the small_gable_shape to the end of the addition, then extrude to a given length. You simply pass the new roof into the existing roof to create the valleys. For most cases, this is both sufficient and efficient for a correct valley situation when viewing from the outside. However, you can also take it a step further to create an intersecting roof system that is viewed correctly from inside and outside the building.

Exercise 2.4.2 Creating an Intersecting Gable with Valleys

1. Open 02_gable_01.max (if it is not already open).
2. Click 3D Snap Toggle to turn it off, and select the 2D small_gable_shape.
3. In the User viewport, use Arc Rotate and Pan until the display looks similar to Figure 2.47.
4. In the Hierarchy panel, click Affect Pivot Only, then click Center to Object, which centers the pivot point on the 2D shape. This is not a critical step for this exercise, but is a good habit to acquire. In the next step, align the 2D shape to the back wall of the addition. However, there are no align tools in MAX R3 that allow aligning 2D shapes to 3D faces in a simple one-step process.

Tip

You can also work with a Reference clone. That allows editing of the original 2D shape to affect the 3D roof that you build in the next steps.

Chapter 2: Architectural Modeling   93

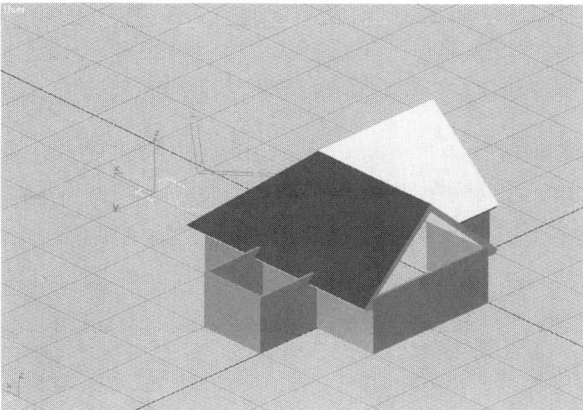

Figure 2.47   View toward the building's addition.

5. In the Modify panel, click the Extrude modifier button, and leave the Height at 0'-0". This creates faces from the 2D shape that have no thickness in the Z-axis.
6. Click and hold the Align button in the Toolbar, and choose Normal Align from the flyout toolbar.
7. Move the cursor over the extruded object. When you get the crosshair cursor, click and hold to reveal a blue normal vector.
8. Move the cursor so the blue normal vector is near the peak of the gable, and release the mouse button. See Figure 2.48.

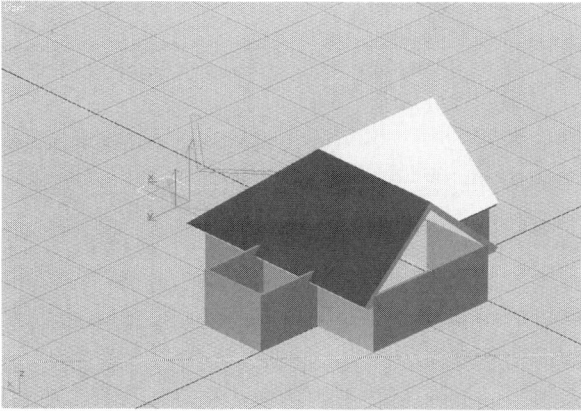

Figure 2.48   Blue normal vector, near gable peak.

9. Move the cursor over the back wall of the addition. When you see the crosshair cursor, click and hold to reveal a green normal vector.

10. Move the cursor so the green normal vector is near the upper-middle of the back wall, and release the mouse button. The Normal Align dialog box appears.
11. Check the Flip check box, and click OK. See Figure 2.49.

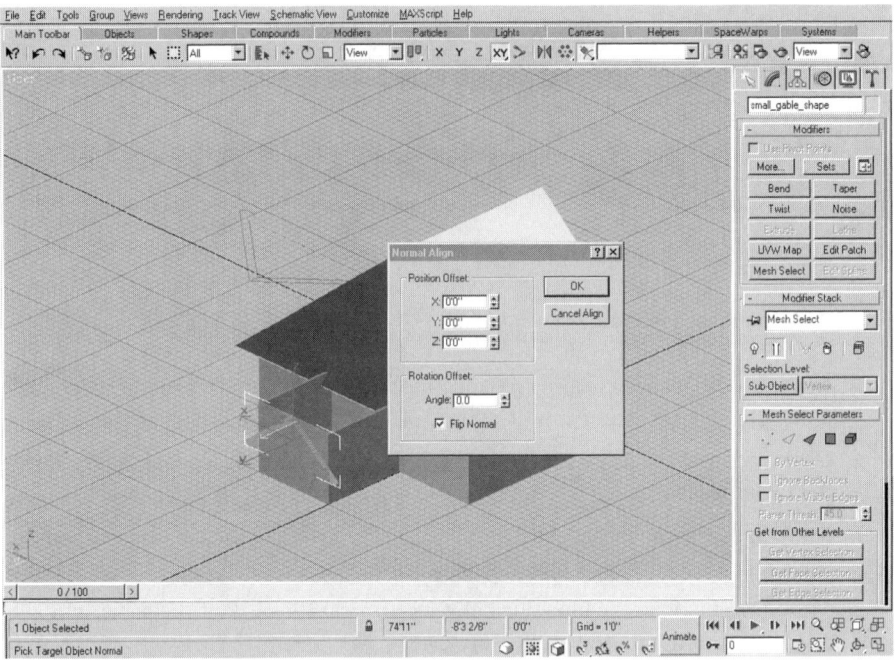

Figure 2.49 Green normal vector, near upper-middle wall.

12. Click, then right-click the 3D Snap Toggle button, and set Snaps to Pivot Point and Midpoint. In the User viewport, zoom in on the addition.
13. Move the small_gable_shape so its pivot point is snapped to the midpoint of the upper-outside wall. This is to ensure that the gable is centered on the wall. Turn Snap Toggle off.
14. Click the Align button, select LARGE_ROOF, check Z Position, check Minimum in Current Object column, and check Minimum in Target Object. This aligns the bottom of small_gable_shape with the bottom of LARGE_ROOF for proper alignment. Click OK. See Figure 2.50.
15. In the Modify panel, enter –20'0" in the Extrude Amount field. In the Parameters rollout, clear the Smooth check box. Rename the roof SMALL_ROOF.
16. Save the file as 02_gable_02. The two roofs intersect and create correct valleys. However, from the inside, the SMALL_ROOF projects into the LARGE_ROOF interior space. (See Figure 2.51.) In the next exercise you correct that.

Chapter 2: Architectural Modeling   95

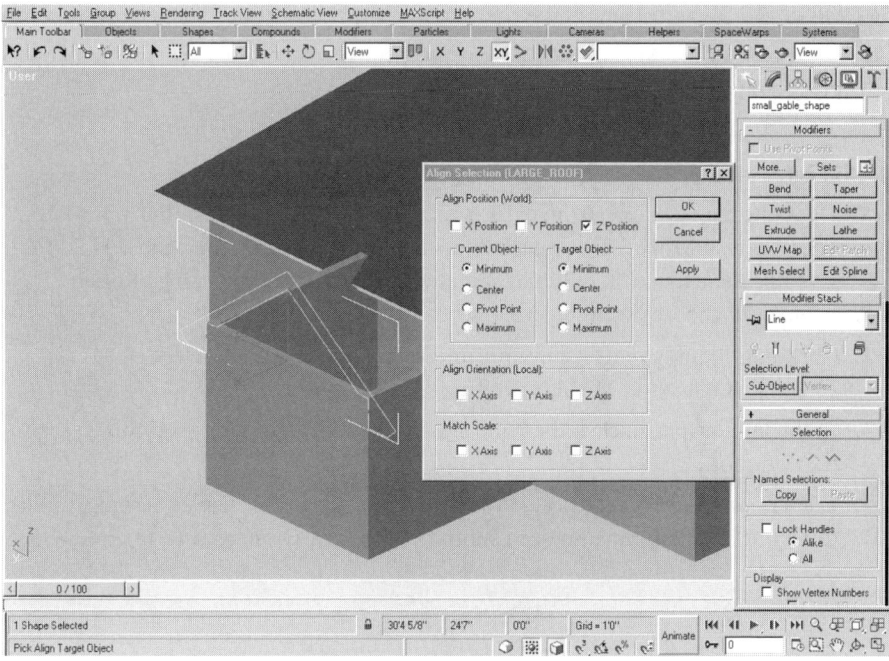

Figure 2.50 Small_gable_shape, aligned to LARGE_ROOF and flush to back wall.

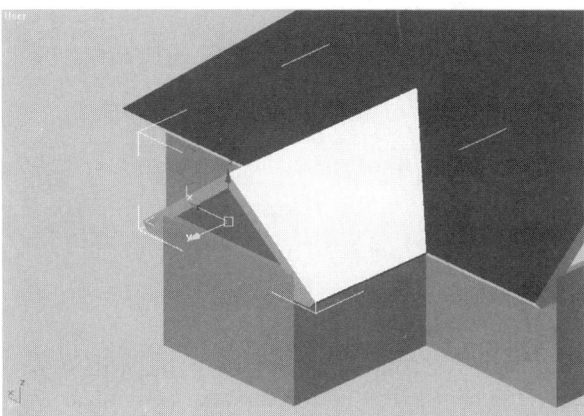

Figure 2.51 Intersecting gable roofs and valleys.

Gable Roof III

There may be times when you need roofs to correctly intersect both exteriorly and interiorly. The next exercise illustrates 3D-Boolean operations and Sub-Object editing to cut the LARGE_ROOF and clean up the small roof at the intersection. The process requires some time-consuming work, so learn the concepts here, then move on. You can always return later and clean up the rest.

Exercise 2.4.3 Using Boolean Operations to Combine Roofs

1. Open the file 02_gable_02.max (if it isn't already open). Performing 3D-Boolean operations in MAX R3 is sometimes risky so in the Edit menu, choose Hold to save the scene to a disk buffer. If something goes wrong, you can go to Edit menu, and choose Fetch to get the scene back—just in case.
2. Click the Zoom Extents All button, and in the Top viewport, select LARGE_ROOF and SMALL_ROOF.
3. In the Display panel, click the Hide Unselected button to hide everything except the two roofs.
4. Click Zoom Extents All Selected to center the roofs in the display. It looks similar to Figure 2.52. You now Boolean subtract SMALL_ROOF from LARGE_ROOF.

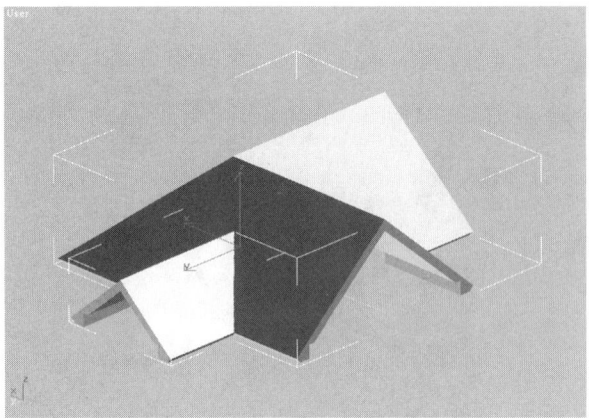

Figure 2.52 Intersecting gable roofs and valleys.

5. In the Edit menu, choose Clone. In the Clone Options dialog box, check Copy, and click OK to accept the default names. This creates copies of both roofs. SMALL_ROOF01 is subtracted from LARGE_ROOF, and LARGE_ROOF01 is subtracted from SMALL_ROOF.
6. Type H, and choose LARGE_ROOF in the Select Objects dialog box. Click the Select button.
7. In the Create panel, click the Geometry button, click Standard Primitives, and choose Compound Objects in the list. Click the Boolean button, and click the Pick Operand B button. Type H, choose SMALL_ROOF01 in the Pick Objects

dialog box, and click the Pick button. This subtracts SMALL_ROOF01 from LARGE_ROOF.

8. Type H, and choose SMALL_ROOF in the Select Objects dialog box. Click the Select button.

9. In the Create panel, click the Boolean button, and click the Pick Operand B button. Type H, choose LARGE_ROOF01 in the Pick Objects dialog box, and click the Pick button. This subtracts LARGE_ROOF01 from SMALL_ROOF.

10. Right-click on the User viewport label and choose Wireframe in the menu. Notice the Boolean operations are created, but there are extra faces in both objects. The roofs were subtracted, but only slices were taken out (see Figure 2.53). Delete the extra faces at the Sub-Object Level.

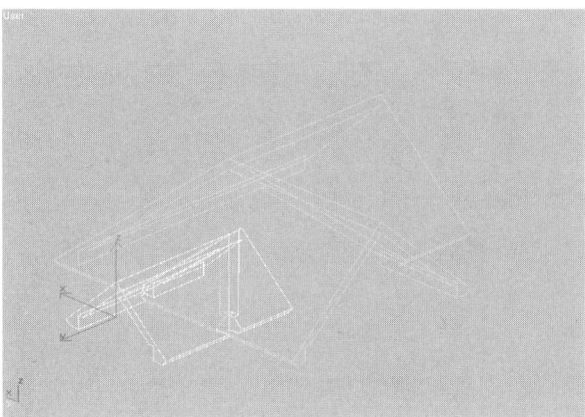

Figure 2.53 Slices booleaned from roofs.

11. In the User viewport, select the SMALL_ROOF, right-click the viewport, and choose Convert to Editable Mesh in the menu.

12. Right-click the Viewport again, select Sub-Object, then choose Element in the new menu. In the User viewport, select the SMALL_ROOF (near the end of the roof that is inside LARGE_ROOF). The Boolean operation split the roof into two elements. The element turns transparent red, similar to Figure 2.54.

13. Press the Delete key on the keyboard, and click the Yes button in the Delete Faces dialog box. In the Modify panel, click the Sub-Object button to exit that mode.

14. In the User viewport, select the LARGE_ROOF, right-click the viewport, and choose Convert to Editable Mesh in the menu.

15. Right-click the Viewport again, and choose Sub-Object. Then choose Element in the new menu. In the User viewport, select the LARGE_ROOF (on the triangular area that is inside SMALL_ROOF). The Boolean operation split the roof into two elements. The element turns transparent red, similar to Figure 2.55.

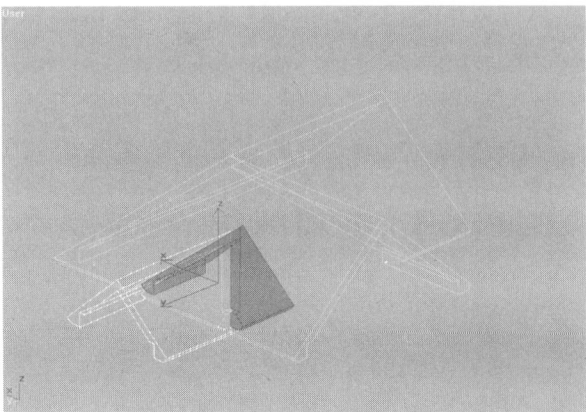

Figure 2.54 Transparent red element of SMALL_ROOF.

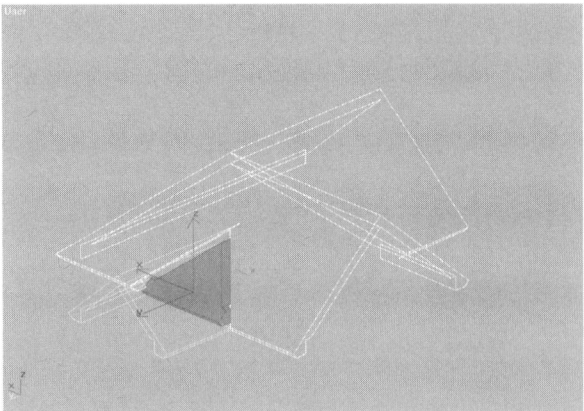

Figure 2.55 Transparent red element of LARGE_ROOF.

16. Press the Delete key, and click the Yes button in the Delete Faces dialog box. In the Modify panel, click the Sub-Object button to exit that mode. The roofs look correct in Wireframe mode, but SMALL_ROOF needs to be extended into the LARGE_ROOF—to match up with the inside roof plane for a flush surface.

17. Type W to switch to multiple viewports. Right-click the Left viewport to activate it, and type W to maximize the Left viewport.

18. Right-click the 3D Snap button, check the Clear All button in the Grid and Snaps Settings dialog box, then check the Vertex option. Close the dialog box, and click the 3D Snap button to turn it on.

19. In the Left viewport, select SMALL_ROOF. Right-click the viewport, and choose Sub-Object mode in the menu. Choose Vertex in the next menu. Drag a selection

window around all the vertices adjacent to LARGE_ROOF. It looks like Figure 2.56.

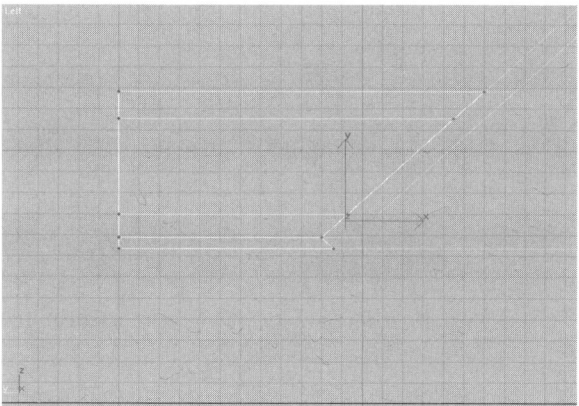

Figure 2.56 Select all vertices adjacent to LARGE_ROOF.

20. Right-click the viewport, and choose Move from the menu. Click and drag the upper-right selected vertex to the right until it snaps to the inside roof-plane vertex. It resembles Figure 2.57. Exit Sub-Object mode.

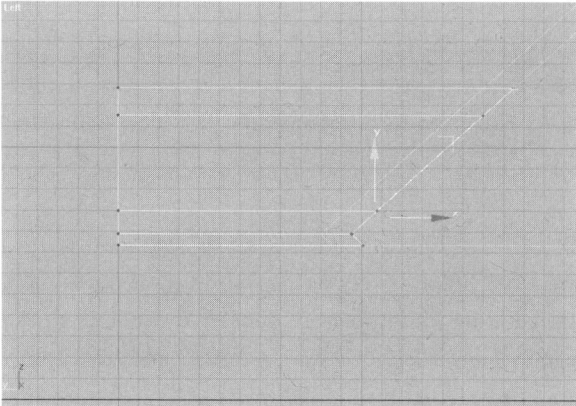

Figure 2.57 Snap upper-right vertex to inside vertex.

21. Type W to see all viewports, activate the User viewport, right-click the User label, and choose Smooth+Highlight in the menu. Use ArcRotate to view the roof from outside and inside, and you see a clean intersection.

22. Save the file as 02_gable_03.max.

Windows and Doors

Doors and windows are, of course, an integral part of any architectural work you do in MAX R3. An option for creating doors and windows is using the parametric doors and windows that ship as part of the bonus files on the MAX R3 CD.

Note
If the Doors and Windows do not show up as options in the Create panel's Geometry drop-down list, do a Custom install from the shipping CD-ROM. Check only the Bonus option in the install routine.

You don't use the parametric doors and windows in this chapter. The process of creating parametric doors and windows is a dragging/clicking session (as with other primitive objects), and the options are easy to understand. The parametric doors and windows are probably sufficient for most of your needs. However, there may be times when you need a custom door or window that the parametric objects cannot handle. In these cases, consider using the:

- Extrude modifier
- Bevel modifier
- Bevel Profile modifier

Each of these methods is essentially extruding along the Z-axis of a 2D shape, but each offers options, advantages, and disadvantages over the other. In the exercises presented below, you work only with windows. Create doors using the same procedure and changing the 2D shape.

Extruded Doors and Windows

Using the Extrude modifier to create a window is very simple, but warrants mentioning because it is also efficient. A large building with numerous doors and windows quickly becomes inefficient if the doors and windows have a few extra vertices and faces in each one. The doors and windows are often viewed from a distance that don't require any detail beyond the shape and glazing layout. For the close-up shots, you create new doors and windows with the required detail. Advantages of extruded 2D doors and windows include:

- Efficient, low face count
- Easy to create
- Easy to modify

Their main disadvantage is they are visually uninteresting at close range. In this next exercise, you create an extruded window from a 2D shape. This is the simplest form of creating 3D custom windows.

Exercise 2.5.1 Creating Extruded Custom Windows

1. Open the file named 02max05.max. It contains three 2D-compound shapes (shapes created with multiple splines) that you use to create 3D windows. There is also one simple 2D shape that is used later in this chapter. See Figure 2.58.
2. Right-click the Front viewport to activate it. From the Main Toolbar, click the Select button, and drag a window around the three 2D shapes to select them. Right-click the viewport again, and choose Move from the pop-up menu. Holding the Shift key, click and drag on the X-axis Transform Gizmo toward the right.
3. In the Clone Options dialog box, check Reference, and click OK to create a set of Reference clones just to the right of the existing shapes.
4. Type W to maximize the Perspective viewport. In the Main Toolbar, click the Select button, and choose the double_hung_sash01 reference shape at the top right of the display.
5. In the Modify panel, click the Extrude button, and enter 0'2" in the Amount field. The Reference clone becomes an extruded 3D object, while the original 2D shape remains unchanged.
6. In the Modify panel's Parameters rollout, clear the Smooth check box at the bottom of the panel.

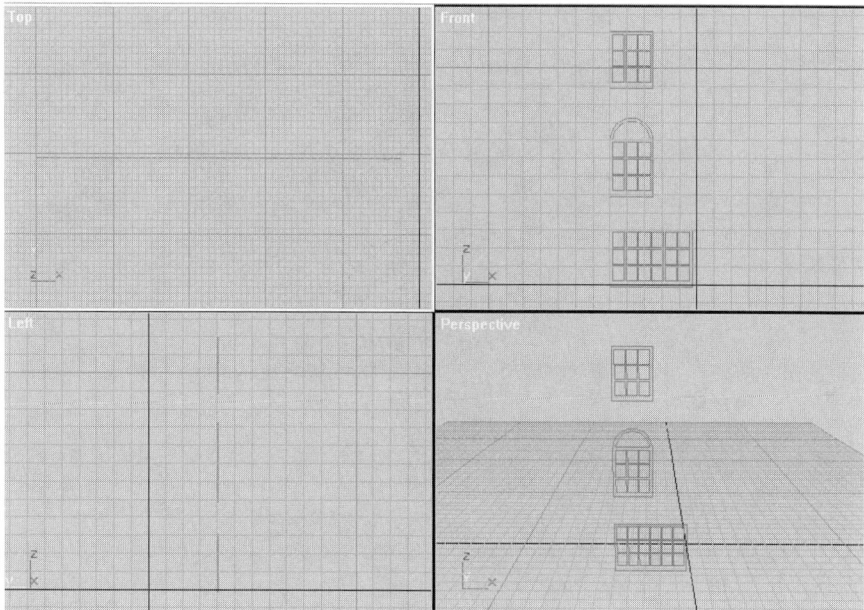

Figure 2.58 Three 2D window mullion shapes.

> **Tip**
> Smoothing can often cause strange shading effects in the rendered image. For objects that are flat surfaces with no curvature, you can usually turn off any smoothing.

 NEW TO R3

7. In the Parameters rollout, check the new Use Shape IDs option. This allows you to quickly change materials by modifying the Material ID assignments of segments on the original 2D shape. Changing material ID at the segment level is discussed in this chapter, Exercise 2.3.3.

8. Right-click the object, and choose Properties in the pop-up menu. Notice the window sash contains only 80 vertices and 192 faces. See Figure 2.59.

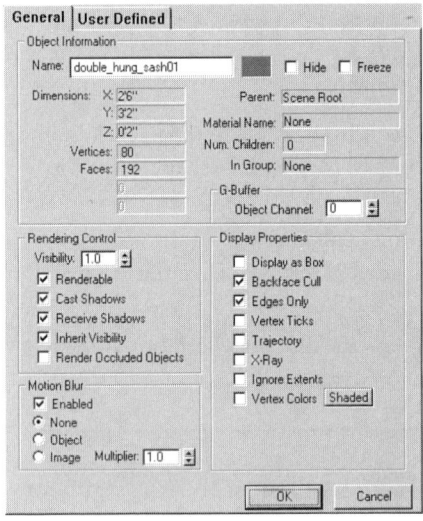

Figure 2.59 Properties dialog box for double_hung_sash01.

9. Rename the object DOUBLE_HUNG_SASH01 because it is now a 3D object, and save the file as 02_windoor_01.max.

 Tip
> The window has no object for the panes of glass. For the glass, create a rectangle slightly smaller than the overall window size, convert it to an Editable Mesh, and use Align to center it in the sash. Then assign a two-sided material with glass properties.

Bevel Doors and Windows

The next step in creating custom doors and windows is to bevel all edges, using the Bevel modifier. This adds more faces and vertices. However, for doors and windows that are viewed up close, the extra chamfer catches the scene's light, making a visually more interesting object. Advantages of beveling 2D doors and windows include:

- Extra surface to catch light
- Easy to create
- Easy to modify

Disadvantages include:

- Added vertices and faces.
- Beveling is added to all edges, including outside edge.

Exercise 2.5.2   Creating Beveled Custom Windows

1. Open 02_windoor_01.max (if it is not already open).
2. In the Perspective viewport, select the Reference clone roundtop_sash01. In the Modify panel, click the More button, and double-click Bevel in the Modifiers list.

Note
The Bevel modifier only appears in the Modifiers list if you selected a 2D shape. If you don't see Bevel in the list, you either selected the incorrect shape or you inadvertently converted it to a 3D mesh.

3. The Bevel modifier allows up to three levels of beveling, letting you chamfer on an object's front and back. In the Bevel Values rollout, enter 0'1/4" in the Level 1 Height and Outline fields. This starts a 1/4 inch, 45 degree chamfer upward in the local Z-axis.

Note
Entering a number in the Start Outline field has the effect of scaling the 2D shape by that amount. Usually you leave the Start Outline field blank.

4. Check the Level 2 check box, and enter 0'1-1/2" in the Height field. You want the side of the window to be straight, so leave the Level 2 Outline field at 0'0".
5. Check the Level 3 check box, and enter 0'1/4" in the Height field, and −0'1/4" (yes, that's minus) in the Outline field to chamfer inward. The total thickness of the sash is two inches.
6. Right-click in the Perspective viewport to activate it, and zoom in on the two 3D windows in the viewport. Slightly Arc Rotate. Observe how the light catches the chamfered edges on the roundtop_sash01, making it visually more interesting. The Perspective viewport looks similar to Figure 2.60.

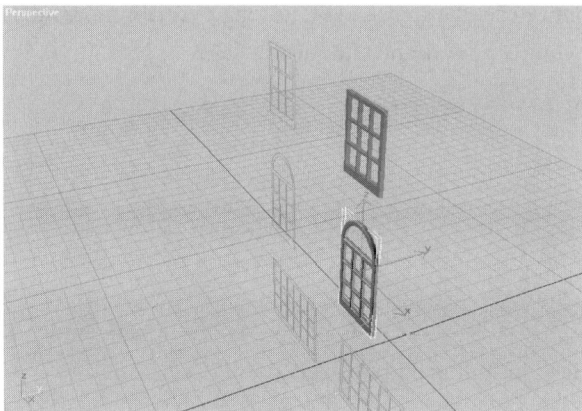

Figure 2.60 A beveled window versus an extruded window—for visual interest.

7. In the Perspective viewport, right-click the selected roundtop_sash01, and click Properties. Notice the vertex/face count is 328/692, considerably higher than the extruded window.

Note
The same Bevel modifier on the double_hung_sash01 creates a face count of 160/352, in direct comparison with the Extrude modifier count of 80/192 (previously mentioned).

8. Rename the object ROUNDTOP_SASH01, and save the file as 02_windoor_02.max.

Bevel Profile Doors and Windows

Bevel Profile is another modifier that works only when applied to 2D shapes. Its function is somewhat different in that it uses a second 2D shape to extrude and bevel the base 2D shape. This allows for complex beveling beyond the capability of the Bevel modifier's three levels. Some of Bevel Profile advantages include:

- Complex chamfers and fillets are possible
- Easy to edit original base 2D shape or the 2D profile

One of the main disadvantages of Bevel Profile is that the Vertex/face counts multiply quickly.

In this next exercise, you apply a Bevel Profile to a 2D-compound shape to create a window sash. The sash is two inches thick, with a chamfer on the back edges and a fillet on the front edges.

Chapter 2: Architectural Modeling   105

Exercise 2.5.3 Creating Bevel Profile Custom Windows

1. Open 02_windoor_02.max (if it is not already open).
2. Type W to switch to multiple viewports. The screen looks similar to Figure 2.61.

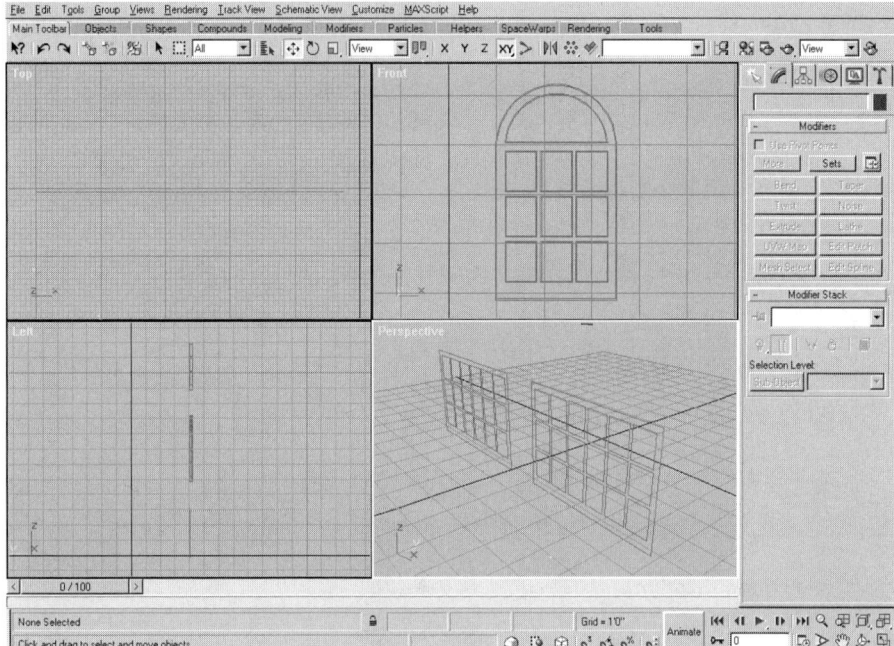

Figure 2.61 Multiple viewports, with curved_sash and curved_sash01 in Perspective viewport.

3. Right-click the Top viewport to activate it, type H, and double-click bevel_profile01 in the list. Click the Zoom Extents Selected button to fill the Top viewport with the shape. Bevel_profile01 looks similar to Figure 2.62.

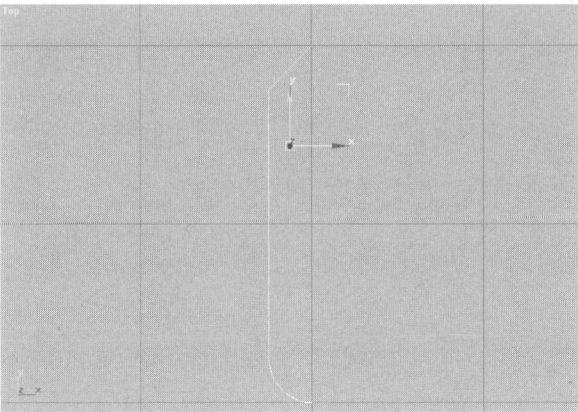

Figure 2.62 Bevel_profile01 2D shape in Top viewport.

4. In the Perspective viewport, select curved_sash01. In the Modify panel, click the More button, and double-click Bevel Profile in the list.

5. In Parameters rollout, click the Pick Profile button, and choose the bevel_profile01 shape in the Top viewport.

6. Zoom in closely in the Left and Perspective viewports. Notice that the window is chamfered on one side and filleted on the other. The window 2D shape is extruded to the height and profile described by the 2D-profile shape. This is used to achieve complex 3D objects from precise 2D shapes. It looks similar to Figure 2.63.

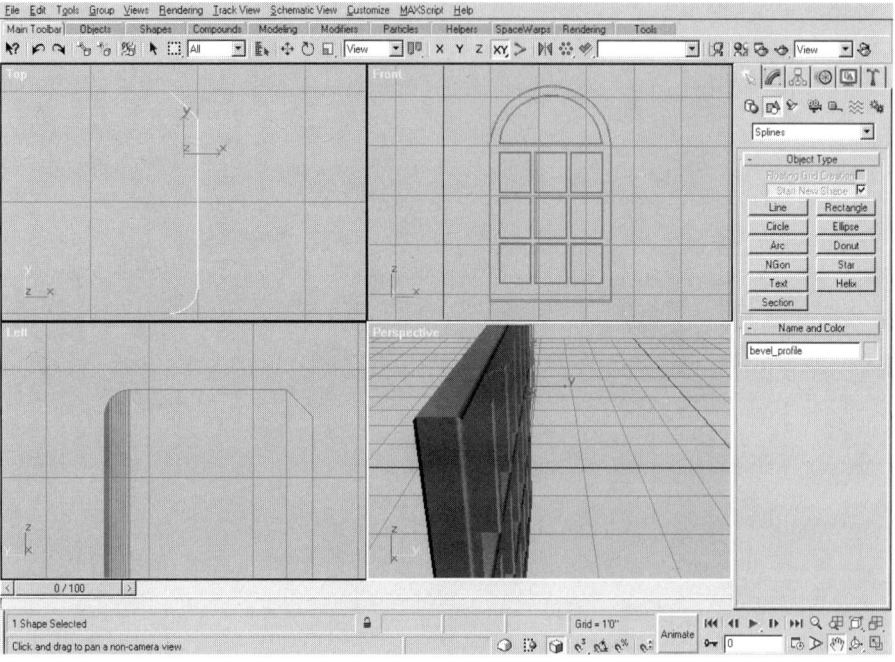

Figure 2.63 Bevel Profile modifier on 2D shape.

7. Rename the object CURVED_SASH01, and save the file as 02_windoor_03.max.

Tip

All the window methods in the previous exercises can create custom doors as well. Just substitute the 2D-door shapes for the 2D-window shapes.

Space Frames

Space frames are a variety of objects constructed from wires or tubes or beams linked together. The following are some typical objects that are considered space frames:

- Wire baskets and shelving
- Mechanical arms
- Highway signage structures
- Structural beams
- Architectural framework/expansion joints

In the next two exercises, you create space frames for a simple wire basket and for expansion joints on a high-rise building. See Figure 2.64 for an example of expansion joints between glass panes in a high-rise building. Perhaps you want to show the building's expansion joint materials with Bump Maps. You usually opt for the mapping solution to reduce the model's number of vertices/faces. However, there are times when the mapping doesn't hold up under close scrutiny, or the contrast of the map creates unwanted rolling edges during animated sequences (caused by image pixels against a contrasting background color).

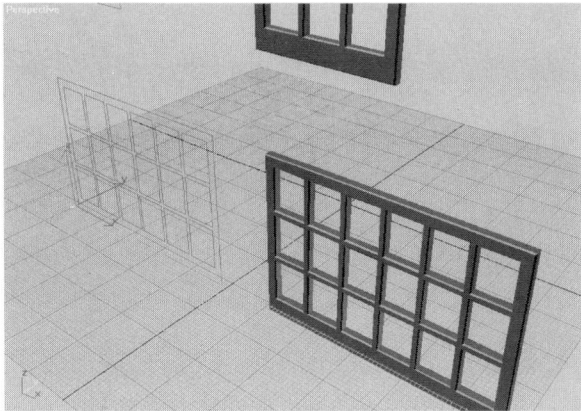

Figure 2.64 Expansion joints between glass panes.

Wire Baskets

In this simple exercise, you work with the Lattice modifier. It is one of the most useful modifiers in MAX R3 and has been around since 3D Studio MAX R2. It's amazing how many users don't know it's there or forget about using it.

108   Part I   Modeling

Exercise 2.6   Using Lattice Modifier for a Space Frame

1. In the File pull-down menu, choose Reset (if prompted, save your work). Then click Yes to reset the display.

2. In the Create panel, choose Standard Primitives, and click the Box button. In the Top viewport, drag a box into the middle of the viewport. Enter Length = 50.0, Width = 50.0, and Height = –1.0. Name the object TABLE.

3. Click the Zoom Extents All button. In the Create panel, click Sphere, and drag a sphere into the middle of the table. Enter 10.0 in the Radius, 24 in the Segments, and 0.5 in the Hemisphere field. Name the object BASKET. The scene looks similar to Figure 2.65.

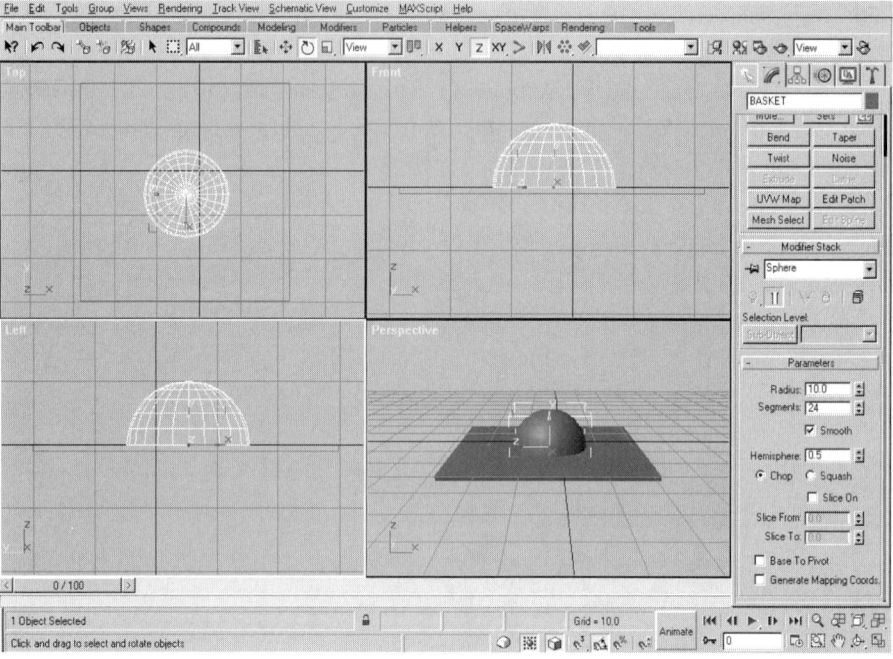

Figure 2.65   Table with hemisphere.

4. In the Toolbar, click the Mirror button, check Z in the Mirror Axis column, and enter 10.0 in the Offset field. Click OK. The Mirror dialog box looks like Figure 2.66.

5. In the Modify panel, click the More button, and double-click Lattice in the list.

6. In the Parameters rollout, check Struts Only From Edges, enter 0.1 in the Struts Radius field, and enter 6 in the Struts Sides field. Check the Smooth option.

Chapter 2: Architectural Modeling   109

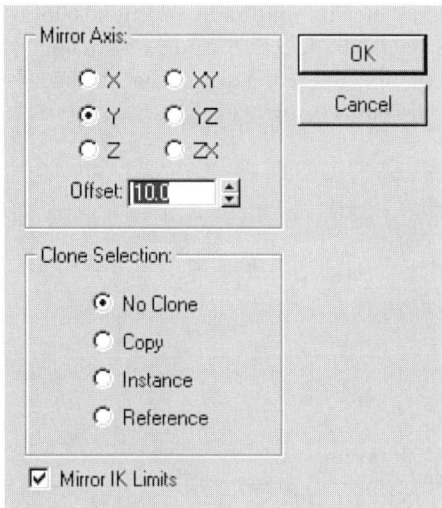

Figure 2.66   The Mirror dialog box settings.

7. Right-click the Perspective viewport, and click the Zoom Extents Selected button to fill the viewport with the basket. Notice the top of the basket has wires. You correct that in the next steps. See Figure 2.67.

Figure 2.67   Lattice basket, with top wires.

8. In the Modify panel, click Edit Stack, choose Lattice in the list, and click the Cut button. Click OK.

 Tip
Cut the Lattice modifier from the Stack, and save its settings in a buffer. This is usually preferable to using the Remove Modifier From Stack button. Later you Paste the Lattice back on the Stack.

9. In the Modify panel, click MeshSelect, click the Edge button in Selection rollout, and check the Ignore Backfaces option. Toggle the selection mode to Crossing Selection. Then drag a window around the sphere's center, where the pie-shaped faces converge. The selected edges look similar to Figure 2.68.

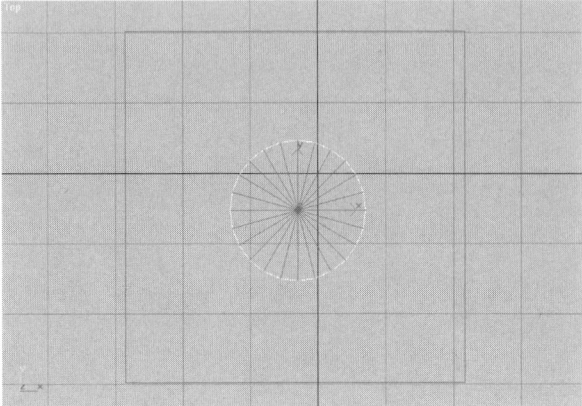

Figure 2.68 Pie-shaped edges selected.

Note
This selection method ensures that you select only the interior edges of the pie-shaped faces and not the edges that form the top-outside rim of the basket.

10. In the Modify panel, click the More button, and double-click DeleteMesh in the list. This removes the edges and adjacent faces, but gives you the option of removing the DeleteMesh modifier at a later date.

Tip
Using a DeleteMesh or a DeleteSpline modifier is a good way to show a client several options in the model. Use several of the modifiers and the Active/Inactive Toggle to reveal each option at a time.

11. In the Modify panel, click the Mesh Select button. Make sure you are out of Sub-Object mode.

Tip
To return control to the entire mesh object, it's always a good idea to apply a MeshSelect modifier and exit Sub-Object mode after Sub-Object selections. Otherwise any subsequent modifier acts only on the last MeshSelect selection set.

12. Click the Edit Stack button, and choose the top MeshSelect. Click the Paste button to paste the Lattice modifier onto the basket. The Edit Modifier Stack dialog box looks like Figure 2.69. Click OK.

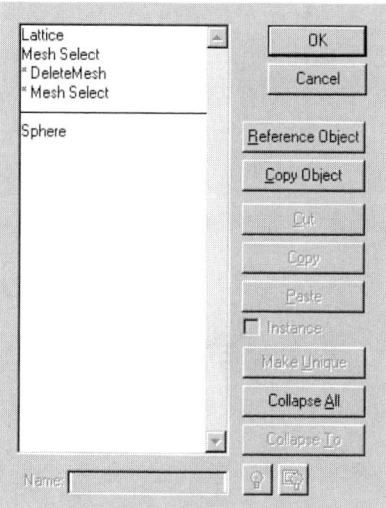

Figure 2.69 The Modifier Stack dialog box, with lattice on top.

13. Save the file as 02_spacfram_01.max.

You now have an open-wire basket, with the option of putting the top back on by removing the DeleteMesh modifier from the stack.

Architectural Framework or Expansion Joints

If you're tired of hearing about the virtues of keeping an object's number of vertices and faces to a minimum, the next exercise is for you. It proves that sometimes the extra geometry *is* worth the overhead. In Exercise 2.7, the building's elliptical glass façade has a Raytrace material with a Bump Map already assigned to it. The Bump Map raises areas of the surface to represent thin framing members for the glazing. Notice that the framing members show aliasing, which undoubtedly causes rolling in animated renderings. Also, if you dolly the camera in from a distant shot to a close-up, the bitmap's resolution causes the bump illusion to appear unconvincing. In the next exercise you use a clone of the glass façade, thus creating a Lattice-modifier framework that holds up in distant or close camera shots.

112   Part I   Modeling

 Note
Remember, this is not an example of an award-winning glass building, rather an illustration of a method for working toward that goal.

Exercise 2.7   Creating a Mesh Frame or Expansion Joint System

1. Open the file called 02max06.max. It is a simple glass structure with a bump material. Also in the scene are landscape and background sky image. The screen looks like Figure 2.70.

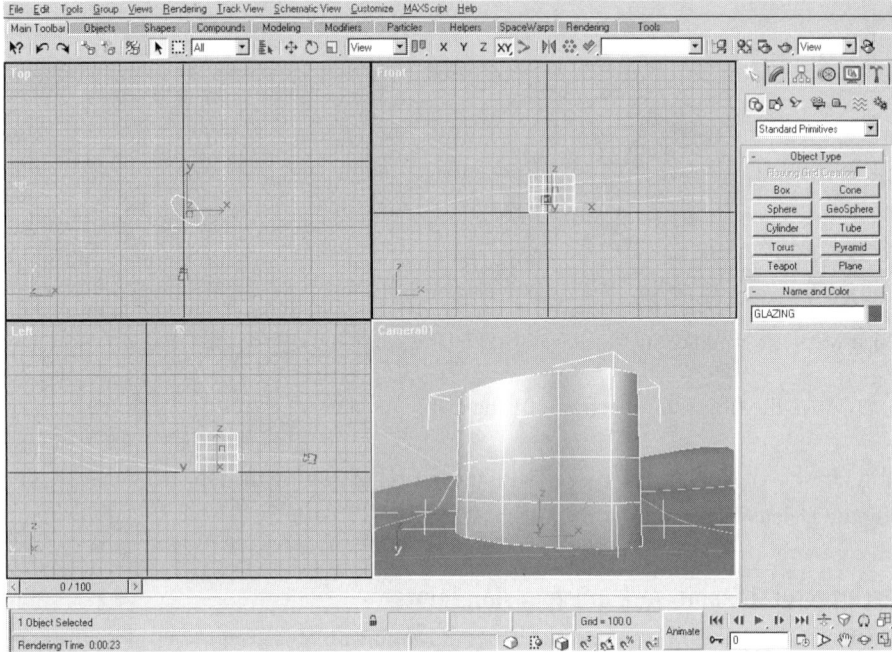

Figure 2.70   The scene with elliptical glass structure in landscape.

2. Right-click the Camera01 viewport to activate it, and click the Quick Render button. The glass structure in the Virtual Frame Buffer shows a reflective surface with an apparent frame (or expansion joint pattern). However, it lacks crispness and punch. There are some material adjustments that help, but essentially the Bump Map gives the look intended in this case. Also, notice the jagged edges along the bitmap joints in the glass. These are bound to cause rolling during animation. The rendered image looks like Figure 2.71.

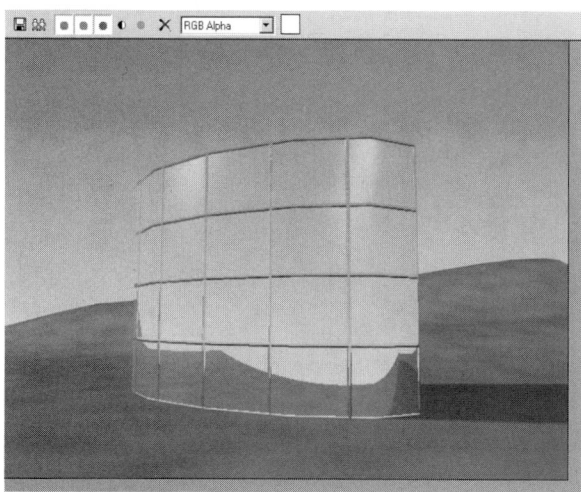

Figure 2.71 Rendered glass structure with bump joints.

3. In Camera01 viewport, select the GLAZING object (if it is not already selected). In the Edit menu, choose Clone, and accept the defaults in the Clone Options dialog box. Click OK. This creates an exact copy of GLAZING.

4. In the Modify panel, click the More button, and double-click Lattice in the list. This creates large struts and junctions over the surface of the glazing.

5. In the Main Toolbar, click the Materials Editor button, then drag and drop the BLACK JOINT material onto the lattice.

6. Click on the GLASS NO BUMP material sample sphere. Then drag and drop it onto the original GLAZING mesh. The bump pattern on the original material doesn't exactly match the lattice pattern so this material shows the same reflectivity without the Bump Map.

7. Select GLAZING01 (if it isn't selected). In the Modify panel's Parameters rollout, check Struts Only from Edges. In the Struts area, enter 0.3 in the Radius field, and 6 in the Sides field.

8. In the Toolbar, click Quick Render. The glass structure now has a crisp, bold expansion joint system. It looks similar to Figure 2.72. Close the Virtual Frame Buffer and the Material Editor.

9. In the Modify panel, click the Edit Stack button. Drag the mouse over Extrude and Ellipse in the list to highlight them. It looks like Figure 2.73.

114   Part I   Modeling

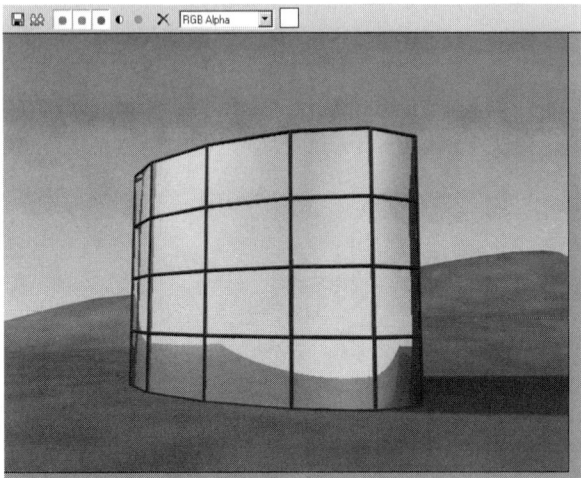

Figure 2.72   Glass structure with lattice expansion joints.

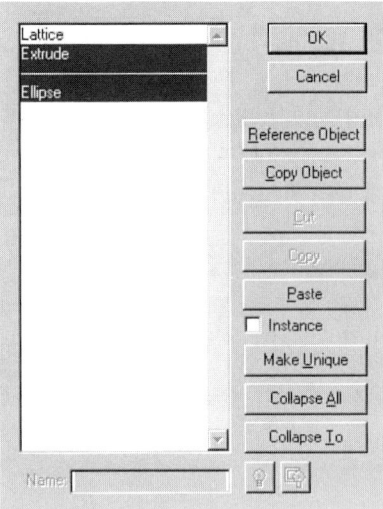

Figure 2.73   The Edit Stack dialog box with Extrude and Ellipse highlighted.

10. Click the Collapse To button, and click Yes in the Warning dialog. Click OK. This collapses the two selected modifiers into an Editable Mesh. This allows you access to Sub-Object editing level while leaving the Lattice modifier intact.

11. In the Modifier Stack, drop to Editable Mesh level, and click the Edge button in the Selection rollout. Click the Zoom Extents All Selected button to fill the orthographic viewports with GLAZING01.

Chapter 2: Architectural Modeling 115

12. Right-click the Front viewport to activate it. Click the Select button, and drag a selection box over the edges between the top and second-from-top horizontal segments. Hold the Ctrl key down, and drag a window over the second segment from the bottom. Selection Crossing mode must be active, and you only select the vertical and diagonal edges between the segments. It appears similar to Figure 2.74.

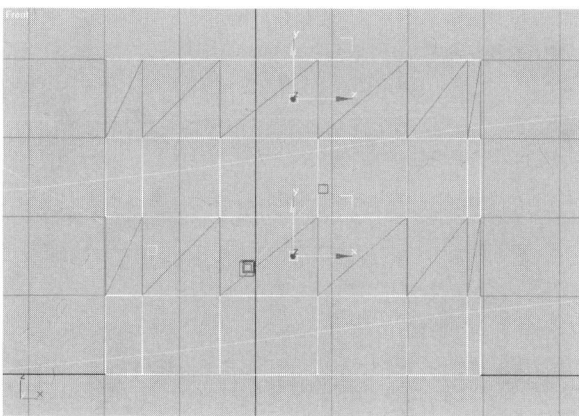

Figure 2.74 Vertical and diagonal edges of top segment selected.

13. In the Modify panel's Surface Properties rollout, click the Visible button. This changes the diagonal edges from invisible to visible or in the viewport, dotted lines to solid.

 Tip
The Lattice modifier works on only the visible mesh edges by default. Adjust the lattice by changing the visibility of edges.

14. Exit Sub-Object mode, click the Modifier Stack, and click Lattice level. Render the Camera01 viewport. Note that you have new lattice structure at the top and the second-from-top segments.
15. Right-click the Top viewport to activate it. Arc Rotate until you are looking at the mesh from an above angled view. The viewport looks like Figure 2.75
16. In the Toolbar, click the Select button. In the Modify panel, drop to Editable Mesh level, and click the Edge button. In the Edit Geometry rollout, check the Ignore Backfacing Option to keep from selecting edges on the object's back by mistake. Click the Turn button, and click every other diagonal edge in the top segment. You must use Arc Rotate to observe the back side and get all the edges. This turns the edge direction for a more realistic brace layout. It looks like Figure 2.76.

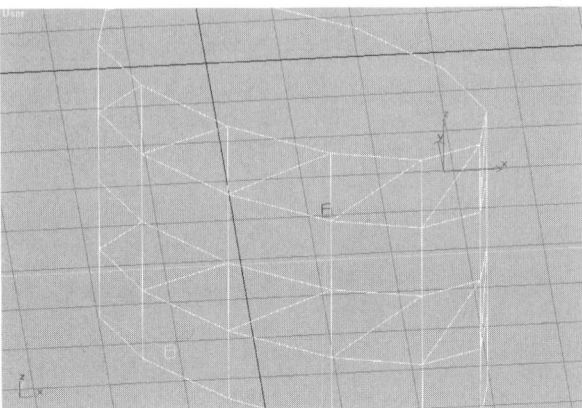

Figure 2.75 GLAZING01, viewed from above in User viewport.

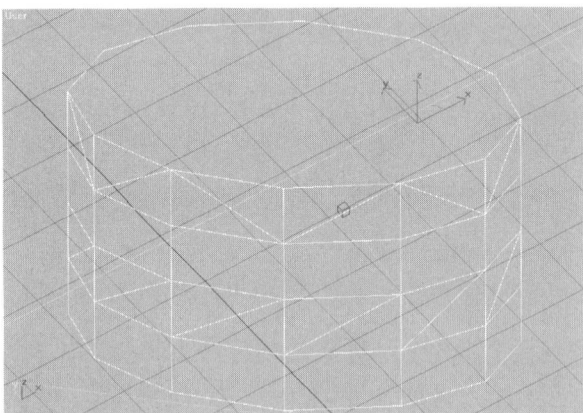

Figure 2.76 Every other edge turned in the top segment.

17. In the Modify panel, exit Sub-Object mode. Return to Lattice level in the Modifier Stack.

18. Activate the Camera01 viewport, and click Quick Render to render the scene. You now have an expansion joint pattern quite different from when you began. The scene looks like Figure 2.77.

19. Save the scene as 02_expjoint_01.max.

 Tip

There are many more edit capabilities at Sub-Object Edge level: You can Divide edges, Cut edges at specific points, or Slice to form continuous new edges, to name a few. Experiment with this model to understand the flexibility of edge-level editing.

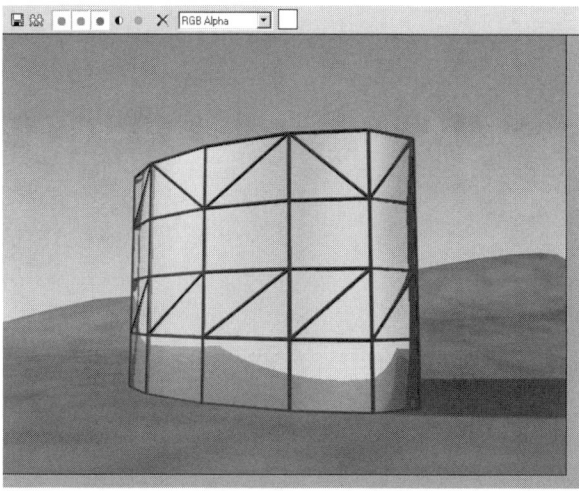

Figure 2.77 Rendered expansion joints.

In Practice: Architectural Modeling

- **Conceptual architectural modeling.** Breaking up projects into smaller parts, and knowing when to model in CAD or Max R3.
- **Level of detail.** Keep face and vertex count to a minimum for the job at hand, thereby speeding up rendering and display screen navigation.
- **Wall systems modeling.** There are several methods of building architectural wall components with flexible editing capabilities.
- **Roofs.** You can choose from several methods of creating roof systems. Use the one that best fits the roof style: gable, hip, or conical.
- **Doors and windows.** Use the Extrude, Bevel, and Bevel Profile modifiers to design custom doors and windows at several levels of detail.
- **Space frames.** Use the Lattice modifier to simulate space frames, as well as to create expansion joints when a bitmap is not sufficient.

Chapter 3

Landscapes and Building Enhancements

Modeling convincing landscapes and trees feels as daunting as cultivating as the real thing. Naturally occurring objects are complex and random, so they can be time consuming to build in a 3D-modeling package. While some plug-ins create complex landscapes and foliage, they often carry the penalty of high-density models that may not be cost effective. This chapter gives you a few alternatives to create landscapes and trees in MAX R3—right out of the box, without buying plug-ins. You even learn a universal method of creating simple trees, trees that are efficient and with enough detail for use in a variety of circumstances. Specifically, this chapter covers the following:

- Tracing contours on a topographic map.
- Using Patch Grid and Edit Patch to create a rolling landscape.
- Using ShapeMerge compound object to project 2D-road outlines into a patch.
- Using PatchDeform modifier to create a loft or an animation path on a patch.

Landscape

Another prevalent architectural project is the landscape. MAX R3 offers several methods of creating landscape forms. Some give more accurate results than others, so choose according to each project's needs for accuracy and realistic contours. Often an art director instructs you to create rolling hills with a small pond or a tropical island and beachfront, but an inviting scene isn't enough. Architects and engineers require more accurate representations of hills and valleys or road cuts and fills. In order of potential accuracy, the common road-building methods are:

- Importing survey data from AutoCAD civil engineering add-ons.
- Using the Terrain modifier.
- Modeling with NURBS surfaces and patch grids.
- Cutting roads into mesh objects with ShapeMerge.
- Lofting a roadbed to conform to a patch grid.

Note
A fifth method of creating landscapes is covered in Chapter 13, "Using MAX 3 as a 2D Paint Tool." There you learn about using displacement mapping in the Material Editor, using the luminance value of map pixels to generate new geometry in a mesh object.

Importing Survey Data from AutoCAD

Achieve an accurate representation of landscapes by importing 3D-mesh objects generated from the engineer's survey data (taken in the field). AutoCAD civil engineering software converts the numeric data collected by surveyors into point data (X, Y, Z) and/or contour-line information. AutoCAD then uses the data to build connected 3D faces to form what is commonly known as a TIN map. That surface information is then imported into MAX R3. If you are doing site or highway presentations, or perhaps forensic animations that require a high degree of accuracy, this is probably the best method to use. Many engineering offices already generate the TIN files in-house or through their usual sub-contractors. If you don't have that capability, check the yellow pages for local engineers with whom you can partner for these projects. If the raw survey data is available, it only takes a few minutes to generate the 3D-terrain mesh.

> **Tip**
> The new compound object called Terrain in MAX R3 uses imported contour lines to generate a smooth surface. The contour lines can be open or closed and must be set to the proper elevation in the Z-axis.

Cut and properly filled roads traversing the hilly landscape in a mesh object is perhaps the biggest advantage of CAD-generated survey data.

Using the Terrain Compound Object

The Terrain compound object is a new feature that was formerly part of 3D Studio VIZ 2.0 and is now included in MAX R3. It uses 2D shapes to define a mesh surface skin. The 2D shapes may be open or closed and must be set at the correct height or elevation.

> **Tip**
> As with all tools in MAX or VIZ, don't put too much weight on the tool's name. While Terrain is intended for creating landscapes, it's useful for building human heads, furniture, and vehicles (to name just a few options). Any object that is defined with a series of cross-sectional shapes is a candidate for Terrain.

> **Note**
> A combination of CrossSection and Surface modifiers creates a similar surface. However, the resultant surface is a patch instead of a mesh.

In the next exercise series, you load a scanned image of a topographic map as a Background image. Then you create a registration reference object, and trace the 250-feet contour lines. In the next step, you move the contours to the correct Z-axis location, and use Terrain to skin the surface mesh.

Part I Modeling

Exercise 3.1.1 Tracing the Contour Lines from a Background Image

1. Open or Reset MAX R3 to a new scene. Right-click Top viewport to activate it, and type W to maximize the viewport.

2. In the Customize pull-down menu, click Units Setup. Select US Standard. Choose Decimal Feet in the list. The dialog box looks like Figure 3.1. Click OK.

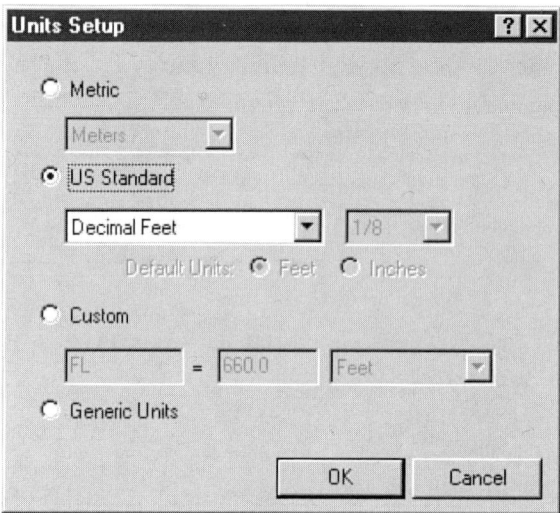

Figure 3.1 The Units Setup dialog box.

3. In the Views pull-down menu, select Viewport Background. Choose Files in the Viewport Background dialog box. Choose topomap.bmp on the CD-ROM. Under Aspect Ratio, check Match Bitmap. The dialog box looks similar to Figure 3.2. Click OK.

 Tip

Using the Match Bitmap Aspect Ratio setting keeps the map image from becoming distorted; it can with Match Rendering Output or Match Viewport.

4. You must determine the real-world distance between two points on the map for scaling purposes. In this map, there is a scale bar in the lower left corner that can be used. The top bar shows 3,000 feet. In the Create panel, choose Shapes and then Rectangle. In the Top viewport, click and drag a rectangle of any size.

5. In the Modify panel, enter 100' in the Length field and 3000' in the Width field. Choose MeshSelect to change the rectangle to a flat plane.

Chapter 3: Landscapes and Building Enhancements   123

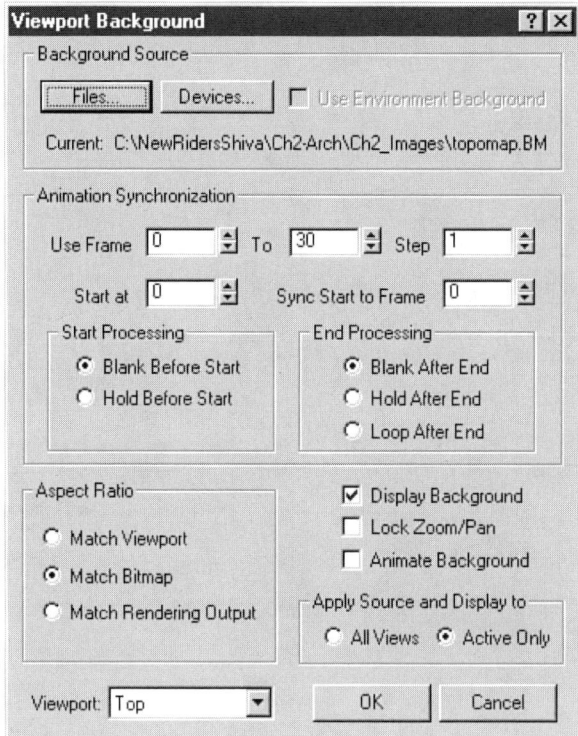

Figure 3.2   The Viewport Background dialog box.

6. Using the Zoom icon and the Pan icon, zoom out to match the new rectangle with the top scale bar. It looks similar to Figure 3.3.

7. In the Views pull-down menu, choose Save Active Top View. This stores the current zoom level and position of the viewport in a buffer. If you change the viewport by zooming or panning, you can restore this view by using Views/Restore Active Top viewport.

Tip
Each viewport can have one view saved in its own buffer.

Caution
You must register an object in the scene with points on the map and zoom to match the two. Otherwise, when the contour shapes are set to the proper height, they are out of scale with the scene's north/south and east/west dimensions.

124   Part I   Modeling

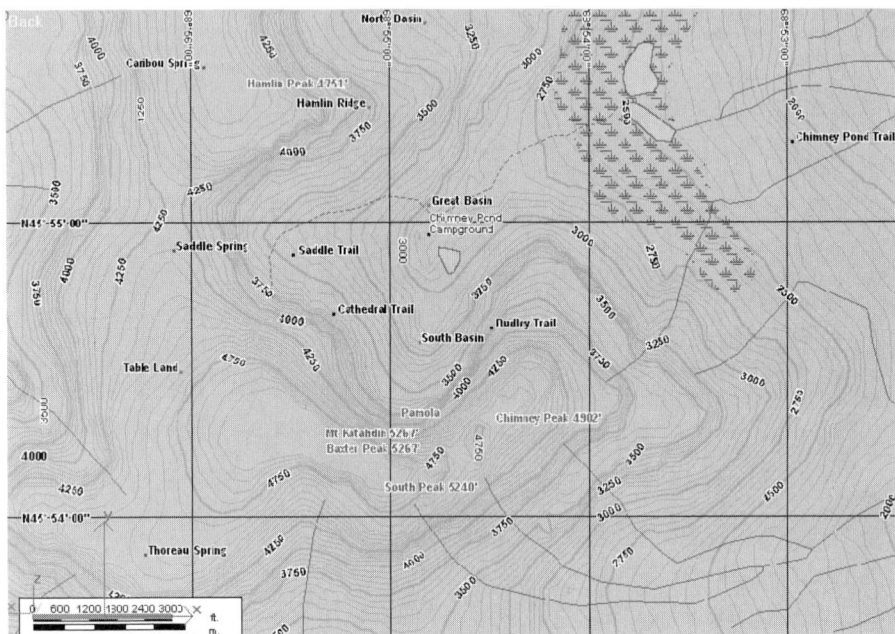

Figure 3.3   Rectangle matched to top scale bar.

8. Starting with the small 4750 contour at Chimney Peak near the map's center in the Top viewport, use the Line command to trace all heavy contour lines at 250' elevations. Name each object by its elevation. Use letters (a, b, c, and so on) to indicate different lines on the same contour for elevations with more than one contour or where you break the line because the contour runs off the map edge. Before you draw the first line, check the Corner option in Creation Method rollout, Drag Type area. This avoids unwanted curvature in the lines (caused by holding down the mouse button). Smooth the contours later. Perform the tracing operation in one sitting. If you make any changes to the viewports, registering the contour lines again is difficult.

 Tip
Trace the contours with as few points as possible (to maintain the accuracy you need). Unnecessary points create extra faces/vertices and slow the workflow.

 Note
There is no 4500' contour on this map.

Chapter 3: Landscapes and Building Enhancements   125

 Caution
In Views/Background Image, select the Lock Zoom/Pan option. Zoom in closer to the background image. Note, however, that this can use enormous amounts of system RAM and potentially throw you out of MAX R3.

9. Right-click the Top viewport label. Clear Show Background (to turn off the map in the viewport). The traced contour lines look similar to Figure 3.4.

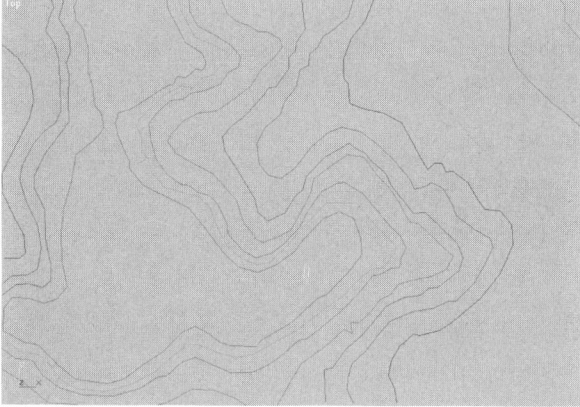

Figure 3.4   Traced contour lines.

10. Save the file as 03_topo_01.max.

In the next exercise, move the contour lines into the correct elevation. Then attach the individual shapes into a single shape of multiple splines. This is necessary for the Terrain compound object to function.

Exercise 3.1.2   Setting the Contours to the Appropriate Elevation

1. Open 03_topo_01.max from the previous exercise or open 03_topo_01.max from the CD-ROM. Type W to switch the display to four viewports.
2. In the Top viewport, type H to view the Select Objects dialog box. Select everything except 1750 and rectangle01. Then choose Select. The Select Object dialog box looks like Figure 3.5.

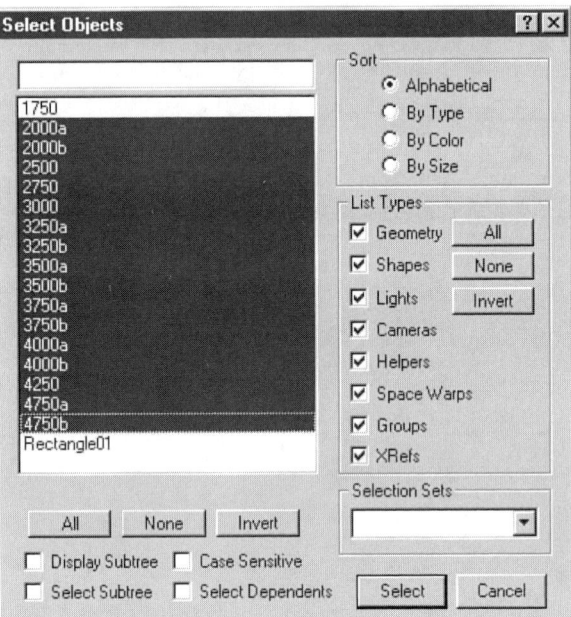

Figure 3.5 The Select Object dialog box with contour names.

3. Click the Move icon, and then right-click it. Enter 250' in the Offset:Screen Z-axis field. This moves the contours 250' above the 1750' contour.

4. Type H. Hold down the Ctrl key, and click on 2000a and 2000b to clear them. Now clear 1750, 2000a, 2000b, and rectangle01. Click Select. Right-click the Move icon and enter 250' in the Offset:Screen Z-axis.

5. Repeat step 4 to move each level of contours 250' in the Z-axis. The viewports look similar to Figure 3.6.

Note

Contours 4750a and 4750b must be moved 500' in the Z-axis, not 250' (like the others).

6. In the Top viewport, select the 1750 contour. Under the Modify pull-down menu, select Geometry. Choose Attach Mult. In the Attach Multiple dialog box, select All. Then select Attach. (See Figure 3.7.) This attaches all shapes into one shape containing multiple splines.

Chapter 3: Landscapes and Building Enhancements   127

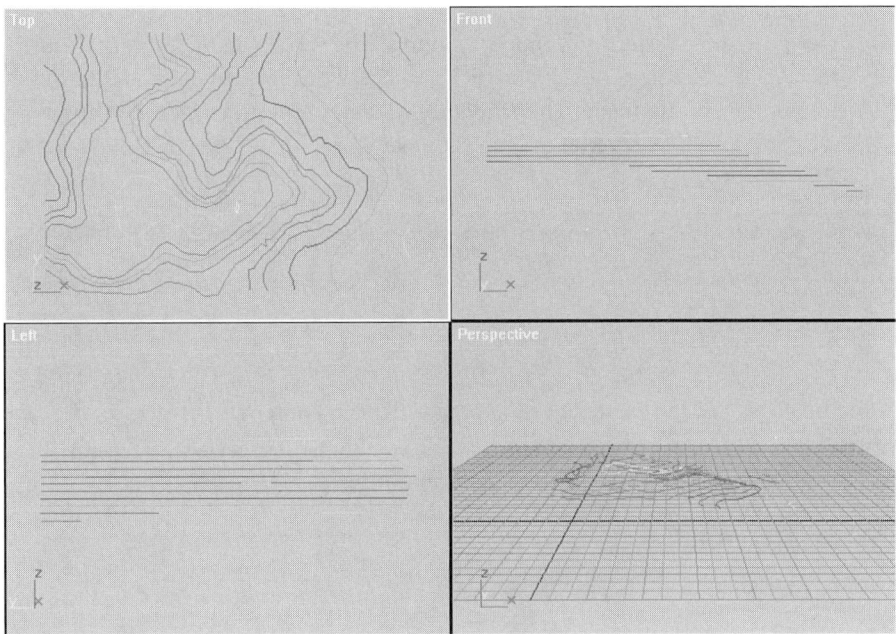

Figure 3.6 Contours moved to the proper elevation.

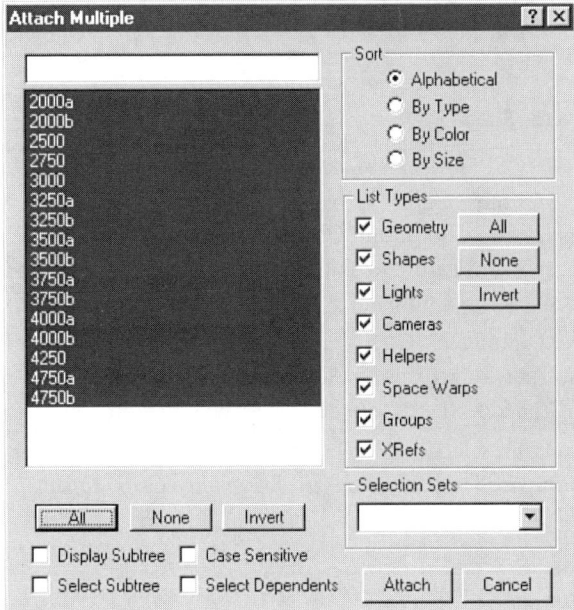

Figure 3.7 The Attach Multiple dialog box.

7. In the Modify pull-down menu, choose Selection. Now choose Vertex. In the Top viewport, drag a selection window around all the vertices in the contours. Move the cursor over any vertex. Right-click and check the Smooth option at the bottom of the pop-up menu. This smoothes all vertex tangency. Click the Vertex selection icon to exit vertex sub-object mode.

Note
When you select all vertices in Step 7, you see a confusing mass of Transform Gizmos in the display. The display clears when you finish the step.

8. Save the file as 03_topo_02.max

In the final stage of the exercise, you apply the Terrain compound object to the shape called 1750. This skins the contours with a mesh that is viewed in several ways. Depending on the information you need, you can view the mesh as a

- Graded surface
- Graded solid
- Layered solid

You can also display the mesh in color—coded to the elevation changes. At the end of the exercise, you apply a material with a diffuse map of the topographic map to see how it all fits together.

Exercise 3.1.3 Applying Terrain to the Shape

1. Open 03_topo_02.max (if it is not already open).
2. In the Top viewport, select the compound shape called 1750. In the Create pull-down menu, choose Geometry and Compound Objects, and then click the Terrain button. The 2D-contour lines are now skinned with a mesh surface. The Perspective viewport looks similar to Figure 3.8.
3. In the Modify rollout, select Parameters. Then choose Graded Solid. This adds a skirt and base to the terrain. Now select Layered Solid (to view it as if it were a foamcore model). Choose Graded Surface again after observing the differences.
4. In the Color by Elevation rollout, select Create Defaults. This shows the elevation changes as color information. Add levels of color (or change the colors) to suit your needs. See Figure 3.9.

Chapter 3: Landscapes and Building Enhancements 129

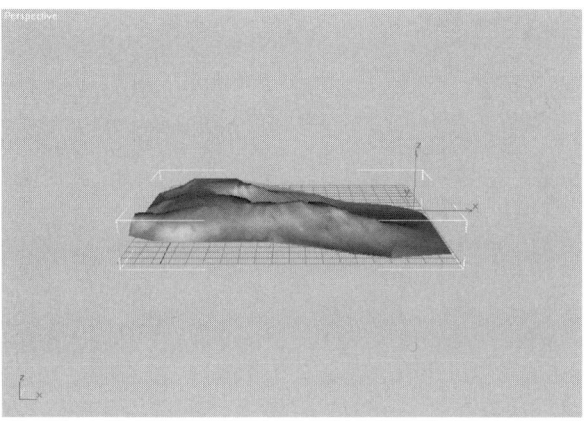

Figure 3.8 Terrain compound object from contour lines.

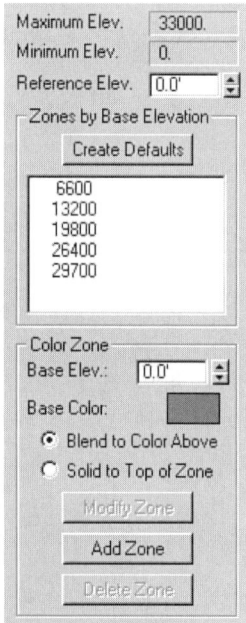

5. Open the Material Editor. Select the small gray Diffuse Map shortcut (on the right of the diffuse color slot). This opens the Material/Map Browser.

 6. Double-click Bitmap, and select topomap.bmp from the CD-ROM. Click the Open button. The new Select Bitmap Image File dialog box looks similar to Figure 3.10.

7. In the Material Editor, open Viewport. Select Show Map. Then drag and drop the new material onto the landscape.

8. In the Modify pull-down menu, select UVW Map. The 'topo' map appears on the mesh surface.

9. Right-click the Perspective viewport, and type U (to switch to a User viewport). Apply ArcRotate Selected, so you view the low corner of the landscape with the lakes and marsh.

10. In the Front viewport, place an Omni light high and right-center of the mesh. Activate the Perspective viewport, and then select Quick Render. The render display looks similar to Figure 3.11, and you see the contours matching the hills' slope.

Figure 3.9 The Color by Elevation rollout.

> **Tip**
> It's nearly impossible to comfortably zoom and pan on large models. Switching to a User viewport makes viewport navigation more manageable. When you're in position, type P (to switch back to a perspective view).

130   Part I   Modeling

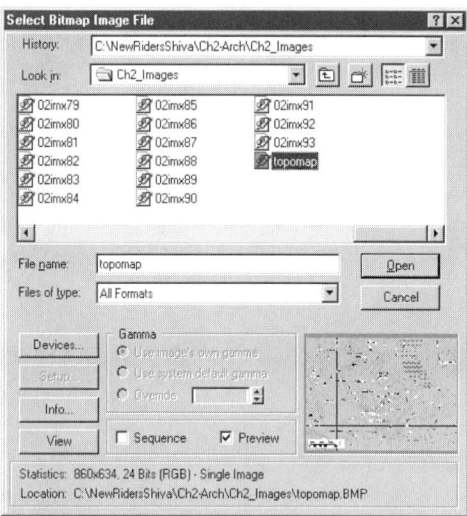

Figure 3.10   New Select Bitmap Image File dialog box.

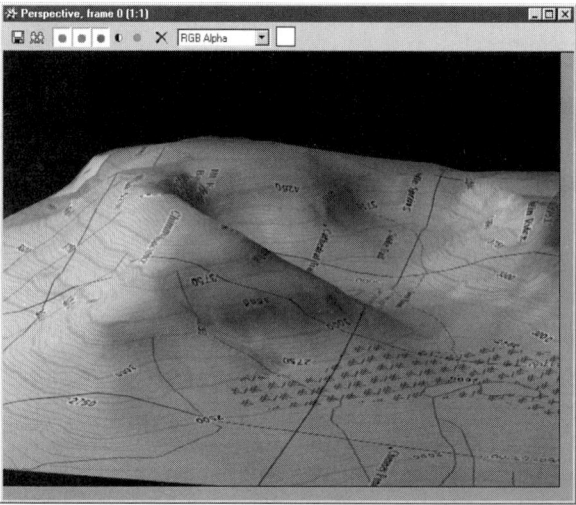

Figure 3.11   A rendered landscape, applied with topographic map.

   11. Save the file as 03_topo_03.max.

Landscape Using NURBS Surface or Patch Grid

Another method of producing landscapes is by creating and modifying NURBS surface or patch grids. To learn this process, use a patch grid to create a hilly landscape. The creation and editing features of NURBS surfaces and patch grids are similar—to a point. Each contains a different set of detailed editing tools, however, that are influential in your choice for landscapes. For example, you can cut holes into a NURBS surface with the Trim tool, and the object remains a NURBS surface. You can cut a hole in a patch with ShapeMerge, but the patch is converted to a mesh object.

Patch grids are more efficient in the use of computer resources than NURBS Surfaces. NURBS are relational. When you pull up on a Control Point to create a hill, areas around the hill drop (to compensate for the new curvature). Patch grids are more predictable. When you pull up on a vertex, only the adjacent area of the patch reacts to the change. In this section, you focus on creating a simple hilly landscape from a patch grid. You then create a 2D shape that is used to animate an object across the landscape, loft a roadbed on the surface, or cut a road into the surface.

Exercise 3.2 Creating a Patch Landscape

1. Open a new MAX R3 session. In the Customize pull-down menu, select Units Setup. Set US Standard to Decimal Feet. Click OK. Right-click 3D Snap, and select Home Grid. Enter 25' in the Grid Spacing field. Close the dialog box.

2. In the Create panel, select Standard Primitives. Now choose Patch Grids, and then select QuadPatch. Click and drag a Patch Grid in the Top viewport.

3. In the Modify pull-down menu, select Parameters. Enter 500' in the Length and Width fields. Enter 3 in the Length and Width Segs fields, to increase the editable vertices in the patch.

4. Right-click the Perspective viewport. Type W (to maximize the viewport to full screen). Select Zoom Extents, and use Zoom to fill the display with the Patch Grid. To speed up the zoom, hold down the Ctrl key while you Zoom.

5. In the Modify pull-down menu, select Edit Patch (to add an Edit Patch modifier to the stack). In the Selection rollout, select Vertex. Notice that 16 blue vertices are on the patch's surface.

6. Make sure 3D Snap is off, and choose Move. Click the back right-corner vertex, and select the Z-axis Transform manipulator. Move the vertex up just a little. Move several vertices, to create a hilly landscape similar to Figure 3.12. Select Vertex to exit Vertex Sub-Object mode. Your scene now contains a hilly landscape.

Caution

It's easy to get confused when working in a Perspective or Camera viewport. If 3D Snap is on and set to Grid (or if the vertex is moving in the XY world plane), the hills appear to be rising. In reality, however, you only slide them in the XY plane. Be sure the vertices are moving in the Z-axis. Work with several visible views, so you get instant feedback on your actions.

132   Part I   Modeling

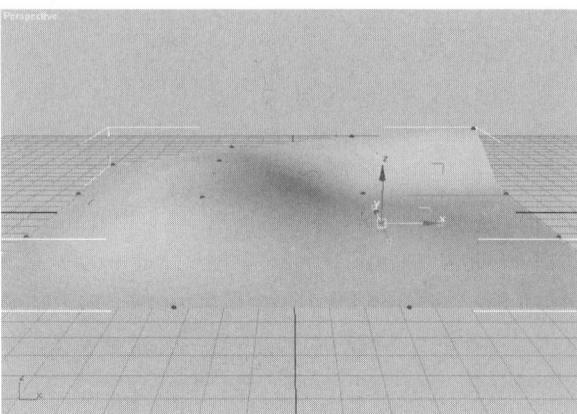

Figure 3.12   Patch grid with Edit Patch, vertices moved in world Z-axis.

7. In the Top viewport, create a curved 2D line similar to the one shown in Figure 3.13. It lies on the world grid plane and is used for animation and lofting.

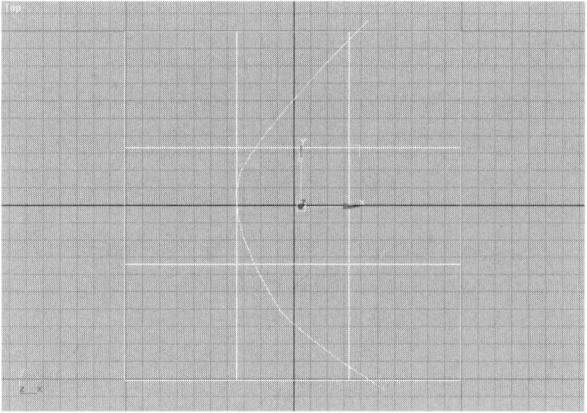

Figure 3.13   Curved 2D line over patch grid.

8. In the Top viewport, select the Move transform icon and, while holding down the Shift key, click and drag the line about 25' to the right. Release the mouse button, and select Copy. Enter 2 in the Number of Copies field. This creates two new copies of the line, offset by 25'. It looks similar to Figure 3.14.

 Tip
Set the Grid Spacing to 25'. Use it to judge the distance to move the line. Or watch the Status line at the bottom as you move the shape.

Chapter 3: Landscapes and Building Enhancements   133

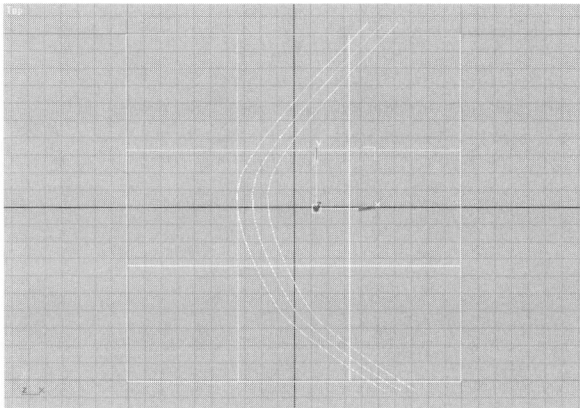

Figure 3.14 A 2D-line, cloned twice.

9. Activate and maximize the Perspective viewport. Select Line01. In the Modify pull-down menu, select More. Double-click the PatchDeform World Space modifier. In the Parameters rollout, choose Pick Patch. Select the patch grid in the viewport. The line conforms to the patch grid's surface.

10. Select Move, and move the line around the patch. The line changes, remaining on the grid surface. The viewport looks similar to Figure 3.15.

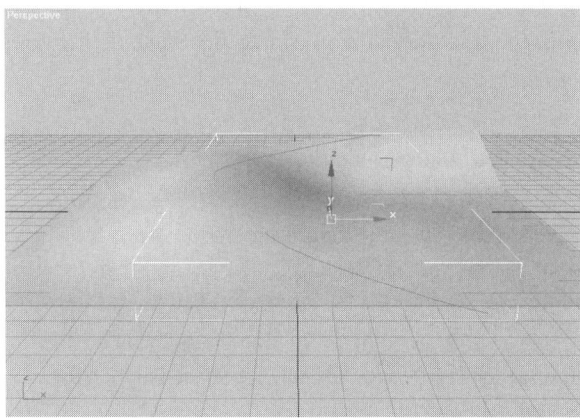

Figure 3.15 Line with World Space PatchDeform modifier.

Tip

The line deformed to the patch can be used as an animation path for objects traveling along the patch's surface.

If the line passes through or rises above the surface, it doesn't contain enough vertices to conform to the surface. Drop to the Line level in the Modifier Stack and, at the Segment Sub-Object level, select all segments. Select Divide to add new vertices. Increase the number of divisions (or click Divide two or three times) for more vertices. Return to the top of the Modifier Stack, and the line conforms more uniformly to the surface.

Caution

PatchDeform can only be used on native patch objects, not on mesh objects converted to patches.

Note

The line with the PathDeform modifier can be used only as an animation path—not as a lofting path—because it is a World Space modifier.

11. Save the file as 03_patch_01.max.

If the steps in Exercise 3.3 seem familiar, you're correct. In it, you repeat the process from Exercise 3.2, this time using a PatchDeform Object Space modifier. An Object Space PatchDeform modifier is similar to World Space, but the line is used as either an animation path or a loft path. However, the line doesn't conform to the patch as it moves because it's bound to local object space.

Exercise 3.3 Applying an Object Space PatchDeform Modifier

1. Activate and maximize the Perspective viewport. Select Line02. In the Modify roll-down menu, select More. Double-click the PatchDeform Object Space Modifier. In the Parameters pull-down menu, select Pick Patch, and then Patch Grid in the viewport. The line conforms to the surface of the Patch Grid.

2. Select Move, and move the line around the patch. The line doesn't stay on the surface but moves through or away from the patch. Object Space PatchDeform shows a control lattice and looks similar to Figure 3.16.

Tip

The PatchDeform control line is used as an animation path for objects that must travel along the patch's surface, as well as a loft path to create roadbeds.

Chapter 3: Landscapes and Building Enhancements   135

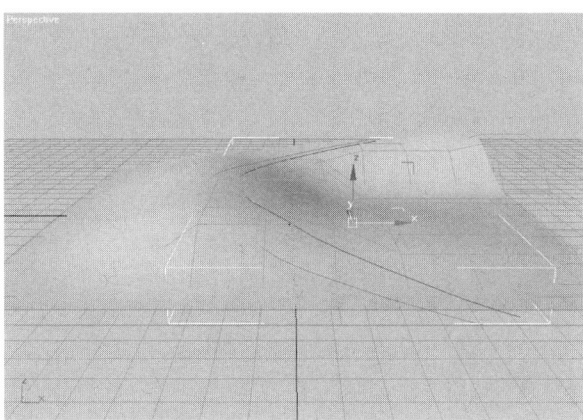

Figure 3.16 Line with Object Space PatchDeform modifier.

 Tip

If the control line passes through (or rises above) the surface, it doesn't contain enough vertices to conform to the surface. Drop to the Line level in the Modifier Stack. At Segment Sub-Object level, select the control line's segments and use Divide to add new vertices. Return to the top of the Modifier Stack and the line conforms more uniformly to the surface.

3. In the Top viewport, select Line03. In the Modify pull-down menu, choose Selection. Select Spline, and choose Line03 in the viewport. It turns red to indicate that you are at Spline level.

4. In the Geometry rollout, enter 40 in the field to the right of the Outline button. Then select Outline. This creates a closed 2D shape that is 40 feet wide. Select Spline to exit Sub-Object mode. The viewport looks similar to Figure 3.17. Use this closed shape to cut new faces in the surface for a road.

5. In the Top viewport, select the QuadPatch01. In the Create panel's Compound Object controls, select ShapeMerge. Choose Pick Shape, and in the Top viewport, select Line03. This projects the shape into the patch, and cuts new edges and faces in the surface.

136   Part I   Modeling

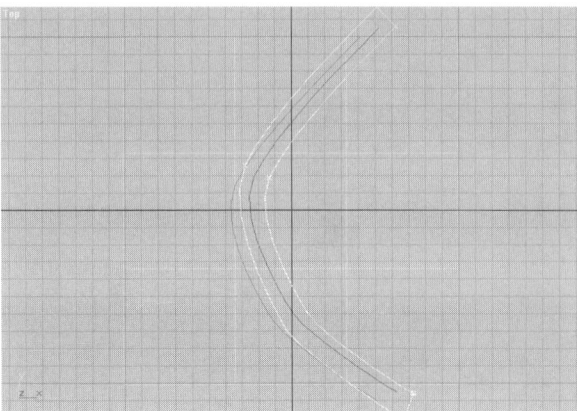

Figure 3.17   Line03 with 40' Outline applied.

NEW TO R3

6. In the Modify panel, click the MeshSelect button and click the Polygon icon in the Selection rollout. The newly cut faces turn red, indicating that they're selected. The viewport looks similar to Figure 3.18

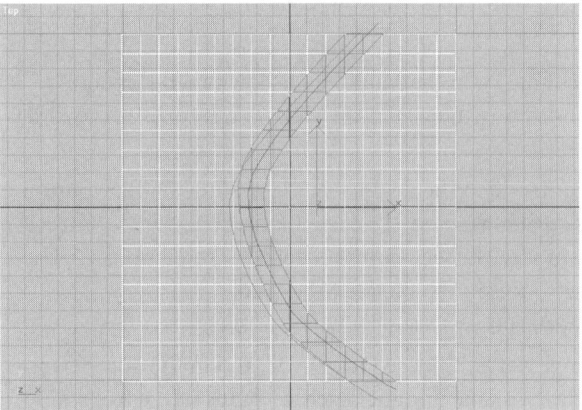

Figure 3.18   MeshSelect of new faces created by ShapeMerge.

7. In the Modify panel, select More. Double-click the Material modifier. In the Parameters rollout, set Material ID to 2. This assigns to the selected faces a Material ID number that corresponds to the submaterials in a Multi/Sub-Object material (that you assign to the landscape).

Caution
Using ShapeMerge on a patch grid automatically converts the patch grid to a mesh object. The two lines with the World Space and Object Space modifiers no longer conform to the surface of this mesh object.

8. In the Modify panel, choose MeshSelect. This MeshSelect should not be in Sub-Object mode and returns control to the whole mesh.

Tip
In the Modify panel, select the Edit Stack. In the Edit Stack dialog box, choose a modifier name. Then append a notation to the chosen name in the field at the bottom of the dialog box. For example, you might select a MeshSelect, and change it to read MeshSelect–road faces. This makes it easier for you and your co-workers to identify the modifiers' functions.

9. Open the Material Editor, and select the first Sample Sphere. Choose Standard. Double-click Multi/Sub-Object, and select Keep Old Material as Sub-Material in the Replace Material dialog box.
10. Select the second material color swatch in the new Multi/Sub-Object Material. Change the color to a bright green.
11. Drag and drop the sample sphere onto the landscape in the Perspective viewport. The land turns maroon while the road is bright green. Faces with Material ID 1 (the default) get Material 1 and faces with Material ID 2 (the Material modifier) get Material 2. Close the Material Editor and other dialogs. The Perspective viewport looks similar to Figure 3.19.

Figure 3.19 ShapeMerge mesh with Multi/Sub-Object material.

Tip
Once you assign the Multi/Sub-Object material, go back to the Material Editor to refine the materials (to be grass and asphalt). They update in the scene.

12. Save the file as 03_patch_02.max.

Trees and Bushes

Trees and bushes are an essential part of many architectural scenes, whether the scenes are accurate representations of building projects or just background scenes in an animation or computer game. The three basic tree-creation options are

- Third-party parametric tree plug-ins
- Opacity-mapped trees on a flat plane
- Modeled trees

Each method has its pluses and minuses, as do most options. The compromise you make is usually one of accuracy and realism verses productive render times. Natural objects (such as foliage and grasses) are incredibly complex and dynamic. One of the beautiful aspects of a real tree is that it never looks the same from minute to minute, depending on lighting, wind, and season. Some of the advantages and disadvantages of the three foliage-creation methods are

- **Third-party parametric tree plug-ins.** These trees offer a wide range of botanically correct species at different growth stages and seasonal variations. They range from the simpler trees generated in 3DS VIZ to the highly detailed, wind-blown trees (from Tree Storm by Onyx). They tend to look realistic and contain various levels of detail to differentiate close trees from distant ones. The biggest disadvantage to this method is that it consumes hefty computer resources to generate and update the trees.

- **Opacity mapped trees on a flat plane.** This uses a tree's photographic image—first as diffuse color information, and then as opacity information (masking the tree's areas from its transparent background). The advantage is that you only have two faces and four vertices for each tree in the scene. The disadvantages are that you can't view the tree from above (or from the side) because it has no thickness. Remember, too, that a scene from a camera looking through several levels of transparent objects uses enormous amounts of computer resources—slowing your render times to a crawl. A variation on simple flat mapping is available with RealPeople plug-in from ArchSoft. The material for the tree is a proprietary animation that ties to the camera in the scene. As you move around or over the flat tree plane, the animation automatically updates to show a tree from that particular camera position.

Tip
You get better results from mapped trees if you use bitmaps (with alpha channel information) in the Opacity slot. Alpha bitmaps produce cleaner opacity, especially at the edges of the image.

Tip
When creating opacity-mapped trees, set Shininess and Shin.Strength to 0. Another suggestion is to use maps to control Shininess and adjust the bitmap blurring lower than the 1.0 default.

- **Modeled trees.** Trees modeled in MAX R3 are a compromise between accuracy and model size, but they are useful in most situations. One advantage is that you control all aspects of the mesh. With a little practice, you can create decent-looking trees in a short time. The disadvantage is the time it takes to create trees of certain species, particularly conifers.

Modeled Generic Hardwood Tree

In the final series of exercises, you grow a tree and add a leaf canopy to it. The first phase is creating a generic hardwood tree. The primary focus is to create a 3D tree that's efficient to scatter about a scene, yet still looks acceptable in most situations. Use this exercise series as a starting point for creating your own library of trees. Remember, however, that unless you keep the face/vertex count to a minimum, you're wasting precious system resources.

Exercise 3.4.1   Modeling a Hardwood Trunk

1. Open a new MAX R3 session, or in the Files pull-down menu, choose Reset (to clear any work in the current scene). In the Customize pull-down menu, choose Unit Setup. Set US Standard/Feet w/Fractional Inches.

2. Select the Top viewport to activate it. In the Create pull-down menu, select Geometry. Now click the Cylinder button and drag a cylinder of any size.

3. In the Modify pull-down menu, select Parameters. Enter 1'0" in Radius, 14'0" in Height, 14 in Height Segments, and 6 in Sides. Clear the Smooth option. This creates a six-sided cylinder with somewhat square segments. Apply Zoom Extents All, and the Front viewport looks similar to Figure 3.20.

140   Part I   Modeling

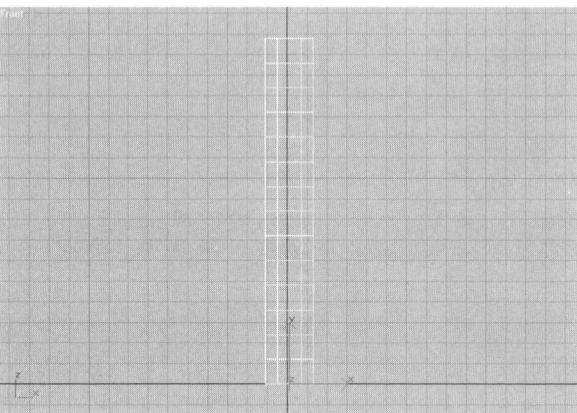

Figure 3.20   Six-sided cylinder with height segments.

4. In the Modify pull-down menu, select Edit Stack. Choose Convert to:Editable Mesh. This removes the base parameters of the cylinder and gives you access to the Sub-Object edit level.

Tip
After you edit the Sub-Object level (to change the size or relationship of faces, vertices, or edges), you can't drop back to the base parameters level and make adjustments. To play it safe, save a version before you convert to Editable Mesh.

5. In the Perspective viewport, select Cylinder01. Right-click Perspective label, and choose Edged Faces. Type W (to maximize the viewport). Edged Faces allows you to see the shaded object *and* the visible edges of each face for easy selection.

6. In the Modify panel's Selection rollout, select Polygon. In the Perspective viewport, choose a segment halfway up the cylinder on the right-hand side. The exact segment is not important, but the segment turns red.

Tip
NEW TO R3   In the Perspective viewport, select the viewport label, and choose Configure. Select the Shade Selected Faces option in the Rendering Options area of the Viewport Configuration dialog. The selected faces turn a semi-transparent red, making them easier to see.

7. In the Modify pull-down menu, select More. Double-click Face Extrude modifier. Set the amount field to 50 and the Scale field to 80. This moves the selected polygon along its local Z-axis and slightly scales it down.

8. Select More, and choose Face Extrude. Set Amount to 40 and Scale to 80.

9. Select More again, and choose Face Extrude. Set the Amount to 25 and Scale to 80. Each time you do this, you extrude the branch's end face. The Perspective viewport looks similar to Figure 3.21.

Chapter 3: Landscapes and Building Enhancements   141

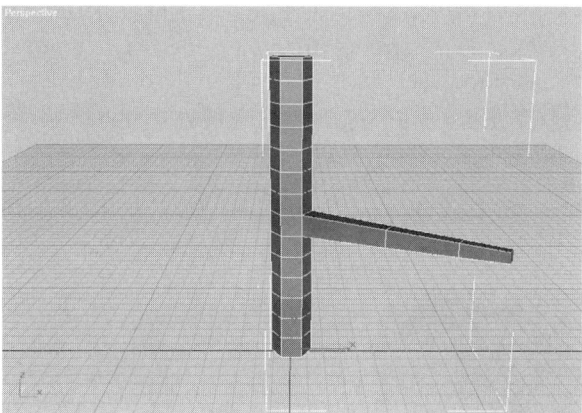

Figure 3.21 Three Face Extrude Modifiers create a branch.

10. In the Modify pull-down menu, select Edit Stack. Drag to highlight the three *Face Extrude entries in the stack. The Edit Modifier Stack dialog box appears similar to Figure 3.22.

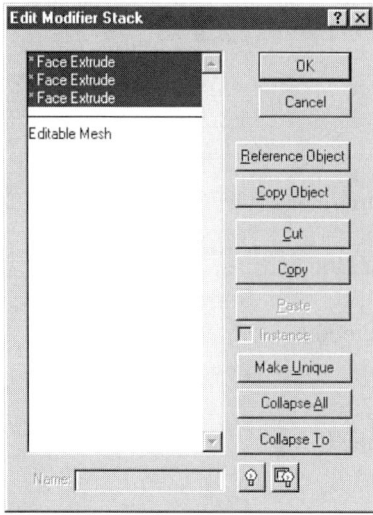

Figure 3.22 The Edit Modifier Stack dialog box.

11. In the Edit Modifier Stack dialog box, select Copy, and then OK. This saves the three Face Extrudes information in a buffer.
12. In the Modify pull-down menu, choose MeshSelect. In the Selection rollout, choose Polygon. Select a polygon two segments higher on the left side of the cylinder.

13. In the Edit Stack dialog box, select the top MeshSelect (to highlight it). Now choose Paste. This pastes the three Face Extrudes (from the buffer) on to the selected polygon, creating a new identical branch. Click OK in the dialog box.

14. Use ArcRotate to go around the tree. Repeat Steps 12 and 13 twice more to create a total of four branches. The scene and Modifier Stack look similar to Figure 3.23.

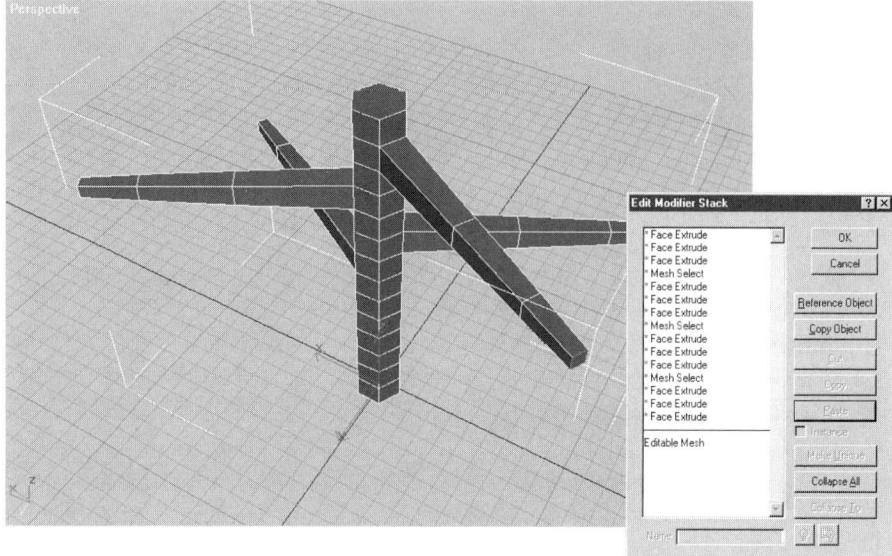

Figure 3.23 Cylinder, with four branches of pasted face extrudes on MeshSelects.

15. Activate the Front or Left viewport, and in the Modify panel, click MeshSelect/Vertex Selection. Then select all the vertices on the branches of one side. Select More, and double-click the Xform modifier. Move and Rotate the Xform Gizmo until the branches are generally pointing upward. It looks similar to Figure 3.24.

16. Repeat Step 15 until all the branches are modified.

 Tip

The amount of detail you go into with these steps is dependent on the tree type you want to create. Try using the Bend modifier on a selected set of faces or vertices. Edge Sub-Object editing and the Cut feature create smaller branches. You also get better results with the Cut feature if you select Ignore Backface (at the top of the panel). This keeps you from cutting edges and faces on the back side of the mesh. At this stage, it's important to keep this tree form as simple as possible.

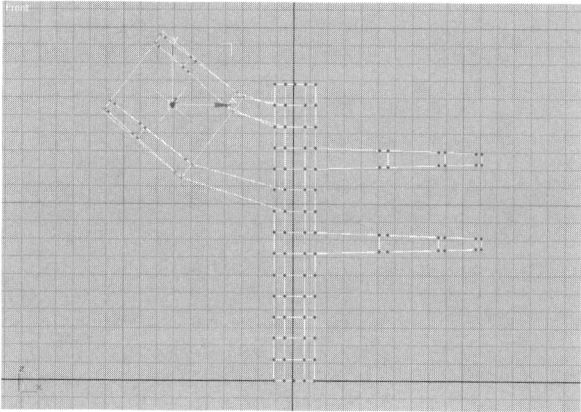

Figure 3.24 The Xform modifier on branch vertices, moved and rotated.

 Caution

After the next step, you can't make adjustments to the modifiers that created the tree branches. If you anticipate later changes, choose Save Selected in the File menu. Save the selected tree (with its Modifier Stack) to disk before collapsing the Modifier Stack.

17. In the Modify pull-down menu, select More. Double-click MeshSmooth. This applies the new NURMS MeshSmooth algorithm to the boxy tree and rounds out the branches.

18. In the Modify pull-down menu, select More again. Double-click Optimize. This reduces the number of faces/vertices in the mesh by combining faces (based on the angle where they meet). In this case, it reduces the number of faces by almost half.

19. In the Modify pull-down menu, select Edit Stack. Choose Collapse All, and then Yes in the warning dialog box. This collapses all modifiers into an Editable Mesh, simplifying the model. The tree looks similar to Figure 3.25.

20. Save the file as 03_tree_01.max.

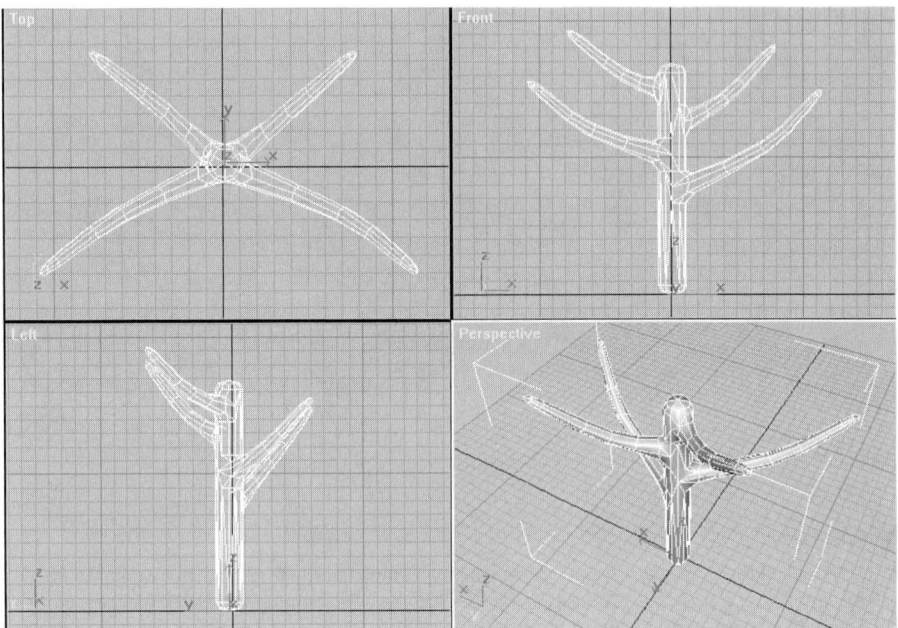

Figure 3.25 The tree, collapsed to Editable Mesh.

Creating Leaf Clusters

In this section you create a single leaf, assign a double-sided material to it, and scatter it across the surface of a hemisphere. Again, collapse the entire cluster to an Editable Mesh (to save on system resources). The initial leaf is extremely simple, but you can create leaves of any complexity to represent various tree species. As with any modeling in MAX R3, don't create detail that is never noticed in the final rendering. If, for example, you want to peer through a tree's branches, make a new model of a more detailed branch with more complex leaves.

Exercise 3.4.2   Creating a Leaf and a Leaf Cluster

1. Open the file 03_tree_01.max. Right-click the Top viewport (to activate it). Type W (to maximize the display).
2. In Create panel's Shapes group, select Line. Choose three points in the Top viewport, to create a triangle similar to Figure 3.26.

Chapter 3: Landscapes and Building Enhancements 145

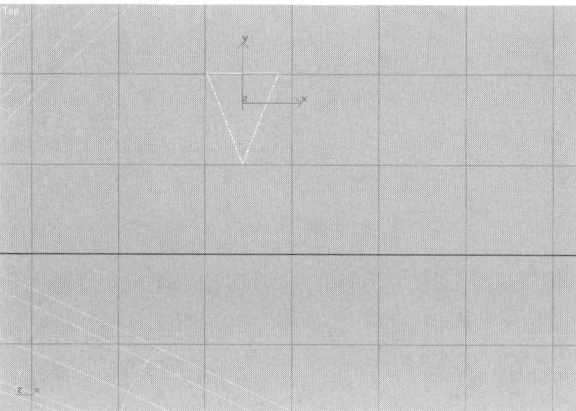

Figure 3.26 Basic leaf, 2D shape.

 Tip

Grid Spacing is still at the default 10 inches, so the triangle is 10 inches high by 8 inches wide. This is a larger leaf than most in nature, but you want to fill the scene and still be efficient.

3. In the Modify pull-down menu, choose MeshSelect. This changes the leaf from a 2D shape to a surface triangle.

4. Open the Material Editor. In the first sample sphere, click the Standard button, and double-click Double-Sided in the Browser list. Check Discard Old Material in the Replace Material dialog box. Double-sided materials allow one material on the face normal side of a mesh and a second material on the back side that doesn't contain face normals. Most leaves have different colors or shades on the front than on the back.

5. Name the material LEAF01, and select Facing Material. Name this material LEAF_FRNT, and change the Diffuse color slot to dark green.

6. In the Material Editor, select Material/Map Navigator, and choose Back Material. Name this material LEAF_BACK, and set the Diffuse color slot to light green. The display looks similar to Figure 3.27.

7. Assign the LEAF01 material to the leaf triangle by choosing Assign Material to Selected.

8. In the Create panel's Geometry group, click the GeoSphere button, and drag out a sphere in the Top viewport. Enter 1'6" in the Radius field, type 2 in the Segments field, clear Smooth, and select Hemisphere (at the bottom of the panel). This is the Distribution object for the Scatter compound object for a leaf cluster. Scatter Objects (see Step 9) allows you to scatter copies of the selected object (in this case, the leaf) over the surface of the distribution object (the geosphere) in a controlled or random pattern.

146   Part I   Modeling

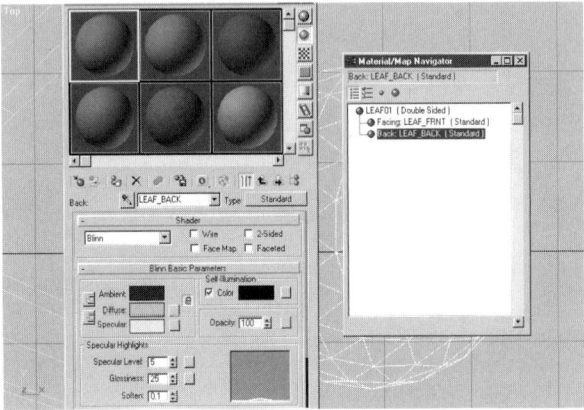

Figure 3.27   Material Editor and Navigator for basic leaf material.

9. Select the leaf. Still in the Geometry panel, choose Standard Primitives, and then Compound Objects. Now select Scatter.

NEW TO R3

> **Tip**
> MAX R3 allows the selected object to be scattered throughout the volume of the distribution object, as well.

10. In the Pick Distribution Object rollout, select Pick Distribution Object. In the Top viewport, choose the GeoSphere hemisphere. The LEAF01 jumps to the sphere surface.

11. In the Source Object Parameters rollout, enter 30 in the Duplicates field. You now have 30 leaves scattered on the sphere surface.

12. In the Transforms rollout, enter 45 in the X-, Y-, and Z-Rotation fields. Enter 20 in the X- and Y-Scaling fields. This randomizes the rotation and scaling of each duplicate.

13. In the Display rollout, select Hide Distribution Object. Scatter made a copy of the Geosphere as the distribution object, and you don't want to see it in the scene. The original Geosphere is also still there.

14. Select the GeoSphere01, and delete it. It is no longer necessary for your tree.

15. Select the leaf cluster. In the Modify pull-down menu, select Edit Stack. Choose Editable Mesh. This converts the Scatter object to an Editable Mesh (to save resources). The leaf cluster in the Perspective viewport looks similar to Figure 3.28.

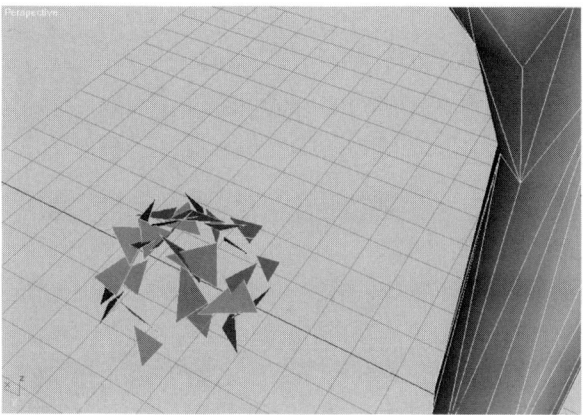

Figure 3.28 The leaf cluster, converted to Editable Mesh.

16. Save the file as 03_tree_02.max.

Creating Tree Leaves from a Leaf Cluster

The final phase of the tree project involves using Scatter (again) to distribute the leaf cluster over a tree canopy object. Create the initial canopy from a GeoSphere primitive, and modify it to fit the tree.

Exercise 3.4.3   Scatter a Leaf Cluster on a Canopy

1. Open 03_tree_02.max (if it is not already open). Type W (if necessary—to view all viewports), and select Zoom Extents All. This fills the viewports with the tree and the leaf cluster.

2. In Create panel's Standard Primitives controls, select GeoSphere. In the Front viewport, drag a GeoSphere. Enter 10'0" in the Radius field, and 3 in the Segments field. Clear the Hemisphere check box (if it's still selected from the previous exercise's Step 8). In the front viewport, move the GeoSphere—center over the tree's upper portion. It looks similar to Figure 3.29.

3. Activate the Front viewport. In the Modify pull-down menu, select Taper. Enter −0.5 in the Amount field. Check Y in the Taper Axis area.

4. In the Modify pull-down menu, select Noise. In the Parameters rollout, enter 20 in the Scale field. Enter 3'0" in Strength X, Y, and Z fields. This tapers and distorts the canopy GeoSphere, giving it a more random look. The Front viewport appears similar to Figure 3.30.

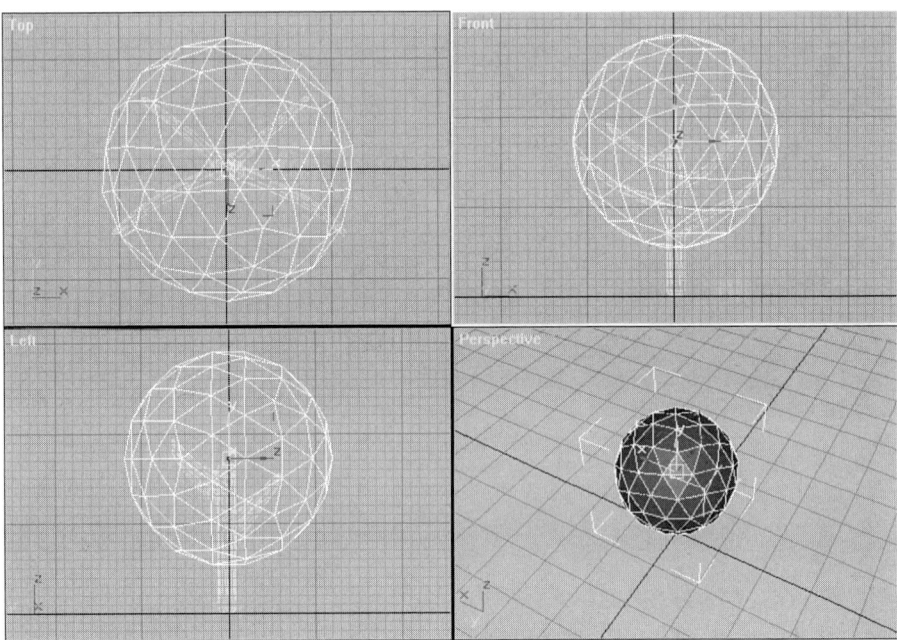

Figure 3.29 Basic GeoSphere canopy.

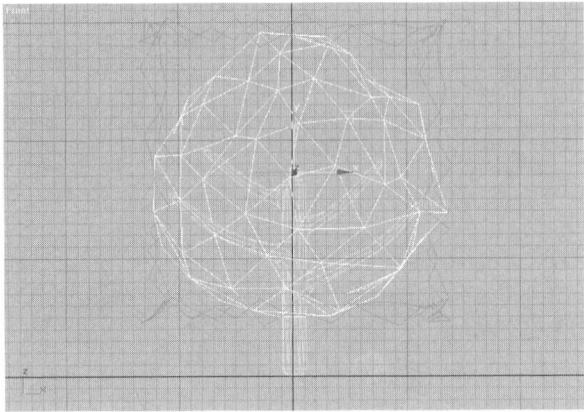

Figure 3.30 Canopy GeoSphere01, with Taper and Noise modifiers.

5. Type H, and choose Line01. Choose Select.

 Caution
The leaf cluster is still called Line01 because you haven't renamed it since creating the triangle. If you saved the cluster as a base object to use later, you should have given it a logical name.

Chapter 3: Landscapes and Building Enhancements   149

6. Under Compound Objects, select Scatter. Choose Pick Distribution Object, and then the GeoSphere canopy. The leaf cluster jumps to the canopy.

7. In the Scatter Objects rollout, enter 100 in the Duplicates field. In the Display rollout, select Hide Distribution Object.

8. In the Modify pull-down menu, select Edit Stack, and convert the canopy to an Editable Mesh. In the Edit Geometry rollout, select Attach. Choose the scene's tree trunk. Name the object HRDWOOD01. This attaches the leaf-cluster canopy and the trunk into a single object.

Tip
The attach process creates one object, but the trunk becomes an element of the object. Use MeshSelect at Face Sub-Object level. Choose Element to apply a Material modifier and UVW Map modifier for the trunk material in a Multi/Sub-Object material.

9. Select GeoSphere01 and delete it from the scene.

10. In the Perspective viewport, right-click Perspective. Clear Edged Faces.

11. Select Quick Render. The rendered Perspective viewport looks similar to Figure 3.31.

Figure 3.31 Rendered Perspective viewport of tree.

12. In the Files pull-down menu, choose Summary Info. Notice that the tree has 3,572 faces. That is quite reasonable for the apparent detail in the mesh. See Figure 3.32 for the Summary Info dialog box.

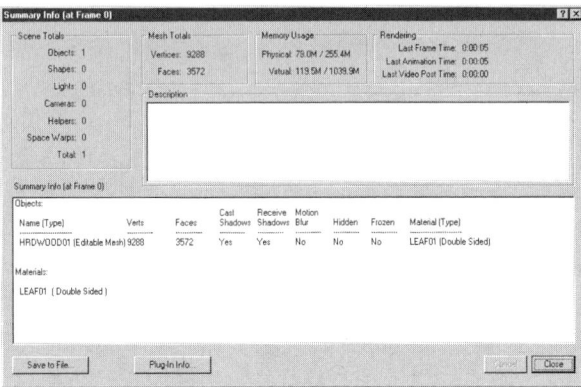

Figure 3.32 The Summary Info dialog box.

13. Close the Summary Info dialog box, and save the file as 03_tree_03.max.

In Practice: Landscapes and Building Enhancements

- **Import survey data from AutoCAD civil engineering add-ons.** A good way to create accurate mesh landscapes for use in MAX R3 is through one of the AutoCAD survey packages designed for road building and landscape design. The mesh conforms to local codes and building conditions, and imports into Max R3 as a polygon mesh object.

- **Use the Terrain compound object.** For close representations of landscape, import a 2D-topographic bitmap in the MAX R3 display's background. Reasonably accurate landscapes are quickly created by tracing contour lines in the bitmap and moving them into the proper elevation. Finally, Terrain compound object skins the contours and you have the finished product.

- **Cut roads into mesh objects with ShapeMerge.** The ShapeMerge compound object is a great tool for projecting 2D splines, defining road and pathway edges into a landscape mesh. Then select and edit the newly created faces and edges (to apply materials and edit the roads and paths).

- **Model with NURBS surfaces and patch grids.** Pulling the Control Vertices of NURBS or vertices of Patches creates rolling landscapes. The surface may not accurately represent any real landscape, but the method is quick and convincing.

- **Loft a roadbed to conform to a patch grid.** If you create a landscape with a patch grid, you then create, line, and conform it to the surface with World Space or Object Space PatchDeform modifiers. Lines with World Space PatchDeform modifiers are used as animation paths and change with the surface (as the line moves over the surface). A line with an Object Space PatchDeform modifier is used as either an animation path or a loft path. However, it holds its original deformed shape if moved over the surface.

- **Pay close attention to the numbers of faces and vertices created in the mesh objects.** Minimizing the complexity of your models is one of the best productivity tools you control. It takes a little thought at first, but soon it's second nature. Before long, you'll be hunting down a single face to purge from your scene.

- **Think beyond the name of the tool in MAX R3.** Don't let a tool's label limit you to one use. For example, Bevel is a great help in making windows. Terrain creates furniture or characters.

Chapter 4

Industrial and Mechanical Design Modeling

Traditionally, mechanical designers create with AutoCAD or Mechanical Desktop, and import their models into MAX R3 for materials, lights, and animation. If the model needs exact tolerances to the nearest, say, 1/1000 inch, the approach seems the best choice—until you make a change.

Changes are a frustrating and time-consuming ritual: Delete the MAX object, edit the original in the CAD program, import the new model into MAX, and reapply and readjust all the materials you thought you tweaked to perfection the first time. An efficient alternative is to import the accurate 2D CAD information into MAX R3—as a basis to create 3D models. This offers a good balance between CAD's accuracy and MAX R3's flexible editing. You can, of course, model entirely in MAX R3 for your mechanical presentation's elements that require realism, but not fanatical accuracy (such as, hoses and cables, knurling and embossing on surfaces, and conceptual industrial objects).

This chapter familiarizes you with MAX modeling techniques that offer more flexible editing during the design visualization process. Some of the covered topics are:

- Simulating surface information with materials and maps.
- Lofting cross-sections along paths.
- Using Xref files for group projects.
- Modeling with Free Form Deformation modifier.
- Modeling with the Surface modifier.

Tip
Don't ignore Chapter 2 just because it's titled "Architectural Modeling." Many of the modeling techniques described there are useful for mechanical design as well. For example, using 2D data to create a flat wall with window openings can be applied to building the cast and drilled side of a printing press (see "2D Wall Elevation Extruded for Thickness"). You can also use the techniques discussed in "Creating a Curtain Wall System" for a thermos bottle with an aluminum body, a rubber gasket, and a plastic cap (instead of a wall system of brick, glass, and concrete). In both instances one object (with multiple elements) receives different materials. Remember: with a little imagination, the modeling techniques we present are adaptable to many different projects.

Mechanical Modeling Issues

Before you begin a project, consider the following four key points:

- **Presentation focus.** Is it conceptual or marketing oriented?
- **Modeling tools.** Is it better to use AutoCAD/Mechanical Desktop, 3D Studio MAX R3, or a combination?

- **Output process.** As the final result, do you need high-resolution still images or an animation?
- **Workflow.** Do you plan to collaborate or work alone?

Answering these questions before you begin helps you work more efficiently and with better results.

Presentation Focus

The focus of your presentation affects everything from the storyboard to the final image output process.

Tip
Make sure your company's management knows what's involved in creating 3D presentations, so they can make informed requests for presentation materials. Often management's only knowledge of 3D animation comes from a MAX R3 sales presentation, leading them to believe that creating fancy 3D animations is *overly* easy.

For example, if you're working on an in-house presentation to convey a new design's concepts to engineers and drafters, you may need only rough or incomplete surface models. These models may illustrate an idea and not require much lighting or materials. The presentation may also just show general motion or the relationship of one mechanical part to another. In that case, animation timing and accuracy are unimportant. This type of presentation may be analogous to a napkin-sketch approach. See Figure 4.1 for a comparison of a basic model and a model with finished materials.

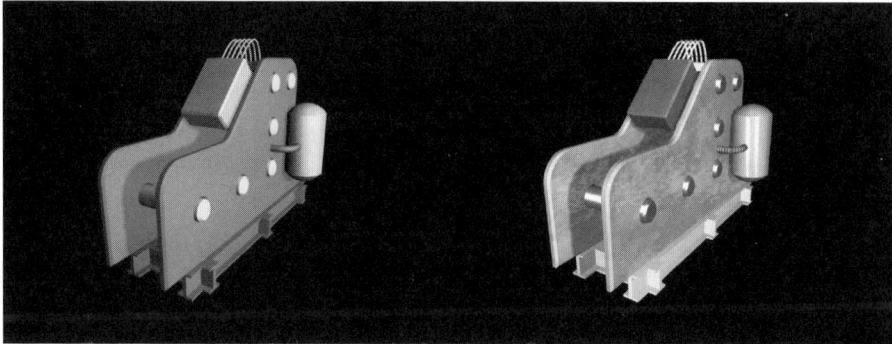

Figure 4.1 A basic color model (left), and a model with materials (right).

Perhaps you're working on a sales or venture-capital raising presentation in which the audience must be entertained, as well as informed. This requires more finished, realistic materials, better lighting, and perhaps, sophisticated animation. The detail is greater and the overall modeling accuracy is higher.

Tip
Don't forget the entertainment element in your presentations. Some humor at a presentation's beginning sharpens the audience's senses and focuses its attention. Special effects (such as glows and highlights, or low camera angles) help maintain attention throughout the presentation.

However, avoid allowing the special effects or humor to become the presentation's main point.

Modeling Tools

Once you know what kind of presentation you need, use the appropriate modeling tools. For instance, AutoCAD or Mechanical Desktop 3D models are not always cost effective in a MAX presentation. Some common issues involved in data imported from other software into MAX are:

- **Excess complexity.** CAD-generated models have thousands of unnecessary faces and vertices that slow MAX R3 during display navigation and rendering.
- **Flipped face normals.** Flipped face normals appear as missing faces in MAX R3 and require forced 2-sided rendering or 2-sided materials. These situations slow rendering.
- **Vertex welding issues.** Incorrectly welded CAD vertices import as flashing faces or shadows in rendered images of 3D objects, and improper extruding and lofting in 2D objects.

Objects modeled in MAX R3 rarely have the above problems. MAX R3 retains the modeling history in the Modifier Stack, so changes are made to the model more quickly and easily than with imported models.

Note
See Appendix A, "AutoCAD and 3D Studio MAX: Sharing Files," for more information on importing AutoCAD data into MAX R3.

MAX R3 materials simulate complex geometry by creating the illusion of raised or relieved surfaces. This is accomplished by simulating a model's transparent areas or by physically displacing a surface (based on the images' information).

It's not necessary to model exclusively in CAD or MAX R3. Mix modeling tasks to suit your company's presentation styles.

Output Process

How you create 3D models depends on the final output, too. Some output options are

- **The Internet.** For presentations viewed over an Internet link, output resolutions are moderate to low (800×600, or less). Animations must be low resolution (320×240, or less). Models must be low polygon, allowing efficient playback speeds.
- **A Computer.** Presentations played from a CD or hard drive need output resolution that is moderate (1024×768 for stills) to low (320×240 for animations). Modeling detail can also be moderate to low.
- **Videotape.** VHS videotape presentations require moderate output resolutions and model detail. Carefully plan your materials and color selection to avoid "blooming," or color bleeding, that occurs when highly saturated colors convert to video signals.
- **Print.** Presentations that are output to paper or film use high to very-high output resolutions (6000×4000, or more). The models contain extra detail, and sometimes simulated geometry appears unrealistic.
- **Combinations of the above.** Presentations commonly combine two or more of the options listed above. Use the methods presented in this book to achieve balance and flexibility in your modeling and materials.

Workflow

MAX R3 offers more flexibility in creating 3D scenes and animations. The modeling process is faster because of the new right-click menus and the customizable interface. Plus, Xref Objects and Scenes will revolutionize the way offices work.

Offices can still employ the traditional single-user concept, where each user is responsible for a complete project or a presentation's segment.

Now, however, collaborative projects are more feasible with the introduction of Xref Objects and Xref Scenes. Teams focus on more specialized processes (such as modeling, materials, lighting, and animation) while retaining exclusive control of any changes. Another team can assemble the presentation, knowing that changes from any team member is reflected automatically or on demand. For a look at Xrefs in action, see the section "Modeling with Xrefs."

Simulating Surface Geometry

Rather than creating physical 3D-mesh objects for everything, take advantage of MAX R3's ability to simulate geometry. Materials in MAX R3 are assigned maps so an object appears bumpy or transparent (based on the pixels' whiteness in the map). White pixels appear as higher bumps or fully opaque areas; black pixels appear as flat or transparent areas. This keeps mesh objects' face and vertex counts to a minimum while creating the illusion of a more complex surface. Rendering times are thus reduced.

Tip
Maps used for geometry simulation materials are usually grayscale images. Colored maps are used, but it's difficult to tell luminance values at a glance. For example, bright green and bright yellow look different to the eye, but the colors may have similar luminance values. Therefore, they have little or no effect when rendered.

Tip
Use Photoshop (or another image software) to convert an image into monochrome or grays, to visualize the actual luminance. Or view the image in MAX R3 file viewer (using the Monochrome button) to see the image gray values. See Figure 4.2 for the file viewer.

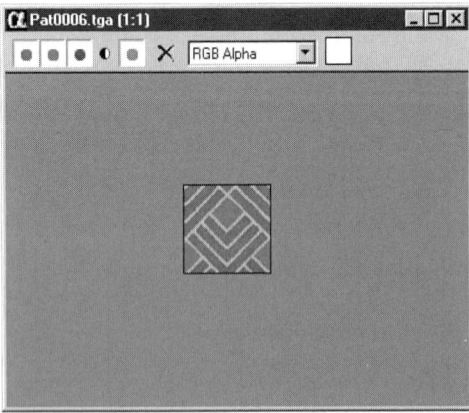

Figure 4.2 MAX R3 file viewer.

Chapter 4: Industrial and Mechanical Design Modeling   159

Tip
To learn more about simulated geometry, consult Chapter 13, "Using MAX 3 as a 2D Paint Tool." For more background on materials and maps, see Chapter 8, "Material Concepts."

The three simple exercises that follow illustrate methods of simulating surface geometry, including:

- **Bump mapping.** You apply a material to an object, giving the illusion of ribbed flexible tubing and a molded rubber anti-slip surface.

- **Opacity mapping.** Simulate holes in a simple mesh object, to make it appear more complex.

- **Displacement mapping.** You create actual new geometry from a map.

Bump Mapping

Bump mapping uses the whiteness, or luminance value, of the pixels in any map to create areas that appear raised from the surface. With bump mapping, black pixels have no effect on surface appearance, and shades of gray appear raised a proportional amount. MAX R3 recognizes 256 levels of gray.

Exercise 4.1   Bump Mapping

1. Open the file called 04max01.max from the CD-ROM. It contains a table, a flashlight, and a flexible light attachment (used for tight spaces). The objects are efficient, with the entire scene composed of 11,546 faces.

2. Right-click the Camera01 viewport (to activate it) and select Quick Render. The flex tube, the flashlight, and the table have plain solid colors, giving the appearance of smooth surfaces. The scene looks like Figure 4.3.

3. Select Material Editor (to open it). Click and drag the material called FLASHLIGHT onto the object called FLASHLIGHT in Camera01 viewport. Click and drag GREEN_PAINT to the TABLE object, and FLEXTUBE onto the FLEXTUBE object.

Caution
Make sure to drag the FLEXTUBE material to the FLEXTUBE 3D-mesh object; not to the Helix01 2D object inside FLEXTUBE. FLEXTUBE turns black and white in the Camera01 viewport when the material is correctly assigned.

160   Part I   Modeling

Figure 4.3 The Flexlight scene, with only plain color.

   4. Select Quick Render while the Camera01 viewport is activated. Notice the segmented appearance of FLEXTUBE and the simulated raised rubber surface on FLASHLIGHT. The raised surfaces are the result of a Gradient map and a Brick map in the Bump map slots of the materials. There is no new geometry. The table has no Bump map, but it has a reflection (making the scene more interesting). The rendered scene looks like Figure 4.4.

Figure 4.4 FLEXTUBE scene with Bump map materials.

   5. Activate the Camera01 viewport (if it is not already active), and type C. Double-click Camera02 in the Select Camera dialog box, to switch to the Camera02 viewpoint. Render Camera02 viewport. Notice that the closer you are to FLEXTUBE, the less convincing the Bump map surface appears. It never shows the bump effect against any background and doesn't appear to significantly raise the surface near the coil's base. The image looks similar to Figure 4.5.

Chapter 4: Industrial and Mechanical Design Modeling   161

Note
Dolly Camera02 closer to the FLEXTUBE several times and render each time. The effect diminishes as you get closer.

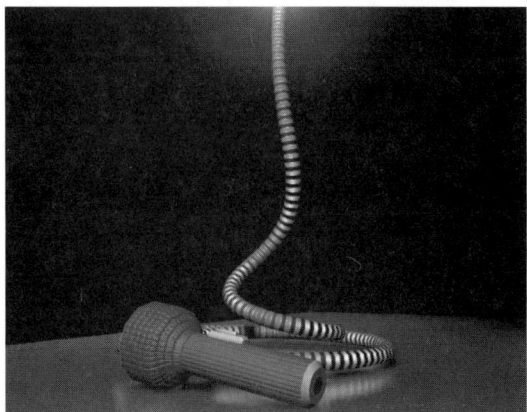

Figure 4.5 FLEXTUBE close-up view.

Tip
For materials that use bitmaps to generate bumps, higher resolution maps create a better bump effect. Using the alpha channel information of bitmap images (when available) also gives better results.

6. Save the file as Ch4_flexlite_01.max. Study the materials in the Material Editor and the creation parameters, noting how the objects were created and the materials mapped to them. Creating the actual detailed 3D geometry for FLEXTUBE and FLASHLIGHT, instead of using bump maps, results in extremely high face and vertex counts. This method slows display navigation and creates long render times. The rendered results are not any more convincing either.

Opacity Mapping

Opacity mapping relies on an image's luminance values to create the illusion of opacity or transparency. White pixels are opaque, black pixels are transparent, and gray pixels are some midlevel of transparency. In this exercise, you apply an Opacity map representing a punched metal plate that shows the colored cylinders inside a stainless-steel box.

Exercise 4.2 Opacity Mapping

1. Open the file called 04max02.max on the CD-ROM. It's a stainless-steel box (with flat metal-end plates) on a table.

2. In Camera01 viewport, select Quick Render (to view the stainless box with flat, painted end plates).

3. In the Material Editor, drag and drop the material called METAL PLATE from the first sample sphere onto BACKPLATE01. The text "tbdesign" repeats over the surface of the plate.

4. Select Quick Render again. Notice that the plate now has the illusion of stamped holes in the surface. The colored cylinders inside the box show through as well. Again, no extra geometry is created, and the illusion is sufficient for many situations. Notice, however, that there is no visible thickness to the plate. The closer the viewer gets to the plate, the less real the effect appears.

Displacement Mapping

Displacement mapping is similar to bump mapping, in that it uses a map's luminance values to affect a mesh surface's height. However, while bump mapping is an illusion, displacement mapping actually creates new polygon faces. The effect holds up well under close examination.

 Caution

Displacement mapping creates dense mesh objects. In the Material Editor Mapping rollout, set the Displacement Mapping Amount spinner to 20 before applying the material to an object. You can then adjust upward to increase the effect. Starting with an amount of 100 creates millions of faces and seemingly locks the machine while it calculates the new geometry.

Exercise 4.3 Displacement Mapping

1. Open the file 04max03.max on the CD-ROM. The file shows a thin metal sheet. You apply a material that displaces the flat mesh into a cone-shaped stamping. This is easier than trying to model with either lofting or lathing methods. The scene also has two lights and a camera.

2. Open the Material Editor. Drag and drop the material called GRADIENT_DISPL onto Plane01 (in the Front viewport). The material used to create the cone has a grayscale radial Gradient Ramp map in the Displacement slot. Open the Maps rollout, and click the Displacement Map button (to view the gradient). The white area displaces the mesh; the black has no effect.

3. Type H, and select Plane01. In the Modify panel, click the More button. Double-click Displace Mesh in the World-Space modifiers. In the Displacement Approx.

rollout, check Custom Settings. The cone appears in the flat plane's surface. Choose Zoom Extents All Selected. Now you see that the mesh is actually displaced in the Top and Left viewports, and you're not seeing a bump map illusion. See Figure 4.6.

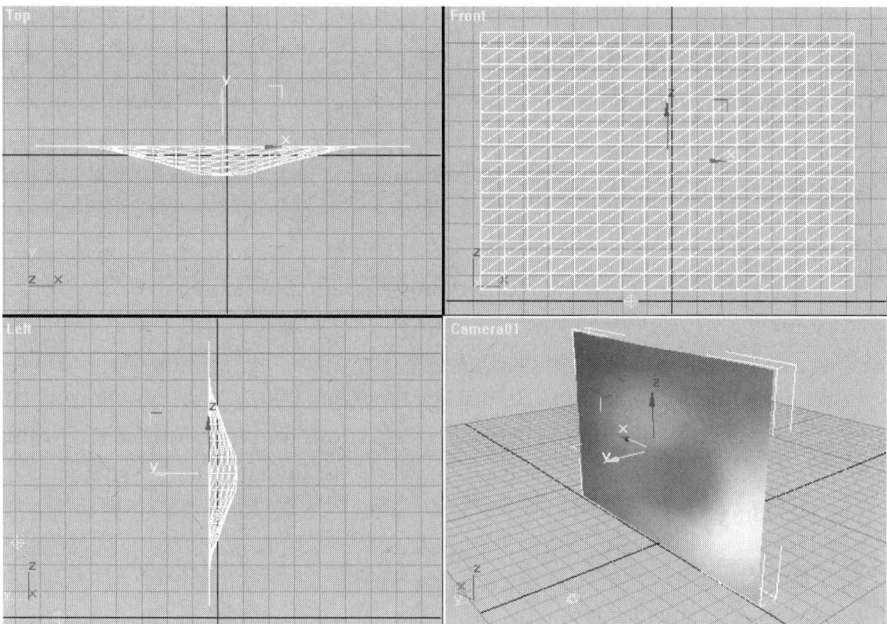

Figure 4.6 Displaced cone.

4. In the Displacement Approx. rollout, the Subdivision method is set to Spatial and Curvature (with Edge at 10, Distance at 10, and Angle at 4). In the Camera01 viewport, right-click the selected Plane01 mesh. Select Properties in the menu, and notice that there are 2,044 faces. The cone's definition is not very good, however.

5. In the Modify panel, choose Low Subdivision Presets. The cone looks somewhat less defined. Select High. The cone edges are well defined, but the mesh now has 8,188 faces.

6. In the Subdivision Methods area, enter 14 in the Edge field, 14 in the Distance field, and 6 in the Angle field. This results in a well-defined cone, with only 2,140 faces.

7. In the Modify panel, select Remove Modifier from the Stack (to remove Displace Mesh). In the Modify panel, choose More. Double-click the Disp Approx Object-Space modifier. In the Spatial and Curvature fields, enter 14 in the Edge field, 14 in the Distance field, and 6 in the Angle field. The plane appears flat in the

viewports. Render the Camera01 viewport. Now notice that the displaced cone renders properly. You have an efficient object in the viewport and an optimized object at render time.

8. Save the file as DISP_CONE_COMPLETE.MAX.

Cross-Sectional Modeling

Cross-sectional modeling is used in MAX R3 in a variety of ways. For example, you can use cross-sections to:

- Loft a threaded bolt.
- Create a Patch surface model from cross-sections.
- Create a free-form model, and export cross-section information to CAD programs.

In many mechanical-design firms, 2D-CAD data exists. With a little editing, you can extract the 2D shapes (to form the basis of cross-sections for use in MAX R3). For this to work efficiently, you must have a basic knowledge of fundamental 2D-editing techniques, including:

- Vertex welding
- Vertex and segment smooth
- Compound shapes
- Spline and segment Attach and Detach commands

The 2D shapes used in this chapter have been created in MAX R3, so you don't need the editing techniques. However, review the 2D-Shape sub-object editing information (in the shipping MAX R3 manuals) if you plan to use CAD 2D data in your own work.

Creating a Threaded Bolt

In this exercise, you use several 2D shapes to create a representative threaded bolt. This is not a bolt that's accurate in every respect, but it's efficient and stands up under close scrutiny. It's made in three parts, which are grouped to create a single bolt.

Making the bolt in three parts allows flexibility in your models. For example, you may need to show the whole bolt turning into a threaded hole. For that animation you need all parts; but suppose you also need other bolts (demonstrating their placement in holding an object together). In that case, you only need copies of the bolt head and not the body or threads. It's extremely inefficient to include the extra geometry if it won't be seen. You may also have a scene where the threads are important for a close-up shot. For that shot, loft a more accurate thread-tooth cross-section along the helix.

Note

Many users try to create a bolt similar to the way it's manufactured (by subtracting 3D threads from a 3D body). This is difficult for MAX R3. The resulting model has numerous faces and problems with missing faces.

Exercise 4.4   Creating a Bolt from 2D Cross-Sections

1. Open the file called 04max04.max from the CD-ROM. Type H, and clear Cameras and Lights in the List Types area. Select Case Sensitive (to see a list of the scene's 2D shapes). The dialog box looks like Figure 4.7. Double-click body_tip_circle in the list.

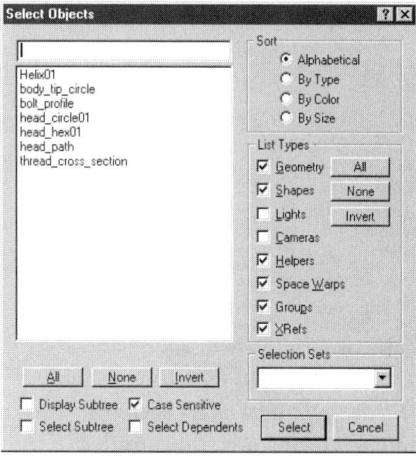

Figure 4.7   The Select Objects dialog box with the 2D cross-sections list.

2. In the Modify panel, select More. In the list of modifiers, double-click Bevel Profile. Bevel Profile requires two valid 2D cross-sections to function: a base shape (body_tip_circle) and a side-profile shape (bolt_profile).

3. Under the Modify pull-down menu, select Parameters. Choose Pick Profile, and select the bolt_profile shape in the Camera01 viewport. To make the model more efficient, clear the End option in the Capping area. This eliminates the faces at the top, where the head is located. The body's face count reduces by more than 25 percent. This is significant if you have numerous bolt bodies in the scene. Rename the object BODY. Save the file as 04_bolt_01.max

> **Tip**
> If you have trouble finding the 2D shape after selecting Pick Profile, type H and select bolt_profile in the list. Click the Pick button (to complete the selection).

4. Loft a simple triangle along a helix path for the threads. The triangle's pivot point is repositioned to the base's midpoint. This lofts it flat against the body. In the Camera01 viewport, select Helix01. In Create panel, click the Geometry button. Select Standard Primitives, then choose Compound Objects. Select Loft button, and then choose Get Shape. Select the thread_cross_section 2D triangle. The triangle is lofted along the helix, but it appears twisted. See Figure 4.8.

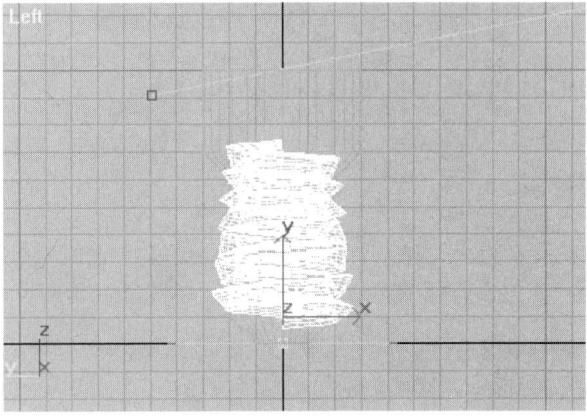

Figure 4.8 The triangle, lofted along helix.

5. In the Modify panel, rename Loft01 to THREADS. In the Skin Parameters rollout, check the Optimize Shapes option, and clear Banking. Optimize Shapes reduces the face count from 6,080 to 1,010. Turning off Banking keeps the thread perpendicular to the body, as it winds up the helix. However, the thread is squared abruptly at each end.

6. In the Deformations rollout, select Scale. Taper the ends of the lofted threads by scaling the shape along the helix. Click the Make Symmetrical button (to turn it off). You don't want the same scaling factor in both the X- and Y-axis. Click and hold Insert Corner Point, and choose the Insert Bézier Point flyout button. Click the red-scale line (approximately 20 percent along the line and 80 percent along the line) to insert new points. Select Move Control Point, and click the left-most point on the red-scale line. At the bottom of the Scale dialog box, enter 0.0 in the left Path Percent field and 50 in the right Scale Amount field. Select the second control point. Enter 20.0 in the Path Percent field and 100.0 in the Scale Amount field. Select the third point. Enter 80.0 and 100.0. Select the last point. Enter 100.0 and 50.0.

7. Select Display Y-Axis (to view the green-scale line). Choose Insert Bézier Point, and insert points near 20 percent and 80 percent. Select Move Point. Starting from the left, enter the following numbers for each point: first, 0.0 and 0.0; second, 20.0 and 100.0; third, 80.0 and 100.0; fourth, 100.0 and 0.0. Select Display XY Axis, and the Scaling dialog box looks similar to Figure 4.9. Close the Scale Deformation dialog box. Save the file as 04_bolt_02.max

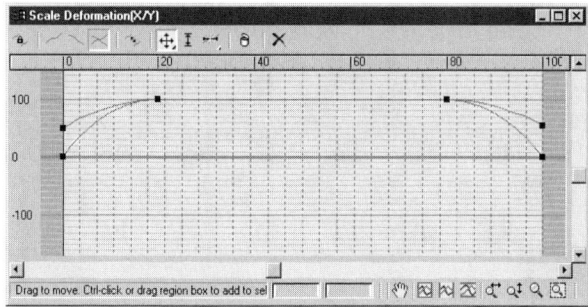

Figure 4.9 Scaling dialog settings to taper threads.

8. Lofting between two cross-section shapes creates the bolt head. In the Perspective viewport, select the 2D line called head_path.
9. In the Create panel, click Geometry. Choose Compound Objects (if it isn't already selected). Click the Loft button, and select Get Shape. Select head_hex01 2D.
10. In the Modify panel, rename the Loft01 object HEAD.
11. In the Skin Parameters rollout, set Path Steps to 0. In the Path Parameters rollout, click the new Path Steps option. Click Yes (to continue at the warning dialog box). This allows you to move from vertex to vertex on the path. In Path Parameters, increment the Path Number to 1, click the Get Shape button (to turn it on), and select head_hex01 again.
12. Increment path Number to 2, click Get Shape (to turn it on), and select head_circle01. The bolt head is a hexagon—until near the top, where it transitions to a circular shape. However, the smoothing is not handled properly by the lofting.
13. In the Surface Parameters rollout, clear Smooth Length and Smooth Width. Use the Smooth modifier for better control.
14. Select Zoom Extents All Selected (to fill the orthographic viewports with the bolt head). Right-click the Front viewport (to activate it).
15. In the Modify panel, choose Mesh Select. Click the Polygon button (to enter Sub-Object mode). From the bottom toolbar, click the Window Selection button (to select only faces inside the selection box). From the Main Toolbar, click the Select

button. In the Front viewport, click and drag to select all the lower faces in the Front viewport. Select More, and double-click Smooth. Check the Auto Smooth option (at the default Threshold of 30 degrees).

16. Choose Mesh Select, choose Polygon Sub-Object mode, and select only the top set of faces. Apply another Smooth modifier. Set the Threshold to 20.0, and check Auto Smooth.

17. Choose Mesh Select again. This applies a Mesh Select at Object level (to give you control of the entire mesh). The bolt head is now smooth, but only around the transition between hex and circular areas. It looks like Figure 4.10.

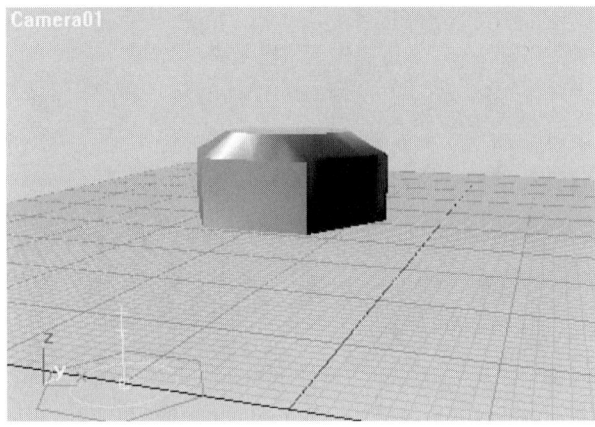

Figure 4.10 Smoothed HEAD mesh.

18. From the Main Toolbar, select Align. Choose BODY (in the Camera01 viewport). In the Align Selection dialog box, check X-Position and Y-Position. Check Center for Current Object and Center for Target Object. Click the Apply button.

19. Check the Z-Position check box. Select Current Object Minimum and Target Object Maximum (to align the HEAD to the BODY's top center. Click OK.

20. Select HEAD, BODY, and THREADS. Select Group, click Group in the menu, and name the group BOLT. Click OK.

21. Open the Material Editor. Drag and drop the BOLT_METAL material onto the bolt. Click OK (to choose Assign to Selection). Render the Camera01 viewport. It looks similar to Figure 4.11.

Figure 4.11 Rendered bolt.

22. Save the file as 04_bolt_03.max.

Creating a Patch Surface from Cross-Sections

Another option of using 2D cross-sectional information is with the new Patch surface tools. There are basically two methods of working with surface tools, using:

- **CrossSection and Surface modifiers**. With this method, you create only cross-sectional 2D shapes. You then apply a CrossSection modifier, to tie the shapes' vertices together with longitudinal Patch edges. Next, you apply a Surface modifier to generate the Patch surface from the edge information. The method works best for objects that are easily described by regular cross-sections alone (such as mechanical parts).

- **Surface modifier alone**. With this method, you create both the cross-sections and the longitudinal 2D edges. You then apply the Surface modifier directly to them. The method works best for objects described by a more complex cage of edges (such as a computer mouse or a human head).

In the next exercise, you use the CrossSection and Surface modifiers method to roughly sketch a ballpoint pen. Then make a few adjustments to shape the form for a more finished design.

Exercise 4.5 Creating a Patch Ballpoint Pen

1. Open the file called 04max05.max from the CD-ROM. It's a series of circular cross-sections, positioned along the axis of (eventually) a pen. The cross-sections are individual shapes, which must be attached before the CrossSection modifier is applied. The User viewport looks similar to Figure 4.12.

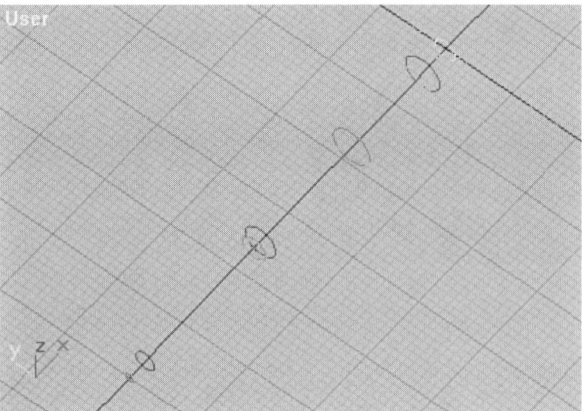

Figure 4.12 Circular cross-sections along a common axis.

Tip

The circular cross-sections are created with the NGon command, as well as the default six sides and the Circular check box checked). This results in a circular 2D shape, with six vertices instead of four. The CrossSection modifier creates longitudinal edge lines from vertex to vertex. Six new edges gives you more control in later editing. Best results are obtained from cross-sections with the same number of vertices. Make sure each shape's first vertex is in alignment (to avoid twisting the surface).

2. Right-click the User viewport (to activate it), and type W (to fill the display with that viewport). Click the Select button, and choose the small NGon (at the display's lower left). It's named NGon01. Right-click the viewport, and choose Convert to Editable Spline.

Caution

Do *not* convert to an Editable Mesh. The shape becomes a 3D object, and the next steps will not function.

3. Right-click the viewport again. Choose Attach. Carefully select each shape (from lower left to upper right) in the order they are created. At the far right, the larger yellow NGon must be selected before the smaller pink NGon.

Chapter 4: Industrial and Mechanical Design Modeling   171

Tip
You can use the H key to select the shapes by name, ensuring the correct order.

Caution
You cannot use Attach Multiple and be assured of getting the shapes attached in the correct order. You must pick them individually.

NEW TO R3

4. In the Modify panel, select More. Double-click the new CrossSection modifier. Notice that white lines appear, running from vertex to vertex, along the cross-section NGons. These lines describe Patch surfaces' edges in the next step. The image looks similar to Figure 4.13.

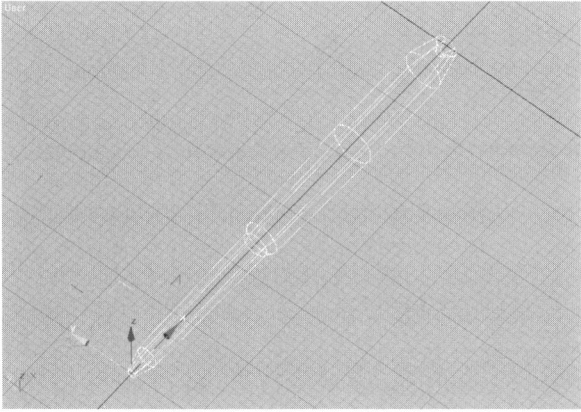

Figure 4.13 New lines formed by CrossSection modifier.

Note
The CrossSection modifier has options for Linear, Smooth, Bézier, and Bézier Corner tangency. This object develops overlapping curves at the tip and barrel-body junctions, with any option except Linear. Make sure you leave this option set to Linear (to avoid unwanted results).

NEW TO R3

5. The pen still has no renderable surface information. Add the new Surface modifier (to create a Patch surface from the edges). In the Modify panel, select More. Double-click the new Surface modifier in the list. In the Parameters rollout, enter 0.1 in the Threshold field. This keeps the surface with small dimensions from collapsing in on itself. Select Remove Interior Patches (to avoid surfaces on each of the circles). In the viewport, right-click the User label. Choose Smooth+Highlight.

6. Now prepare the new Patch surfaces for material assignments. Type W (to return to the default four views). Right-click the Front viewport (to activate it). In the

Modify panel, select EditPatch, and go to Sub-Object Patch. Choose Select. Click and drag a selection window around the body portion of the pen. It looks similar to Figure 4.14.

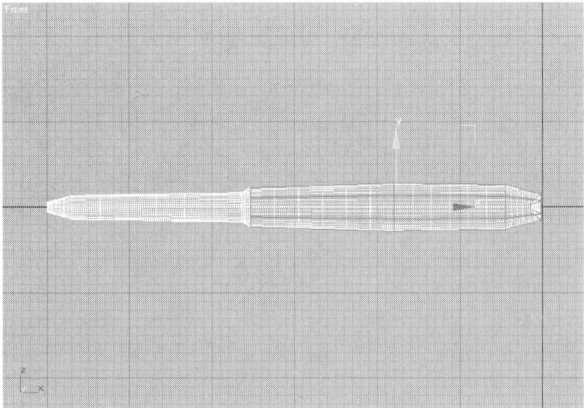

Figure 4.14 The pen body with Patch surfaces selected.

7. In the Surface Properties rollout, make sure that the Material ID field reads 1. Drag a selection window around the narrow ring of faces (that make up the bezel between body and grip). Enter 2 in the Material ID field. Next, select the grip surfaces, and enter 3 in the Material ID field. Refer to Figure 4.14 (to identify the pen's body portion).

8. With the grip surfaces still selected, click the UVW Map modifier button. Check Cylindrical as the mapping type. Select EditPatch (adding a new modifier to the top of the Modifier Stack). This returns control to the entire object.

9. In Material Editor, drag and drop the BALLPOINT material onto the pen. The User viewport looks similar to Figure 4.15.

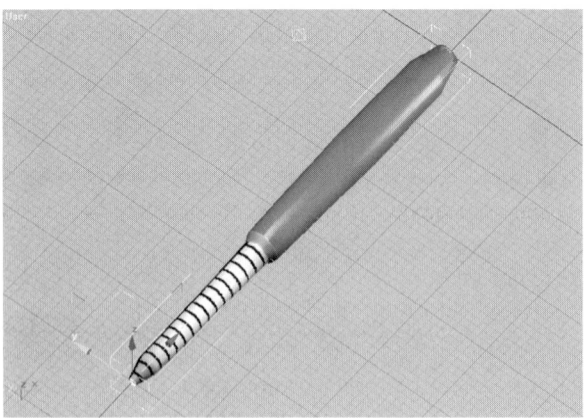

Figure 4.15 The pen, with BALLPOINT material in shaded viewport.

Chapter 4: Industrial and Mechanical Design Modeling   173

10. In the Modify panel, go to Sub-Object Edge. In the Front viewport, select the body's two top edges. Move and rotate the two edges to form a raised crown, similar to Figure 4.16.

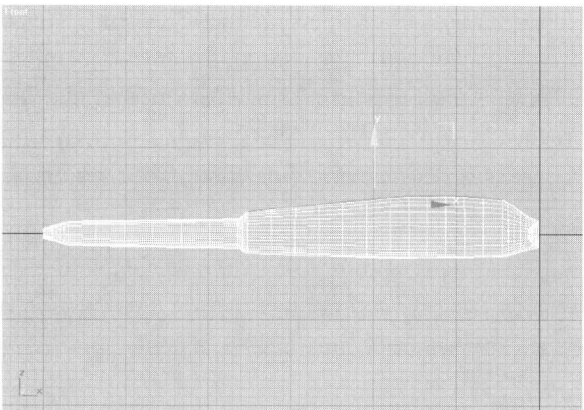

Figure 4.16 Top body edge, moved upward and rotated into a crown.

11. Go to Sub-Object Vertex. Adjust the Bézier handles on the previously selected edges' right-most vertex. This smoothes the new crown's transition and exits Sub-Object mode, returning control to the entire object.

Note

Steps 10 and 11 illustrate how the pen is molded into shape (much like clay) and is not intended to create any specific form. Use your imagination for what makes the crown look good. You are the designer.

12. Right-click the User viewport (to activate it). Select Quick Render. The rendered image looks similar to Figure 4.17.

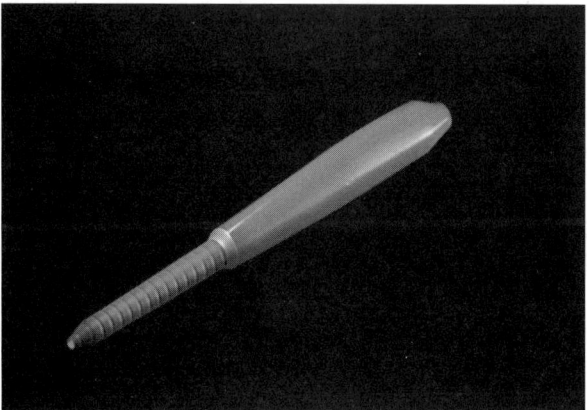

Figure 4.17 Rendered ballpoint pen.

13. Save the file as 04_pen_01.max.

Generating Cross-Sections from Free-Form Mesh Objects

You may be asked to design a conceptual model of a new product. The design process gives you freedom to shape a flowing object with little concern for exact dimensions. Once you have the design worked out, you have to send information to the machine shop for them to manufacture the product. MAX R3 has tools that allow you to freely work (as if modeling with clay), and then to slice and export sectional information ready to be dimensioned in a CAD program.

In the next exercise, you start with a simple filleted-box primitive and mold it into shape with several modifiers. After the object looks the way you want it, pull 2D sections from several points along the mesh (in a form that exports to a CAD program).

Exercise 4.6 A Motorcycle Fuel Tank

1. Open the file called 04max06.max from the CD-ROM. It appears empty, but it actually has several hidden objects and lights (that you reveal later in the exercise).

2. In the Create panel, select Geometry. Choose Extended Primitives from the drop-down list. Click the ChamferBox button. In the Top viewport, click and drag a box of any size. Rename the object TANK.

3. In the Modify panel, enter the information shown in Figure 4.18 into the proper fields. Enter 16 in the Length field, 24 in the Width field, 8 in the Height field, and 2 in the Fillet field. Enter 8 in the Length Segs field, 12 in the Width Segs field, 4 in the Height Segs field, and 4 in the Fillet Segs field. This creates a filleted box that is the basis of the tank. Select Zoom Extents All.

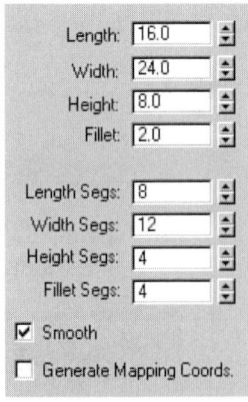

Figure 4.18 Parameters for ChamferBox.

4. In the Modify panel, select Taper. Enter 0.1 in the Amount field, 0.75 in the Curve field, and check the Primary X-Axis option. The tank looks like Figure 4.19.

5. In the Modify panel, select More. Double-click Skew. Enter 3.0 in the Amount field. This tilts the tank forward on its base. The Front viewport looks like Figure 4.20.

Chapter 4: Industrial and Mechanical Design Modeling   175

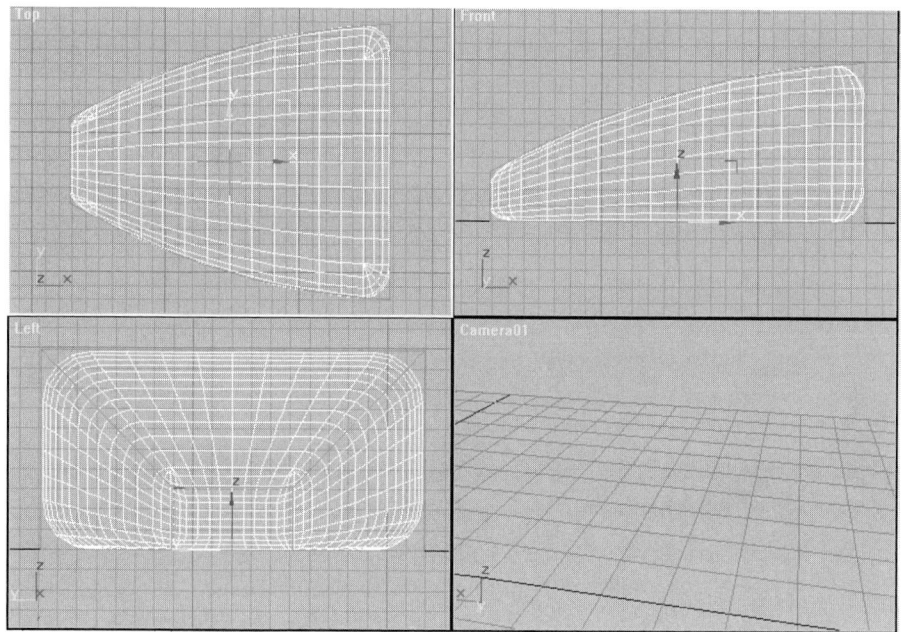

Figure 4.19 ChamferBox with Taper modifier.

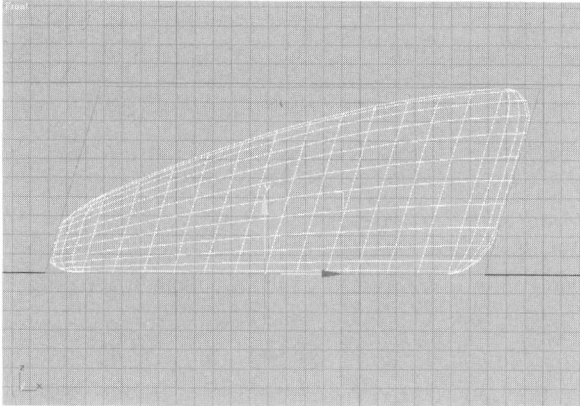

Figure 4.20 ChamferBox with Taper and Skew modifiers.

   6. In the Modify panel, select More. Double-click FFD (box). In the FFD Parameters rollout, choose Set Number of Points. Enter 10 in the Length field, and click OK. The resulting box-shaped lattice of control points allows you to mold the mesh into a curved form (by transforming the control points).

7. Right-click the Camera01 viewport (to activate it). Type U (to switch to a User viewport). Select Zoom Extents All (to zoom where you can see the next step's effect). Right-click the Left viewport (to activate it).

8. In the Modify panel, select Sub-Object Control Points. In the Left viewport, click and drag a selection window around the top-center's two sets of control points. Press Ctrl while clicking and dragging the bottom-center's control points (to add them to the selection set). The Left viewport look similar to Figure 4.21.

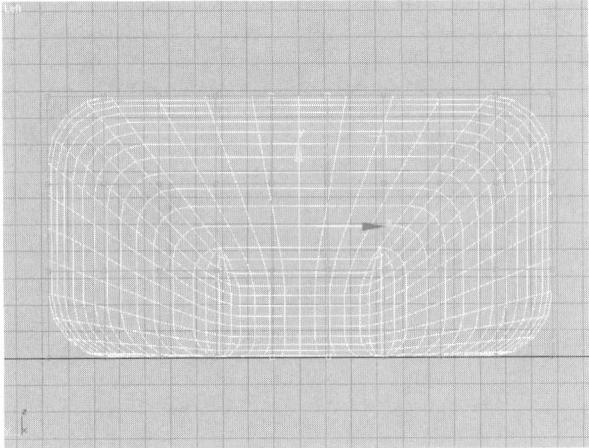

Figure 4.21 Top- and bottom-center control points selected.

9. Choose Select and Move. Right-click the button. In the Transform Type-In dialog box, enter 2.0 in the Offset:Screen Y-axis field.

10. Click and drag in the Left viewport, selecting the four top-center control points. Choose Select and Move. Then enter 2.0 in the Offset:Screen Y-axis field again. Exit Sub-Object mode. Close the Transform Type-In dialog box. Save the file as 04_tank_01.max. This a good point to take a break. You have the tank looking the way you want it. The Left viewport looks like Figure 4.22.

11. Open the file 04_tank_01.max (if you closed it since the last step). Right-click the User viewport (to activate it), and type W (to fill the display). In the Create panel, select Shapes. Then choose Section. In the User viewport, click and drag in the display's lower left. You drag out a small four-panel section plane. The plane's size is not important, but its position is pivotal.

Chapter 4: Industrial and Mechanical Design Modeling   177

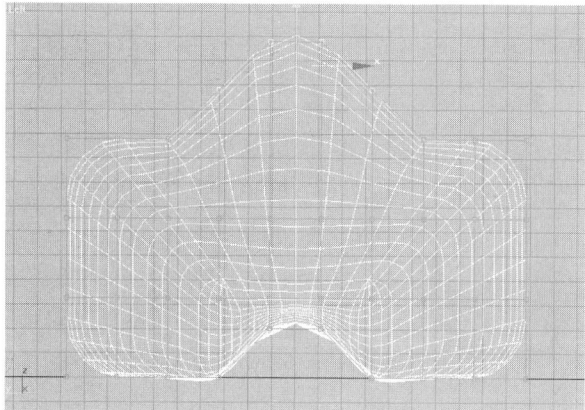

Figure 4.22   FFD control points, moved upward to finish rounding out the tank.

12. Choose Select and Rotate. Click the Angle Snap button (to turn it on). Click and drag the Transform Gizmo Y-axis (to rotate the section plane 90 degrees). A yellow line appears on the tank. That is the section's new location. It looks similar to Figure 4.23.

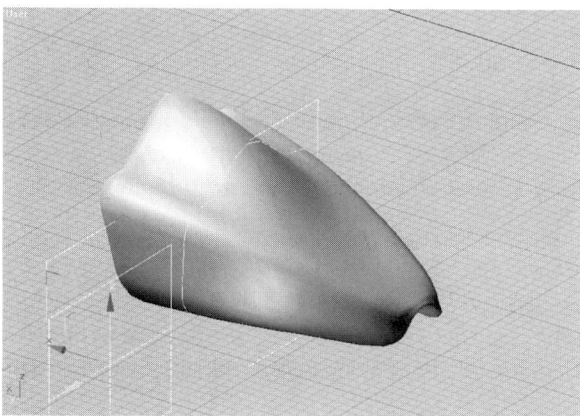

Figure 4.23   Section plane, rotated 90 degrees in Y-axis.

13. Position the plane where you want the first section located. In the Modify panel, select Section Parameters. Then choose Create Shape. In the Name Section Shape dialog box, click OK (to accept the name SShape01).

14. Move the section plane along the X-axis toward the back of the tank. Choose Create Shape again, and accept the name by clicking OK. Move the section plane again, and create another section shape.

178   Part I   Modeling

> **Tip**
> Use Align to align the section plane at the tank's end. Clone the section plane, and use Transform Type-In (to position the section plane's copies at exact points along the tank).

15. Type H, and select the three SShape objects in the list. Choose Select and Move, which translates the three shapes to one side of the tank. It's similar to Figure 2.24.

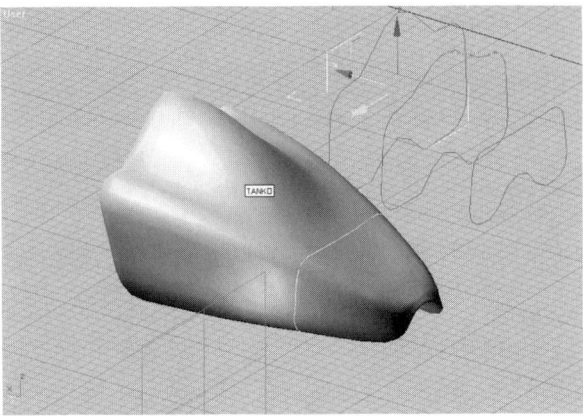

Figure 4.24 Three selected 2D cross-section shapes.

16. Make sure all three shapes are still selected. Click the File pull-down menu, and choose the new Export Selected. Set the file type to DXF, enter a name for the file, and save it to disk. The DXF file may now be imported into AutoCAD for adjusting and dimensioning.

17. Open the Material Editor. Drag and drop the METALFLAKE material onto the tank. In the Display panel, select Unhide All (to reveal the frame and gas cap).

18. Using Align, Move, and Rotate, move the tank and gas cap into position on the frame. Click Quick Render (to render the Camera01 viewport). It looks similar to Figure 4.25.

19. Save the file as 04_tank_02.max.

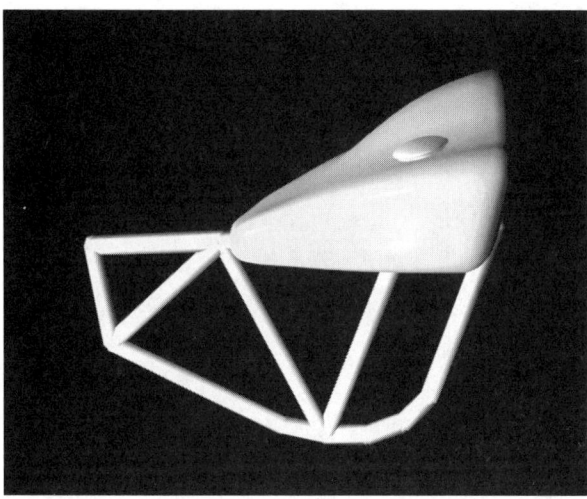

Figure 4.25 Rendered frame, tank, and gas cap.

Sectional Views

Sectional cut-away views of mesh objects can be generated as well. This does not result in 2D information that is sent to CAD (as in the previous exercise). It is, however, a method of removing mesh portions and revealing the internal structure, if any. In the next exercise, you slice open the fuel tank (to show how it fits to the motorcycle's frame).

Exercise 4.7   Using Slice for Cut-Away Views

1. Open the file 04_tank_02.max (that you saved from the last exercise), or get it from the CD-ROM. It contains the motorcycle fuel tank, gas cap, and frame.

2. In the Camera01 viewport, select the TANK mesh object. In the Modify panel, choose More. Double-click Slice. The Slice modifier shows as an orange, flat plane gizmo. It's positioned at the mesh's Pivot Point and aligns with the local axis system.

3. In the Modifier panel, select Sub-Object Slice Plane. The gizmo turns yellow. Click the Angle Snap button (to toggle it on). Right-click the Camera01 viewport, and choose Rotate. Select View Reference Coordinate System, and set it to Local. Click and drag downward on the X-Transform Gizmo axis, rotating the Slice Plane 90 degrees. The viewport looks similar to Figure 4.26.

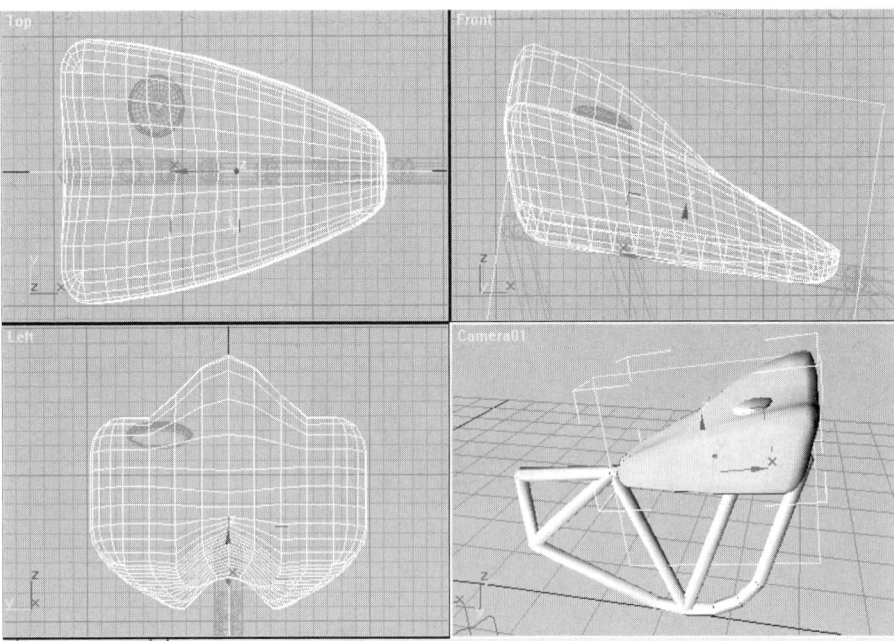

Figure 4.26 The Slice Plane, rotated 90 degrees.

4. In the Slice Parameters rollout, select Remove Top. This slices away the portion of the tank toward you. It only slices away the faces, however. Because the tank mesh has no thickness, it may look strange as you look at the inside surfaces.

5. In the Modify panel, select More. Double-click Cap Holes. This modifier closes the sliced object (with a new set of faces that makes it appear as though the tank were a solid object). It looks similar to Figure 4.27.

Figure 4.27 The Tank Slice modifier and Cap Holes modifier.

Chapter 4: Industrial and Mechanical Design Modeling   181

Tip
You can apply a MeshSelect modifier to select the new faces. Then apply a Material modifier, and change the ID number. By converting the METALFLAKE material to a Multi/Sub-Object material, you apply a different color or material to make the slice more apparent.

6. Change the Camera01 viewport (so it's more from the back of the frame). Select Quick Render, and it should look similar to Figure 4.27. Save the file as 04_tank_03.max.

Modeling with XRefs

NEW TO R3 The Xref command set is one of MAX R3's new features that offers the greatest promise for increased productivity. Xrefs, or external references, are similar to Reference cloning results. The Xref commands establish a one-way link from the original object to the Xref file. This allows the the original file's editing to transfer to each file with Xref objects or scenes. The file containing the Xref objects or scenes automatically updates whenever the file is opened, or updates on command.

Xrefs promote collaborative work within a company or even between companies. Work on animated sequences and materials development now begin before the modeling is completed. Each object or scene updates, to reflect progress as it happens. This cuts project time considerably as more steps are performed concurrently.

Production is also enhanced because externally referenced objects and scenes use less computer resources than original objects merged into the master file. XRef objects can also be represented in a file by proxy objects. These proxy objects are extremely low-resolution versions of the original. The computer runs more efficiently during display navigation because fewer faces are displayed. Rendering can use the proxy object for test renders, or default to the original mesh during final renders.

The Xref commands are:

- **XRef Scenes.** XRef Scene allows complete use of MAX R3 files in a new scene. However, the referenced scenes can't be altered or edited in the new file.
- **XRef Objects.** Using the XRef Objects command, you can bring objects into a new scene as individual objects for further editing. The original objects are protected from any changes, as a result of modifying the Xref.

In Exercise 4.8 you use XRef Objects and XRef Scenes to assemble a project composed of several files. The scene is a room, with a prototype printing press. Imagine that a different group within the company develops a portion of the final file. You are the lead designer in charge of the finished product. You're responsible for blending the various files into a single scene, with the press rotating in the display room.

Exercise 4.8   A Project Using XRef Scenes and XRef Objects

1. Open the file called 04max07.max. It's an empty file, with the units set to Feet with Fractional Inches. Your task is to build a printing press scene, with MAX R3 files from coworkers, and animate the press turning.

2. In the File menu, choose XRef Objects to access the XRef Objects dialog box. The first step is to choose a Max file from which to import objects. Select Add (in the upper-right corner of the dialog box). Find and highlight the file called 04_press_base on the CD-ROM. In the Open File dialog box, click Open. You see an XRef Merge dialog box. Highlight STEELBEAM, and click OK. The steel-beam base appears in the scene. The viewports and dialog box look like Figure 4.28.

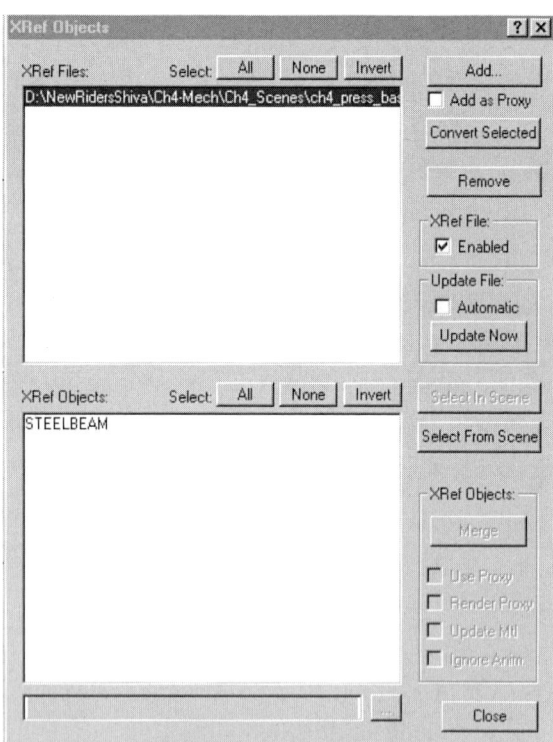

Figure 4.28   XRef Objects dialog box for steel-beam base.

Chapter 4: Industrial and Mechanical Design Modeling   183

3. Assume STEELBEAM mesh is relatively complex. You increase your production by substituting the beam work with a simple box object in the display, but you want the beams to render in the final scene. In the lower XRef Objects panel, highlight STEELBEAM. Check the Set Proxy check box (at the upper right of the dialog box, and click the Set button. Double-click 04_press_base.max in the Open File dialog box. Double-click base_proxy. The XRef Objects dialog box looks like Figure 4.29. The beam base is replaced by a simple box. Close the XRef Objects dialog box.

Note

At this point you can also work with the XRef and Proxy in the Modify panel, which make changes to the objects and proxies.

4. Right-click the Perspective viewport (to activate it), and select Quick Render. The scene renders with the complete base, but the viewport displays only the proxy. If you select the proxy in the viewport, it's fully accessible. It can be moved and modified, if necessary.

5. There are situations where you don't have access for making modifications on XRef files. From the Files pull-down menu, choose XRef Scenes. In the XRef Scenes dialog box, select Add. Double-click the file called 04_press_room.max on the CD-ROM. This externally references the entire file and does not prompt object selection in the scene. The screen looks similar to Figure 4.30. Close the dialog box, and select Zoom Extents All. If you try to select the walls in the display or in the Select by Name dialog box, they won't select or appear in the list. There is no way to directly select the walls.

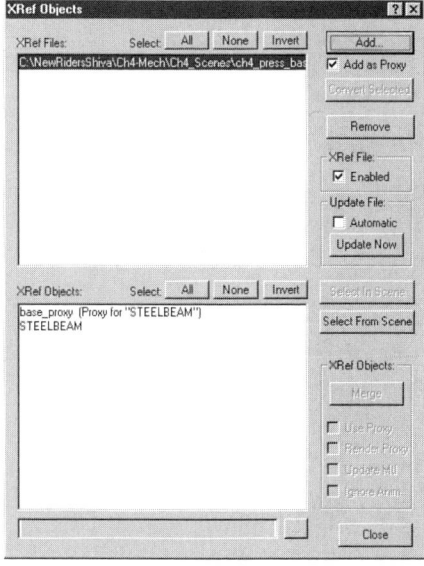 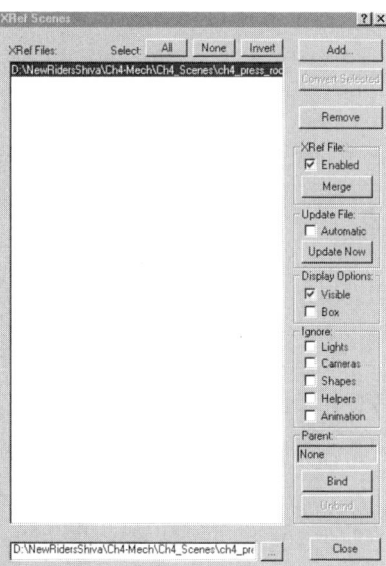

Figure 4.29 Xref Objects with proxy.   **Figure 4.30** The Xref Scenes dialog box.

6. In the viewports, notice that the base_proxy box is outside the room and you want it in the center of the room. It's possible to move the base_proxy into place, but in this case it makes more sense to move the room. You accomplish this by binding the room to another object—a dummy object. Select 3D Snap (to turn it off). Activate the Top viewport. In the Create panel, select Helpers, and click the Dummy button. Click and drag a small dummy in the Top viewport, and move it close to the room's center.

7. In the File menu, choose XRef Scenes. Highlight it in the XRef Files list. In the parent section, select Bind. Next, choose the dummy in the Top viewport. The room is now a child of the dummy parent. Close the XRef Scenes dialog box.

8. In the Top viewport, select the Dummy. On the Toolbar, choose Align, and select base_proxy (in the Top viewport). Check the X-Position and Y-Position check boxes, and check Center in both columns. Click OK. This centers the dummy in the World X- and Y-axis. Select Zoom Extents All. The screen looks similar to Figure 4.31.

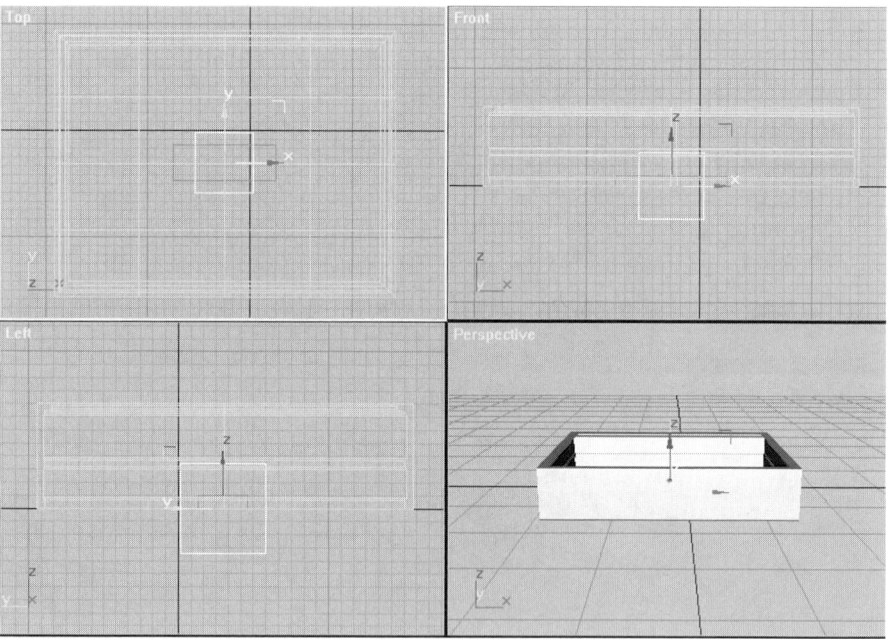

Figure 4.31 The Dummy and room, aligned with base_proxy.

9. Activate the Perspective viewport, and type C. This shows a Camera01 viewport of a camera that is in the room scene.

10. In the File menu, choose XRef Objects. Select Add, and double-click the file called 04_press_sides.max. In the XRef Merge dialog box, choose All, and click

Chapter 4: Industrial and Mechanical Design Modeling   185

OK. Repeat the process for the files called 04_press_motor.max, 04_press_nozzles.max, 04_press_roller, and 04_press_tanks.max. When you get a Duplicate Material Name dialog box, select Use Merged Materials (to keep materials separate). Notice the scene in the Camera01 viewport doesn't look quite right. The press is taller than the room and sticks through the ceiling. Your display looks similar to Figure 4.32. Save the file as 04_press_comp.max.

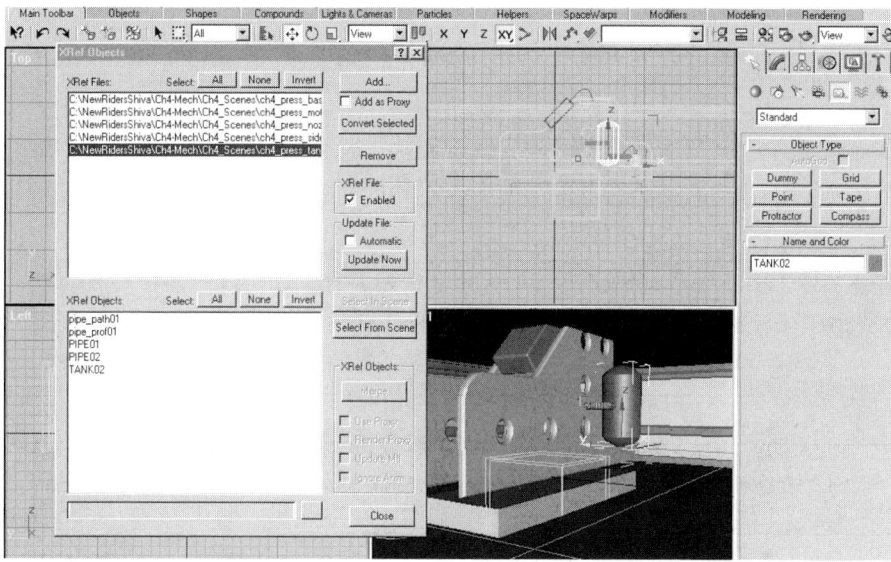

Figure 4.32 Xref Scenes and Objects.

11. Open the file called 04_press_room.max on the CD-ROM. Save changes to the current file (if you are prompted). Activate the Front viewport, and choose Select. Type H, and double-click wall_shape.

12. In the Modify panel, choose Vertex. Drag a selection window around all the vertices at the top of the wall_shape, including the cove-molding trim.

13. Choose Select and Move. Then right-click the button. Enter 2'–0" in the Offset:Screen Y-axis field of the Transform Type-In dialog box. Close the dialog box, and select Vertex (to exit that mode). The walls are two feet taller.

14. Type H, and double-click CEILING in the list. Use Transform Type-In to move it 2'–0" in the Y-axis, also. Save the file.

15. Open 04_press_comp.max (that you saved to disk). Activate the Perspective viewport, and type C (to switch to Camera01 viewport). The room's walls are two feet taller, and the ceiling is in the correct place (due to XRef Scenes' automatic update). In a real-world scenario, a co-worker calls you, reports a change in the room file, and you click the Update button in the XRef Scenes dialog box.

16. Save the file as 04_press_comp.max.

In Practice: Industrial and Mechanical Design Modeling

- **Simulate geometry when possible.** Simulating surface information with materials and maps reduces the number of faces and vertices needed for some complex surfaces. It also speeds render times and display response.

- **Use the new CrossSection modifier to turn 2D shapes into a framework for Patch surfaces.** Create 2D cross-sections, and move them into position. Apply a CrossSection modifier to connect the vertices with edges that define the edges of Patch surfaces.

- **The new Surface modifier creates Patch surfaces that are worked like clay.** A Surface modifier (applied to shapes with a CrossSection modifier or to shapes on which you create connecting edges) is a flexible method for efficiently building smooth-flowing surfaces.

- **Mold and shape simple 3D-mesh objects with Free Form Deformation modifiers.** Create complex flowing objects by manipulating the Control Points of a FFD modifier. Then apply 2D-Section objects, taking section cuts through the object for export to CAD software.

- **Collaborative work is much simpler with XRef Objects and XRef Scenes.** Groups of animators build different objects and scenes for referencing into a master file. The workgroups then alter the original files, and the files update automatically in the master file. However, no group changes the work of another group. Using Xref Proxy objects reduces the display overhead while ensuring that the original mesh always renders.

- **Keep vertex and face counts low for efficiency.** To work productively with MAX R3, model only the parts that show in the scene. Keep all models to a minimum face and vertex count for the purposes of your presentation. It is important to use materials to simulate geometry whenever you can, by using bump and opacity maps.

Chapter 5

Modeling for Real-Time 3D Games

No area of 3D graphics is garnering as much attention as real-time gaming—and no other area shows as much potential for massive growth in the next few years.

Unlike prerendered graphics, real-time 3D is generated on demand. In other words, when the viewer requests to look to the left in a 3D world, the real-time processor (usually called the *engine*) creates the graphics necessary to move the view to the left. A prerendered image doesn't have that luxury since it's generated by the artist long before the viewer sees it. The trade-offs are that prerendered images are more rich in color depth, complexity, and special effects whereas real-time graphics are usually low detail, limited textures and colors, and minimal special effects.

Real-time 3D is reaching its teenage years in the consumer market. In other words, more consumers see it in their daily lives, whether it is on television or through the latest 3D games. Set-top gaming systems that support real-time are in their first generation. With the sudden popularity of real-time 3D video game cards for PCs, developers are now producing more games that involve real-time 3D graphics. Renderware, OpenGL, Brender, Multi-Gen, and Microsoft's DirectDraw (a software engine for Windows 95/98 graphics) are among the real-time graphics engines gaining popularity.

The massive influx of Internet games is also fueling the drive to real-time 3D games. Real-time 3D games using various technologies are popping up all over the world. Whole companies are building around the concept of 3D multi-player games available to anyone on the Internet.

The skills of the real-time 3D artist are broad and varied. In addition to in-depth knowledge of the software used to generate source materials (3D meshes, texture maps, animations, and so on), a real-time artist must have a firm grasp of the programmatic principles that make real-time 3D possible. This does not mean that one should be a computer programmer—far from it, in fact. The excitement of real-time games lies in the artist's creations, generated on the spot and in instant response to the user's whims, with a life and a personality of their own.

Modeling and realistic texturing are the key issues and the most critical part of creating graphics for real-time games. The myriad issues and technical details that go into making a model efficient (low-polygon count), believable, aesthetically pleasing, and poised to behave and display properly in the real-time world are issues that face the real-time artist alone. After all, real-time engines rely on only the most basic elements of 3D graphics to create their illusion. (See Figure 5.1.)

Fortunately, 3D Studio MAX contains some of the best polygonal modeling and texturing features anywhere. It not only provides excellent tools to control every facet of working on a model, but also provides real-time 3D shaded views as the model is created. This enables the user to accurately preview the "look" of the finished product in the game itself.

Figure 5.1 A real-time 3D environment modeled in MAX and ready for export. Special thanks to Frank DeLise for the model.

Although all real-time game engines vary slightly in structure, capability, and the technologies used to squeeze the most speed out of the system, the principles behind each engine remain the same.

This chapter covers the following topics:

- 2D versus real-time 3D graphics.
- The basics of real-time 3D.
- The differences between real-time and prerendered 3D graphics.
- Principles and techniques for using 3D Studio MAX in modeling real-time objects.
- The future of real-time 3D graphics.

2D Versus Real-Time 3D Graphics

Although real-time 3D graphics have really just begun to appear on the PC, arcade games using 3D vector graphics (such as Tempest and Star Wars) first appeared in the mid-1980s. Military simulations have used real-time 3D on high-end machines for training purposes for quite some time. Only recently, however, could these graphics be nicely shaded and texture mapped on a PC at a speed that could match 2D animated graphics.

To fully appreciate the speed difficulty, you need to understand the difference between 2D and 3D animation at the computational level.

2D animation relies on the principles of traditional cel animation. A huge number of pictures are created, and then captured in sequence for playback in the chosen medium—in this case, a computer of some kind (including PCs, set-top gaming systems, custom-designed arcade systems, and so forth). The computer pulls the pictures from memory and displays them on-screen as fast as necessary to give the illusion of movement. The factors critical to 2D animation are data storage space (which accounts for the rise of the CD-ROM as the preferred gaming medium), the speed at which that data can be read, and how fast that data can be displayed. The computer does not have to do much "thinking" to display 2D animation.

3D graphics require much less storage than their 2D counterparts because the 3D pictures are not predrawn (with the exception of texture maps). The "recipe" for the 3D picture (meshes and animation) is stored as a mass of formulas and called up when needed. Because the pictures are drawn on-screen by the program as they are seen—and not before—the computer must "think" much more and much faster than it does with 2D images.

Let's look at a more concrete example. Imagine someone pulling nicely arranged pictures from a stack. That's 2D graphics. Now imagine another person trying to accurately draw, at the same speed as the person who's pulling pictures, a collection of objects that yet *another* person is moving around. That's your PC when it is trying to draw 3D. Imagining such a scenario should help you grasp the difference in what is demanded of a machine running a real-time application. Only the current high-speed processors are capable of meeting these extreme demands. Even then, the geometry drawn must be simple and have a low polygon count to make the process fast enough to meet acceptable display speeds.

Note

3D game accelerator cards are one of the most popular items for consumer PCs these days. These cards help reduce the 3D calculation burden on the CPU by offloading them to the card's own processor. Due to this technology, both developers and users alike can enjoy faster, richer 3D environments at a relatively low cost.

As a 3D real-time artist, your increasing challenge is to produce convincing 3D worlds that immerse your customers and keep them coming back for more. There are many 3D titles on the market, but only a few have succeeded with capturing the customer's attention for more than a few plays. With 3D accelerator cards, customers are becoming pickier about which 3D games they buy. The "Wow, it's fast 3D" factor is no longer an issue. The mindset is now more like, "Wow, when I turned the corner, that monster almost gave me a heart attack!"

Real-Time 3D Basics

Modeling for real-time graphics is a delicate process. You must have an accurate picture of what the result will be after the modeled object is exported into the real-time engine. The more you know about how the average real-time engine thinks, the better your initial efforts are, and the more time and frustration you save yourself.

Real-time 3D and high-end, prerendered 3D graphics have many elements in common. To achieve the speed necessary for presentable game play, however, real-time must use only the most necessary elements—namely, the geometry, the transform, and the surface properties of the mesh. Most of the time, these elements are created by the export program (a third-party application that converts the source model into a language the game engine can read). They are then put into some kind of text file (or a c-language file, before compilation into binary code) so that they can be manually edited, if necessary. Sometimes, these elements can be parceled out to a number of separate files (one for geometry, one for surface properties, and one for the transform) that are combined when the file is compiled for the game engine.

Currently there are plug-ins that enable the user to export directly from 3D Studio MAX into console systems, such as Playstation, Sega Saturn/Dreamcast, Nintendo 64, and DirectDraw formats. PC game developers, such as Sierra Studios and ID, have produced exporting tools so that you can design 3D maps in MAX and then export them to their game formats for Quake and Half-life. More plug-ins are always under construction to support the myriad real-time formats used in gaming. Most pre-made, real-time 3D *application programming interfaces* (APIs) provide a proprietary converter that works with the 3DS or DXF format. Freeware converters for exporting OBJ and VRML files are available from several web sites on the Internet.

Note

The API (application programming interface) for a real-time engine usually consists of a set of tools, commands, or both, so that independent developers can "plug-in" to a company's product. For a real-time game, an API gives game developers the ability to use the 3D game engine as a base and then build on top of it using their own custom commands that are hooked in via the API.

In many ways this is how MAX functions when developers wish to write plug-ins for it. MAX's API consists of specific commands, named *calls*, that allows a developer to directly control MAX through their own custom code. APIs also allow developers to create controls, such as buttons and spinners, in exactly the same manner as MAX. This helps provide consistent user interfaces, allowing the developer to focus on the functionality of the plug-in instead of its UI.

The geometry is exactly what you would expect: A list of numbered vertex positions in 3D space, followed by a list of how to connect these vertices into coherent triangular polygons. The normal (or visible solid) side of the polygon is determined either by the order in which the vertices that comprise the polygon are chosen or by a separate list of vertex normals, also attached to the polygon construction list.

Most real-time engines use triangular faces, as does 3D Studio MAX. Some systems use quadrilateral, or four-sided, polygons for modeling. Still other systems let you define quads and other types of polygons, but break them down into triangles at rendering time. Even though these other methods exist, the best results seem to come from predefined triangular faces. Although they require more storage than quadrilateral or other types of polygons, predefined triangular faces tend to render faster, and always display as intended. The .3DS file format exports only triangles, which is why it is so widely supported among real-time engines.

Warning

3D Studio MAX has two sub-object selection and editing modes that could be easily confused: face and polygon. The Face level in MAX is simply three vertices connected together to create a closed triangle. The Polygon level is two or more adjacent faces that form a four-sided polygonal object. While the Polygon level appears to be selecting four-sided faces (or quads), it's really just selecting all of the faces present to create a closed, four-sided polygon.

A smooth export of the source model into the game engine always proves a bit tricky and often requires a great deal of tweaking. High-powered modeling programs, such as 3D Studio MAX, frequently add unusable information to the relatively simplistic real-time game engine through proprietary formats. Most of this information is *invisible* (it may or may not be apparent when you look at the model in 3D Studio MAX). This information can have drastic effects on the exported real-time model, causing it to be drawn in the wrong orientation or position, or to behave improperly when animated in the game engine. The biggest trouble areas for export are generally the transform and the surface properties. However, when a developer writes a custom export tool that works directly from within MAX, these types of obstacles can often be overcome.

Tip

The MAX file format is not something that's entirely usable to a game engine. The primary reason for this is that it doesn't contain all of the necessary information needed to display outside of MAX. MAX files rely on the .DLLs located in your "STDPLUGS" directory. DLLs are usually plug-ins or even core features that MAX uses. You can see MAX loading those plug-ins when you start and the "splash screen" appears. Unless those plug-ins are both present and readable by your game engine, the MAX file contains only a fraction of the data necessary to display the geometry. For this reason, you almost always need to convert the data directly in MAX to a more basic file format that your real-time engine understands. As mentioned before, .3DS works fine, but you can also have a programmer on your development team write a custom exporter to export to your proprietary format.

The Transform Matrix

The *transform matrix,* or TM, is a numerical matrix that describes the orientation, position, and often the scale of an object in 3D space. This number is applied to every vertex in the object, and therefore acts as the object's center. In practice, imagine that every object you create is written as though it was centered at the global origin (0,0,0). To create this object farther off in 3D space, you could rewrite every vertex to the new location, or you could add to each vertex the distance (X, Y, and Z) the object must travel to reach the new position. Clearly, the latter method is the more efficient: Even though it takes two processes to achieve the new position, only one number is being created on-the-fly. The same process can be used to rotate or scale the object. This matrix may change syntax from program to program, but it will always be there because it is critical to controlling objects in 3D space.

When an object is moved in a 3D game, it is the TM that is actually affected. Prescripted animations, such as a character walking or the wheels of a car turning, are performed as if the object were standing still. To move the main object through space, the player's input is translated into a series of numbers that is combined with the TM to propel the object in the desired directions. In this way, a simple series of numbers is generated from whatever input device is used (keyboard, joystick, and so on) to create fast, responsive actions.

As mentioned earlier, the TM is usually an invisible number set in the modeling program and a numerical string in the data file(s) created by the export program. In 3D Studio MAX, however, the transform is also a visual tool that shows exactly how the physical geometry of the object is written.

When you select the object whose transform you want to see, and then select Reset Xform from the drop-down menu of the MAX Utilities panel, a bounding box that represents the object appears. When an object is created, it is automatically aligned to the orthographic viewports. If you rotate this object, scale it, or move it, the bounding box goes with it and maintains its relative location and orientation. If, however, the object is reoriented away from its orthographic alignment, and then has its transform reset, the bounding box moves back into orthographic alignment. This effectively rewrites the object geometry and resets the axis of the object, causing the object to behave differently than expected. The results will be obvious when you animate the object in a real-time game.

Normally, the transform is not something you have to worry about. When you work with primitives, MAX automatically generates them properly aligned. The only time a transform can get misaligned with primitives is when they are cloned or mirrored. When you perform these operations, always check the object's transform immediately after the modification. If a transform is off on an object that is part of a hierarchical model, to correct the transform you must detach the hierarchy, realign the object, and re-create the hierarchy. Figure 5.2 shows an object with a properly aligned transform. Figure 5.3 shows an object whose transform will cause problems when animation is applied to it.

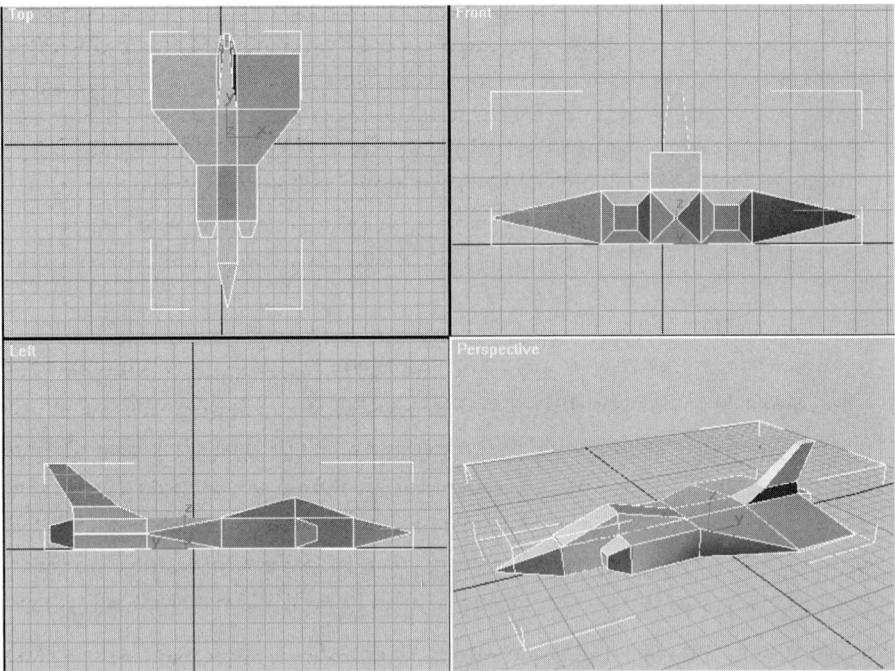

Figure 5.2 An object with a correctly aligned transform. Notice how the bounding box appears to fit properly and is correctly oriented.

The only other time transforms can be generated differently than what you might want is when you loft objects that are naturally skewed. Remember that, by default, MAX automatically sets an object's local coordinates to align with those of the global coordinate system. If a Loft object is created askew to the global system, its local transform matrix will be misaligned. If an object must be created this way, manipulate it after it has been completed, so that it comes as close as possible to orthographic alignment; then reset the transform and proceed with the rest of the model and animation.

You may be thinking that realigning the object center would accomplish the same thing as resetting the object's transform. That is correct when you are not exporting the object into a real-time engine. Unfortunately, most exporters are not able to use this bit of information. It does not rewrite the actual geometry of the object—as does performing a "reset transform." In fact, to ensure that an object performs in the real-time engine in the same way it performs in MAX, make certain that the *pivot point* is aligned to the object. The pivot point dictates the origin of the object, but its alignment corresponding to the object ensures that rotational alignment and values will be the same in the game engine.

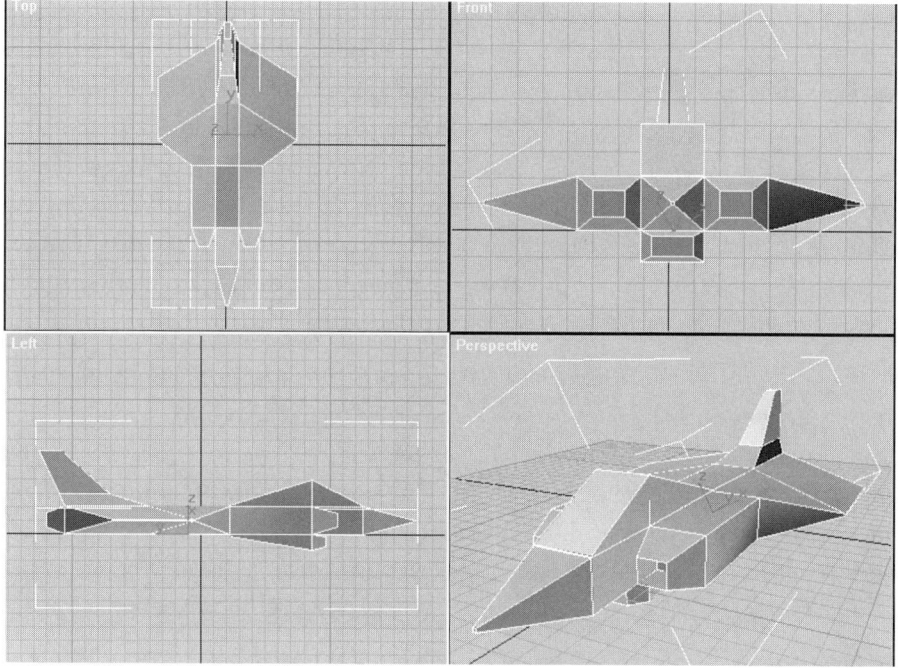

Figure 5.3 An object with an incorrectly aligned transform. You can see how the bounding box doesn't appear to "sit" right on the model, as if it's not the best fit. This is almost always your visual clue that the TM is misaligned and needs to be corrected.

Tip

It is important to note that the pivot point is the point around which animation is defined, and that the transformation matrix is that around which the object is created. These points need not be the same in MAX and can be a frequent cause of confusion. If you choose the Affect Pivot Only button in the Hierarchy panel, you can move and orient the pivot point relative to the object and its transform. If you choose the Affect Object Only button, you can move and orient the object relative to its transform.

Surface Properties

Surface properties in a real-time engine are almost identical to those in the MAX viewports—namely, the smoothing algorithm (flat or Phong shading). In addition, many surface properties, such as the color of the polygon, the shininess, opacity, self-illumination, and the texture map applied are also similar. These properties generally are applied to the vertex list rather than to the faces themselves.

In addition, most real-time engines allow colors to be assigned to the vertices themselves, which can create the illusion of the object being lit, without direct lighting applied to the model. Because most of the surface attributes are translated into numerical data, some strange translations happen during the exporting process. Colors, for example, are translated from a 0–255 scale to a 0–1 scale. No hard and fast rules dictate how to minimize problems when exporting source materials from MAX. Generally, these materials must be manually adjusted in the real-time text file, unless a third-party visual exporting system is used (such as those used with most set-top gaming systems). The best approach here is to be aware that surface properties are sometimes a trouble area during exporting, and examine the final product closely.

Again, MAX proves to be an excellent real-time tool. It provides flat and Gouraud shaded viewing options, enabling the artist to view an object (before the object is exported) in a manner that closely represents what the object will look like in a real-time gaming engine. Using a 3D accelerator card, you can also get a better idea of the interactivity of an environment. Just by using the Arc-Rotate command, you can look all around you to see if an object is misplaced or a texture looks strange—without having to export first.

Differences Between Real-Time and Prerendered 3D

The way real-time games and prerendered 3D graphics are created differ in five major areas:

- Z-buffering
- Levels of detail (LODs)
- Shadows
- Texture map size (and color depth)
- Shading modes

The basic difference in these systems is a result of what they are intended to do: Prerendered graphics need to look as realistic as possible, whereas real-time graphics need to be as fast as possible.

Z-Buffering

Z-buffering is a computationally intensive process of determining which polygons are behind which other ones (from the active viewpoint), so that a scene is correctly drawn with the proper depth. When you render a scene from MAX, visible portions of objects with correct mapping, shadows, and so on are produced for a near-photorealistic reproduction of the way the physical world is perceived. This process can be much too slow for real-time games. Most game engines do have the capability to perform modified z-buffering (a faster, but less accurate, process than in MAX). For fastest performance, however, *binary separation planes* (or BSPs) are created to give the processor a simple decision process as to what gets drawn in front of what. These planes divide concave (self-overdrawing) objects into convex pieces (more on this coming up). These pieces, combined with the transform of the object, are quickly evaluated by the computer to determine proper placement of objects.

Most real-time games also have a *far clipping plane*—a predetermined distance from the user's viewpoint, beyond which no objects are rendered even though they are stored in memory. The far clipping plane allows the designer to greatly increase the number of objects in a game world because the computer doesn't always have to draw everything simultaneously.

Often, far clipping planes are disguised by fog so objects don't just "pop" into the universe but appear to arrive out of a misty veil.

Levels of Detail

Levels of detail (LODs) also are critical in achieving the speed necessary to create an enjoyable game. In short, they are "stand-in" objects used to represent the real object at a greater distance from the user's viewpoint. When the object is close to the player, the highest-resolution model available is drawn. When the object takes up a small portion of the screen, a lower polygon count model is substituted. Very often—at the greatest distances at which the object can still be seen—a colored box is used to represent the object. The increase in speed is dramatic, because the processor does not have to calculate all the faces of the full object, but still draws the same number of pixels the object would take up on-screen. Figure 5.4 shows a model with its high, medium, and low LODs.

NEW TO R3 MAX R3 now has a script that can be run from the MAXScript pull-down menus called the LOD Tester. In it, you can assign level of detail data before exporting to a real-time format.

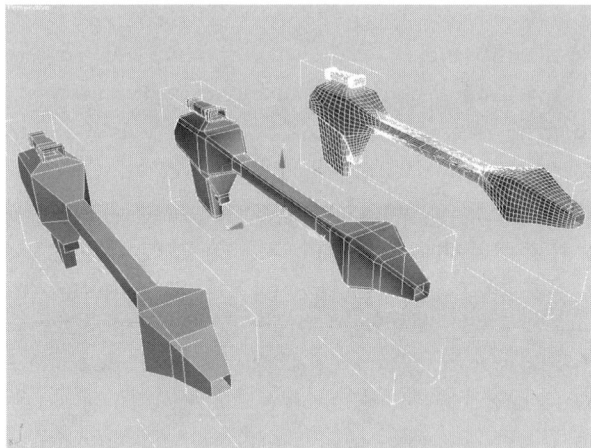

Figure 5.4 A cannon model with low, medium, and high levels of detail (LODs).

Complex objects (such as trees), which require a large number of polygons even to approximate, are represented by an x-shaped arrangement of quads. This arrangement is mapped with a picture of a high-resolution object and an opacity map (or "cookie cutter" map) that makes everything outside the desired object invisible. This technique is also used effectively with LODs or complex game *sprites* (2D animated objects). Figure 5.5 shows a tree model created with this cookie-cutter method for use in a real-time environment. Figure 5.6 shows the rendered version of the tree.

Level of Detail Utility

In MAX R3, you can use the LOD utility (see Figure 5.7) to effectively switch between different levels of detail, based on the object's distance from the camera or viewpoint. Using either rendering resolution or a percent of screen size, the LOD utility chooses which object of several in a group to display. This utility can be extremely helpful in managing face count for prerendered scenes, although it's not intended to be used for real-time output unless the engine you're using supports the code generated by the utility.

Chapter 5: Modeling for Real-Time 3D Games   201

Figure 5.5 A real-time tree model. The image of the tree is a simple rendered image with an alpha channel mapped onto a plane object. The image looks essentially the same from all angles, with the exception of extreme vertical angles. This saves a great deal of rendering time when compared to even a low-polygonal tree.

Figure 5.6 The rendered version of the tree. Notice how the tree casts shadows. This is done by using a raytraced spotlight. The shadows are received by a plane object with a Matte/Shadow material applied to it.

Part I Modeling

Using the LOD utility takes a little time to get used to because the documentation is rather scarce on it, and there's no real tutorial to speak of. To remedy that, let's do a small exercise with the Level of Detail utility.

Exercise 5.1   Using the Level of Detail Utility

1. Load 05imx01.max from the Inside 3D Studio MAX CD-ROM.
2. In the Create panel, select Sphere. In the Perspective viewport, interactively create a sphere that's about 75 units in radius.
3. Select Clone from the Edit pull-down menu, choose Copy, then click OK.
4. Repeat Step 3 to create another clone. You should have a total of three spheres.
5. Go to the Modify panel. The name at the top of the Panel should read Sphere03. If it doesn't, select it by name.
6. Set the number of segments to 4.
7. Press the H key on your keyboard, and select Sphere02.
8. Change Sphere02's segments to 16.
9. Press the H key, and select the three spheres.
10. Choose Group from the Group pull-down menu and name the group LOD Group, and then click OK.
11. Go to the Utility panel, and click on the More button.
12. Select Level of Detail, then click OK.
13. Make sure the Sphere is selected, and click the Create New Set button in the Level of Detail options panel.
14. By default, the LOD utility will opt to display one object in the viewports. Usually it's the lowest detail object. Click the Quick Render button from the Main Toolbar tab of the Tab panel. Notice that the high-detail sphere is rendered.
15. Move to frame 15, and click Quick Render. Notice the medium-detail object is now rendered.

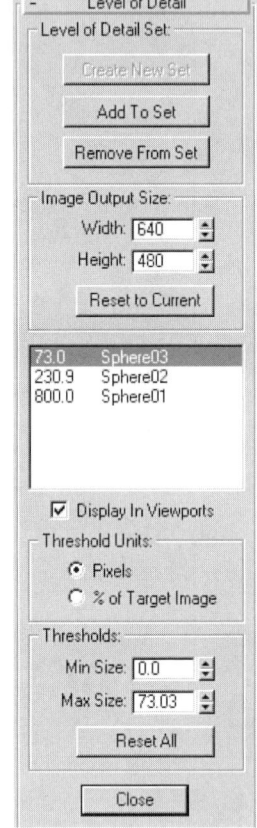

Figure 5.7 The interface of the Level of Detail (LOD) utility. With the LOD utility, you can select a certain object of a group to be displayed, depending on the distance from the camera.

 Tip

The LOD utility only works with objects in a group. So in order for you to use the LOD utility, you need to arrange your objects into a group first, then you launch the LOD utility.

16. Move to frame 30, and Quick Render. Notice that the lowest detail object is visible now.
17. If you don't see the low-detail sphere on frame 30, chances are the default Max threshold is too low. Select Sphere03 from the list, and increase the Max Size value to at least 15.
18. When you're done, render out an animation to see how the LOD utility handles the changing of objects over time. Figure 5.8 shows the animation at frames 0, 7, 15, 23, and 30.

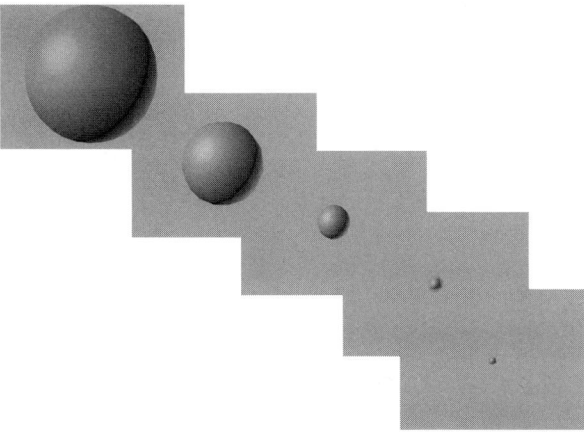

Figure 5.8 A sphere's progression from high detail to low as it travels away from the camera. The detail changes are handled by the Level of Detail utility built into MAX.

Shadows

Although shadows add a great deal of realism to any 3D scene, they require far too much calculation time to be feasible in a real-time engine. Instead, shadows are generally created one of two ways:

- By mapping a silhouette onto a semitransparent polygon. The same cookie-cutter technique mentioned earlier for trees is used for simulating shadows.
- By using Vertex coloring to simulate shadows. With the new vertex color generator in MAX R3, this becomes a very simple process. Figure 5.9 shows the output using the new Vertex Color generator. The next section talks about the Assign Vertex Color utility in more detail.

Figure 5.9 This viewport image is a result of selecting all the geometry in the scene and applying the vertex color generator.

Vertex Coloring and Shading

The Assign Vertex Color utility does a number of things to help make your models appear to be shaded with shadows in a real-time engine. It can:

- Automatically generate shadows using MAX's lighting and vertex coloring system.
- Blend vertex colors to provide a smoother shading transition from vertex to vertex.
- Blend vertex colors with texture maps applied to the objects, effectively creating shaded textures.

By using the Assign Vertex Color utility, you save a great amount of time by having MAX automatically generate the necessary colors for the vertices of the selected objects. Combine that with the fact that it also blends texture maps with vertex coloring and you have a powerful tool inside of MAX. Figure 5.10 shows the interface of the Assign Vertex Color utility. The steps to use the Vertex Color Assignment utility are simple:

1. Create your model for real-time output. You need to find the right balance of vertices so that your model not only moves quickly throughout the engine, but also so it doesn't sacrifice too much image quality.
2. Apply your texture maps and make sure they're shown in the viewport.

3. Select all the geometry in your scene, go to the Display panel and turn on Vertex Color display. Click the Shaded button, too.

4. Go to the Utility panel, and click the More button. Choose Assign Vertex Colors.

5. Select whether or not you want to use Scene Lights, which calculates illumination from the scene, or Diffuse, which simply uses the object color. If you desire, activate vertex color mixing, shadow calculation, and the maps applied. Click Assign to Selected to calculate the colors.

6. Later on, if you make changes, you can update the assignments you created earlier by clicking the Update All.

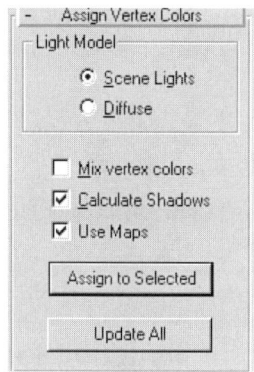

Figure 5.10 This is the interface for the Assign Vertex Color utility, accessed by the More button of the Utility panel. By using this feature in MAX, you can easily color the vertices of a model based on texture maps and shadows, then export it to your real-time engine.

Let's take a quick look at a few of the options available in the Assign Vertex Color utility. The Mix Vertex Color option will blend or interpolate the colors of the shaded polygons between vertices. With Mix on, you get a result like in MAX R2.5—where the colors blend from one side of a face to the other adjacent face. With Mix off, each face retains its own color. The Calculate Shadows utility is the true power of this utility. When turned on, it will calculate how the shadows fall on the model in a normal rendering and tries to match it as closely as possible with vertex coloring. With enough vertices to show the color detail, you get very impressive results. The selection Use Maps colors the vertices, based on the map's color that is applied to the model. If this option is off, then the vertex color is shaded based on the diffuse color of the material assigned to the model.

Map Size and Color Depth

Because of active memory limitations (RAM) and the processor demands of calculating true color (24-bit) images, most real-time engines use smaller texture maps at a smaller color depth (usually 8 bit). Most systems use texture maps sized from 16 × 16 pixels up to 128 × 128 pixels. As a result, texture maps can be stored in RAM for quickest access whenever necessary (up to 60 times a second, depending on the platform).

Although some set-top gaming platforms can use 24-bit color maps, most systems use 8-bit color for texture maps. On many PCs, 8-bit color is the average display color depth. Because this is 3D, however, remember that light sampling is still calculated in some form, and colors will vary. On systems that display higher color modes, your 8-bit map reaches true color levels when different lighting is applied.

Shading Modes

Real-time engines currently support only two shading modes: Flat shading (which makes an object look faceted) and Gouraud shading (which smoothes out most edges). Phong shading is too processor intensive to be fast enough for real-time games.

Modeling for Real Time

With all the limitations of real-time games, modeling for real time involves a great deal of thought and precision. Real-time models must achieve the right balance of detail and low geometric complexity to make them fast, recognizable, and believable elements of the gaming experience.

Although modeling varies from platform to platform, several basic principles need to be considered at the start of a gaming project:

- Put the detail in the map, not in the mesh.
- Don't build what you don't need.
- Model convex (whenever possible).
- High-res for low-res modeling.

Put the Detail in the Map, Not in the Mesh

Every polygon added to a real-time mesh takes a certain amount of time to render. Even if it is less than 1,000th of a second, that time adds up and diminishes the possible frame rate during game play. Texture maps are drawn much faster than the polygons needed to create the details, which are "painted" into the texture map. To be effective, an object's texture maps must fit into RAM. Therefore any detail that can be effectively simulated—by adding it to the texture map—should be mapped, not modeled—as should any detail that is too mesh intensive to be effective (such as the "cookie cutter" trees discussed earlier).

A great example of when to use mapping instead of modeling is the muscle tone in a character. Nice, rounded muscle structure is far too polygon intensive to accomplish in real time. When muscles are added to a texture map, however, a similar effect can be achieved through careful use of simulated highlights and shadows, with almost no cost in frame rate.

A helpful process when you create real-time models is to create a fully detailed, high-face-count model first. Then construct the low-resolution model over the high-res model, using the latter as a template. You then take individual orthographic renderings from the high-count model, tweak them in a paint program, and use them as texture maps for the low-res model. (This process is discussed in more detail in the "Dealing with Texture Limitations" section later in this chapter.)

Another related process is to load two images (preferably scanned pictures) of the object you're creating, seen from the side and the front, as a texture map to be placed on a two-quad "tree" in MAX. This tree can then be displayed as a shaded template to be built over. This technique is quite handy as a reference for building real-time characters.

Other techniques for mapping simple models with complex maps are as follows:

- **Use a single map and crop it for different parts of a model.** For instance, a car has five main views: top, front, back, left, and right. A single texture map may have all five views in it, which you crop using the Bitmap Crop feature. This means one texture map per model versus five or six maps.

- **Use the Unwrap UVW modifier.** With this modifier, you explicitly position the mapping coordinates on an object, so that your map matches the model exactly. Figure 5.11 demonstrates a real-time model with the Unwrap UVW modifier applied to control the placement of the texture.

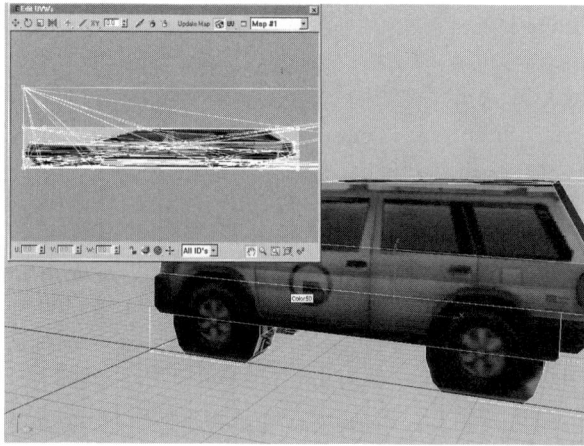

Figure 5.11 A real-time model of a vehicle built using polygonal modeling, then mapped with a single texture map. The placement of the texture map on the model is controlled by the Unwrap UVW modifier.

Don't Build What You Don't Need

Do not model unnecessary objects. This principle seems obvious, but it is important to remember to ensure that your objects maintain the lowest possible polygon count.

Real-time game environments are more akin to Hollywood movie sets than to real-life environments. Like a movie set, they are seen only from limited viewpoints. Specific knowledge of where your objects and environments are seen by the player is critical to efficient modeling. Figure 5.12 shows a real-time environment from a top-down view (a view the player can never see) that illustrates set-like construction.

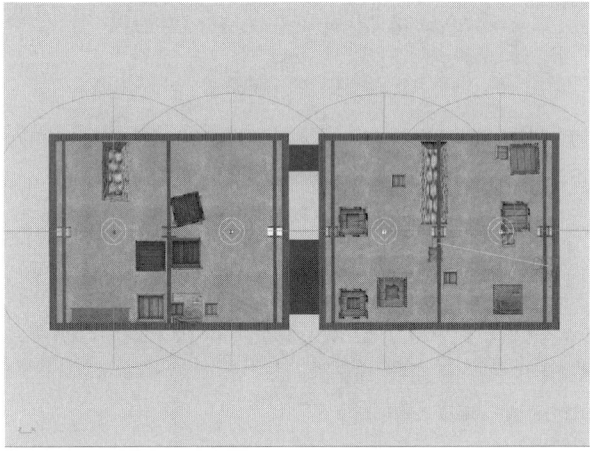

Figure 5.12 "God's eye" view of a real-time set.

If you build the cars for a racing game, for example, you need to know whether the cars flip over, exposing the undercarriage. If not, you eliminate that part of the mesh and add detail (if necessary) to the parts of the vehicles that are seen most often.

Segmented real-time characters offer another example. Normally the segments are modeled solidly at the joints so that no holes appear in the mesh throughout a full range of motion. In a game setting, your model may not need a full range of motion, or different versions of the model may be swapped in, depending on the action, damage to the character, and so forth. By eliminating the "capping" polygons inside the joints (which are never seen) you lower the total face count of the model, and make rendering more efficient.

Model Convex (Whenever Possible)

I discussed the differences between z-buffering and using BSPs in real-time gaming systems earlier in this chapter. *BSPs* are a system where game designers "pre-make" decisions for the game hardware, such as which objects (or parts of an object) will be drawn on-screen last (over the other screen objects) to create the illusion of depth. The use of BSPs creates a dramatic speed increase over z-buffering (which not only keeps the movement of the game going, but also determines object placement on-screen) based on the position of every polygon in the scene.

Effective BSPs divide objects into pieces that are drawn correctly on their own, without any sort of depth information. This means that you must make convex pieces—where all the face normals of the object face away from the center of the object and do not point into each other. Convex pieces are absolutely critical to real-time game engines because they are rendered at the maximum speed possible and still display correctly. Figure 5.13 shows a model with its BSPs visible. The data is invisible in the real-time game engine.

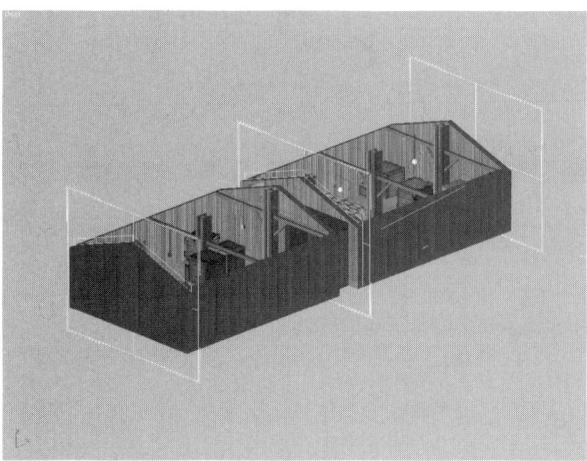

Figure 5.13 A model with visible BSPs inserted. A BSP is placed at every point where an object potentially obscures itself, so that the engine relies on BSP data rather than z-buffers to determine what parts do not need rendering.

The best test of convexity is to look at the object in a shaded, perspective view (smooth or faceted), hide the faces on opposing sides of the object (top and bottom, left and right, or front and back), and rotate the object in multiple directions. If you see a solid face through an empty space in the model (where the normals face away, making the polygons invisible), the object is not convex and needs modifications (or more dividing) before it is used effectively in a BSP sorting engine. Repeat the process for each opposing pair of sides. Figure 5.14 shows the visible differences between a convex and a concave object.

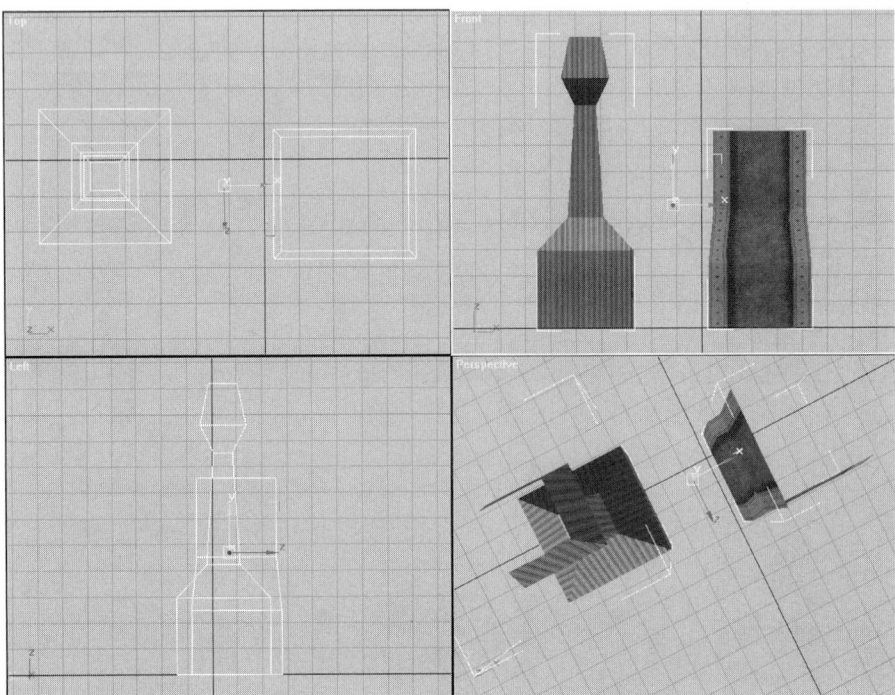

Figure 5.14 A convex object section (left) and a concave object section (right). Notice that when you look down into the 4-sided cylinder, you see the mid-level faces of the convex object.

High-Res for Low-Res Modeling

When working with low polygon counts, it is extremely difficult to determine a proper level of detail to make the object clearly recognizable and distinguishable from similar objects. It is helpful, therefore, to build a high poly-count "template" object (with as much detail as possible) over which to construct a low-count model. This process clarifies where detail is needed in the low-count object, and where to omit it and place it in the texture map. And, as mentioned before, the high-detail model generates intricate texture maps for the low-count model later on.

Warning

Do not use the Optimize modifier in MAX to lower the polygon count of the high-detail mesh to acceptable real-time levels. The Optimize modifier is an excellent tool to make a complex mesh more efficient or to use on a real-time model to check for unnecessary polygons. However, it creates unpredictable losses in detail when you're drastically reducing a high-count model.

The Optimize modifier works by eliminating faces that are determined to be coplanar, based on the entered face and edge threshold angles. The Optimize modifier cannot prioritize details; it just uses a straight numerical algorithm. When an entered parameter is high enough to bring drastic face count reductions, the Optimize modifier also eliminates most of the nice smooth areas created to round out certain edges.

Real-Time Modeling Techniques

The best way to ensure that your model has appropriate detail and the lowest-possible polygon count is to create the model with a low polygon count to begin with, then add detail and subtract faces only where necessary. The sub-object editing tools of the Edit Mesh and Editable Mesh become your best friends when you finalize a real-time model.

Modifying Primitives for Low-Resolution Models

The other popular way of creating an efficient real-time mesh is to start with a primitive (preferably a multi-segmented cylinder or box) and manipulate the individual vertices to match the template object. Modeling this way allows you to start with any detail model you want and either reduce or add geometry as needed. For modelers who prefer to model from the "inside-out," using primitives for modeling is ideal.

Exercise 5.2 demonstrates how to modify primitives to produce low-resolution models. In the exercise, you will build an imaginary fighter jet from a box and see how to model just from a box that is converted into an Editable Mesh.

Exercise 5.2 Modeling a Jet from a Primitive

1. Reset 3D Studio MAX.
2. In the Top or Perspective viewport, create a box that's approximately 180 units long, 75 units wide, and 20 units high. Set the number of Length and Width segments to 3.

Tip

You can turn on the Edged Faces option in the shaded viewports, so that you can see the faces of the box you need to edit. (See Figure 5.15.) Otherwise, you must constantly switch between wireframe and shaded modes.

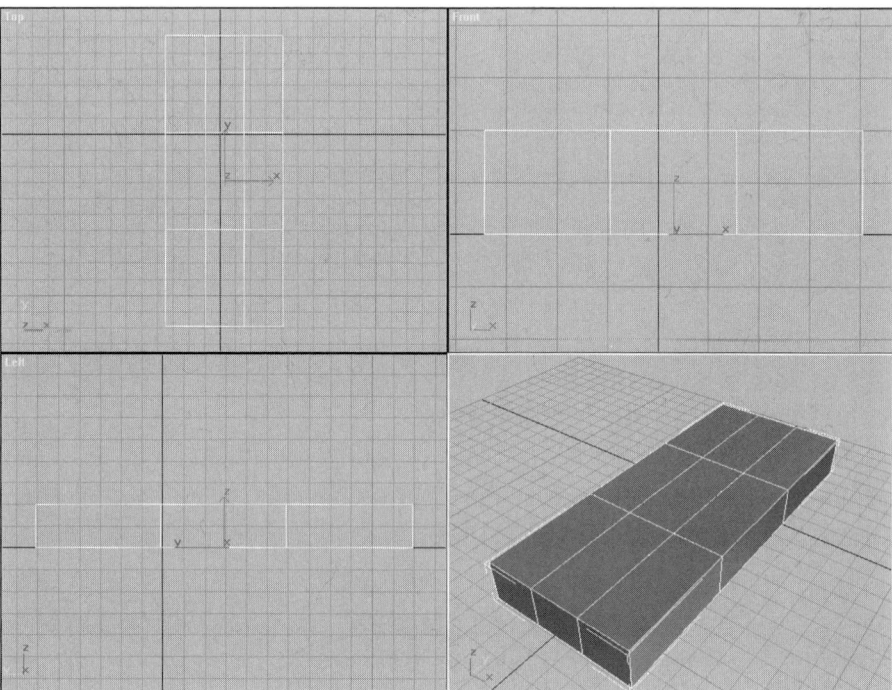

Figure 5.15 The box in the viewports with Edged Faces turned on.

3. Right-click on the Box, and choose Convert to Editable Mesh.
4. In the Modify panel, click the Polygon button.
5. In the Perspective viewport, click the middle segment of the box at the "front" end of the plane to select it.
6. In the Extrude Amount field in the Modify Panel, type 40, press Enter, and then type 40 again, and press Enter. This will create a two-segment "extension" on the plane that will be its nose.
7. Click the Vertex selection button at the top of the Editable Mesh Selection panel, and select the four vertices at the end of the last segment you created. Then click the Collapse button in the Edit Geometry section in the Modify panel. The result of Steps 5 through 7 are shown in Figure 5.16.
8. Switch back to Polygon mode and select the other two segments on the box on either side of the nose. (You can do both at the same time by holding down the Ctrl key during the selection process.) Extrude them 20 units.
9. Use the Outlining value to set the bevel amount to –5.
10. Use the Extrude command again, but extrude –15 units. This will create the intake "holes."

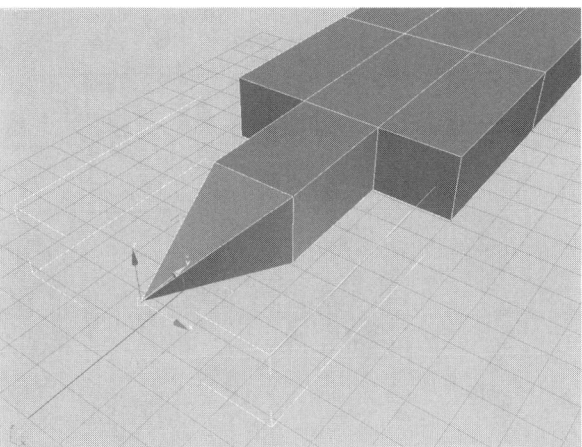

Figure 5.16 The plane is beginning to take shape with the nose extruded and scaled from the front of the box.

Note
While you can interactively extrude and bevel faces in the viewport in a positive direction, you cannot negatively extrude or bevel. You must use the spinners or numerical input field in the modify panel to do this.

11. To Create the Canopy, first select the top face on the nose *and* the face immediately behind it on the "body" of the aircraft and extrude them 20 units.

12. Click the Vertex selection button, and select the vertices at the top of the "canopy," but exclude the middle two.

13. To finish, use the Move command to move the selected vertices down, so that they're level with the body of the aircraft. Figure 5.17 shows the sequential actions of Steps 11 through 13.

Tip
While modeling this way, it's always a good idea to keep a shaded Perspective viewport active, checking it often to make certain that a vertex is where you intended. If it isn't, use the Undo feature until it reaches the place where the error occurred. (The more often you check, the less you have to undo in case of an error.)

By using simple extrusions and transforms on a standard primitive, such as a box, you can basically create anything. Remember to first convert the geometry to an Editable Mesh before working at the Face or Vertex sub-object level. This method helps maintain the low polygon counts required for gaming environments. Try using the same techniques to create the wings, tail, and exhaust port. To see a completed version of the jet, see the 05max02.max file on the CD-ROM.

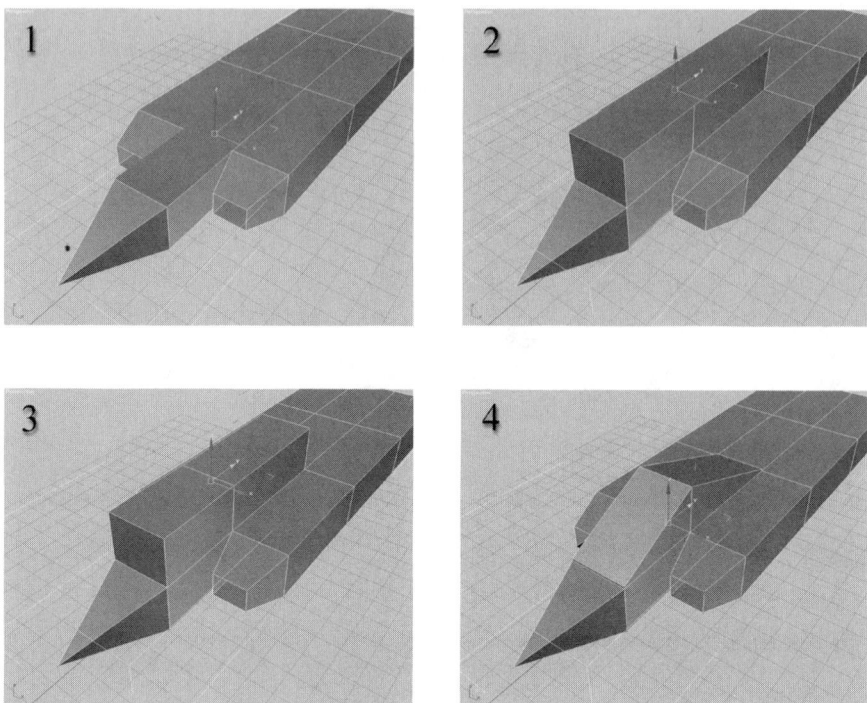

Figure 5.17 Using a combination of face selection/extrusion and vertex translation, you create a canopy for the jet fighter.

Dealing with Texture Limitations

As you have already seen, quite a bit of detail can be accomplished with limited meshes. To get the most out of limited geometry, however, you must rely on texture maps. Maps have their own limitations—either limited size, limited color depth (usually 8-bit), or both. Fortunately, you can work around these limitations and still produce excellent results.

Dealing with Limited Colors

Opinions abound on the subject of how to create a real-time environment by using 256 colors. Many people favor starting with a limited palette (pre-picking the colors to be used) and making all texture maps from those colors. Others believe that better results derive from creating the maps with the full 16.7 million colors available, then using another program to evaluate the texture maps and remap them into the 256 most-used colors.

Generally, however, when you create texture maps with 16.7 million colors, you don't use them all (or even a significant percentage of them). To achieve a happy medium between the two previously mentioned methods, decide on a general scheme (based on the scene, time of day, mood, and so on), then paint in 24-bit color, focusing on the selected color scheme. This method provides a better distillation to 256 colors when you create the final game palette, while still keeping the scene focused toward the visual goals identified with the color scheme.

If you don't have access to a program capable of distilling a 256-color palette from multiple images (and re-mapping the colors in those images to the new palette), your best choice is to start with a predetermined 8-bit palette.

Tip

MAX is capable of outputting to a specific palette or set amount of colors by saving to the .FLC file format. When saving to that file format, click the Setup button in the Save dialog box to customize how you want the palette generated.

Limited Map Size

All gaming platforms today use small texture maps, ranging from 16 × 16 pixels to 128 × 128 pixels. Although this may be intimidating for those whose smallest maps are 320 × 240 pixels (one quarter the size of the average monitor display at low resolution)—after a bit of practice, you will discover how much detail you can achieve in a very small area. You may even find that texture mapping with small maps opens new techniques for creating larger maps when creating prerendered 3D images.

A great temptation is to create a texture map at a high resolution and then scale it down to the parameters of whatever real-time engine with which you are working. This seldom performs well. Scaling, in most paint programs, is done by a mathematical elimination of pixels, based on the percentage of down-scaling. When you reach real-time limits, where every pixel counts, this process can make quite a mess of an originally great texture map—filling it with scattered, color-cycling pixels and making an otherwise smooth map look rocky or rough.

Your best bet to be sure that the exact detail you want (and nothing else) appears on-screen during game-play is to start with the same size texture map that will occur in the game. This technique leaves no room for extraneous information, and enables you to be precise about what amount of detail goes where. And, you can use multiple maps (or a large map carved into real-time sizes) on an object, with very little impact on the speed of the game.

Adding "Impossible" Detail

As you probably gathered from everything discussed in this chapter so far, real-time is mostly a matter of creating the best illusion with what is technologically possible. Most of the model creation process, so far, has been accomplished by using limited versions of what is already available in 3D Studio MAX, and using simple planning and efficiency to achieve results. Some things, however, cannot be done in real time. Certain mapping types (bump mapping, shininess, and specular mapping), specific lighting design, and many other techniques are beyond the limitations of real-time games—at this point—because of the bare-bone shading limitations needed to create speed. These more complex maps require the computationally expensive Phong shading mode, and must simply be "faked." Here again, a little planning goes a long way.

Faking a Bump Map

Bump maps, in prerendered 3D, are a way to create the illusion of limited surface relief on an object. Artists have been doing this in flat images for hundreds of years by creating highlights and shadows in still images. The same techniques work well for creating "fake" bump maps. Determine the angle of your light source (high and right always creates a believable, recognizable source), and paint in the highlights and shadows. The only difference is that your shadows do not move in response to the real-time light source, and the "bumps" are not visible from the edge of the faces to which they are applied. Figure 5.18 shows a "faked" bump map with faked lighting (discussed in the next section).

If creating bumps through painting feels a bit intimidating, create your bump-mapped material, apply it to a flat plane in 3D Studio MAX, add lighting, and render the image out to a file for use on your real-time mesh. But remember the earlier comment about map sizes: Render the image to the size it will be in the game, instead of rendering the image larger and scaling it down later.

NEW TO R3   When you now render texture maps for real-time environments, use MAX R3's new Render Crop or Render Box Selected feature to get specific resolutions and aspect ratios for your texture maps. Let's take a look at how Render Cropped works:

1. Set your maximum resolution in the Render Properties dialog box.
2. From the Main Toolbar in the Tab Panel, select Crop in the Render Type pop-down.
3. Click any render button and a dotted selection box will appear in your active viewport, much like Render Region. Select the boundary that you wish to crop to, then click OK.

MAX renders just the selected area to a resolution of that area, rather than the maximum resolution. This saves one extra step by not forcing you to use a paint tool to crop your textures!

Render Box Selected works by rendering the bounding box extents of your object. It works a little differently than Render Cropped:

1. Select an object or group of objects that you wish to render the extents.
2. From the Main Toolbar in the Tab panel, select Box Selected in the Render Type pop-down.
3. MAX will now ask for the resolution of your rendering and whether you wish to constrain the aspect ratio. Choose your resolution, and then click Render.

Now you see a similar result to what Render Cropped does. However, Box Selected rendering automatically calculates the extents of your rendering—based on the selected objects and outputs to a resolution independent of the resolution specified in the Render Settings dialog box.

Tip
Save your rendering from the Virtual Frame Buffer (VFB) when using the Render Box Selected mode. Otherwise the image cannot be saved to the specific resolution and aspect ratio that you specify.

Faking Lighting

To create spotlight effects (such as under-lighting or light pooling), repeat the preceding "create it in MAX" technique or use the lighting filters available in many image-editing packages (such as Adobe Photoshop or MetaCreation's Painter) to get similar results. Moving a MAX light around in 3D space can give you a much more specific effect than using a light fixed to a two-dimensional plane. You can see an example of faked lighting in Figure 5.18.

Curved Surfaces

Creating a curved surface with geometry is an almost impossible accomplishment in real-time because curves require a high number of polygons.

Fortunately, creating the illusion of a curved surface in a texture map is not difficult. It is painted into the map—using a highlight for the highest point on the surface, and blending that into half-tone at the sides of the curve, with shadows reacting to the light source. Again, rendering a fully mapped, highly detailed curved surface in MAX and then using it as a texture map for the flat-surfaced real-time object yields great results.

Exercise 5.3 demonstrates most of the previously mentioned concerns when texture mapping.

Figure 5.18 A 3D rendering of a texture that, when applied in a 3D environment, gives the illusion of both a bumpy and a lit/shadowed surface. This particular model was rendered using the Render Crop feature that automatically crops a rendering to a specific size.

Exercise 5.3   Real-Time Texture Mapping

1. From the accompanying CD, open the file called 05imx03.max. This is a sporty mag-wheel (see Figure 5.19) that would add a nice bit of detail to your real-time sports car. Modeled in high detail, it is much too complex to be used in real-time, especially considering that it must be multiplied by four. The chrome reflection map on the spokes of the wheel are also impossible in real-time, but renders very nicely in MAX.
2. In the left view, select all the objects.
3. Choose Box Selected in the Render Type list.
4. Click Quick Render.
5. In the Render Bounding Box/Selected dialog, verify that Constrain Aspect Ratio is checked and enter 64 in the width field. The height field will automatically update to match.
6. Click the Render button. The wheel renders into the Video Frame Buffer.

Chapter 5: Modeling for Real-Time 3D Games   219

7. In the Video Frame Buffer, click the Save Image button. Select an image type of Targa Image File, and enter the file name Wheel64. Click Save. In the Targa Image Control dialog, choose 24 Bits-Per-Pixel and check Compress, Alpha Split, and Pre-Multiplied Alpha. Click OK. This creates two images—Wheel64.tga (your new texture map) and A_Wheel64.tga (its alpha channel).

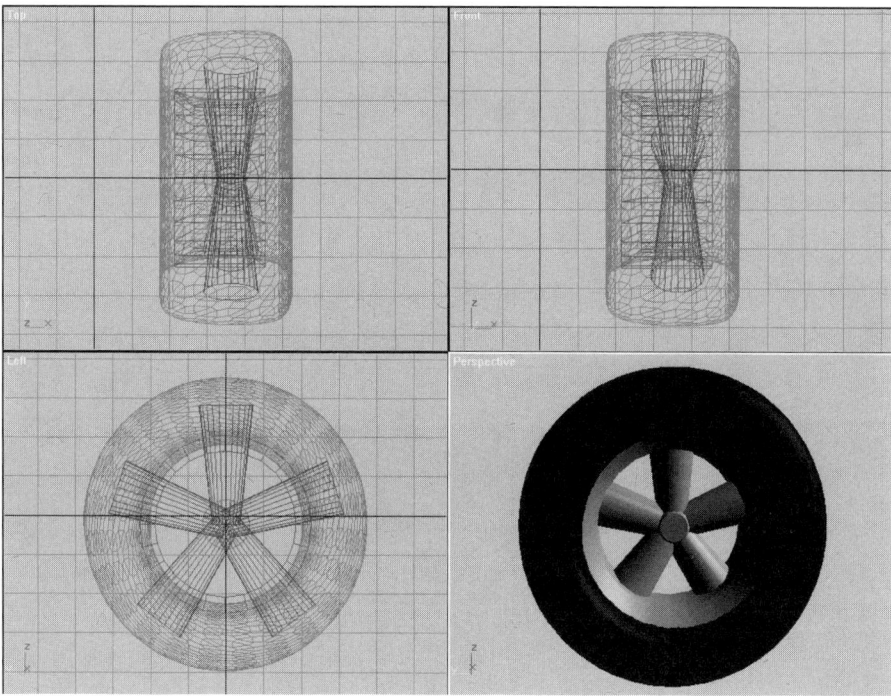

Figure 5.19   The high-detail wheel mesh in MAX.

8. Open the file called 05max031. At one of the wheel-wells, create an eight-sided cylinder with one height segment to be used as a wheel for your car (use the existing wheel as a reference). Make the depth and radius the appropriate size for your vehicle (see Figure 5.20). Keep the new Wheel object selected, and choose the UVW Map modifier from the Modify panel. Make certain that the mapping type is Planar, that the top is aligned with the top of your newly created wheel, then choose the Fit option to fit the mapping coordinates to the bounding box of your wheel.

9. Open the Material Editor and create a new material that is faceted, and has no Specular Level and no Glossiness. Apply the material to the wheel.

10. In the maps area of the Material rollout, load wheel64.tga into the Diffuse channel. Go to Parent level, and assign A_wheel64.tga into the Opacity channel. Change the material sample type from a sphere to a cube, so that you see exactly what the map looks like on the wheel.

220   Part I   Modeling

11. Render a clean view of the newly mapped wheel, and adjust it until it has a nice rounded feel on the edge of the tire and you see through the spokes. Clone this object three times, and place the copies into the other wheel-wells (see Figure 5.21).

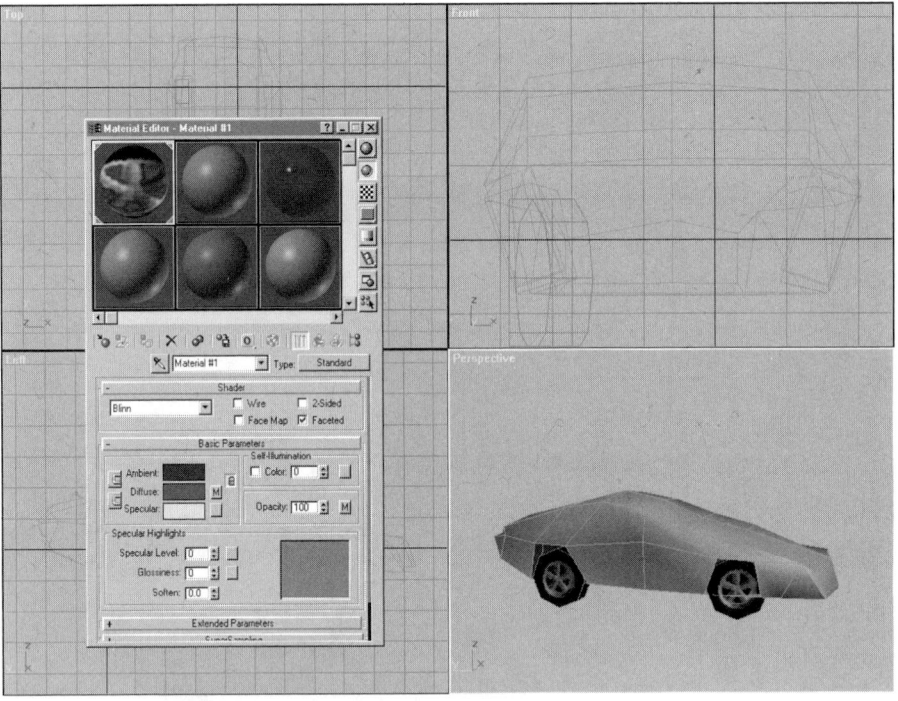

Figure 5.20   The real-time car with the passenger-side wheels added.

Figure 5.21   All four wheels in place on the vehicle.

Working with real-time models often requires a balanced usage of both low-detail geometry and convincing maps. You'll find that most real-time interactive titles on the market do this very well. This exercise demonstrates that you don't even have to be a 2D artist to create those convincing maps. Use your 3D skills whenever possible. With the right lighting, materials, and geometry, your renderings serve very well as 2D maps for lower-detail models. The final result of Exercise 5.3 is shown in Figure 5.22.

Figure 5.22   The finished wheels on the low-res car.

Using Opacity for "Impossible Detail"

Sometimes, an object is far too complex to be modeled convincingly in a low-polygon fashion. When using 3D Studio MAX to create models of objects with holes and complex edges—objects so detailed that you cannot efficiently make them recognizable—use a simple opacity map to create the effect.

Fortunately, almost all real-time systems have some capacity for using opacity maps—whether they are 8-bit grayscale maps or just 1-bit black-and-white, cookie-cutter type maps. This capability enables the model maker to add detail that is otherwise impossible. The effect is not quite as clean as in 3D Studio MAX, but the result is still effective. Try this technique on the wheels created in the last exercise so that you see through the spokes.

Other Tricks

One of the most common things for real-time artists to look for in modeling is workarounds for tough problems. For instance, why model a face when you can put a mask over it? Or if you need a face, you can always hide the eyes with sunglasses. An example of this is shown in Figure 5.23.

You can also blend certain elements of your geometry. The earlier example of modeling and texturing a tire is avoided if the tires aren't moving. If your vehicle is parked and designed to be just scenery or cover for the players, there's no need to make the wheels separately. Simply make four "bumps" where the tires appear, and then map a texture of the entire side of the vehicle onto the side of the polygonal object, as in Figure 5.24. Use your image editing tool and the UVW Map modifier to place the texture accurately. You can also use the Unwrap UVW modifier to adjust the mapping coordinates explicitly.

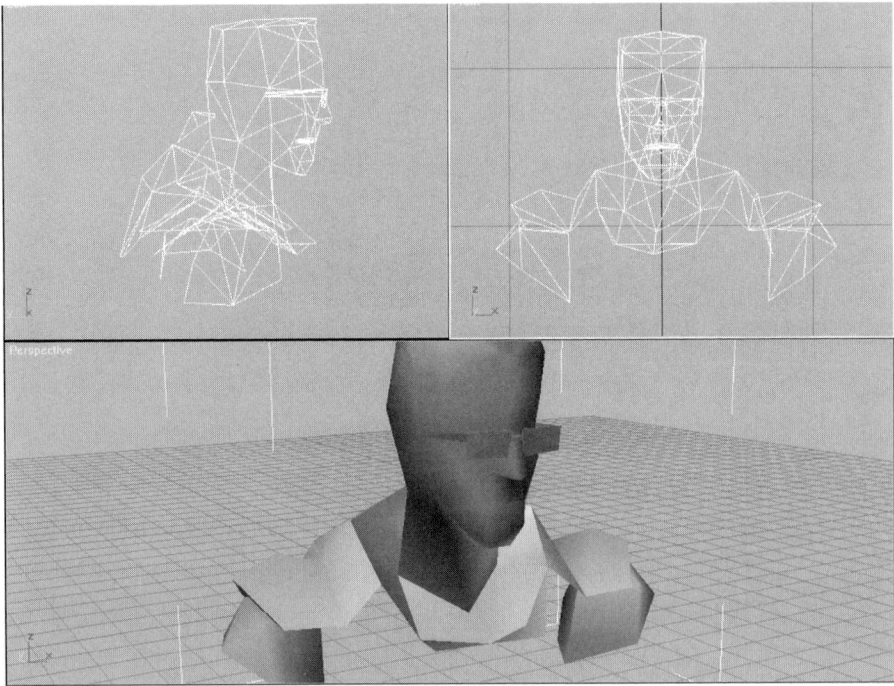

Figure 5.23 A low-polygon head that avoids surface detail around the eyes by using a simple shape of sunglasses. From the Half-life SDK by Valve.

If you're in the gaming field and already using MAX, you have quite a few advantages. There are other polygonal tools on the market, but none really have the necessary functionality to get the whole job done. With new features such as the Assign Vertex Color utility and enhanced Unwrap UVW modifier, many tasks that were considered tedious are much more reasonable.

Figure 5.24 A scenery vehicle that uses one model to represent several different objects. For instance, the tires are actually mapped on to the vehicle rather than as separate objects. This helps reduce the face count of the tires by half. From the Half-life SDK, by Valve.

Note
This chapter deals mainly with the issues and work-arounds for getting the best performance out of your real-time engine from the models you create in MAX. For more information on mapping, material application, or just more modeling, check out the other chapters in this book. Although they may apply to another discipline, you can still use those techniques for real-time modeling and design.

Simplifying Things with Scripting

There's no question that modeling for a real-time environment involves a great deal of work, including several people working on many teams. As a 3D artist, making your models and textures as streamlined as possible for real-time is the key to building great environments and characters that contain depth and challenge.

With MAX R3, the process of streamlining your models and textures is simplified through the new enhancements to come along in MAXScript. In this section, we take a look at how to use MAXScript to create your own toolbar of textures and apply them to any model on a project. Once you get the gist of it, you'll see how easy it is to translate these techniques into a real project.

NEW TO R3

Using the Macro Recorder

MAXScript now has a tool that records every action you perform while working within MAX. This feature is called the Macro Recorder and is located in the MAXScript pull-down menu. While we're not going to go through every detail of the Macro Recorder here, you will see how easy it is to use for real-time game development.

The Macro Recorder has two modes:

- **Explicit Mode:** Records everything you do and also remembers object names, which is useful if you're creating objects with specific names or you need to refer to an object with a specific name when executed in a script.

- **Relative Mode**: More useful for repetitive tasks that will be executed via a script. For instance, while recording, apply a specific material and map coordinates to an object. Then you can repeat that task set on any other object. We'll take a closer look at this example.

The following is a multi-part exercise intended to show you how to create your own toolbar of textures. While there are several steps to do this right, it becomes much easier to do after you run through it a couple of times.

Exercise 5.4.1 Creating a Macro Button

1. Open 05imx041.max from the Inside 3D Studio MAX R3 CD-ROM.
2. From the Customize pull-down menu, select Load Custom UI and choose 05imx041.cui from the Inside 3D Studio MAX R3 CD-ROM.
3. Open the Material Editor, and take note of the materials present. If necessary, right-click a sample sphere and choose to view 6×4 Sample Windows.
4. Go to the Create panel, and click the Box button.
5. Create a small box in the viewport.
6. Choose Macro Recorder from the MAXScript pull-down menu, if it isn't already checked.
7. Select the Box in the viewport, click the Gray Wood material in the Material Editor, and click the Assign to Selected button. Note that you must use the button and *not* drag and drop.
8. Go to the Modify panel, and click the UVW Map button. Choose the Box mapping type.
9. Choose Macro Recorder again from the MAXScript pull-down menu to turn off the macro recording feature of MAXScript.

10. From the MAXScript pull-down menu, choose MAXScript Listener (see Figure 5.25). The window should be horizontally divided into a pink area and a white one. If not, drag the divider bar to reveal both windows.

11. The code present contains all that's necessary to apply the Gray Wood material and UVW Map modifier with Box mapping to any object. However, there's some extraneous code. Using standard editing commands, edit the code down to where it looks something like this:

```
$.material = meditMaterials[2]
addModifier $ (Uvwmap ())
             $.UVW_Mapping.maptype = 4
```

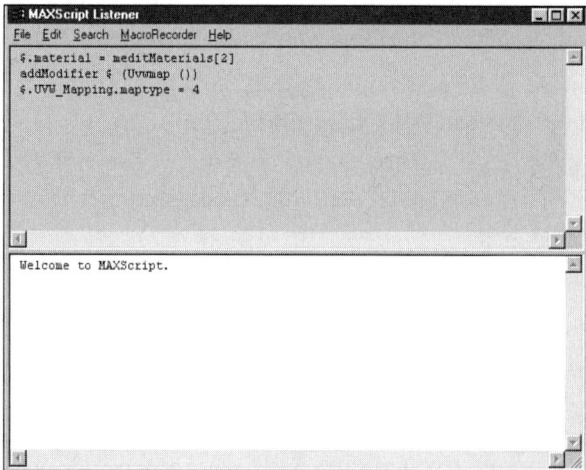

Figure 5.25 The MAXScript Listener window after cleaning up the code, as stated in Step 11.

12. Select the cleaned-up code and drag to the blank toolbar along the left side of the interface. Release over the toolbar to create a new button. MAX will create a stand-in icon for the button.

13. You can now repeat Steps 7 through 12 to create buttons for the "Old Wood" and "Steel Plate" materials.

14. When you are finished, select Save Custom UI from the Customize pull-down menu.

The first part of this exercise covers some important steps in creating a macro button. Here, we got the chance to see how you simply drag code created by the Macro Recorder in MAXScript right into a toolbar. While this in itself is a great feature, it does require some vigilance on your part to create useful streamlined scripts. Sometimes just copying and pasting code into a button is not the best way to create custom buttons. Take the time to edit down or streamline the code so that MAXScript does only what it needs to do to get your job done.

At this point in the book, while we're looking at how to create custom buttons for real-time output, use this information anywhere you need a custom button. For instance, use it to create any number of objects with specific materials or to launch a pop-up window to edit the faces on just a selected object. The basic rule is that if it can be a script, it can be a button in the user interface.

Let's take a look at exactly what this exercise covered:

- You can now record almost any action in MAX in the MAXScript Recorder window. Use this feature to, as its name implies, create your own macros. You can also use it to see how MAX writes code to do a specific operation. If writing your own script, this is very handy to observe the proper code command.

- Creating a custom button in MAX R3 is as simple as dragging code from the Macro Recorder window into a toolbar. While this works for almost any situation, be careful to paste only the code you need. If you do just drag, however, you can always edit the content of a button by right-clicking it and selecting Edit Macro Script from the pop-up menu.

- It's always a good idea to save your custom user interface after creating your own macro buttons (or any other buttons, for that matter). Just choose Save Custom UI from the Customize pull-down menu before you exit MAX. If you like, you can also save the custom UI to another file so you don't overwrite your old one.

At this point you now have three very similar looking buttons in MAX. While they all do different things, they still look the same and you'll eventually find yourself clicking the wrong button because you don't have a good visual clue as to what the button does. Fortunately, MAX R3 ships with a nice script utility that will create custom icons that you use in your buttons.

This next exercise takes a look at how to create your own custom icons using this new feature. Because the three macro buttons you created apply materials, it stands to reason that you want graphical representations of those materials in the buttons. The easiest way to do that is to render the diffuse map of the material as a background image. The icon-making script will handle the details for turning it into a button icon that you use in your custom buttons.

Exercise 5.4.2 Creating Custom Icons for Macro Buttons

1. From the Edit pull-down menu, choose Select None.
2. Delete the box you created in exercise 5.4.1 to return to an empty scene.

Chapter 5: Modeling for Real-Time 3D Games   227

3. If the Material Editor isn't open already, open it and click the Gray Wood material.

4. From the Rendering pull-down menu, select Environment.

5. Drag the M button next to the Diffuse color swatch to the Environment Map button. When you release, choose Copy from the new dialog.

6. Go to the Utility panel, and click the MAXScript button. Select Run Script.

7. Select the script called "makeicon.ms" located in your 3DSMAX3/Scripts/samples directory.

8. Select Custom Icon Maker from the Utilities pop-down list.

9. In the Create New Library section, type in a library name called "Tutorial," then click the Create Library button.

10. Next, click the Render Icons button to render the current scene, which is the Gray Wood background. This now appears in the preview window.

11. Click Put to Library to write the icon to its own location in the new library.

12. Repeat Steps 3 through 11 for the Old Wood and Steel Plate materials. Note that you don't have to create a new library for each new icon as stated in Step 7. Creating a library is a one-time process for each series of icons going into it. (See Figure 5.26.)

Figure 5.26 After you complete Step 12 the first time, you'll see a result in MAX similar to this figure.

228   Part I Modeling

This exercise showed only the beginning of how much you can actually customize MAX R3. Not only do you have the ability to create custom macro buttons, but also you can put your own icons into the buttons, which are, in turn, created by yet another script extension to the product. If you just take a moment to think about that, there's really no limit to what you can do with scripting in MAX. As a matter of fact, it's safe to say that the vast majority of users in MAX can code a script that does a specific function in a much shorter time than it takes a developer to write a specific plug-in.

While this exercise didn't focus on new features, it did cover a specific item worth reviewing:

- The icon maker in MAX R3 allows you to create custom icons for using in your macro scripts or any other button within MAX. You don't like the Box create icon? Create your own—using the icon maker script. It's a really simple process, and you can always revert to the old MAX icons if you don't like your new creation.

Building custom buttons goes beyond just cool icons. You need to make icons that are easy to associate with the button's commands, especially if you're in a shared environment. Squeezing the features that a script or macro button contains into an image that's only 32 × 32 pixels in size is often difficult to do. You have to think of the main things that the script does and come up with a reasonable graphical representation of it. For instance, if your script applies Box mapping coordinates, perhaps an icon with a small box that has the letters UVW on all sides is appropriate.

And you don't *have* to use icons either. MAX also lets you add in any text you like instead of an image. Sometimes this can be even better than an icon representation of a feature.

> **Note**
> You don't necessarily need to use the icon-maker script. If you want to learn how to create your own custom icon images, refer to the MAX documentation. There it discusses the process of creating a series of named images that can be used as custom icons.

The icon maker derives its icons from the MAX rendering engine. This means that whatever settings you currently have in the MAX renderer will be used to render your button. If an icon looks too blurry, turn off anti-aliasing. If there's too much clutter, hide objects. If there's not enough depth, add shadows against a matte-shadow object. Since all the buttons in MAX use alpha (both default and ones created by the icon maker), shadows will look good in almost any setting.

After you've labored to create your icons, now it's just a matter of adding them to the custom buttons you created in Exercise 5.4.1. MAX makes it a simple operation that's covered in the next exercise.

Exercise 5.4.3 Adding the Finishing Touches to a Macro Button

1. Restart MAX from the Customize pull-down menu, select Load Custom UI and choose 05imx041.cui from the Inside 3D Studio MAX R3 CD-ROM.
2. Right-click the first button you created in the new toolbar.
3. Choose Edit Button Appearance.
4. When the Edit Macro Button dialog box appears, click the Group pop-down list and find your tutorial library.
5. Select your Gray Wood icon image, then click OK. Your custom macro button should now have a new graphic.
6. Repeat Steps 2 to 5 for the other two buttons. When you're done, proceed to the next exercise. The toolbar should look similar to Figure 5.27.

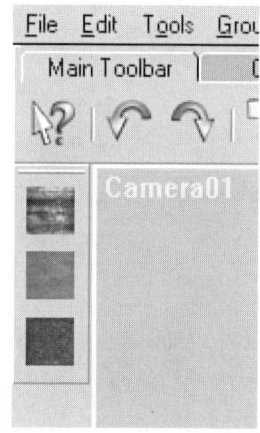

Figure 5.27 The custom toolbar created during Exercise 5.4. The button commands were created using Macro Scripts, and the icons were created using the icon-maker script.

See? There's nothing to it. Adding your own icons or customizing the existing MAX icons is really simple to do. Just right-click the button and select the Edit Button Appearance option, or select Customize from the right-click menu for the Tab panel. You now have a set of custom buttons for use in applying texture maps to objects in your scene.

NEW TO R3

- The ability to customize menu button icons greatly enhances your ability to adjust MAX's look and feel to suit your needs. This series of exercises explored how to create a small palette of icons for a real-time application. It's easy to see how a group of artists use a common palette of materials that they apply across a map. Once the toolbar is set, they just use it on their own machine. There's never the question of whether the material is valid, or if they can use it in the map or level.

Now it's time to realize the fruits of your labor. This next exercise looks at how you use the custom toolbar you just created. Load the same file, and quickly discover that there is much more there than you originally thought!

Exercise 5.5 Using Your New Toolbars in a Real Application.

1. Open 05max041.max from the CD-ROM.
2. Go to the Display panel, and select Unhide All.
3. Using your new toolbar, assign materials to the real-time model. Select an object, then click a Macro button to assign a material. You can also assign more materials from the Material Editor to other parts of the model by creating custom buttons similar to these. Add in a few Box objects, and use the toolbar to give them some standard materials. It's fun! When you're done, you should have something that looks like Figure 5.28.

Warning

In order for these new buttons to work, you must have an object selected. Otherwise, MAXScript gives you an error message.

Figure 5.28 The final result using the new custom toolbar and other materials on a real-time scene.

Final Thoughts

After looking through this chapter, we see that MAX really has a great set of tools for doing game development. While it may not ship with all of the custom export tools or even some key modeling functions, MAX R3 has the best overall feature set of any other tool on the market.

Modeling for real-time games has several constraints that you don't find in other 3D disciplines. Fortunately, you can usually stick within these boundaries when working in

MAX. The things that you'll find yourself using a great deal will be Editable Mesh and the Unwrap UVW modifier. Take some time to play with them and get comfortable. Once you do, you'll find that MAX is a great tool for doing your real-time worlds.

In Practice: Modeling for Real-Time 3D Games

- **Real-time 3D gaming relies on speed and must use only the bare basics of 3D to accommodate the extensive necessary calculations.** These basics include limited geometry, limited texture map sizes and color depths, and often, the use of Binary Separation Planes (BSPs), rather than slower z-buffering calculations for depth.

- **Modeling is the most critical process in real-time 3D.** If your models are too detailed, the real-time game engine is simply unable to process the data fast enough for the players. If it's too simple, then the interactive title doesn't look professional—or worse, the models don't look anything like what they're supposed to represent. Either way, effective modeling makes a title. Poor modeling breaks it.

- **Use templates when possible.** Creating a 3D template over which to model is a useful procedure for creating real-time objects with enough detail in the right places. This way, you can construct the lower-detail models as close as possible to the originals, yet have a low-enough polygon count to be usable in a real-time environment.

- **Be conscientious and primitive in your modeling.** The basic procedures in creating a real-time model are selecting the proper primitives, followed by the manipulation and editing of those primitives. With primitives and the Editable Mesh object, you can push and pull on the faces or vertices of an object to build interesting, low-detail models that work great for real-time engines.

- **Texture maps are the key to realism in real-time.** Detail that cannot be accomplished with mesh can be created with texture maps, using opacity, "faked" bump maps, and rendered images of high-detail meshes manipulated for real-time use.

- **Use the Macro button to streamline the design process.** Creating your own series of toolbars for use in a single or shared environment can help save time in developing levels.

Chapter 6

Cinematics and High-Detail Modeling

If there's one thing that almost every person associates with, it's cinematic 3D graphics. These days we are completely surrounded by all kinds of computer-generated items—digital actors, props, even complete films. Furthermore, the game industry brings Hollywood to the monitor. You now experience games as if you are watching a movie. Many are produced with budgets that surpass those of films! Where is all of this money and effort really spent? The producers buy into computer technology and artists go along with it.

Whether you are already an animator in the "biz" or are thinking about it, there's one thing that you must have: impatient patience. This means knowing when something is feasible and when something is completely beyond the scope of what a computer does—and figuring out a way around it. Anyone can shove a project through with brut force. However, this often leads to excessive spending on both people and resources. A skillful animator knows when a project, as it's currently defined, is simply beyond the scope of the software and how to adjust the approach to get the same result through different means.

While the preceding paragraphs aren't necessarily unique to the film or game industry, you tend to find much more of this impatient-patience behavior in these industries. Why? Tight deadlines and incredible goals. As an animator in these industries, you're always given a heap of shots to complete and not enough time to complete them.

The trick of working as an animator in this business is knowing your plan of attack *before* you get into a project. This mentality is outlined here. Start not so much by learning the modeling process but rather learning what to avoid *before* you start to model. You'll be more efficient in the long run, and you may even be able to finish a project in time. To that end, let's explore the following topics in this chapter:

- Hardware considerations
- Texture mapping for detail
- Starting with primitives or lofts
- Using new features in MeshSmooth
- Scene optimization

While quite a bit of cinematic and film modeling information is contained within the chapter, notice that there's information for anyone needing to know more about high-detail modeling. Let's start with the bad news.

High-Resolution Modeling Pitfalls

Many new digital artists wonder, "Why do those animators need all of that expensive workstation hardware to get the job done? Everyone says that MAX can do it on a well-equipped PC." Well, if you've ever tried to work with a high-detail scene, you know the answer: processing power. Whenever you throw a bunch of triangles at your system's processor (CPU) and say, "Chew on these and give me a model," it taxes the system's resources to the limit. The more highly detailed a scene, the more processing power you need. This is, perhaps, the most serious pitfall of doing high-resolution work. Even the fastest computer isn't fast enough for richly detailed scenes.

While the PC has come of age in terms of its status as a workstation-quality computer, it still faces the same problems that more expensive workstations face: processing power. As an animator, you need to know where the bottlenecks are, so that you can minimize the "slow-CPU syndrome" as much as possible.

Hardware Limitations

When you talk about a workstation—in the case of MAX, a PC workstation—you're actually talking about several components. Even though they are independent of each other, they all must work together to give the best performance possible. These components include:

- CPU
- RAM
- 3D graphics accelerator cards

Although this book isn't an advertisement for hardware manufacturers, hardware is king in this business. If you don't have the top-of-the-line in all three categories, you may face longer production schedules. The one time you sell yourself short on hardware is the one time that you lose a bid for a job because you can't complete it on time. Like a Boy Scout, "Always be prepared."

The question is *how* to do that. If you have to upgrade, what do you upgrade first? To find the answer, evaluate what about your computer seems slow. Is it the display, the rendering time, or just a general "slowness" that you can't quite isolate to one component? Whatever the case, there are three steps to upgrading (or buying a new computer)—and they should be followed religiously. Upgrade the

1. RAM
2. CPU
3. Display

RAM

The absolutely *last* thing you want to happen is for your computer to start using its hard drive as virtual RAM. As you already know, your high-end workstation can turn into a high-end "sloth" that moves about as fast as you do when you wake up in the morning. To avoid this, get as much RAM as you can afford or that the computer can take. Realistically, you need a minimum of 256MB of RAM to do most cinematic projects. However, don't be surprised if you need more. It's not uncommon these days for workstation PCs to have 512MB to 1GB of RAM. If there's one thing to remember about the importance of RAM, it's this: Even the fastest CPU becomes unimaginably slow if it doesn't have enough *physical* RAM.

NEW TO R3   Currently not in the market for RAM? Then MAX R3 introduces a saving grace—not just for RAM, but also for the CPU and display components. This new savior comes in the form of externally referencing scenes and objects. External references, or *Xrefs*, are objects within your scene that point to, or reference, another file. They consist of either the actual object or a proxy representation. Using Xrefs enables you to see an entire scene or a single object for reference. It saves RAM by loading only the part of the scene on which you are working. Take a character, for example. While working on its torso, you want to see the arms and legs, but you don't need to edit them. By making the arms and legs Xrefs, you conserve RAM and improve system performance. See Figure 6.1 for a sample scene using Xrefs. More on Xrefs later in this chapter.

Figure 6.1 An example of a scene that uses Xrefs. The starship was created by a professional modeler and the animator—a different person—is animating the proxy Xref for speed reasons. A nice benefit of this method is that if the modeler changes the starship in any way, it usually doesn't affect the way it was animated. (Thanks to Frank DeLise for the scene.)

CPU

The next consideration is the CPU, or processor. The CPU is almost as important as RAM, so don't skimp here either. The first thing to consider is a single or multiple CPU solution. For most cinematic work, you want a dual-CPU system as your workstation. I say dual because of the way MAX works with the CPUs in your computer.

- MAX will perform nearly twice as fast when running a dual-CPU computer versus a single-processor model, with respect to interactivity—that is, your interaction with the MAX interface. Adding more than two CPUs is not as beneficial in the interface.

- MAX gains from more than two CPUs in mainly rendering speed. Complex scenes using environmental effects and high-detail geometry exercise the CPUs more than a simpler scene.

So if you're doing the modeling/animation *and* rendering on one computer, load up on CPUs. If you're modeling on the computer and sending the rendering off to a rendering farm (a network of rendering-only computers), then two CPUs are fine. Because speeds change so quickly, it's pointless to mention a specific speed to get. The easiest thing to remember is that if you can afford the fastest, get it.

3D Acceleration

There's been a ton of progression in the 3D-acceleration market since NT became more prominent in the 3D-animation industry. PC users were restricted to fast 2D-acceleration video cards. It wasn't until about 1993 that 3D-acceleration manufacturers began to produce for the PC. Since then, many technologies have come along. In fact, some are already gone.

When modeling for cinematics or anything high-resolution, a 3D-acceleration card is a must. The primary reason for this is that an accelerator card helps to relieve the CPU from making the calculations to display geometry in the viewports. If the CPU worries less about what to display and more about what to do with the geometry, you work more efficiently. The key to accelerators is that they take some or all of these processing tasks to their own processor and free up the CPU to work on other tasks. When they are designed to take on more, the display is faster.

MAX R3 supports the following three technologies for 3D acceleration:

- HDI, or Heidi
- OpenGL
- Direct3D

All three technologies are faster than just using a standard VGA card—even a 2D-accelerated one. Many cards on the market support at least one of the technologies—many support all three.

Heidi Versus OpenGL

When MAX R2 shipped, there was much debate as to which would be best: Autodesk's new Heidi technology or the already established OpenGL technology. Now it is obvious which is winning. The most prominent current technology is OpenGL. The interesting thing is that OpenGL came from Silicon Graphics. OpenGL actually began as an acceleration technology for workstations. Today, it is the fastest way to accelerate your 3D display. If you want a card that accelerates your display, make sure that it supports OpenGL.

Heidi is still a viable solution. However, because Heidi is an Autodesk-developed technology, it isn't as prominent in much of the industry. Heidi is supported in Windows 95/98 and NT 4/5.

Note

Windows NT/2000 provides OpenGL emulation that works with most cards, accelerated or not. If you select the OpenGL option, you may believe you have 3D acceleration—when in fact you don't. Likewise, Heidi, with specific hardware drivers, provided 3D acceleration for R1 (but no manufacturer is presently developing R2 Heidi drivers). Software Z-Buffer is also part of Heidi and is strictly software based. Be sure to refer to your card's documentation to verify its capabilities. Also check the current driver in the About dialog of the Help pull-down menu.

Direct3D

Direct3D is an acceleration technology developed by Microsoft for Windows 9x and Windows 2000. While it's still in its infancy for the workstation market, many game developers have supported it for their real-time 3D-interactive games in Windows 9x. Because Microsoft is the owner of both OpenGL (a licensed technology) and Direct3D (Microsoft's own), it eventually comes down to choosing one of them to support upcoming versions of Windows. To be safe, get a card that at least supports OpenGL. Then check to see if the manufacturer supports Direct3D. Most do already. It's important to note that many cards support all three acceleration technologies.

Editing Issues

So why all this talk about hardware? Simply put, it comes down to how fast you work on the PC. If your computer is slower than your thought processes, you're not at your peak productivity level, especially for editing. If you want to change the look of a model or an entire scene, you need a high-powered machine. However, there are other steps to make modeling on high-detail scenes a bit easier.

Hide Geometry

The most obvious method of speeding up the editing process is to hide objects on which you aren't working. This is done in two ways. One way is using the Display panel. The Display panel is where you control which objects or object types are displayed and how they're displayed. The other method is using the Display floater. Both function the same way. Depending on what you're doing in MAX, one may be preferable over the other.

Using the Display Floater

Rather than having to access a panel, call up the Display floater and keep it up; regardless of what you're doing to an object in a viewport. This saves a great deal of time by not switching back and forth between panels. The Display floater comes in handy in full-screen or Expert mode. Figure 6.2 shows MAX R3 in Expert mode with the Display floater active and the floating command panel.

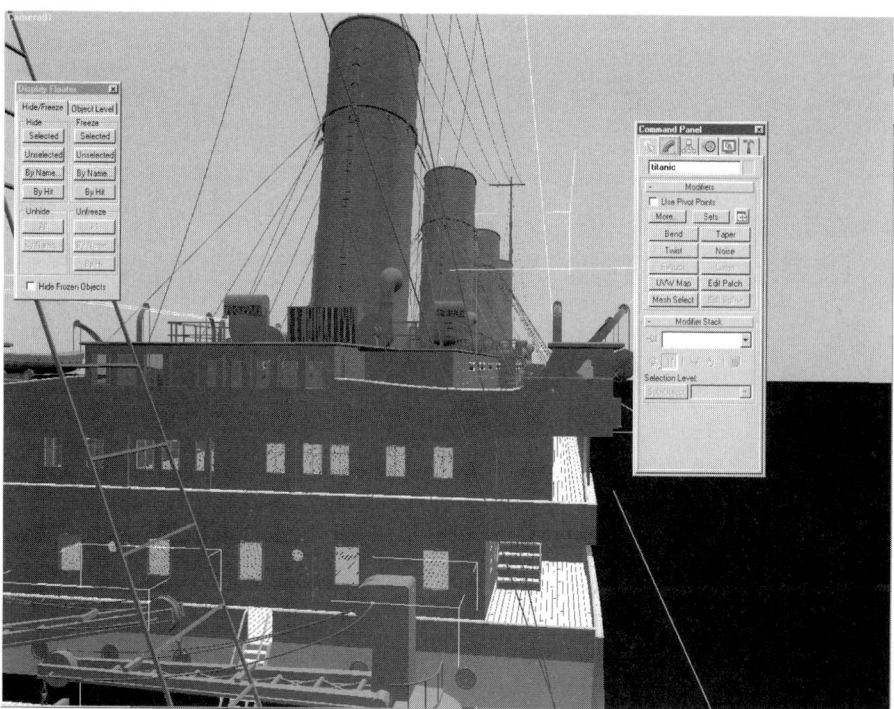

Figure 6.2 A shot of the Titanic model in Expert mode. The Display floater helps control which elements are displayed without going to the Display panel.

You launch the Display floater from the Tools menu, but not, however, in Expert mode. Alleviate this problem by assigning a keyboard alternate to call the Display floater. This is especially crucial because you often find yourself closing the Display floater. Unlike most floaters, the Display floater cannot be minimized. Figure 6.3 shows the Tools menu displaying a good keyboard alternate for the Display floater.

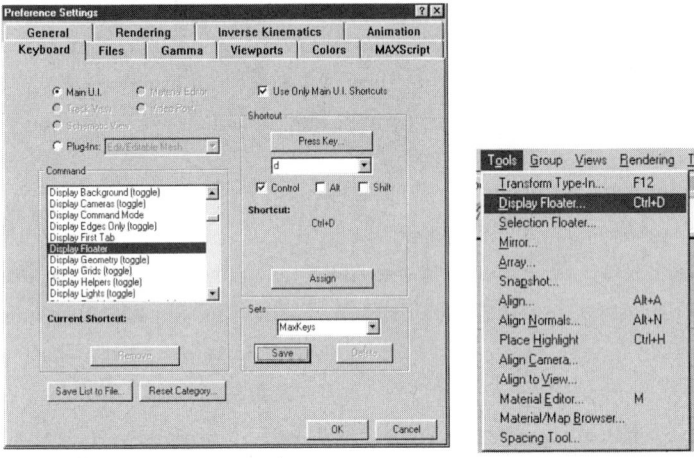

Figure 6.3 The Display floater option in the Tools menu with a keyboard alternate assigned to it. A keyboard alternate, assigned in the Keyboard tab of the Preferences dialog, helps speed access to this critical function.

Creating Keyboard Alternates

If you haven't already begun to set up your keyboard alternates, this is a good time to do so. Apply this technique to any of the topics discussed in this book as long as the feature is supported by MAX's keyboard alternate system. Here are some quick steps to creating a keyboard alternate:

1. Select Preferences from the Customize menu.
2. Click the Keyboard tab in the Preferences dialog box.

 Tip
Right-clicking the Plug-in Shortcut Toggle button at the bottom of the main interface immediately brings you to the Preferences dialog and Keyboard tab.

3. Select a command you wish to apply a keyboard alternate to on the left side of the dialog box.
4. On the right side, click in the Shortcut entry field and type in the key you want to use. Clicking the arrow next to the field produces a drop-down list containing

special keystrokes, like the arrow keys or F-keys. Click the respective check boxes to see whether or not you want Ctrl, Alt, or Shift to be part of the keyboard alternate. (The Press Key button, when clicked, reads a keyboard combination directly from the keyboard and automatically fills in the field and check boxes.) Now click the Assign button.

5. If there's a conflict, MAX notifies you. Just select a new alternate or change the conflicting alternate.

6. Save to the MAX default keyboard alternates by clicking the Save button. If you wish, type in your own custom name and save the existing set—and your new alternate—to a new name. This new alternate list will be used for successive sessions of MAX.

7. Click OK, and get working again.

Note

MAX automatically displays assigned keyboard alternates for pull-down menu items. Once you assign a keyboard alternate to a MAX command that's present in the pull-down menus, you see the new keyboard alternate appear to the right side of the command.

Setting Up Display Groups

Hiding geometry is the easiest way to speed the editing process. However it is also tedious, if your scene isn't properly organized. An easy thing to do is arrange your objects into "display groups." These groups consist of objects that you hide or unhide, collectively. Because you instruct MAX to display and hide objects by name, the "display group" technique is very effective. The only downside is that you cannot *hide* objects in Expert mode using this method—only restore them. Otherwise, this method works great for just about any high-detail scene.

Creating Display Groups

Display groups, a combination of Named Selection sets, are relatively easy to create as a specific case of Named Selection Sets. In the following exercise, you create display groups to manage the manipulation of a high-detail model of a Formula-1 racecar.

Exercise 6.1   Creating and Managing Display Groups

1. Load 06imx01.max from the CD-ROM.
2. Select all four tires by clicking each one while holding down the Ctrl key.

3. In the Named Selection Sets field in the Main Toolbar, type in Tires, and press Enter.
4. From the Tools menu, select Display Floater.
5. Click the Hide Selected button.
6. Select the front wing. In the Named Selection Sets field, enter Spoilers.
7. Mistakes in named selections are easily fixed. Add the rear spoilers to the selection set, as well. This is easy to do by selecting Edit Named Selections from the Edit menu.
8. Click Spoilers in the Named Selections field in the Edit Named Selections dialog. Click the Add button. From the object list, choose [RearSpoilers], click Add, and then click OK to exit the dialog.
9. Choose Spoilers from the Named Selection Sets drop-down list and click the Hide Selected button in the Display Floater.
10. Click any one of the four struts. They're grouped, so that they all select at the same time. In the Named Selection Sets field, enter Struts.
11. Click the Hide Selected button in the Display Floater.
12. Select the body of the race car. In the Named Selection Set field, enter Body.
13. Now, using the Display Floater, hide and unhide objects based on name. To unhide an entire selection set, click the Unhide By Name button (see Figure 6.4).
14. In the Unhide Objects dialog box, click the arrow in the Selection Sets field to show a list of named selections. Choose Spoilers, then click Unhide. Hide By Name offers the same functionality for hiding selections.

This exercise demonstrates how you create some high-level display groups. As demonstrated, named selections are easy to access in the display commands. This model was already grouped by major sections prior to you doing the exercise. You have to decide how the model is organized at a high level, and then use Named Selection Sets to create your display groups accordingly. Display groups are just one way in MAX R3 for you to effectively manage system performance on high-detail models. In a later section, you use Xrefs and proxy graphics as another way to optimize your display.

Note

Some developers created special organizational plug-ins or scripts that help organize scenes better than just through display groups. Check some of the MAX-related Web sites such as max3d.com or 3dcafe.com to see what's available.

Chapter 6: Cinematics and High-Detail Modeling   243

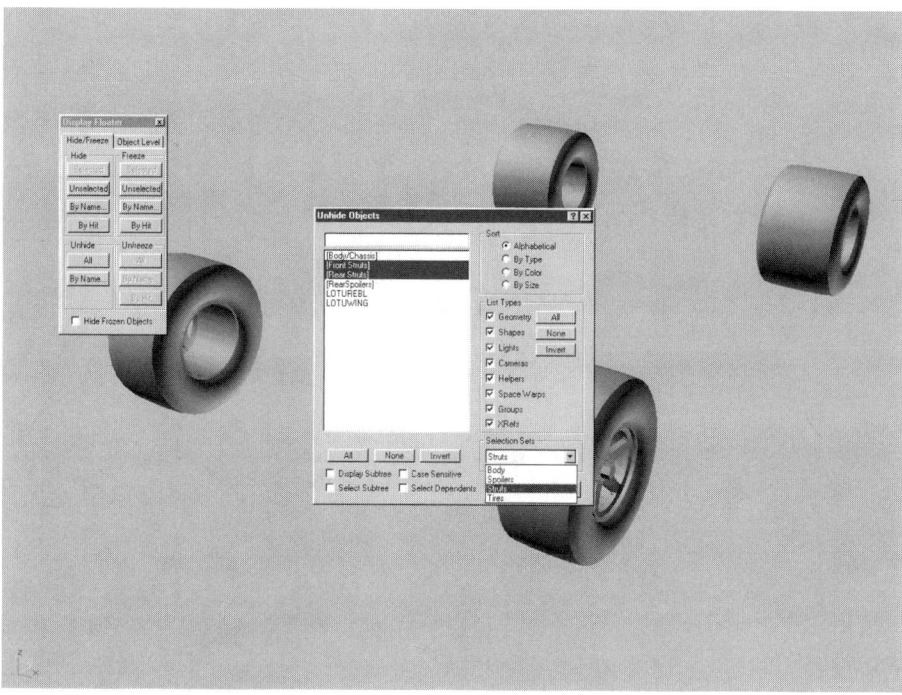

Figure 6.4 A sample of using the Display Floater in Expert mode to control display groups either shown or hidden.

Using Object Xrefs

One method for working with high-detail scenes is to use proxies—or stand-in objects. Instead of having every piece of the original geometry in the scene, you replace them with simple geometric primitives. This way, you have an idea of the shape, size, orientation, and animation of an object without the complete object's overhead. Hiding or unhiding objects does not have this benefit. Once you're ready to render, the proxy mesh is replaced by the real object, using the Object Xref command—new to MAX R3.

NEW TO R3   Object Xrefs let you work in your scene with objects from an external source file. While this was somewhat possible in the past with the Replace command, the convenience of Xrefs makes them far easier to use. With Xrefs, you work either with the original geometry or with a lower-detail, proxy representation. The proxy is any object in the source scene or from a completely different .max file. In a typical situation, you use both the original object and the proxy at the same time. The proxy is used in your viewports, and the original, more detailed object, is used in the rendering. Figure 6.5 shows the Object Xref dialog and proxy control in the command panel.

Figure 6.5 Using Object Xrefs, insert either the actual object or stand-in geometry.

Streamline Texture Mapping

Textures are an essential part of any scene, especially high-resolution models. Since MAX R1, you've been able to display those textures in your viewports. This invaluable feature makes placing decals and the like on objects extra easy. As an animator, it is a critical component of the scene design process.

The downsides of displaying maps in the viewport do exist, but are outweighed by the benefits. When working with high-detail scenes, notice that it isn't difficult to push the limits of your computer or video card by displaying many textures in the viewports. In MAX R3, there are some features designed to help you out in the texture-display department.

Display Maps

By clicking the Material Editor's Display Maps button, you display the most common map types, such as Bitmap, in viewports.

If using Heidi through the standard Software Z-Buffer option, use the computer's memory to display textures. While this is a great thing if you have a good amount of RAM, it also means that there's less RAM for other MAX operations.

If you're using hardware acceleration in the viewports, the hardware usually has texture memory on-board. This form of texture memory is often much quicker than the computer's generic RAM, but it is limited. In high-detail scenes, it's not uncommon to reach your card's upper limit of texture memory. When you do reach that limit, the card now takes on the process of both loading and clearing its memory in order to display the textures. This swapping process is analogous to your computer using the hard drive to swap RAM data, although it's not as dramatic. It results in similar, but not equal, performance degradation.

So the golden rule should be: Display only what you need. Let's face it, the only *real* reason you need to display textures in the viewports is for placement on a 3D mesh. After that, you're usually done. If you are done, turn off the Display Map option in the Material Editor. This will speed up performance all around.

Deactivate All Maps and Disable TEXTURES

There are two other ways to switch off maps in your viewports. One is more permanent, while the other is designed to be temporary. The Deactivate All Maps option (see Figure 6.6) turns off the Display Maps button for *every* material that is currently displaying a map in the viewport. The key thing to remember about this option is that it is *not* a toggle. It's a one-way trip. The only way to re-activate the maps is to turn them all on again, one by one. Use this feature only when you need to turn off all the maps in the viewports. MAX will confirm the operation.

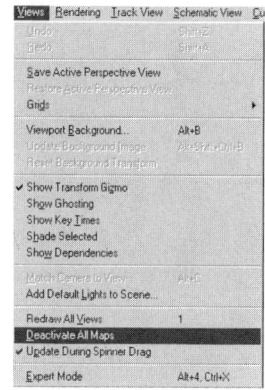

Figure 6.6 The Deactivate All Maps option in the Views pull-down menu. Use this feature to turn off the Display Maps option for every material used in the scene.

Tip
Sometimes you load a model with the texture map display on, but the maps aren't available to MAX for one reason or another. Because MAX is looking for those maps, it's also trying to figure out a way to display the material in the viewport. This almost always causes a serious slow-down in interactivity. To clean things up a bit, use the Deactivate All Maps feature to instruct MAX to not worry about the texture maps. Doing so improves performance—sometimes dramatically.

A less permanent option for turning off maps is Disable Textures, located in the Viewport Configuration dialog. To get there, right-click on any viewport label, and choose Configure. Disable Textures is in the Viewport Configuration dialog's Rendering

Method tab. The default is off. Turn this feature on to temporarily disable textures in your viewports. Turning on Disable Textures enables you to keep the Display Maps option on for your materials, while it is still able to turn off the display of the map in the viewports. Figure 6.7 shows this dialog box.

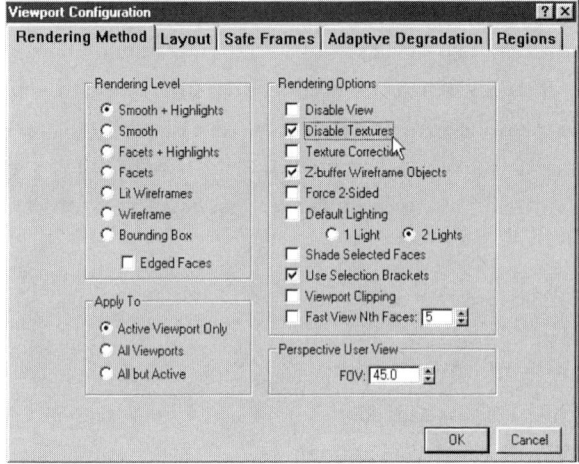

Figure 6.7 The Viewport Configuration dialog, where the Disable Textures option is located. Use this feature to temporarily turn off texture displays in your viewports.

Level of Detail Utility

As mentioned in Chapter 4, the Level of Detail utility allows you to control the rendered level of detail for an object based on its distance from the camera. This feature helps high-detail scenes by forcing geometry that's too far from the camera to render in a lower-detail version. This feature is primarily for the benefit of optimizing your rendering time; however, you use it to optimize the performance in the viewport, as well.

Level of Detail has a switch that allows you to select which of the embedded objects in the group are displayed in your viewport. For the best performance, choose the lowest-detail version. This has no effect on the object that's rendered. Those calculations are based on the object's distance from the camera. Figure 6.8 shows the Level of Detail utility with the lowest-detail version of a high-resolution object displayed in the viewport.

Inactive in Viewport Toggle

Before we get into the actual modeling section, there's one other display option that's worth discussing: the Inactive in Viewport toggle for modifiers. There are times when you want to shut off certain modifiers that are applied to objects, in order to speed up

Chapter 6: Cinematics and High-Detail Modeling   247

the display performance of your viewports using the Active/Inactive modifier toggle. This is a handy toggle to have. It affects your rendering as well, which means that you have to re-enable the modifier in order to render the modifications it makes. Usually this isn't a big deal, merely a nuisance, for most smaller models. With larger models, however, turning a modifier on and off sometimes takes time as MAX processes the new calculations. To avoid this hang-up, use the other button embedded within the Active/Inactive Modifier toggle button, called the Active/Inactive in Viewport toggle.

Present since MAX R2, the Active/Inactive in Viewport toggle simply shuts off the display that a particular modifier shows on your object in the viewport. When you render, however, the modifier renders in the "active" state, meaning it renders as if it were on in the viewports. To access the Active/Inactive in Viewport toggle, just click and hold the Active/Inactive Modifier toggle button until the flyout appears. The only other button is the Active/Inactive in Viewport toggle. Turn it on to disable the display of that particular modifier in the viewport.

Modifiers with their viewport display inactive show up as a faint blue in the Modifier Stack. If they display as a faint gray, then the modifier is also set to inactive, instead of just inactive in the viewport.

This feature works best when used on models that are complete or nearly complete. Unlike the Show End Result toggle, Active/Inactive in Viewport is intended to improve performance rather than act as a modeling enhancement tool. And it's really useful when you apply:

- A MeshSmooth modifier with several iterations.
- The Tessellate modifier.

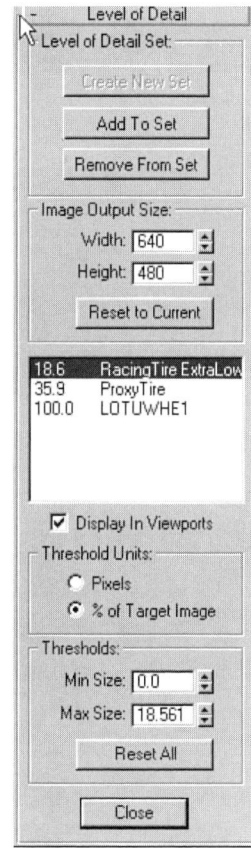

Figure 6.8 The Level of Detail utility with the Display in Viewports option, checked on for the lowest-detail model. While primarily a rendering optimization tool, this particular option within the utility allows you to speed up interactive performance in the viewports, as well.

 Tip
You can access the functions of both the Active/Inactive modifier and Active/Inactive in Viewport toggles through the Edit Stack button in the Modify panel. That way, you set modifiers to active or inactive without having to jump to them in the stack—sometimes avoiding a costly redraw.

Figure 6.9 shows a model with the MeshSmooth modifier turned off in the viewport, but calculated for the rendering. Note that the Active/Inactive is set to Inactive in Viewport—indicated by the fact that the button is pushed in and that the light bulb is gray instead of white.

Figure 6.9 A sample situation where the Active/Inactive in Viewport toggle works well. The model is low detail in the viewports, but when rendered, the MeshSmooth modifier is calculated to produce the higher detail version.

Building the Basic Model

Now that you've seen how to get the most from your workstation's hardware when modeling, let's get into how to actually *use* MAX for high-detail scene design.

Models that you build for cinematic sequences more than likely start from simpler objects. As a matter of fact, this is often easiest to do. Depending on your background, you may find it easier "building" a model from a simple object or "sculpting" a more complex model from a simple piece of geometry. In either case, with MAX you have the luxury of starting simple and getting complex only when and where you need it.

In this section, you explore some of the more common ways to model in MAX. Later on, you'll see how you apply some of these techniques to more complex modeling techniques.

Starting with Primitives

Modeling with primitive objects is, by far, the easiest way to create in 3D. The trick is to think ahead to determine what you want in the end. When modeling for high-detail models, don't rely on just one primitive object to complete your model. Instead, you want to think of your model in terms of smaller pieces that you put together later to produce the final result. This is especially true if the camera is going to closely examine a particular surface.

Knowing which primitive to start with and what detail level is appropriate is the challenge. Let's first talk about which primitive works best for a given situation.

The Box Primitive

It is said that almost anything can be modeled from a box. For the most part, it's true. With a box, you can push, pull, rotate, or whatever to any detail level to produce a more complex model.

The biggest benefit of using a box model is that the faces extrude at right angles. This means that shaping a model into some other complex geometry is much easier to do. Instead of faces extruding in every direction, as it often happens with rounded primitives, the faces of a box extrude in the direction you intend them to extrude.

Non-Box Primitives

You often find yourself using primitives other than a box for a more rounded look. For instance, a very common model to build from a sphere is a head. Figure 6.10 shows what's possible using the Displace modifier to push and pull on the vertices of a GeoSphere.

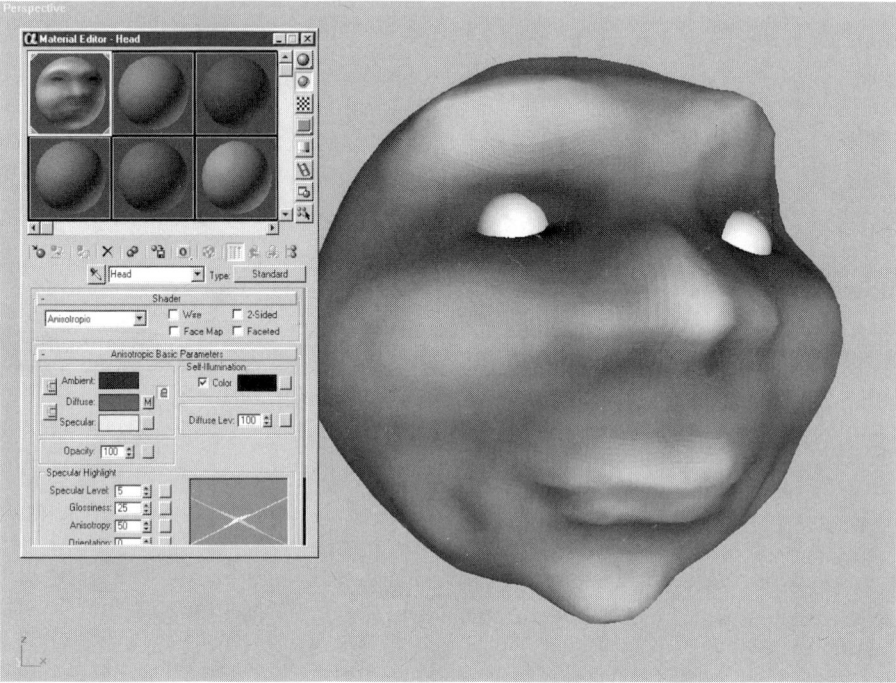

Figure 6.10 A GeoSphere shaped by the Displace modifier. Using this method, however, requires that the model is somewhat detailed in order to deform properly. Displacement map by Glenn Melenhorst.

Loft Objects

Building from Loft Objects is sometimes a better way to design a model. You have more control over the way an object is surfaced. You also custom design the style and shape of your model by using different cross sections along the extrusion path. For instance, if you design the exhaust pipe of a truck, you want to use lofting. Figure 6.11 shows what this looks like. Producing the complex twists, scaling, and turns of the pipe is not as easy if you use a primitive.

Chapter 6: Cinematics and High-Detail Modeling   251

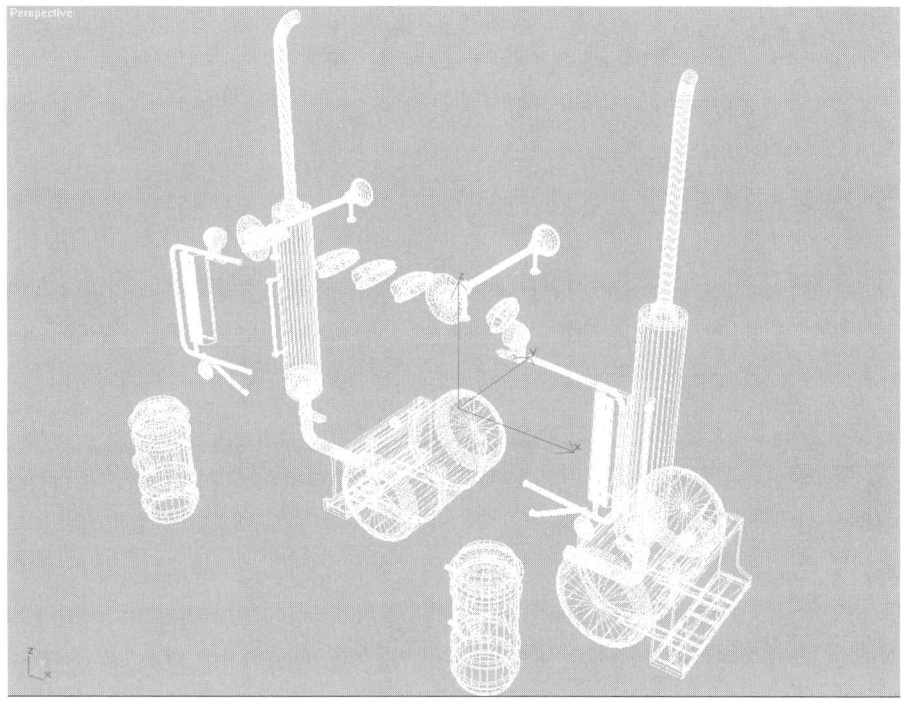

Figure 6.11 Complex exhaust pipes produced through the lofting process. Through lofting, it's possible to deform a single shape along a path into more complex-looking objects, like you see here.

MeshSmooth

NEW TO R3

MeshSmooth turns out to be the sleeper hit for MAX. Since the later days of MAX R1, people have discovered its usefulness as a tool for turning low-detail models into high-detail ones. Whether you're building a character or designing a spaceship, it's fair to say that MeshSmooth should be part of your modeling arsenal. If you're not familiar with MeshSmooth already, it does two basic things. It adds faces to the mesh, like Tessellate, and it softens the edges, like Relax. In effect, it smoothes the topology of the mesh, while also giving you a control lattice to push and pull on the smoothed object.

In MAX R3, MeshSmooth is enhanced, giving you the most flexible modeling tool for smooth or organic-looking polygonal objects. The enhancements are:

- NURMS output (Non-Uniform Rational Mesh Smooth).
- Editing the control mesh vertex weights (Sub-Object mode).

- Restricting to Convex Output (constant face count).
- Uses Show End Result while at the Editable Mesh level.
- Explicit control of iterations.

Probably the most significant feature of MeshSmooth in MAX R3 is the NURMS-output method. Rather than just giving you smoothness and iterations values like Quad Output and Classic do, NURMS also gives you control points that you weight to shape the model. Much like control vertices (CVs) on NURBS objects, NURMS control points each have their own weight that can push or pull on the MeshSmoothed model. By default, MAX R3's MeshSmooth automatically outputs NURMS. However, unlike the older MeshSmooth in R2, R3's MeshSmooth now contains a Sub-Object mode that allows you to pick the vertex points or edges between two vertices. After you pick a point or an edge, you then control its weight in the Display/Weighting section of the MeshSmooth modifier.

You can't, however, move the points or edges within the MeshSmooth modifier. To move faces, edges, or vertices, you must go back to the Editable Mesh object, to which you applied MeshSmooth. However, unlike R2, you now display the end result while editing—that is, you see the smoothed model at all times while you're moving geometry around at the Editable Mesh level.

NURMS also gives you explicit control over the detail of the model when rendered, versus how it's displayed in the viewports. This allows you to model with a relatively low-detail object and render with a much higher detail version. This feature, called *Subdivision Amount*, subdivides the surfaces at render time to a specific amount. And now you specify any value for iterations, rather than having just four choices. Be careful, though. High iteration values make face counts sky rocket.

Warning

MeshSmooth in R3 now allows you to input just about any value for iterations. While more flexible, it also means that you have the chance to seriously slow down your system. As a rule, try to never go above 3 in the viewport and 5 in the renderer. While the maximum is 10 for either the viewport or renderer, 10 could cause the system to run out of RAM—both real and virtual.

If you're modeling for games or for graphics engines that require convex-only polygons, use the new Keep Faces convex check box. When checked, MeshSmooth ensures that the smoothed faces it generates remain convex. It does not, however, check your model to see if any of the faces are convex prior to smoothing. It only checks to make sure the faces are convex after they are smoothed.

If you're familiar with MeshSmooth from R2, some of the older features are still there:

- **Operate On.** Toggle buttons to indicate whether MeshSmooth operates on triangular faces or N-sided polygons. (This feature is identical to the Eliminate Hidden Edges feature of MeshSmooth in MAX 1.2.) Essentially, working on faces produces a result that is tessellated, based on all edges of your mesh—even the invisible ones. The result is that you have a mesh that looks like a bunch of interconnecting triangles. It also means that your polygon count increases dramatically. Use this option when working with very smooth, rounded geometry. Otherwise use the second option—Operate on Polygons. Operate on Polygons forces MeshSmooth to work only on the visible edges of your mesh. The result works really well for shapes such as box and cube-like objects. This option also keeps your face count down. You can usually get away with using Operate on Polygons.

- **Quad Output.** Produces a mesh that is built from quadrilateral facets. Although the mesh itself is still made from triangles, you see what appears to be quadrilateral faces. Figure 6.12 shows this feature with Operate on Quads on, as well. Notice how uniform the mesh looks. This is because the mesh is built from a box primitive. The MeshSmooth modifier is restricted to operate only on visible edges and produce only quadrilateral faces. The end result is what you see in the figure. It almost looks as if the mesh is scanned in, using a 3D scanner versus building from a box primitive.

When building high-detail models for cinematics, MeshSmooth is a great tool. Later on in this section, you explore some of the ways to use MeshSmooth in your day-to-day modeling techniques.

Applying MeshSmooth to Your Model

There are a few ways to deal with MeshSmooth on your model. The first is to apply the MeshSmooth modifier to the whole mesh. The other option is to apply MeshSmooth to a specific section of your model. Using one versus the other completely depends on your intended final result. Exercises 6.2 and 6.3 explore the usage of each option on the same model.

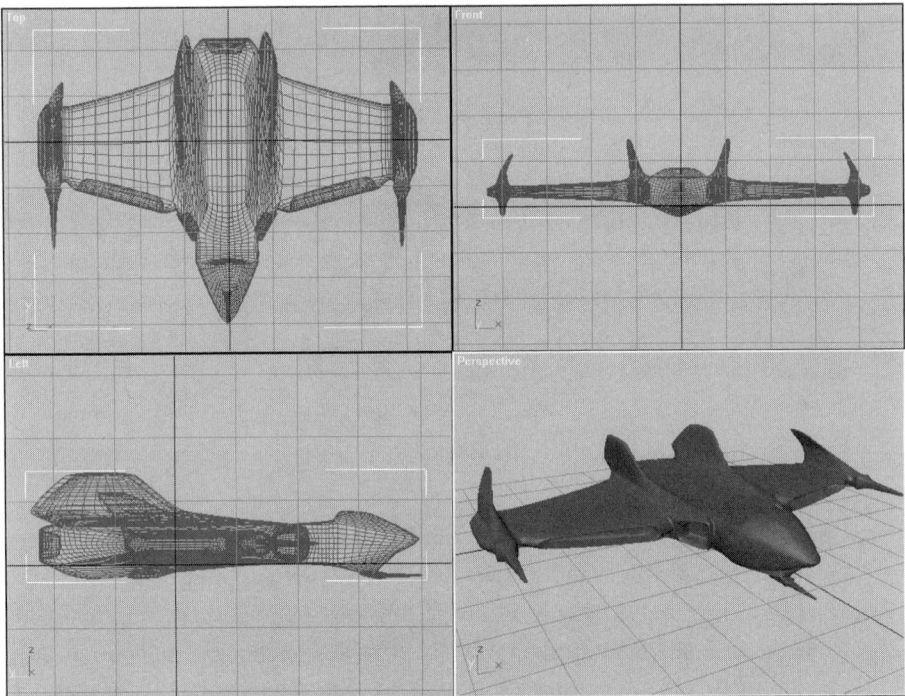

Figure 6.12 A model built from a box primitive. The quadrilateral mesh produced is a result of using MeshSmooth, with Operate on Polygons and Quad Output.

Using Apply to Whole Mesh

MeshSmooth's Apply to Whole Mesh option allows you to apply the modifier to the whole model, regardless of what sub-object elements you selected on the geometry. This means that you work on any area of the model without worrying about the wrong selection getting passed up the Modifier Stack to the MeshSmooth modifier.

To illustrate this, take a look at a "how to" model using MeshSmooth and Apply to Whole Mesh. Exercise 6.2 demonstrates using MeshSmooth on an entire model, while working on only one area of the model at a time. In the exercise, we create a smooth-skinned, winged space fighter.

Exercise 6.2   MeshSmooth on an Entire Model

  1. Load 06max02.max from the CD-ROM. This contains a scene with a simple box primitive converted to an Editable Mesh.
  2. Select the box. Go to the Modify panel, and click the More button. Choose MeshSmooth.

3. In the MeshSmooth Type, select Classic. Select the Operate on Polygons button, and turn on the Apply to Whole Mesh option. Under Smoothing Parameters, set strength to 0.25. Under Subdivision Amount, set Iterations to 3. This will produce a slightly smoothed box.

4. Using the Modifier Stack pop-down menu, return to the Editable Mesh object, and switch to Sub-Object mode at the Polygon level. Turn on Show End Result.

5. Select the "Sides" named selection set from the Named Selection Sets pop-down list in the main toolbar. Right-click over either one of the faces, and choose Chamfer/Bevel, and then Bevel Polygon.

6. Interactively drag the sides out about 6 units. When you release the mouse, bevel the faces about −1.3 units. (Note that you can see these values in the Modify panel while you're doing the operation.)

7. Next, while still using the Bevel polygon command, extrude the selected faces about 25 units. (Note that you may want to lock the selection using the Space Bar because you are working with these faces for a few more steps.) When you release the mouse button after extruding, bevel the faces about −1 unit. You should now have wings projecting from the ship.

8. Choose the Move command, and using the Transform Gizmo, move the selected faces back, so that they are nearly parallel to the back of the craft.

9. Render the viewport. (See Figure 6.13.) Notice that with the Apply to Whole Mesh option on, it doesn't matter what elements you selected in Editable Mesh. The whole mesh is still deformed by MeshSmooth. Go back in the stack to MeshSmooth, and turn off Apply to Whole Mesh. Observe that most of the smoothing disappears from the model and is only applied to the wings. Save your work when you're done.

This is the classic way to work with MeshSmooth—by moving faces and edges exactly to where you want them and only utilizing the mesh smoothing capabilities of MeshSmooth. In the next exercise, take a look at how to use the new NURMS output to shape your model, using control points.

MeshSmooth for Sections

Sometimes you want to control the smoothness of a specific area of your model. For instance, you may select the wing tips of the ship model and smooth them less, or more, than the rest of the model. MeshSmooth works the exact same way on a selected area of a model as it does on the entire model. Using MeshSmooth in combination with the MeshSelect modifier does this fairly easily. Select contains the same ability as VolumeSelect to select the faces, edges, and vertices of a 3D mesh. Unlike VolumeSelect, which selects objects based on what's contained within its volume, MeshSelect allows you to select non-contiguous areas of a model. However, MeshSelect does *not* allow you to animate your selection—unlike the VolumeSelect modifier. MeshSelect is also dependent upon mesh topology. This means that if you alter the number of faces in the model somewhere in the stack before the MeshSelect modifier, you destroy your selection.

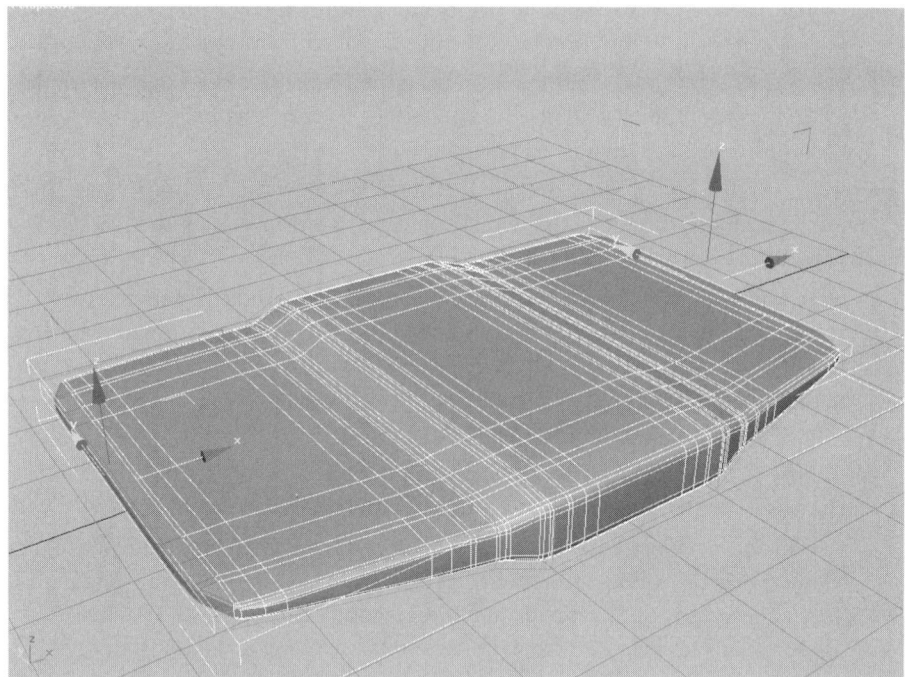

Figure 6.13 The mesh result from Exercise 6.2. The tapered "wings" are a result of using the extrude and bevel commands on the polygons of a box primitive. Then the box is rounded using the MeshSmooth modifier.

A big feature gained with the MeshSelect modifier is the ability to grab sub-object selections from other selection levels. For instance, if you have vertices selected on a mesh, and then switch to the Face selection level, you can use the Get Vertex Selection button to select faces that are based on the selection of vertices.

In Exercise 6.3, come back to the ship now modeled a bit more. At this point, use the MeshSelect modifier to select the wing tips to smooth them at different levels from the rest of the body. Also work with the new NURMS control mesh to pull on the wing tips more.

Exercise 6.3 MeshSelect and MeshSmooth on the Wing Tips

1. Open 06max03.max from the CD-ROM. This scene contains two views of the same ship. Start by working in the Front viewport.
2. Select the ship model, and go to the Modify panel.
3. Apply the MeshSelect modifier, and click the Polygon selection level. At this point, select the wing tips one of two ways. You either use the Select Invert command *or* you manually select the wingtips. Which one do you think is easier?
4. From the Edit pull-down menu, choose Select Invert.
5. Click the More button in the Modify panel. Choose MeshSmooth.
6. Turn off Apply to Whole Mesh; set Iterations to 2 and Smoothness to 1.
7. Click the Sub-Object button to enter Sub-Object selection and editing mode.
8. In the Front viewport, select the wing tip vertices. Refer to Figure 6.14 to determine which ones.

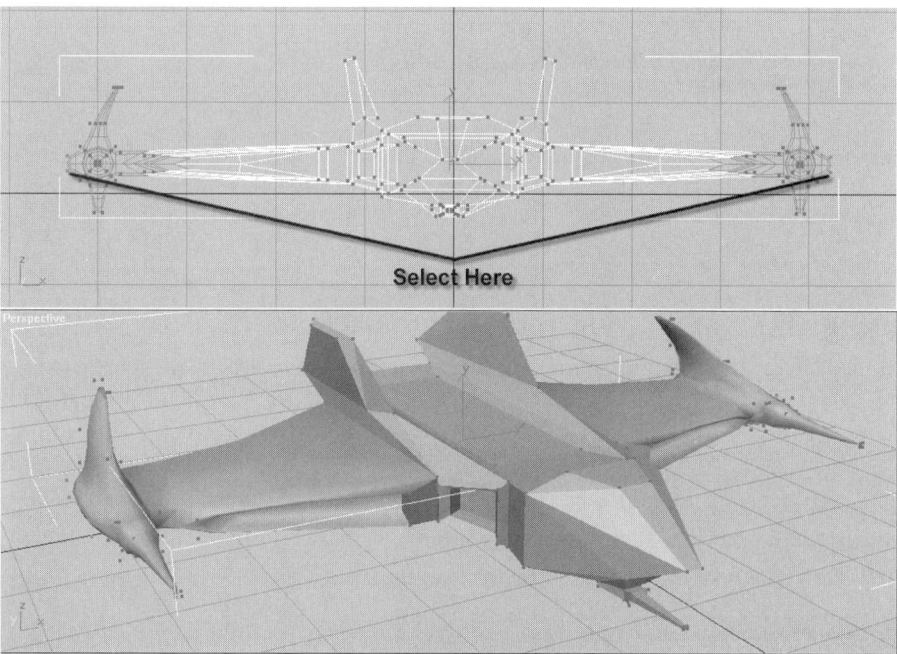

Figure 6.14 When performing Step 8 in exercise 6.3, select the vertices indicated in this figure.

9. In the Display/Weighting section of the MeshSmooth modifier, it should say 8 vertices selected. In the Weight field, enter 200.
10. Using the Modifier Stack pop-down menu, go back to the MeshSelect modifier, and choose Select Invert from the Edit pull-down menu.

11. Click the Show End Result button. Notice that the smoothing is now applied to your new selection set.
12. Choose Select Invert from the Edit pull-down menu again. Notice that the smoothing is transferred to your old selection set, and the vertex weights that you set up earlier are remembered. This is a good thing to remember. You smooth various sections of the model at different times without losing weight information.

By manipulating the vertex weights for different parts of the model, you shape the model as if it were like clay rather than made up of vertices. As you can see, by using a combination of MeshSelect and MeshSmooth on specific sections of the model, it is fairly easy to specify where the smoothing occurs on the model.

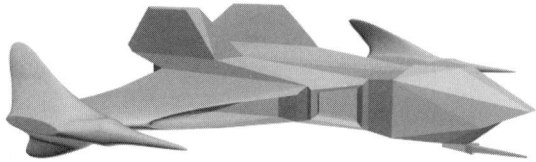

Figure 6.15 The completed result from Exercise 6.3. The varying levels of mesh smoothing are a result of using multiple MeshSelect and MeshSmooth modifiers, along with NURMS vertex weighting on the model.

Using MAX's Animation Tools to Create Models

MAX contains an enormous amount of built-in animation tools. Use these tools to your advantage to create interesting models, which might otherwise be tedious or impossible to create.

The Snapshot tool, developed in the days of 3D Studio DOS, actually creates a clone of your selected objects as they appear in a specific frame. The snapshot doesn't animate; it's merely a copy of that object's state on that frame.

In the past, MAX has offered several deformation tools that produced some interesting models through animation and using snapshot, but now with recent additions such as Flex, MAX takes the tools to a new level. With Flex, your models potentially look incredibly fluid and, if you like, realistic.

While this book doesn't focus on animation, the tools that are available to you while you're modeling involve both keyframe and other modifier-based animation methods. For instance, look at Figure 6.16. The flower petals' irregular look is the result of deforming a patch using the Flex modifier. The Flex modifier is capable of using force-based space warps to deform a mesh in addition to its soft-body-like dynamics. Using the Motor space warp as a force within Flex, as well as applying Wind and Gravity just to give more deformation, you create the twisted shape of the petals.

Figure 6.16 A flower modeled using the Snapshot feature on patch objects, deformed over time using the Motor space warp in the Flex modifier.

This next exercise focuses on using Snapshot to create a series of petals. Look at the final version of the flower on the Inside 3D Studio MAX CD-ROM.

Exercise 6.4 Creating Models Through Animation

1. Open 06imx04.max from the CD-ROM. The scene contains a patch surface with the Flex modifier applied. If you play the animation, notice that not much happens.
2. Select the blue patch object, and go to the Modify panel.
3. Click the More button at the top of the panel, then choose Flex from the list of Object-Space modifiers.
4. Scroll down the panel to the Advanced Parameters section, click the Add Force button, press H, and select Motor01 from the list.
5. Scroll the Time Slider to see that the patch is now getting radically deformed over the course of 100 frames.
6. Click the Add Force button again to add the Gravity01 and Wind01 objects, respectively. Note that if you can't select them visually, use the H key to select them by name.
7. Scroll to about frame 29 or 30, then click and hold the Array button in the Main Toolbar tab of the Tab panel until the Snapshot button is visible. Select it.
8. When the Snapshot Options dialog appears, just accept the defaults of a single snapshot and the Clone Method of a Mesh.

260 Part I Modeling

9. This creates an Editable Mesh snapshot of your deformed patch. Hide your patch by going to the Display tab and choosing Hide By Name. Hide Plane01.
10. Use the Clone and Rotate Selected commands to create two additional copies of the petals created so far.

Tip
In Step 10, you created the clone after you created the snapshot object. If you create the clone before the snapshot, you get varying petals because they're still being deformed in real-time by the Flex modifier. If you're looking for more randomness, create the clones first, then snapshot them all on frame 29 or 30.

11. Select all the petals and Apply, then return to the Modify panel.
12. Click the More button, and select the Affect Region modifier.
13. Set the Falloff Amount to 480, then click the Sub-Object button. In the viewport, select the arrowhead point of the Sub-Object gizmo. If you have trouble selecting it, just zoom in and select it. Drag the arrowhead on the Y-axis to about 275 units, or use the Transform Type In dialog. Right-click the Move button, and type in 275 in the Y, Absolute:World coordinate area.
14. Click the Material Editor button in the Main Toolbar tab of the Tab Panel.
15. Assign the Petal material to all the petal objects.
16. In the Modify panel, click the More button, and select the *MapScaler modifier. Then select just one of the petals in the viewport. Set the Scale amount of the MapScaler to 800 in the modify panel.
17. Render the scene.

Figure 6.17 The rendering created in Exercise 6.4. The petals were created using animation tools, rather than through traditional modeling. With high details, soft deformations such as this are quite easy to do.

Using the Clone System

When it comes to modeling, cloning multiple-repeating geometry, such as a swarm of bees, is often the quickest way to edit your scene. As a matter of fact, it's sometimes the *only* way to model efficiently enough to get a project done by deadline time.

Cloning an object refers to making some sort of duplication. This duplication results in a straight copy of the object, a Reference copy of the object, or an Instance. All three types have their own benefits. However, the Instance is proving itself to be a valuable clone object. Figure 6.18 shows both stair and column objects that are Instances.

Figure 6.18 The stairway and columns are all Instances of each other. This makes high-detail, repetitive modeling much simpler in the editing stages.

An Instance is an *exact* duplicate of the original object. They each behave the same way; they look the same. The only things that are different are the material they use and their position, rotation, and scaling data. Figure 6.18 is a good example of a typical scene needing Instances. The following are some tips for dealing with Instances:

- *Use the Array operation when necessary.* Use the Array tool whenever possible. Array makes multiple clones—as Copies, Instances, or References—at calculated distances in both 2D and 3D directions.

- *Use named selection sets when possible.* The example in Figure 6.18 is well suited for this. You create one named selection containing the columns and another for the stairs. That makes applying materials and hiding objects for editing purposes very efficient.

Lofting for Detail

Most of your modeling is done without lofting these days. Instead of lofting representing one of the few ways to model, it's now one of many. Because careless lofting of shapes results in a great amount of detail in the model, most animators avoid it. Most objects are built using both the lathe and loft methods. However, without careful planning, the resultant geometry created with a loft object is usually much more detailed compared to a lathed object. For instance, one of the columns shown in Figure 6.18, is easily lathed and is roughly 3,000 faces. A lathed object, using default settings, has over half the faces.

However, there are times when lofting is beneficial. Using the columns again as an example, you want to add finer detail to the column, itself, than a Lathe operation does. The only way to build an object like a column with more detail than the Lathe modifier provides is with lofting.

Exercise 6.5 enhances the columns in this scene. Use a Loft object to build a new column, and then replace the columns in the scene with new Instances.

Exercise 6.5 Building a Complex Column Using Lofts

1. Open 06max05.max from the CD-ROM. Render the scene. You see an image very similar to Figure 6.18.
2. From the Tools menu, choose Display Floater.
3. Select Unhide All to reveal the hidden Loft object.
4. From the Named Selection Sets list, choose Instances.
5. In the Display Floater dialog Hide section, click Hide Selected. Then click on the Object Level tab.
6. Uncheck the Shapes category, and close the Display floater.
7. Select the Loft object, and go to the Modify panel.
8. In the Path Parameters section, type 5 in the Path field. Then in the Creation Method section, click Get Shape and select the circle shape in the viewport. By

repeating this technique, you get shapes for several path levels and define the contour of the loft. (Use Zoom Extents if you need to see more of the scene.)

9. Type in 8 in the Path field, and select the circle shape again. (Note, it might be easier to select the circle if you switch to a 4-viewport configuration rather than a single viewport.)
10. Type in 10, and select the rounded star shape, Star01. Select the star again at Path level 85.
11. Type in 90, and select the circle shape again to complete the column.
12. Render the scene to see the completed column, then save the file. (See Figure 6.19.)

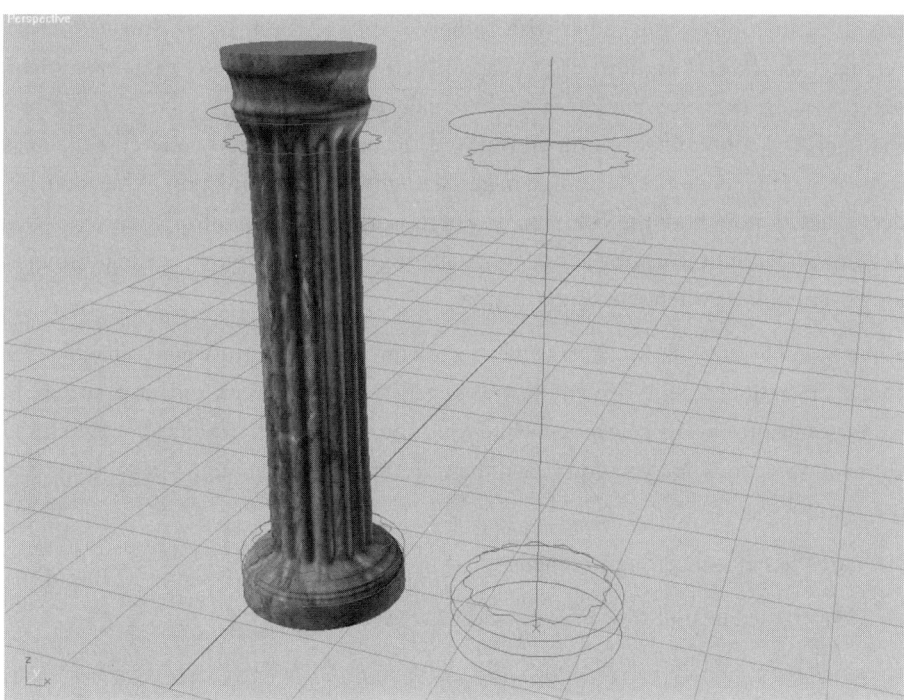

Figure 6.19 A view of the completed, more complex-looking column, created using loft objects versus a lathe. The shapes used to make the loft object are visible on the right side.

The completed rendering in Figure 6.19 demonstrates that lofting a column produces a much more realistic result. In Exercise 6.7 notice how the Object Xref management system helps you keep the system performance high, even though you created new, more complex geometry.

Creating and Working with Xrefs

Earlier in this chapter, I introduced you to the benefits of using the new Xref system in MAX. There are actually two methods of externally referencing files through this new system. One is through Scene Xrefs, and the other is through Object Xrefs. I talk about both here, but primarily focus on how you work best with the Object Xref system.

Scene Xrefs

There are times that, as a digital 3D artist, you need to be either working alone on large projects or collaboratively with others. In either case, you sometimes need to work on the smaller parts of the whole scene. In MAX R2 and earlier, you had to load the whole scene, then hide the objects you didn't wish to have displayed. Even worse, you needed the geometry displayed, but didn't want to accidentally select it while working on your current project. Now with Scene Xrefs, you externally reference the "big picture" of the project while still continuing to work on your specific part. This allows you to use the main scene as a visual reference, including materials, lighting, and animation. When you render, you also note how the component you're working on fits into the current scene design—all without worrying about either altering the main scene or sorting through a long list of objects when selecting by name.

Scene Xrefs basically allow many people to work on the parts of the whole while they reference the entire scene. When you just need general positional information, switch the whole scene into Box display mode while you continue to work in Shaded or Wireframe with your model. When you don't need the scene anymore, just remove it from the Xref list.

Here are the steps to getting a Scene Xref into your current scene:

1. From the File pull-down menu, select Xref Scenes.
2. Click the Add button, and select any .max file as your external reference.
3. MAX loads the file into your current scene and displays it. You can now turn on things like Box display mode and whether you wish to respect such elements as lights or animation.
4. If the scene gets updated, click the Update Now to reload the scene information.

Warning
Updating a Scene Xref takes a while for large scenes. In most cases, it's recommended that you leave Automatic Update off.

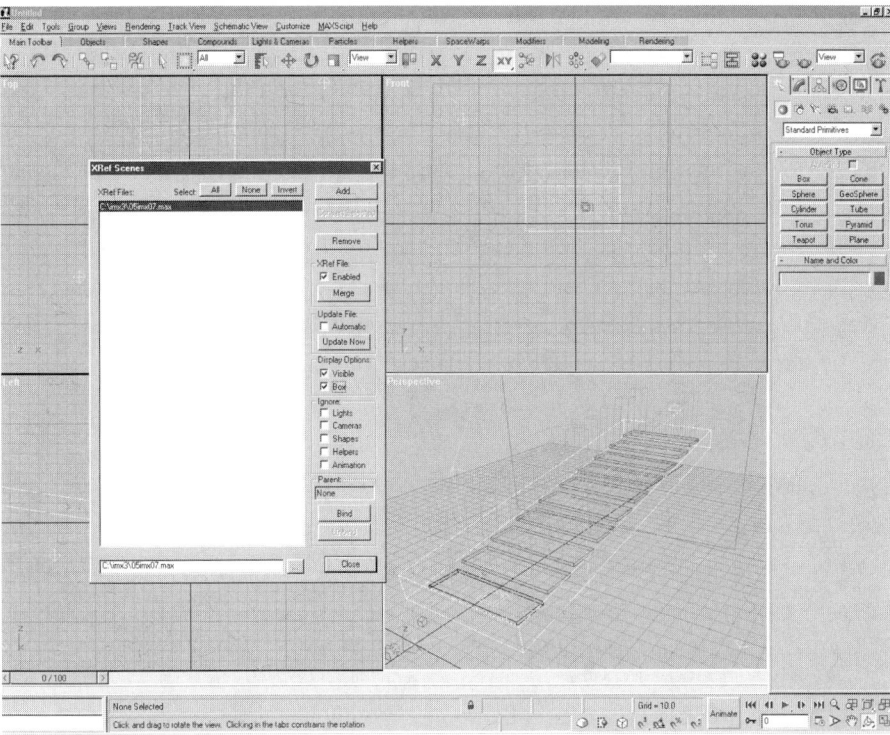

Figure 6.20   A Scene Xref and the Xref Scenes control dialog. With Scene Xrefs, you use the whole design as a reference while you work on the smaller parts. This makes the scene only a reference and won't clutter your Named Selection list or slow down your display if you put it in Box display mode.

Object Xrefs

Much like Scene Xrefs, Object Xrefs allow you to externally reference a .max file. The primary difference is that you usually want Scene Xrefs when working on the whole scene—or a larger part than just one object—and you need to externally reference work created in another file. Object Xrefs work best when you need to insert, and perhaps replace, individual elements into an entire scene.

When thinking about the differences between Object Xrefs and Scene Xrefs, it's best to think of a virtual set design. Scene Xrefs act as a sort of 3D background, like a stage on which your animated actors perform. The key is that you get the whole scene and can't modify any of it. Object Xrefs are best thought of as an object replacement tool. You work with a simple proxy object and at render time, it will automatically replace itself with the more detailed model. Both of these serve as collaborative design tools, allowing multiple people to work on the same project.

Using the stage analogy, in the modeling team, one person models the stage, another works on the actor (character mesh), and another creates the props. The animator begins combining the elements into a finished project before any of the other components is finished. In the animated scene, the animator brings in a Scene Xref of the "stage" and Object Xrefs for the character and props. Using either Automatic Update or the Update Now buttons, the animator gets the latest versions of the models saved by the other members of the team. Object Xrefs appear in the stack like any other primitive. Stack up modifiers on top of an Xref and deform it like any other object. As the source file changes, the modifications carry up through the stack. In the next two exercises, learn how Object Xrefs are created and then managed.

Exercise 6.6 Creating Object Xrefs

1. Open 06imx06.max from the Inside 3D Studio MAX CD-ROM.
2. From the File menu, choose Xref Objects.
3. When the Xref Objects dialog appears, click the Add button and add a file called RacingTire.max.
4. MAX asks which object from RacingTire.max you want to Xref. Select the object LOTUWE1, and click OK.
5. You now see the tire appear in the scene. If you don't, just move the Xref Objects dialog box over a little, and select the wheel.
6. While holding down the Shift key, use the Transform Gizmo to make an instance of the front wheel on the back strut. (You may need to move a little on the X-axis, too.)
7. Use MAX's Mirror command to mirror both the front and rear tires to the other side of the race car. Make them instances.
8. Select any of the tires, then go to the Modify panel.
9. In the Object Name section of the Xref object, click the button next to the LOTUWHE1 name field.
10. In the Object's list, select JXJ_WH1L, then click OK.
11. As Figure 6.21 shows, your cool racing tires are replaced! To switch back, click the button next to the JXJ_WH1L name, and select the LOTUWE1.

With Xrefs, you have the ability to change your objects with just about anything else. If you look at the original RacingTire.max file, you see that the two tires are in different locations within the scene. This doesn't matter to Object Xrefs. They rely on the position of the object in the scene you're currently working in.

Tip

When you replace an object, the internal transforms of the objects are aligned with one another. If you create one object in the Front view and another in the Top or Side view, you may find that objects have different orientations when swapped. Keep this in mind when designing your objects to be swapped. If the objects are already created and you are experiencing this "flipping," align the objects' pivot points, then Reset Xform from the Utility panel.

Figure 6.21 The race car, after having its tires swapped out using Object Xrefs. Using Object Xrefs, you externally reference a .max file that contains a number of different tire objects and cycle through them until you find the ones you like.

In this next exercise, let's say that you already replaced the old columns with the new ones you created in Exercise 6.5. Unfortunately, you found that your interactive performance dropped significantly. This is a case-in-point for using Object Xrefs with their proxy objects. Fortunately the new columns were inserted as Object Xrefs. All you need to do now is specify the proxy setup.

Exercise 6.7 Setting Up Proxies Using Xrefs

1. Open 06max07.max, the updated column scene.
2. Click the Orbit button, and orbit the viewport to test the interactive viewport performance. It should be fairly slow.

3. Select any of the columns, and go to the Modify panel.
4. In the Xref: Viewport Proxy section, turn on the Use Proxy check box option. (Note that the current columns will disappear.)
5. In the File Name section, click the button with the three dotted lines in it—the File Pick button.
6. On the CD, choose SimpleColumn.max. From the Merge dialog, choose Line02. The viewports are now replaced by the simple column.
7. Test the interactive viewport again by using Arc Rotate. You should see a significant improvement.
8. Render the viewport. It should look something like Figure 6.22.

This method is a clever way to easily replace multiple objects in a scene with one incoming object. By working with just one of the columns, you affect all columns in the scene because they are all instances. It's also a timesaver, since the instanced copies let one operation handle all of the objects. When working with complex, repeating geometry, this can be a big time saver. Figure 6.22 shows the completed rendering from Exercise 6.7.

Figure 6.22 The completed rendering from Exercise 6.7. The more complex columns, which are Object Xrefs, are using more simple columns to keep viewport interactivity high. However, the complex columns are still rendered in the final rendering.

>  **Note**
> Object Xrefs also allow you to render the proxy object instead of the original Xref. Use this option when you want to see the location/animation of your Object Xref, but aren't interested in detail for the moment.

NURBS U-Lofts and UV-Lofts

The object created with the loft process described in the previous section is a polygonal mesh. As a result, you must primarily perform Sub-Object level operations on the geometry to edit it. Since MAX R2, you can create similar types of NURBS-based surfaces, called U-Lofts and UV-Lofts. Both surfaces rely on NURBS curves to work properly.

The process for creating U- and U-lofts is similar to creating a Loft object. However the primary difference is that there is no path—only cross sections. Use U- and UV-Lofts to build all sorts of geometry. However for cinematics, you often find yourself using NURBS to create characters and complex organic-looking surfaces.

Cinematics benefit greatly by using NURBS surfaces. The primary reason for this is that the level of complexity in the viewports is far less than what is actually rendered. Consider Figure 6.23. The engine was modeled from a photograph of a real jet engine. The curves are accurate, as well as the cross-sections. However, the viewport model is relatively low detail when compared to the model that is rendered.

For most uses, you need to work with the Surface Approximation values for the surface to render smoothly. There are two options for the way the surfaces approximate, either in the viewports or the renderer. Typically you leave the viewport settings to their defaults. However, the defaults for rendering rarely work well for highly detailed models. Figure 6.24 shows the Surface Approximation section in a NURBS surface object level edit parameters.

Curvature-based approximation works the best for smoothly contoured models. Make the default values for Distance and Angle along the lines of 0.5 and 5, respectively. (Note, this will produce a *much* more detailed mesh at lower settings.) If your rendering time is already long, consider reducing face counts in other areas of your scene before proceeding to increase the detail of your model. For more information on the various settings for the NURBS surfaces within MAX R3, consult the on-line help.

270   Part I   Modeling

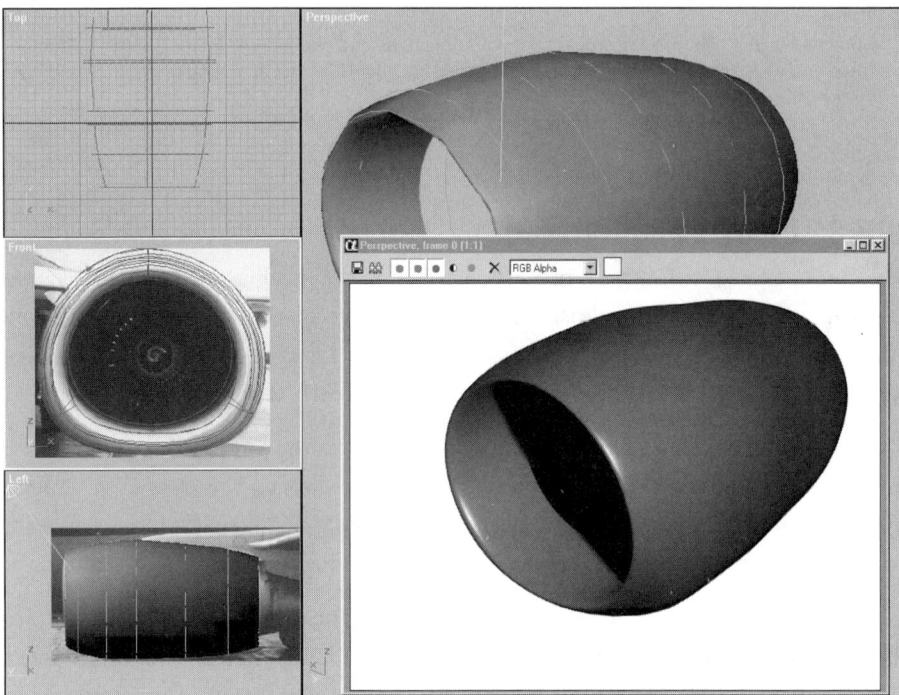

Figure 6.23   A 737 engine, modeled from photographs of an actual engine using NURBS U-Lofts.

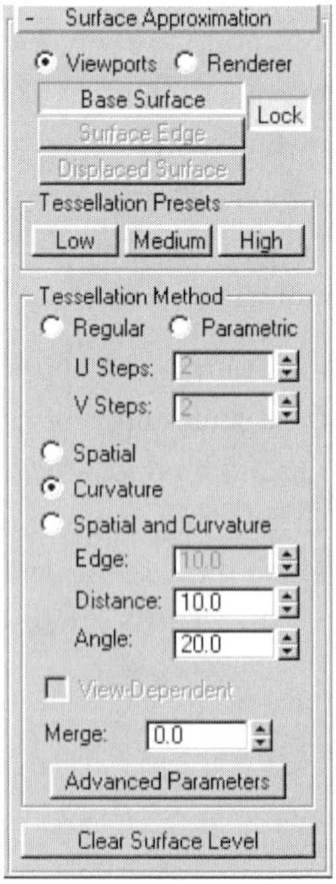

Figure 6.24   The Surface Approximation rollout of a NURBS surface. You often need to set the Rendering values lower to produce a smooth mesh.

Optimizing the Model for Animation

When building high-detail geometry, chances are you are viewing it from different angles, as well as for different lengths of time in your animation. Because high-detail models get a bit unwieldy during complex sequences, try to evaluate what is absolutely critical for the scene to pass without the viewers noticing. For instance, there's no need to model people in a stadium if you're not getting close to every one of them. Even if you are, swap low detail versus high detail as you get closer or farther away.

These aren't really cheats but rather optimizations. There's no need to overload the computer with a highly detailed model if you're viewing only one section of it for a particular shot. Studios don't build entire buildings just so they can shoot one room on one floor. To do such a thing breaks the budget and is just plain impractical. Even though a computer can theoretically handle an entire high-detail model, there's no practical reason to do it. When working with an animated shot, you're going to find yourself taking advantage of some of these optimizations.

Determining Animated Entities

The first step in working with high-detail animated scenes is determining which parts of it are actually animated. For instance, is there an asteroid somewhere in the scene that comes hurtling past the camera? Is there a character that is in the scene for a second or two? Run through the shot to see which parts of it are animated in the camera's view. This will help you figure out which areas of the scene to optimize. Let's take a look at the following possibilities for optimizing your scene:

- Go back to the asteroid example and think about the asteroids themselves. Are they all individual objects? If so, think about using a particle system instead. Not only do you control an asteroid field a bit more easily this way, you also randomize the animation much better. Fewer individual objects means less transform data that MAX has to keep track of, and consequently, less resource usage.

- If you are animating several of the same pieces of geometry, are you using the Scatter compound object? This is a *much* more efficient way to model and animate if your scene contains several of the same object. The Scatter compound object even has the ability to display proxy geometry instead of the actual mesh. This is a *huge* time saver. For more information on the features of the Scatter Object, refer to the MAX R3 on-line documentation.

Note
The Scatter compound object is great for randomly distributing multiple iterations of the same object across the surface of some other object. However, each instance of the scattered object will not have its own transformation matrix. This means it cannot be moved, rotated, or scaled independently of the distribution object.

By figuring out which areas to cut down with respect to objects, notice that both your scene editing process and the rendering times are greatly reduced. The principle of "Less is More" holds true for high-detail scenes and animation.

Removing Nonessential Animated Components

There will be times when you realize that a particular element within your scene can be eliminated—at least as geometry—from the rendered shot. Determining this takes rendering a few previews of your animation or perhaps even a thumbnail 320 × 200 rendering of the shot. Those elements which pass by the camera too quickly for the viewer to notice should be eliminated or replaced by lower detail components.

For instance, many less-experienced animators tend to model every small element of a detailed model. While this is fine for still and close-up shots, there's no need to have some of the more minor elements present for an animated shot. Nor is there a need to have a highly detailed model of a pilot in a fighter ship that's flying quickly past. You can often get away with a small-bitmap representation of the pilot instead.

Camera Angle Optimization

How do you optimize the camera angle? Include those elements in the scene that are *critical* to the shot and eliminate everything else. (Of course, if you're not the director of the piece, then you may not have any control over this.) Some beginning animators worry about every component that *may* be present in a shot rather than what *is* in the shot. By reducing the area that the camera sees and focusing on the subject more, you get rid of elements outside the camera and therefore increase rendering performance.

Warning
Sometimes "out of sight" elements in the scene still influence the rendering. Be careful not to remove objects that cast shadows or are reflected in other visible objects.

Texture Map Considerations

Most animators learn early on that if you can do it with a texture map, don't model it. For animators who do high-resolution film cinematic work, this is often impossible to do. Texture maps tend to fall apart—visually—as you get closer. The only work-around is to model it.

However, as a cinematic animator, take advantage of the fact that the camera, the objects, or both are often moving. Where possible, substitute texture maps for your geometry—especially for models that are far off in the distance or moving rapidly. Again, think of particle systems. Particle systems are capable of emitting texture-mapped flat planes. These planes render very quickly and provide a level of realism that you would normally achieve only through models.

In Practice: Cinematics and High-Detail Modeling

- **Don't sell yourself short on hardware.** Clients don't care that your PC wasn't fast enough to render the project on time. It's up to you to make sure that the hardware you have meets the deadlines you accept.

- **RAM is king.** Before all other components, invest in RAM. A high-end workstation computer without sufficient RAM for cinematic modeling is like a Porsche without gas.

- **Hide geometry when possible.** Even with the most sophisticated hardware, your computer eventually slows down in more detailed scenes. A great way around this is to hide extra geometry. You'll find that MAX is much more responsive that way.

- **Apply MeshSmooth to geometry for smoother surfaces.** While not the same as applying smoothing groups, the MeshSmooth modifier actually adds faces to the edges of your object to produce a smoother model. Rendering times are longer, but often worth it.

- **Use Object Xrefs for repeating or high-detail objects.** Object Xrefs allow you to control the content in the scene just by updating the original object. In the case of the columns, it's much easier to change one rather than all.

- **Use Object Xrefs proxy graphics to control detail levels.** Proxy objects help speed up your interactive viewports while still allowing you to render a more complex version. They're also great for keeping rendering times down when you're just checking location/animation characteristics of the model.

- **Cull down your scene for animations.** Whether reducing geometry count in a model, hiding nonessential objects or liberal use of texture maps, you can always find ways to optimize your animations before rendering.

Chapter 7

Character Modeling

Character modeling is perhaps one of the most challenging types of 3D designs to create, because we, as an audience, expect characters to look and behave a certain way.

If they don't, we notice. Character models are probably the most scrutinized of all model types because a large number of characters are human or based on humans. Getting character models right takes practice. Understanding the nuances of how a wrinkled forehead looks as it's animating, or how the torso deforms as a character runs, are just some of the things you must take into consideration when designing.

3D-digital character creation has actually been around for many years. You see the results in everything from full-length feature films to airline safety videos. Obviously, characters differ based on a number of factors, which you'll read about later in this chapter. You'll then see what MAX has to offer in terms of tools to make digital characters possible.

With MAX R3, Discreet has clearly addressed several of the issues that disturbed character modelers in the past. Additions (such as Surface Tools and the Skin modifier) and enhancements to NURBS and some polygonal tools (such as MeshSmooth) make modeling characters in MAX easier than ever. It's just a matter of knowing where everything is, and where to begin. While this chapter explores character modeling in MAX R3, you'll learn about

- Character modeling basics
- The Skin modifier
- Building characters using NURBS
- Building characters using patches
- Building characters using polygons

The discussion focuses not so much on techniques building character components but rather on the various modeling technologies available in MAX R3, and how you use them to build characters. For a more in-depth discussion on character modeling and animation, look at *Inside 3D Studio MAX 3 Animation*.

Character Modeling Basics

No matter what type of character you build, all characters have the same foundation: basic shapes. By beginning from 2D shapes or 3D primitives, you start from a simple object that eventually turns into a complex character. Where you start on your character, however, depends on your targeted end result.

Types of Characters

As mentioned before, there are many different types of characters created by artists. And it's not just the basic shape—two or four legs, and so on—but how the character is presented to the audience. In other words, how will your audience view the character? Will the character be in a real-time, first-person, shooter game (see Figure 7.1), or will it be a true-to-life character that interacts with real actors in a film? (See Figure 7.2.)

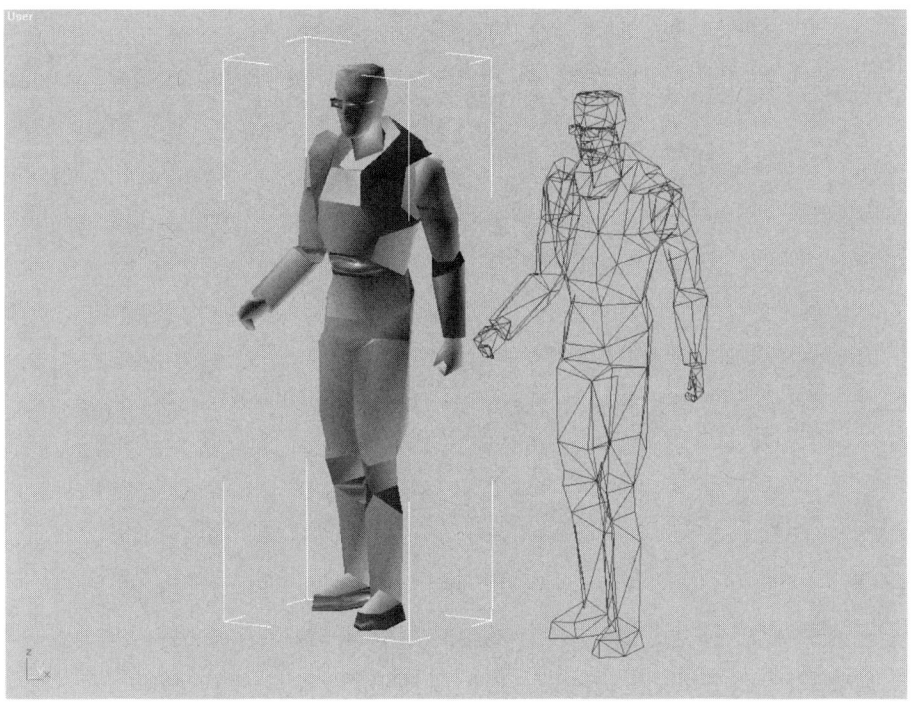

Figure 7.1 A character created for real-time games. Notice that the texture maps make up for the low-polygon count of the model. From Half-Life, Sierra Studios/Valve.

Each type of character has its special modeling considerations. For instance, you typically don't want to build a character for a real-time game using patches, but rather polygons. Conversely, a high-detail polygonal model creates problems for animators who want to realistically deform the character for video or film output.

278   Part I   Modeling

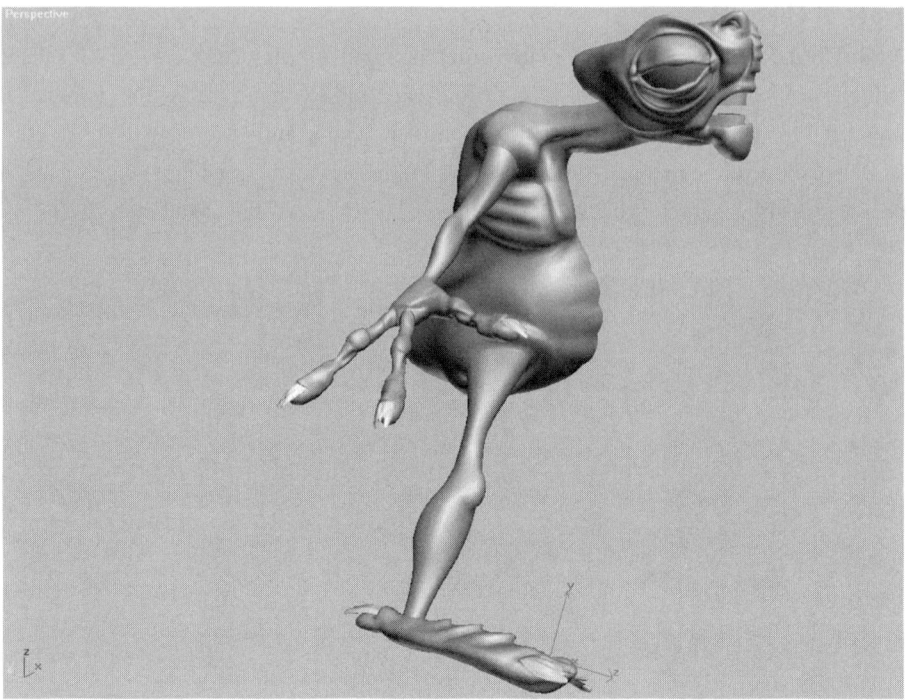

Figure 7.2 Another type of character designed for film/video. This character is made primarily out of patch objects created with the new Surface Tools feature found in MAX R3.

The following are a few guidelines for designing characters digitally:

- **Start with a rough sketch.** Get an idea of what you want by first just drawing it out. It need not be perfect, just a quick idea of what you have in mind. You may go through several revisions on paper before you even open the 3D viewports of MAX. Even if you're not great at hand-drawing, this process helps save time when you actually get to the modeling process.

- **Use your sketch to pick a starting point.** Finding a place to start is often the most difficult part of modeling. For characters, the starting point varies, depending on what you feel comfortable with and the type of character. Use your sketch to help you pick your starting place. There's no hard and fast rule for what part of a character is the best place to start, but it's usually easiest to start with a simple part of a character first and work out from there.

- **Start simple and get more detailed as you go along.** By working with a more simple design, it's easier to quickly make changes. As you feel more comfortable with the simple design, start to add detail to the model by adding more faces to a polygonal object, curves and surfaces to a NURBS object, or patches to a patch object. MAX works well this way, by offering some great tools for automatically adding detail to simple models. Such features as Displacement and MeshSmooth, which use unique, but similar output Subdivision Surface technology, add the detail where you need it to make a character organic looking or smoother.

- **Model with animation in mind.** With only a very few exceptions, most character models eventually come to life through animation. Designing a joined model versus a segmented model makes a difference when it comes to animation. Even if the model is never animated, taking care in how you create things that may animate, such as joints and facial features, goes a long way towards making a character appear more believable. It also goes without saying to pay more attention to the areas of a character that animates than those areas that don't. For example, if all you see most of the time is the character in motion, then focusing on how the body looks while in motion is more critical than the detail of the face.

Common Starting Points

Characters can be built from several starting points. The most common is to begin with the body and model outward. In the case of a character modeled to have a humanoid form, this is the hip and torso area. By starting from the body, you then add on arms, legs, and a head. For many animators, this method proves the easiest. Figure 7.3 shows an example of a character modeled with the body-outward approach. The hips and torso are part of one object. The arms, legs, and head are all separate objects that are added on later. The only major downfall of this method is that when the character animates, the seams where the limbs meet the body become evident. You can, however, work around this problem. For polygonal models, use the Connect compound object to join shapes.

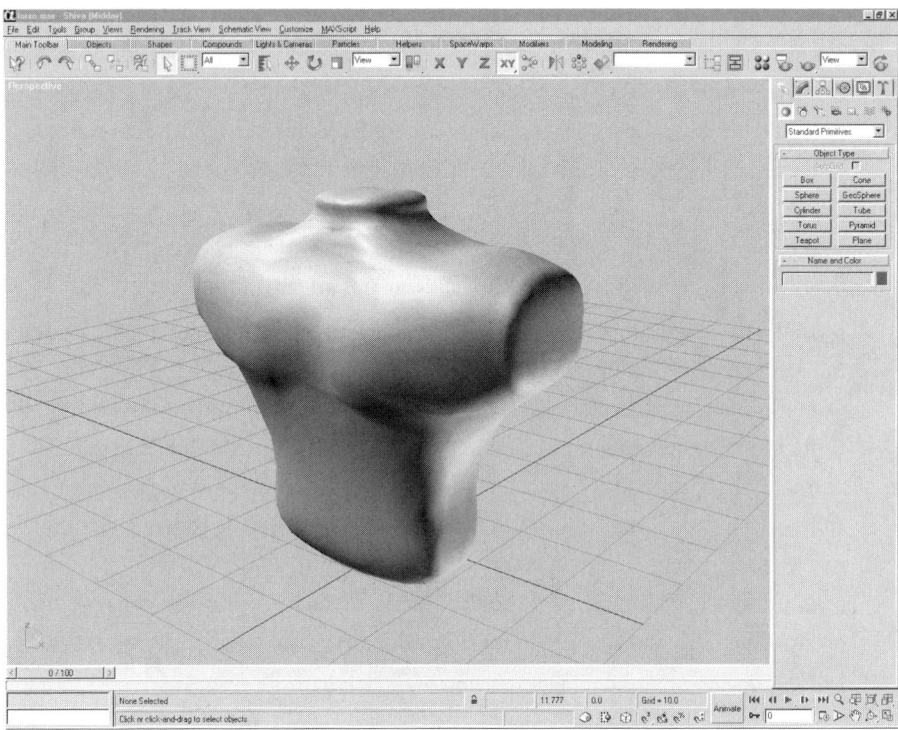

Figure 7.3 Modeling a character using the body-outward method. This torso was created from a box primitive, with MeshSmooth, NURMS, and FFD modifications applied.

Another method for building characters is by breaking the body into an upper and lower half. If your character has an obvious waist, then this type of modeling may work best. Essentially use one or two objects for the top half and a similar method for the bottom half. Then using either Boolean Union or just attaching via Editable Mesh, connect the character at the waistline. Figure 7.4 shows how the top half of a character is built using this approach. This method also animates the best, especially if you hide the waistline through clothing or a belt or something similar.

 Note

Modeling characters using Boolean methods, especially for low-polygon characters, isn't a common practice. Most people prefer to manually weld two objects, rather than have the Boolean object calculate the union between two objects. A Boolean typically produces too many faces for a low-polygon character to be useful because it adds the necessary faces to create the proper junction between two operands.

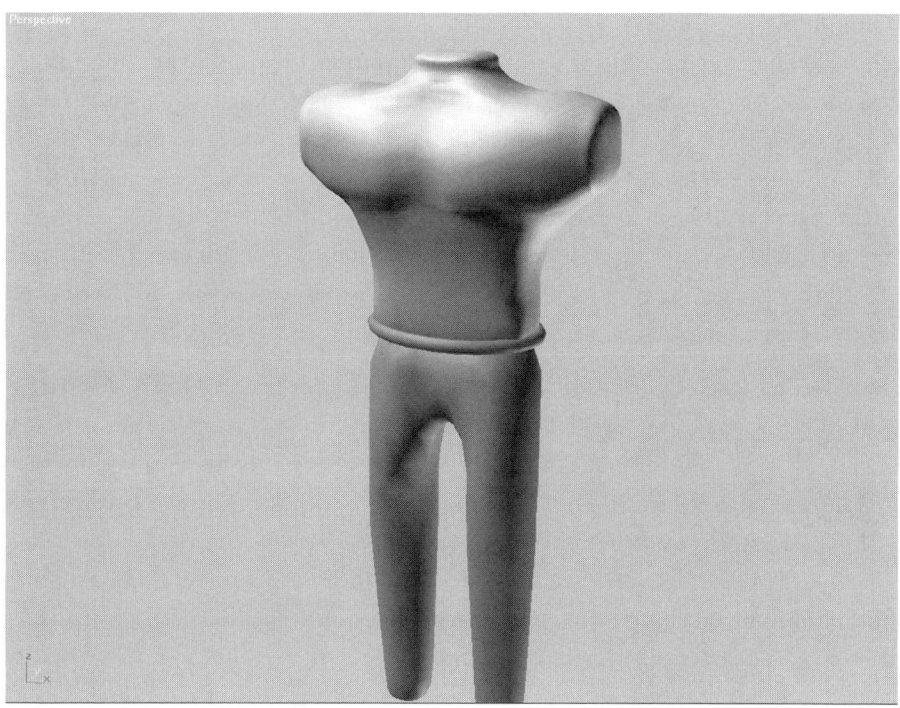

Figure 7.4 A character modeled with separate top and bottom halves. The seam at the waist is easily hidden with some other object, such as a belt.

Now build a character one side at a time—basically splitting it right up the middle. Some animators find this method easier because it means that you simply mirror over the entire model, and you have a complete character. The primary fault with this type of modeling is that it restricts your character to being symmetrical. Of course you can always edit one side of the body afterwards, but that is time consuming, especially if you spent a great deal of time already modeling the first side. The second problem is that because the seam runs right down the middle of the character, it may be noticeable when the character is animated.

Finding which technique works best is a matter of trial and error. After some time, you'll discover which technique is better for the type of character you usually model, and you'll stick with it. And remember, you don't have to build the whole character at one time. Many modelers prefer to model a character piece-by-piece. You can still apply the methods discussed in this section, but just on a smaller scale. For instance, a palm of a hand may be considered the base from which you will build outward to produce the fingers.

Modeling Various Forms

You can create all kinds of characters. Don't limit yourself to people or animals. You can turn a microwave into a character just by giving it a bit a personality. If the folks at beer companies can turn a few bottles into a football team, then anything is possible! The key is the animation component. This chapter focuses mainly on modeling a character, but you're almost always going to want to animate the character in one form or another. If that's the case, then model with animation in mind. How will the character move? Where will it bend? From what angle will it be viewed? Answering these questions helps you determine exactly where you need to concentrate your modeling efforts.

Characters are generally classified as either typical or unusual. A typical character is something that you expect to see animated like a character, such as a person. An unusual character is something that you don't normally think of as possessing a personality, such as that microwave. While we're not focusing on giving either one an animated personality in this chapter, you set a "tone" for your character just through its static appearance. As a matter of fact, characters are often viewed in their "freeze frame" form almost as much as the animated form. How many times have you seen a character from a show that's on a billboard, at a bus stop advertisement, a Web site, or just about anywhere else animation is not possible? The way the characters pose and their facial expressions all play a part in the message conveyed to the audience. As a modeler, you convey all sorts of feelings through your characters just by the way they look on a single frame.

Typical Characters

All of us relate to typical characters, whether human or otherwise. For instance, if you look at a cartoon, the facial features and movements of the characters are usually very human-like. In that sense, we relate to the character. If nothing else, the movements are familiar to us. Creating a typical character is actually the most difficult for this very reason. Reality is one of those elements that is still very difficult for computers to re-create. For the best in realism, you need to use a combination of modeling and mapping. Through effective materials, you create a realistic skin and even folds in the skin through bump mapping. Often there isn't a need to model every component.

Unusual Characters

Unusual characters represent something that we wouldn't normally think of as being animated or having a personality. Although they're equally challenging to bring to life, you aren't limited to what the audience "expects" to see because your model is not based on real life—necessarily. Think of a stapler; you expect it to animate the way it works. A stapler gets pushed down from the top while the base remains flat on the table. Naturally you expect the stapler to almost walk like a kangaroo or rabbit by hopping around.

When modeling these types of characters, take into account how you build their components. For instance, take a look at Figure 7.5. If you wanted to animate the stapler, you probably want it opening and closing much like the mouth of an alligator. Therefore you make sure that you modeled the components in such a way that when the stapler opened and closed, both the model and the movement looked correct. We all know what a stapler looks like and even how it operates. However, no one knows how it would "live" because it's not possible—except in the digital world. From a modeling standpoint, it's just a matter of building the stapler from a real-world prop. From there, all you need to do is to make the model animate correctly by placing pivot points in the proper location.

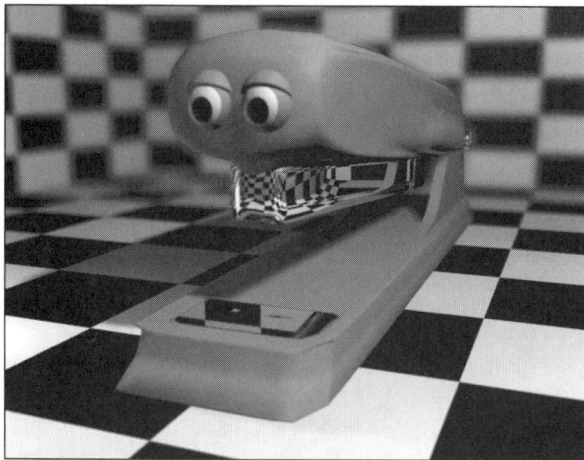

Figure 7.5 A polygonal stapler character modeled using polygons and the MeshSmooth modifier.

Let's suppose you wanted to have the "head" of the stapler twist and turn so that it's less like a hard plastic and more like a clay stapler. You need to add enough detail so that the stapler bends properly. Figure 7.6 shows how this is done via the MeshSmooth modifier.

Figure 7.6 The stapler with a more "clay-like" composition. This makes objects like a stapler appear more organic. In order for the stapler to bend realistically, however, there must be enough detail in the model where it bends the most.

Character Modeling with NURBS

A very common approach to modeling high-detail characters is using NURBS. NURBS models work well because they are smooth and organic without much detail in the geometry—something that is a major limitation for polygonal models. This is easily demonstrated with a sphere primitive. Looking at Figure 7.7, you see that the head on the left, which is made of polygons, must be much higher detail to achieve the same level of smoothness of the NURBS head on the right.

NURBS modeling provides you with several options for building character geometry. From the head all the way down to individual toes, NURBS models work best. MAX R3 gives you several options for creating your characters. In the coming sections you learn how to use the various modeling technologies to construct different components of a character.

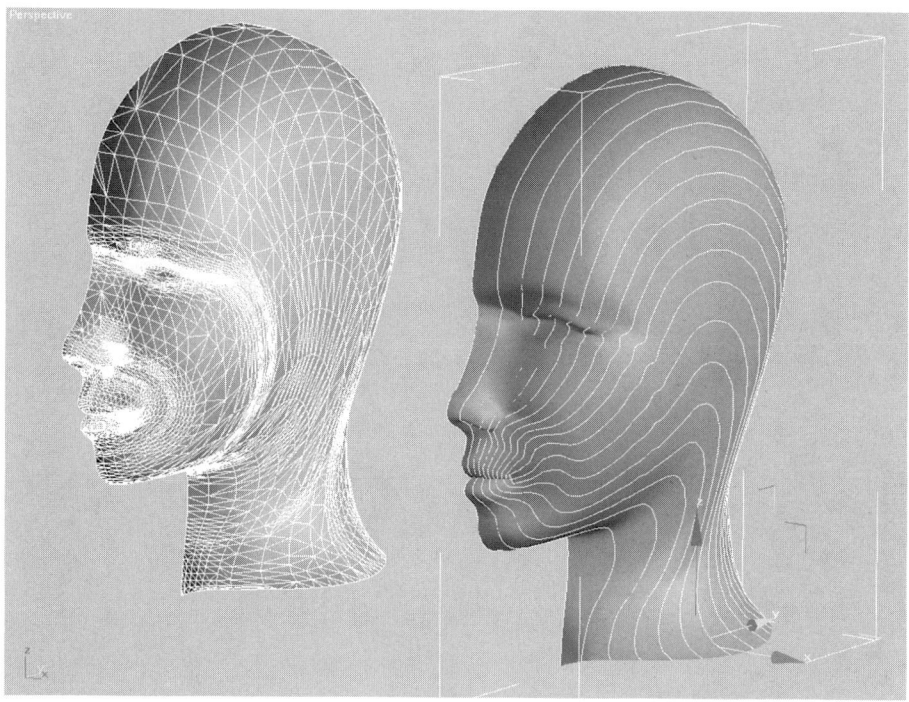

Figure 7.7 A simple example of polygonal geometry versus NURBS U-Loft. Notice how much more detailed the polygonal head is compared to the NURBS model.

U/UV-Lofts and Ruled Surfaces

NURBS lofts (U and UV) are created by "draping" a surface over a series of NURBS curves. The surface itself is interpolated across several curves in order to produce a "flowing" look. This means that you never see where the cross sections exist. They act more as framework to which the surface loosely adheres.

NURBS lofts work best when trying to create a complex shape from a series of similarly shaped curves; an arm, for instance. The arm is essentially a circular shape created down a long axis. Figure 7.8 shows an arm created with U-Lofts. You build incredibly complex surfaces this way. The primary limitation is that the loft cannot split. This means that when you get to the end of the arm, you need to stop at the palm, then join the fingers.

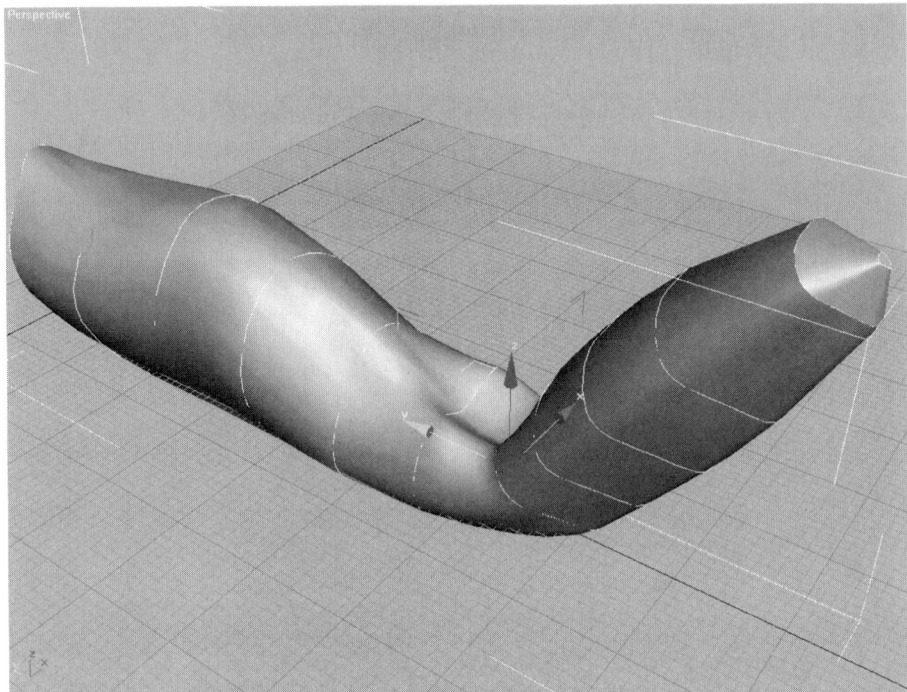

Figure 7.8 An arm created from a series of NURBS curves used together to form a U-Loft surface. You'll create this arm in a later exercise.

Building Cross-Sections

In order for the example in Figure 7.8 to work properly, you need to build cross sections to make up the overall shape of the arm. This is best achieved by using one shape, and then copying it multiple times until you have enough cross sections to build the object you want. With MAX R3, there's no need to convert curves into surfaces anymore. When you begin the creation of a NURBS surface from a series of curves, MAX automatically converts it into a NURBS surface. From there, you use the U-Loft command to loft across the cross sections to create the object.

In the next exercise, you create cross sections from a simple NURBS curve. Using the processes described in this section, you create the upper arm of a character.

Exercise 7.1.1 Creating an Arm Using Cross Sections

1. Open 07imx01.max from the CD-ROM. This scene consists of one NURBS curve that serves as the starting point for your cross sections.

2. Select the Curve in the Left viewport, then right-click to select Move.

3. While holding down the Shift key on your keyboard, select the curve and drag about 100 units to the right, using the X-axis lock on the Transform Gizmo (about the equivalent to one grid square). Take note of the numeric display in the status area to see exactly how far you're moving the object.

4. When the Clone Options dialog appears, set the number of clones to 5. Make sure Copy is the clone type selected, and click OK.

5. Select the four inner curves, then right-click to choose Scale. By default, MAX wants to use the selection center to scale. Click the Selection Center button in the main toolbar, and select the Pivot Point Center button. Scale the middle curves so that they are about 150% larger than the end curves. You're creating the bicep/tricep shape. This works best in the Left viewport. In the Attach Multiple dialog, select all the curves, then click OK.

NEW TO R3 MAX R3 no longer requires you to first attach NURBS curves or convert them to a surface prior to creating a U-Loft. Simply click the U-Loft button and start lofting!

6. Click on the NURBS Creation Toolbox button if the dialog isn't already on the screen.

7. Click the U-Loft button, then click each one of the cross sections, in order, from one end to the other. (If the normals are flipped, select the Flip Normals check box in the Modify panel.)

8. You now have a surfaced arm. However, you need to shape the muscles by editing control points. Switch to Sub-Object at the Point selection level by either right-clicking on the NURBS object, and selecting Point Level or by pressing Alt-Shift-P. (Note that your plug-in keyboard shortcut toggle must be on for the keyboard alternates to work.)

9. Using the Move command, select and move various points on the upper arm until you have something that looks like Figure 7.9.

10. Render the upper arm object, and save the file.

Using the U-Loft surfaces, you easily create smooth, contoured objects through the use of cross sections. While a similar result is generated using the polygonal Loft Object, the NURBS equivalent requires less geometric detail, and it's much easier to animate.

288   Part I   Modeling

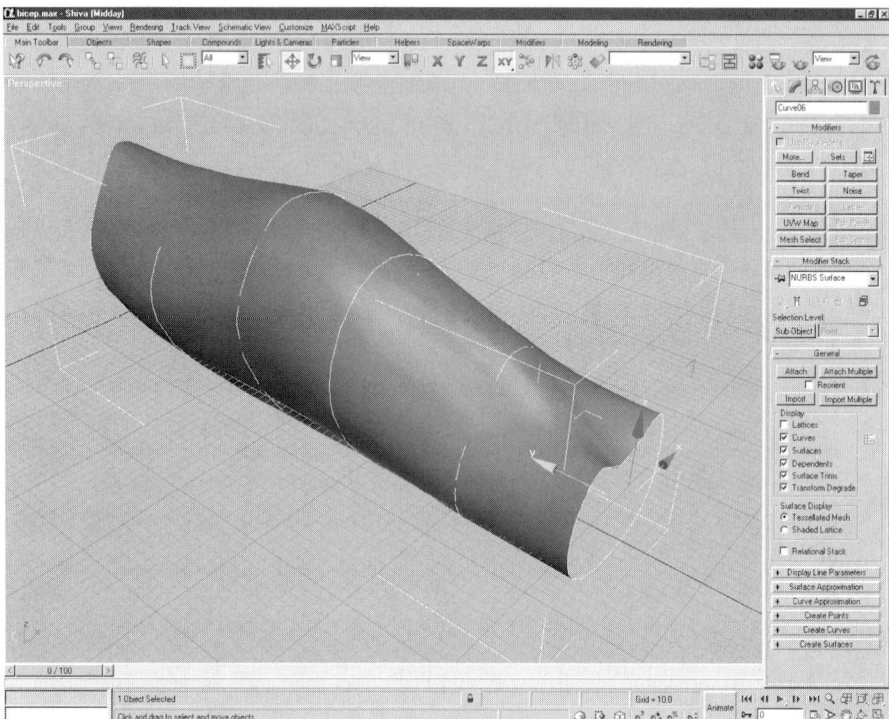

Figure 7.9   The completed result from Exercise 7.1. The upper arm was created using cross-sectional NURBS curves and a U-Loft surface.

Ruled Surfaces

Ruled surfaces work a bit differently from NURBS lofts. Essentially, a ruled surface is drawn by connecting two curves. Rather than selecting multiple curves like a Loft surface, a Ruled surface only works by picking two curves. The result is that, while two Ruled surfaces can be adjacent to each other, there is no blending, so an obvious seam exists. The resultant complete surface looks much more like a series of sections rather than one continuous surface. For smooth flowing surfaces, a Ruled surface is not as ideal as a U-Loft surface. (See Figure 7.10.) However, you used Ruled surfaces for items such as clothes or where two curves define a surface. In Figure 7.11 you see how a cape-like object is easily built using a Ruled surface from two curves.

The steps for creating a ruled surface are as follows:

1. Create two NURBS curve objects—either CV or Point.
2. Use the Attach button on the Modify panel to attach one of the curves to the other.
3. Click the Ruled Surface button in the NURBS toolbox.
4. Select the first curve, then pick the second. Again, if the normals are flipped, simply select the Flip Normals check box to reverse them.

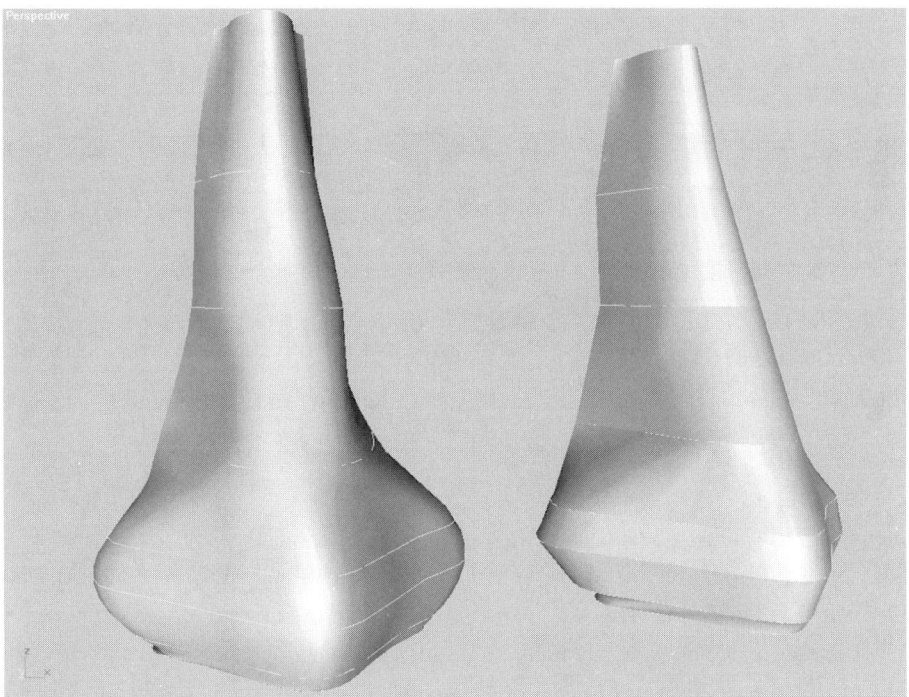

Figure 7.10 A nose created on the left using NURBS Loft surfaces and NURBS Ruled surfaces on the right. The difference between the two is easy to distinguish. A Loft surface uses multiple curves to build the contour of the surface, whereas a ruled surface only uses two curves. The nose of the left contains one surface, and the nose on the right contains seven.

Figure 7.11 A simple cape object created from two NURBS curves and a Ruled surface.

Blend Surfaces

Blend surfaces allow you to join two existing surfaces together by connecting their adjacent curves. The Blend surface, much like a Loft or Ruled surface, is dependent—meaning that it relies on the position and orientation of the two curves used to create it. The surface created also has no apparent seams, unlike a U-Loft or ruled surface. This means that the connection of the two surfaces is not only physical, but is also visually apparent by creating a new surface in your rendering, as well. Because the Blend is dependent, if you alter the two surfaces in any way, the Blend updates.

You use Blend surfaces all over a character. Any time you need to connect two surfaces together but cannot via a U-Loft or Ruled surface, use Blend surface to connect them. For instance, in Figure 7.12, you use Blend to connect the forearm and upper arm. Contained within the Blend are parameters for adjusting the tension between the two surfaces. This allows you to adjust the overall "tightness" of the Blend.

In the Exercise 7.1.2, return to the arm example. Using the Blend surface, connect the two arm components. From there, adjust the tension of the Blend to create a better-looking elbow joint.

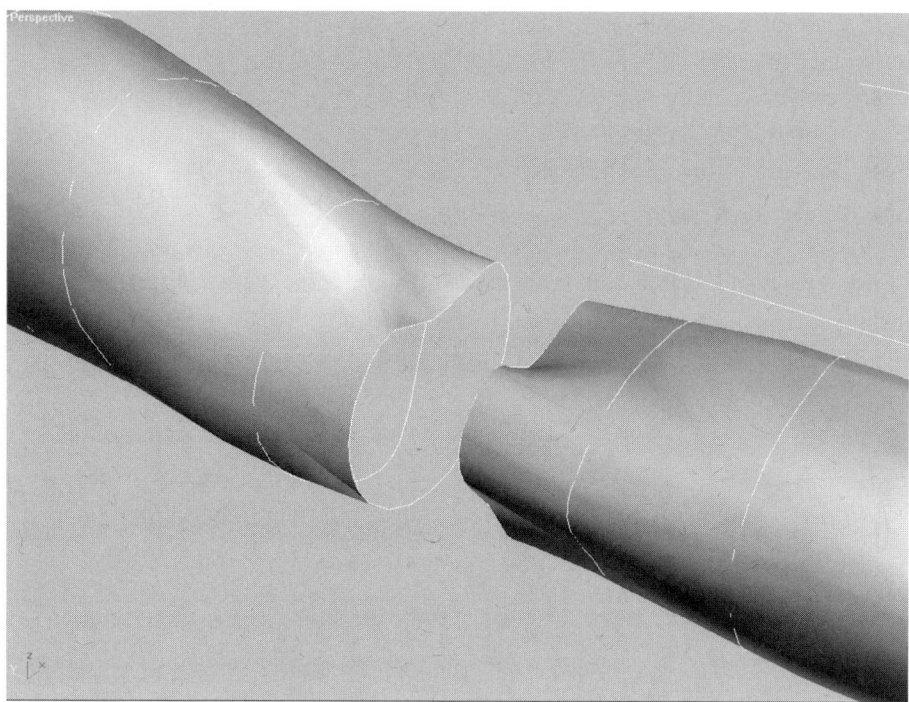

Figure 7.12 These two arm segments represent an ideal candidate for using the Blend surface. Not only are they separate surfaces, but they also help "shape" the Blend surface through their own contours.

Exercise 7.1.2   Creating an Elbow with Blend

1. Open 07max02.max from the CD-ROM.
2. Click the upper-arm object, go to the Modify panel, then choose Attach. Click the forearm object. This attaches the two together. The forearm switches colors to the upper-arm's color.
3. Click the NURBS Creation Toolbox button to activate the dialog if it isn't already on the screen.
4. Click the Create Blend Surface button and move your cursor over the last cross-section curve of the upper arm (closest to the forearm). It should turn blue.
5. While the surface is orange and the end curve is blue, click and drag your cursor to the first curve of the forearm (closest to the upper arm), and when that surface turns orange and the curve turns blue, release the mouse button. A surface appears now.
6. Click the Sub-Object button, and set to the Surface selection level.

7. Click the new Blend surface that you just created. Switch to Wireframe mode if you're having trouble selecting the surface.
8. Scroll down to the bottom of the Modify panel until you see the values for Tension 1 and Tension 2.
9. Set Tension 1 to 1.3 and Tension 2 to 0.9.
10. Render the scene.

By using the Blend surface, you create a smooth and flexible transition surface between the upper arm and forearm. The end result is something that animates very well—and you don't need to worry about it staying connected. It deforms as necessary, remaining connected to the two arm components. The final result is shown in Figure 7.13.

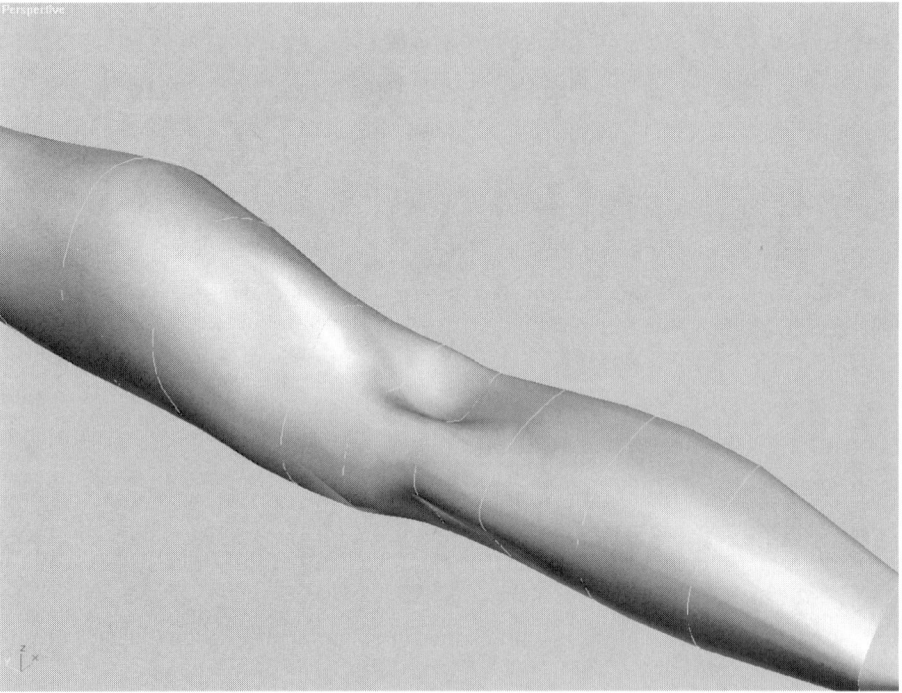

Figure 7.13 The arm pieces sewn together through the use of the Blend object. Notice how the surface properly deforms to create the divot at the elbow joint.

Blend surfaces are used in other ways, as well—for instance, when you connect the arm to a torso. Blends also work well when you connect fingers to a palm. Simply trim away the areas on the palm and fingers that you want to eliminate and then connect using the Blend command.

As with any dependent surface, both Blend and Ruled surfaces can be made independent. This disassociates the Blend or Ruled surface from the other two surfaces or curves that originally created it.

Character Modeling with Patches

Before NURBS modeling was available within MAX, the only way to get smooth, complex surfaces without too much polygonal detail was via the patch surface. Patches come from a similar background as NURBS, and they behave much like a NURBS surface. However, NURBS surfaces evolved, within MAX, to be much more complex than patches. In MAX R3 you now use either patch primitives or the Surface Tools feature to create your patch objects. While patches require a somewhat different modeling-thought process, with the addition of Surface Tools, there are quite a few similarities.

Building patches in MAX is done through

- Patch surfaces
- Primitives
- Surface tools

Primitives give you the ability to start with a more complex shape from which to build. For instance, building an arm from a patch cylinder is much easier than building from a series of Quad Patch objects.

Warning

While it is possible to turn any type of nonprimitive geometry into a patch surface using Edit Patch, this technique is highly inadvisable. Doing so creates an enormous amount of control points that are extremely difficult to edit. The best way to build patches is from patch surfaces, from cross sections, or by converting a primitive into an Editable Patch object.

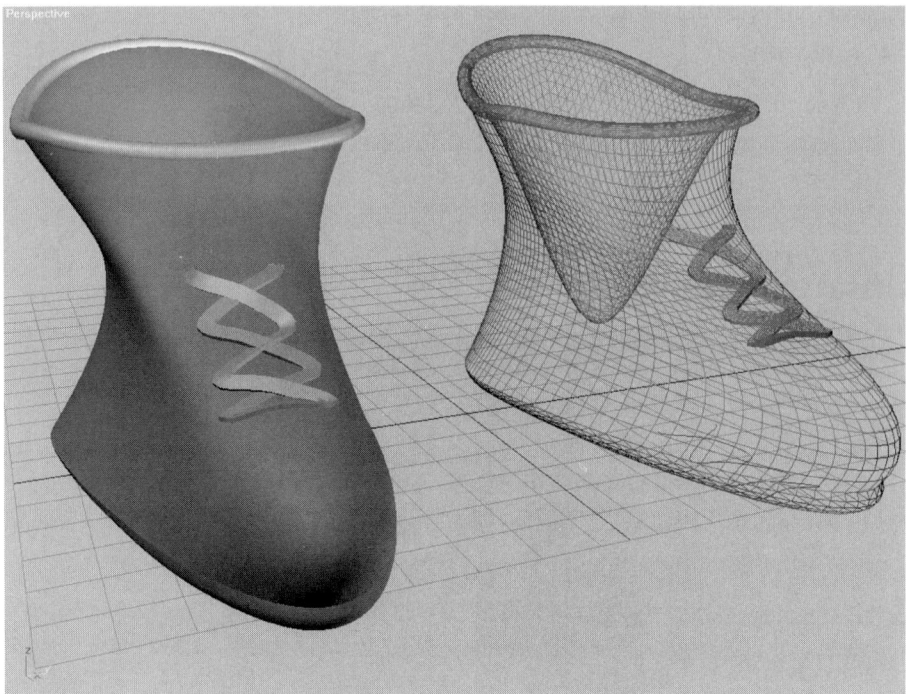

Figure 7.14 A simple ski boot created from a Cylinder primitive. The cylinder was converted into an Editable Patch object, which allows you to manipulate patches, vertices, or edges just like an Editable Mesh object does for polygons.

Quad Versus Tri

If you decide to use patch surfaces as your foundation for patches, you have two choices: *Quad* or *Tri* Patches. Both types of patches initially create the same geometry. Looking at Figure 7.15, you see what happens when you create a Quad or Tri Patch: They look very similar. The visual difference is that the Tri Patch is made up of triangles, whereas the Quad Patch is made up of four-sided shapes. The main geometric difference between using either one is what happens when you add to an existing patch. When you add a Quad Patch, you add another square-like patch. When you add a Tri Patch, you add a three-sided Patch object—that is, a patch that comes to a point. When adding massive sections to an overall object, use Quad Patches. When adding in a patch to cover a small area for detail, use a Tri Patch. The results of using Add Tri and Add Quad are shown in Figure 7.16.

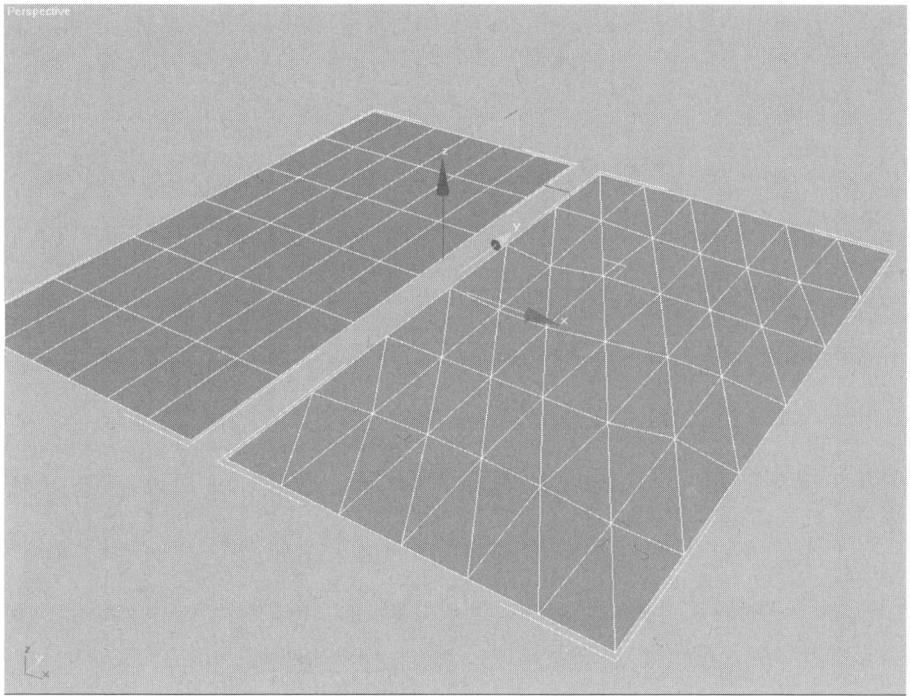

Figure 7.15 A Quad Patch (left) and a Tri Patch (right). Note that the base objects are essentially the same shape.

 Note

Add either type of patch to existing Quad and Tri Patches. This means that if you prefer to use Quad Patches most of the time, you can always add a Tri Patch where you need it.

Choosing Quad Patches

Quad Patches are best for large sections of geometry. When building the cheeks of a face or a forehead, you can usually get away with Quad Patches. As a matter of fact, it's better to start with Quad Patches, and *add* Tri Patches where you need them. This is primarily due to what happens when you use a patch as a flat surface. Quad Patches have less geometric detail information to bend with and produce more faces in order to bend properly. Therefore, if your surface requires little curvature, stick with Quad Patches. They work better when it comes to editing.

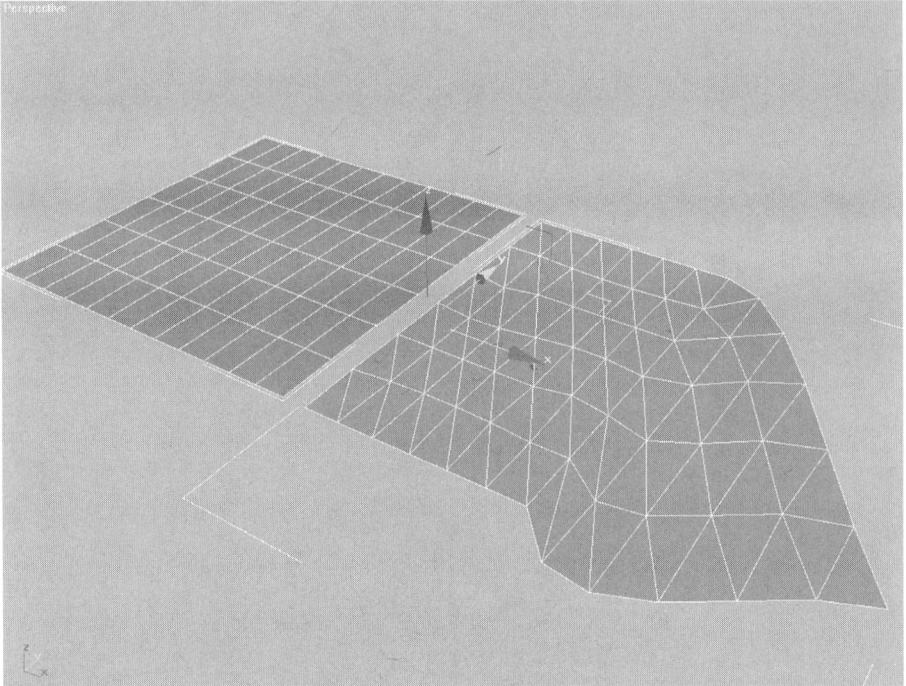

Figure 7.16 The same patches shown in figure 7.15 but with added edges. The Quad Patch has another Quad Patch added to it (left), and the Tri Patch has another Tri Patch Added to it (right). The Quad Patch always produces a quadrilateral patch, and a Tri Patch always produces a trilateral patch.

Choosing Tri Patches

Tri Patches already contain enough built-in detail information to bend more efficiently. Therefore, flatter surfaces should use Quad Patches, and more intricate surfaces should rely on Tri Patches.

Building in Sections

Because the patch objects limit you to either building with flat surfaces or primitives, you often need to build in small sections, one at a time. This also allows you to focus in on detailed areas much more easily because there's less "extraneous" geometry with which to deal. With this method, however, you must eventually put the pieces together.

Stitching Via Weld Operations

Combine pieces of your patches with the Weld operation. This process of welding vertices together is sometimes called *stitching*. When you weld vertices together, the seam between two patches virtually disappears from the model. By combining two vertices into one, you not only join the surfaces, you also reduce the number of Bézier handles that are present. In a way, this helps to better control the geometry. Figure 7.17 shows what happens when the vertices along the edges of one patch are welded to an adjoining patch.

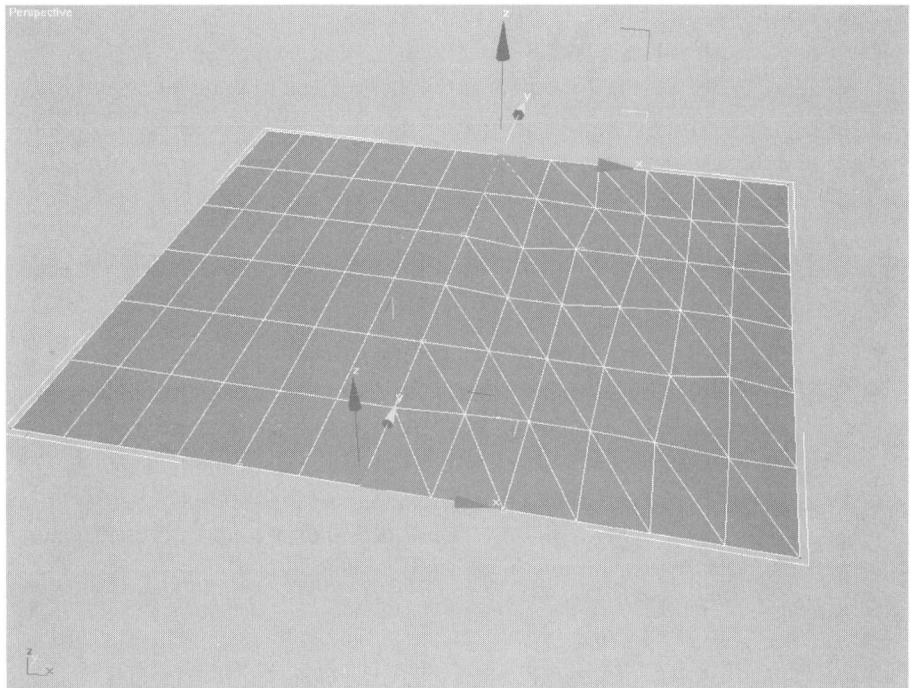

Figure 7.17 The result of two patches with adjoining vertices welded together. Note that one patch is a Quad Patch (left) and the other is a Tri Patch (right).

Note

When you add a Tri or Quad Patch to an edge of an existing patch, there's no need to weld vertices because MAX does this automatically. The main difference is that Add Tri and Quad just adds a default patch. Manually welding vertices of patches together allows you to connect patches that you have already shaped and formed for the character.

NEW TO R3   In Exercise 7.2, we explore how to weld two independent Patch objects together using the Edit Patch modifier. The objects started out from two cylinder primitives and were then collapsed to Editable Patch objects. With MAX R3, when you collapse to a patch, you now get a fully editable patch surface, much like Editable Mesh or Editable NURBS. To edit the vertices or edges of a patch, you need to apply an Edit Patch modifier.

Exercise 7.2 Stitching Two Patches Together

1. Open 07max03.max from the CD-ROM. This scene contains two independent patch objects.
2. Select the larger (beige) patch, and go to the Modify Panel.
3. Click the Attach button, and select the other patch in the current viewport. The attached patch changes to the color of the original patch. Click the Attach button to turn Attach mode off.
4. Click the Patch selection level button. From the Edit menu, choose Region Window, or depress the Window Selection button next to the status area.
5. In the Top or Front viewport, use the Window Selection mode to draw a window around the "gap" area that exists between the two patches. (Make sure you select the ends of the patches that are facing each other.)
6. The end-cap patches are highlighted in red. Press the Delete key to remove the selected patches.
7. Using the same window selection method, select either complete patch.
8. Move the selected patch closer to the other patch, so that they almost touch.
9. Switch to the Vertex Sub-Object selection level by clicking the Vertex button in the Modify panel, and select all of the vertices on the ends that you just moved closer to each other.
10. In the Topology section of the Geometry rollout, set the Weld Threshold value to 2.0, and then click the Weld button. The vertices should connect. If they do not, raise the Weld Threshold value, and click Weld. Repeat until they do.
11. Render the Perspective viewport, then save the file.

This is a simple example of how to weld patches together, but it does show that the patches can be joined to eliminate the seam. Unlike drawing a Blend surface between two existing NURBS surfaces, you must physically join patches together via the Weld command. The final rendering of Exercise 7.2 is shown in Figure 7.18.

Using Surface Tools to Build Characters

Constructing characters using patches is now significantly easier, thanks to the Surface Tools modifiers in R3. With Surface Tools, you construct the framework for the patches, and then it wraps a patch around that framework. There are some rules to doing this, but all-in-all, you may find that constructing characters with Surface Tools and patches is your new favorite way.

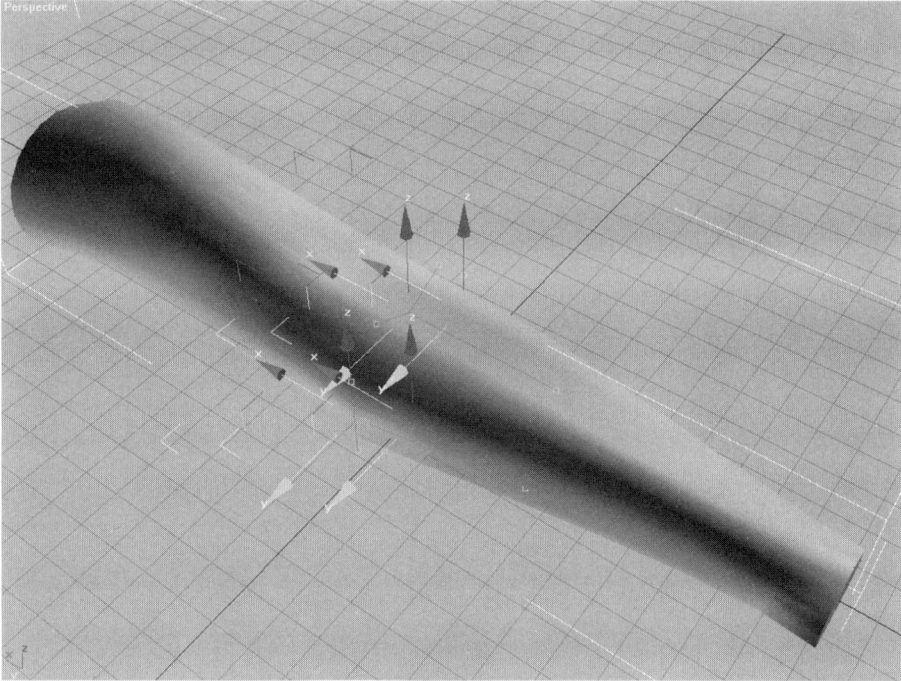

Figure 7.18 The resultant object from Exercise 7.2. This figure shows how two independent patches are welded together, not only to join them but also to remove the seams.

This section talks about the two modifiers that make up Surface Tools—the Surface modifier and the Cross Section modifier. Take a look at the Surface modifier first because you probably use that one more frequently. Later on, look at how to use the Cross Section modifier as a prep tool for the Surface modifier.

Creating Characters with the Surface Modifier

Remember the discussion on Quad Patches and Tri Patches? The Surface Tools feature relies on patch technology to do its magic. Rather than building surfaces or converting primitives, you draw spline shapes that define the edges of either a Quad or a Tri Patch object. This is a much more flexible way to model patches, once you get the hang of it. As mentioned before, though, there are some rules:

- The shapes must be made out of no more than three or four vertices.
- Vertices don't have to be welded, but need to be coincident if they define an intersection.

While these rules may sound a little restrictive at first, they are far from it. As a matter of fact, some of the best character modeling work to come from MAX to date has been using Surface Tools. Why? Mainly because you get the benefit of working with simple objects like splines to design your models, but you get the smoothness of NURBS when you apply the Surface Modifier to it.

Figure 7.19 contains a the framework of a hand. The version on the left is the spline framework. The one on the right is the patch surface generated by applying the Surface modifier to the framework. See how it works? The arm is comprised of several three- and four-point sections, from which the Surface modifier is able to create a patch surface. By connecting all the patches together, you produce the arm on the right. A closer look at the fingertip in Figure 7.20 reveals that the points of the fingertip are nothing more than two spline curves with coincident vertices. The fingertips themselves are tri patches, and the finger is a series of quad patches.

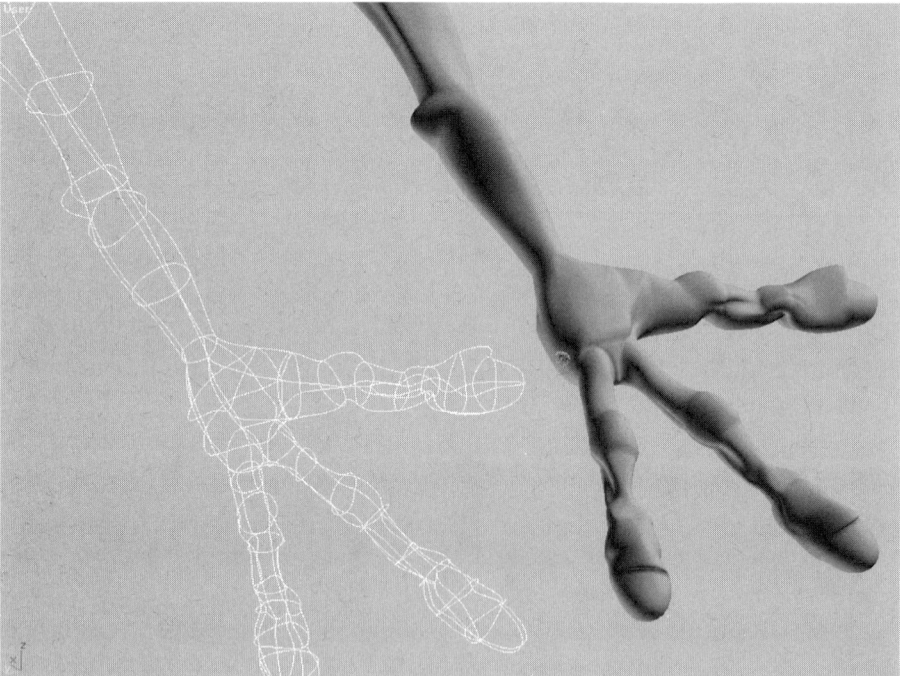

Figure 7.19 A patch hand created by building the framework (left), and then applying the Surface modifier (right). The created surface consists of both Quad and Tri Patches, automatically created by the Surface modifier.

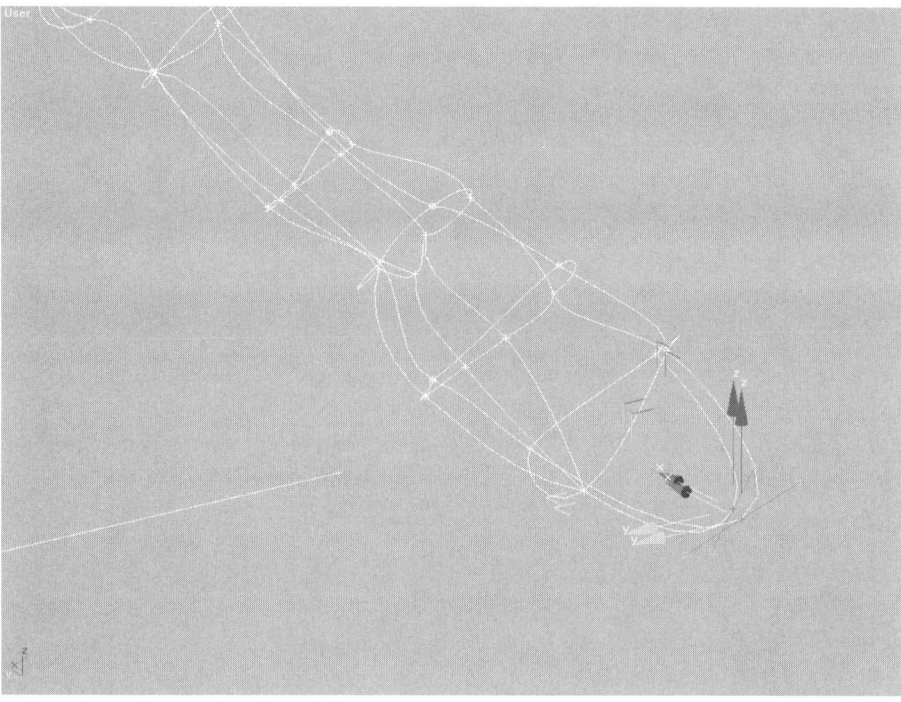

Figure 7.20 Upon closer inspection of the fingertip, notice that although the vertices aren't welded, they still produce a surface. The Surface modifier automatically treats vertices as welded if they lie within a specified threshold distance from each other.

Note
The rule about coincident vertices applies to how the Surface modifier works. When two vertices lie within a certain distance from each other, the Surface modifier treats them as welded, even though they remain separate. This helps when creating shape objects that you plan to use as framework pieces for a patch surface, and the patch surface is created with the Surface modifier.

A good way to see how the Surface modifier works is to play with it a bit. In this next exercise, apply the Surface modifier to a spline object that consists of several independent spline shapes, which are treated as welded when you apply the Surface modifier.

Exercise 7.3   Using the Surface Modifier

1. Open 07imx04.max from the CD-ROM.
2. Select the green spline object, then go to the Modify panel.
3. Click the More button, and select the Surface modifier. A surface is now applied to the patch.

4. Set the Threshold to 0.1
5. Select the Remove Interior Patches option.
6. Set the Patch Topology Steps to 5.
7. Use the Modifier Stack pop-down list to choose the Editable Spline object.
8. Click on the Vertex selection button.
9. Select any of the vertex points, and use the Transform Gizmo to move it away from the other vertices.
10. Click and hold down the Show End Result button. Some of the patches may disappear, due to the fact that some of the vertices are no longer within the set threshold of the Surface modifier.
11. Click the Undo button to return the patch to its previous state.
12. Render the viewport. The rendering looks decent, but you can do better. To get a better quality rendering, just increase the Patch Topology Steps amount.
13. Save your work.

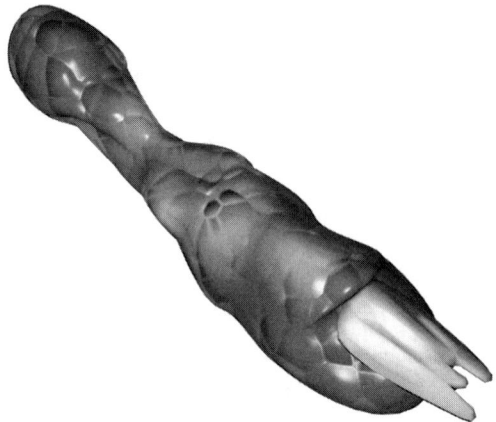

Figure 7.21 The completed rendering from Exercise 7.4. The patch model is created using the new Surface modifier from the surface tools feature in MAX R3.

 Tip

When your patches aren't capped properly, it's usually because you have a series of splines that exceed the three- or four-vertex limit needed to create a patch surface. If that's the case, simply draw a line, using the Editable Spline Create Line feature, between two of the vertices in question that results in the creation of a three- or four-sided spline. In other words, a six-point polygon could become two four-point polygons just by drawing a line between two opposing vertices.

Using the Cross Section Modifier for Characters

The intent of the Cross Section modifier is to prep your model for the application of the Surface modifier. Cross Section connects a series of spline shapes in a spline object to produce a framework lattice that the Surface modifier uses.

It also has some rules that you must adhere to so that it works properly.

- All splines must reside within the same spline object.
- The spline shapes connect in the order in which they were attached to the spline object.
- While you don't need the same number of vertices in each cross section, it's a good rule of thumb because Cross Section guesses which vertex gets connected to the orphaned vertex.

The Cross Section modifier contains four useful settings to control how the cross sections connect with splines. The four settings control what types of vertices are created at each intersection. Those choices match the exact same set of choices as those for a regular vertex:

- Corner
- Smooth
- Bézier
- Bézier Corner

Typically, all the vertex types (with the exception of Linear) give you the same *looking* results. Although they all create different types of vertex points, Smooth, Bézier, and Bézier Corner offer the same visual result, due to the way the Cross Section modifier creates the cross sections.

Polygonal Character Modeling

In the past, character modelers mainly relied on patches and polygons to develop their models in MAX. As a result, quite a few tools were designed to make character modeling both easier and more powerful in MAX R3. A new and improved Editable Mesh object is a prime example. In addition to better polygonal modeling features in R3, Editable Mesh also sports a handy, new right-click menu system. In addition, further enhancements made to the MeshSmooth modifier make designing characters even easier.

With all of these improvements, you probably wonder why polygonal modeling isn't the best way to model characters. After all, if you're already familiar with creating and manipulating polygons, why reinvent the wheel? It all boils down to how much detail you need on your model. If you're looking for high-resolution, high-detail models, try to work with NURBS as much as possible. And with the new features introduced for R3 from Surface tools and patches, you have yet another way to model characters. NURBS and patch models are a convenient way to model complex, organic surfaces. However, if you want to build a character that either requires less detail or has components on it that aren't NURBS or patch-friendly (such as hard edges), polygonal models probably work best.

Using Editable Mesh and MeshSmooth

The Editable Mesh object allows you to work on just about any piece of geometry as a polygonal object. You can even convert NURBS and patch surfaces to an Editable Mesh. The primary benefit of using Editable Mesh is that it requires less memory than a parametric object with the Edit Mesh modifier applied, and it's probably the most natural way to model with polygonal objects. When this object is used in combination with MeshSmooth, the results are quite amazing.

In the Exercise 7.4 series, we use Editable Mesh and MeshSmooth to create the right half of a character's torso. Not only do you model the torso, but you also organize it so you can properly edit the model later when you want to deform sections of the mesh.

Exercise 7.4.1 Creating a Torso with Editable Mesh

1. Reset MAX. Create a box primitive in the Top or Perspective viewport with the dimensions of Length: 15, Width: 20, and Height: 33. Give the box two height segments, as well.
2. Right-click on the Object, and select Convert to Editable Mesh.
3. Click the Vertex selection button, then select the middle row of vertices in the Front viewport.
4. Move the vertices to about 2/3 of the way up the box. (You may want to use the Transform Gizmo to lock to the Y-axis, so that you don't move the vertices out of their X-axis orientation.) This step basically divides the chest from the abdomen.

5. Click the Polygon selection button, and select the bottom face (the waist) of the box. Press the Spacebar to lock the selection. (You may need to use Arc-Rotate to see the bottom face.)
6. Right-click the face, and select Scale; scale the face to 65%. Right-click again, and choose Move. Use the Transform Gizmo to move the face so the left side is vertical in the front viewport. Press the Spacebar to unlock the selection.
7. Turn on Edged Faces display mode in the Perspective viewport, and rotate the viewport until you see the left side of the body.
8. Select the top-half side polygon (the faces just above the obliques) along the tapered side of the box. This is the beginning of the arm socket.
9. Right-click over the face, and select Extrude/Polygon to extrude the face 4 units. To do this, just scroll down in the Modify panel until you see the Extrusion parameters, then type in 4 for the extrusion amount.
10. Click the Bevel button in the Modify panel, and in the viewport, interactively extrude the face about 15 units. When you release, Bevel the face about −1.5 units.
11. Click the Extrude button, and interactively Extrude another 4 units. Now choose Bevel. Interactively extrude another 15 units, and bevel the end of the arm down to −1.5. Deselect the face. (Note that you alternate between right-clicking to do Extrude/Bevel and to use the buttons in the Modify panel. Use whichever is convenient for you.)
12. Select the faces on the untapered side of the torso. You do this by dragging a window along the left edge of the torso in the front view. Press the Delete key to remove the faces.
13. Save the model, which should look similar to Figure 7.22. If you wish, use the saved model in the next exercise.

While the result isn't all that impressive at this point, you do have a good model that serves as a foundation for more editing in the next exercise. This is also where you add named Sub-Object selection sets to the model.

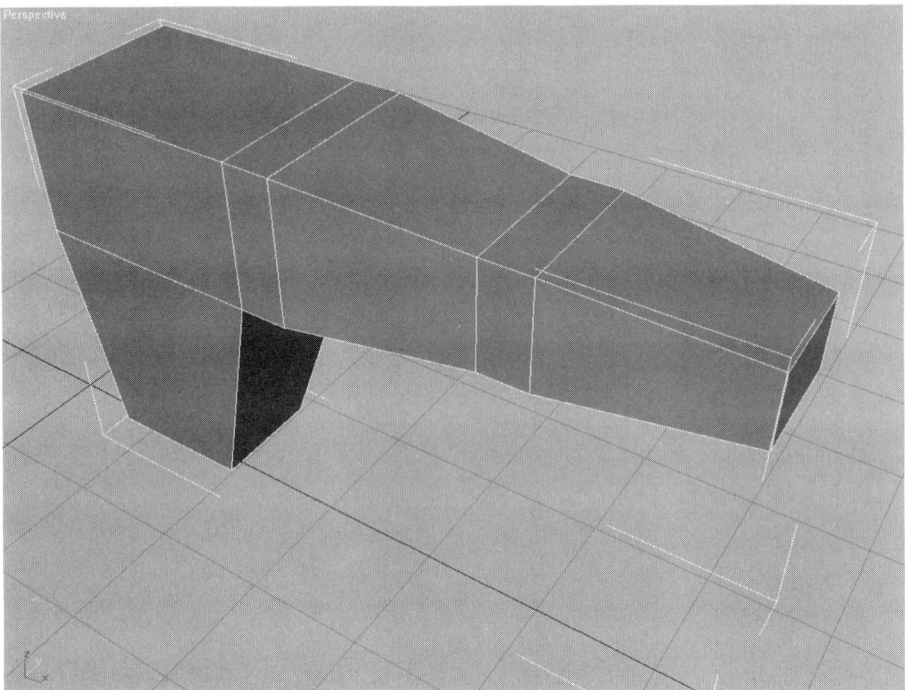

Figure 7.22 The result of Exercise 7.4.1. This box-looking torso is created just by using the Editable Mesh object on a box primitive.

Exercise 7.4.2   Adding Detail to the Torso with MeshSmooth

1. Open the file 07imx05.max from the CD-ROM. This is the model that you built in the last part of this exercise or, if you wish, use the file you saved.
2. Select the model, and go to the Modify panel. Click the More button. Select MeshSmooth.
3. Set the MeshSmooth values to NURMS Output; Iterations: 3, Smoothness: 1.0, and turn on Display Control Mesh.
4. Save the file.

To see the changes you just made, see Figure 7.23.

Chapter 7: Character Modeling   307

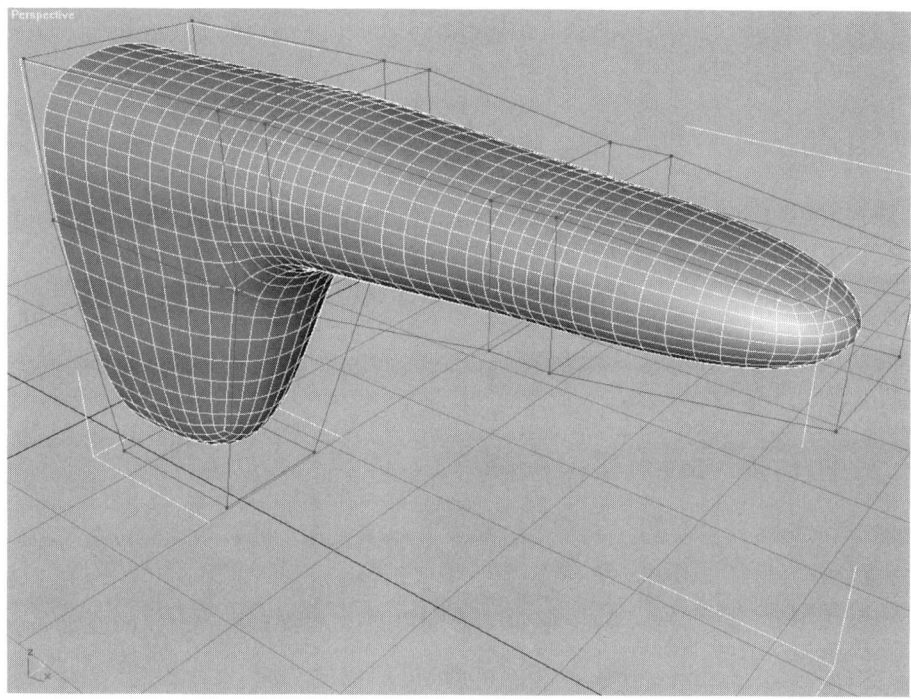

Figure 7.23 The result of Exercise 7.4.2. The mesh model is smoothed using the new NURMS feature of the MeshSmooth modifier.

 Note
> By using MeshSmooth and Editable Mesh together, you easily create any component of a character. Although the model looks fairly simple at this point, it serves as a good foundation for modeling more complex geometry later. The only hitch about Exercise 7.4.2 is that you may want to add or remove detail to the torso later in the MeshSmooth modifier. This will destroy your Sub-Object selection sets. To prevent this, use the Vol. Select modifier instead. Because Vol. Select selects geometry based on what's inside it, you add or remove detail as needed.

NURMS in MeshSmooth

NEW TO R3 A great new feature embedded within the MeshSmooth modifier is *NURMS*, or *Non-Uniform Rational MeshSmooth*. Now whether or not the name is strange, the feature is great! NURMS relies on the original mesh that is smoothed to create a series of control points at the same location as the vertices of the underlying mesh.

Much like a NURBS CV, NURMS vertices have weights whose values can change. Higher values cause the smoothed geometry to gravitate towards that vertex. Lower values push the mesh away. In a way, NURMS vertices are much like little magnets placed all over your mesh. See Figure 7.24.

Figure 7.24 A MeshSmoothed model with just the NURMS control points displayed. Each control point acts like a magnet that pushes and pulls on the smoothed mesh. In this example, the NURMS vertices that make up the eyebrows can change weight values to raise or lower the eyebrows. Courtesy Andy Murdock.

Because NURMS may very well become the way you alter your smoothed models, now is a good time to get familiar with them. In this next exercise, you edit the torso you've been working so the body is shaped more. Because the number of control points is low, you don't have much control over where you edit. However, use this exercise to get a feel for how NURMS behaves. In the following exercise, you'll see how to use FFDs to better shape the body.

Exercise 7.4.3 Working with NURMS

1. Open 07imx07.max from the CD-ROM, or the file you saved in Exercise 7.4.2.
2. Go to the Modify panel, and click the Sub-Object button.
3. Select the vertices near the armpit of the Torso in the front viewport. They turn blue—like the vertices of Editable Mesh.
4. Enter 0.25 for a weight value in the Display/Weighting section of the MeshSmooth modifier.

5. Select the vertices near the elbow and set their weight to 5. (Think of this character in the typical prone position where its arms are outstretched, with the elbows facing the back of the scene. That helps you determine what vertices to select.)
6. Select the vertices on the opposite side of the elbow (the inside of the arm) in the top viewport, and enter a value of 0.5. This adds some curvature to the elbow.
7. Select the four vertices at the end of the arm, and type in a value of 5 for the weight. This pulls the vertices back towards the end of the arm, creating a more squared-off shape.
8. Save the file.

Now select the vertices at the base of the torso, and enter in a value of 5 for the weight. The final result looks similar to Figure 7.25.

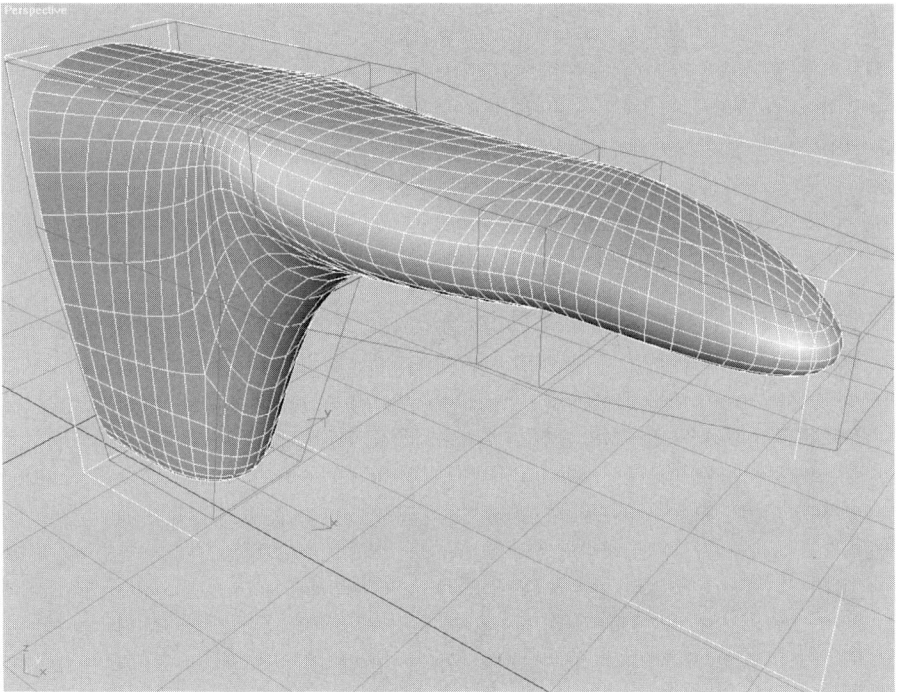

Figure 7.25 The torso after changing the weights of several of the NURMS points. By editing the weights of the NURMS points, you control the general shape of the torso.

Overall, having NURMS in MeshSmooth gives you the ability to work with smoother models because it controls the level of detail needed to produce the curvature you desire. Enter the Smoothness setting you like, specify the iterations, then just start pushing and pulling on the NURMS vertices. There is tremendous power in going down the stack to the Editable Mesh object and dividing edges with a cut or a slice. Add detail where you need it and immediately see a smoothed result. This gives you localized control you don't find in any other modeling technique. However, also look to the FFD modifiers to further manipulate higher-detail polygon models created from MeshSmooth, by controlling regions rather than specific points directly related to the model's topology.

Using FFDs on Polygonal Objects

The easiest way to alter polygonal geometry is to use any of the FFD modifiers. MAX contains several FFD modifiers that help you alter the surface of a model. In all, you have five FFD modifiers to apply to your geometry. All are located in the More button by default. They are:

- FFD 2×2×2
- FFD 3×3×3
- FFD 4×4×4
- FFD Cylinder
- FFD Box

Two FFD modifiers—FFD Cylinder and FFD Box—have configurable points. That is, you set the number of points that you use to alter the shape of the underlying geometry. As you may know, the concept behind FFD modifiers is simple. Upon applying the FFD modifier to an object, MAX places a lattice around the object. The lattice is connected by a series of points, called *control points*. As you move the location of one or more points, the model reacts as if the points are magnets pushing and pulling on the surface of the geometry. It's much like shaping a lump of clay.

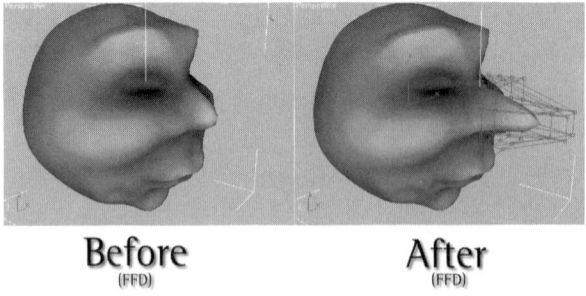

Figure 7.26 Getting an FFD nose job. The model of a head from an earlier chapter with an FFD box applied to it. When you move the control points, as seen in the figure, you push and pull the model as if it were a lump of clay.

FFD modifiers are applied at the Object or Sub-Object level. In either case, the control points affect only those faces to which they are applied. The points also store their own position, rotation, and scaling data, so that you can animate them. However, they cannot be assigned to named selection sets.

For character modeling, FFDs work great to complement NURMS for shaping basic models, much like the one you worked with in the past few exercises. By applying FFDs to Sub-Object selections on basic characters, you shape each desired area at a time. This means that you can vary levels of detail in different portions of the model, getting more control where you need it and less where you don't. FFDs don't actually add detail to your model—that's your job. What they do allow you to do, however, is control high-detail regions through lattices, rather than direct vertex manipulation.

To selectively control where FFDs are applied to your object, it's often a good idea to create selection sets of the areas where you wish to apply FFDs *before* shaping the model.

In this next exercise, use the updated MeshSelect modifier to select certain areas of your torso and create named selection sets as a result. A later exercise in this chapter uses the named selection sets that you create here.

Exercise 7.4.4 Creating Named Selection Sets for FFDs

1. Open 07imx08.max from the CD-ROM or the file you saved in Exercise 7.4.3.
2. Begin adding selection sets by applying the MeshSelect modifier, and clicking the Polygon selection button.
3. Select the forearm portion of the model first, and name it Forearm in the Named Selection Sets pop-down list in the top toolbar.
4. Repeat Step 3 for the upper arm, the upper torso, and lower torso. (You can also load 07imx09.max from the CD-ROM to see the completed result.)
5. Save the model, which looks like Figure 7.27. You'll need it for another exercise later in this chapter.

Exercise 7.4.5 continues with the torso and arm that you created earlier. Apply the FFD modifier to the forearm first, then to the upper arm. This way, you shape the arm so it looks more muscular and less like Gumby's arm.

312   Part I   Modeling

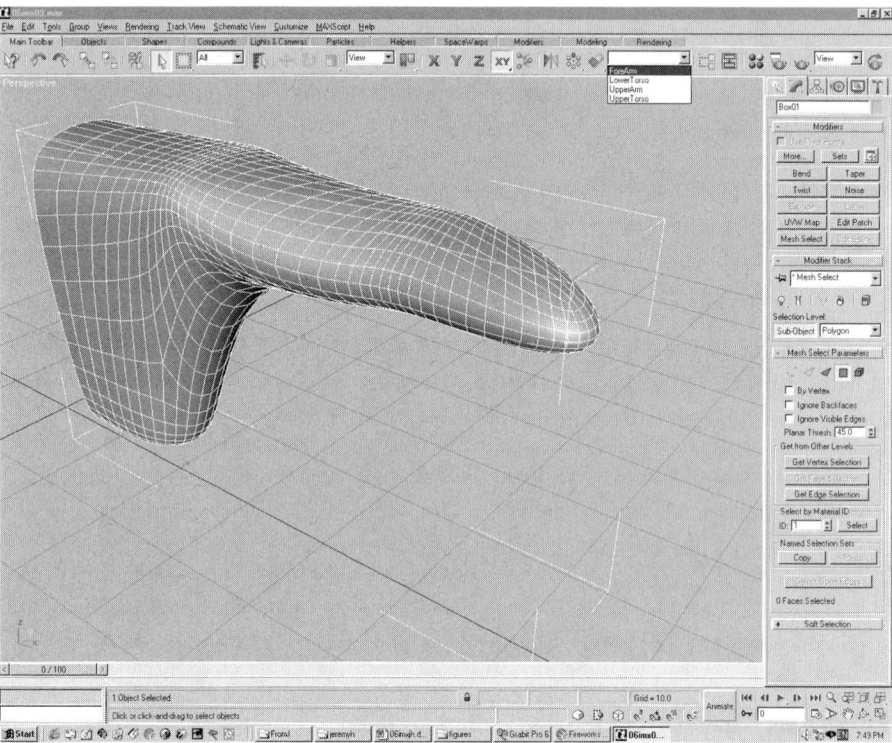

Figure 7.27 Use Named Selection Sets to control where you apply modifiers. In this exercise, the torso has four major parts that will have FFD modifiers applied to them in a later exercise.

Exercise 7.4.5 Shaping the Arm with the FFD modifier

1. Open 07imx09.max from the CD-ROM, or use your saved file.
2. Select the Object, and go to the Modify panel. Click the Polygon Sub-Object editing button.
3. In the MeshSelect parameters in the Modify panel, click the Copy button for Named Selection Sets. Choose Upper Arm. You'll use this later.
4. Select Forearm from the Named Selections pop-down list in the top toolbar.
5. Click the More button in the Modify panel, and choose FFD (box). This applies a 4×4×4 lattice around the forearm selection set.
6. Click the Sub-Object button to enter the Control Point Selection Level.
7. Using Move and Scale, shape the forearm by selecting the control points on the lattice, so that it looks more like a human forearm. Use your own arm as a guide.
8. After shaping the forearm, apply another MeshSelect modifier to your object.

9. In the Named Selection Sets section of the MeshSelect modifier, click Paste.
10. Open the Named Selection pop-down list, and observe that the Upper Arm is successfully pasted. If it is not presently selected, select the Upper Arm now.

 Note
Sub-object named selections are stored on a per modifier basis, unlike Object-level named selections. While you can't select sub-object selections between modifiers, you can copy and paste between any modifier that supports copy and paste operations, as in Step 9.

11. Click the More button in the Modify panel, and choose FFD (box).
12. Click the Sub-Object button to enter the control point selection level mode.
13. Using Move and Scale, shape the upper arm so it looks more like a human bicep/tricep. Again, use your own arm as a guide.
14. Render the Perspective viewport.

After shaping the arm, you can repeat the process on the upper torso and lower torso. Then apply the MeshSmooth modifier to the entire model to further round out the geometry. The result is quite believable. The end result of your model may look like Figure 7.28.

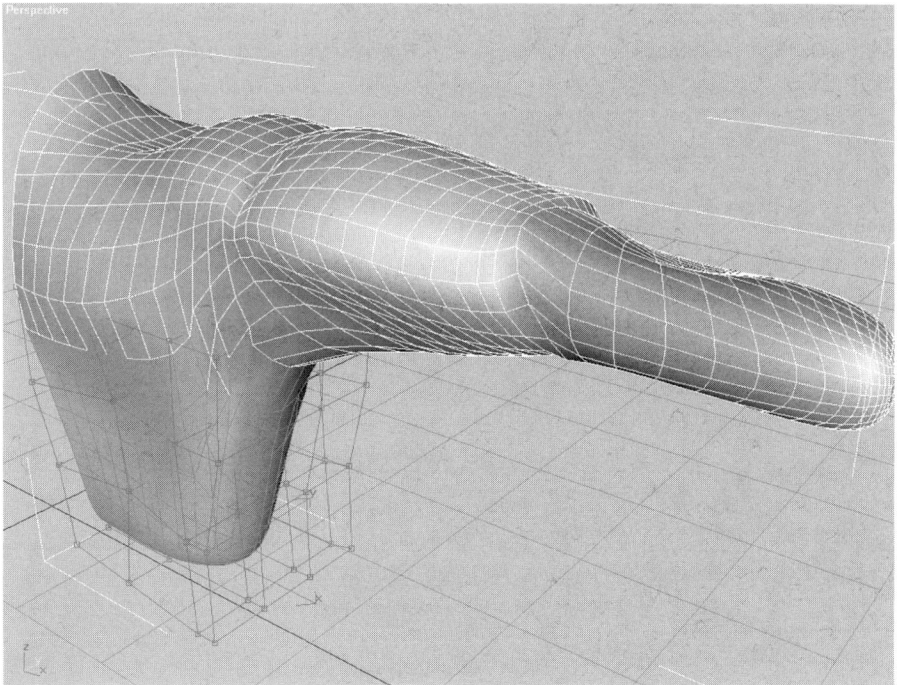

Figure 7.28 A box primitive converted to an editable mesh with MeshSmooth and FFD modifiers applied to produce the right half of a human character's torso.

Although polygonal models aren't the most efficient way to model characters, they prove useful for building richly detailed models that look great close up. Using a combination of Editable Mesh, MeshSmooth with NURMS, and FFDs, you can build just about anything out of polygonal primitives.

NEW TO R3

Skinning a Model

Perhaps the biggest feature to hit MAX in terms of character animation is the addition of the Skin modifier. Not unlike the Physique modifier that ships with the Character Studio plug-in, Skin in MAX R3 allows you to deform a mesh, based on an underlying "bone" system.

This means that now your characters can walk, dance, or just pose by positioning bones that exist already in MAX. Using the bone system that you create in the Create panel, Skin automatically determines what areas of the applied mesh are assigned to a particular bone. Almost always, it's at least 90 percent what you want—and sometimes higher, if the bones are set up correctly.

Envelopes

The meat of Skin (pardon the pun) exists in the Sub-Object selection level. Called *envelopes*, their function is for each envelope to wrap themselves around one bone object. That means for every bone in the Skin modifier, there's an associated envelope that goes with it. To understand envelopes, you must understand what Skin is actually doing.

Each bone in a Skin modifier controls a certain set of vertices in the object to which it's applied. Which vertices is determined by the proximity of the bone to the vertex, and then by user definition (if you wish to change it). Those selected vertices fall within the bone's envelope, or area of influence. You size and shape envelopes to perfectly fit your model, although they're always rounded shapes. Figure 7.29 shows what happens to vertices—for a selected bone—that fall within the envelope versus those that don't.

Tip
If you prefer, you can also use linked objects as your bones. Some people prefer this method to using MAX's bone system. Still others use splines as their "bones." That way, you have the powerful spline editing tools to shape the skinned model just about any way you want.

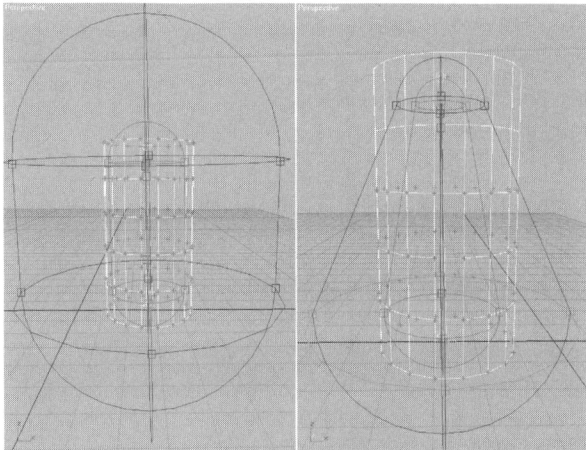

Figure 7.29 Envelopes, the cylindrical shapes with spherical end caps, determine which vertices get deformed by the bone object with which they're associated. In this example, the envelope on the left is controlling all the vertices while the envelope on the right controls only about half. Its top radius is reduced, so that it no longer encompasses any vertices. Those that aren't controlled by the envelope are either controlled by other bones or they aren't deformed at all.

When you look at the vertices affected by envelopes, you see that they're color coded. Notice that vertices close to the bone object are colored red and go to yellow, then green, then blue. Red means that those vertices are directly affected by the movement of the bone. Blue means that they're minimally affected: It takes pretty drastic bone movement to see them deform very much. Think of envelopes and the color-coded vertices as nothing more than a colorized version of the Affect Region modifier or a direct relation to the new Soft Selection feature of the Mesh Select and Vol. Select modifiers.

To apply the Skin modifier to an object, you just need to have some things in place:

- **Check to see if your model contains any parts that aren't moving.** If so, only apply Skin to a sub-object selection of your model. You'll get better interactive performance as a result.
- **Use the bones system to place bone joints at the corresponding joints of your model.** Doing this ensures not only that the model deforms in the right places, but also that the envelopes are placed in the correct spots as well.

Once you take a few steps to prepare your model, just add the bone structure, and then apply the Skin modifier. In this next exercise, take a look at applying the Skin modifier to an object and see what results you get.

Exercise 7.4.6 Using Skin on Your Model

1. Open 07imx11.max from the CD-ROM.
2. Select the Torso object, and go to the Modify panel.
3. Click the More button, and choose Skin from the list.
4. In the Skin parameters within the Modify panel, click the Add Bone button. Select all the objects in the list, then click Select.
5. Using the Rotate Transform Gizmo, rotate the right upper-arm bone (cylinder) on the Z-axis. As you see, the envelope is too large and causing the chest to cave in when the arm gets close to it. Leave the arm rotated down, so that it hangs alongside the chest. (Note that if you have trouble selecting the bone, just use the Select By Name feature (the H key on your keyboard) to select the Right Upper object.)
6. Select the torso again. Click the Sub-Object button, and choose Right Upper from the list of bones.
7. Each envelope has 4 radii to work with: one hotspot and one falloff area for each end. Select the outer ring nearest the armpit by clicking one of the handles. In the Radius field of the Modify panel, enter 13.
8. Next select the inner circle, and enter 7 for its value. When you complete this step, click the small C button in the Modify panel to copy this envelope's values.
9. Select Left Upper from the list, then click the small P button next to the C you just clicked to paste the envelope's values to the left arm. The chest should no longer be caving in on itself, as before. (See Figure 7.30.)

It takes a little getting used to when working with the new Skin modifier. As you note from the previous exercise, not only do the envelopes need to be tweaked sometimes, but the models do too, in order to work better with Skin. As you spend more time with Skin, you'll see that it's a nice way to pose your characters. If you're interested in designing a model for animation using Skin, check out *Inside 3D Studio MAX 3 Animation*.

In this chapter, you saw that there are many features within MAX that are used specifically for character modeling. New features for R3, such as MeshSmooth with NURMS and the new Skin modifier, make modeling characters in MAX all the easier. Channeling these features into a character just takes time, effort, and—most of all—patience. With enough of each, producing characters like the ones you see in this chapter are possible.

Chapter 7: Character Modeling   317

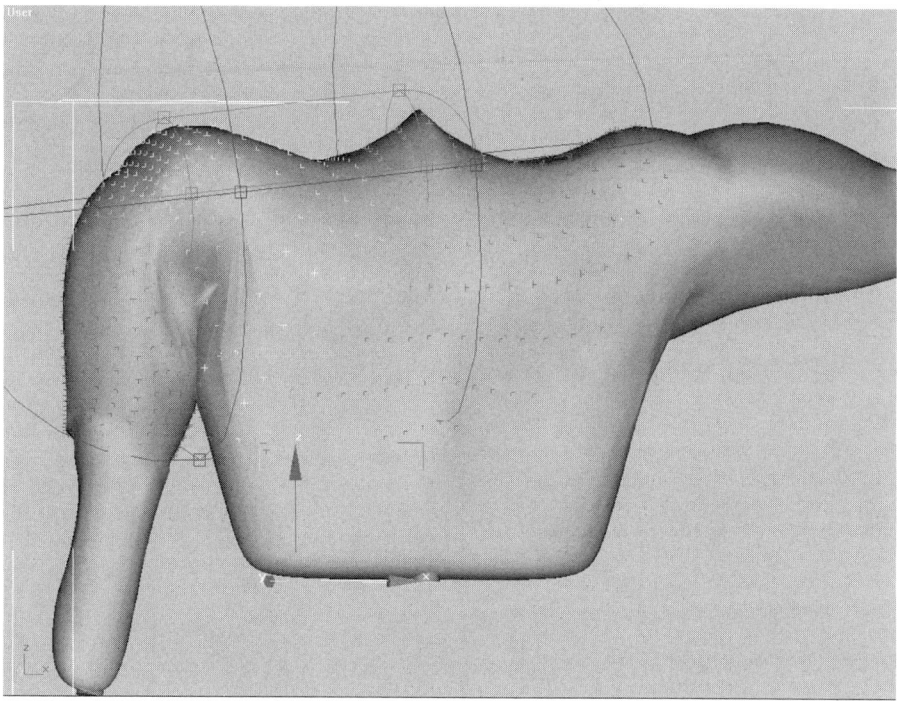

Figure 7.30 After completing the last exercise of this chapter, you now see how the new Skin system works in MAX. Creating models that work well with skin deformations takes practice, but the ability to animate a model through a bones system is well worth the time invested.

In Practice: Character Modeling

- **NURBS produce the high-detail animatable characters.** Pound for pound, NURBS models work best for high-detail characters. Because they produce relatively complex models with the least amount of geometry in your viewports, NURBS models are the ideal way to build a character.

- **Use Lofts and Blends to build NURBS characters.** By building characters in sections, you then use MAX's NURBS editing tools to piece everything together. NURBS Loft and Blend surfaces are the optimal surfaces with which to model when using this technique.

- **Polygonal models are easy to make but require more faces for higher detail models.** MAX's polygonal modeling tools are superb. Build just about anything you want using the Editable Mesh, MeshSmooth, and FFD modifiers. You then use the Skin modifier to deform them.

- **MeshSmooth and NURMS make polygonal modeling easier.** Much of the flexibility in modeling that NURBS offers is now found, in part, in the updated MeshSmooth modifier and the NURMS output. By editing the weights of the NURMS points, you can push and pull on the smoothed object, much like a CV on a NURBS surface.
- **Avoid using Booleans and other compound objects for characters.** While compound objects, such as Booleans, are easy to make, they often create too many faces in places you don't need them. Instead, spend the time extruding, beveling, adding, and deleting faces to create your model. You almost always get better results with half the faces.

Materials

8   **Material Concepts**

9   **Designing Naturally Occurring Materials**

10   **Designing Man-Made Materials**

11   **Designing Fictional and Special Effects Materials**

12   **Animated Materials**

13   **Using MAX 3 as a 2D Paint Tool**

Chapter 8

Material Concepts

Perhaps the most critical element of any scene, realistic or otherwise, is the type of material applied to the geometry. Surfaces can be shiny, dull, reflective, transparent, translucent, or just about any other surface property you envision. If you built materials in previous versions of 3D Studio or any other product, you know how creating your own materials is both challenging and even slightly frustrating. The flip side is that when you get the material right, the rendered image looks incredible.

When building materials from scratch, you need to understand and apply three somewhat obvious rules:

1. Know the tools you have at your disposal for material creation.
2. Understand how those tools work.
3. Practice, practice, practice with those tools to find the settings and techniques that work best for you.

Fortunately, this chapter helps take some of the guesswork out of Rule 3, explaining how MAX R3's material creation tools work and the optimum settings to provide the best results—for most cases. You get a chance to see both the pros and cons of the various tools in the Material Editor. In particular, the chapter covers:

- What are materials and shaders.
- Procedural maps versus Raster maps.
- Raytracing—the good and the bad.
- Organizing your materials.

There is one caveat, though. Working with and designing materials is purely subjective, and you must expect that what works for one scene doesn't necessarily work for another. However, as you spend more time designing materials, you overcome this situation just by taking more time to carefully create them from the start. This way, you build a material once, eventually developing nice libraries that are used over and over again. That said, the examples in this chapter provide general, but solid, foundations for understanding the material creation tools in MAX.

Shaders

For several years, most animation software has referred to the definition of how a rendered surface looks as a *shader*. Shaders are essentially mathematical algorithms that, through various parameters, make surfaces on geometry appear as water, wood, or even fur. You, the user, adjust the settings to produce the right look. Depending on the software, your interaction in the user interface may be visual or strictly through numbers.

If you used the 3D Studio product line for several years, you knew shaders as *materials and maps*. Materials are defined by properties, such as shininess, opacity, or reflectivity. This is essentially another way to work with shaders. MAX R3 comes closer to the traditional definition of shaders and exposes algorithms that give a material a certain look. These algorithms are now called *shaders* in MAX and combine with other information to form a material. The Standard material is now *plug-able*, meaning that shading and SuperSampling algorithms, as well as map types, are inserted into the material itself—they no longer need a new material type written. As a user, this doesn't translate to much, except that now you go to one place in the Material Editor to create a multitude of materials—all in a common interface.

Types of Materials

Ten default materials ship with MAX R3. (See Figure 8.1.) Some function as *rendering materials*, which actually produce the color information that you see when you render. A second type, *root materials*, acts as a foundation for other materials that are embedded within. They render nothing unless they contain rendering sub-materials. The materials that ship with MAX (and their functions) are:

- Blend—Root
- Composite—Root
- Double Sided—Root
- Matte/Shadow—Rendering
- Morpher—Root
- Multi/Sub-Object—Root
- Raytrace—Rendering
- Shellac—Root
- Standard—Rendering
- Top/Bottom—Root

This chapter focuses on the inner-workings of the Standard and Raytrace materials. Although the other materials are important, the only way they function is through the Standard or Raytrace materials embedded within them (with the exception of the special purpose Matte/Shadow material).

Figure 8.1 The Material/Map Browser window with the ten default material types. This chapter focuses primarily on the Standard and Raytrace materials because they serve as the foundation for the other material types.

Map Types and Map Channels

Throughout this chapter and section, there are various discussions on two terms—"map types" and "map channels". If you're unfamiliar with what they mean, basically think of *map types* as the electrical cord and *map channels* as the electrical socket. You plug map types into the map channel to create a certain effect in the material.

So where are the two located within MAX? For starters, the map channels are all of the categories you see in the Maps rollout of the Standard or Raytrace material. If you click the None button for one of the map channels, you see a complete listing of all of the map types available in MAX in a modeless window called the Material/Map Browser. So the process is this:

1. Select the map channel to which you wish to add a map type by clicking the None button next to the category name.

2. When the Material/Map Browser appears, select the map type you wish to add.

3. To edit the map, just click its name (where the "None" used to be).

While the above steps don't cover every situation where you add or edit map types for a material, they do give you a basic rundown of how you apply map types to your material. For the remainder of this chapter, the term "maps" will refer to all map types, and map channels will be referred to by "map channel."

Bitmap Maps

The most common and easily understood of the different images, or maps, that you use for a material is a *bitmap*. Basically, a bitmap is an image that's usually something like a digital picture or scanned photograph. Image file formats, such as JPG, TGA, and BMP, are common file types for bitmaps. Bitmaps also come from image editing or paint programs, such as Discreet's Paint or Adobe Photoshop.

MAX makes use of bitmaps in a variety of ways through the Material Editor. For instance, use a bitmap image of wood to give the decks of an old battleship a wood appearance. However, you also use bitmaps in other capacities, such as giving a surface a bumpy look. An image of polka dots, for example, gives your rendered surface the appearance of having dotted bumps across it when you use the bitmap as a Bump map (more on this later).

While MAX's materials contain many different maps that can be used, the Bitmap map type is the only one that allows for using bitmap images in it.

Procedural Maps

In the digital imagery field, the term "procedural" now means the "automatic" or "computer-generated" way of producing renderings. Rather than defined by bitmaps, *procedural maps* (see Figure 8.2) work by the user adjusting various numerical settings. The renderer calls the map that, in turn, processes those settings and turns them into a correctly colored image. For instance, suppose you have a wooden-plank map with the sole purpose of procedurally rendering wooden planks. As the user, you adjust the base color of the planks, maybe a default spacing for the planks, and then the average size. The renderer would, in turn, render a series of wooden planks (usually randomly generated) on the geometry where you applied the map.

Procedural maps can be used in any map channel, such as Bump, Diffuse, or Opacity. An example of a procedural map is Perlin Marble. Rather than creating a bitmap image of marble through scanning or painting, specify two colors and a size variable, and the

Perlin algorithm automatically creates a marble surface. A benefit of procedural maps is that you don't assign mapping coordinates. Since you're not using bitmaps to define how the material looks, there's no need to tell MAX how to apply it. Instead, the procedural map knows how to evenly distribute itself across the surface, or in the case of 3D procedural maps, through the volume of an object. MAX R3 offers several other procedural maps, such as Noise, Dent, and Wood. Refer to the MAX manuals for more information on the procedural maps that ship with the product.

Figure 8.2 The result of using procedural maps instead of bitmapped images. The only bitmap used in this scene is for masking the procedural Marble map to give the appearance of tiles used for the counter top.

Materials in MAX

In MAX, the main material used is known as the Standard material. Rather than completely procedural, this material consists, first, of a shading algorithm—an illumination model or how the material will appear when lit—and second, maps that allow you to use digital images, such as bitmaps, to represent various attributes of the surface. With the Standard material, you essentially combine a shading algorithm with a mapped image to produce the complete material. The shading algorithm dictates how the rendered surface looks, overall, such as shininess. The maps specify the material's surface quality, such as the color and bumpiness. For clarity, the term "shader" will be used to define the shading algorithm throughout this book.

As an alternative material type, you can also select the Raytrace material. While the Standard material gives you the best "general purpose" surface characteristics, the

Raytrace material focuses on special features, such as reflectivity and illumination. With the Raytrace material, it's easy to create such things as a shiny cocktail glass or an illuminated lampshade.

When you design scenes in MAX, you almost always apply either the Standard material or the Raytrace material. Either one provides you with the ability to apply rendered surface characteristics to your geometry. In some ways, the Standard material and Raytrace material are the same, but in many they are different—especially with MAX R3. Deciding which one works best for you is determined only by understanding which features each material produces.

The Standard Material

The Standard material is made up of several sections:

- Shader
- Basic Parameters
- Extended Parameters
- SuperSampling
- Maps
- Dynamics Properties

All play roles in how the material performs in the MAX scene. This book focuses on all but one of the sections—Dynamics Properties. For more information on Dynamics and animation within MAX, please consult *Inside 3D Studio MAX R3: Animation* from New Riders Publishing.

Rather than demonstrating a feature-by-feature rundown of the Standard material, this section discusses the way the material works. After all, that's what really matters. It's not so much how high a spinner value goes, but rather how changing that value affects the look of your material.

NEW TO R3

Shader

The Shader section (see Figure 8.3), introduced in R3, provides you with the ability to easily change the rendered characteristics of a material. In the past, this section was part of the basic parameters section in the Standard material. Before R3, the shader (the algorithm to determine the illumination characteristics of the rendered model) stayed completely within the material. You only had limited access to a portion of the shader that essentially controlled the gradation of color across the faces and the specular highlight.

This control choice offered Constant, Phong, Blinn, or Metal shading. Each of these was a variant of a similar algorithm. The roots of the shading tree were deeply buried and not exposed to you. You were only allowed to work on the exposed branches. To make a significantly different shader required developing a complete plug-in material. R3 dug deeper to expose the roots. The shader itself is now "plug-able," allowing you to change the most basic material characteristics. Blinn, Phong, and Metal still appear in the shader list with their common basic parameters, but several other entries have been added, which essentially redefine the entire material.

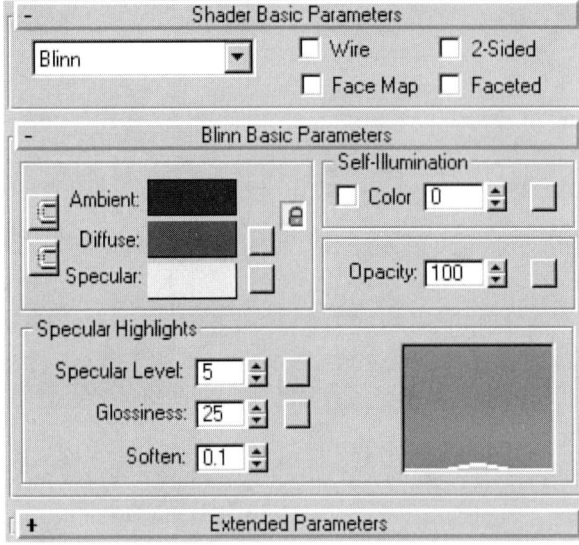

Figure 8.3 The Shader Basic Parameters rollout in the Standard material.

NEW TO R3 MAX R3 removes the old Constant method of shading and replaces it with the Faceted Rendering check box in the Shader Basic Parameters rollout. Rather than selecting only one shading mode to get faceted materials, as with Constant, now you have a faceted material for any of the shaders available in MAX. SuperSampling, which used to be located in this spot, has been moved to its own rollout, which is discussed later.

 Note
Smoothing groups eliminate facets between adjoining polygons at render time. On geometry without smoothing applied, all materials, regardless of shading setting, render with facets.

> **Note**
> The new shaders in MAX R3 are simply plug-ins. It's now much easier for developers to port existing shaders from other tools or write new ones that plug right into this list.

In this section, I discuss the shaders available in MAX R3, as well as their use in a typical situation. Keep in mind, however, that it's really up to you to be creative with the features in each one.

NEW TO R3

Anisotropic

The Anisotropic shader (shown in Figure 8.4) provides much of the same functionality that you see in the Blinn or Phong shader, with the exception of the specular highlight area. Rather than having a circular highlight, Anisotropic gives you the ability to squeeze the highlight so it appears more "linear" and less circular (See Figure 8.5). You can also rotate the highlight to any angle. So rather than having all of the highlights in your scene, objects that are more elongated in shape have stretched highlights. A simple example is a sheet of brushed aluminum. By creating an elongated, noncircular highlight, your rendered image looks much more realistic. Note that the Multi-Layer shader also supports anisotropic highlights.

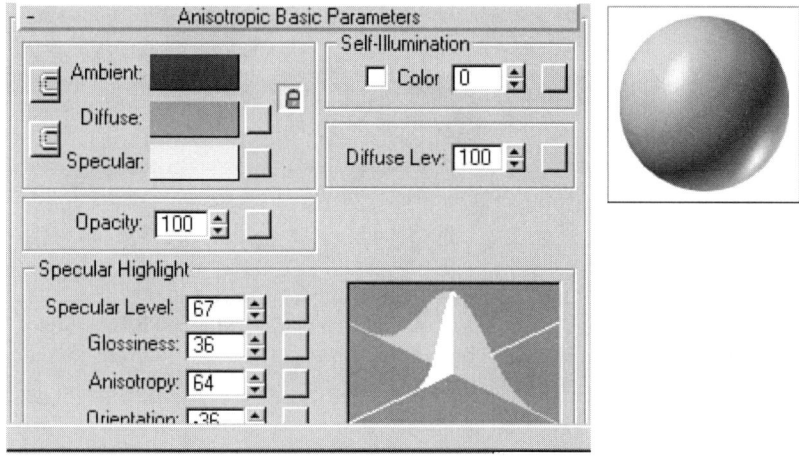

Figures 8.4 and 8.5 The Anisotropic shader interface and a sample of an Anisotropic material. Notice that the specular highlight is defined by two specular curves, rather than one resulting in highlights that are elongated.

Note

Terminology in the MAX R3 Standard Material has changed a bit from R2. Specifically, Shininess and Shininess Strength are renamed to Glossiness and Specular Level, respectively. Their positions have changed, too. Specular Level, the old Shininess Strength, is now located above Glossiness, the old Shininess setting.

Blinn

The Blinn shader acts much like the old Phong shader, discussed later, except that Blinn-shaded surfaces have softer specular highlights on the back side of a material. The result is that the material looks "flatter," with little Glossiness. See Figures 8.6 and 8.7.

Note

Using Blinn shading is one way to soften glancing highlights of backlit objects. The Soften field in the Material Editor Basic Parameters rollout also has an obvious effect on the backlit portion of a material. Unless the value is set very close to 1, the soften feature has little effect on the specular highlight directly facing the camera.

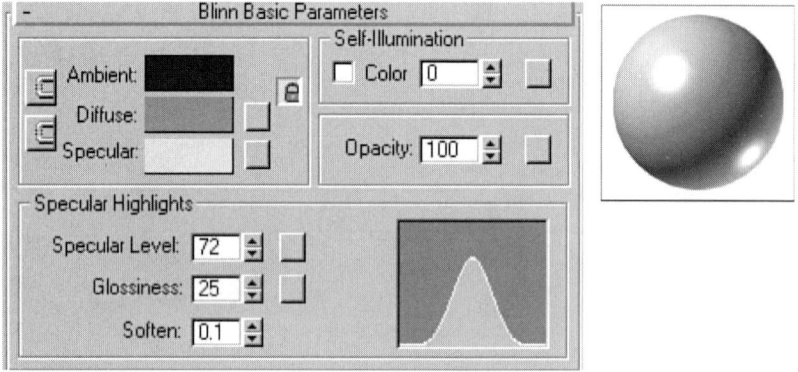

Figures 8.6 and 8.7 The Blinn shader interface and a sample material. Notice that the specular highlights of the Blinn material are round on both sides. Contrast this with the Phong shading method, which produces elongated highlights on the back side.

Metal

The Metal shader uses the Diffuse color property (map or color) to dictate the color of the specular highlight. Another difference is that when you increase the Glossiness value for a metal-shaded material, you also increase the intensity of the specular highlight. Conversely, when you increase Specular Level, you decrease the intensity of the Diffuse color. So what's going on here? Well, the assumption is that if a metallic surface is incredibly shiny, then it reflects more of its environment, rather than its inherent Diffuse color. However, that's the assumption, not the rule. In fact, the material reflects *nothing* unless you apply some sort of reflective characteristic to the material. Metal materials actually produce a very nice shiny glass-like surface. While metal surfaces look good using Metal shading, the fact is that the Raytrace material does a much better job of reproducing metal with *Blinn* shading. See Figures 8.8 and 8.9.

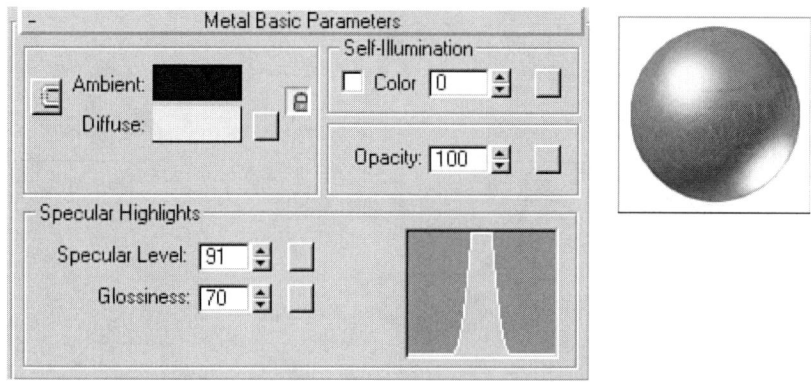

Figures 8.8 and 8.9 The metal shader interface along with a sample. The interface appears much simpler because the metal shader requires less information to work properly—more specifically, specular information that is derived from the Diffuse color and highlight settings.

Multi-Layer

NEW TO R3

A Multi-Layer shader works on the same principles as an Anisotropic-shaded material, except for an additional specular layer with its own parameters independent of the first layer. By using two different specular layers, you specify different colors, Glossiness, Anisotropy, Levels, and Orientation to produce more complex-looking specular highlights. This works well for surfaces, such as faceted diamonds or any particular material types with more intricate highlights. It also serves as a great way to create deeply glossy metals. For example, if you set the one specular highlight to a similar color of the Diffuse, and then the other as a bright white, you easily achieve a glossy painted surface. See Figures 8.10 and 8.11.

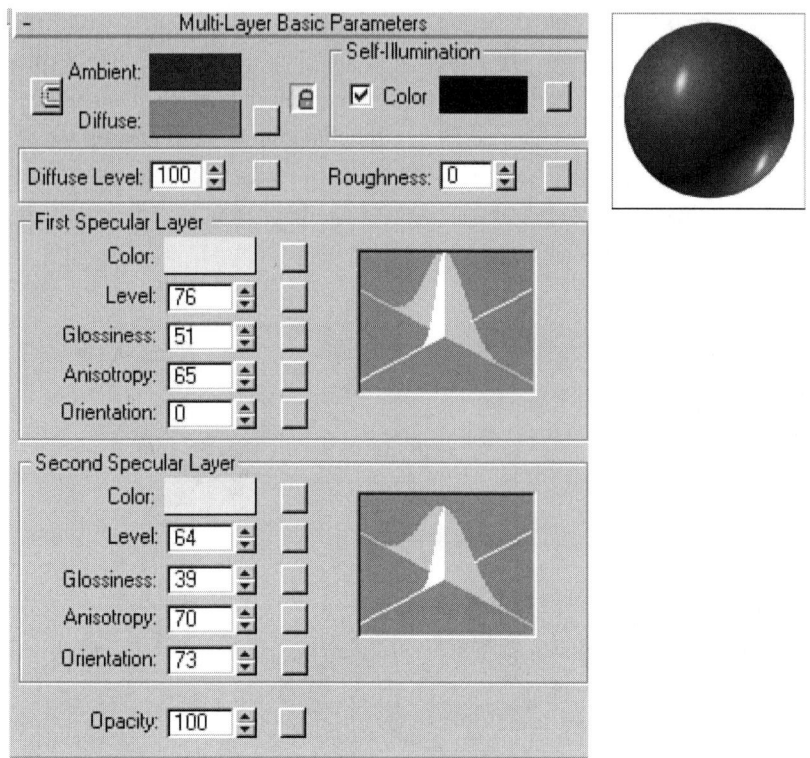

Figures 8.10 and 8.11 Similar to the Anisotropic shader, Multi-Layer allows you to have Anisotropic highlights, the main difference being that you can have two instead of one. In the example, the highlight is actually two highlights 90 degrees to each other.

Oren-Nayar-Blinn

NEW TO R3

Oren-Nayar-Blinn functions similarly to the Blinn shader, but has additional controls for handling the Diffuse Level and Roughness of the diffuse color (see Figure 8.12). Diffuse Level affects the intensity of the Diffuse color component in relation to the Ambient and Specular levels. A high setting acts much like a multiplier on the Diffuse color, making it incredibly bright. Values below 100 blend in more of the ambient color.

The Roughness setting controls the blending between the Ambient and Diffuse areas of the material. With a low setting, you see a distinct band between the two areas, whereas a high setting produces a much softer transition (see Figure 8.13).

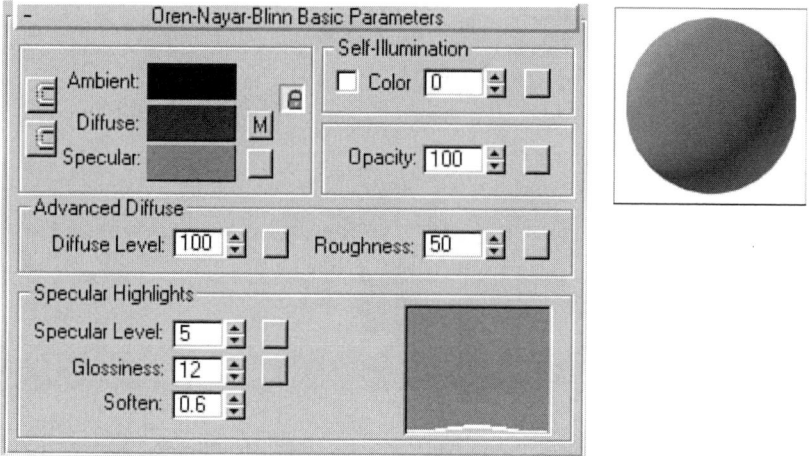

Figures 8.12 and 8.13 The Oren-Nayar-Blinn shader interface and sample. This shader excels at producing surfaces, such as skin and fabric textures. By increasing the Roughness value, you scatter more of the Ambient and Diffuse colors, producing a softer-looking surface.

Phong

Phong has been around since the early days of the 3D Studio family and even longer outside of 3D Studio. Phong consists mainly of color, specular, and transparency settings, much like the Blinn shader. However, Phong's backlight-specular highlights are broader and more intense than Blinn's. Actually, the backlight-specular highlight on a Phong material is just more elongated than a Blinn material. This often results in a specular highlight on the back side that may be too bright. If that's the case, use the Soften spinner to reduce the intensity of your backlit highlight. Phong works great for plastic materials. It also works well as a more general purpose material, much like Blinn. Because its controls are simple and straightforward, it's easy to set the parameters in Phong to quickly get decent-looking materials. See Figures 8.14 and 8.15.

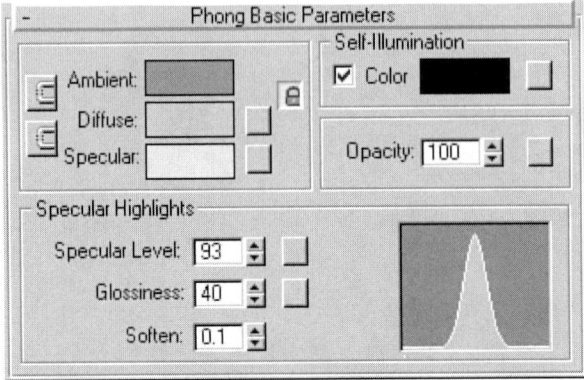

Figures 8.14 and 8.15 The Phong shader interface and a sample. Similar to the Blinn shader, with the specular highlights as the primary exception. When compared to the Blinn sample, you see that the Phong's backlight-specular highlight is elliptical, rather than round like Blinn.

Strauss

NEW TO R3

Take all of the things that are great about the Metal shader, reduce it into an easier interface, and you have the Strauss shader. Think of the Strauss shader as a metal material "wizard." Just define your color, then dial in the "metalness" of the shader. If all you want is a good-looking metal surface, start using Strauss. Metal materials come much more easily and are easier to tweak. See Figures 8.16 and 8.17.

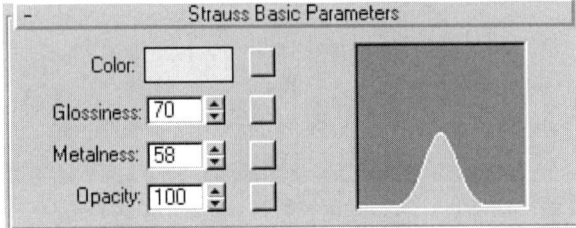

Figures 8.16 and 8.17 The Strauss shader and an example. Rather than dealing with several spinners, the Strauss shader combines many controls into a few parameters that are adjustable, achieving a realistic-looking metal material.

 Warning

Because you can switch shaders at any time for a given material, MAX does its best to carry the values over from one shader to the next. This works well for importing old material libraries or converting simple shaders into more complex ones. However, when the newly-selected shader doesn't contain the parameters of the outgoing shader, those values are lost. Settings, such as Anisotropy, not supported in Phong are lost when switching from Anisotropic to Phong.

Note

In case you wondered, most of the shader names in MAX are derived from individuals who developed the algorithms that produce the shading you see in a rendering. These publicly available algorithms were developed to advance 3D rendering technology, regardless of the tool. That's why it's quite common to see shading such as Phong and Blinn as part of many 3D tools today.

Basic Parameters

The *basic parameters* of the Standard material are essentially the "core" of the material. By altering the settings in the Standard materials Basic Parameters rollout, you change the very basic look of the material when it's rendered. The effect of changing these values is global for the material—meaning the changes affect every part of the rendered surface. The Maps rollout, discussed later, allows you to specifically control many of the values in Basic Parameters through maps. So remember, Basic Parameters=Global Control; Maps=Precise Control. For more complex and interesting materials, use a mixture of the two, (more on this later). In this section, take a look at the general descriptions for the types of items you find in the Basic Parameters section of the Standard material. Note that you won't see every one of these parameters for every shader. The shader determines what parameters are necessary for display.

Color Swatches

The color swatches in the Material Editor represent the color of light reflected back to the eye (camera) off the object's surface. While we won't go into detail as to what the various color swatches mean (that's in the MAX manuals and just about every other fundamental book on MAX), consider their role with respect to lighting and maps.

Each of the three color swatches available—Ambient, Diffuse, and Specular—determines the color of the surface as it is illuminated and sent to the eye. A fourth swatch, Filter, located in Extended Parameters, controls the color perceived by the viewer when peering through a transparent material. By using both material and light combinations, rendered scenes take on much more depth. Seasoned animators rarely use pure white lights in their scenes. For more information on lighting setups, refer to Chapter 14, "Cameras, Camera Effects, and Lighting." Finally, a fifth swatch allows you to define a constant Self-illumination color. Rather than using the Diffuse color to self-illuminate the material, dial in a specific color to create special effects, such as iridescence.

Tip

If you shine lights using Raytraced shadows on mostly transparent surfaces, the Filter color is transmitted with the light onto the surface receiving the shadow. Hence, you tint your shadows with this method.

Diffuse Level

The Diffuse Level parameter, available only in the Anisotropic, Oren-Nayar-Blinn, and Multilayer shaders, controls the intensity of the diffuse channel. At a setting of 100, the diffuse level is normal, based on the map or color specified. At a level of 400—the maximum—the intensity of the Diffuse map or color is increased fourfold. Values below 100 produce a darker material, all the way down to the Ambient color.

The real benefit of the Diffuse Level setting is the ability to use maps instead of a constant value. Mapping the Diffuse Level changes the way the object reflects light back to the eye. Imagine how a smooth plastic ball shows a clear distinction from the bright specular highlight to the main diffuse color, which in turn falls off to the Ambient color away from the light. If the same plastic ball has some rough scuffed-up spots or greasy smears on it, despite the whole ball being the same color, you then see dark spots on the diffuse area due to the scuff or grease causing the light to be absorbed or reflected away from the eye. The result is that more of the Ambient color shows. In short, it is easy to "dirty-up" your material and make it look more natural.

Roughness

Roughness is a value unique to the Oren-Nayar-Blinn shader. By adjusting its value from 0 to 100, you increase the flatness, or matte look, of a material. This works great for matte-like objects, such as clothing or dull surfaces. A value of 0 makes the surface look much like a normal Blinn-shaded surface. A value of 100 flattens out the effect of the diffuse channel, actually giving the material a less-defined diffuse and ambient border. If you use a map in this slot, the grayscale values work much the same as any other parameter. Pure black is a value of 0, and pure white is a value of 100 on the spinner. For a really noticeable (and cool) effect, place a 5×5–tiled checker map in the Roughness slot and render the view.

Specular Highlights

One of the greatly improved sections in MAX R3 is the control of specular highlights. Not all controls are available in each shader, but common controls work similarly. This hopefully makes it easier to remember what effect a parameter has when you adjust it.

Both the Glossiness and Specular Level fields in the Standard Material work together to produce the specular highlight on the surface of an object using the material. Glossiness controls the broadness of the highlight, while Specular Level controls the highlight's intensity. The Glossiness bell-curve display is an excellent tool for determining the size and intensity of the highlight itself.

By default, the Glossiness and Specular Level settings are set too low, resulting in default materials that are "dull" in their look. The primary reason for this is that most beginning animators don't bother much with adjusting the sample materials' Glossiness settings, and consequently, renderings have bright specular highlights that usually look too much like plastic. With MAX R3, you need to "dial-in" glossiness, if you want it. The key with glossiness is moderation in use—much like anything else in MAX. Surfaces that are too shiny not only look bad in a rendering, they also distract attention from your subject—not a good thing.

A feature unique to the Anisotropic and Multi-Layer shaders, Anisotropy controls the roundness of a specular highlight. Essentially it alters the X-axis, independent of the Y-axis, allowing you to give your highlights a more oval shape. If you want to control the anisotropy with a map, it uses the map's intensity values to control the anisotropy between 0 and 100.

The Orientation parameter controls the orientation of the specular highlight. In order to see the effect of this setting, you need to have the Anisotropy value set at least to something higher than 0. The value starts at 0 and goes as high as you want. Just note that you are really only rotating the highlight in multiples of 180 degrees. If you use a map for this parameter, pure black is 0 degrees rotation and pure white is 180 degrees.

Tip
You control exactly where a highlight appears on the surface of an object by using the Place Highlight icon in the toolbar Align icon flyouts. Use it in a Perspective or Camera viewport to reposition a light, relative to the view's line of sight. Note that the highlight is a result of the light's position and that "placing the highlight" is a function of the light rather than the material.

Tip
An interesting technique for creating highlights on an object without over-illuminating it is to add an extra light, using its Affect Specular feature—found in the Modify Panel/General Parameters rollout of any light object— while not using the Affect Diffuse. This adds highlights to your object without blowing out the scene's diffuse colors.

Self-Illumination

When creating materials to represent an object that is illuminated from within, use the Self-Illumination option. It's a fact that a self-illuminated object does not actually cast light—it just appears to be lit. A point about Self-Illumination: It essentially removes the Ambient color component of a material while making the Diffuse component disregard light sources. Basically light does not affect the intensity of the Diffuse color, and there is no more Ambient component. The effect is convincing for many uses, such as neon tubing.

With MAX R3, self-illumination is no longer just a 0 to 100 value, but is now based on a color. With a color value of 0,0,0 for R, G, and B, respectively, the object has no self-illumination properties. However, as you increase the value from black to white, the material appears more and more self-illuminated. This now gives you 256 levels of grayscale self-illumination. You can also tint the self-illuminated color by using a value other than some grayscale. In other words, if a neon tube is a deep red when off, but bright pink when on, set the Diffuse color to red and the Self-Illumination color to a bright pink. If the Self-Illumination color is something other than somewhere between pure black and pure white on a grayscale, the Self-Illumination color is tinted whatever color you have in the swatch. If you like, use a map instead to tint or control the level of self-illumination.

The Self-Illumination value only specifies how a rendered surface appears. It doesn't cause the object to which it's assigned to cast light. It also doesn't react to light objects that are in your scene. So, using self-illumination for a lampshade with a light on inside doesn't look all that realistic. However, the Raytrace material has some parameters that are useful for having materials react to light. See the section, "Raytrace Material," for more information on its features.

Note
There's no way to make a nonlight object in MAX cast light without a plug-in. If you're creating things such as fluorescent light tubes, you need to either fake it with projection maps or use a tool like LumaObject from Cebas.

Opacity

Opacity in Basic Parameters gives you global control over the opacity of a material. Lower values make an object more transparent and higher values make it more opaque. It does not, however, attempt to simulate refractive effects when looking through many transparent surfaces. For that, use a Refraction map, or better yet, use the Raytrace material, instead. If you have a flat plane of glass, there is no real perceived refraction, so using the Opacity value is prudent here. In the section on maps, we discuss examples for using Opacity maps.

Warning
If you are using a Refraction map to simulate refraction, don't drop the Opacity below 100 percent. It ruins the refraction effect. Refraction mapping is an illusion and not an actual refraction of a scene through a transparent object.

Extended Parameters

The Extended Parameters rollout gives you more precise control over many of the settings contained within both Basic Parameters and Maps. For instance, using the Out setting for Opacity Falloff produces a great looking light bulb or any self-illuminated source, where the light emanates from the center out. With MAX R3, the Extended Parameters are now shader-dependent and change if the shader model is changed as well.

Advanced Transparency

Transparent objects in MAX, by default, only give you see-through renderings. Transparent objects really don't act like their real-world counterparts, providing refractive or falloff qualities. However, in the Advanced Transparency section of the Extended Parameters rollout, notice that you have quite a few more controls for changing that transparent look.

Falloff controls the transparency of a material, depending on the angle of the surface to the viewer. By default, the material appears completely transparent, regardless of the angle from which you're looking. By increasing the Falloff Amount spinner, you increase the amount of transparency falloff, either from the inside of the object outward or from the outside of the object inward. Where the Opacity value controls the overall opacity value of a material, the Falloff amount controls how the opacity falls off of an object. By setting the value to In, notice that the material becomes more transparent the more you look at the center of the object (or at the faces, whose normals point directly at you). By setting the value to Out, the reverse happens. Use In for things like cola bottles and Out for objects like light bulbs.

The Filter color swatch is somewhat of an exception to the reflected-color rule of the Ambient, Diffuse, and Specular color swatches. The Filter color acts more like the colored film, called a *gel*, placed in front of a stage light. The only time you see the Filter color is if the object is mostly transparent. Higher Opacity values (less transparent) are less obvious. The Filter color is the color that is perceived by the viewer when looking through a mostly transparent surface.

In older versions of 3D Studio (prior to MAX), the Filter color was the same as the Diffuse color. Not only was this inflexible to use, but also wrong. Many materials exist in the world that reflect one color on the surface while tinting objects behind them a different color. For instance, consider an F-16's canopy. The canopy's surface contains a thin, gold film designed to reflect the sun. However, the film covers the canopy glass, which is a smoked color. Therefore, when looking at the surface of the canopy, especially in direct sunlight, you see a golden surface. If you look through the canopy to the other side, everything appears darker because of the smoked glass. This rather lengthy example is designed to demonstrate why Diffuse and Filter colors are separate in MAX. Using the two independently of each other gives you more realistic looking rendered surfaces.

Using the various transparency methods—Filter, Subtractive, or Additive—helps the realism of a transparent material. For instance, light bulbs and light beams that are geometry make great candidates for Additive transparency. Subtractive transparency works well for unlit objects, such as a soap bubble. Filter transparency, by the way, is the default. Rather than adding or subtracting pixel whiteness values behind the transparent object, it simply tints them the Filter color.

Wire (the right section of the rollout) is a method of simulating open mesh objects, such as wire baskets, radio transmission towers, open Web beams, and so on. When the Wire option is checked, MAX uses the visible edges of a mesh object to represent wires, and the faces become invisible. The apparent thickness of the wire edge is adjusted in the Wire section of the Extended Parameters rollout. The wire thickness is based on pixels, in which case the wire always appears the same size, no matter how close or far from the viewer. Wires are also set as unit sizes, and the closer you come to the object, the larger the wire appears. Wire-material attributes are an efficient method of simulating complex open-mesh objects.

Note

Generally check the 2-Sided option above the Wire option, so that the back side of an open mesh object is visible.

In this section is also the Index of Refraction value. Here you specify how light is bent as it passes through a translucent material. This setting is only effective with maps that respect refraction—either the Raytrace map or the Thin Wall Refraction map.

Reflection Dimming, a feature added in MAX R2, overcomes a rather difficult problem associated with using reflection maps—reflection maps don't respect light sources all that well. If you've ever tried to render a chrome object in darkness or darker scenes, you know the problem. Essentially the reflection-mapped material appears somewhat illuminated. Reflection Dimming corrects this problem. As a rule of thumb, it's a good idea to turn this on for just about every material using a Reflection map. This instantly improves the rendering quality of your scenes. Use Reflection Dimming to your advantage in other ways, too. Exercise 8.1 shows how to use Reflection Dimming to accentuate the sun illuminating the surface of the Earth.

Exercise 8.1 Sunrise with Reflection Dimming

1. Open the file 08max01.max, and render the scene. Notice how the Earth looks okay, but the clouds could be much brighter where the sun is hitting the planet.
2. Click on the Material Editor button in the toolbar.
3. Choose the Earth material in the lower right material slot.
4. Expand the Maps rollout.
5. To add a Reflection map, click and drag earthy.jpg to the Reflection map slot. When prompted, select Copy Map.
6. Set the Reflection amount to 50.
7. Render the scene. Here you see the problem associated with using reflection mapping. The dark side of the Earth is now completely gone—the lighting hasn't changed.
8. Go back to the Material Editor, and expand out the Extended Parameters section.
9. Check the Apply check box on for Reflection Dimming.
10. Set the Reflection Level to 2.0. Dim Level should be 0.0.
11. Render the scene again. (See Figure 8.18.)

Figure 8.18 The sun illuminating the surface of the Earth. The intense clouds are a result of using a reflection map, in conjunction with the Reflection Dimming feature in the Extended Parameters section.

You now see a much more believable planet by adding a Reflection map and using the Reflection Dimming feature. While this feature can be used in other ways, this example clearly shows how the problem of using reflection mapping creeps up and how you solve it.

SuperSampling

SuperSampling was introduced in MAX R2 to counteract the problems associated with using maps that radically changed color values from one pixel to the next. For instance, a checker map has a white pixel right next to a black pixel. When used for something like a Bump map, you often had aliasing along that edge between the black and white values because the renderer couldn't effectively interpolate the rendered surface. SuperSampling is much like an antialiasing engine for the material. The SuperSampling algorithm traverses the object that has the material applied to it and does its best to smooth out the surface where the aforementioned problem areas occur. Your rendering quality and speeds vary, depending on the sampling algorithm chosen. See Figures 8.19 and 8.20.

> **Note**
>
> In the case of computer graphics, a smooth line can't be accurately rendered across the rows and columns of pixels that make up the image. *Antialiasing* is the general term for techniques used to provide a closer representation to the smooth edge. SuperSampling is one type of antialiasing that looks at neighboring pixels and in some way, averages the values together.

Figures 8.19 and 8.20 The effects of SuperSampling. On the left, an image of tile bumps are rendered without SuperSampling. If you look closely at the edges of the tiles in the image, you see the obvious aliasing. The image to the right is using Halton Adaptive SuperSampling, resulting in a much smoother rendering. The quality comes at a price, however. The renderings on both left and right took 0:27 and 4:58, respectively, on a Dual Pentium II with 256MB of RAM.

SuperSampling Check Boxes

In these three check boxes, you alter three main states of the SuperSampling engine. Enable is obvious; it turns the SuperSampling on or off for that material. SuperSample Texture also analyzes and SuperSamples the maps that are used in your material. Leave this set to the default because maps often cause the need for SuperSampling. The Adaptive check box is active only if your chosen sampling algorithm supports adaptive SuperSampling.

MAX ships with two types of adaptive SuperSampling—Adaptive Halton and Adaptive Uniform. Using Adaptive allows the supersampler to analyze where it actually needs to do the sampling, rather than just passing over the whole material. Since this option limits the sampling only to areas that need it, your rendering times are often much better than if the whole image was SuperSampled. However, this is only true if your Threshold value is set low enough. Adaptive works by analyzing the difference in color between adjacent pixels. If the difference is great enough, it SuperSamples between them. If not, it leaves them alone. The Threshold value tells the material just how much difference is allowed between two pixels before the SuperSampler needs to step in. The higher the value, the greater the difference between the pixels. With the default of 0.1, you'll notice some difference between Adaptive on and off. However, the greatest difference and speed gains are at the 0.5 to 1.0 level. You just need to do a few test renderings to get the best look.

SuperSampling Algorithms

MAX ships with four built-in SuperSampling algorithms, so that you can decide which one works best for you. This feature is plug-able by developers, so new sampling algorithms can be written as people's needs change. The default MAX 2.5 Star method is the old way of SuperSampling. It's nonadaptive, meaning that it works from set parameters, regardless of the pixels it's SuperSampling. As a pixel is rendered, it essentially blurs the difference between the adjacent pixels to soften the edge. While it works fairly well for straight surfaces, curved surfaces often present a problem.

The other nonadaptive method, Hammersley, works by going along the horizontal axis of your rendering and SuperSampling along the Y-axis in a random fashion. The amount of samples are controlled by the Quality setting. This often provides great results, again, for rendered surfaces without much curvature, but provides better results than the MAX 2.5 Star method because it's more random.

The other two methods work with the Adaptive parameter discussed earlier. The main difference between the two is how they scan the rendered image. Adaptive Halton randomly samples in different directions around a pixel to determine the SuperSampling, whereas the Adaptive Uniform method scans equally in X- and Y-directions around the pixel. Adaptive Halton does a much better job at handling curved surfaces than Adaptive Uniform; however, Adaptive Uniform tends to excel on straighter surfaces or surfaces with linear angles.

While it's difficult to demonstrate SuperSampling in print, it is possible to quote statistics. On a tiled floor rendering, similar to Figure 8.20, using the defaults for MAX 2.5 Star

(Hammersley, Adaptive Uniform, and Adaptive Halton), the rendering times were 0:21, 1:23, :41, and 1:24, respectively. Not surprisingly, Adaptive Halton and Hammersley looked the best, but the MAX 2.5 Star method also faired well. The Adaptive Uniform method just didn't work well on an angled pattern, and only cleaned up the aliasing a small amount. (See supersampletest.max on the book's CD for some examples.)

Maps

The Maps rollout contains slots where Maps are used to control many of the Standard material's parameters, rather than just numerical values set by a spinner (see Figure 8.21). On a basic level, some slots provide color information to the material, such as Ambient, Diffuse, Specular, Filter Color, Reflection, and Refraction. The others—Shininess, Shin.Strength, Self-Illumination, Opacity, and Bump—use the intensity of a map to alter surface characteristics of the material. By adding a map you gain precise control over various areas of the material surface. Note that if you use a 2D map in any slot, you need to apply UVW mapping to your object or enable default mapping coordinates. Now in MAX R3, there are several empty map slots. Don't worry, you're not missing other features. Much like expansion slots on a computer, these slots are reserved for developers, so that they can plug in their own map types to expand and enhance the capabilities of the Standard material—or any other material type that uses maps. In all, there are twelve additional slots for new map types in MAX.

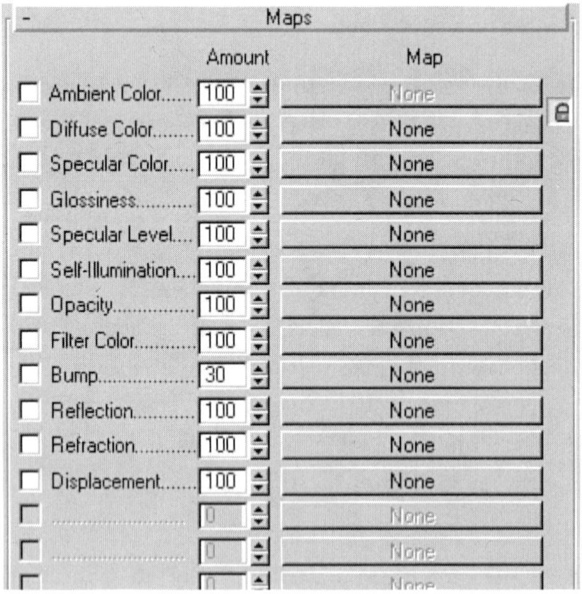

Figure 8.21 The Maps rollout in MAX R3. Notice that, as of R3, there are several blank slots that developers can plug into and write their own custom map types.

Summary

The Standard material provides you with several options for creating outstanding materials. The fundamental concept that every animator must first master is *control*. It's both tempting and easy to alter several parameters at once. If you're just getting the hang of the Material Editor, that probably isn't a good idea. Instead, adjust one parameter at a time to analyze its effect. Granted, production schedules don't often allow for close analysis of every little thing you do; however, you may find that by just taking the time to "stop and smell the roses," you discover a subtle function of the Standard material that you never knew existed. You can also work from the large material library that ships with MAX. By using these materials as a foundation, you can build on and enhance them to suit your liking. Sometimes it's better to start with someone else's material and make it better.

The Raytrace Material

The Raytrace material, introduced in MAX R2, has been enhanced in R3 to give you more explicit control over the parameters. Ideal for many transparent or translucent objects, the Raytrace material automatically uses the Raytrace rendering engine when you wish to render materials that are reflective, refractive, or both. While there are many interface similarities between the Raytrace material and the Standard material, their underlying code varies greatly in the areas where transparency and reflection are concerned. If you haven't spent much time with the Standard material, try to do so before taking on the Raytrace material. Take some time to learn the interface and how the various map channels work. When you feel comfortable with the Standard material, come back to this section to get up to speed on the Raytrace material.

Basic Parameters

The Raytrace material is an extension or enhancement of the Standard material. At first glance, you probably think the Raytrace interface (see Figure 8.22) is just Standard's interface shuffled around a bit with certain items renamed. Fortunately (and unfortunately), this is not the case—not at all, as a matter of fact.

The Raytrace material requires that you think beyond just normal color theory to the physics of how light is transmitted, absorbed, and reflected in your rendered scene. As with learning the Standard material, learning and understanding the Raytrace material means adjusting one parameter at a time to see its effect. While many of the concepts map from the Standard material to the Raytrace material, some concepts that center around how the light is reflected or absorbed are different.

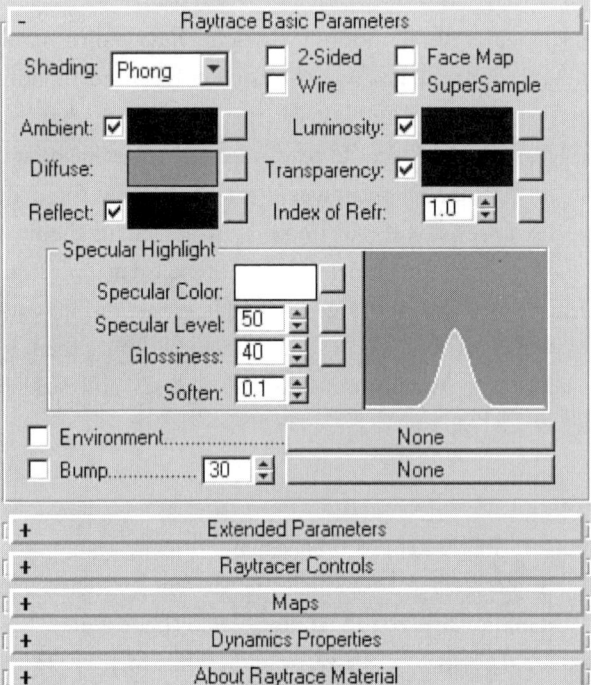

Figure 8.22 The Raytrace material's Basic Parameters. Notice that while the layout is slightly different from the Standard material, the controls are essentially located in the same position. Tread lightly though, things don't behave the same in the Raytrace material as they do in the Standard material.

Shading

Most of the new shaders that are available in the Standard material aren't present in the Raytrace material. As a matter of fact, one of the older shaders, Constant, is back. Constant works similarly to using a Phong shader with the Faceted check box on in the Standard material. The other shaders behave as their counterparts in the Standard material, mentioned in a previous section.

Ambient and Diffuse

Under the Raytrace material, Ambient and Diffuse have different relationships to each other than in the Standard material. Rather than Ambient just known as the "dark side" of a material, it is now the amount of ambient light that the material absorbs. Black means it *absorbs* all the ambient light, whereas pure white means that it *reflects* all the ambient light (and the Ambient color is now the same as the Diffuse). Changing the hue of the Ambient color means that you tint the reflection of Ambient light.

In MAX, if you wish, you can alter the ambient intensity on a grayscale from white to black, just by clearing the check box between the Ambient label and its color swatch. You can't specify a color, but rather just a grayscale ramp in the ambient component of a material.

Reflection

Reflection is, by default, defined as a color. By increasing the whiteness value of the Reflect color, you increase the amount of the environment reflected around your object. At full intensity, you don't see *any* of the Diffuse color properties in the material. If you use any color above R0, G0, B0, you are using the Raytracing engine. Therefore renderings take more time. To tint the reflection of a material a certain color, just increase any or all of the R, G, and B color values. Doing so means that the material reflects back that color to the camera rather than absorbing it.

> **Note**
> Assigning Raytrace materials to all objects in a scene does not necessarily result in a "Raytraced scene." The render algorithms are selectively applied during rendering, giving a balance of speed and quality. More Raytrace detail is included in following sections.

> **Note**
> When not using reflection or refraction features of a Raytrace material, rendering times are nearly identical to using a Standard material for the same surface.

Luminosity

Luminosity is the equivalent of Self-Illumination, available in the Standard material. As a matter of fact, MAX R3's Self-Illumination feature adopted the mechanism for determining self-illumination from the R2 Raytrace material's Luminosity parameter. As with Self-Illumination in the Standard material, you get some great effects by tinting the Luminosity a color other than the diffuse color of the object.

Transparency

Transparency has much of the same control as the Reflect color: Black means no transparency, and white means full transparency (and any amount of transparency invokes Raytracing). However, if you want true refraction values, alter the index of refraction by entering a value in the Basic Parameters rollout's Index of Refr field. (For a complete discussion of indices of refraction, see the "Transparency and Reflective Surfaces" section.)

Warning
Remember that in a Standard material, if you use a Refraction map to simulate refraction, don't drop the Opacity below 100 percent, as it ruins the refraction effect. Refraction mapping is an illusion and not an actual refraction of a scene through a transparent object.

In contrast, for the Raytracing renderer to calculate refraction, the material *must* be transparent. This is a difference of simulated refraction versus calculated refraction.

Specular Highlights

While not much different than their Standard material counterparts, the Raytrace material's Specular Highlights have some minor differences that make them worth using. Many of the spinners go well beyond the settings of the Standard material. Specular Level goes as high as 100, and Glossiness goes as high 200. This means you can have an incredibly shiny surface—more so than the Standard material. The result is that the highlights are intentionally "blown out" or pushed to intense, over-exposed white-like highlights on many metallic surfaces. Instead of using the Metal or Strauss shading method of the Standard material, you can use the Raytrace material's shininess settings to produce shiny glass or metal. Soften goes as high as 10, although values higher than 1 diffuse the highlight so much that it's not even discernible in a rendering. The values for Soften don't correspond one-to-one with the Standard material's setting.

Environment and Bump Map

A new map type that appears in the Basic Parameters section (and not in Maps) is the Environment map. This allows you to use some maps, other than the scene's environment, to reflect and refract. Why would you use this? Well, both the Raytrace material and the Raytrace map require that you have some sort of environment to reflect. If you don't have one, as in a case where you use a Screen Mapped background, you need to fake it. Often, just use the same map as your environment.

The Bump Map setting is identical to the Standard material Bump Map settings and capabilities.

Extended Parameters

The R3 Raytrace material's Extended Parameters rollout (see Figure 8.23) exposes not only several more controls, but also what may be unfamiliar controls that don't exist in any of the other material shader types. The first section, Special Effects, contains some controls unique to the Raytrace material. Advanced Transparency is completely tuned to work with the Raytrace material's special transparency features. The same goes for the Reflections settings.

Chapter 8: Material Concepts   351

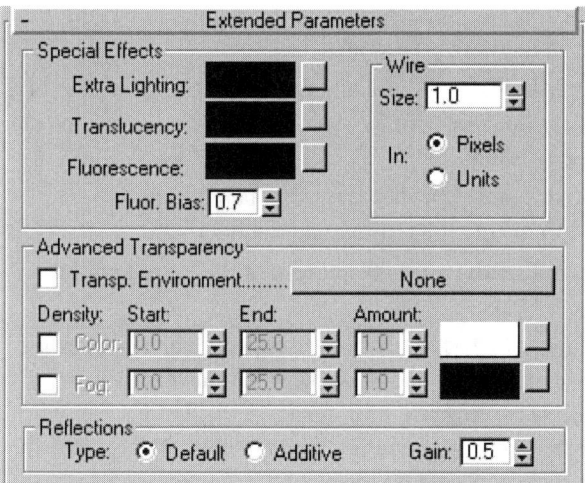

Figure 8.23 With the Extended Parameters section of the Raytrace material, you create special effects that aren't possible in the Standard material. You also control transparency effects with a much finer control.

Extra Lighting

Extra Lighting actually adds light of whatever color you choose to the Ambient color area of a material. The result is an effect that closely *simulates* radiosity. However, to get the proper control to simulate radiosity, use a map. In the following exercise, you learn how to use this feature.

Note

Radiosity is the process of distributing light throughout a scene, based on physical properties of both the light and surfaces it hits. Rather than a light beam illuminating just the first surface it hits, a radiosity-based rendering bounces a light beam many more times, depending on the energy of the source and the reflectance of the surface it hits. The result is a more realistic-looking rendering, especially for interiors.

Exercise 8.2   Using Extra Lighting for Radiosity Effects

1. Open 08max02.max and render the scene. This is a small room with white, stucco walls and a blue carpet.
2. Select RAM Player from the Rendering pull-down menu. Then click the Open Last Rendered Image in Channel A button. Just click OK when the RAM Player Configuration dialog appears. For now minimize the RAM Player window.
3. Click the Material Editor button, and select the lower-right material slot, called Room Material. Then click any one of the Walls sub-materials.
4. Expand the Extended Parameters rollout.
5. Click the blank, square button to the right of the Extra Lighting color swatch.

352 Part II Materials

6. When the Material/Map Browser appears, double-click Gradient to put the Gradient Map into the Extra Lighting map swatch.

7. The material is too bright. Make Color 1 pure black. Colors 2 and 3 need to be lighter and darker shades of blue, respectively. Make the hues similar to the color of the carpet in your first rendering.

8. Set the Color 2 position to 0.2, and then click the Go to Parent button in the Material Editor to go back to the main Raytrace material interface.

9. Expand the Maps rollout, and set the intensity amount of the Extra Lighting map to 50.

10. Render the scene. (See Figure 8.24.) Then restore the RAM Player, and click the Last Rendered Image in Channel B button. Click OK when the RAM Player Configuration dialog appears. By dragging your cursor in the RAM Player window, notice the difference between using and not using the Extra Lighting map.

Note
Extra Lighting is pretty sensitive. It only takes a little bit of light to tint a material whatever color you want. It's also very easy to blow out the brightness values of your rendering when using bright colors for extra lighting. For best results in well-lit areas, use muted colors.

As you can see from the results of the rendering, the image gets a bit lighter, but there's now much more blue on the walls. The upshot is that it appears as if the color of the carpet is tinting the color of the walls—but more along the bottom of the wall versus the top.

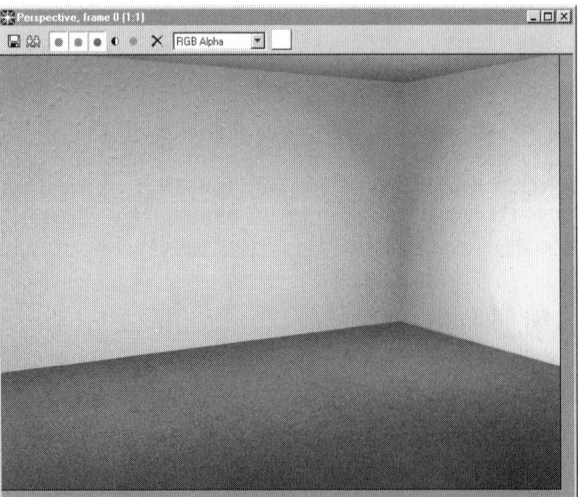

Figure 8.24 The completed result from Exercise 8.2. While not readily apparent in a black-and-white image, the Extra Lighting feature of the Raytrace material allows you to tint objects a specific color, based on the amount of light they receive. This example uses a gradient map for the lighting effects. The gradient allows you to gradually blend from the blue of the carpet near the floor to the white of the stucco walls.

Translucency

Perhaps one of the best features of the Raytrace material is its ability to simulate the transmission of light through translucent surfaces. If you're not familiar with the concept of translucency, it's actually pretty easy. Think of a lit candle. The wax closest to the flame allows a given amount of light to pass through it. However, the density of the candle is such that the light only passes through to a certain point from the flame. Then it's simply not bright enough to travel further. With the translucency feature of the Raytrace material, you can duplicate this effect. Simulating candle wax that is illuminated by a lit candle is easy with translucency. For finer control, use a map instead of just a global color. (Consult Chapter 11, "Designing Fictional and Special Effects Materials," for more information on translucency and for examples on how to use it.)

Tip
You don't need bright colors for good translucency. As a matter of fact, brighter colors look less realistic. If a color is too bright, just use the Value slider to decrease its brightness.

Fluorescence

The Fluorescence parameter allows you to create cool (albeit of limited usage) black-light effects. To produce something akin to a black-light effect, you need to use both the Fluorescence color and Bias settings. Values of 0.5 and higher create black-light effects. However, you need to get pretty close to 1.0 for this to happen. The best effects happen between 0.5 and 1.0. As an experiment, try setting the Fluorescence color to pure blue with a bias of 0.75. Then set both the Ambient and Diffuse color swatches to pure red. The rendered surface looks amazing.

Advanced Transparency

The Advanced Transparency section allows you to fine tune a transparent material. Since the Raytrace material works differently than the Standard material, you need more specific controls to define how a transparent material refracts light and blends the colors of other objects near it. To do this, there are three options—the Transp. Environment map, Color, and Fog color. The Transp. Environment map refracts whatever map is placed in the slot. It's kind of a cheat because all the Raytrace material has to do is project the image through the transparent surface. However, it works well when all you're doing is simulating refraction, or when the real refraction just doesn't look good.

The other two options allow you to tint the color of a transparent material through color values and falloff parameters. Here's how both Color and Fog work: The start value is the Start Distance of a ray leaving a surface; the End Distance is the distance that the ray travels to fully achieve the color or fog effect. Think of them as environmental range settings for a camera or, better yet, like a hotspot and falloff setting. The distance between Start and End is how long a ray travels (in MAX units) before the pixel it affects is fully tinted or made opaque (through fog). For instance, use this for a thick piece of glass. FogDensity.max, located on your Inside 3D Studio MAX CD, demonstrates what happens when you look at a piece of glass, both head-on and along the edge using the fog parameters.

Reflections

Since the Reflection amount in the Raytrace material controls how much light is absorbed versus how much is reflected, the Diffuse color component of a Raytrace material always has the appearance of fading away with higher reflection amounts. If you want to mimic the Standard material's reflection behavior, however, select Additive. This adds the reflection amount on top of the Diffuse color and makes the material appear brighter. Be careful with the Gain parameter. While you might think the higher values produce a brighter reflection, the reverse is true. For brighter reflections, set the value closer to 0. For more dim reflections, *increase* the number closer to 1. While this appears to contradict normal logic of "gain," it's actually controlling the amount of Diffuse color that's blended in with the reflection. At a value of 1, or 100 percent, the Diffuse color is blended at the maximum amount, completely obscuring the reflection.

Raytracer Controls

The Raytracer Controls section is designed to give you access to almost all of the functionality of the Raytrace map type. The main feature that's missing is attenuation control. You have falloff capabilities, but not explicit. If you need that level of control, you need to use the map for reflections or refractions.

NEW TO R3

New to the Raytrace material is the ability to pick a custom or plug-in antialiasing engine just for calculating reflective and refractive surfaces in a rendering. Two antialiasing algorithms ship with MAX:

- Fast Adaptive Antialiaser
- Multiresolution Adaptive Antialiaser

As its name implies, the Fast Adaptive Antialiaser is fast. Its primary purpose is to antialias reflections and refractions as much as possible with minimal hit in performance. The Multiresolution Adaptive Antialiaser takes far longer to render but usually produces higher quality reflections and refractions on larger scenes. It does this by taking more time to analyze the areas that need antialiasing.

A more in-depth look at some of the other parameters of the Raytracer Controls section is covered later in this chapter.

Other Material Types

As mentioned previously, several other material types ship with MAX R3. They are:

- Blend
- Composite
- Double Sided
- Matte/Shadow
- Morpher
- Multi/Sub-Object
- Shellac
- Top/Bottom

The main difference between these materials and both the Standard material and the Raytrace material is that they require the Standard material, the Raytrace material, or an equivalent to function. While going into functionality of the other material types is not in the scope of this book, you can find more information on them by consulting the MAX online help or *Inside 3D Studio MAX 3* (New Riders Publishing).

Reflection and Refraction Concepts

Raytracing has come to be known as the *de facto* way to calculate reflections and refractions in computer-generated renderings. Through raytracing, you achieve a higher level of realism that isn't possible with simple Reflection maps and transparency. However, this realism comes at the price of both speed and ramp-up time for mastery—as you recently experienced in the introductory sections. You can literally spend days working with and tweaking the raytracing settings for just one scene.

One of the most common difficulties for people just learning raytracing is the fundamental concept of how it works. Raytracing is based largely upon simple angular math. There are, however, many fine-tuning variables associated with that math that, at first, makes learning either the Raytrace map or material a bit daunting.

To better understand what's going on internally with the Raytracer, let's first look at some basic, foundation-building concepts.

Light Rays and Illumination

For you to see anything, whether in real life or on the computer, you need light. Light travels through *rays*, infinitely small trajectories from the source. Rays travel in a constant direction until they encounter another atmospheric condition or a surface. In real life, rays not only alter their trajectory when encountering another atmospheric condition, but they also may change their grouping. For instance, imagine light entering an outdoor swimming pool. As the rays enter the water, they change direction and grouping, altering the way the light falls on the floor of the pool. That effect is known as *caustics*.

While MAX is capable of altering the direction of a ray based on the index of refraction on a transparent surface, it has no way of doing caustics with the default Scanline Renderer. You can, however, achieve these effects through plug-in renderers, such as Mental Ray and Renderman.

Reflection and Reflective Surfaces

Light, except when hitting a pure black surface, is always reflected, in some way, back to the eye. Think of reflective surfaces as reflective in two ways:

- **Reflecting Color.** Any surface other than matte black reflects light in some way back to the eye. The colors perceived by the eye are the color of the light spectrum not absorbed by the surface of the object.
- **Reflecting the Environment.** Surfaces also reflect the environment, depending on their surface characteristics—normally very shiny. Fully reflective surfaces are black. Other than that, there's always some sort of a mixed diffuse color in the reflection.

Transparency and Refractive Surfaces

When a surface allows light to pass through it (and you see through it), it is referred to as *transparent*. An easy real-world example is glass. If you look at the glass, you see right through it. In MAX, this is equivalent to setting the Opacity to near 0 in the Standard material or the transparency to pure white in the Raytrace material.

As the light ray enters a transparent surface, its course alters, depending on the difference of the density between where the ray came from and where it's entering. The angle at which the light ray strikes the surface also alters its trajectory as it enters the surface. (See Figure 8.25.)

Chapter 8: Material Concepts 357

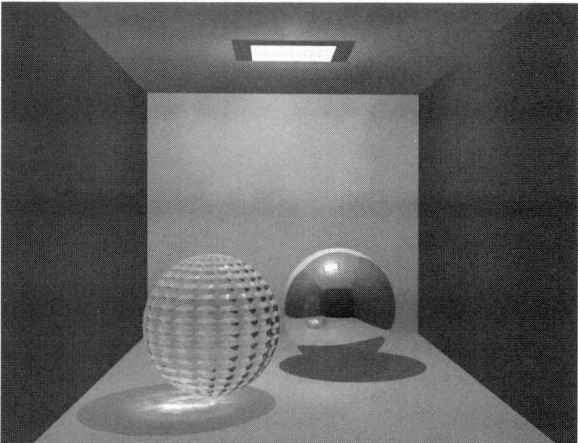

Figure 8.25 A refracted light ray as it hits the glass surface. Notice how the beam is bent as it enters and leaves the glass object. This bending of light is due to the Index of Refraction (IOR) for a given material. This particular image was rendered using the Mental Ray renderer, in order to achieve the effect of caustics. Special thanks to Frank DeLise, Discreet.

The index of refraction is the ability of a medium to alter the trajectory of a ray as it enters the surface. The number is actually a coefficient. Common indices of refraction are 1.5 for glass and 1.33 for water. There are several other indices of refraction to use in MAX besides these two. Table 8.1 lists several other indices of refraction that you use in MAX. Note: all items except Vacuum are in alphabetical order, and STP stands for Standard Temperature and Pressure.

Table 8.1 Indices of Refraction

Material	Index
Vacuum	1.00000 (exactly)
Acetone	1.36
Air (STP)	1.00029
Alcohol	1.329
Amber	1.54
Amorphous Selenium	2.92
Barium borosilicate	1.554
Calspar1	1.66
Calspar2	1.486
Carbon Disulfide	1.63
Chromium Oxide	2.705
Copper Oxide	2.705
Crown Glass	1.52

continues ▶

Table 8.1 (Continued)

Material	Index
Crystal	2.00
Cubic Zirconia	2.15
Diamond	2.417
Emerald	1.57
Ethyl Alcohol	1.36
Flourite	1.434
Fluorapatite, synthetic	1.633
Fused Quartz	1.46
Garnet	1.73–1.89
Glass	1.5
Heaviest Flint Glass	1.89
Heavy Flint Glass	1.65
Hydroxyapatite, synthetic	1.649
Ice	1.309
Iodine Crystal	3.34
Lapis Lazuli	1.61
Light Flint Glass	1.575
Liquid Carbon Dioxide	1.20
Lucite or Plexiglass	1.51
Opal	1.44–1.46
Polystyrene	1.55
Porcelain, feldspathic	1.504
Quartz 1	1.644
Quartz 2	1.553
Ruby	1.77
Salt	1.644
Sapphire	1.77
Sodium Chloride (Salt) 1	1.544
Sodium Chloride (Salt) 2	1.644
Strontium glass	1.550
Sugar Solution (30%)	1.38
Sugar Solution (80%)	1.49
Tooth structure, enamel	1.655
Topaz	1.61
Triethyleneglycol dimethacylate	1.457
Urethane dimethacrylate	1.481
Water (20 C)	1.333
Ytterbium trifluoride	1.530
Zinc Crown Glass	1.517
Zirconium glass	1.520

Note that many animators disregard these values and simply go by what looks right. If you're just getting started with refraction, start with Table 8.1, and then make adjustments to the values to get your "right look."

What Is Raytracing?

Generally speaking, raytracing is the calculation of a ray from the point of view or camera to the light source or the reverse (from the light to the camera/point of view) for *backwards raytracing*. Raytracing technology is typically noted for its ability to generate super-realistic reflections and refractions in renderings. However, the concept of raytracing is taken much further to include effects such as soft shadows and caustics (light refraction in water).

In the next few sections, we explore some concepts surrounding raytracing and, more specifically, raytracing in MAX's raytrace rendering engine.

Recursive Raytracing

The method of *backwards raytracing* closely emulates the physics of light in the real world. Essentially, infinitely thin light rays are emitted from all light sources in all directions. Of the millions of rays cast, some that bounce or intersect surfaces eventually end up hitting the camera. The result is that each rendered pixel on the screen is made up of several rays traced from one or more light sources—each ray interacting with one or more objects in your scene. More importantly, millions of rays are cast in directions that never approached the camera. As you can imagine, computational times would be outlandishly high if you traced from the light source to the camera because lights cast rays in *all* directions.

Since we're only concerned with the rays that actually hit the screen, MAX works from the camera out, and only figures out the rays that determine each pixel. More specifically, MAX uses the most popular raytracing technique, called *Recursive Raytracing*. In Recursive Raytracing, each time a ray bounces or intersects some surface, it spawns a new ray—usually traveling in another direction. Each bounce or intersection is called a *recursion*. In MAX, you control the number of recursions by setting the Ray Depth variable, as seen in Figure 8.26. The default is 9, but you may need more, depending on the complexity of your scene.

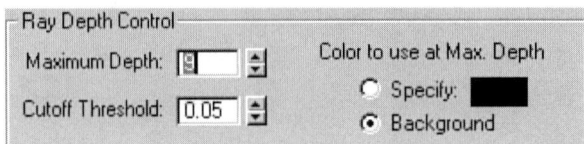

Figure 8.26 The Ray Depth controls in the Raytrace Global Options button. You access this feature in the Raytrace Map or Material.

There is a quick way to see if you have a high enough setting for Ray Depth. To the right of the Maximum Depth setting is an option for what the raytracer does if a ray reaches its maximum depth and never gets to a light source. Under Color to Use at Max Depth, choose to render the background, or you can specify a certain color. The only time you need to use this feature is to test if your Ray Depth setting is too low. By attaching a bright color to a pixel whose ray never reaches the light source, you quickly determine if your Ray Depth setting is too low for your scene.

MAX's raytracing engine is adaptive, so there's no need to specify a minimum value—the raytracer will automatically find the lowest possible number of ray bounces each pixel needs. Believe it or not, most surfaces need only one or two bounces.

Note

You can "clamp" the number of ray bounces to a very low setting. However, there's no real need to do this for speed purposes because the MAX raytracer automatically determines the minimum number of bounces needed.

Lighting and Raytracing

Raytracing is dependent upon lighting to work properly. Remember, rays are traced from the camera or point of view to the light source. Good placement of lights always makes renderings using raytracing look better.

NEW TO R3   MAX's raytracing engine is not capable of tracing light color through a transparent surface. This means that colors are not projected in shadows—only the shadow itself. Whether you use Shadow Mapped or Raytrace Shadow lights, the resulting projected shadow is gray. MAX R3 compensates for this by altering the shadow color of the light. This works well, since all you're doing is tinting the shadow some color other than gray. However, if you use this method, remember that all of the shadows cast by that light will be tinted. More than likely, you need to exclude objects from receiving illumination and casting shadows from lights that use unique shadow colors. The process of excluding objects from lights is much easier through the Include/Exclude tool (see Figure 8.27), available in the Lights & Cameras tab of the Tab panel.

Scanline Rendering Versus Raytraced Rendering

MAX R3 ships with a scanline rendering engine. However, MAX also allows for raytracing, using the Raytrace map or Raytrace material. For the purposes of this book, we explore the primary differences of how a raytrace rendering engine works versus how a scanline rendering engine works, with respect to reflections and refractions.

In a scanline rendering engine, the render prepares the entire scene prior to the actual rendering process. First, it starts by arranging a long list of all of the vertices in the scene and their positions in space. Next, it calculates all light source locations and maps—both texture and shadow. While preparing the rendering takes from less than a second to several minutes, the rendering process itself is very quick. The only exception is for Raytraced shadows, which are calculated for each scanline. During the rendering process, a scanline renderer works its way down an image line-by-line. If you watch the process, it's much like a watching a scanner scan down a photograph—hence the name.

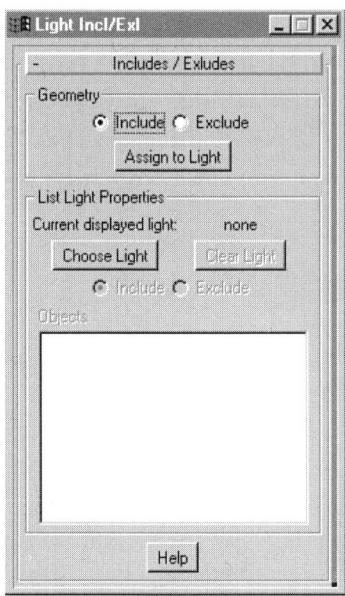

Figure 8.27 The Light Include/Exclude utility dialog box. With this tool, select geometry from the scene and choose to include or exclude it from a light source. This tool is handy because you work by selecting the objects, rather than the light sources, for determining exclusion lists.

A raytrace rendering engine works a bit differently. Depending on the implementation, there is usually some up front processing by the raytracer prior to the rendering process. However, the main difference is that such items as reflections and refractions are calculated when the renderer reaches the pixel containing a reflection or refraction. If the whole scene is being Raytraced, as in many renderers, this takes an enormous amount of time.

MAX's implementation of raytracing is a bit different. MAX uses what's known as a *hybrid raytracer* that plugs itself into the scanline renderer. This means that the scene is Raytraced only where a surface uses the Raytrace map or Raytrace material. This greatly speeds up rendering times. With MAX R3, you now see a small window pop-up the first time the renderer hits a pixel that requires the raytracing engine. This window shows you that the raytracer is, in fact, activated and is now calculating the scene to continue the rendering. Don't worry if you see this dialog box; it's just letting you know everything is OK. If you don't see it, however, and you expect Raytraced reflections or refractions, then more than likely one of the parameters in the map or material is not set correctly. Usually, you just need to set either the reflection or refraction amounts to something other than 0.

Antialiasing

Antialiasing has been around since the early days of graphics. Ever since you saw the "stair-stepping" effect of thin diagonal lines on a computer screen, there were ways to smooth them out. The "stair-step" effect is called *aliasing*. To counter the effect, programs use *antialiasing*. Antialiasing employs an averaging method around a given pixel. In MAX, the antialiasing component of the rendering engine first analyzes a pixel, its color, and the color of the pixels around it. It then averages the colors of surrounding pixels to produce a softer edge. Figure 8.28 demonstrates the example of an aliased versus non-antialiased geometry in an image.

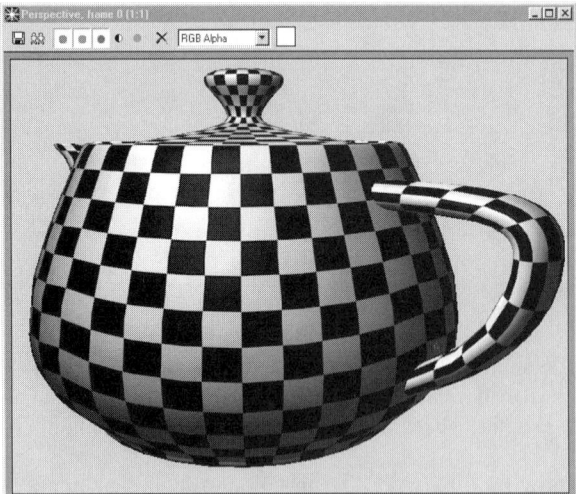

Figure 8.28 The aliasing of the edges of a teapot. With MAX's master antialiasing switch turned off, all geometry is aliased along their edges—most noticeably along the dark side of this teapot rendering. However, notice that the checker map is not aliased. This is due to the map's own Blur setting, which is independent of antialiasing. To alias the map, just set its Blur to 0 or turn off the Filter Maps check box in the Rendering Options dialog box.

Chapter 8: Material Concepts

Note
Generally antialiasing is designed to work with geometry. It doesn't usually affect texture mapping. Most texture maps have a *Blur* setting that allows you to smooth the rendering of a texture map on the geometry. However, when SuperSample is checked in Standard or Raytrace materials (see SuperSample in the Standard materials section of this chapter), MAX antialiases any objects using those materials in the scene.

Raytracing and Antialiasing

Objects with Raytrace maps or materials use one type of antialiasing for their reflections and refractions. Unlike other fully Raytraced renderers, MAX uses adaptive and analytical algorithms to accelerate the process and yield better results. The scanline renderer is fully analytical, with a host of new antialias filters designed to give you more options for countering the effects of aliasing. All methods require only one pass over the rendered image to provide the necessary antialiasing. The final result is what you see in the virtual frame buffer.

Tip
If your scanline rendering's antialiasing is looking less than perfect, try increasing the Filter Size of your rendering. This actually increases the size of the averaged pixels. (Increasing Filter Size increases rendering times but it's not available in all of the filters.)

Antialiasing Within an Antialiased Image?

If you haven't noticed yet, when you use raytracing, there are actually two different settings for antialiasing—one for the scanline renderer and one for the raytrace renderer. Managing the two isn't really all that difficult. First and foremost, set your scene antialiasing to a suitable algorithm. Filters such as Video tend to blur the scene enough to where antialiasing isn't even needed in Raytraced reflections and refractions. For more information on the filters available in MAX and how they work, refer to the MAX online reference.

Why and When to Use Antialiasing

Antialiasing greatly improves image quality in your scenes. It is even truer when using antialiasing with reflections and refractions. If you render a scene with scanline, but not Raytraced antialiasing, areas where reflections and refractions occur are aliased and usually noticeable. If you turn both antialiasing options on, however, your reflections and refractions look much better. Of course, it is here where you see the major problem with Raytraced antialiasing—speed. As soon as you enable antialiasing in your Raytraced map or material, your rendering performance takes a nosedive. It's important to point out that this performance hit, while sometimes major, is a necessity in anything but the simplest of renderings.

The best suggestion for using antialiasing with raytracing is to use it only when and where you need it. We'll discuss the "where" later on. For now, let's take a look at the "when."

Still-Life Imagery

A still life is perhaps the most critical time where you want to use raytrace antialiasing. Still-life images are subject to very close scrutiny and, therefore, must be antialiased at all times. Fortunately you usually don't have to worry about turning antialiasing on until you're near the final rendering stages. Make it a point to use antialiasing on objects only where you need it. See the "Raytracing Optimizations" section for advice on how to control where antialiasing happens and to what degree.

Tip
Minimize the need for antialiasing in a scene by employing depth-of-field blurring. See Chapter 17, "Focal Effects," for techniques on how to use the Lens Effect Focus module.

Detailed Geometry

Detailed Raytraced geometry often requires antialiasing. The primary reason is the amount of reflection or refraction that takes place on geometry with higher face counts. Raytraced reflections and refractions rely on faces to work. (Refer to the section on Voxel Trees for more information.) The more faces a Raytraced renderer works with, the better are the reflections and refractions. Consequently, rendering times are much longer. There is no real way around this, however, because you want accurate reflections. You can, however, alter the adaptive settings on the materials only applied to the detailed geometry that is independent of the rest of the scene. That way, you optimize the antialiasing just for the surface.

Animations

Typically you want to use antialiasing on animations. You may think that with enough motion and motion blur, you don't need to use much antialiasing. This may be true in some cases, where the object that's reflective or refractive is the one in motion, and it is sufficiently blurred. Generally, however, you want to use antialiasing simply for the fact that pixel "crawling" is an issue. (Crawling is the effect you see in a rendering where edges appear buzzy or ropy and appear to move like an escalator in high-contrast video.) When aliased pixels move, you really notice it—even small amounts. When those same pixels are blurred through antialiasing, those noticeable pixels all but disappear.

Raytracing Optimizations

At this point, you're probably thinking that you'll never finish another project on time if you use raytracing. While it's true that raytracing dramatically slows down rendering speeds, there are also some ways to maximize the usage of built-in optimizations of the raytracing engine, itself.

You see, out of the gate, the raytracer is designed to work optimally for every scene that you throw at it. This means that the default settings are general enough so no one scene is all that much faster than another—or slower, for that matter. Just as you set up your own general preferences in MAX, you probably need to alter various settings of the raytracer for the best possible performance out of each and every scene.

While it's not absolutely critical that you know every setting for optimizing the raytracer, the next few sections give you an idea of when to use them.

Voxel Trees

When a raytracer processes the scene before rendering, it breaks the scene into small, cubical areas called *voxels*. Pixel is short for pixel element; voxel is short for volume area.

As mentioned before, the raytracer relies on faces to determine where the rays will hit. The problem is that if every ray was tested against every face in the scene, processing times would increase significantly—something almost every animator dreads. Instead, the raytracer breaks down the scene into smaller areas: the voxels. A voxel first starts out by encasing an object, much like a bounding box. Next, depending on where the detail is on an object, the voxel is further broken down to isolate small, concentrated packs of faces. The result is something that's much like a tree of addresses. The easiest comparison to think of is a state/city/street/street-number relationship. An object is the state. Areas of concentrations of faces are broken down into cities. If there is enough detail to break a city down in to streets, the city is subdivided, and so on.

This elaborate system of breaking down a scene by objects and faces helps the raytracer isolate where a ray travels during the course of its life. This, in turn, eliminates unnecessary hit testing where the ray does not travel. It's much easier to say that the ray travels through these cities and hits these streets, rather than just saying it travels somewhere in the world. Tracking it down would just be a pain. Voxel trees help eliminate this problem. See Figure 8.29.

Many raytracers use what's known as *Octrees*. As its name implies, the tree is divided eight times. While this works for some scenes, it often leads to voxels that vary a great deal in size. If a small object is left in a large voxel, there's quite a bit of hit testing to do by the raytracer, checking where the object lies within the voxel.

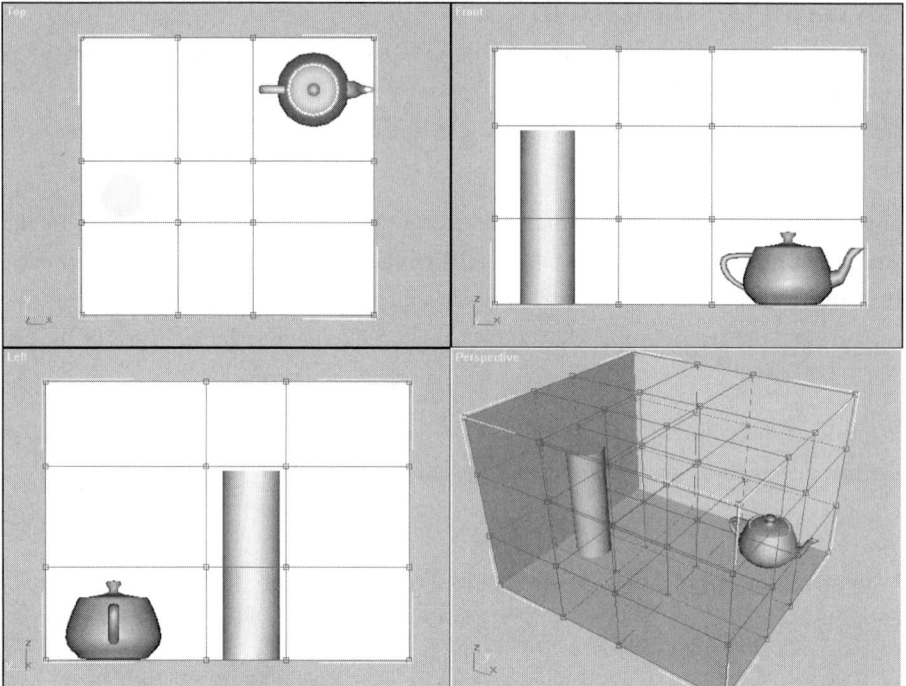

Figure 8.29 A graphical example of what a voxel tree looks like. This single pipe example shows a scene, represented by the extents of the box, being divided into sections. Notice that while the volume is a 4×4 grid, it is spaced such that the objects within the scene fit in as few voxels as possible, thereby optimizing raytrace calculations.

In MAX, voxels are adaptive. This means that *you* determine how far the voxel trees are divided by setting up limits—much like the Ray Depth control discussed earlier. In the next section, you learn how to control the usage of voxel trees.

Single Versus Dual-Pipe Acceleration

In the Global Parameters section of the Raytrace material or map, there is a grayed-out section towards the bottom of the dialog box (see Figure 8.30). If you check on the Manual Acceleration check box, the whole area becomes active. You just tapped into the voxel tree controls of the raytracer. Normally, you leave it up to the raytracer to decide things. Sometimes it's better that you take the controls and determine where acceleration takes place. There are two sections to Manual Acceleration:

- Single Pipe
- Double Pipe

Chapter 8: Material Concepts

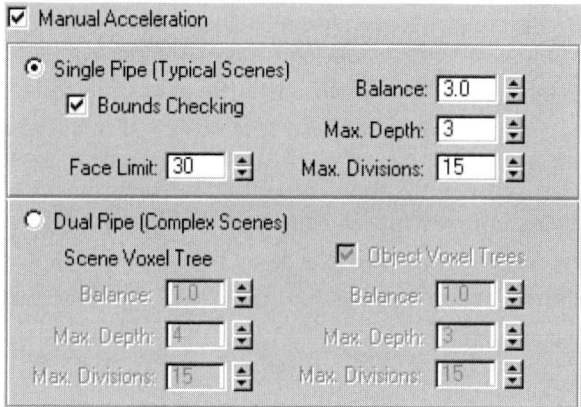

Figure 8.30 The Manual Acceleration area of the Global Raytracer Settings dialog box. Single Pipe works by breaking down the entire scene into voxel trees, while Dual Pipe works by breaking down the scene, then the objects in the scene.

Single Pipe breaks down your scene by faces. The end result is that most scenes with low face and object counts benefit from this acceleration. During the initial raytracing process, your scene gets broken down at the face level into a structured voxel tree. The division of the tree is determined by the Max Depth setting (a setting of 4 will create a 4×4×4 tree). The Max Divisions setting sets how far the tree is subdivided. Face Limit sets how many faces occupy a voxel before the voxel is divided again. There are fewer subdivisions when this number is set higher. However, this also results in more hit tests per voxel in order for the raytracer to determine what face it's actually hitting in the voxel. Balance allows you to control how evenly the subdivision is calculated for the scene. Since most scenes are not evenly distributed (object wise), a low Balance setting results in a large voxel, which contains only one small object. If you think this is the case for you, try increasing the balance. Your scene will divide a bit better. Just remember that it also uses more RAM as you increase the number. You'll find that Single Pipe acceleration works for most scenes because it's primarily designed to handle scenes of less than 300 objects.

If your scene is a bit meatier, try using Dual Pipe. Dual Pipe forces the raytracer to break down a scene first into one big voxel tree and then, if checked, each object into its own voxel tree. Rather than relying solely on where faces concentrate in the scene, Dual Pipe first looks at the objects. It then subdivides those voxels based on object complexity. The end result is a potentially complex tree, but efficient for ray hit testing. All of the settings work the same as Single Pipe. The primary thing to remember with Dual Pipe is that it works much better on larger scenes because it breaks down first by scene, then by object.

Global Exclude

Global Exclude is designed for you to eliminate an object or objects from calculation in any raytracing. Use this feature when you don't want any of the materials rendering a certain object through Raytraced reflections or refractions. This works well when you exclude large, complex objects or many small objects.

Think of a shiny flying saucer flying low over the desert terrain. The highly polished underside of the saucer tends to reflect every feature of the desert floor. By using Global Exclude, you eliminate small features of the terrain, such as those pesky Jacob's Trees, from factoring in to the raytracing calculations.

Local Exclude

Local Exclude allows you to isolate an object or objects from raytracing just for the particular map or material you're using. This means that other materials using raytracing still reflect/refract the excluded object—but not the locally excluded material.

Local Exclude works well to isolate small or complex objects from being Raytraced by a particular material. For instance, if you have a small, ornate wine glass next to a chrome wine chiller, consider eliminating the chiller from the refraction and/or the reflection calculations of the glass. Whenever you have small, intricate detail in an object, evaluate the practicality of using Raytraced reflections and refractions. The golden rule is: The more detail there is, the longer it takes to raytrace—no matter what.

Global Ray Antialiaser

NEW TO R3

At the beginning of the Raytrace material discussion, you saw that the raytracing engine now incorporates two antialiasing algorithms that are selected in the Global Ray Antialiaser section (see Figure 8.31). The default Fast Adaptive Antialiaser generally works well for all scenes, whereas the Multiresolution Adaptive Antialiaser works better for scenes that have several objects in them that either reflect or refract. Regardless of which one you choose, both are adaptive—they analyze what they're antialiasing before they do it—and contain parameters to control adaptivity of the antialiaser.

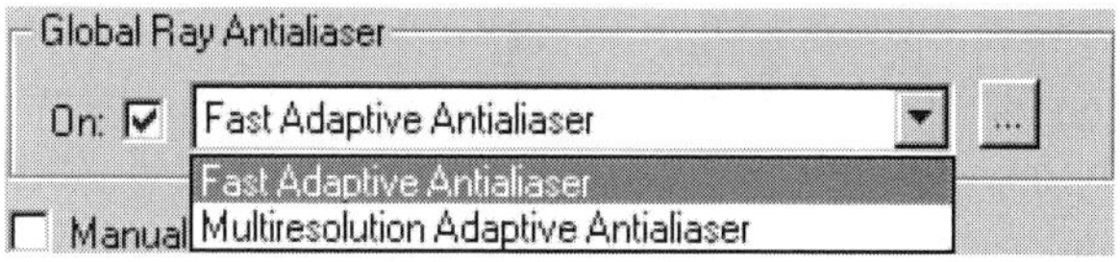

Chapter 8: Material Concepts 369

Figure 8.31 The Global Ray Antialiaser controls of the raytrace engine. This feature is located in the Global Settings button of both the Raytrace map and the Raytrace material.

Fast Adaptive Antialiaser

Control settings for the Fast Adaptive Antialiaser by clicking the small button marked with three dots, which is next to the pop-down list of antialiasing methods (see Figure 8.32). The settings, contained within the Fast Adaptive Antialiaser, control the amount of blurring or defocusing that occurs on a pixel when antialiased. Blurring is a general blur that applies to all pixels contained within a reflection or a refraction. Increasing the Blur Offset value increases the amount of offset each blurred pixel travels from the original antialiased pixel. The Blur Aspect controls the ratio of width to height that pixels are blurred. At 1.0, pixels blur at an equal amount in the X- and Y-directions. Higher than 1.0, and pixels blur more in the X-direction than Y. Lower than 1.0, the reverse is true. By distorting the blurring values, you achieve effects of elongated or warped mirrors, such as you find in a fun house.

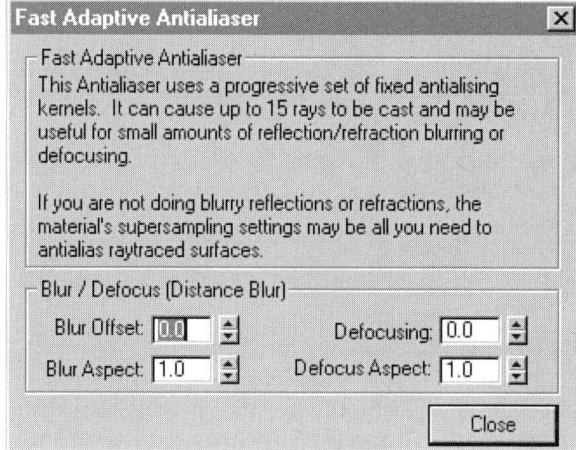

Figure 8.32 The settings dialog box for the Fast Adaptive Antialiaser. When antialiasing using this method, you basically control the amount of blurring or defocusing that occurs on aliased pixels.

Defocusing increases blur in pixels, as the rays used to create them are longer. In other words, as the reflection of an object gets farther from the object it's reflecting, it becomes blurrier. Using this in conjunction with the Blur Offset Values make the initial pixels blurry in the entire reflection, and then pixels further from the source are blurred even more. Much like Blur Aspect, Defocus Aspect blurs more in the X- or Y-direction, depending on the set amount of greater or less than 1.0.

Multiresolution Adaptive Antialiaser

This antialiaser has many of the controls that you saw in the Fast Adaptive Antialiaser. However, there are additional settings for explicitly controlling how many rays are fired by the raytracer to the pixel. The Threshold value sets the sensitivity for the adaptive controls. Higher threshold values allow for greater variation between adjacent pixel colors. In other words, the higher the threshold value, the less sensitive the antialiaser and the faster things render.

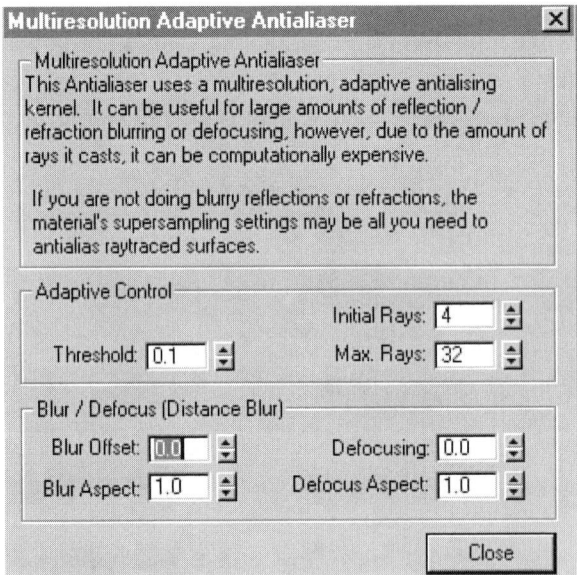

Figure 8.33 The settings dialog box for the Multiresolution Adaptive Antialiaser. Multiresolution allows you to control the amount of rays fired at an aliased pixel. By keeping these values small, you usually get better results than the Fast Adaptive Antialiaser.

The Initial and Max. Rays' values specify the absolute minimum and acceptable maximum number of antialiasing rays that are calculated for a single pixel, respectively. The defaults, 4 and 32, bracket too wide a range for most scenes. Instead, it's always a good idea to start with these values close to each other, and add a few more to the Max. Rays until your rendering looks good enough. Left at the default settings, a 640×480 rendering with every pixel Raytraced and antialiased results in as much as 9,830,400 calculated rays! By just setting the initial and maximum values to 4, you reduce that number by almost 90 percent, translating into faster rendering times. See Figure 8.34.

Figure 8.34 This shows what little difference exists between regular Raytraced antialiasing (left) versus adaptive raytracing with Initial and Maximum Ray values set to Low (right). Darker scenes such as this don't require much antialiasing. If this scene was brighter, however, it would show which image is using antialiasing and which one isn't.

 Tip

The Antialiasing Settings dialog box notes that by using SuperSampling, you get decent results without using antialiasing. This is very true. The power of the antialiasing in raytracing is its ability to blur or defocus pixels a user-specified amount. When you don't need this level of control, you often get away with just enabling SuperSampling.

Using Blurs and Attenuation

Use Blur, Defocusing, and Attenuation to your advantage to improve antialiasing quality. To begin with, the raytracer has two decent antialiasing engines. Sometimes, however, they are fine-tuned by using the Blur, Defocusing, and Attenuation settings.

Blur and Defocus basically blur an antialiased material more than it is already. As mentioned before, Blur adds a general blur across the entire Raytrace material/map. Defocusing blurs a reflection or a refraction more and more as the reflected surface's distance is farther and farther away from the material. The end result is that Raytraced reflections and refractions do not appear as sharp. However, the raytracer tends to produce crisp, hyper-real images anyway. By using Blur and Defocus, you "dirty" up the reflections and refractions. Be careful, however, not to add too much blurring or defocusing. At higher settings, blurring is overwhelming for most scenes. Lower offset values, anywhere between 0.1 and 0.3, often work fine. See Figures 8.35 and 8.36.

Attenuation helps to control the amount of reflections or refractions taking place on your material by limiting the distance that it reflects or refracts the environment. Since there is less of the environment to reflect, there is less to antialias. This also means that rendering times are shorter when a material is more attenuated. Attenuation has its own section within the raytrace map. The material has only check boxes for attenuation, called Reflect Falloff and Refract Falloff. If you desire a great deal of control over the attenuation of your Raytraced reflections or refractions, you need to use the map versus the material. When it comes to reflection control, this is one of the primary differences between the Raytrace material and the Raytrace map.

Tip

The most realistic Attenuation type to use is Exponential. Set the Start and End Ranges to values that reflect objects and the environment in the immediate vicinity of the reflective/refractive surface. The Exponent value acts as a multiplier. The higher the value, the more attenuation occurs. Take care, though. Much like the realistic Inverse Squared falloff-attenuation type of the lights, Exponential attenuates reflections over a very short distance.

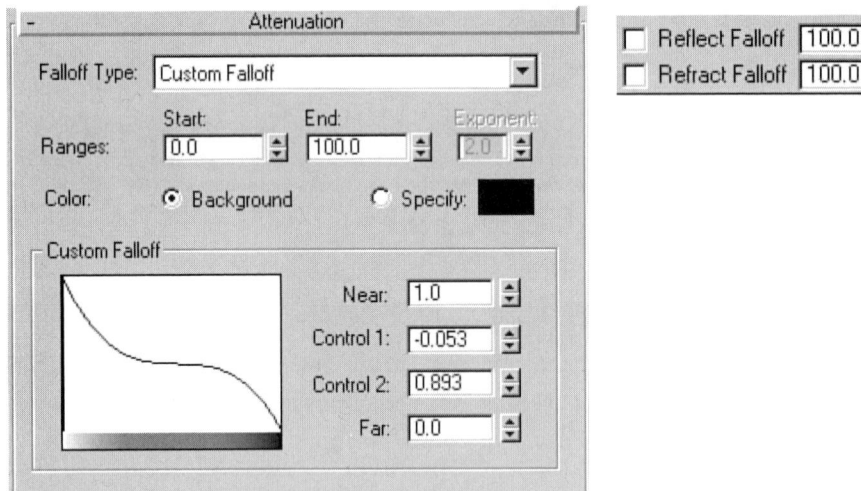

Figure 8.35 and 8.36 The attenuation controls of the map in Figure 8.35 versus the material in Figure 8.36. Because there are so many other controls for reflection amount in the Material, there is less of a need for increased control over attenuation.

Rendering Limitations and Problem Areas

Every great feature always has a downside. With antialiasing, we already know that slow rendering speeds are a major downside. As an animator and 3D artist, you must determine when and where to take advantage of this feature.

Knowing when you should and should not use a feature takes a little trial and error—no matter what type of scene on which you work. However, there are some items you should be aware of when rendering scenes with Raytraced materials and maps. By knowing what's good and what's bad for the raytracer, you take pre-emptive measures to control longer-than-normal rendering times.

Antialiasing Speed Hits

Antialiasing is at its worst, speed wise, when it encounters complex geometry or surfaces that are both reflective and refractive. Unfortunately, the best reflections and refractions are produced on geometry that is of high detail. An easy way to test this is to render a default-polygonal teapot. Then convert it to a NURBS teapot and compare the quality. The NURBS surface looks much better, but takes over twice as long to render.

Because geometry detail is critical for close-up shots, there's not much you can do to avoid long rendering times. However, there are a couple things you can do to minimize potential problem areas:

- **Animate antialiasing settings.** It's not widely known that you animate not only the antialiasing on/off settings but also any of the Adaptive settings. This means that if your shot starts up close and backs out, you can lower the antialiasing calculations as the camera gets farther away.
- **When possible, avoid both reflective and refractive surfaces.** There are alternatives. If the material is glass, use a raytrace map in the refraction slot and a bitmap or automatic reflection map in the reflection channel. This isolates the raytrace calculations to only focus on the refractive qualities of a material.

SuperSampling

While not as much of a slowdown as antialiasing, SuperSampling can and does increase your rendering times. Fortunately, it occurs on a per-material basis, and you must turn it on in order to use it. SuperSampling works well in basically two situations:

- **For materials that use maps with wild pixel value variations from pixel to pixel.** The border between colors in a checker map, for instance.

- **When precise control of antialiasing isn't needed, or the antialiasing engine is too much for your scene.** You often increase your rendering times by turning off antialiasing for a specific material and changing it to supersampled. Better results are not always guaranteed, but it's worth experimenting if Raytraced reflections and refractions are just taking too long.

Organizing Your Materials

No matter what rendering engine you use, one of the absolutely critical techniques to master early on—or to start mastering now, if you're a seasoned animator—is organizing your material libraries. As you build more and more scenes, you often find that you spent hours building a material some time back that you plan to use on a current project. The problem is that you don't know what scene you used it in, and possibly worse, where the scene is now stored.

The 3D Studio product line, even since the DOS days, has organized materials into libraries. With MAX, browsing material libraries and assigning materials to objects is greatly improved. You don't have to use the Material Editor to assign materials. You can also browse materials as they're constructed—meaning, of what maps is the material comprised—in a tree-like fashion. Figure 8.37 shows the Material/Map Browser with the *3dsviz.mat* material library file broken down into material/map trees.

Since building and assigning materials is now so much better in MAX, why not take advantage of organizing them, as well? Organization involves many aspects, which are outlined below. Depending on how many custom materials you have, a large project may lay ahead of you if you plan to organize them. This is a good way to "condition" yourself in the future when building scenes. Granted—organizing materials may go against the very grain of the person you are. However, when you're under a critical deadline and you want to find a great material that you built a while back, a little organization goes a long way.

Building Libraries

Building libraries is the first, and most tedious, step to organizing your materials. Libraries are nothing more than binary files with the .MAT extension that contain named materials, their settings, and the names of the maps they use—not the actual maps, themselves. Material libraries are saved, by default, in the Matlibs directory.

Chapter 8: Material Concepts   375

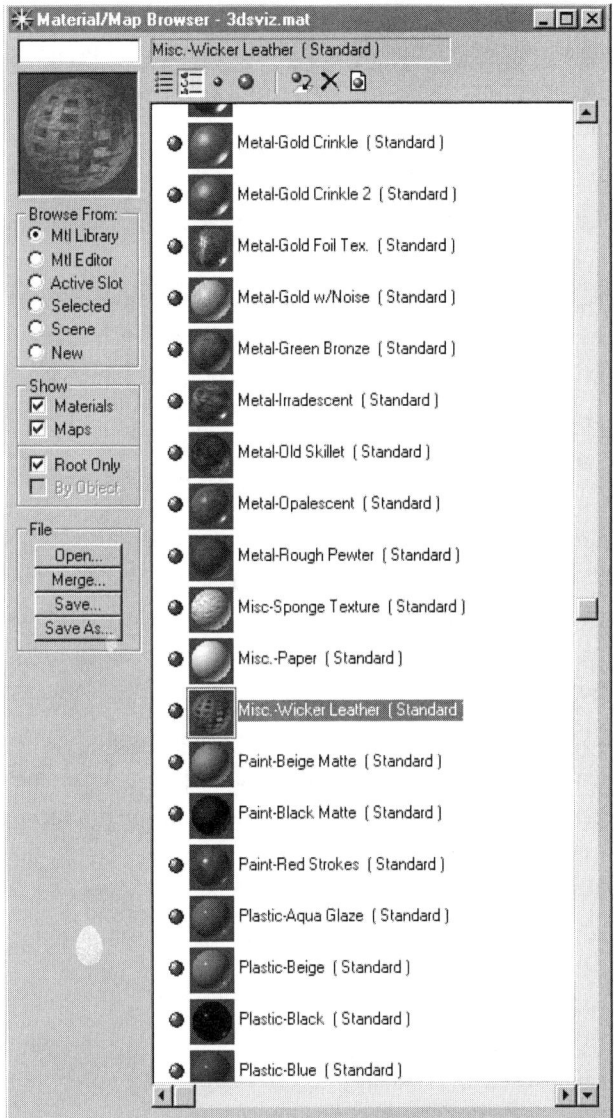

Figure 8.37 A sample material library from 3D Studio VIZ that is categorized first by type, and then alphabetically by name. Without creating separate libraries, this is a decent way to organize and sort through many types of materials that you have in a library.

> **Note**
> You save thumbnail images of your materials and their maps. Thumbnails get saved automatically with the library, if you save the material library after viewing the thumbnail images in the Material/Map Browser.

How you build a library is dependent upon how you remember your materials. Some artists/animators prefer categories, some prefer by material type (Standard, Multi/Sub-Object, and so on), and yet others by project. Which system works best is determined by the user—you. Here are three ideas to help you organize material libraries:

- **By Category.** This is the simplest way to think about putting your materials together. All metals go in one library, all animated materials go into another library, and so on. The benefit of this method is that if you know you need a specific material type, you easily identify where it is by looking at the categories you built. The downside is that you have to open a new material library each time you need a material from a different category.

- **By Type.** If you built many Multi/Sub-Object materials, it would be nice to go to a library of only Multi/Sub-Object materials to find what you need. Same thing with the new Raytrace material: If you know that you want some kind of reflective metal, but are not sure what kind out of all of the Raytrace materials you want to use, this method works great. The downside, as opposed to the category method, is that all types of materials—woods, glass, metals—could all potentially reside in the same library. This makes browsing a library quite time consuming.

- **By Project.** This method works well if you know what types of materials you used on a project. If you remember that, "Hey, I created a great textured alien skin for that Project X game," then looking up that material by project would be a snap. Since many projects are documented down to this level during production, it shouldn't be a problem finding a material from a project that you did several years ago. However, this method suffers from one fatal flaw—projects often involve hundreds of materials. If you don't have or don't remember that material's name, or where it was used in a project, you probably have a few hours ahead of you, searching for the material.

While each of these methods can be used individually, you may find that a combination of two or all three works well for you. The whole point is that it's much easier to have materials in a place where you know where to go to find them. Having materials scattered across .MAX files is just not efficient 3D design.

Naming Materials

Perhaps one of the most common mistakes of many novices is to accept the default material name that MAX gives you. How many Material #1s have you built? This is painfully obvious if you have multiple Material #1s in your Material Editor, and you try to assign them to two different objects. MAX likes unique material names in a scene. This means that you need to spend some time creating material names as you use them in your scene. Fortunately, if you get in the habit of at least giving the whole material a unique name, you avoid a major amount of the confusion.

However, did you know that MAX allows you to not only name materials, but also sub-materials and even maps? Most animators don't realize this. So their materials are littered with Map #1's, and the like. How easy is it to recognize a map named that when browsing with the Material/Map Browser?

Figure 8.38 shows a properly named material with a map versus a material/map combination that uses the defaults. Which one would you rather use when browsing several materials looking for the right "Stucco Wall"?

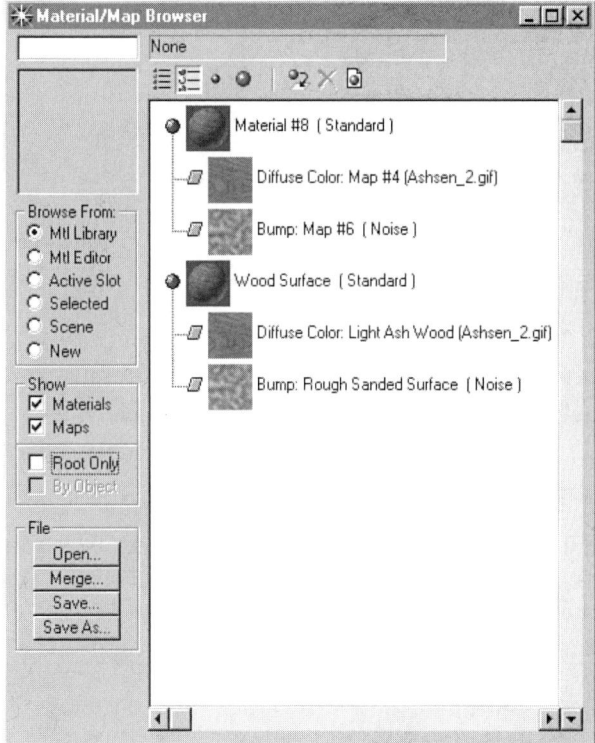

Figure 8.38 The Material/Map Browser view of two materials. The top material and map use the MAX-default naming scheme. The lower material uses more descriptive names to indicate what the material looks like and of what it contains. (The lower material took a few more seconds to create by adding in the names.)

How you name materials is entirely up to you. The only guideline to follow is to name the material something descriptive enough that you can come back to it several months later and recognize it. Other than that, use any naming scheme you want. When you browse materials from the library, they're always listed alphabetically. So if you use certain materials frequently, you could give them names that put them at the top of the list. Using the number "1" puts any material at the top.

Creating a Macroscript to Launch Your Libraries

With MAX R3, it's simple to call a specific material library from a macroscript, rather than using the traditional method in the Material/Map Browser. You have an entire toolbar or tab in the Tab panel dedicated to your libraries. By clicking the button associated with a material library, the macroscript both loads the material library and activates the Material Map Browser, so that you drag and drop materials directly on to your objects. The following is an example code for a macroscript to do this.

```
macroscript loadMyMatLib category:"Custom" tooltip:"Loads my custom library
(
if loadMaterialLibrary "mymatlib.mat" == false then messageBox "Can't find material library!"
else
shortcuts.RunShortcut "Material/Map Browser"
)
```

The first line of the code defines the actual name and category of the macroscript. The first line of the macroscript, itself, tests to see if the material library is present. If it can't find the library, the macroscript alerts the user. Otherwise, it loads the material library, and then displays the Material/Map Browser dialog box.

By using this script, or one similar, you assemble your own palette of material libraries that are called from their own buttons in the MAX-user interface.

Warning
Material libraries are stored in the matlibs directory below the max root directory. By default, the *loadMaterialLibary* function searches all bitmap paths for the material library if an explicit path isn't specified. To alleviate this problem, just add the matlibs directory to your bitmap search path list.

The contents of this chapter dealt mainly with the concepts behind materials. As you progress through this section, you enjoy the opportunity to put these concepts into practice. If you get stumped by an exercise or don't quite get why something is working the way it is, just refer back this chapter.

In Practice: Material Concepts

- **MAX's materials utilize shaders.** In most tools, a shader is an entire material. In MAX, however, the shader is only one element of the material. Features, such as maps and SuperSampling, have their own independent controls that exist for not just one, but all shaders.
- **Use the Standard material for most situations.** The Standard material contains most of the elements you need to design convincing materials. To get nice, Raytraced reflections or refractions in the Standard material, just use the Raytrace map in the Reflection or Refraction map slots.
- **Use the Raytrace material for enhanced highlights and special effects.** The Raytrace material contains features that the Standard material doesn't, such as Translucency and Fluorescence. When your needs call for more specialized effects or looks, the Raytrace material is the best choice.
- **Raytracing is great for hyper-realism.** One of the best qualities of a Raytraced image is that it looks extremely convincing. Reflections and refractions are believable. Specular highlights make metals and glass look more realistic than ever.
- **Raytracing is bad for speed.** Although raytracing produces great imagery, it comes at a price—slower rendering times. However, there are many optimizations for both rendering quality and antialiasing that help reduce your rendering bottom line.
- **Keep material libraries organized**. After three releases of MAX, material libraries are growing larger and larger. Use the naming techniques described in this chapter to keep your libraries from getting out of hand. Use the power of macroscripts to condense your material libraries to a button or icon that loads the library and launches the Material/Map Browser.

Chapter 9

Designing Naturally Occurring Materials

Nature never makes things easy, especially when it comes to simulating materials from the outside world. The randomness of nature and the dynamics of natural light and atmosphere are more complex, mathematically speaking, than personal computers and workstations can currently handle.

In this chapter you explore some concepts that add to the randomness and natural look of materials in your outdoor scenes. Some of the material groups you experiment with are

- Ground cover
- Sky
- Water
- Trees
- Vegetation
- Mapping natural materials

Use these examples as starting points for your own creations. The best way to distinguish your work from that of others is to use materials that you build from scratch. Capture or paint your own bitmaps or modify the procedural maps (such as Noise, Smoke, Cellular, and Dents) in conjunction with Blend materials; and Mix or Mask map types to form endless variations on a theme.

General Tips for Mimicking Nature

One thing that helps create natural materials is training yourself to observe your surroundings with a more critical eye. Did you notice, for example, that the leaves in midsummer are often quite blue? The high shininess of leaves reflects the blue of the sky and at times, makes a tree appear quite blue. This is true of pine and other needled trees, as well. Take the time to examine the way light plays off plants and grasses. Study the sky over the course of a week—in each season—to determine what typical sky conditions are for your locale. Pay attention to the cloud types and the amount of haze in the atmosphere.

An important fact of creating scenes in MAX R3 (or any software for that matter) is that materials do not stand on their own. Scene lighting makes or breaks your materials. Low, raking lights enhance materials with Bump maps. Colored lights enhance or destroy the effect of a material. Lighting and reflections radically change the appearance of water. For example, foreground to background lighting makes the water flat, while background to foreground lighting creates dramatic highlights on the surface and gives an illusion of depth and dimension.

Trees and vegetation require complex models, as well as complex materials, to be effective. The shadow casting qualities of plants also affect the realism in a scene. While mapped trees appear most efficient, the combination of rendering overlapping opacity mapped objects and complex raytrace shadows may mean that 3D-mesh trees are more efficient.

The use of the Double-Sided material type is effective for vegetation. Double-Sided materials ignore face normals, placing one material on the facing side (the side with the face normal) and another material on the back side. This reduces geometry by allowing you to loft open 2D shapes along paths to create simple leaves.

Because of the complexity of realistically rendering plants, you may be better off (in many instances) to use lighting and camera angles that draw the viewer's attention away from the details. Unless you're a landscape designer or botanist, your audience is probably focused on other aspects of your presentation.

Creating Ground Cover

If you have a copy of *Toy Story, Antz,* or *A Bug's Life*, study the grass and dirt mapping used in those feature films. In *Toy Story*, for example, the grass and dirt in Sid's backyard appear similar to a Blend material with yellows and greens for the grass and browns for the dirt. You use such techniques to create a meadow with wildflowers in Exercise 9.2. *A Bug's Life* has some good examples of lofted grass and plants, probably with Double-Sided materials for efficiency, similar to what you create in Exercise 9.12. *Antz* has lots of dirt materials that appear to make use of blending, masking, and Mix diffuse maps. Many of the details can be applied to your own simulated ground covers—from rough ground to manicured lawns. The examples you practice here are for fairly long distance shots and are not for realistic close-ups of lawns and grass. For added realism and depth, add a variety of natural objects (such as rocks and 3D grasses) to the mapped surfaces in the coming exercises.

Rough Ground

As in the real world, the best way to digitally landscape is from the ground up: Build on a simple base material that can be used for many types of ground cover. In Exercise 9.1 you create such a material and apply it to a fairly large tract of land. If your projects are on a smaller scale, however, adjust the material's map-scale factors accordingly.

Exercise 9.1 Patchy Ground Cover

1. Open the file from the CD-ROM called 09max01.max. It's a hemisphere skydome with a hilly landscape, made from a QuadPatch. There is a Sun light for the landscape and an Omni light for the skydome (set to include only their respective objects).

2. Open the Material Editor, and enter ROUGH_GROUND in the name field. This material is a grassy field with dirt patches. The idea is to create a randomness with the illusion of texture, using several levels of color information and some bump mapping. The material is a Standard-material type (for simplicity at the material level), but you can add flexibility by using several levels of Noise, Smoke, and Mask maps.

3. Click the Diffuse map button to drop to that level. In the Material/Map Browser, double-click Noise. This defines the overall pattern of grass area and dirt area. Name this level *colors*. In the Noise Parameters rollout, enter the numbers as shown in Figure 9.1. This increases the scale of the noise pattern to fit the scene's scale. It more clearly defines the transition between white and black with the High (0.75) and Low (0.45) Threshold settings.

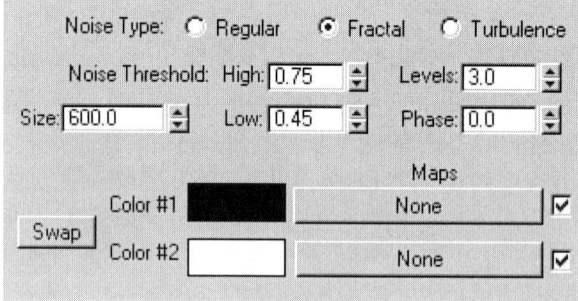

Figure 9.1 Noise parameters for top-level Noise map.

4. Drag and drop the ROUGH_GROUND sample sphere onto the GROUND mesh object in the Camera01 viewport. Select Quick Render, and you see a grayscale pattern on the landscape. Where the pattern is black, the green shades appear; where the pattern is white, the browns appear. The scene looks similar to Figure 9.2.

 Note

You are not able to view procedural map types in the viewport. Rendering is the only way to see the pattern.

Chapter 9: Designing Naturally Occurring Materials 385

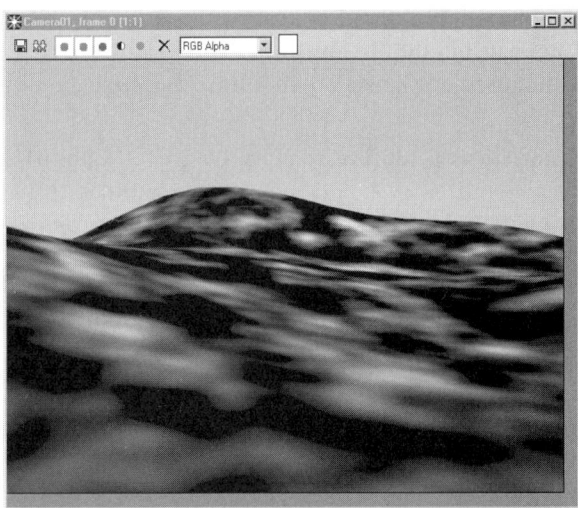

Figure 9.2 Noise pattern on landscape.

5. Next replace the black-and-white Noise colors—not with plain colors—but with a Smoke map to define multiple greens. Select the None map button for Color #1, and double-click Smoke. Name the map *greens*, and in the Smoke Parameters rollout, enter 400 in the Size field. Change Color #1 to a middle green (R50, G110, B50) and Color #2 to a lighter green (R95, G160, B100).

6. In the Material Editor, select Material/Map Navigator. Choose Diffuse Color. Now you add a Noise map in Color #2, to define multiple brown colors. Click the None map button for Color #2, and double-click Noise. Name the map *browns*, and in the Noise Parameters rollout, enter the values shown in Figure 9.3. Change Color #1 to light brown (R150, G140, B80) and Color #2 to dark brown (R40, G35, B12).

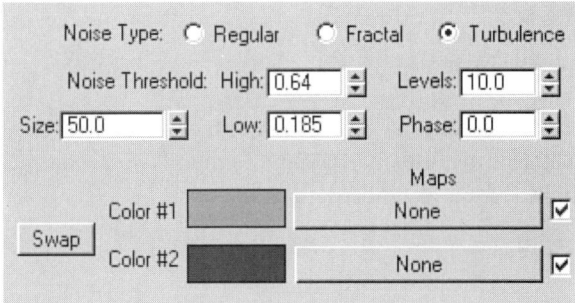

Figure 9.3 Noise parameters for brown colors.

7. Select Render Last. The pattern changes to mottled green, with patches of tan and brown. The pattern is not bad, but the dirt areas need some texture. In the next step add a bump map and use a Mask map, so the bumps show only in the material's brown dirt areas.

8. In the Material/Map Navigator, click the top level (named ROUGH_GROUND). In the Material Editor's Maps rollout, enter 500 in the Bump Amount field. Now select None for the Bump map. Double-click Noise. Name this level *noise bump*. Click the Render Last button, and notice that the whole landscape appears bumpy. You want bumps in the dirt area only, so use the same Noise that defines the overall color pattern and masks out the effects of the Bump map. Where the mask is white, bumps appear; where the mask is black, there are no bumps. Close the Virtual Frame Buffer.

9. In the Material/Map Navigator, select the bump noise level. Click the Noise map-type button, and double-click Mask. Select Keep Old Map as Sub-Map in the Replace Map dialog box, and click OK.

10. Click the Mask None button, and double-click Noise. Name this level *noise mask*. In the Noise Parameters rollout, enter the settings shown in Figure 9.4. Click the Render Last button. Notice that the green areas are smooth while the brown areas are bumpy. The Material/Map Navigator for the ROUGH_GROUND material looks similar to Figure 9.5.

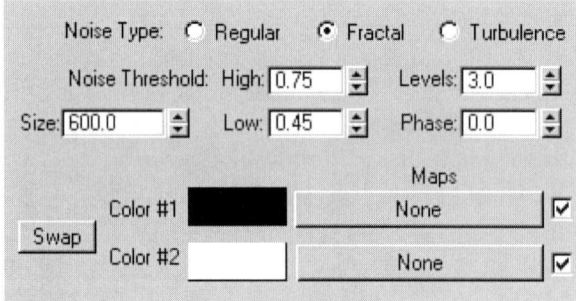

Figure 9.4 Noise parameters for Mask level Noise map.

11. Save the file as 09_ground_01.max. You can experiment with different combinations of color and bump patterns to create many types of ground cover. The material is not overly complex, as it is a Standard material.

Chapter 9: Designing Naturally Occurring Materials   387

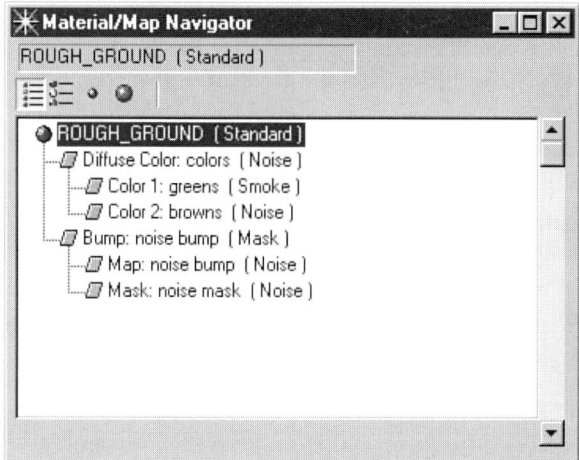

Figure 9.5 Material/Map Navigator for ROUGH_GROUND material.

Wildflowers

By using a Blend material type instead of a Standard material, you increase the complexity of your scene. The Blend material is composed of two completely separate Standard (or any other type) materials. Mix these two together (in percentages) or apply a mask by using a map's luminance values (whiteness) to reveal one material or the other. Exercise 9.2 starts with the same hilly landscape as Exercise 9.1. However, Exercise 9.2 uses a Blend material, thus producing more complex colors. It also generates an extra layer of Noise and Cellular maps, plus each material has its own bump pattern. The grassy areas appear as short, tight bumps while the wildflower areas appear more lumpy.

Exercise 9.2   A Meadow with Wildflowers

1. Reopen the file called 09max01.max from the CD-ROM. It is the same base file used in the previous exercise.

2. In the Material Editor, click the Standard material type button. Double-click Blend, and select Discard Old Material Click OK. Enter WILDFLOWERS in the name field. Drag and drop the sample sphere on to the GROUND object in the Camera01 viewport. Save the scene as 09_flowers_01.max. The Blend material contains two Standard materials and a Mask slot.

3. Select Material 1, and enter GRASSES as the material name. This material's greenish-yellow diffuse color is determined by a Smoke map. This Smoke map consists of two Noise maps—one with two shades of green, the other with two shades of yellow. Click on the map shortcut button at the right of the Diffuse color slot to drop to that level. Choose Smoke. Name the map *greenyellow*. Change the settings in the Smoke Parameters rollout, as shown in Figure 9.6.

4. Now add a Noise map in both Color #1 and Color #2 slots to create varying shades of greens and yellows. Click the None button for Color #1, and double-click Noise. Name this level *greens*. In the Noise Parameters rollout, enter the values shown in Figure 9.7. Set Color #1 to light green (R100, G165, B100) and Color #2 to medium green (R35, G120, B35).

Tip

As a general rule, keep Saturation levels below 160 for natural materials. Colors that are too saturated tend to look artificial; natural materials are usually muted by a layer of dirt and film.

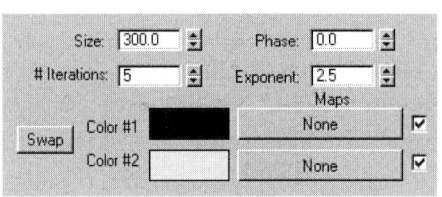

Figure 9.6 Smoke map parameters for *greenyellow* map level.

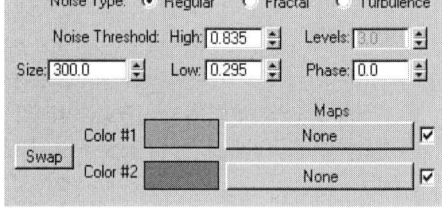

Figure 9.7 Noise map parameters for *greens* map level.

5. In the Material Editor, select Go Forward to Sibling, and enter *yellows* in the Name field. Enter the Noise parameter values shown in Figure 9.8, and change Color #1 to dark yellow (R85, G85, B55) and Color #2 to light yellow (R215, G215, B150).

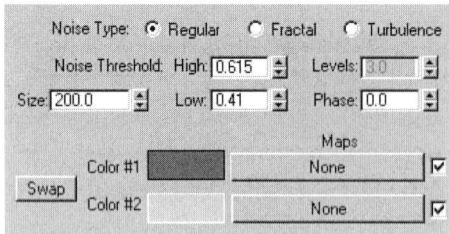

Figure 9.8 Noise parameters for *yellows* map level.

Chapter 9: Designing Naturally Occurring Materials   389

6. Select Quick Render to render the Camera01 viewport. Notice the random pattern of four colors making up the diffuse component of this material. Now add a Bump map to this material.

7. In the Material/Map Navigator, click Material 1:GRASSES (Standard) (to go to that level). In the Maps rollout, enter 45 in the Bump Amount field, and select None for Bumps. Double-click Speckle. Name this level *speckle bump*. Change Color #1 to pure white and Color #2 to pure black. Click the Render Last button, and the ground has a tight bump pattern everywhere.

8. You now want to create a second material that appears to be areas of wildflowers randomly scattered around the hillside. In the Material/Map Navigator, click the bottom level that takes you to Material 2. Name this material FLOWERS. It's also a standard-material type. The Diffuse color component of this material is made of a Cellular-map type with blue and brown, and a submap of red and yellow (to represent the blossoms). In Material 2, click the Diffuse-map shortcut button, and double-click Cellular. Name this level *bluebrown*. Set the values in Cell Characteristics area to those shown in Figure 9.9.

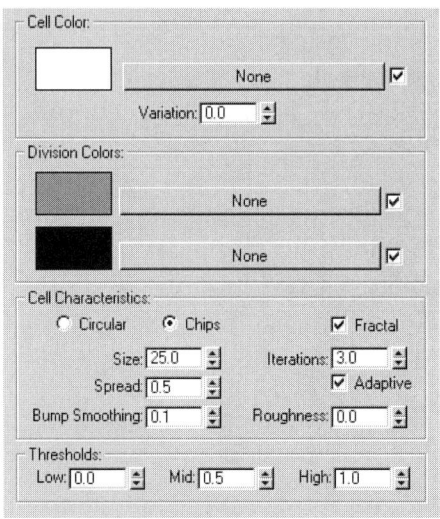

Figure 9.9 Cell Characteristics values.

9. Set the top Division Colors slot to bright blue (R90, G50, B255) and the bottom slot to muddy brown (R95, G80, B50). In the Cell Color area, click the None map button. Then double-click Noise. Name this level *redyellow*. Set the Noise parameters to the values shown in Figure 9.10. Set Color #1 to bright yellow (R255, G255, B105) and Color #2 to bright red (R255, G25, B25).

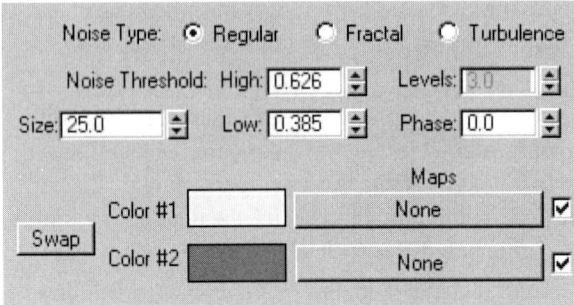

Figure 9.10 Noise parameter, *redyellow* level map.

 Tip

None of this color information shows up on the sample sphere because the Mix amount for this Blend material is 0.0. This allows you to see only Material 1. To view the progress of the color changes, select Show End Result to toggle it off. Then click Go to Parent several times, to step up through each level of mapping.

10. In the Material/Map Navigator, select Material 2:FLOWERS(Standard). In the Maps rollout, enter 200 in the Bump Amount field. Choose Bump None, and double-click Cellular. Name this level *cellular bump*. Set the Cell Characteristics values to those shown in Figure 9.11.

Figure 9.11 Cell Characteristics settings for *cellular bump*.

11. The final step is to add a mask to the Blend material, allowing the flowers to show through the grassy meadow. In the Material/Map Navigator, click the top level, WILDFLOWERS(Blend). Select Mask None, and double-click Noise. Name this level *noise mask*. Set the values in the Noise Parameters rollout to those shown in Figure 9.12.

Chapter 9: Designing Naturally Occurring Materials   391

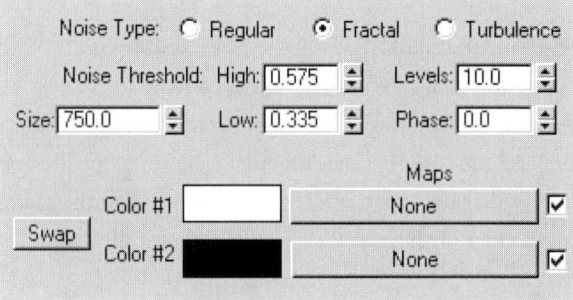

Figure 9.12 Noise parameters for *noise mask* level.

12. Make sure Camera01 viewport is active, and select Quick Render. This hillside is covered with brightly colored wildflowers. At the *noise mask* level, in Noise Parameters rollout, choose Swap (to swap the black-and-white color swatches). Render the scene again, and you have fewer flowers. Where the mask is white, Material 1:GRASSES shows; where the mask is black, Material 2:FLOWERS shows. Any gray in the mask shows a mix of GRASSES and FLOWERS.

13. Save the file. It's already named 09_flowers_01.max. The final rendering looks similar to Figure 9.13.

Figure 9.13 WILDFLOWERS Blend material on a hillside.

Striped Lawn

Sometimes a scene needs a more manicured look. The next exercise walks you through the steps of making a material that simulates a carefully mowed lawn (similar to grass on a golf course). You use the Blend material type again for the mowed lawn. Instead of using a mask, try Mix amount to blend the two materials together. This gives the illusion that mowers went one way, then mowed again in perpendicular swaths. One of the materials has a bump map to simulate the nap of the grass, lying in a different direction, for each pass of the mower.

One advantage of this striped material type is that it accentuates the distant convergence, giving the scene an impression of more depth.

Exercise 9.3   A Striped Lawn

1. Reopen the file called 09max01.max. Again, it's the same hilly landscape from previous exercises in this chapter. Save the file as 09_mowed_01.max.

2. Open the Material Editor. Select Standard material type, and double-click Blend. In the Replace Material dialog box, check Discard This Material. Click OK. Name this material MOWED_LAWN.

3. Select Material 1, and name this material GRASS01. It's a Standard material type. In the Blinn Basic Parameters rollout, choose Specular Highlights. Enter 50 in the Specular Level field and 10 in the Glossiness field.

NEW TO R3
4. Click the Diffuse-map shortcut button. Double-click Gradient Ramp, and name this level *diffuse ramp*. The new Gradient Ramp map type is a flexible procedural map that allows a variety of gradient forms and transitions. Use it to define a two-colored, hard-edged map, once an impossibility with gradient maps in MAX's previous versions. In the Gradient Ramp Parameters rollout, click and then right-click the left flag arrow. Choose Edit Properties. Select the color swatch in the Flag Properties dialog box, and set the color to medium green (R75, G145, B60). In the Flag Properties dialog box, click the 'up' spinner arrow to advance to Flag #2. Now change the color to a lighter green (R80, G180, B95). Close the Flag Parameters dialog box. The ramp is now a smooth transition between three shades of green.

Caution

Starting from the left, Flag 1, Flag 3, and Flag 2 is the three flags' default numbering (in the Gradient ramp). This is confusing, so carefully follow Step 4 to avoid unwanted results.

5. Click and then right-click on the ramp's flag, farthest to the right. Choose Copy. Click and then right-click on the middle flag. Choose Paste (to paste the right flag's color on the middle flag).

6. In the Gradient Ramp Parameters rollout, click Linear in the Interpolation box. Choose Solid. This creates a hard-edged transition between the two shades of green. It looks similar to Figure 9.14.

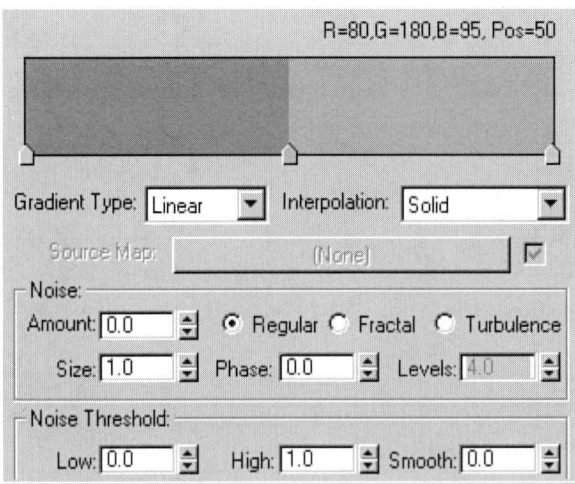

Figure 9.14 Gradient Ramp Parameters rollout.

7. In the Material Editor, drag and drop the material on to the object named GROUND. In Viewport, select Show Map. The hilly landscape turns gray. This map doesn't show in the viewport because GROUND contains no mapping coordinates.

8. Select the GROUND object. Now in the Modify panel, click the UVW Map button. In the Parameters rollout, enter 10'0" in both the Length and Width fields. You see green stripes running from front to back in the shaded Camera01 viewport's landscape. Select Quick Render (to render the Camera01 viewport). The scene looks similar to Figure 9.15.

394   Part II   Materials

Figure 9.15   The striped lawn, running front to back.

 Tip

This material is an effective illusion of freshly mowed lawns in a scene. Creating realistic grass is extremely difficult, and this simple treatment works well in many cases.

9. In the Material/Map Navigator, select Material 1:GRASS01. Apply a Bump map (with a mask) to show bumps on only every other stripe of grass. In the Maps rollout, enter 10 in the Bump Amount field, and then select Bump None. Now double-click Mask. Name this level *bump mask*. In the Mask Parameters rollout, select Map None, and double-click Speckle. Name this level *speckle bump*. In the Speckle Parameters rollout, enter 1.0 in the Size field. Change Color #1 to pure black and Color #2 to pure white.

10. Choose Go to Parent (to go up one level). In the Material/Map Navigator, drag and drop the Diffuse Color:Gradient Ramp map on to the Mask None button. Choose Copy in the dialog box, and click OK. This copies the color information into the mask slot. However, the mask is ineffective because the two green shades maintain similar luminance values.

11. In the Material/Map Navigator, click the Mask (Gradient Ramp) level. Name this level *mask gradient*. In the Gradient Ramp Parameters rollout, change Flag #1 to pure black, and Flag #2 and Flag #3 to pure white. This creates bumps in the light-green stripes, but no bumps in the dark-green stripes. Select Render Last to view the effect on the landscape.

12. Now enhance the striped-grass material by copying Material 1 into the Material 2 slot of the Blend material. This gives you two grass materials—one hidden by the other. In the Material/Map Navigator, click the top level, MOWED_LAWN (Blend). In the Material Editor, drag and drop the GRASS01 button on to the Material 2 button. Choose Copy in the dialog box, and click OK. In the Navigator, select Material 2. Name this material GRASS02. In the Maps rollout, drag and drop one of the None buttons onto the Bump slot button. This deletes the bump for this material.

13. In Navigator, select Diffuse Color. In the Coordinates rollout, enter 90 in the W angle field. This rotates the stripes 90 degrees to the other Material 1.

14. Now blend one material in to the other by adjusting the Mix Amount for a 50–50 mix. In the Material/Map Navigator, click the MOWED_LAWN level. In the Material Editor, enter 50 in the Mix Amount field. Close the Material Editor and all dialog boxes. Choose Render Last, and the scene looks similar to Figure 9.16.

Figure 9.16 MOWED_LAWN material on a hilly landscape.

15. Save this file. It's already named 09_mowed_01.max.

Creating Sky Materials

The biggest problem with skies in computer-generated scenes is not the image used but rather that the perspective of the sky doesn't match the perspective of the scene. Most cloud images must be photographed with camera points 20 degrees to 30 degrees *above* the horizon. However, the most common camera angle in outdoor scenes tends to be from an elevated position, looking *down* at the horizon. The two just don't match. Cloud images are often taken with a 50mm lens on a 35mm camera. This only covers about 45 degrees, horizontally, and the computer's image is made to cover 135 degrees or more. This stretches the map and makes it look unrealistic.

Tip
For computer scenes that encompass more than a 60-degree horizontal view, find panoramic cloud images (or stitch your own) in many of the available paint software packages.

One key to making sky materials look correct in a scene is for clouds to converge at the horizon. For example, on a partly cloudy day with 50 percent of the sky covered with puffy clouds, you look straight up. You see 50 percent clouds and 50 percent blue sky. However, as your view nears the horizon, the sky appears completely cloudy because of the view's angle. This convergence is missing in many scenes. While viewers may not know what's wrong, they sense that something is amiss.

There are three popular methods for creating sky materials:

- Cloud mapping
- Gradient Ramp mapping
- Using a Blend material with a mask

The exercises that follow illustrate each of these, and demonstrate how to apply the material to the inside of a hemisphere. For added realism, you also investigate simulating cloud shadows.

Cloud Map Skies

The cloud mapping method uses a bitmap image of clouds in your scene. MAX R3 ships with several cloud images. The one you use in Exercise 9.4 was originally photographed with a standard lens camera, at a 25-degree angle above the horizon. From it, you create a material. Then you resize it on the hemisphere (to fit the horizontal view of the scene's camera), thus enhancing the convergence effect near the horizon.

Exercise 9.4   Cloud-Map Sky Material

1. Open the file 09_mowed_01.max from the last exercise or from the CD-ROM. It's the hilly landscape with the material simulating mowed grass. You simulate a partly cloudy day by placing a material on the hemisphere. Save the file as 09_cloudmap_01.max.

Chapter 9: Designing Naturally Occurring Materials   397

2. Open the Material Editor, and select an available sample sphere. Name the material CLOUDMAP. Choose Map Shortcut for the diffuse level, and double-click Bitmap. Use the Select Bitmap Image File dialog box to load a map—called Cloud2.jpg—from the CD-ROM. Name this level *diffuse cloud*.

3. In the Material Editor, select Show Map in the Viewport. Drag and drop the material on to the SKYDOME object in the Camera01 viewport. The Camera01 viewport looks like Figure 9.17. There is an obvious seam in the clouds, and the clouds are stretched horizontally. You see only a narrow portion of the image, vertically, as well.

Figure 9.17 Cloud2.jpg, mapped to the inside of SKYDOME.

4. In the Top viewport, select the SKYDOME object. In the Modify panel, choose UVW Map. In the Parameters rollout, check the Spherical mapping option. Click the Sub-Object Gizmo button. and in the Top viewport, rotate the Gizmo 180 degrees in the View Z-axis. In the Front viewport, move the Gizmo downward in the View Y-axis so the Gizmo's horizon is at the GROUND object's base. It looks similar to Figure 9.18. This places the seam behind the camera, but the clouds are still too stretched. In the Modify panel, select Sub-Object (to exit that mode).

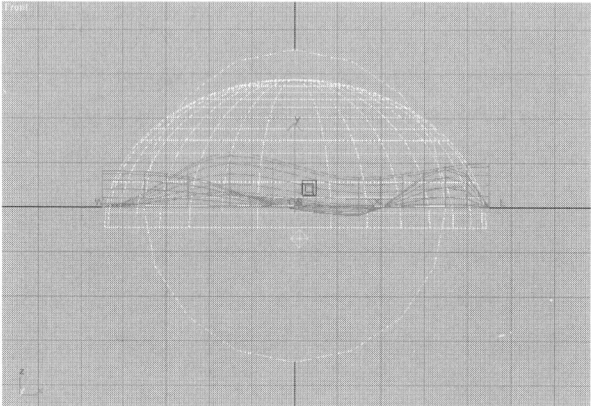

Figure 9.18 UVW Map Gizmo horizon at GROUND's base.

5. Now position the cloud map to fill the visible sky area in the Camera01 viewport. In the Material Editor, select Coordinates. Clear the U Tile and V Tile check boxes. Enter 2.5 in the U Tiling field. The map compresses horizontally in the Camera01 viewport. Enter 2.5 in the V Tiling field, and the cloud map compresses vertically (toward the mapping Gizmo's horizon). To move the map up toward the zenith, enter 0.2 in the V Offset field. The clouds now fit the view and have a more natural perspective. Close the Material Editor. The Camera01 viewport looks similar to Figure 9.19.

Figure 9.19 The Cloud map, compressed horizontally and vertically.

Chapter 9: Designing Naturally Occurring Materials   399

6. Save the file. It's already named 09_cloudmap_01.max.

Gradient Map Skies

The cloud map sky (from Exercise 9.4) is boring. You can't turn the camera very far (left or right) before you reach the map's edge and ruin the effect, by displaying the default color on the SKYDOME mesh object. In Exercise 9.5, you use the new Gradient Ramp map type to create a sky image that allows 360-degree views. Using the Gradient Ramp map to generate skies, you can evoke a particular mood—from a warm hazy summer sky to a violent other-worldly atmosphere.

Exercise 9.5 Gradient-Map Sky Material

1. Open the file 09_cloudmap_01.max, from the last exercise or from the CD-ROM. Save the file as 09_gradient_01.max.

NEW TO R3

2. Open the Material Editor, and select the next sample sphere. Name this material GRADIENT_SKY. Click the Diffuse map shortcut button, and double-click Gradient Ramp. Name this level *diffuse gradient*. Drag and drop the sample sphere on to the SKYDOME object in the Camera01 viewport. In the Material Editor, select Show Map in Viewport. This replaces the current cloud map with the new Gradient Ramp. Only the green portion of the gradient appears because you still have the Spherical mapping coordinates from the previous exercise. The new map is also stretched, to cover the entire inside of the SKYDOME.

3. In the Material Editor, enter the information in the Coordinates rollout, shown in Figure 9.20. The Tiling and Offset values are the same as you used in Exercise 9.4 (2.5 for U and V), but the W Angle value is set to 90 degrees (rotating the ramp to run from zenith to horizon).

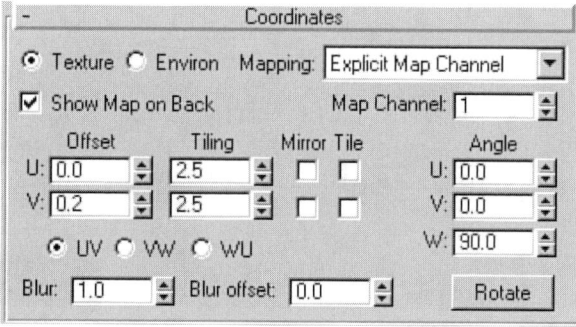

Figure 9.20 Coordinates rollout settings.

4. In the Gradient Ramp Parameters rollout, click and then right-click the left-most flag at the gradient window's base. In the Flag Parameters dialog box, click the

Flag #1 color swatch. Set it to pale yellow (R255, G250, B180). Click the 'down' spinner arrow (to jump to Flag #3). Set it to grayish blue (R125, G165, B210). Set Flag #2 to very light reddish blue (R220, G220, B255). See Figure 9.21. This map makes an agreeably hazy sky for many scenes, but you can make it more interesting.

Tip

Adjust the V:Offset spinner in the Coordinates rollout, to see the colors of the sky gradient move up and down in the scene. Set it back to 0.2 when you have seen the effect.

5. In the Gradient Ramp Parameters rollout, select Noise. Set the Amount to 0.2 and the Size to 2.0. This gives the appearance of slightly puffy clouds on the distant horizon.

6. Click and drag the middle Gradient Ramp Flag to the right, until Pos=70 appears just above the gradient-ramp colors. This compresses the white clouds closer to the horizon, and yellowish clouds appear near the zenith.

7. In the Gradient Ramp Parameters rollout, select Noise. Check the Fractal option. The rendered Camera01 viewport looks similar to Figure 9.22. Save this file. It's already named 09_gradient_01.max.

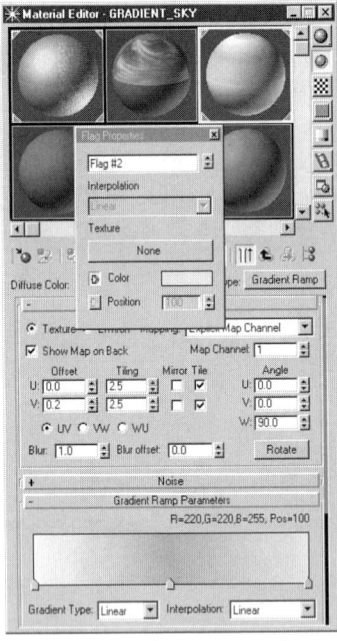

Figure 9.21 Gradient Ramp rollout settings.

Figure 9.22 Rendered Camera01 viewport with Gradient Ramp sky.

Tip

If you reset the V Tiling to 1.0, this material can be used as a 360-degree sky material.

Chapter 9: Designing Naturally Occurring Materials   401

Note
The reason you adjust the V Tiling option (causing the map to wrap horizontally on the SKY-DOME) is because you rotated the map 90 degrees in Step 3.

Experiment with ramp colors and positions, and adjust the Noise parameters. You can create a wide variety of convincing skies with the Gradient Ramp material. Experimenting with the U-spinner values, which adjust the vertical setting because of the 90-degree map rotation, increases or decreases the amount of white cloud effect.

Blend Material with a Mask

For added realism blend the two sky materials you created in the previous two exercises, and add a mask to reveal gradient areas through cloud-image areas. This allows you to alter the mood of any cloud image, giving your skies a more dramatic look or toning down a sky that is too clear. This method is also used for the illusion of haze near the horizon. This way, your scene indicates distance without using MAX R3 atmospherics—which slow render times.

Exercise 9.6   Blend Material Skies

1. Open the file 09_gradient_01.max, from the last exercise or from the CD-ROM. Save the file as 09_skyblend_01.max.

2. Open the Material Editor, and select the next available sample sphere. Click the Standard material type button, and double-click Blend. Check Discard Old Material in the dialog box, and click OK. Name this material SKYBLEND.

3. In the Material Editor, select Get Material. In Browse From, choose Mtl Editor. This shows a list of materials currently in the editor and looks similar to Figure 9.23.

4. From the Material/Map Browser, drag and drop CLOUDMAP material on to Material 1 in the Material Editor. In the Instance Material dialog box, select Copy. Click OK. Next drag and drop GRADIENT_SKY material from the Browser onto the Material 2 button. Choose Copy in the dialog box, and click OK. Close the Material/Map Browser dialog box. This copies the two existing materials in to your new material.

Note
You are dragging from the Material/Map *Browser* dialog box, not from the Material/Map *Navigator* dialog box.

402   Part II   Materials

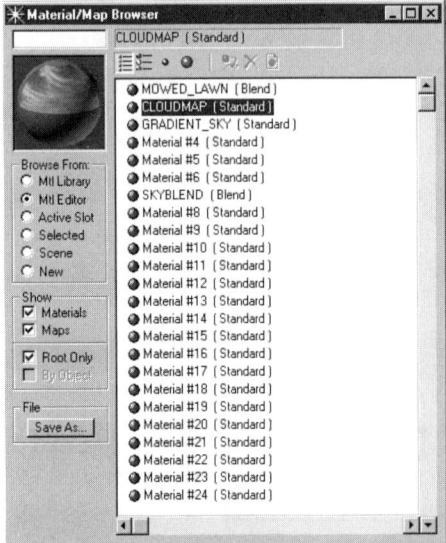

Figure 9.23   Material/Map Browser dialog box.

5. In the Material/Map Navigator, click Material 1, and rename this material CLOUDMAP. In the Navigator, click Material 2, and rename this material GRADIENT_SKY. In the Navigator again, click to return to this material's top level. In the Material Editor, drag and drop SKYBLEND on to the scene's SKY-DOME object. If you rendered the Camera01 viewport now, you'd see only the CLOUDMAP material on SKYDOME. This is because there is no mixing or masking set for this Blend material. If set the Mix Amount to 50 percent, you'd see a muddy-looking sky.

6. In the Material Editor, select Blend Basic Parameters. Choose Mask. Double-click Gradient, and name this level *gradient mask*. This is a simple black-to-white gradient, not the elaborate Gradient Ramp you used earlier. Select Show Map in Viewport. In the shaded viewport, Gradient is applied over the entire dome.

7. In the Coordinates rollout, adjust the values to those shown in Figure 9.24 (2.5 in U and V Tiling, 0.2 in V Offset). In Gradient Parameters, select Noise. Enter 0.2 in the Noise Amount field, and check the Fractal option. This resizes the gradient mask to fit the same area as the other two maps and adds rough noise to the mask.

Chapter 9: Designing Naturally Occurring Materials   403

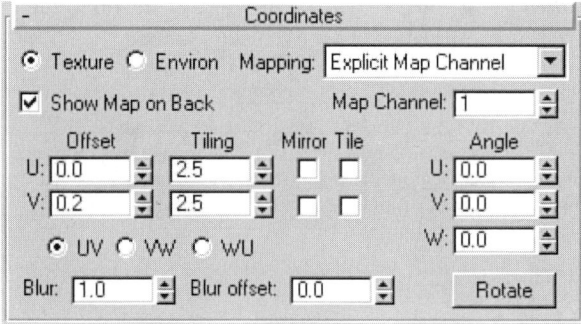

Figure 9.24 Coordinates rollout settings.

8. Render the Camera01 viewport. A fairly blue, partly cloudy sky is near the zenith, and sky with almost no blue and hazy clouds is near the horizon. In the Gradient Parameters rollout, adjust the gradient's Color #2 to a much darker gray. Render again, and more blue sky shows through the mask.

9. In the Material/Map Navigator, click the Diffuse Color diffuse-gradient level of Material 2. In the Material Editor's Gradient Ramp Parameters rollout, click and then right-click the far-right Flag #2. Set its color slot to a deep orange (R240, G150, B90). Close all dialog boxes.

10. Right-click the Camera01 viewport (if it's not already active), and select Quick Render. The rendered scene appears as though there is an orange gas cloud, approaching over the horizon. It looks similar to Figure 9.25.

Figure 9.25 Orange clouds on the horizon.

404   Part II   Materials

11. Save the file. It's already named 09_skyblend_01.max. As you can see, different colors and different noise settings completely change the sky's mood.

NEW TO R3

Tip

In the Material Editor map level, use the controls in Output to subtly or radically adjust various aspects of that map. Enabling the new Color Map feature helps adjust a curve to alter the colors in your map (see Figure 9.26), or it helps adjust the Output level to make a more saturated image.

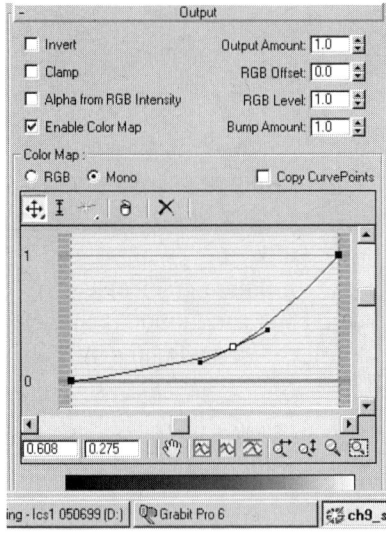

Figure 9.26   Map level Output rollout.

Simulate Cloud Shadows

An important component in conveying realism is usually missing from simulated outdoor scenes: cloud shadows. Although present in nature, they're almost always missing in computer reproductions. In this next exercise you add a projector map in the Sun01 direct light, giving the illusion of clouds casting shadows on the ground. Cloud shadows also add depth to your scene. Viewers can't put their finger on what's wrong with the scene, but they sense something is missing. The next time you see a nature scene that doesn't look natural, check for cloud shadows.

Exercise 9.7   Simulating Cloud Shadows

1. Open the file 09_skyblend_01.max, from the last exercise or from the CD-ROM. It is a scene with the rolling landscape. Save the file as 09_shadow_01.max.

2. Open the Material Editor, and select a new sample sphere (to activate it). Name the slot SHADOW_PROJ. Choose Get Material. In the Material/Map Browser, select Browse From, and check New. Double-click Smoke. Name this level *smoke proj*. Close the Browser dialog box.

3. Click the Select button, and type H. In the Select Objects dialog box, double-click Sun01. In the Modify panel, go to the Directional Parameters rollout. From the Material Editor, drag and drop the SHADOW_PROJ sample sphere on to the None button (in the Projector Map area). In the Instance Map dialog box, check Instance, and click OK.

4. In the Material Editor's Smoke Parameters rollout, enter 1000 in the Size field. Select Swap (to swap black for white in the color slots). The light shows through the white areas of the projector map and is blocked by the black areas.

5. Render the Camera01 viewport, and the scene looks similar to Figure 9.27. It appears as though clouds are casting shadows across the landscape.

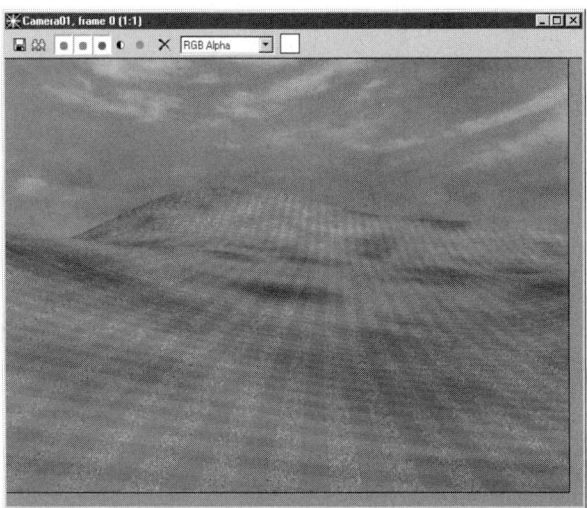

Figure 9.27 Simulated clouds on the landscape.

6. Close all the dialog boxes, and save the file. It's already called 09_shadow_01.max.

Over the course of the last few exercises, you created a decent-looking outdoor scene, without using expensive plug-ins or MaxScripts. The effect is fully scalable for differently sized scenes. Once you create a few basic materials, it's easy to make minor adjustments to radically change your scene's look.

Creating Water Materials

Specular highlights and reflectivity distinguish water from other natural materials. In this section you create pond water on a breezy day and rougher seas on a windy day. The pond water is fairly simple. The rough seas are a bit more complex, taking advantage of multiple mapping channels. There are also fantastic new shaders (shipped with MAX R3) that help control the specular highlights.

Pond Water

Little ripples can lead to something bigger. For Exercise 9.8, the little ripples are on a small pond on a breezy day. Use the landscape you created in Exercise 9.6. Unhide a flat plane, representing the pond's surface. For specular highlights coming from the bright sky, add a light that is just over the horizon (in front of the camera). Such highlights are an important part of most water scenes. The bright sky must be factored in (as part of the lighting scheme) and is simulated with an Omni light that excludes everything but the pond's surface.

Exercise 9.8   Pond Water

1. Open the file 09_skyblend_01.max, from Exercise 9.6 or from the CD-ROM. Save the file as 09_pond_01.max.

> **Note**
> Don't use the scene from Exercise 9.7 (with the simulated shadows). It's easier to see the materials' changes without the cloud shadows.

2. In the Display panel, select Hide. Click Unhide All. This reveals a flat plane that becomes the pond's surface. Open the Material Editor, and select the next available sample sphere. Name this material POND_WATER.

NEW TO R3

3. Use a Standard material, but instead of using the Blinn shader, use one of the new shaders (called Multi-Layer). This new shader allows you to use two specular highlights (opposed to each other), creating highlights with an elongated crossing effect. In the Shader Basic Parameters rollout, select Blinn, and then choose Multi-Layer.

4. In the Multi-Layer Basic Parameters rollout, click the Diffuse map shortcut button, and double-click Noise. In the Noise Parameters rollout, enter 300 in the Size field. Set Color #1 to dark blue (R60, G60, B100) and Color #2 to dark green (R50, G100, B50). Name this level *diffuse noise*.

5. In the Material Editor, drag and drop the sample sphere onto POND. Render the Camera01 viewport, and notice that the surface is dark blue-green and flat.

6. Add some ripples to the surface with a Noise bump map. However, use a Mask map with Noise, making the ripples more irregular across the pond. In the Material/Map Navigator, click the top level. In the Maps rollout, enter 15 in the Bump Amount field. Click the Bump None button, and double-click Mask. Name this level *noise mask*. Select Map None, and double-click Noise again. Name this level *noise bump*.

7. In the Coordinates rollout, enter 3.0 in the Y-axis Tiling field. This elongates the ripples. In the Noise Parameter rollout, enter 75.0 in the Size field, 0.75 in the High Threshold field, and 0.275 in the Low Threshold field. These settings create a moderate bump with a smooth transition between white and black for smooth-sided bumps. Render the Camera01 viewport again, and notice the evenly spaced faint ripples on the surface.

8. Select Go to Parent. In the Mask Parameters rollout, choose Mask None. Double-click Noise, and name this level *noise mask*. In the Noise Parameters rollout, enter 300 in the Size, 0.635 in the High Threshold, and 0.385 in the Low Threshold. This causes the ripples to appear only in some surface areas by masking out the bump effect.

9. In the Material/Map Navigator, click the top level. In the Multi-Layer Basic Parameters rollout, enter the values shown in Figure 9.28. These values adjust the specular highlights of the material and its glossiness. Render the Camera01 viewport, and the water's surface shows more definition.

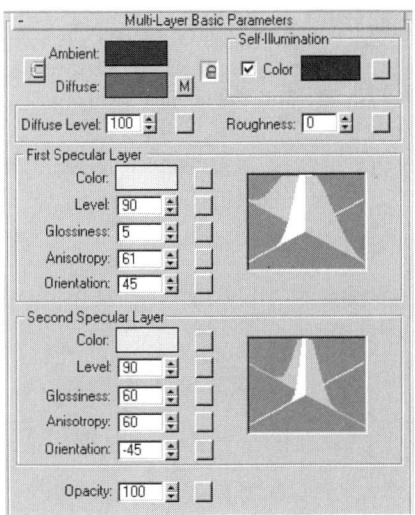

Figure 9.28 Multi-Layer Shader values.

10. In the Maps rollout, enter 30 in the Reflection Amount field. Select Reflection None, and double-click Raytrace. Name this level *raytrace refl*.

11. Now you need something to make it appear as though the bright sky background is causing specular highlights in the water. Right-click the Front viewport. In the Create panel, choose Lights, and then Omni. Click just above the hill (in the Front viewport's center. In the Top viewport, move the new Omni light to the GROUND object's back edge. The viewports look similar to Figure 9.29.

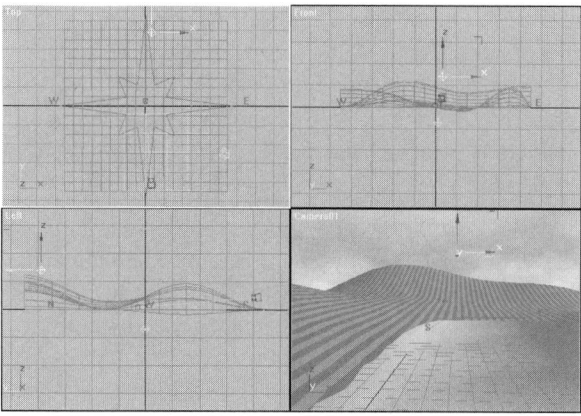

Figure 9.29 Omni Light, in Back of Scene and Above Hill.

12. In the Modify panel, select General Parameters, and check Exclude. Choose POND in the left column, and click the arrow button (to move it to the right column). Select Include (located in the top right of the dialog box), and click OK. In the Modify panel, enter 20 in the Contrast field. Under Affect Surfaces, clear Diffuse. Now the light affects the water surface and the surface's specular portion, with higher contrast results.
13. Render the Camera01 viewport, and the result looks similar to Figure 9.30. Save the file. It's already named 09_pond_01.max.

Chapter 9: Designing Naturally Occurring Materials   409

Figure 9.30 Rendered pond scene.

Rough Water

NEW TO R3 The waves and the water are getting larger: In Exercise 9.9, you tackle an ocean—with moderate waves rolling across the surface and wind rippling the waves. The modeling of the water is already done, and you create a material for the finishing touch. The water mesh is a new Plane object with high segmentation. A Volume Select modifier is applied, with a new option by Texture Map. A Noise map selects vertices in the white areas for the full Wave modifier effect, areas of gray for partial Wave modifier effect, and areas of black for no Wave modifier effect. This results in an irregular wave pattern that was difficult to achieve before MAX R3. Use the multiple map-channels feature to apply color information and ripple bumps with one UVW Map, and self-illumination (with another UVW map) to a single object.

Exercise 9.9 Creating Rough Water

1. Open the file 09max09.max, from the CD-ROM. It's the SKYDOME from the previous exercises. It contains a high-density Plane, deformed with a Wave modifier. It deformed on vertices using a Vol.Select modifier and Noise map. Save the file as 09_wave_01.max.

2. Open the Material Editor, and set the cursor between two sample spheres. When the hand cursor appears, click and drag it to the left (to reveal new sample spheres). Select a new sample sphere to activate it. Choose Standard type, and double-click Blend. Check Discard Old Material in the dialog box, and click OK. Name the material ROUGH_WAVE. Drag and drop the sample sphere onto WATER (located in the Top viewport).

3. Select Material 1, and name this material BLUES. Click the Blinn shader name, and choose Multi-Layer. In the Multi-Layer Basic Parameters rollout, click the Diffuse map shortcut button. Then double-click Smoke. Name this level *diffuse smoke*. In the Smoke Parameters rollout, enter 400 in the Size field, Change Color #1 to dark blue (R30, G30, B90) and Color #2 to a darker blue (R20, G20, B60).

4. Select Go to Parent button (to go up one level). In the Multi-Layer Basic Parameters rollout, change both specular Color swatches to pure white, and change the settings as shown in Figure 9.31. (Level=90, Glossiness=25, Anisotropy=85, Orientation=–45 in First Specular Layer; and Level=80, Glossiness=60, Anisotropy=85, Orientation=45 in Second Specular Layer.)

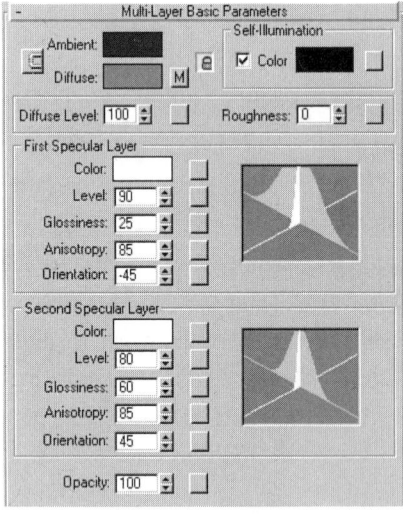

Figure 9.31 Multi-Layer settings.

5. In the Navigator, select Material 1. In the Maps rollout, enter 30 in the Reflection Amount field. Choose Reflection None, and double-click Raytrace. Name this level *raytrace refl*.

6. Select Go to Parent. Enter 20 in the Bump Amount field, and click the Bump None button. Double-click Noise. Name this level *noise bump*. In the Coordinates rollout, change the Source to Explicit Map Channel, and leave the Channel at default 1. In the Noise Parameters, enter the values shown in Figure 9.32.

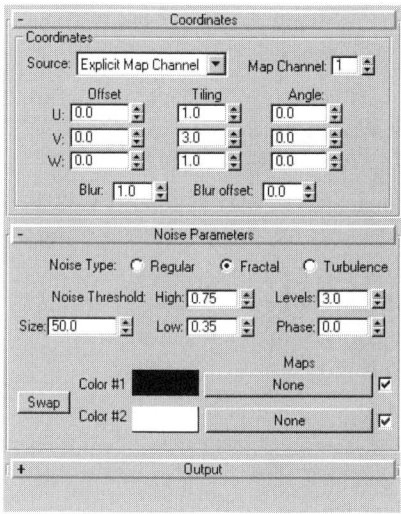

Figure 9.32 Noise bump parameter settings.

7. Select Material/Map Navigator, and click the top level. In the Blend Basic Parameters rollout, drag and drop BLUES (Standard) onto Material 2. Choose Copy in the dialog box, and click OK. Select Material 2, and name this material GREENS. In the Material/Map Navigator, select Diffuse Color for Material 2. Change Color #1 to dark green (R35, G90, B45) and Color #2 to a lighter green (R70, G150, B90).

8. Select the scene's WATER object. Now in the Modify panel, click the UVW Map button. In the Parameters rollout, enter 0'4" in the Length and Width fields. Notice the Map Channel is set to use Channel 1.

9. In the Material/Map Navigator, click the top level. In the Material Editor, select Blend Basic Parameters. Choose Mask, and double-click Smoke. Name this level *smoke mask*. In the Smoke Parameters rollout, enter 500 in the Size field. Render the Camera01 viewport. You have a bluish green sea, with moderate waves and wind ripples on the surface. The sky is also reflected on the surface. In the real world, however, wave tops are thinner than the troughs, so more light passes

through and is refracted. This makes the wave tops appear lighter. You simulate this effect over the next four steps.

10. In the Material/Map Navigator, select Material 1:BLUES. In the Maps rollout, choose Self-illumination None, and double-click Gradient. Name this level *self-illum gradient*. Check Show Map in Viewport. In the Coordinates rollout, set the map to use Explicit Map Channel 2.

11. In the Camera01 viewport, select WATER. In the Modify panel, choose UVW Map. Now in the Parameters rollout, set the Map Channel to 2. WATER is a gradient, with light color in the foreground and darker color in the background. However, you want the top of the waves to be light and the troughs to be dark.

12. Right-click the Front viewport (to activate it). In the Modify panel, select Alignment, and then View Align. Choose Fit. This flips the map gizmo up, projecting to WATER's side and resizing it to fit WATER from that view. The waves in the Camera01 shaded viewport are dark on top and light at the base.

13. In the Material Editor, select Gradient Parameters. Set Color #1 to R60, G60, B60; Color #2 to R30, G30, B30; and Color #3 to R0, G0, B0. Enter 0.8 in the Color #2 Position field. This reduces the self-illumination amount and pushes the greater effect toward the wave top. Render the Camera01 viewport to view the result. The material isn't too bad, but as mentioned earlier, materials are only part of the story. Lighting usually makes the materials more finished.

14. There is still an Omni light in the scene that lit the pond in the previous exercise. When you created it, however, you set it to include an object called POND. There is no POND in this scene, so the light does nothing. Choose Select, and type H. Double-click Omni01. In the Modify panel, select General Parameters. Choose Include. Now select WATER in the left column, and click the arrow (to send it to the right column) Check OK. Enter 2.0 in the Multiplier field, boosting the light's intensity. You add one extra effect to the scene.

NEW TO R3

15. In MAX R3 add atmospheric effects to lights from the Modify panel, and preview the results without rendering. Right-click Camera01 viewport (to activate it). In the Modify panel, go to the Atmospheres and Effects rollout, and Add. Double-click Lens Effects. Select Lens Effects in the window, and choose Setup. In the Lens Effects Parameters rollout, select Glow (in the left column). Click the right arrow, sending it to the right column. In Preview, check Interactive. Wait while a preview of the active viewport is rendered, complete with a small glowing sun near the horizon.

16. In the Glow Element rollout, enter 100 in the Parameters Tab Size field. Note that the glowing sun got larger, without re-rendering the scene. Close all the dialog boxes, and render Camera01 viewport. It looks similar to Figure 9.33.

Figure 9.33 Rendered ocean scene, with hazy sun.

17. Save the file. It's already called 09_wave_01.max.

Beachfront Surf

In Exercise 9.10 you use yet another form of material mapping—mapping coordinates. Mapping coordinates are applied during the loft process, creating the illusion of surf crashing on a beach. Waves on a curving shoreline usually hit the shore at a nearly perpendicular angle. The landscape has a simple Gradient Ramp material mapped to the side of GROUND, giving the illusion of a beach. You create the material for the water.

Exercise 9.10   Beach Surf

1. Open the file 09max10.max from the CD-ROM. The file contains a beach and a straight line (lofted along a curved line), which becomes the water. It's important that the water is a lofted object. This lets you take advantage of the lofted mapping coordinates. These coordinates are located under Surface Parameters, in the Modify panel. These lofting coordinates make the material follow the shoreline.

2. Open the Material Editor, and select an available sample sphere. Name this material SURF. Drag and drop the SURF material onto the SURF object in the scene. Click the Diffuse map shortcut button, and double-click Gradient Ramp. Name this level *diffuse gradient*. Select Show Map in Viewport, and you see the Gradient Ramp on the water (with the red component following the shoreline).

414   Part II   Materials

3. In the Gradient Ramp Parameters rollout, click and then right-click the left-most Flag #1. Choose Edit Properties. In the Flag Properties dialog box, change the color swatch to very light blue (R235, G240, B255). In the Flag Properties dialog box, click the 'up' arrow on the spinner. The cursor jumps to Flag #2. Set it to dark blue (R25, G30, B110). Click the 'up' arrow to jump to Flag #3, and set it to dark teal (R45, G150, B110). Close the Flag Properties dialog box. The colors are okay, but the surface distribution is too even. You want to squeeze the colors toward the shore.

4. In the Gradient Ramp Parameters rollout, click beside each flag (along the ramp's base). This allows you to more easily control the colors' position and transition. Click and drag the two center flags to the left, close to the flags already on the left. Move the next-to-the-last flag on the right (just left of center). In the Noise area, enter 0.1 in the Amount field and 0.2 in the Size field. The rollout looks similar to Figure 9.34.

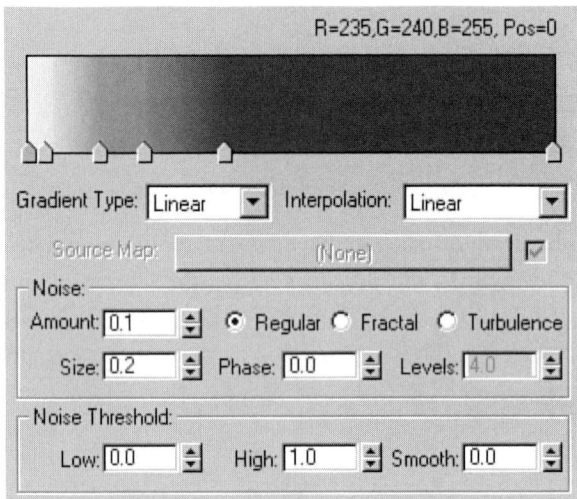

Figure 9.34   Flags moved left.

5. In the Material/Map Navigator, click the top level. Enter 75 in the Specular Level field and 50 in the Glossiness field. In the Maps rollout, drag and drop the Diffuse color map button onto the Bump None button. Check Instance in the dialog box, and click OK. Enter 1 in the Bump Amount field.

6. In the Maps rollout, enter 20 in the Reflection Amount field. Select Reflection None, and double-click Raytrace. Render the Camera01 viewport. The image looks similar to Figure 9.35.

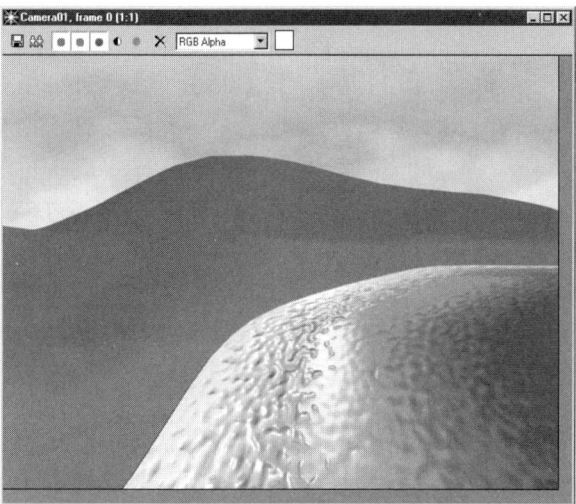

Figure 9.35 Simulated surf along a beach.

7. Save the file. It's already named 09_surf_01.max.

For different variations on this scene's landscape and surf, apply some of the material settings from the previous exercises. Also, study how the SURF object is lofted using the loft-mapping coordinates so that the surf follows the shore. It's a straight line, lofted along a curving line. In the Surface Parameters rollout, Apply Mapping is checked. This same process (using the lofted mapping coordinates) allows a road striped-line map to follow the curve of a lofted road, or a brick pattern map to follow a circular lofted patio.

Trees

Creating trees using the Material Editor is a simple process that you may know from other books. So why go through the steps again? Because even the simple can be troublesome. Here you focus on a few common problems you may encounter, when creating trees mapped to flat planes. The often-seen problems with mapped trees are

- The plane is visible in the scene.
- The plane's edge flashes in the light.
- The scene renders slowly.

Mapped Trees on Plane

Faking tree objects by mapping a material onto a flat plane is a great shortcut, until the plane is visible. The material in the next exercise needs a diffuse component (to give the tree color) and an alpha channel opacity component (to show only the tree and not the rectangular plane). In certain light the whole plane appears, as the specular highlight plays across the surface. To avoid this use the map's alpha channel in the Glossiness slot. At other times just the plane's edges show (when the light is right). Often too much blurring on the bitmap shows a few stray pixels at the edges. Reducing the Blur setting avoids this problem.

Exercise 9.11 Mapped Trees

NEW TO R3

1. Open the file 09max11.max from the CD-ROM. It's a simple ground QuadPatch and a new primitive Plane object. You create a material for application to the Plane, making it appear like a free-standing tree. Save the file as 09_treeplane_01.max.

2. Open the Material Editor, and name the active sample sphere TREE. In the Maps rollout, select Diffuse None. Double-click Bitmap, and load the image file called 4morpap0.tif. Name this level *diffuse tree*. In the Coordinates rollout, right-click the Blur field spinner, setting it to 0.01 (its lowest amount). This eliminates any stray pixels from showing up on the plane's edge. Select Show Map in Viewport, and choose Go to Parent. Drag and drop the material on to the TREE object. Render the Camera01 viewport. It appears like a tree pictured on a billboard, similar to Figure 9.36.

Figure 9.36 Tree image on flat plane.

Chapter 9: Designing Naturally Occurring Materials   417

3. In the Maps rollout, drag and drop Diffuse Color onto Opacity None. Check Copy in the dialog box, and click OK. This uses the image as an opacity map, but you obtain better results by using the image's alpha channel as the opacity.

4. In the Maps rollout, select Opacity map, and name the level *opacity tree*. In the Bitmap Parameters rollout, select Mono Channel Output, and check Alpha. Render the scene. The tree remains, but the plane is transparent.

5. In the Maps rollout, drag and drop the Opacity map onto the Glossiness button. Choose Copy in the dialog box, and click OK. This uses the alpha channel, which keeps specular highlights from showing on the plane's transparent portions and ruining the effect. Close all dialog boxes.

6. Select TREE01 in the Camera01 viewport, and choose Array. Enter 1'6" in the X-Move field, and 2'0" in the Y-Move field. In the Type of Object rollout, check Instance. Then click OK. The Array dialog box looks like Figure 9.37. You see a diagonal array of trees.

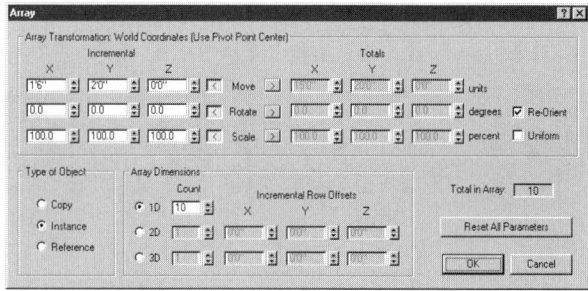

Figure 9.37 The Array dialog box.

7. In the Files pull-down menu, select Summary Info. Under Rendering, note the Last Frame Time. Close the Summary Info dialog box. Render the Camera01 viewport. The render time is substantially longer, even though you only added a few extra faces and vertices. The longer render time illustrates the third problem with mapped trees: Multiple levels of Opacity take a long time to calculate and render.

 Caution
Watch the objects with transparency in your scene. Simple mapped trees are quite effective in saving render times—if *they do not overlap* from the viewer's point of view. Overlapping transparent objects are much slower than some mesh geometry trees.

8. Notice the light rectangular areas around each tree. Step 5 only partially corrected the visible-plane problem. Open the Material Editor. Use the Material/Map Navigator, and go to the glossiness tree map level. In the Output rollout, select Invert. This inverts the black-and-white values of the alpha

418   Part II   Materials

channel. Render the Camera01 viewport again, and you see the problem is now corrected.

9. Save the file. It's already named 09_treeplane_01.max.

Vegetation

Grass and leaves viewed close up require a combination of geometry and materials, unlike the grasses you created earlier in this chapter. Those grasses and flowers were just the color representations over a large surface. In this section you learn to make two types of vegetation:

- Thin, reed-like grasses blowing in the wind.
- House-plant style leaves.

Again, the exercises are only a starting point. Expand the principles taught here and use elements of previous exercises to create vegetation that meets your needs.

Note
When creating vegetation geometry, pay close attention to the face/vertex counts. It's quite easy to let the mesh density get out of control and to overload any computer system with unnecessary detail.

Blowing Grass

With simple geometry and a simple material, you can quickly represent a patch of grass. Add MAX R3's new Flex modifier, and you animate the grasses (as if they're blowing in the wind).

Exercise 9.12   Blowing Grass

1. Open the file 09max12.max from the CD-ROM. It's a small sandy mound, with several 2D shapes and a Wind SpaceWarp. Loft a blade of grass, apply a material to it, and then use Flex modifier and Wind to animate grass that's blown by a breeze. Save the file as 09_grass_01.max.

2. Right-click the Front viewport (to activate it), and type H. In the dialog box, double-click a 2D shape called grass_path. It's a line whose pivot point is moved to the base, and three segments are added between the end vertices.

Tip
The extra vertices give the lofted object enough segments to bend correctly. Take control of all mesh objects' density and don't rely on the default settings.

Chapter 9: Designing Naturally Occurring Materials   419

3. In the Geometry menu, select Create. Click Standard Primitives, and choose Compound Objects. Select Loft. In the Creation Method rollout, choose Get Shape. Type H, and double-click grass_shape. Grass_shape is a triangle and gets lofted the length of the grass_path. Name the object BLADE01.

4. In the Modify panel, select Deformations, and choose Scale. In the Scale Deformation(X) dialog box, click and drag the right control point (on the red line) downward, until the lower right-hand numeric field reads 10. The Deformation dialog box looks like Figure 9.38. This tapers the grass to a blunt point at the top.

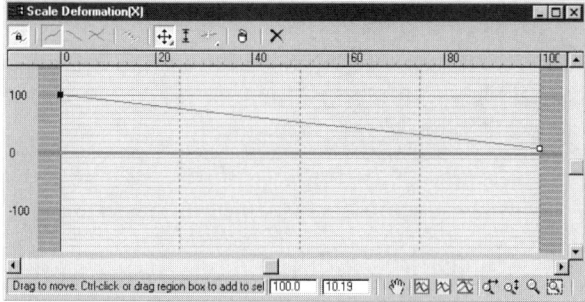

Figure 9.38 The Scale Deformation(X) dialog box.

5. In the Skin Parameters rollout, enter 0 in the Shape Steps field and 2 in the Path Steps field. This reduces the mesh faces to the minimum necessary for this exercise.

 Tip
In this case, selecting Optimize Shapes has the same results as setting Shape Steps to 0.

6. Open the Material Editor, and click the second sample sphere (in the top row). It's named GRASS. Now choose Assign to Selected, which puts the material on the BLADE01 object. The material is very simple, just a Noise map in the Diffuse slot with two shades of greens. Close the Material Editor.

7. Select BLADE01, and move it middle-left of the Camera01 viewport. Render the scene, which looks similar to Figure 9.39.

8. BLADE01 is too rectangular, but you don't want to increase its complexity. Close the Virtual Frame Buffer. In the Modify panel, select More, and double-click Smooth. In the Parameters rollout, check the Auto Smooth check box. Type 90 in the Threshold field, and press Enter. This makes the blade look rounded, by applying a common smoothing group to the faces.

420   Part II   Materials

Figure 9.39   BLADE01, in middle foreground.

NEW TO R3

9. In the Modify panel, select More, and double-click Flex. In the Parameters rollout, choose Add Force. Click on the round, yellow Wind gizmo (near the top of the mound) in the Camera01 viewport. This is a spherical Wind space warp. Scrub the Animation Slider back and forth, and you see BLADE01 bend at its mid-point. In the Modifier Stack rollout, select Sub-Object to enter Center mode. Choose Align, and then BLADE01 in Camera01 viewport. In the Align dialog box, check Z-Position. In the Target Object column, check Minimum. This puts the Flex center at BLADE01's base. Scrub the Animations slider, and notice that the grass flexes at its base.

10. In the Camera01 viewport, hold the Shift key and right-click the viewport. Select Move. Move BLADE01 a bit to the right. Check Instance in the dialog box, and click OK. This makes an instanced copy, which you now scatter over selected faces on the ground object.

 Tip

You can use Scatter on the original blade of grass, but it's easier to edit the blades later (by modifying an instance object) than it is to work your way down in the Scatter Compound Object.

11. Now scatter the BLADE02 over a few selected faces on the GROUND object. Select BLADE02. In the Create panel, select Compound Objects, and then Scatter. In the Pick Distribution Object rollout, choose Pick Distribution Object. Select GROUND in the Camera01 viewport. In the Source Object Parameters area, enter 50 in the Duplicates field. In the Distribution Object Parameters area, check the Perpendicular check box and the Use Selected Faces Only check box. In the Display rollout, check the Hide Distribution Object check box.

Chapter 9: Designing Naturally Occurring Materials   421

Note
The Use Selected Faces Only option is confusing. The distribution object is not selected at this point, so you can't see any selected faces. The selected faces can be from a MeshSelect, located at the Modifer Stack's top on the distribution object. Scatter finds those faces.

12. Scrub the Animation slider, and notice the grass blades flex out away from the wind gizmo. Select Render Scene. In the Render Scene dialog box, check Active Time Segment. Click the 640×480 resolution button, and select Files. Render the animation as grass.avi.

Tip
The Cinepak codec by Radius is a good choice for this animation.

13. Save this file. It's already called 09_grass_01.max.

NEW TO R3
14. In the Rendering pull-down menu, click RAM Player. In the RAM Player dialog box, select Open Channel A, and open grass.avi. In the RAM Player Configuration dialog box, click OK, and wait for the animation to load. In the RAM Player dialog box, click Playback Forward, and watch the animation at 30 frames per second. (A pre-rendered grass.avi is found on the CD-ROM, as well.)

The scene certainly needs a lot of work, but you get the idea and have starting point. With a little work you can make an interesting animation in a short time.

Leaves

In this exercise you learn to create leaves similar to those on many potted plants. This method can also create grasses for close-up shots. Use Double-Sided materials, and take advantage of loft-mapping coordinates to create leaf ribs.

Double-Sided materials use face normals to determine which side of an object gets which material. It's a way to create objects with low face/vertex count that have no thickness. A box object isn't be a good candidate for Double-Sided materials, unless you must see the box's inside faces. A plane primitive is ideal for Double-Sided material (to create page one and two of a book, for example).

Exercise 9.13 Leaves

1. Open the file 09max13.max from the CD-ROM. It's a low dirt mound with two 2D shapes. Loft a leaf, and apply a Double-Sided material that has a light green top (with ribs) and a darker green back.

2. In the Camera01 viewport, type H, and double-click leaf_path. In the Create panel, select Standard Primitives, and click Compound Objects. Choose Loft. In

the Creation Method rollout, select Get Shape. Type H, and double-click leaf_shape. An open V-shaped line is lofting along a curved line. Name the object LEAF01. The result is a mesh object with no thickness. The leaf doesn't appear in the Shaded viewport because the normals point away from the camera.

3. Open the Material Editor. Select the third sample sphere (in the top row), called LEAF, and choose Assign to Selected. You see the leaf appear because of the Double-Sided material. Close the Material Editor.

4. Activate the Top viewport. Select Zoom Extents All Selected, zooming in on LEAF01 in all orthogonal viewports. In the Modify panel, select Modifier Stack, and choose Sub-Object. Select the shape at the bottom of LEAF01 (in the Top viewport).

 Caution
Do not select the original V-shaped line. When you select the Sub-Object shape at the loft's base, the shape turns red.

5. Select Rotate, and rotate the shape 90 degrees on the path. Choose Sub-Object (to exit that mode). The viewports look similar to Figure 9.40.

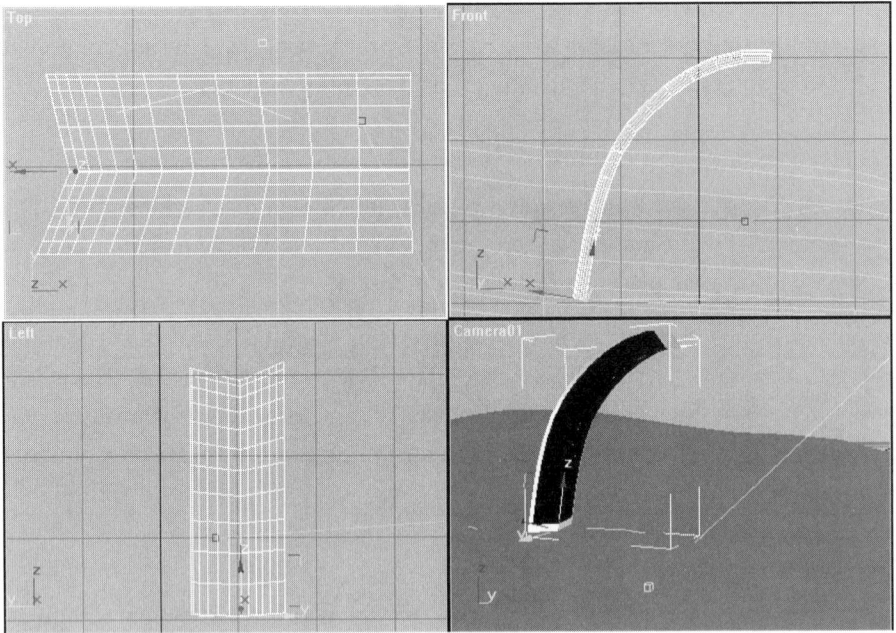

Figure 9.40 Shape, rotated 90 degrees on path.

Chapter 9: Designing Naturally Occurring Materials   423

6. In the Surface Parameters rollout, select Mapping. Now enter 10 in the Width Repeat field. This repeats a Bump map ten times across the leaf's face, creating ribs in the rendered scene. The ribs are only on the Facing material.

Note
You never see both materials in the shaded viewports. You must render the scene to see the results of a Double-Sided material.

7. In the Deformations rollout, select Scale. In the Scale Deformation(X) dialog box, choose Add Insert Bézier Point (beneath Insert Corner Point). Select the red scale line near the dotted vertical line. In the Scale Deformation dialog box, select Move Control Point. Move the right control point downward to the gray 0 line, and the left control point about half-way to the gray 0 line. It looks like Figure 9.41. You can create a variety of leaves by using different scaling modifications.

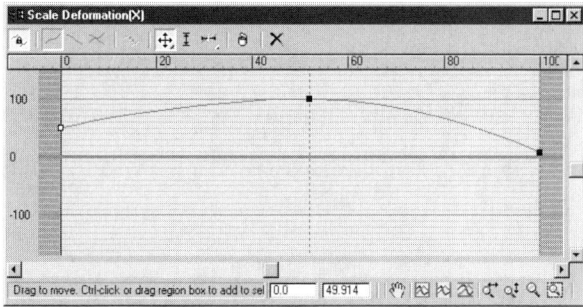

Figure 9.41 The Scale Deformation(X) dialog box.

Caution
Each Control Point you add in the Deformation dialog boxes adds to the mesh object's density. The face and vertex count can quickly get out of control.

8. Render the Camera01 viewport, and you see the leaf from the back. In the Camera01 viewport, hold the Shift key, and click the Rotate button. The leaf rotates about 45 degrees in the World Z-axis. Release the mouse button, and check Instance. Enter 4 in the Number of Copies field, and click OK.

9. Adjust the camera in Camera01 viewport, so you look down on the new leaves. Now render the scene. You see the light-green ribbed material on the leaf tops and the darker green underneath. It looks similar to Figure 9.42.

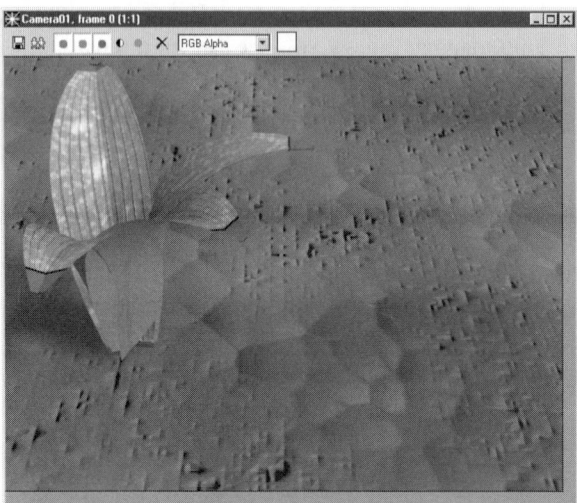

Figure 9.42 Rendered leaves, with Double-Sided material.

10. Close all dialog boxes, and save the file. It's already named 09_leaf_01.max.

This method of creating leaves and applying Double-Sided material has wide-ranging applications, from leaves to book pages to cloth and fabric. Use your imagination.

In Practice: Designing Naturally Occurring Materials

- **Procedural maps add randomness to your scenes.** Map types (such as Noise, Smoke, and Cellular) are generated with random patterns that make rough ground look more convincing. They create color information or masks (to bleed one map through another).

- **Blend materials add another level of complexity to your materials.** The Blend material type further randomizes the look of your environment. Use it with a Mix Amount for bleeding, or a Mask map for random or controlled masking. It allows combinations of color, bumpiness, glossiness, and so on.

- **Skies are created with bitmaps or procedural maps.** Photographic bitmaps don't always make the best skies in a scene. In this chapter you tried blend bitmaps and procedural maps to modify a dull photograph. You also scaled the cloud photo, creating the illusion of convergence (often missing in computer-generated skies). You created a dramatic sky with only a Gradient Ramp map, as well.

- **Clouds are more convincing with shadows on the ground.** You learned a method of applying a Projector map to the Sun light, simulating shadows from clouds overhead.

- **Water, water everywhere.** You learned to create flat water with ripples; then to adjust a light in the scene to enhance the backlit specular highlights for more realistic water. You also used multiple map channels to apply color bump mapping to an ocean scene from above, as well as a separate Self-Illumination map from the side (giving the illusion of lighter wave tops).

- **Opacity mapped trees are efficient.** You learned how to use maps on flat planes to give color and transparency. When viewed from a distance, this makes good-looking trees. You also learned caution regarding multiple overlapping opacity-mapped trees. The render time is exponential to the number of trees that overlap from a given viewpoint. You also learned that material Glossiness and bitmap blurring cause problems with opacity-mapped trees.

- **Blowing in the wind.** You used the new Flex modifier and Wind space warp to bend a lofted blade of grass in the wind. While not a material technique, the effect is impressive for other plants and trees you created in this chapter.

- **Real-world map scaling makes more convincing images.** To calculate the sizes to enter in UVW Map mapping gizmo fields, first analyze the pattern being mapped and determine how much area one repetition of the pattern covers. Then enter the mapping-gizmo size amounts for that area.

NEW TO R3
- **Paint accurate maps with Box Select rendering.** Box Select is a new rendering option that renders an image that is the resolution of the object's bounding box. This resolution is selected at render time. That image imports into a paint program, and a pattern is painted on top of it. When the image is saved from the paint program and applied in the scene as a material map, it perfectly fits the object.

- **Complex curved, lofted objects have loft-generated mapping.** Using the Loft-generated mapping coordinates allows the material pattern to follow the contours of the lofted object. This is critical for fitting a pattern to odd-shaped objects.

- **Take advantage of Double-Sided materials for efficient mesh objects.** The biggest advantage of using Double-Sided materials is reducing the face and vertex count of mesh objects. To be productive always create the most efficient scenes possible.

NEW TO R3
- **Use multiple Map Channels for flexible mapping.** MAX R3 allows up to 99 map channels per object. These many channels have their own UVW Map modifier, to adjust the pattern on any single object.

Chapter 10

Designing Man-Made Materials

Creating the illusion of plastics, metals, fabrics, paper, and other man-made materials has its own set of challenges, most of which hinge on surface specular highlights.

Look carefully around you. The amount and quality of light scattered from an object's surface are the most important clues to determine the materials of that object.

Surface reflectivity also has some bearing on determining the type of material. For example, some metals have similar reflectivity to water, but radically different specular highlights. Other important factors that affect the look of man-made materials are:

- Quality and quantity of light in the scene
- Reflectivity and objects reflected
- Flatness or curvature of surface
- Roughness or smoothness of surface
- Color and brightness of background

The condition of the surface of objects also affects the overall illusion of the material applied to the object. For example, suppose you create a beautiful old parchment material, and apply it to a default flat Plane object. It won't have nearly as much effect as applying it to a torn and tattered piece of geometry. (See Figure 10.1.)

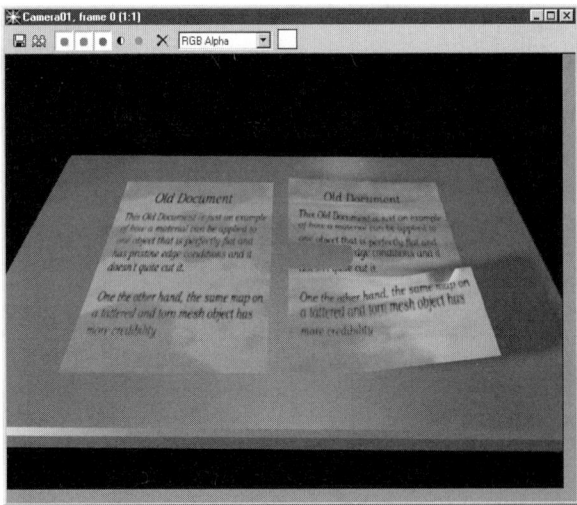

Figure 10.1 Document material on a flat plane and a tattered plane.

In this chapter, you learn about:

- The impact of geometry on realistic materials
- Material corruption techniques

- Creating paper and cardboard
- Creating paint
- Creating glass
- Creating metal
- Creating black plastic

One aspect that is often missing or underplayed in computer images is the most important one for making an image appear convincing: wear and tear. You must take the time to create surface imperfections, even when you are representing brand-new objects. Wear and tear is introduced in the manufacturing process and shows as slight imperfections in most things. This chapter focuses on methods of bringing those imperfections into your materials. In the following exercises, the imperfections are often exaggerated to illustrate the point. In your materials, you adjust the effect to get the look you need for your project.

New Shaders for Specular Highlights

As mentioned earlier, realistic specular highlights are the key to replicating believable man-made materials. In MAX R3, two components are involved in the quality of the specular highlights: the whiteness, or *Specular Level*, and the diffusion, or *Glossiness*. MAX R3 offers several new shaders that give you much more control of a material's specular highlights. The new shaders are:

NEW TO R3

- **Anisotropic.** Allows you to elongate a material's specular highlight. The specular highlight is an important element in metals, especially stainless steel and brushed aluminum-type metals.
- **Multi-Layer.** Similar to Anisotropic, but allows two elongated specular highlights at varying angles. Again, good for metals and some plastics.
- **Oren-Nayer-Blinn.** Has a very flat specular component and is good for rubber, paper, or fabric.
- **Strauss.** Has a specular component that uses the shader from the material's diffuse color. It is also good for metals and plastics.

Most specular highlights are white—regardless of the object's color. However, both Metal and Strauss shaders use the material's Diffuse color to calculate the specular color. Metals (such as anodized aluminum) exhibit this quality.

The color and the whiteness of the specular highlights are important, and the transition from specular to diffuse varies for different materials and alters a viewer's perception of a material. Figure 10.2 offers several boxes and spheres with the new shaders applied. All Glossiness and Specular Level settings are about the same for each material. The material on the objects at the left uses the default Blinn shader for comparison.

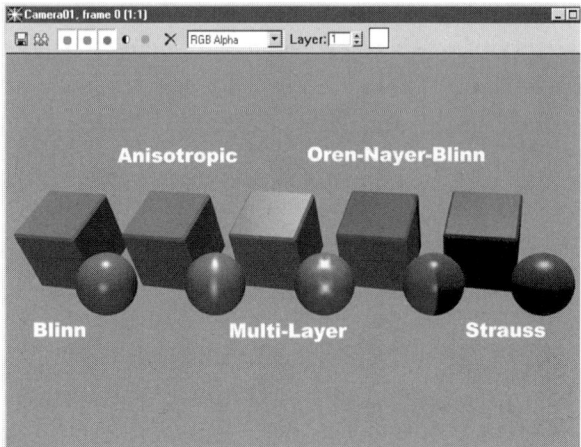

Figure 10.2 Comparison of new shaders.

Creating Material Imperfections

Objects in the real world are seldom perfectly flat, perfectly square, or without blemish. Even if you're creating a scene to show a client a new invention, include some imperfections to the table or background objects to add some realism. Slight variations in a surface or color may not be *noticed* by the viewer, but will be *perceived* by the brain for a more convincing image. As illustrated in Figure 10.2, there are two methods used to create imperfect surface representations:

- Mesh Distortion
- Material Corruption

Mesh Distortions

For even moderately corrupted materials, affect the geometry to an appropriate extent for the used material. For example, aluminum dents quite easily and some rubber is designed to be flexible; hard plastic seldom dents, but may crack. Mesh distortions appear as variations in the object's physical shape, caused by day-to-day wear and tear. Distortions on some objects are even introduced in the manufacturing process or during shipping. Some distortions you may utilize are:

- Edge warps and tears
- Surface dents and cracks
- Surface wrinkles and folds
- Bulges

Using Bump and Opacity maps is a great way to simulate the effects mentioned above, but in some cases it isn't enough. For example, a surface's Bump map gives the illusion of a distorted surface. Where the bump mapping meets the background, however, the effect is lost because bump mapping does not actually change the surface.

Objects that are more severely distorted or objects where the camera is very close must show a more convincing distortion. To physically distort geometry, use the following tools:

- FFD modifiers
- Noise modifier
- DeleteMesh modifier
- Wave and Ripple modifiers
- Patch Deform and Path Deform modifiers
- Xform and Vol.Select modifiers at Sub-Object level
- Conform compound object
- Displacement mapping

Some of the modifiers mentioned above are applied to the whole object, such as FFD, Noise, Wave, and Ripple. They may also be applied to just a portion of the object by first using a MeshSelect or Vol.Select modifier to select a set of faces, edges, or vertices, which apply the modifier. The Patch and Path Deform modifiers use native patch objects or splines to describe deformations of objects. The DeleteMesh modifier, in conjunction with MeshSelect or Vol.Select, remove faces to create holes in a surface. Because it's a modifier in the stack, it is easily removed or disabled if you change your mind. Displacement mapping allows you to paint the distortions in a paint software package (for example, good control of wrinkles or folds in fabric).

Note

Displacement mapping was available on Patch and NURBS surfaces in MAX 2.5. You can now apply displacement mapping in MAX R3 to polygon mesh objects, as well. Displacement mapping uses the luminance value (whiteness) of pixels to actually displace vertices in space. The effect of the Displacement map is viewed in the display viewports, applying a Displace Mesh World Space modifier and adjusting the Displacement Approximation settings.

Caution

Displacement mapping creates high face and vertex counts. After you have the displacement you need, it's sometimes wise to use Snapshot to create a new mesh. Then apply an Optimize modifier to reduce the mesh's density.

Material Corruption

Mesh distortions usually require fairly dense mesh objects before they have any noticeable effect. Dense mesh objects, of course, are best avoided unless absolutely necessary. Material corruption simulates mesh distortions much more efficiently than extra faces and vertices. Use it whenever possible, but many other corruption types are introduced by:

- Surface roughness and dents
- Discoloration
- Smudges and blurring
- Dust and dirt
- Weathering and corrosion

Good material corruption techniques are accomplished with some of the procedural map types. For example, Noise, Smoke, Stucco, Dents, Cellular, and Speckle contain at least two color channels to break up a homogenous surface. The best results, however, are often obtained when Mix and Mask mapping and Blend materials are used in conjunction with the procedural maps.

Use maps in other channels besides Color to corrupt a surface's look in other ways. A simple Smoke map in the Glossiness channel of a material does wonders toward making the material look more realistic. Reflections also look much better through masking techniques.

Creating Man-Made Materials

While learning to create realistic materials in MAX R3, concentrate on the base material first. After you have a firm base, apply the corruption. In this section, you create several

Chapter 10: Designing Man-Made Materials 433

materials that form the basis of man-made surfaces. The objects that you use in the exercises are straight-forward, with minimal surface perturbations. The materials illustrate the fundamentals of:

- **Paper and Cardboard.** The technique you use can also be applied to other soft materials such as fabrics.
- **Paint.** The tools you use are adaptable with plastics.
- **Glass.** Hard polished plastics can be made to look like glass.
- **Metal.** The example exercise is on chrome materials, but other metals are similar.

Remember, the specular highlights and the reflective qualities are the most obvious indications of an object's material.

Paper and Cardboard

Paper and cardboard come in a wide variety of surface styles. In many cases, they look like other materials, such as metals or plastics. What gives a paper its unique quality is often the amount of clay used in the manufacturing process. High-clay content papers have very glossy surfaces. Look around your office; notice the different highlights on the surfaces of cardboard boxes, newspaper, color-print paper, or stationery. Specular highlights are not very bright compared to the diffusely lit areas, and the highlights are quite broad. On some papers (such as newspaper) the specular highlights are almost nonexistent. A level of softness is a clue that defines paper. In Exercise 10.1 you create a slightly distressed, common cardboard box.

Note
Printed paper, such as shipping boxes and book covers, are defined more by the ink on the surface rather than the quality of paper itself.

Exercise 10.1   Creating Cardboard and Paper

1. Open the file called 10max01.MAX from the CD-ROM. Save the file as ch10_crdbrd_01.MAX. The scene is a simple cardboard box on a flat plane. There is a kitchen photo as a background image, and the flat plane has an assigned material. You will look at the material later in the exercise.

Tip
The cardboard box is created from several rectangular shapes that are extruded, then attached to each other to make one object. Two of the flaps are selected at Element Sub-Object mode and had Xform modifiers applied. The flaps can be animated with this technique. Check the Modifier Stack for more detail.

2. Open the Material Editor, and select the first sample sphere. Click the Assign Material to Selected button to assign this CARDBOARD_BOX material to the cardboard box. Click the Quick Render button. Notice that it's just a plain gray box against the photo background.

3. First, build up the color on the box to look like a used brown cardboard box. Click the Diffuse Color slot. Change the Diffuse color to a light brown (R165, G155, B130). Render the scene again. Notice the color changed, but it doesn't look like cardboard. It is much too flat, too clean, and too homogeneous; in other words—boring. Close the VFB. Drag and drop the Diffuse Color slot onto the Ambient Color slot. Pick Copy in the dialog box. In the Color Picker, drag the Value slider left to a value of 55. This adds contrast to the material.

4. Because cardboard is cheaply made, the color is not usually consistent. Often it's wet or dirty as well. Change the Diffuse color to reflect those qualities. Click the Diffuse Map shortcut button, and double-click Smoke. Render the Camera01 viewport. Notice that the box is now black with blotchy gray patches. Continue changing the colors to resemble cardboard. You already created a good brown. To reuse that color, click the Go to Parent button. In the Modify panel, click the Utilities button. Then click the Color Clipboard button, and click the New Floater button. The Color Clipboard floater is a palette to transfer colors that you created. It looks like Figure 10.3.

Tip

At this point, you can introduce another level of color control by modifying the Diffuse color and using the Diffuse Amount field in the Maps rollout. This bleeds the new Diffuse color into the Smoke map colors. This has the effect of tinting the Smoke colors.

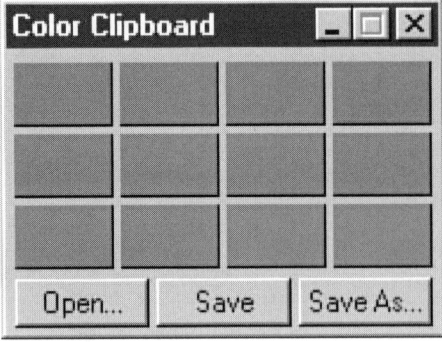

Figure 10.3 Color Clipboard floater.

5. Drag and drop the Diffuse color swatch onto the first swatch of the Color Clipboard. Select Copy in the dialog box. In the Material Editor, click the Map shortcut button for the Diffuse swatch. Drag and drop the brown from the Color Clipboard onto the Color #1 swatch for the Smoke map. Click Copy in the dialog box. Name this level *diffuse smoke*. In the Smoke Parameters rollout, drag the brown Color #1 swatch onto the Color #2 swatch. Select Copy. In the Color Selector, drag the Value slider left to about 110, or a darker brown. Render Camera01 viewport. The cardboard now has a slightly mottled brown look.

> **Tip**
> The Color Clipboard palettes are saved from the floater as .ccb files and called up at any time from any file.

NEW TO R3

6. In the Blinn Basic Parameters rollout, enter 40 in the Specular Level field and 15 in the Glossiness field. The sample sphere appears quite shiny, but in a "plastic" sense. Because cardboard has a softness to the surface that is defined by the fiber content, use the new Oren-Nayer-Blinn shader. This shader is intended for soft materials. In the Shader Basic Parameters rollout, click Blinn. Select Oren-Nayer-Blinn. The sample sphere takes on new shininess qualities. Render the Camera01 viewport. Notice that the box looks softer and has an overall gray cast, caused by the flat shininess. Again, because of wear and tear on the box, the surface is probably not consistently shiny.

7. In the Oren-Nayer-Blinn Basic Parameters rollout, click the Map shortcut button to the right of the Glossiness field. Double-click Noise. Name this level *gloss noise*. Where the Noise map is black, the glossiness is high. Where the map is white, there is no glossiness. The current levels are a bit too high, so change Color #1 to dark gray (R70, G70, B70). Render the scene. Notice that the shininess is inconsistent across the surface, more like the look of real cardboard.

> **Tip**
> You can also adjust the Roughness spinner in the Advanced Diffuse area. Higher makes the material less shiny or rougher looking.

> **Tip**
> Most materials benefit from the addition of a map in the Glossiness field. This is a good method of simulating the effects of dust or smudges on a shiny surface, to show simulated nap on carpets, or to show the difference in shininess on a painted object (from brush strokes catching the light).

8. For an old cardboard box, it is in pretty good shape. Now add a Bump map to rough up the surface, giving it a more realistic look. The bumps also change the shininess, as the light is calculated based on the simulated bumps. In the Material Editor's Maps rollout, click the None button to the right of Bumps. Double-click

Noise. Name this level *bump noise*. Render the Camera01 viewport. You hardly notice a change in the surface. There are several possible reasons for the lack of change: the scale of the Noise bitmap, the Bump amount is too low, or improper lighting.

9. In the Noise Parameters rollout, enter 10.0 in the Size field. Render the scene. In the Material Editor, click the Go to Parent button (or use Material/Map Navigator) to go to the top level. Enter 60 in the Bump Amount field. Render the scene. Now you begin to see a bumpy surface appear, so a combination of map Size and Bump Amount helped. Close Material Editor, and all the dialog boxes.

10. Get ready to use the Place Highlights alignment tool to create a specular highlight on the object. This makes it jump out from its surrounding materials. Right-click the Camera01 viewport (if it is not already active). Click the Zoom Extents All button, type H, and double-click Omni01 in the list to select it. In the Toolbar, click and hold the Align button. Choose the Place Highlight button. In the Camera01 viewport, click and hold the long front face of the box and move the mouse. A blue normals vector appears. This moves the Omni01 light to a 90-degree angle from the viewer (to force the position of the highlights caused by this Omni light). Render the Camera01 viewport. The material now looks like plastic and is much too bumpy. The placements of the lights in the scene have a profound effect on the material's appearance.

11. In the Modify panel, reduce the intensity of the Omni01 light to 150, by changing the V value to 150. In the Material Editor, set the Bump Amount back to 30 and the Noise map size up to 25. Render Camera01 viewport again. In the Material/Map Navigator, click the gloss noise level. Set Color #1 to R130, G130, B130 to reduce the glossiness. Render the scene. Now the cardboard appears to have bulges, similar to Figure 10.4.

Figure 10.4 Cardboard material on box.

Chapter 10: Designing Man-Made Materials   437

Tip
In a scene where the box is important to the story, it probably makes sense to create lights that use the Exclude option to include just the cardboard box object. You can then fine-tune the scene, using the lights without adversely affecting other objects.

12. The material and lights are not enough to make this a convincing old cardboard box. The edges and surface are too straight and flat. Select BOX01 in the scene. In the Modify panel, click the More button, and double-click Tessellate in the list. In the Parameters rollout, enter 5 in the Tension field. Render the Camera01 viewport. Edge tessellation divides the existing edges with distortion (based on the Tension amount), so the box appears more tattered and worn. Compare Figure 10.5 with Figure 10.4.

Figure 10.5   The Tessellate modifier creates a tattered look.

Caution
The Tessellate modifier significantly increases the face/vertex count of a mesh. You may want to use the Optimize modifier after the Tessellate to reduce some of those extra faces.

13. In the photograph notice how the box casts a shadow and has a reflection on the countertop. There is an object in the scene called SHELF_PLANE, with a material called SHELF_PLANE. In the Material Editor, click the SHELF_PLANE sample sphere to activate it. The material type is Matte/Shadow. The Matte/Shadow material is invisible in the rendering, but always allows the background image to show through objects that have the material assigned to them. In addition to the Receive Shadows option, MAX R3 offers a new option that allows for a

Reflection map. This material has the Raytrace map set to 20 percent. Render the scene and look at the reflection. In the photograph, it appears as though the 3D mesh is sitting on the countertop. Open the Material Editor. Study how the Matte/Shadow material is created. Enter 35 in the Reflection Amount field, and render the scene again to see the difference in the reflection. The dialog box looks similar to Figure 10.6.

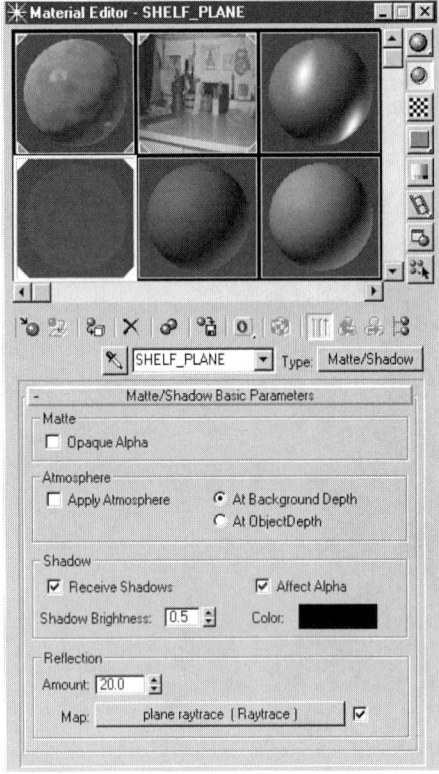

Figure 10.6 The Matte/Shadow material settings.

 Tip

Two other factors contribute to a better scene. First, adjust the scene lighting to more closely match the lighting in the photograph. The right side of the box is very dark while the right side of the small cutting board is very light. Then use the Camera Match utility to accurately adjust the scene camera to the viewpoint and lens used in the photograph.

14. Save the File. It's already labeled ch10_crdbrd_01.MAX.

Paint

Paint comes in almost unlimited variety and is affected by the underlying material on which it is applied. Multiple layers of paint look different than just one coat, especially if each layer is sanded or buffed. Additives are mixed with paint to create special effects. Factors, such as glossy or satin finish and (of course) lighting, alter the end results. In Exercise 10.2, you create a paint material for a car. The underlying material is metal, with coats of some form of primer. High gloss and luster are important, and you want the paint to be noticed in a crowd of other automobiles. It will be a coppertone candy-apple, hand-rubbed lacquer finish. The scene is a sport coupe in a hilly meadow under blue skies.

Exercise 10.2 Creating Glossy Paint

1. Open the file called 10max02.MAX. It is the coupe in a meadow. The car has chrome wheels and headlights, and glass in the windows. The tires have a new rubber look, like you see on show cars. Save the file as ch10_paint_01.MAX. Render the Camera01 viewport, and study the look of the scene. Open the Material Editor. Click the second sample sphere, called BODY, to activate (if it is not already active).

2. The base Diffuse color for the material is bright red. While you can change the Diffuse color to a coppery orange, it's difficult to get the finish used in high-end automotive paint. That paint uses additives to give a deep shellac-like finish. You will use the new MAX R3 material type called Shellac. In the Material Editor, click the Standard type button for BODY, and double-click Shellac. Select Keep This Material as Sub-material in the dialog box, and click OK. Name this level SHELLAC. Shellac is made of a base material and a Shellac material, with a Shellac Color Blend spinner to blend the two together. Increasing the number in the spinner blends the amount of Shellac material in the diffuse areas without equally affecting the ambient areas.

Note

True shellac is a special finish that is mixed with the ground-up wings of a beetle found in India. The quality of the light reflecting off the tiny particles suspended in the finish changes with changing light and the viewer's sight angle.

3. Because the paint is applied to metal, the car's underlying metal influences the specular highlights. Use the Anisotropic shader to create a more metallic specular highlight. In the Material/Map Navigator, click the Base Material:BODY level. In the Shader Basic Parameters rollout, click Blinn, and select Anisotropic. In the Anisotropic Basic Parameters rollout, change the Specular color swatch to pure white. Enter 85 in the Specular Level field, and 75 in the Anisotropic field. This increases the whiteness of the highlight and elongates it. Leave Glossiness at 25,

to give a broad specular highlight. Render the Camera01 viewport, and you now see a material that is beginning to look like dull plastic.

Tip

Even though you perceive paint as having high gloss, a high Glossiness setting often causes the highlight to become too small or disappear. Start with lower Glossiness amounts in all materials. Work the amount higher (as needed).

4. Reflections are important to the quality of your paint. In the Maps rollout, enter 35 in the Reflection amount field. Click the None button to the right of that field. Double-click Raytrace. Name this level *refl raytrace*. Render the Camera01 viewport. Notice that the material has a very shiny metallic look because of the reflections.

Note

The reflections work well in this scene because there is plenty for the surface to reflect. The visible portion of the sky is a cloud image, while the portion of the skydome behind the camera is pure white. This white is reflecting off the car's body, defining the curvature with contrasting reflections.

5. Now you add the Shellac effect. In the Material/Map Navigator, click the Shellac material level, and name this material OVERTONE. In the Shader Basic Parameters rollout, click Blinn. Select Anisotropic. In the Anisotropic Basic Parameters rollout, set the Diffuse and Ambient colors to bright yellow (R255, G220, B0) and the Specular color to pure white. Enter 50 in Specular Level, 75 in Anisotropy, and 45 in the Orientation fields. There is no difference in the sample sphere or in the scene because the yellow OVERTONE material is not blended with the red BODY material.

6. In the Material/Map Navigator, click the top level. In the Shellac Basic Parameters rollout, enter 50 in the Shellac Color Blend field. The sample sphere turns a rich orange-red. Render the scene. The paint looks metallic copper, with plenty of depth. The reflections are strongest in the base material (or the ambient areas).

7. In the Material/Map Navigator, click the Shellac Mat:OVERTONE level. In the Maps rollout, enter 35 in the Reflections field. Now click the None button, and double-click Raytrace. Name this level *refl raytrace2*. Render the Camera01 viewport, and now you see the added reflections in the most brightly lit or diffuse areas.

Caution

On a computer with limited resources, render times can be quite long. You may want to render at 320×240 resolution to speed render time.

8. Click the Select button in the Toolbar, type H, and double-click Omni01. This is an Omni light that is set to contain only the car body. It is turned off. In the Modify panel, General Parameters rollout, select On. The light also has the Diffuse check box cleared at the bottom of the rollout. The light only affects the Specular areas and is only used to make the car stand out against the background. Render the scene again to see the effect. The scene looks similar to Figure 10.7.

Figure 10.7 Coupe with copper Shellac paint.

Tip

Backlighting is an effective tool in film and photography to make your objects stand out against the background. Study films and photographs; observe the bright edges of objects and characters created by strong lighting aimed at the side away from the viewer. The Place Highlight command is ideal for creating this effect in MAX R3.

9. Save the file. It's already named ch10_paint_01.MAX.

Glass

Hold a wine glass or goblet. Walk around your house, and look closely at the glass in different settings and lighting. Look at the glass as a painter might, by defining the glass by the light and dark areas projected into a 2D plane.

While both transparency and background have an effect on glass objects, window glass in buildings is perceived almost entirely on reflection. If you have any glass-walled buildings in your area, study the reflections and note the way the surroundings and the sky change with varying weather conditions and time of day.

Lighting is also critical to getting good representations of glass objects. If a glass object is central to your image, you want extra lighting that excludes all other objects in the scene and is adjusted to bring out the best in the glass.

Note

To be proficient with MAX R3, it is important that you master paint and imaging software. This is so you can alter the images used in your materials and so you can create masks. Masks are one of the easiest ways to add patina to your scenes that distinguish your images from those of your competition. Essentially, a mask is a grayscale image that hides a portion of one material (or map) and reveals another, based on the whiteness of the pixels in the mask image. Masks are used in Blend materials and Mask maps.

Another problem occurs with materials related to reflections. "How do I create good-looking glass?" is a frequent question. First you must ask another question. What do you mean by "good-looking" glass? Glass, itself, is not much different than any other material. The problem of good-looking glass lies in the reflective properties of the glass, and most importantly, what is reflected. It is possible to create beautiful glass in one scene, move the object and material to another scene, and end up with flat, boring results.

Glass, black paint, and (to some extent) all shiny objects are subject to the same problem: Without something to reflect back to the viewer, the effect doesn't work.

Take your cue from traditional photography. Several years ago, many automobile ads (especially on TV) used black cars. If you look at those ads with a critical eye, you notice that a black car shows up as more than 75 percent pure white. Your brain compensates for the white because you know that it is a black car. However, if you point spotlights at a black car, all you get is very tiny white dots on what appears (to the viewer) as a black void. To elude this effect, photographers use bounce cards or light tents. It is the reflection of bright white cards of fabric that defines the contours of the object. The same is true of glass and metal in photography; without an artificially intense reflection, the material appears flat.

Tip

It's important to remember that realism is not always the best choice. Many times reality is cluttered and rather boring. What you want to strive for in your computer-generated images is that the image is *convincing*. Often you need to use lights and materials that cannot exist in reality; but when applied to a scene, make the viewer feel comfortable with the effect. An example is the fire balls and explosions used in space scenes. They have no bearing on reality, but without them the viewer feels cheated.

In this exercise, you work with a glass object on a table and use several variations of both materials and objects.

Exercise 10.3 Creating a Glass Vase

  1. Open the file called 10max03.MAX from the CD-ROM. It is a lofted glass vase on a plain painted tabletop. The vase is formed by lofting a circle on a straight

line and uses the Scale Deformations of the Loft command. The glass, itself, has no thickness, and you can see through the back of the vase at the top because of face normals. You usually want to use a 2-Sided material on glass objects, especially when they are lofted from a simple shape. Save the file as ch10_glass_01.MAX.

2. Open the Material Editor. Notice that the first sample sphere is active, and the material called GLASS is assigned to the VASE in the scene. Click the Standard type button, and double-click Raytrace. Raytrace is a good option for many glass objects because of the extra controls it offers for mixing various color attributes with the reflections. In the Raytrace Basic Parameters rollout, check the 2-Sided option. You now see the inside top of the vase in the shaded Camera01 viewport.

Note
You can use another material type with a Raytrace map to get similar reflections, but the reflections are applied on top of the color information. In the Raytrace material, the color attributes and the reflections are blended, allowing more control.

Tip
It's not absolutely necessary to call on the intensive raytrace calculations of a Raytrace material. You can still use a Bitmap or Reflect/Refract map for speed, and leave the Reflect color swatch to 0. Take advantage of Extended Parameters, such as Extra Lighting, Florescence, and Translucency. With the Reflect color swatch set to 0, the added raytrace time is negligible, and no reflections are created.

3. In the Raytrace Basic Parameters rollout, change the Diffuse color swatch to a very light blue (R200, G215, B240). This is the primary color attribute of the glass, which in glassmaking is controlled by adding lead, magnesium, and so on. Change the Reflectivity color swatch to a value of R100, G100, B100 and the Transparency color swatch to a value of R140, G140, B140. Render the Camera01 viewport. Notice that Reflectivity and Transparency alone do not make good glass.

Tip
Reflectivity has a tendency to cancel out transparency. You cannot have a highly reflective, very transparent material displaying both attributes.

4. We perceive glass as containing a shiny material, so naturally you make your glass shiny. In the Raytrace Basic Parameters rollout, enter 115 in the Specular Level field and 25 in the Glossiness field. This gives a broad, white specular quality. Render the scene again. With the new specular highlights, the vase contrasts more vividly against the dark background.

Tip

Specular Level is often set too high for glass materials, and the specular highlights are lost. Try starting at lower levels and increase as needed.

5. Notice that the center of the vase and the edges of the vase are equally transparent. This is not the case in reality, because you look through more glass at the edges than in the center. In a Raytrace material, this effect is simulated with a Falloff map in the Transparency slot. In the Raytrace Basic Parameters rollout, click the Map shortcut button to the right of the Transparency color swatch. Double click Falloff. Name this level *trans falloff*. In the Material Editor, click the Background button to show the checkered pattern behind the sample sphere. Notice the sample sphere appears *less* transparent in the center, especially in the neck of the vase. In the Falloff Parameters rollout, drag and drop the black color swatch onto the white swatch. Select Swap in the dialog box. The sample sphere is now completely transparent in the center and opaque on the edges. Render the Camera01 viewport. The glass looks better, but still needs work.

Tip

If you have trouble seeing the effect of the Falloff map, set the Reflect color swatch to R0, G0, B0 (black) to turn off the reflections. Don't forget to set the Reflect color swatch back to R100, G100, B100 when you are done. Remember, high transparency is diminished with reflections.

6. One problem is that the lighting in the scene is not conducive to good glass. The table is dark and the background is black, so the transparency and reflections don't have much effect. In the Front viewport, select the Spot02 light, directly above the vase. It is not lighting the tabletop due to Exclude. In the Modify panel, General Parameters rollout, click the Exclude button. In the Exclude/Include dialog box, select TABLE in the right panel, and then the left arrow button to send TABLE into the left panel. (See Figure 10.8.) Render the Camera01 viewport. Notice the lighter table showing through the glass as it is picked up by the reflections.

7. As mentioned previously, reflective objects need something to reflect. This scene, with all the surrounding black, doesn't produce good reflective objects. In the Display panel, Hide rollout, click the Unhide All button. This reveals an extruded arc in the scene, called Arc01. It has a Normal modifier that points the face normals toward the arc's center. It also has a Look-at animation controller with the vase as a look-at target. This object acts like a photographer's bounce card. Click the Zoom Extents All button to view the object in the scene. Then click the Select button, and choose the Arc01 in any viewport.

Chapter 10: Designing Man-Made Materials 445

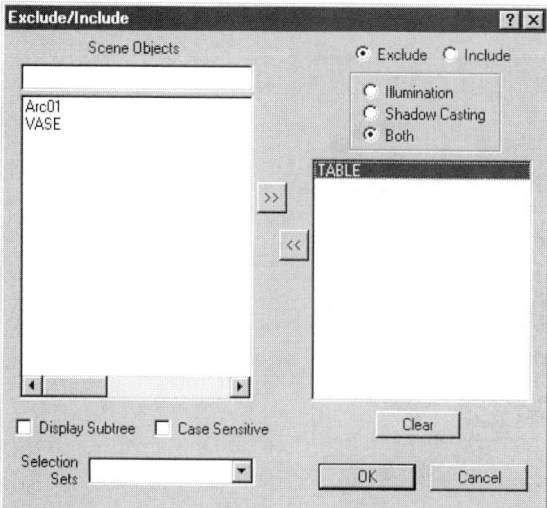

Figure 10.8 TABLE selected in Exclude/Include dialog box.

8. In the Material Editor, select the second sample sphere to activate it. In the Blinn Basic Parameters rollout, change the Specular, Diffuse, Ambient, and Self-Illumination color swatches to pure white. Click the Assign Material to Selected button. Render the Camera01 viewport. Now the glass looks more like the way you expect glass to appear. It's all in the reflection.

9. Refraction also helps define glass by giving an indication of its thickness. In the Material Editor, Raytrace Basic Parameters rollout, enter 1.5 in the Index of Refr. Field. Render the scene. Notice the changes through the material at the table's edge and at the bottom of the vase. The added distortion makes the vase look as if its glass is thicker.

10. The background has an effect on the glass as well. In the Material Editor, click the third sample sphere. In the Anisotropic Basic Parameters rollout, click the Map shortcut button to the right of the Diffuse color swatch. Double-click Checker. In the Coordinates rollout, enter 4.0 in the U and V Tiling fields. In the Checker Parameters rollout, change the Color #1 swatch to dark red and Color #2 to dark green. Render Camera01 viewport. Notice the difference the color makes in the reflection.

11. Geometry is another change. This object appears to be a smooth, thick blown-glass vase. You want to see what it looks like as a cut-glass vase. Close the Material Editor and all dialog boxes. In the Camera01 viewport, select VASE. In the Modify panel's Creation Methods rollout, click the Get Shape button. Type H, and double-click Star01. This substitutes a star shape for the original circle on the loft path. Render the Camera01 viewport. Notice that the vase takes on a different character because of the facets reflecting and refracting the scene. The rendered image looks similar to Figure 10.9.

Figure 10.9 Rendered cut-glass vase.

12. Save the file. It should already be named ch10_glass_01.MAX.

Again—when you use reflective materials, include enough well-lit objects in the scene to adequately reflect back to the viewer. Lighting of the whole scene is also crucial for getting good results. The glass vase created here appears totally different in another scene, based on its surroundings.

Metal

Metal materials, especially the more reflective metals, share similar attributes to glass materials. The lighting is important, and the reflected elements in the scene make or break a metal material. Metals have one major difference from other materials—the way light scatters from the surface to form a specular highlight. Most metals have a *grain* similar to that of wood. The grain, in conjunction with surface marks from the machining or finishing process, tend to line up the specular highlights in one or two directions. The underlying metal grain runs in one direction, and the surface scoring runs in another. This creates star-shaped specular highlights. In previous versions of 3D Studio MAX, elongated specular highlights are approached with only complex specular-mapping methods.

NEW TO R3 The specular component is not white in metals, as in other materials. This is due to the dielectric properties of metal. The Specular color is derived from the object's Diffuse color. This gives gold its peculiar sheen. MAX R3 still uses the Metal shader for this effect. It also adds a new Strauss shader, with a Metalness adjustment to vary the effect.

In Exercise 10.4 you create a chrome material for a toaster. Because chrome is highly reflective, lighting and other scene elements are important for a good effect. The toaster has elongated specular highlights due to the metal's metallic coating.

> **Tip**
>
> The Raytrace material type doesn't use the new Anisotropic and Multi-Level shaders. However, use the Blend material with the Raytrace material in one slot and the Standard material with Anisotropic or Multi-Level shaders in the other. Use the same information in both materials for the Diffuse and Ambient colors. Set the Blend Amount to 50 percent.

The reflections in the following exercise offer a combination of reflected bitmap images and reflections from objects in the scene. You accomplish this with a Mix map type in the Reflection slot, composed of a Raytrace map and a bitmap (with a Mix Amount of 50 percent to 60 percent).

Exercise 10.4   Creating a Chrome Material

1. Open the file called 10max04.MAX from the CD-ROM. It is a tabletop with a toaster and several lights. There is also a background image of a kitchen in both the Camera01 viewport and in the Render Environment background slot. Save the file as ch10_chrome_01.MAX.

2. Open the Material Editor. Drag and drop the first sample sphere onto the toaster (called CHROME_BODY) in the Camera01 viewport. This changes the Blinn shader to Anisotropic, to allow elongated specular highlights. Click Blinn in the Shader Basic Parameters rollout, and choose Anisotropic. Set the Specular Highlight area fields to those shown in Figure 10.10. (Specular Level 225, Glossiness 20, Anistrophy 76, and Orientation 45.)

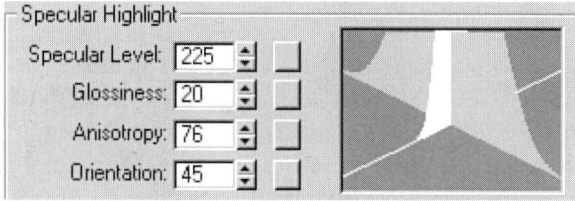

Figure 10.10   Anisotropic Specular Highlight settings.

3. Because of surface variations in the thin metal toaster, the color is probably not consistent across the entire surface. Add a Noise map to the diffuse color swatch, adding shades of gray. In the Anisotropic Basic Parameters rollout, click the Map shortcut button (to the Diffuse color swatch's right). Double-click Noise. In the

Noise Parameters rollout, enter 12 in the Size field and change the Color #2 swatch to HSV of 0, 0, 150. Name this level *diffuse noise*. Render the Camera01 viewport. There is now a soft-gray shiny toaster, similar to the one in Figure 10.11.

Figure 10.11   Gray shiny material on toaster.

4. The toaster carries the maker's name stamped on the side. In the Material Editor, click the Go to Parent button. In the Maps rollout, enter 40 in the Bump Amount field. click the None button to the right. Double-click Bitmap. In the Bitmap Parameters rollout, click the Bitmap button. In the Select Bitmap Image File dialog box, locate the GenToast.png file on the CD-ROM and double-click it. In the Coordinates rollout, clear the U and V Tile options. Name this level *text bitmap*.

5. Now apply mapping coordinates to the toaster to position the text on its side. In the Camera01 viewport, select CHROME_BODY. In the Modify panel, click the UVW Map button. In the Parameters rollout's Alignment group, click the Normal Align button. In the Camera01 viewport, left-click in the middle of the toaster and move the mouse while pressing its left button. Notice that the orange map Gizmo flips to align itself with the face currently hosting the cursor. Position the cursor roughly in the center of the side of the toaster and release the mouse button. In the Parameters rollout, click the Fit button and the Gizmo will resize to fit the toaster in the new orientation.

6. Reduce the size of the Gizmo by 10 percent in Length and Width. Enter 55.34 in the Length field and 72.13 in the Width field. Render the Camera01 viewport. You now see raised text on the toaster's side.

Chapter 10: Designing Man-Made Materials 449

Tip

Calculate Gizmo's reduction by highlighting the numeric value in the Length field, and typing Ctrl-N. This opens the Numeric Expression Evaluator, where you enter mathematical expressions instead of just numbers in any field. In the Evaluator field, enter the formula 61.486*0.9 (your actual number may be different). Click the Paste button to transfer the amount to the field. Repeat the process for the Width field, using the number currently in the field. See Figure 10.12 for an example of the Numeric Expression Evaluator.

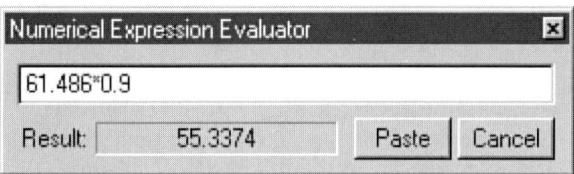

Figure 10.12 Numerical Expression Evaluator with expression.

Tip

You can right-click on the current value in the field and use the pop-down menu Copy and Paste feature to transfer the value to the Expression Evaluator.

7. The rendered toaster looks sort of metallic but more like pewter, and certainly not like chrome. The reflections are missing. To make this scene more convincing, the toaster must reflect the tabletop and another wall of the kitchen. Raytrace reflection mapping is the easy way to reflect the background image. That doesn't work here because that image is not behind the viewer. The way you get around this restriction is with a Mix map, using Raytrace and Bitmap as sub-maps and mixing the two together. In the Material Editor, Material/Map Navigator, click the top level. In the Maps rollout, click on the Reflection None button, and double-click Mix. Name this level *refl mix*.

Note

The Mix map is similar to the Blend material. However, Mix works only at the map level, whereas Blend material allows the blending of two complete materials.

8. In the Mix Parameters rollout, click the None button to the right of Color #1. Double-click Raytrace. Use the default Raytrace map settings. Name this level *mix raytrace*.

9. Click the Go to Parent button. In the Mix Parameters rollout, click the None button to the right of Color #2. Double-click Bitmap. Name this level *mix bitmap*.

10. In the Bitmap Parameters rollout, click the Bitmap button. Open the Kitchen2.jpg file on the CD-ROM. Name this level *mix bitmap*. Render the

Camera01 viewport. The toaster appears transparent because Raytrace map is set to reflect the background image.

11. In the Material/Map Navigator, click the *mix raytrace* level. In the Raytrace Parameters rollout's Background area, select the check box to the None button's left.

Tip
You can select the None button, entering the Kitchen2.jpg file here. However, to decide whether the Bitmap map or the Raytrace map has the most effect, use Mix mapping.

12. In the Material/Map Navigator, click the *refl mix* level. In the Mix Parameters rollout, enter 50 in the Mix Amount field. This uses 50 percent Bitmap map and 50 percent Raytrace map to calculate the reflections. Render the Camera01 viewport. The toaster is now a metallic chrome material. The table reflects in the bottom and the back wall of the kitchen (which doesn't exist) reflects overall. The long specular highlights on the toaster's corners are created by the Anisotropic shader. The image looks similar to Figure 10.13.

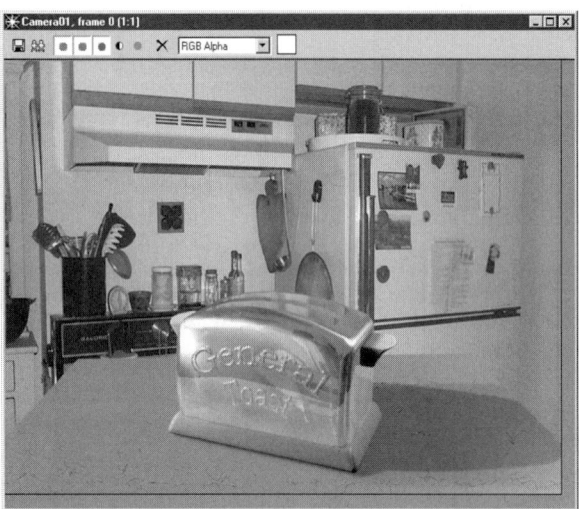

Figure 10.13 Rendered chrome toaster.

Note
Reflections make this material a convincing chrome color, just as they created a convincing glass material in the previous exercise. Without skillful reflections the material is like dull pewter. With the wrong reflections it looks out of place.

13. Save the file. It's already labeled ch10_chrome_01.MAX.

Black Plastic

One of the most difficult materials to simulate is an object's black surface. Because black surfaces absorb light, only the specular highlights and reflections define the shape of the object. In the next exercise, you create a black plastic material for the toaster's base and handles. Use an Oren-Nayer-Blinn shader to achieve a soft look. You also use the Reflection Dimming feature, which creates minimized reflections in areas with less light (similar to reflections in the real world).

Exercise 10.5   Creating Black Plastic

1. Open the ch10_chrome_01.MAX file that you saved from the last exercise, or open it from the CD-ROM. It's the chrome toaster in a kitchen background. Save the file as ch10_chrome_02.MAX.

2. Open the Material Editor, and select the first sample sphere in the second row. It is labeled BLACK PLASTIC. In the Shader Basic Parameters rollout, click Blinn. Choose Oren-Nayer-Blinn. This shader gives a softer look to a material.

3. In the Oren-Nayer-Blinn Parameters rollout, drag and drop the Ambient color swatch onto the Diffuse color swatch. Select Copy in the dialog box. Select the Specular color swatch and set it to pure white.

4. Choose the Select button, and type H. Choose HANDLE01, HANDLE02, and PLASTIC BASE, and click the Select button.

5. In the Material Editor, click the Assign Material to Selection button. Render the Camera01 viewport. Notice that the plastic parts appear more like voids in the image rather that parts on a toaster. They need glossiness and reflections. In Specular Highlights, enter 130 in the Specular Level field and 30 in the Glossiness field. Render the scene again. Now you see some definition on the edges where the specular highlights are strongest.

6. In the Maps rollout, enter 60 in the Reflection Amount field. Click on the None button to the right. Double-click Bitmap. In the Select Bitmap Image File dialog box, locate the Kitchen2.jpg bitmap on the CD-ROM, and double-click it. Name this level *refl bitmap*.

7. In the Coordinates rollout, enter 0.05 in the Blur Offset field to slightly blur the reflection. Render the Camera01 viewport. The handles and base appear lighter because of the reflected bitmap. The problem is the front of the base, which is in direct light. It has the same reflectivity as the base's side, which is in less light.

 Tip

The Blur Offset setting blurs all pixels in the image while the Blur setting blurs only edges of contrasting color fields in the image.

8. In the Material Editor, click the Go to Parent button. Click the Extended Parameters rollout bar to expand it. In the Reflection Dimming area, check the Apply check box, and enter 1.5 in the Refl. Level field. With the Dim Level set to 0 and Apply on, the reflection shows in areas of diffuse light but not in areas of ambient light. Setting Dim Level to 1 is the same as turning off Apply. The Refl. Level spinner increases or decreases the reflection in the diffuse lighting areas. Render the Camera01 viewport again. The reflection shows on the top of the handles and the front of the base, but not on the sides of either. The rendered image looks like Figure 10.14.

Figure 10.14 Rendered chrome toaster with black plastic parts.

9. Save the file. It's already labeled ch10_chrome_02.MAX.

In Practice: Designing Man-Made Materials

- **Mesh distortions.** A burned and dirty material on a perfectly smooth object looks out of place. Physically distorting an object to give it a less-than-perfect surface helps your scenes look more realistic. However, be careful not to overdo the effect.

- **Material corruption techniques.** Fingerprints, dust, static electricity, dirt, and other variations also make any surface imperfect. While sometimes less noticeable than surface distortions, these effects are important to make the material more believable. For example, just a slight change in shininess over a surface radically changes the effect the object has on the viewer.

- **Creating paper and cardboard.** Paper and cardboard have a glossiness and texture that (while variable) is always distinguishable to the viewer's eye. The common component is a softness and wide specular highlight that the new Oren-Nayer-Blinn shader replicates.
- **Creating paint.** Paint also varies widely in its impression on the viewer. In this chapter, you created paint with high gloss and luster using the new Shellac material type. Shellac gives a dynamic surface effect that depends on the relationship of lights and viewpoints to the surface.
- **Creating glass.** Glass is mostly transparent. In this chapter, you used reflections to bring out the surface attributes. Without something in the scene for the glass to reflect, the material never has the punch to look like real glass.
- **Creating metal.** In this chapter, you created a metal toaster with a chrome finish. This exercise illustrates the importance of specular highlight quality in conveying a metallic look. The new Anisotropic shader simulates the elongated specular highlight, caused by the metal grain and machining process. Reflections are an equally important component of achieving realistic metal.
- **Creating black plastic.** Black plastic is one of the most difficult materials to create. This chapter explains that, once again, reflections have a profound effect on illusion. A black plastic material without reflections appears as a black hole in your scene.

Chapter 11

Designing Fictional and Special Effects Materials

Whether working with MAX for a few weeks or since the early days of 3D Studio DOS, you've already created at least one fictional material—or at least tried it.

Fictional and special effects materials are the most taxing to create for one simple reason—they stretch our creative thinking to the limits. Time after time, we need to come up with materials that are both creative and fresh.

While this chapter won't solve your creative-thinking problems, you may find that it helps you push the envelope of what you think is possible in MAX. With MAX, creating fictional materials is not all that difficult. Knowing the available tools and how they operate greatly helps the creation process. In this chapter, we explore fictional and special effects material techniques through several key items:

- Fictional planet building
- Fictional skin
- Simulating real-world light
- Special effects using noise
- Working with mirrors

There's quite a bit to explore in both fictional and special effects materials. Let's start by first taking a look at building two different fictional materials—one for an alien and one for the planet on which it lives.

Building a Fictional Material

A fictional material is anything that your mind dreams up—even if it's based on something that exists in the real world. Whatever the case, we often find ourselves facing a task that seems a bit daunting—building a material from scratch. Fortunately, there are many techniques for building fictional materials that help you in almost every situation. And with the new shaders and map types available within MAX R3, the ease and speed with which you create these materials is significantly greater than in R2.

Use the Real World as a Starting Point

The real world is chock-full of great ideas for fictional materials. How many times have you stared at a cloud's shape and thought about what it resembled in the real world? Look around you. Even the objects on your desk make for some interesting starting points for materials. For instance, take a look at some wood. Look closely at the grain. Now imagine the dark areas of the grain receding into the wood and the lighter areas raising. Now skim a highly shiny, slimy coating on top of that and you have a nice organic alien muscle.

By looking at the real world, there is an unlimited number of ideas for building materials. The key trick is to know what tools you have at your disposal, so that you can easily re-create them. When building organic, fictional materials, for example, it's often a good idea to start with procedural maps—such as Noise or Cellular.

Start from a Concept

Sometimes the real world just won't do, and nothing you see provides an inspiration or foundation for building a fictional material. If that's the case, you need to rely on your creativity. Unfortunately, that's not always easy. If you haven't been to an alien planet or never met an alien, your experience in designing a material for either one can be a bit frustrating.

Fortunately people have gone through many of these mental exercises already. Some have produced works on it, books, movies, tabloid articles, and so on. If you're strapped for material, the best solution is to base your work on something already done. This doesn't mean to copy someone else's work. Not only is this unethical, it's illegal. You can, however, look at another's work and come up with *your own* ideas for your work. Why re-invent the wheel, right?

Use Procedural Maps

Procedural maps, as mentioned earlier, are great for building organic surfaces. Why? Procedural maps are, by nature, random in their effect. This means that you can design a great, complex, organic surface without even a remotely repeating pattern. Rather than worry about a map that tiles across the surface of an object, a procedural map distributes itself—without mapping coordinates.

Using procedural maps, however, takes away some of your control when using mapped materials. Because there are no mapping coordinates, you can't specify that a puff of smoke from the Smoke map appears in an exact location without spending some time fiddling with the parameters. Animating procedural maps can also be a challenge. For instance, if you want the water in a Water map to crest at a certain time, the only way to achieve this is through trial and error. The water's movement is controlled by its phase-and-offset values, not by some user-specified value for crest timing. While these limitations seem a bit difficult to work with, they really aren't all that bad. As a matter of fact, most people don't even think about them since they're so minor. It's only at those certain times when you want explicit control that you actually notice the limitations.

Procedural maps are the best armament in your fictional material arsenal. Let's take a look at a few of the more prominent maps.

Noise

What do you call the most popular map of all time in the 3D Studio MAX user community? Noise! Noise is, perhaps, the most used (and sometimes overused) map within the MAX material arsenal. Noise is pretty uninteresting just looking at it bare, meaning while it is not being utilized as a map anywhere. Essentially Noise uses two colors—any colors—and blends them together, using one of three algorithms. Don't let the term "algorithm" scare you off. You don't have to know any math, much less how the algorithms work. Noise is a visual map. This means that you're looking very closely at the random mixing pattern it produces. It is this very randomization that gives Noise its well deserved status as the most popular map.

Beyond the Noise Map

Noise is not just limited to a singular map, either. There are other instances where noise is used within MAX. The Noise modifier is an example. However, Noise is also embedded in most of the other map types that you use in the Material Editor (such as Bitmap). In this case, the Noise parameters are consolidated into a single rollout within the map. Looking at Figure 11.1, notice that although you're working with the Bitmap map type, Noise can also be added to produce a random distortion. Also note that the controls available in the Noise parameters of the Bitmap map type are somewhat limited compared to those of the Noise map, as seen in Figure 11.3. This isn't really a limitation. The Bitmap rollout basically contains just the controls you need to create a random distortion in your map using the Noise function. For this section, we're focusing mainly on the Noise map. However, you can easily transfer the things you learn here over to the Noise parameters located in other map types.

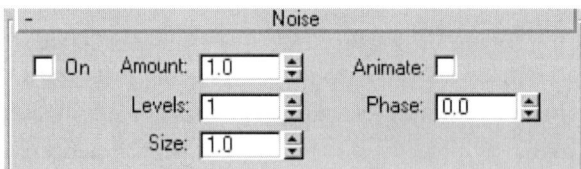

Figure 11.1 The Noise parameters rollout in the Bitmap map type. These parameters, located in other map types besides Noise, are specific to map distortion and therefore provide more limited functionality.

Use Noise for just about anything. In this chapter, you learn how to use it to create a complex-looking alien-planet surface. However, you can use Noise for other purposes, too—blotchy transparency, muddled refractions, or even star fields. Noise truly is the multipurpose map. Figure 11.2 shows how Noise produces a nice water surface when used as a bump map. In Chapter 12, you'll re-create this very scene.

Figure 11.2 A rolling sea surface created with the help of the Noise map used in the Bump Map channel of a material.

Noise Parameters

Noise has several parameters that allows you to control how it performs. Some of the terminology is a bit strange, but use this section to get more of a "real-world" idea of how the various settings work in production. Figure 11.3 shows the Noise map's parameters.

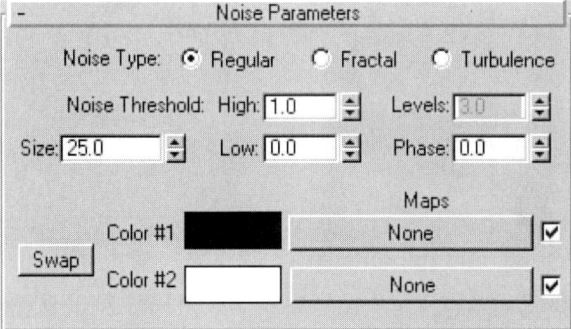

Figure 11.3 The Noise map parameters. The two color swatches are black and white by default, providing a great grayscale ramp that works well for intensity map channels—such as Bump and Opacity. However, if you tint the colors a different hue, you produce some great random color distribution across a surface. You can also add maps to the color swatches for more complex effects.

Across the top of the Noise Parameters section are checkboxes for the three types of Noise that you can use. They are Regular, Fractal, and Turbulence.

Before you get hung up on the names, there is an easy way to remember which type of noise is good for what occasion. The easiest way to see how Noise affects a material is to use it as a Bump map. With that in mind, here's how to look at the three Noise types:

- **Regular produces a nice rolling hills look.** The ramping between the two colors is smooth, meaning there's a nice gradient produced between areas of Color #1 and areas of Color #2.

- **Fractal looks like a mountain range.** Much like Regular, Fractal produces ramped gradients between the colors that are somewhat smooth. However, this is interspersed with sharp changes between Color #1 and Color #2. When used as a Bump map, for instance, it produces a good combination of both smooth and sharp edges on a surface.

- **Turbulence creates a great moonscape-like surface.** Rather than evenly distributing Colors #1 and #2 across a surface, Turbulence creates "chunky" areas on your surface that give an object a pitted appearance.

Even though these are geological references, you clearly see how the three types work. In case you're having a bit of trouble visualizing the three examples, Figure 11.4 demonstrates the same material using the Noise map with all three types.

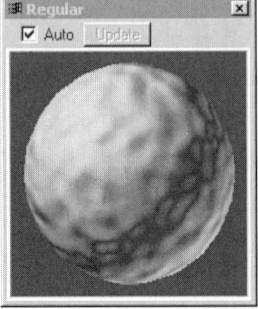 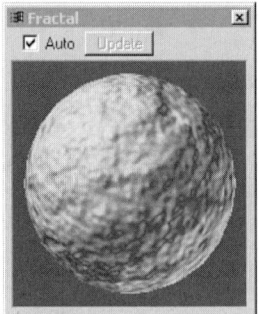 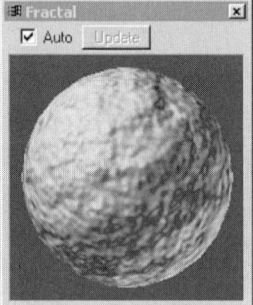

Figure 11.4 This figure shows how the three types of Noise work on the same material. They are Regular (left), Fractal (middle), and Turbulence (right).

Once you chose the style of randomization (Regular, Fractal, or Turbulence), you then begin to alter some of the other settings. The most common setting to adjust is Size. The

Size field controls the overall size of the noise effect, based on MAX-world units. This means that the size of the object does not matter.

High and Low for the Noise Threshold allows you to control the predominance of either color by "ramping" between Color #1 and Color #2 (shown at the bottom of the panel). Ramping is most easily understood when working with black and white. To transition smoothly from black to white, you need a grayscale gradient. That gradient is called the *ramp* and equates to the difference between the High and Low values. Longer ramps mean more gradient colors exist. Shorter ramps mean that fewer colors are used in the gradient. The Thresholds not only allow you to control the size of the ramp, but also which color is more weighted. This means that by reducing the High Threshold, you shorten the length of the ramp—but you also shorten it in favor of the Low Threshold's color (since it's remaining at 0). When you alter the Threshold values, you're basically just telling Noise you want to use less of one color and more of the other.

Technically, noise is similar to a mathematical wave, which varies in a random manner between values of 0 and 1. The lower the number goes, the more Color #1 is shown. The closer it gets to 1, the more Color #2 is shown. The High threshold is the point above which Color #2 is shown. Decrease the High, and more of the mid-range values on the curve turn to Color #2. Increase the Low, and more mid-range values turn to Color #1. Once those colors are filled in, the area between them is filled with a ramp of colors 1 to 2. It helps if you think of Color #1 as the low color and Color #2 as the high color. Draw a zigzag scribble on a piece of paper. Across the page at the bottom peak, draw a line marked "0 = Low Color" and across the top "1 = High Color." As the high line moves down, more of the zigzag gets the high color. The same is true of the low color and moving the low line up.

The Swap button allows you to easily switch Colors #1 and #2 with each other. This way, you don't worry about copying colors between swatches or writing down the values—a timesaver, to say the least.

Lastly alter the Phase of the noise. Phase controls the shifting of the positions of Color #1 and Color #2 within the map itself. By animating Phase, you make the Noise map appear to undulate on the material.

Notice that you can also substitute maps for Colors #1 or #2. This means that you use multiple colors from a map instead of a solid color. Using maps in Noise is great for textures like freckles on skin or similar items. The check boxes next to the Maps button allow you to turn a map on or off if you've already defined one. Use this as a troubleshooting feature to test the effect a map has on the Noise's output.

Cellular

Cellular is the first runner-up in the map-popularity contest. Rather than randomly mixing two colors to produce an effect, Cellular works by producing small cell-like patterns. The distribution of the pattern is completely procedural—meaning that it's based on numerical values that create a random distribution. As a result Cellular works great for creating organic surfaces. As a Diffuse map, it creates terrific dried-out textures, such as a desert lakebed. As a Bump map, it is excellent for creating a scaly surface. Figure 11.5 shows how you use Cellular. The image comes from the alien-skin exercise later in this chapter.

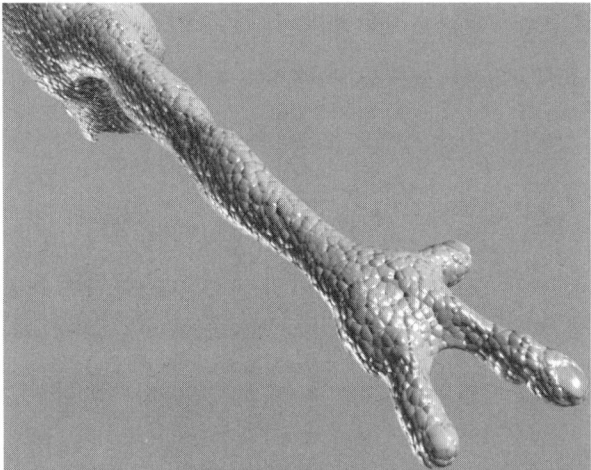

Figure 11.5 This is an example of using Cellular to produce the small scaly bumps you see on this alien's arm. Cellular is used as Bump map that's set to a high amount to show the example. Typically, the effect of Cellular should be a little less obvious.

The Cellular interface resembles nothing of the Noise map's interface. As with the Noise map, however, the primary way to manipulate Cellular is by visual reference and not getting hung up on all the technical terms. Some nomenclature is carried over from the Noise map. Figure 11.6 shows the Cellular map's interface.

The three colors allow you to control the colors of the cells (Cell Color) and the colors that exist between the cells, which are called *divisions* (Division Colors). The default colors work well for most bump map usage, but more than likely you need to change the colors or add a color map—such as a bitmap—for using Cellular as a Diffuse map.

The Cell Characteristics section alters the overall shape and size of the cells and the amount of space between them. Circular works great for scaly, bumpy surfaces while

Chips works well for dry, cracked surfaces, such as dry lakebeds. By increasing or decreasing Spread, you increase or decrease the spacing between the cells, respectively.

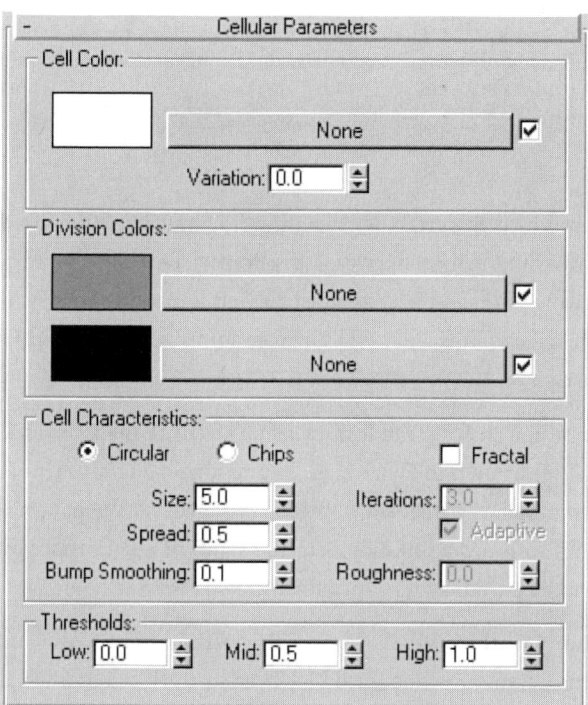

Figure 11.6 The Cellular map's parameters. Like the Noise map, Cellular uses color values to produce its random effect. The colors can be solid (selected from the color swatch) or multiple (using a map).

The cells have no variation of the color within themselves. The Fractal check box allows you to introduce a noise-like pattern into the cells and their divisions. This produces a more splotchy pattern that you might use to distribute something across a surface, such as rashes across skin.

The only hitch about the Cellular map is the rendering speed. Since the effect is more complex than Noise, it typically takes longer to render. Keep that in mind when using the map in both the Diffuse and Bump map channels. Not only does Cellular get calculated twice, but also SuperSampling is used to counter the aliasing effects of the Bump map.

> **Tip**
> Rendering a material that uses a Cellular map often takes as much as *four times longer* than the same material that uses a bitmap instead. For that reason, you might consider using the Material Editor's Render Map feature. That way, you render the Cellular map to a bitmap and use the Bitmap map versus the Cellular map. Because MAX doesn't need to do any underlying calculations during rendering time, your rendering speed improves significantly. For more information on the Render Map command, see MAX's online help.

NEW TO R3

Swirl

The Swirl map allows you to produce materials with a random, multi-colored swirl effect. You can use it to create anything from a hurricane/typhoon-type object to warp effects. Swirl, being procedural, works the same way as Noise or Cellular—with color values or colors from color maps. However, it is a 2D effect that requires mapping coordinates in order to function properly.

While Noise and Cellular are good for creating random color or intensity maps, Swirl is a bit more specialized. You won't typically find Swirl used as much in a general-purpose capacity. Nevertheless Swirl works well as a distortion effect. And since all the parameters are animatable, there are quite a few possibilities as to the types of effects that you can create. In Figure 11.7, notice the parameters rollout for the Swirl map.

The first section, Swirl Color Setup, works similarly to the color definition of Noise and Cellular. Notice, however, that the default is orange and black versus the black and white that both Noise and Cellular have. Like Cellular, the colors are also labeled specifically—Base and Swirl—to help identify where they occur in the map. This is because you are more likely to use this as a color map (possibly in a Diffuse channel) rather than as an intensity map. Swirl works well in either situation.

Beyond the map and color definitions lay three main controls that affect the color blending that makes up the swirl. Color Contrast works by affecting the contrast between the two colors. By increasing the number, you increase the contrast between the Base and Swirl colors. Higher contrast values produce a definitive boundary between the colors, but the intensity of the colors is also increased (much like using the Contrast adjustment in Photoshop). Swirl Intensity specifically boosts the output of the Swirl color. This helps "bring out" the color by increasing its output value. This setting can go between –10 and 10, which means that you intensify the output of the base color by using a negative value. The controller of everything, though, is the Swirl Amount. Think of this value as the multiplier for the whole effect. At 1.0, the effects of the color, the contrast, and the intensity are all at their normal values. However, to achieve more muted effects, decrease the Swirl Amount value below 1.0. Values above 1.0 boost the output of color, contrast, and intensity.

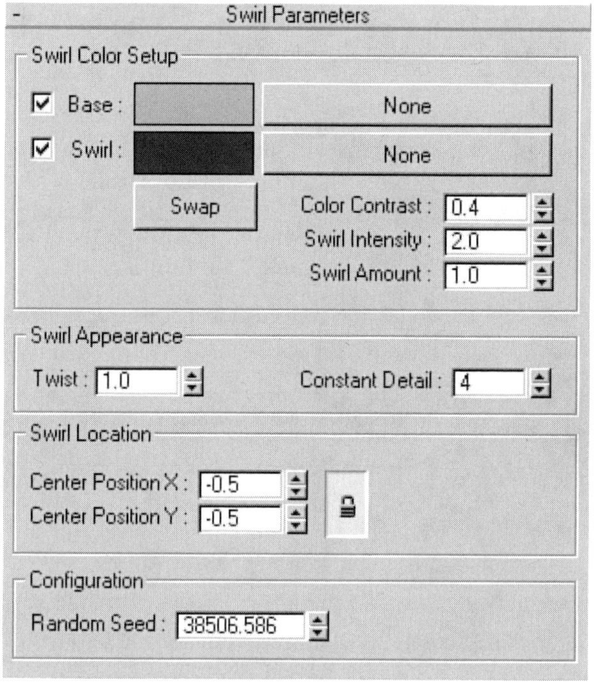

Chapter 11: Designing Fictional and Special Effects Materials   465

Figure 11.7 The Swirl map parameters. Much like Noise and Cellular, Swirl works through blending multiple colors or color maps to produce its effect. Unlike Noise and Cellular, however, Swirl requires mapping coordinates in order to render properly.

The preceding parameters controlled the color of the swirl. To alter the number of revolutions or the crispness of a swirl's appearance, you need to change the Twist and Constant Detail values, respectively. Twist just controls how many revolutions the colors make around the center. The Constant Detail value works much like other Detail settings within MAX. By increasing the value, your Swirl appears to be more crisp. Lower values produce a "muddier" look for the swirl colors.

The remaining parameters simply allow you to control the location of the swirl's center and how the colors are randomly generated and distributed. An interesting effect is to animate both the Twist and Random seed using small values to produce swirling, gaseous clouds. Be sure to use only small values, however. Large changes over short time frames produce rapidly changing effects.

Splat

Imagine a bored painter. One day the painter just dips the paintbrush into the can, and then violently shakes the brush around the room. The end result (besides a mess) is little paint splats all over. This is exactly what the Splat map does—except you're the painter. Figure 11.8 shows the Splat map's capability, when used as a Texture map.

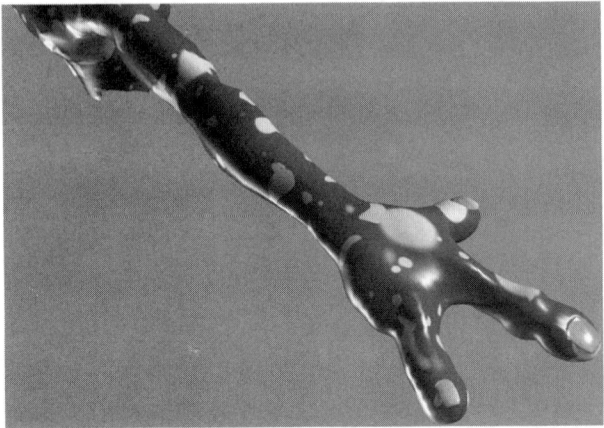

Figure 11.8 The Splat map, used to create a nice reptilian look on the alien's arm.

The Splat interface (shown in Figure 11.9) is relatively simple. Some of the parameter names, such as Iterations and Threshold, are not designed for the artist (or painter, in this case) so a little deciphering is necessary.

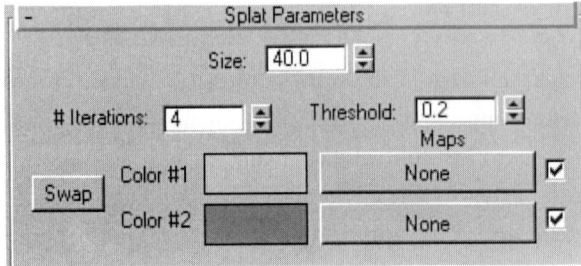

Figure 11.9 The Splat map's interface. Notice that the controls, while technically named, are few—and even easy to use!

The Size function controls the maximum size of the splats. Some splats can be smaller, but none can be larger than the Size value. Iterations control how much paint is on the brush. The more iterations you use, the more splats you see. However, you also see more tiny splats. Threshold, as in other maps, specifies which color is more predominant—#1 or #2. At 0, Color #1 is predominant; while at 1, Color #2 is more predominant.

> **Note**
> Color #2 controls the color of the splats. Color #1 controls the "other" color used to fill in the areas where the splats do not exist. Think of Color #1 as the wall color before the painter started waving the brush around.

You can use Splat for all kinds of wacky tricks. A great thing to try is to use the same Splat map in both the Diffuse and Bump map channels. This produces raised splats—a nice effect if you're trying for nice, thick splats!

Water

The Water map comes to us from the days of 3D Studio DOS, where it first started as an IPAS plug-in. Use it to create the obvious—water. It also works very well for such effects as opacity and bumpiness. For clarity, however, let's refer to the map as if it were used as a liquid-based material within the scene. You can apply any of the concepts or techniques discussed here to just about any situation that calls for the Water map.

The map has several adjustable parameters. The strength of the Water map is not so much the static version of the map—actually Noise produces a much better "still" water—but rather how it animates. Just by animating the Phase value over time, you produce some pretty incredible organic motion. Figure 11.10 shows the interface of the Water map.

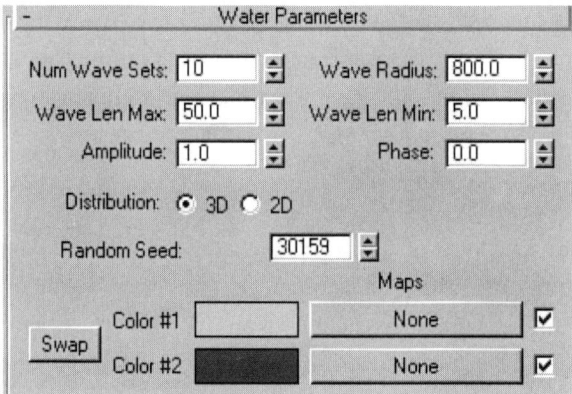

Figure 11.10 The Water map's interface. While Water works well when used as a combination of Diffuse, Bump, and Glossiness in a material, its versatile control set allows you to create surfaces that also use opacity or reflection channels.

If you observe the way ripples move on the surface of the water, you may see that there are actually many sets of crossing ripples—sometimes they're even crossing each other or moving in the opposite direction. The reasons for this are many—wind, interaction with still objects—but you simulate this by increasing Water's Num Wave Sets value. The default of 10 works well for many situations but may prove too cluttered for calmer effects. The distribution of the waves is completely random.

The wave-length fields (Wave Len Min and Wave Len Max) control the biggest and smallest sizes of the wave sets. Wave sets, themselves, are many sizes. By specifying a different Min and Max value, you give the Water map some leeway in randomizing the sizes of the sets. If these two values are the same, the sizes of the sets are the same and probably look a bit unrealistic. For the best random effect, put at least a 20-unit difference between Wave Len Min and Wave Len Max.

Amplitude is a sneaky value—you're controlling a single threshold value. Believe it or not, it's actually controlling the predominance between Colors #1 and #2. At 0, Color #1 is predominant. As you increase the Amplitude, Color #2 becomes more predominant. The default setting of 1.0 works for most situations.

Wave Radius allows you to control the overall size of the water ripples. Setting the radius to 0 sets the Water map's waves to the smallest size possible. Increasing this value enlarges the size of the effect across the surface of your object. You notice this most easily if you set the number of Wave Sets to 1.

Animating Phase is the most powerful part of the Water map. The Phase value moves the wave sets around the material over time. For most animations, you only need to use *small values* when animating Phase. For instance, a 100-frame animation requires only about a 5-unit change in phase. This produces nice, brisk water. Anything higher approaches a rapids-like speed. Slower results produce more bayou-like, slow moving water.

Wood

Wood, in itself, does not produce a fictional or special-effect material. However when you use the Wood map outside of its intended context, you begin to see its possibilities. For instance, use the Wood map in the Bump map channel to produce grainy scales for a snake-like skin. If you use Wood as a Diffuse map, you simulate geological layers on the surface of a planet. Figure 11.11 shows a rendering from Exercise 11.1 (later in this chapter). The rendering depicts a fictional planet with geological layers etched into the surface and visible along the sides of the canyon walls. These layers are created by the Wood map.

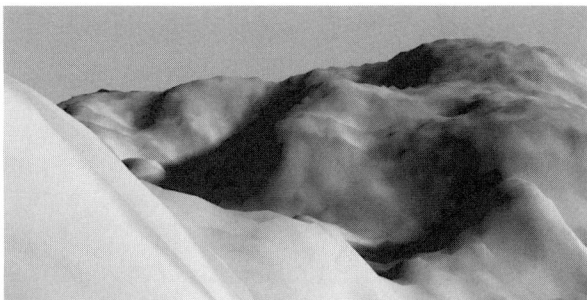

Figure 11.11 The Wood map is used in this rendering as a texture map for the surface of the planet. The grain-like nature of the Wood map gives the planet's surface nice geological layers.

The Wood map's parameters are fairly straightforward, at least a little more so than some of the other maps. Instead of a "Size" parameter, there is a Grain Thickness field. It essentially controls the size of the Wood map. Where the confusion often comes in is the difference between what is Radial and Axial noise. Before you break those down, take a look at how the Wood map works. In Figure 11.12, note the Wood map applied to a block of, well—wood. Notice the circular ripple pattern on one side of the box. The Radial axis travels in the same direction of that ripple. Wood is, however, a 3D effect. The wood grain gets projected all the way through the object. That axis of projection is the Axial value. Therefore, the following is true:

- Radial Noise controls the distortion of the wood grain along the rings of the grain.
- Axial Noise controls the distortion of the grain as it is projected through the wood.

Ironically you *don't* rely on the Wood map for making realistic wood materials. The map parameters are just too limited to make this possible. You really need to use a bitmap image of wood instead. You can use the Wood map, however, in many other ways to produce complex, concentric material effects.

Smoke

Smoke, like Water, comes from the old IPAS collection of the 3D Studio DOS days. Its intended function is to create the appearance of a smoky-like surface on whatever object to which it is applied. However, the smoke map serves as other great effects, such as clouds or other gaseous anomalies.

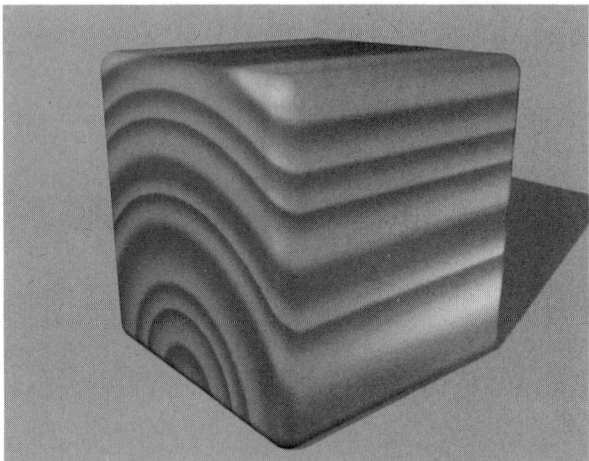

Figure 11.12 A cross-section view of the Wood map. The circular pattern is the Radial Axis. The grains traveling through the block comprise the Axial Axis.

The interface of Smoke is very simple. Note the various parameters in Figure 11.13. By now, you are noticing a pattern in the interfaces. There are some small differences in the naming of the various parameters, but you basically control the same thing. The only item that is really changing is the mathematical function (or algorithm) that controls the random behavior of the map.

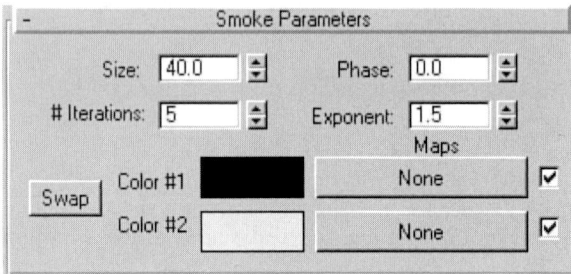

Figure 11.13 The Smoke map's parameters. Notice how closely they resemble parameters for other maps discussed in this chapter.

For instance, the Exponent parameter controls the threshold between Color #1 and Color #2. For the most part it works just like the Amplitude parameter of the Water map. The Iterations parameter closely resembles the Iterations of the Splat map. The more iterations you create, the more puffs of "smoke" appear.

Dent

Dent—as its name implies—creates a nice, pitted surface on your material when used as a Bump map. Ported from an old IPAS plug-in for 3D Studio DOS, the Dent map's functionality has not changed all that much. And like many of the other maps, the parameters are fairly simplistic. Figure 11.14 shows the interface of Dent.

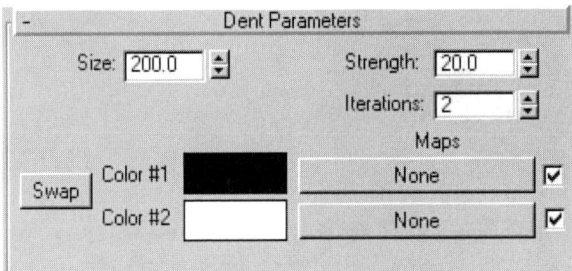

Figure 11.14 The Dent map's interface. Dent creates a simple random distribution of Colors #1 and #2. There is virtually no ramp between the colors, so the effect when used as a bump map is a heavily pitted surface.

A quick overview is that Size controls the size of the Dent map, Strength is the threshold (predominance) value between Colors #1 and #2, and Iterations controls the number of dents.

The Dent map isn't all that exciting when just used as a Bump map. Instead of limiting it to the Bump map channel, try using it with the Self-Illumination map channel and even Shininess. Dent also works well as a component of a Mask map for creating splotchy "Shroud of Turin" texture effects. For Dent to look good, you need to increase the size. The default of 200 produces too small of a dent pattern that almost looks like it's tiling. Instead, increase the size to around 500. The result is much better. Figure 11.15 shows Dent used in several map channels.

 Tip
It's always a good idea to use SuperSampling with Dent because there is little or no ramping between the colors. If you choose not to do so, aliasing along the "pits" of your surface occurs.

Procedural Map Tutorials

In the exercises that follow, you'll apply some of the techniques and maps discussed in this chapter to produce an extra-terrestrial planet surface and an alien to inhabit it. Exercise 11.1 includes using various maps for the planet's surface. Exercise 11.1.2 uses

Figure 11.15 The Dent map used in several map channels of a material. They include Shininess, Shin.Strength, Self-Illumination, and Bump.

the same type of maps for creating a nice haze/fog effect. Finally, Exercise 11.2 shows you how to map skin to an alien body.

Exercise 11.1   Creating an Alien Planet Surface

1. Open 11imx01.max, and render the scene. Notice that the file is just a simple terrain model.
2. Click the Material Editor button in the toolbar, and select the upper-left material. Roll out the Maps section.
3. Click the None map for the Bump map channel. Select Noise.
4. In the Noise Parameters section, set the Noise type to Fractal and the Size to 0.5.
5. Use the Go To Parent button to go back up to the Maps rollout. Set the Bump map's Strength to 60.
6. Apply the material to the Planet Surface object, and render the scene. Notice the bumpy look of the terrain surface.
7. Click the None map for the Diffuse map channel, and choose Swirl. Set the Swirl Intensity to 0.5 and Twist to 5.0.
8. Click the None map for the Swirl map , and choose Mix. Set the Mix Amount to 50.
9. In the Mix map's parameters, click the None map for Color #1.
10. In the Material/Map Browser's Browse From section, choose Material Editor. Select the Noise map that appears in the list to the right. When asked about making a copy or instance, choose Copy.

Chapter 11: Designing Fictional and Special Effects Materials

11. Change the Noise map Size to 1, and alter the color of both Color #1 and #2 to dark shades of brown (R87, G45, BO, and some variation). Note: Make the two colors somewhat different.

12. Now add the Wood map as the other map within the material. Use the Go To Parent button to return to the Mix map's parameters, and click the None map for Color #2.

13. In the Material/Map Browser's Browse From section, choose New. Select the Wood map.

14. In the Coordinates section, change the Z Angle parameter to 90.

15. In the Wood Parameters section, set the Grain Thickness to about 18, and change both Color #1 and Color #2 to darker shades of brown—similar to the Noise map's colors, but noticeably different.

16. Re-render the Camera01 viewport. You now see a much more convincing alien-planet surface (Figure 11.16). Save your file before moving to the next exercise.

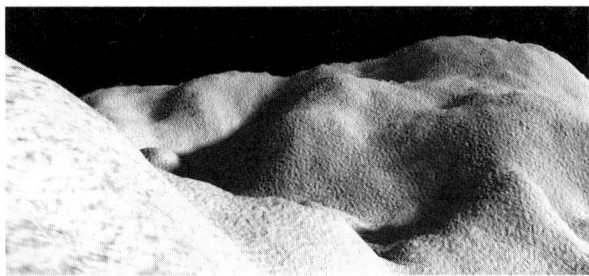

Figure 11.16 The results from Exercise 11.1. The planet surface is using a combination of Noise and Wood maps for the surface.

The terrain looks great in Figure 11.16, but the atmospherics are nonexistent. To make this look more like a planet, you need to add some sort of sky, some haze, and some "clumpy" ground fog. Use the same type of techniques in the previous exercise to create believable environments in your scene. In the Exercise 11.1.2, use Noise and Gradient to produce these effects.

Exercise 11.1.2   Adding Fog to the Alien-Planet Atmosphere

1. Open the file 11imx02.max. This is the completed planet surface from the previous exercise.

2. To add Haze to the Scene, choose Environment from the Rendering pull-down menu.

3. Click the Add button in the Atmosphere section, and choose Fog.

4. In the Name field, enter Haze.
5. Set the Color of the fog to a light brown. A value of R192, G149, B66 works well.
6. Set Far% to 45, and render the scene. Notice the nice haze now applied in the distance.
7. Click the Add button again, and add another Fog effect. Name this one Ground Fog.
8. Set the color of this fog to about the same as the Haze effect. Then set the type to Layered. Uncheck Fog Background, as well.
9. When the Layered parameters appear at the bottom of the fog interface, set the Falloff to Top, the Top value to 15, and the Density to 75.
10. Turn on Horizon Noise. Set the Size to 5.
11. To create the clumpy fog effect, click the None map for the Environment Opacity map. Choose Noise.
12. First open the Material Editor, if it isn't open already. Then drag the Noise map from the Environment dialog to any unused material slot in the Material Editor.
13. When prompted for Cloning options, select Instance.
14. To alter the clumpiness, you need to alter some parameters of the Noise map. Set the type to Fractal and the Size to 7.
15. In the Environment dialog, check Use Map in the Background section. This will activate the Alien Sky map already designed in the scene.
16. Re-render the scene and save the file (see Figure 11.17). Your alien planet is complete!

Figure 11.17   The final rendering from Exercise 11.1.2. The atmospherics are all generated by using procedural maps and fog effects.

As you can see, many different settings are used within the maps discussed to create convincing effects. Although you don't create the sky, take some time to analyze how the material is built. Notice that it simply incorporates the compositing of the Gradient Map and the Noise map to produce a sunset and cloud effect.

If you want to build a great alien planet, you need to build a great alien to live on it. In Exercise 11.2, you use some of the other maps discussed in this chapter to build the skin on an alien body. Pay close attention to how the maps are used in multiple channels, instead of just one. By copying or instancing one map throughout a material, you can create some great-looking complex surfaces.

Exercise 11.2   Creating an Alien Skin with Maps

1. Open 11imx03.max. Render the scene. This is the right side of an alien's upper body. Let's apply various materials to it to give a more "scaly" look.
2. Open the Material Editor, and select the upper-left hand sample sphere.
3. First build the splattered looking surface. Roll out the Maps section, and click None for the Diffuse map.
4. Select the Splat map. Set the Size of the Splat map to 5 and Iterations to 5. Finally adjust the Threshold value to 0.27.
5. Alter Color #1 to a dark green and Color #2 to a muted yellow. Use the Go To Parent button to return to the Maps rollout.
6. Click None for the Bump map channel. Select Cellular.
7. Set the size of the Cellular map to 0.2, then click the Go To Parent button. Set the Intensity Amount of Bump map channel to 65.
8. Drag the Cellular map to the Glossiness and Specular level map channels, both times making instances of the map. This mutes the shininess in the "grooves" of the scales.
9. Roll out the SuperSampling check box, and check Enable SuperSampler. This prevents harsh aliasing around the scales. Drag and drop the material onto the skin object.
10. Render the scene, and save your file.

Just by using two maps, you create a convincing alien skin to apply to just about any object (see Figure 11.18). Something else to try in this scene—add a Noise map into the yellow color of the Splat map in the Diffuse channel. This "breaks up" the edges of the splats. You can also mix another map, such as Gradient or Wood, with the Cellular map in the Bump channel to increase the scaly look. Figure 11.19 shows what happens when you add Noise to the Splat and mix a Gradient map into the Bump channel.

476   Part II   Materials

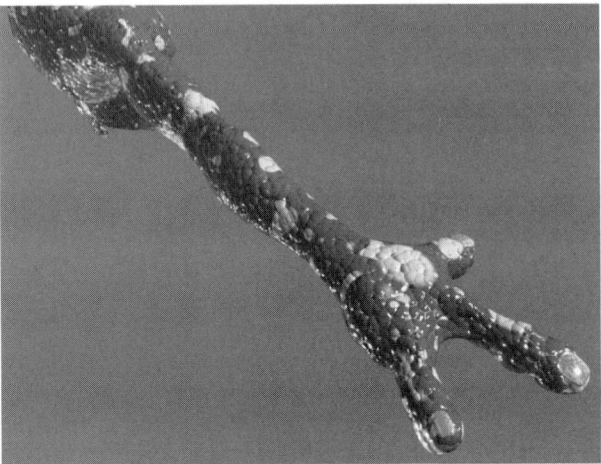

Figure 11.18 The final rendering from Exercise 11.2. The skin was produced just with the Splat and Cellular maps.

Figure 11.19 By adding Noise to the splat colors, you effectively randomize the color of the splats, themselves. Adding a gradient map to the Bump channel helps add a more scale-like effect.

Illumination Effects

Time to get back to reality—at least a little. In MAX R3, there are actually several features, materials wise, that help you with illumination. This section talks about how to use various components of both the Standard and Raytrace materials to produce lighting effects from the materials themselves.

Clear and Soft Light Bulbs

Light bulbs are always a challenge to get just right. They differ so much in size, shape, and intensity that creating a "catch-all" material for all lights just isn't possible. However there are some basic rules for light bulbs.

- **Use Opacity Falloff.** When a bulb is lit, you effectively simulate the falloff of light within the bulb by using Opacity Falloff.

- **Use Additive Transparency.** Additive Transparency helps when the light source needs to appear to be lit. Basically it brightens the color of the pixels behind the semi-transparent light. This makes the light appear to be all the more bright. Note that this isn't really effective if the light is not illuminated.

- **Don't use a strong Self-Illumination value.** By keeping Self-Illumination somewhere around 70–90, you retain some of the ambient color of a material. This is very effective for materials that are using Opacity Falloff.

- **Use Reflection maps.** Reflection maps effectively brighten your material. Using a map like sky.jpg in the reflection channel works very well. To keep from overpowering a material with a Reflection map, only use them at about a strength of 10–20.

Note

If you use a Reflection map for an unlit bulb, remember to use Reflection Dimming! Otherwise your bulb still appears to be lit—even when you turn off Self-Illumination.

- **Use high Specular Level and Glossiness values.** Remember, these bulbs are made out of glass. They should be shiny.

- **Use Lens Effects Glow in Video Post.** Glow in Video Post helps diffuse the light immediately around the light source—or at least appears like it. You must use subtle values for the Glow effect so it looks appropriate.

- **Use raytracing only when necessary.** Sure, raytracing looks good—especially on glass. But remember that it adds a great deal of rendering time to your scene, and it can actually make light bulbs look worse. The only time you really want to use raytracing is for an unlit bulb when you look at it up close.

Figure 11.20 shows what a good illuminated and nonilluminated light bulb might look like. Find this file on your CD as Bulb.max.

Figure 11.20 Two light bulbs—one lit, the other unlit. Both use Standard materials. The main difference, besides the illumination, is that the right light bulb uses a Raytrace map for refraction.

Candles and Other Light Sources

Lit candles are often very difficult to make as a material. For instance, think about a lit candle. The primary problem is that because candle wax is translucent, it appears to be somewhat lit when the wick is lit. There has never been an easy way to re-create this in MAX—if at all. However, in MAX R3, you have the Translucency value in the Raytrace material to simulate this effect very well. Similar to dealing with light bulbs, there are several tips for dealing with translucent materials.

- **Lights illuminate translucent materials.** Remember that if a light source is near a translucent material, it will appear to be lit unless you exclude it from that source. Note that this includes lights that reside within objects containing a translucent material.

- **Light intensity affects translucent materials.** The brighter the light, the brighter the translucent material. Extremely bright lights wash out the subtleties of a translucent material. Be careful not to overpower your lights.

Chapter 11: Designing Fictional and Special Effects Materials   479

- **Use darker colors for translucency.** Translucency is affected by a global color or a map. In either case, take care not to use maps with high brightness values. This overpowers the translucent material.

- **Translucency does not take long to render.** Even though Translucency is part of the Raytrace material, it does not require the calculations that reflections or refractions require. Unless your translucent material is using either reflection or refraction, your rendering time is not seriously impacted.

Figure 11.21 shows how you use translucency to make candle wax appear more realistic. Note that two lights are used to get better translucency effects. One light uses attenuation, while the other excludes the candle but provides more illumination to the room. The example is included on your CD-ROM as candle.max. See Figure 11.22 for the settings used in Figure 11.21.

Figure 11.21 Use a translucent material on an object, such as a candle, to simulate the transmission of light through the wax when the candle is lit.

480   Part II   Materials

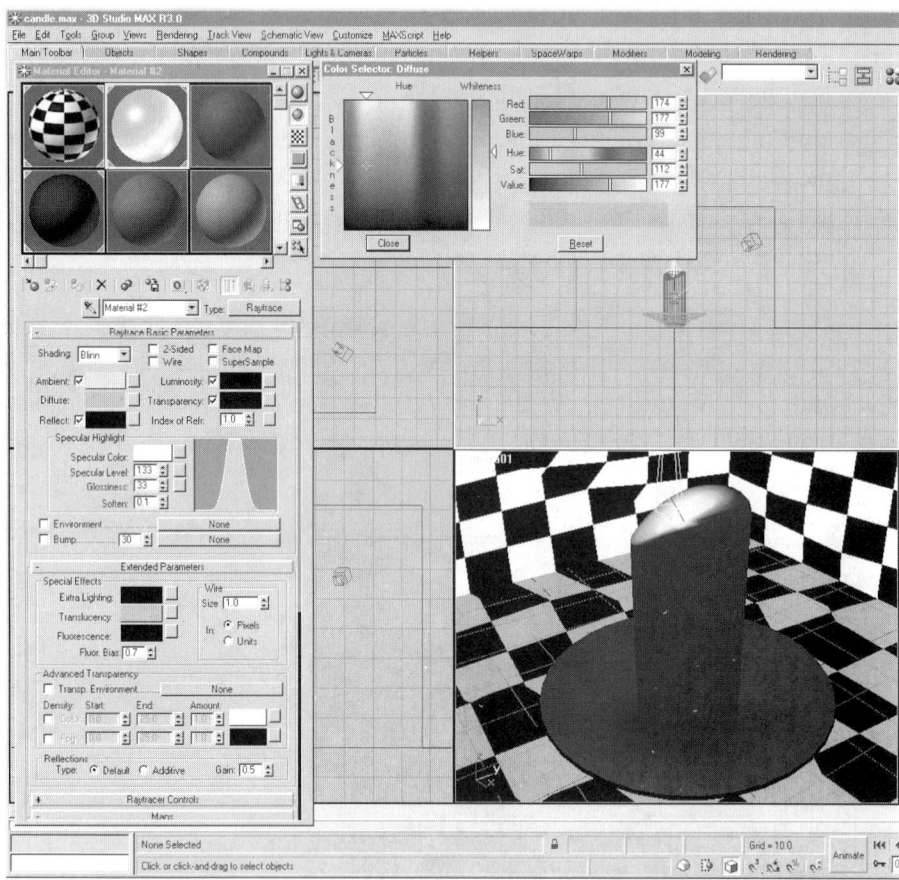

Figure 11.22 The settings in the MAX scene for the previous example. The translucency color is the same as the Diffuse color. One omni light is used with attenuation for the translucency effect. Another is used for general illumination.

In Practice: Designing Fictional and Special Effects Materials

- **Use the real-world as a foundation.** A great deal of good source material is available from the world around us for fictional materials.

- **Procedural maps work for organic materials.** Because procedural maps are random in their effect, they're quite easy to use within an organic material. Create complex, organic surfaces just by using one (or a combination of) procedural map(s).

- **Noise is *still* the undisputed king of procedural maps.** You can use Noise just about everywhere in a scene when there's a need for randomization. Using combinations of Noise within itself or with other maps greatly enhances a material.

- **Light sources require several steps to build.** There are many things to consider when building a light-source material. In this chapter, you created both a lit and unlit source just by making minor adjustments to the same material.
- **Use Translucency in the Raytrace Material.** Translucency really makes a difference for such objects as lamp shades or candle wax. Anytime you have an object that normally allows some light to pass through, use the Translucency feature of the Raytrace material.

Chapter 12

Animated Materials

As a MAX user, you're probably well aware of the ability to animate materials. As with anything else in MAX, if it has a spinner, you can animate it. Furthermore, any animatable parameter within the Material

Editor uses special animation controllers, as well as the new Motion Capture feature. For more information on Motion Capture, see *Inside 3D Studio MAX 3 Animation*. The animation power of MAX is truly amazing. With this raw power, however, comes unrefined capabilities that you must manipulate to get the effects you desire. Translation: MAX's presets are very limited. You can't say, "Give me water," and expect MAX to do it perfectly right out of the gate. You need to tweak the values quite a bit to get it "just right."

Note
Don't let the fact that MAX has few preset values discourage you. Not only does MAX ship with several materials, it's fairly easy to create your own library of materials to use over and over again.

When it comes to animating materials, there are quite a few directions to go. Before you dive into this chapter, familiarize yourself with the animation capabilities of MAX, as well as basic material-animation concepts. This chapter doesn't cover such basic topics as animating the Diffuse color of a material. Refer to the online MAX reference for more information on basic material editing.

In this chapter, you explore topics such as

- Animating naturally occurring materials
- Animating man-made materials
- Maps to use with either man-made materials or naturally occurring materials

Tip
Whenever you work with animated materials, remember to use the Material Preview function. That way, you preview the animations of materials in your scene without doing a full rendering.

Natural Animated Materials

As discussed in Chapter 11, "Designing Fictional and Special Effects Materials," a slew of procedural maps helps you easily design both fictional and natural organic materials. Any procedural map that is available for stills is also used in an animation. Almost all the maps have a Phase value that you can animate. Depending on the map, animating Phase has a different effect, but essentially it causes any procedural map to move.

In the sections that follow, study which procedural maps to use with different naturally occurring materials. While several maps are covered, keep in mind that these are just starting points. Another map may work better for another natural material. The best thing is to try one. The possibilities are limited only by your imagination. Figure 12.1 demonstrates what's possible: Artist Frank DeLise used materials with particles to produce a realistic waterfall.

Figure 12.1 An animated waterfall, created using both natural materials and particle systems. Image courtesy of Frank DeLise, Discreet.

Maps to Use with Natural Materials

Procedural materials provide the greatest flexibility for organic surfaces due to their randomness. However, you can also use other maps for natural materials. Bitmaps are obvious candidates because they use images, such as actual photographs and paintings. For more on bitmap usage, see the section later in this chapter, "Maps to Use with Man-Made Materials." However, in the end, the combination of both mapped materials and procedural materials looks the best.

> **Tip**
> Most procedural maps allow for other map types to be plugged into them. For instance, Noise can have maps, instead of colors, used for the Color #1 and Color #2 parameters. By placing bitmap images within those map channels, you can use the procedural maps to create random effects (with bitmap images as their foundation).

All the procedural maps discussed here are animated through the map's Offset, Tiling, and Angle values. You animate along the world's X-, Y-, and Z-axis, initially, or based upon the UVW mapping coordinates applied to the object. Using the XYZ method, your map remains oriented to the object's local coordinate system. If the object transforms, so does the map on the surface. However, if you use a modifier, such as Bend, the map remains oriented to the object's local coordinate system. This makes the map appear to "pass through" the geometry as it is bent rather than bending with it. If you use the UVW map method, specify how the Noise map, for example, is applied to the surface of your geometry through mapping coordinates. This gives you more control over the map, but it also requires you to use mapping coordinates that often look bad on more complex shapes. Unlike XYZ mapping, UVW mapping deforms with the object—providing that the mapping coordinates are applied before the deforming modifier. For most applications, stick with the XYZ method and use UVW only if XYZ doesn't work right or you need more explicit control of the map.

Noise

As mentioned in Chapter 8, "Material Concepts," Noise is the king of random, organic maps. Use Noise just about anywhere to get a great natural-looking material with static surfaces. However, animating Noise is just as much fun. Depending on the desired effect, you need to animate different parameters. Following are some helpful guidelines:

- **Animate the Offset to "move" the Noise effect.** By animating the Offset values you just translate the noise along the object's surface that you assigned the material. Use this effect later in the chapter to move the "waves" in water.

- **Animate Blur and Blur Offset to smooth the Noise effect over time.** Blur and Blur Offset just blur the noise effect. However, if you animate the blurring over time, you give your material a more distorted appearance.

- **Animate Phase for churning.** Phase actually controls the shifting around of Color #1 and Color #2. By animating Phase, you animate where the two colors exist over time. Where the shift occurs (meaning where the colors move from one place to the next) is completely dependent upon the type of noise you select.

- **Animate the colors or maps.** This has the greatest effect of all—especially when using Noise in an Intensity map channel, such as Opacity or Specular Level. By animating the shifting in colors, you control the intensity of that channel's effect on the material. By animating the colors along with Phase, over time you churn the effect and alter its intensity.

Cellular

The Cellular map is a close second to the Noise map for great random effects. The Cellular map animates such effects as moving skin on a slithering snake. The primary difference between Cellular and the other maps is that it doesn't have a phase value. This means you animate it through Offset, Tiling, Angle, and maps. While this isn't necessarily a problem, it proves a bit of a hindrance when you just need a quick, randomly animated surface. When animating Cellular, follow these guidelines to get the best results:

- **Use maps.** The best part about maps is that you throw an easily animated value into one of the color slots of the Cellular map—even Noise. Remember that the map affects only that particular color slot of the Cellular map—such as the Cell color.

- **Animate the Offset values.** By changing Offset over time, you move the cells around the material. While they move in unison, use the previous technique to vary the cellular map's components for a more random-looking translation along a surface.

- **Use and animate Fractal cells.** The Fractal option gives your cells a more "rough around the edges" look. By altering the number of iterations or the amount of roughness, you easily add random animation to the cell's characteristics.

Planet

The Planet map works differently than most of the other maps. Rather than applying math to two colors to produce a random effect, Planet creates something that looks like a topographical map from eight colors. Planet works well as a map within other maps. It is not as effective as a stand-alone map. Figure 12.2 shows the Planet interface.

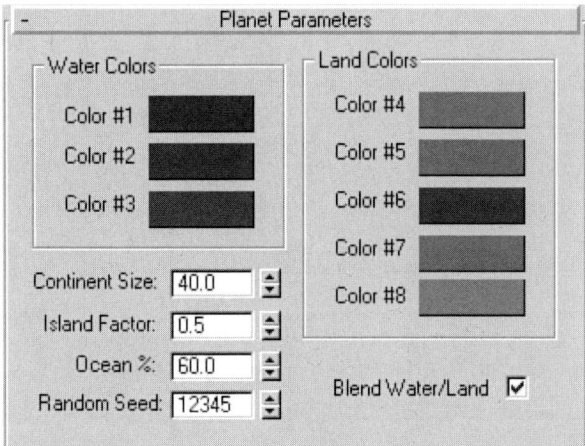

Figure 12.2 The Planet map's interface. While animating the colors of Planet map produces nice effects, animating other parameters (such as Offset and Angle) produces similar effects without managing 24 independent color channels.

The obvious way to animate the Planet map is to animate the colors. However this is the most inefficient way, as well. If you've ever tried to control colors animating over time, you know exactly how quickly things get complicated. Each color actually has its own track—*and* each track is broken into three different animatable parameters. That's a total of 24 individual animatable parameters per map. That gets unmanageable, even for seasoned animators.

If you use the Planet map, try animating the Offset and Angle values. Either one produces an excellent effect. When you animate Offset, the planet effect morphs as it moves over the surface of the object. Animating the Angle value simply rotates the map along each of the axes, as with other map types. On the other hand if you animate the Continent Size value, you create some interesting fractal patterns. The default value of 40 is fine for stills. However, if you animate anywhere between 15 and 60, you get good results.

Splat

Splat gives great results when animated. However, you may not want to use it in the traditional "splat manner"—to simulate paint splatting against the side of a wall. With Splat, there are a few functions for animation:

- **Animate the Offset.** Rather than just moving the splat effect around an object's surface, the Splat map actually "morphs" as it moves (just like Planet on curved surfaces). Since Splat doesn't contain a phase value, this is a way to create churning. This most prominently affects rounded surfaces. For surfaces where the map is parallel (flat), the map simply moves.

- **Animate Iterations.** The higher this field goes, the more little splats appear. Since this value makes more splats, use it for a surface with tiny water droplets on it. As time goes on, more droplets develop.

- **Use Maps.** As with many of the other maps, you place maps within Splat's Colors #1 and #2. Just by placing the Noise map within the map slots, you randomize the splat pattern even further. As a bonus, you can animate Noise's Phase value.

Smoke

The Smoke map is just begging to be animated. The map can be used in almost any channel, but there are three main channels where it's most appropriate. Following is a quick way to properly set up Smoke:

1. Apply the Smoke map first to the Diffuse map channel. When using Smoke there, the Diffuse colors are affected by the map.
2. Instance the Smoke map to the Opacity channel and turn on 2 Sided. This gives the smoke a transparent look.
3. Instance the Smoke map to the Reflection map.
4. For an enhanced effect, turn on Reflection Dimming, so the smoke appears brighter in direct light.

After you set up Smoke, there are two main values you animate to get a good effect. The first is the Offset value. By animating Offset in the direction you want the smoke to travel, you can make it rise, blow sideways, or whatever you decide. As with the other maps, you can animate the Phase value to make the smoke appear to churn. Small Phase changes work well for most situations.

Animated Water

In Exercise 12.1, you create a water material from scratch, and then animate it. The end result is believable seawater that you can use for a variety of situations.

Exercise 12.1 Animating Water with Noise

1. Open 12imx01.max from the CD-ROM. First, render the scene to see the current set up. At this point, you basically have a sea object and a sky.
2. Open the Material Editor, and select the upper-left material in the sample window.
3. Set the Ambient color to R51, G51, B89, and set the Diffuse color to pure black.
4. Set the Specular Level to 40 and Glossiness to 30.
5. Rollout the Maps section, and click None in the Reflection map channel. Select Bitmap, then select sky.jpg.
6. Click the Go to Parent button to return to the Maps level. Set the Reflection Amount to 40.
7. Click on None in the Bump map channel. Select Noise.
8. At this point, you see a decent-looking Bump map. Try some further refinements. In the Noise map parameters section, set the Size to 5, and the Noise Type to Fractal.
9. Turn on the Animate button in the main MAX interface, and move the Frame slider to frame 100.
10. In the Coordinates section of the Noise map, set the Z Offset value to 20.

11. In the Noise parameters section, set the Phase to 2.
12. Click the Go to Parent button to return to the Maps level. Click the None button in the Displacement channel, and select Noise.
13. While still at frame 100, set the Z Offset value back to 0. Turn off the Animate button, and set the size to 20. Set the Low Threshold value to .575, as well.
14. Click the Go to Parent button in the Material Editor, and set the Displacement amount to 10.
15. Render the scene to an AVI file to view the animation.

Figure 12.3 The Water, from Exercise 12.1, is created from just a material using Noise and a Reflection map.

After the animation is rendered, you know how easy it is to create realistic-looking water. You see one frame of the animation in Figure 12.3. The best part is that you don't use Raytracing. Rather than just using a Bump map to create the disturbed surface, use Displacement mapping to alter the geometry, as well. This especially helps when objects intersect with the water's surface. Remember: Bump mapping only affects the surface appearance in the rendering, whereas Displacement mapping actually alters the geometry (based on pixel values from a map).

Man-Made Animated Materials

Man-made materials are far easier to create and animate. Why? Well, if you look around, you're surrounded with all kinds of ideas for materials. Some materials are animated; some are not. Whatever the case, almost every material that occurs as a result of human intervention is re-creatable within MAX. Just take a look at the your desktop. With a digital camera, you take a snapshot of the surface, use it as a Diffuse map, and apply it to a 3D object that renders nearly identical to the "real thing."

While you can use any of the maps discussed earlier in this chapter to create man-made materials, some other specific maps assist you in creating more realistic materials.

Maps to Use with Man-Made Materials

When designing a man-made material within MAX, you can use several different kinds of maps. However, you typically need to be more precise with man-made materials because they are often based upon exacting figures. For instance, a steel plate that has bolts around the edges is easily re-created, using a map like Bitmap in the Diffuse channel. In any case, you learn that certain maps work particularly well for reproducing real-world materials in MAX. The first, and perhaps most used, is the Bitmap.

Bitmaps

If you've gone through the tutorials and even through the other sections in this book, you have already used the Bitmap map type. Bitmap essentially allows you to use an image (in one of several supported image-file types) as a color or rendering property of a material. Images include anything from scans of objects or pictures to animations from MAX or other programs. Figure 12.4 shows the Bitmap Parameters section.

As with other maps, you can animate Bitmap's values of Offset, Tiling, and Angle. Generally animating the Offset of a Bitmap—especially for decals—is more practical than for procedural maps.

By scaling down a Bitmap, you also maintain the ability to crop it or place it anywhere within a material. The Crop and Place controls eliminate the need for a paint program for cropping and scaling (their only functions). Another benefit of cropping with MAX is that it animates. This works well for situations like the one in Figure 12.5 and Exercise 12.2. The stripes on the Bitmap are vertical, but that is easily adjusted with the Angle parameter. Animating the cropping rectangle moves the stripes as if the pole were spinning. The Place feature works by using the entire Bitmap. The window, rather than acting as a cropping window, allows you to scale and place the entire map on an object's surface.

492   Part II   Materials

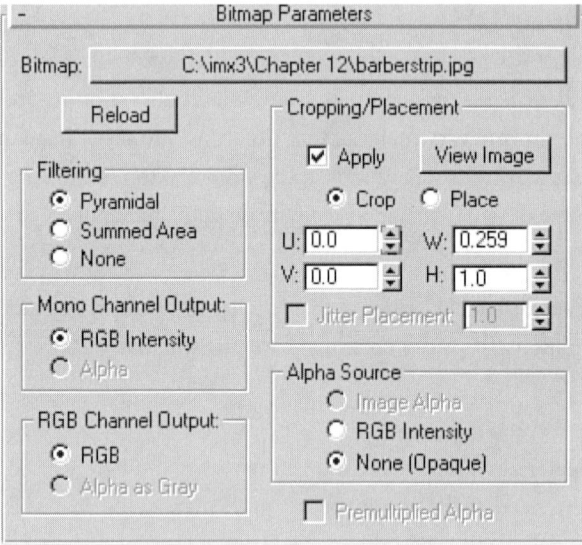

Figure 12.4 The Bitmap map's parameters. With cropping, you can select the parts of an image that you want to use as a texture. With cropping animated, you produce intriguing effects as the cropping window passes over a Bitmap during an animation.

Exercise 12.2   Using Animated Cropping

1. Open 12imx02.max from the CD-ROM, and click the Material Editor button in the main toolbar.
2. Click the upper-left material slot (called Pole), then click the small button next to the Diffuse color swatch.
3. Select Bitmap from the Map Type list, then select barberstrip.jpg from the Inside 3D Studio MAX CD-ROM. Click OK.
4. Set the W:angle parameter to 45. Click the View Image button in the Crop/Place section of the Bitmap parameters.
5. Size the cropping window so that it occupies the left one-quarter of the image. Use coordinates of U, V, W, and H of 0.0, 0.0, .0259, and 1.0, respectively, for exact placement.
6. Turn on the Animate button, and move the Frame slider to frame 100.
7. Move the cropping window to the right, so that it occupies the other half of the image. Or use coordinates U, V, W, and H of 0.741, 0.0, 0.259, and 1.0, respectively, for exact placement.
8. Click the Show map in Viewport icon, and move the Frame slider back and forth to see the effects of the cropping window currently animating in your viewport.

9. Select the Apply check box in the Cropping/Placement parameters section. Then render the Camera viewport to see the result (See figure 12.5). You can also view the completed file on your CD.

Figure 12.5 The completed rendering from Exercise 12.2. The pole stripes were animated by using a single Bitmap and cropping over time.

Another benefit of using the Bitmap map type for man-made materials is that you use animation files—such as AVI or sequential still frames. This means that you use both computer-generated animations and high-resolution captured video as a texture for a material. In Exercise 12.3, you learn how this is done.

Marbles

The Marble map, while procedural, offers a more realistic-looking version of its name than some of its Bitmap counterparts provide. MAX offers two marble maps, the generic Marble and the Perlin Marble. Figures 12.6 and 12.7 show their interfaces.

The generic Marble is not all that useful as a texture; however, it functions very well for Bump maps. Perlin Marble does well as a Diffuse map, an Opacity map, and even as a Bump map, if the Levels are set to a low number. In the Color sections of both marble maps, use Maps versus a solid color to control the colors. You animate both marble maps most effectively when changing the Offset values over time. As with some of the other procedural maps, animating the Offset values actually changes the look of the map itself—not just moving it across a curved surface. Of course, you can also animate the maps you use in the color slots. Just remember to keep the number of extra maps low. The more maps you use in the material, the more animatable parameters you must track.

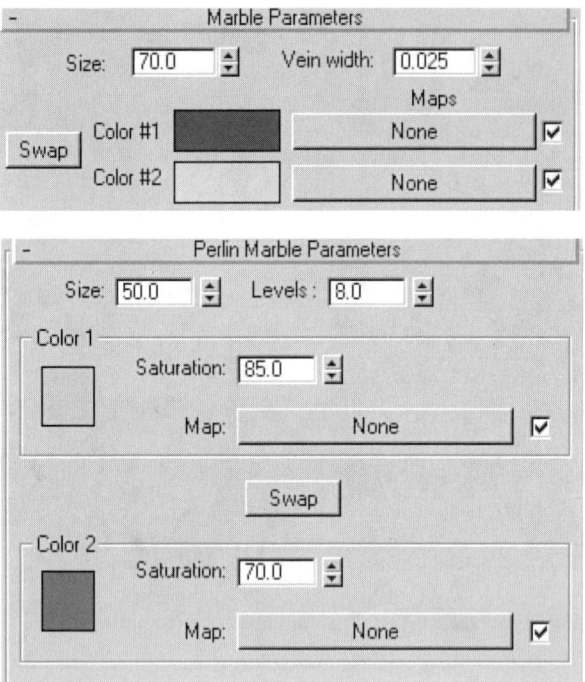

Figure 12.6 and Figure 12.7 The Marble (top) and Perlin Marble (bottom) map interfaces.

Perlin Marble is used quite well as an Opacity map. As an alternative to the Smoke map, you make a nice smoke by changing Color #1 and Color #2 to grayscale colors. By animating the Z Offset value in a negative direction, you make the smoke rise.

The Ballpark Sign

In Exercise 12.3, you create a material that simulates an animated ballpark sign. The sign is a progressively lit series of bulbs with several starting points along the text. The Blend material uses two masks: One is a still image of the text itself, and the other is a line of animated dots. The dots are in a single line only to speed creation and render times. They are tiled to give the appearance of an array of bulbs. Use Video Post to apply a glow to the bulbs.

Exercise 12.3 An Animated Ballpark Sign

1. Open the file 12imx03.max on the CD-ROM. The scene is a painted iron framework with a flat signboard mounted on top. Mapping coordinates are already applied to the signboard and a paint material is on the framework. The display looks like Figure 12.8.

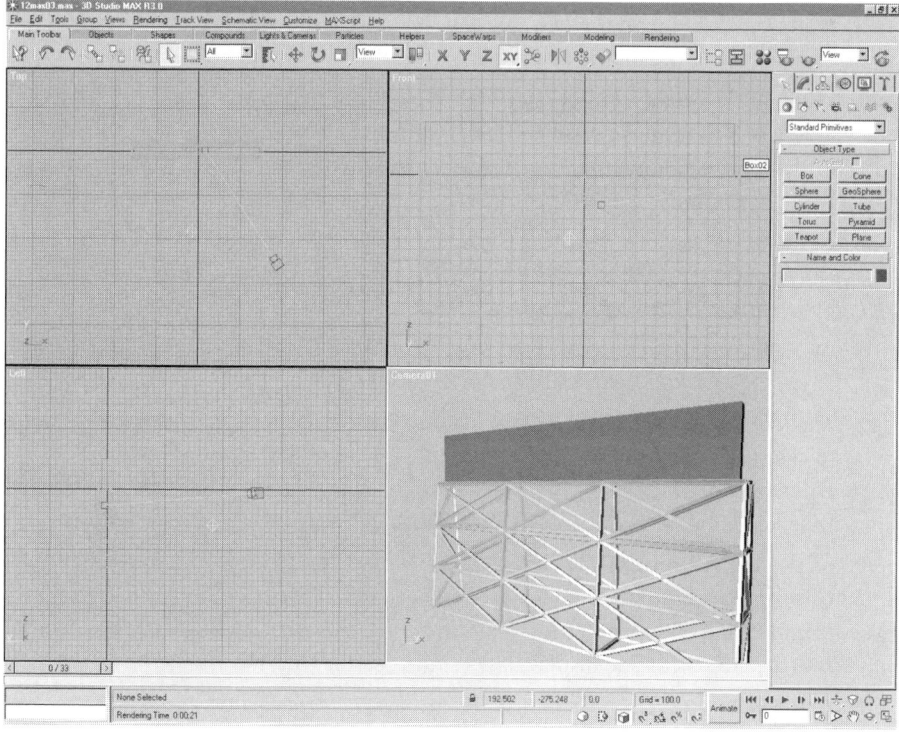

Figure 12.8 Basic ballpark sign.

2. In the Material Editor, click the first sample sphere, named DOTS TEXT. Click the Material/Map Navigator icon to open it.

3. Click the Type button, and double-click Blend in the Browser list. Select Discard Old Material, then click OK.

4. Click the Material 1 button, and name this material TEXT. In the Basic Parameters rollout, click the gray box on the Diffuse color swatch's right. Double-click Bitmap in the Browser list, then select the CD-ROM file called ballpark.jpg. Name this Level ballpark diff. Click Show Map in Viewport icon, and the map appears on the signboard in the shaded viewport. In the Coordinates rollout, drag the Blur spinner until the field reads 0.01.

Tip

Neither the sign nor the camera is animated in this scene. Setting the Bitmap to Minimum Blur keeps its edge's crisp. If there were motion in the scene, however, the edges of the text might show a rolling effect and blur would have to be added.

5. In the Navigator, click Material 2, and name this material DOTS. In the Maps rollout, click None in the Diffuse map slot, and double-click Bitmap in the Browser. Click the file called DOTS2.AVI from the CD-ROM, but don't click OK.

6. While in the Select Bitmap Image File dialog (after choosing DOTS2.AVI), click the View button to view the AVI file. It is a single row of dots animated from left to right. Close the Viewer, click OK to accept the file, and click the Show Map in Viewport icon.

7. Name this Map Level dots diff. Click and hold the Material Effects Channel icon, and select 1 from the numbers menu. This Material Effects Channel is used in Rendering Effects to cue a glow effect.

8. In the Coordinates rollout, enter 0.01 in the Blur field, 0.02 in the U:Offset field, 2.0 in the U:Tiling field, and 12.0 in the V:Tiling field.

9. The DOTS2.AVI file is made of white dots on a black background, and you want to change the color of the dots (lightbulbs) in your sign to red. This is the Diffuse map for the dots, so now is the time to change the color. You don't want to recreate the dots' animation, however.

10. Click the Type:Bitmap button, and double-click RGB Tint in the Browser list. Check Keep Old Map as Sub-map, and click OK. This RGB Tint map type allows you to change the color of existing Bitmaps. Change the green-and-blue color swatches to black. The display looks similar to Figure 12.9.

11. In the Navigator, click Material 2:DOTS. From the Navigator, drag and drop Map:dots diff (DOTS2.AVI) to the Self-Illuminaton slot in Maps rollout. Check Instance in the dialog, and click OK. Drag and drop the new Self-Illumination slot onto the Bump slot, check Instance in the dialog, and click OK.

12. In the Navigator, click the top Material Level, DOTS TEXT (Blend). In the Navigator, drag and drop Diffuse: ballpark diff (ballpark.jpg) onto the Mask slot. Check Instance in the dialog, and click OK. Drag the Frame slider to frame 17, and the display looks similar to Figure 12.10.

13. Render frame 17. Notice partial letters on the sign made up of red dots and a faint white outline for the letters. Close all dialog boxes.

14. In the Rendering pull-down menu, click Render Effects. In the Render Effects dialog, you see a place to set your queue up. Click the Add button, and select Lens Effects. When Lens Effects appears below, double-click Glow on the left-hand list of effects to add it to the scene.

Chapter 12: Animated Materials 497

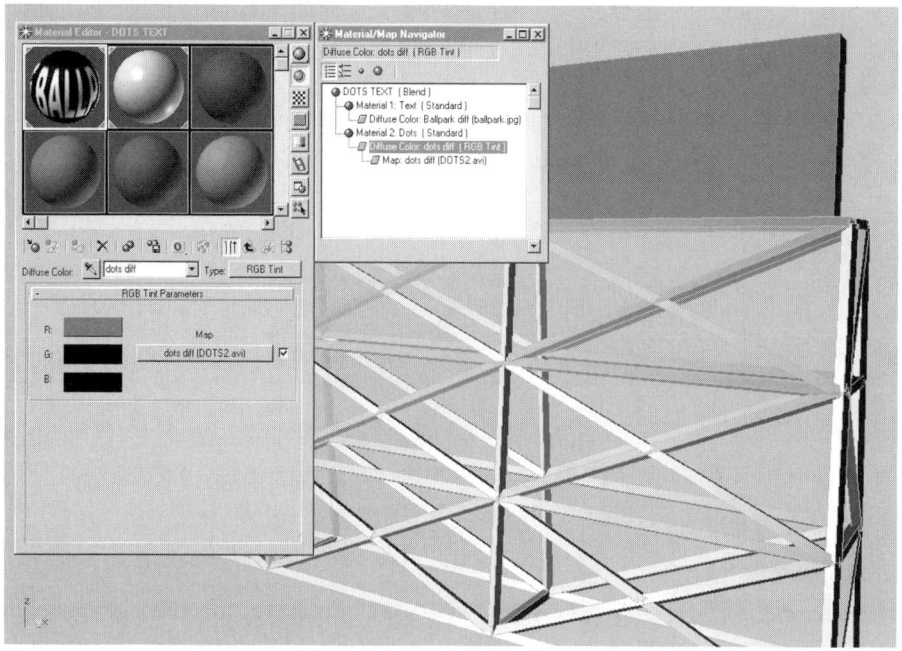

Figure 12.9 Material Editor and Material/Map Navigator.

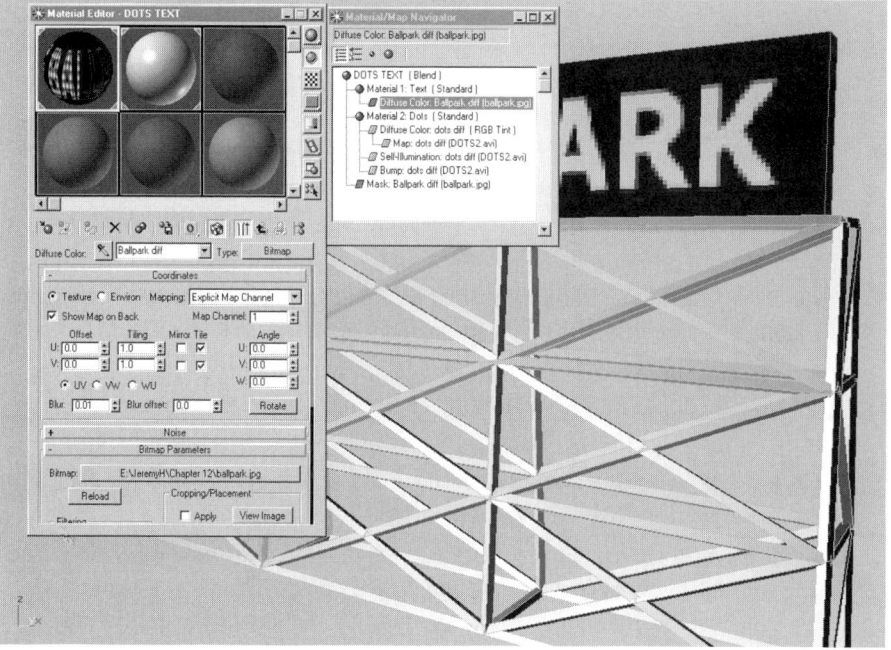

Figure 12.10 Material Editor and Material/Map Navigator at Frame 17.

498 Part II Materials

15. In the Glow Element section, set the Size to 2.0, and Intensity to 5. Set the Use Source Color parameter to 20.

16. Click the Options tab and note that Effects ID is checked and set to 1. Next, check Bright as your image filter, and set the parameter for Bright to 50.

17. Render the sequence of frames to an .AVI file. (Use the Cinepak codec for the best results.)

Tip
You can adjust the way the letters light up by changing the U:Offset and U:Tiling of the DOTS2.AVI maps. They must all change the same amount because they are instances. You can also create a new DOTS2.AVI file by opening DOTS.MAX and making changes to the animation of the dots themselves.

In Exercise 12.3, you created a Blend material by using animated and still Bitmaps to reveal the underlying materials of the Blend material type. To make the image more realistic, you used a Material Effects Channel to cue a glow in Render Effects.

Dropping a Bomb

In Exercise 12.4, you create a material to be used as a burning fuse on a classic bomb. The material is a complex Blend-Within-a-Blend, similar to the material used on text in Chapter 13, "Using MAX 3 as a 2D Paint Tool." Lens Effects Glow and a particle system round out the effect.

Exercise 12.4   A Burning Fuse

1. Open the file 12imx04 from the CD-ROM. The scene contains a bomb with a fuse. There is also a Particle System, a Particle Array (PArray), and a Combustion Atmospheric Apparatus in the scene (for special effects). The fuse object is a circle, lofted on a helical path with Apply Mapping checked in the Surface Parameters rollout. In this exercise you focus on creating the fuse material.

2. In the Material Editor, click the Material/Map Navigator icon. The first sample sphere is a Blend material type named BURNING FUSE. In the Basic Parameters rollout, click the Material 1 slot, and name this material FUSE SURFACE.

3. In the Maps rollout, click the Diffuse color swatch, and make it a dark brown color. In the Basic Parameters rollout, check the 2-Sided check box.

4. In the Navigator, click Material 2:(Standard), name the material INVISIBLE. Click the Type Button, double-click Blend in the Browser list, and check Discard old material in the Replace Material dialog. Click OK.

5. In the Navigator, click the new Material 1:(Standard), and name it Invisible. Enter 0 in the Glossiness, Specular Level, and Opacity fields. This creates a completely invisible material that doesn't show any specular highlights due to shininess.

6. In the Navigator, click Material 2:(Standard). Set Specular, Diffuse, and Ambient color swatches to pure white. Then click the Self-Illumination swatch, and set its

color to pure white. Click and hold the Material Effects Channel icon, and choose 1 from the number menu. In the Shader Basic Parameters rollout, check the 2-Sided check box. Name this material GLOWREVEAL. This creates a material to cue a glow and highlight effect in Render Effects.

7. In the Navigator, click Material 2:INVISIBLE (Blend), and in the Basic Parameters rollout, click None in the Mask slot. Double-click Bitmap in the Browser list, then select GLOWMASK.AVI from the CD-ROM. In the Basic Parameters rollout, enter 0.01 in the Blur field. Name this Level glow mask.

8. Click the Show Map in Viewport button, and drag the Frame slider back and forth. In the Shaded viewport, you see a particle system moving down the fuse and a thin white line moving up the fuse. You want these two to be in sync with each other, but the GLOWMASK.AVI was created from bottom to top.

9. In the Coordinates rollout, enter 180 in the W:Angle field, and drag the slider. The white line now stays with the particle system.

10. In the Navigator, click BURNING FUSE, click None in the Mask slot, and load a Bitmap called MATLMASK.AVI. Name this Level material mask. Enter 180.0 in the W:Angle field to reverse the direction to top to bottom. Enter 0.01 in the Blur field. The display now looks similar to Figure 12.11. Close the Material Editor and the Material/Map Navigator.

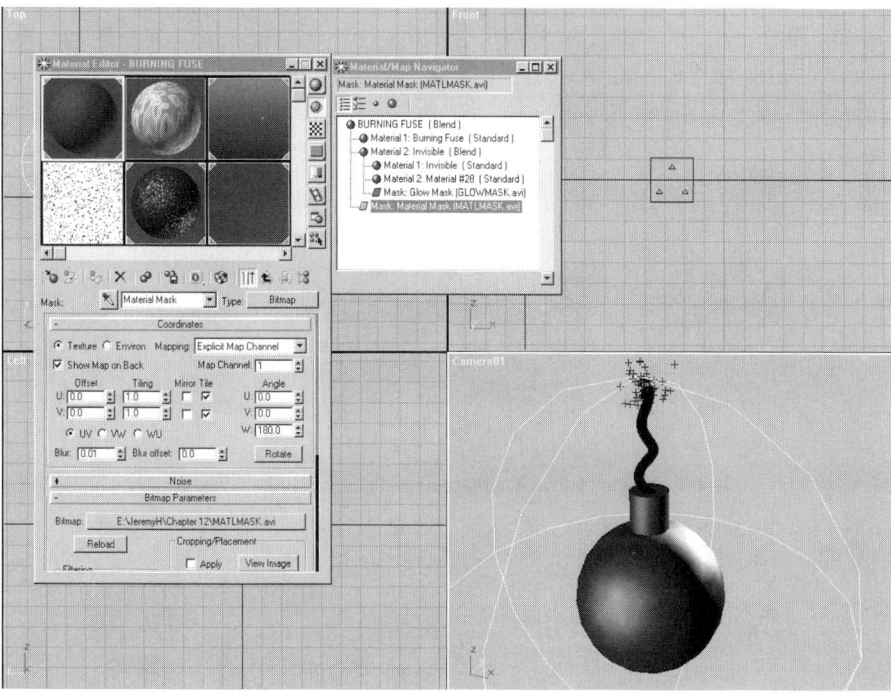

Figure 12.11 Material Editor and Material/Map Navigator for BURNING FUSE.

11. Render the scene. There are several rendering effects added to enhance the look of a burning fuse. You can take a look at them by selecting the Rendering Effects option in the Rendering pull-down menu.

Warning

Many frames from this exercise take a significant time to render—even on fast computers. Plan to leave an evening free for your computer to render the final result.

In Exercise 12.4, you created a compound Blend-Within-a-Blend material. You also used animated masks to reveal a material with Material Effects Channel to cue a glow and a highlight in Video Post. Material 2 in the Blend is a fully invisible material that gives the illusion of a burning fuse.

Take the time to analyze the other materials and objects in the scene to study how that bomb object exploded (PArray) and how the fiery blast was made (Combustion). The smoke material is simply another invisible material with Material Effects Channel 2, to cue the smoke glow in Video Post.

Fictional Animated Materials

Fortunately for artists and animators, the realm of fiction is easy to create on the computer. Maybe that's why there are so many movies about space that are produced with computer animation software. In MAX, you plug just about any map into any Map channel and by animating it, create some wild effects.

The next exercise focuses on what's possible with the Raytrace material and MAX's maps. By adding Noise to the Luminosity channel, the effect is intensified tenfold.

"Plasma Engine" Exercise

In this exercise, you use the Raytrace material with various settings to give a spaceship's plasma engines the illusion that they're actually working as the ship leaves Earth.

Exercise 12.5 Plasma Engines Using Raytrace Material and Noise

1. Open the file 12imx05.max. Move to frame 40, and render the viewport to see the current scene. Notice that the engines are nothing more than a hot-pink color.

2. Open the Material Editor, and choose the upper-left material. The material is called Plasma, and is a Raytrace material with several colors already set.

3. Set Glossiness to 63 and Specular Level to 71.

4. Click the Empty button on the Luminosity color swatch's right. Choose Noise.
5. In the Noise Map parameters, set the Type to Turbulence and the Size to 10.
6. The High Threshold reads 0.525, and the Low reads 0.125.
7. Set Color #2 to a hot-pink color, approximately R255, G127, B253.
8. You now have a nice, hot-pink, plasma-looking material. The next step is to animate it. Start by turning on the Animate button.
9. Move the Frame slider to frame 200.
10. In the Noise Parameters section, set the Phase value to 0.5. In the Coordinates section, set the Z Angle value to 90.
11. Render out the scene to an AVI file at 320 × 240 resolution.

Figure 12.12 shows the result of Exercise 12.5. By animating just a few values, you easily create some incredible fictional materials. When you get the time, examine both the Raytrace material used and the scene's set up. There are actually several elements to this scene—not just the engines—that make it look good.

Figure 12.12 A single frame from Exercise 12.5. In this exercise, you add a plasma-like glow to the ship's engines just by using animated Noise.

In Practice: Animated Materials

- **Flexibility often means complexity.** The greatest thing about MAX's materials is that it animates everything. It is also its worst quality. Use discretion when creating animated materials. With so many possibilities, the material quickly gets away from you.

- **Procedural maps work well for animation.** Procedural maps contain the ability to animate the offset. Some also have a phase value. By animating one or both of these values, you create wonderful organic-looking materials.

- **Bitmaps are king for man-made materials.** Let's face it—the best way to re-create a man-made material in MAX is to scan an image of it and use it as a bitmap. There's certainly no shame in doing things the "easy" way. Just remember that you can also animate many of the Bitmap's values—this includes the Cropping/Placement function.

- **Fictional materials can use, well—anything.** There's no limit to how you can design a fictional material. The Raytrace material, however, lends itself to creating great fictional materials because there are several special-effects parameters to use. By working with items such as Translucency and Luminosity, you design some superb fictional materials.

Chapter 13

Using MAX 3 as a 2D Paint Tool

What do you usually do when you need a 2D image to use as a map or a mask for a MAX material or in Video Post? You probably open a program such as Discreet

Paint*, Adobe Photoshop, or Spaceward Satori Paint; paint the image you need; save the file; and import the image file into MAX R3. This is not, of course, a bad way to work and is often critical to getting the project out the door. Why turn to those other packages when you already have a powerful 2D-image program open already: 3D Studio MAX R3? Yes, paint with MAX R3. With it, you create still images or animated maps and masks.

In this chapter's exercises, you use MAX R3 to create bitmaps for application in several different ways. The bitmaps are used for:

- **Exterior night lighting.** In a night scene of a building on a hilly landscape, you must create the illusion of night lighting from several fixtures. The fixtures light a pathway, and you must also show the beams of light as if there were a haze in the air. Efficient rendering is of prime importance. You learn to use a single light with a projector map, created in MAX R3, to simulate multiple lights. You also use physical mesh objects to simulate light beams, instead of multiple lights with Volume Light effects. This is quite efficient.

- **Valley landscape.** You need a scene with a deep river valley running through a flat plain. The valley is formed with a 2D image you create in MAX R3, and applied to the surface as a Displacement map.

- **Burning fuse.** You must animate a glowing fuse burning on a bomb. In this exercise, you create two 2D animations in MAX R3. This exercise illustrates how to reveal one material under another and to cue a glow effect.

- **Animated valley landscape.** The client wants to see the valley landscape as an alien machine digs it. In this exercise, you create an animated version of the previous valley Displacement map.

Still Image Maps and Masks

Still images for maps and masks are created quickly and accurately in MAX, using the underlying model as a target to control the images' size and placement. Generally, higher resolution images work best. However, if your 2D elements are hidden in place when you don't need them, you can always unhide them and rerender them at a new resolution.

Exterior Night Lighting

In the first exercise, your goal is to give a scene convincing night lighting while adding only minimal rendering time. One approach is to place a Spot light in each of the scene's light fixtures to make pools of light on the ground. Then show the beams of light using the Volume Light Atmospheric effect. Because a couple of trees are near the lights, the lights must cast shadows.

This method poses potential problems on several fronts. First, the pools of light overlap in some areas. Without attenuation, the area of overlap is twice as bright and is unrealistic. The attenuation needs adjustment on each light. The process may not look badly in a scene with only a few lights, but it is time consuming in large scenes. Second, the Volume Light effect adds considerably to rendering times. For realistic lights, you spend time adjusting the Volume Light effect attenuation. Another problem is that each light must cast shadows from the trees, and that also adds to the render time.

Exercise 13.1 offers a better solution. You create 2D geometry assigned a pure white material with full self-illumination. When rendered, this type of material is not affected by the scene's lighting. Rendering the 2D objects against a black background creates a pure black-and-white image with the option of an alpha channel. Saved as a TGA or PNG file, it makes an excellent map. You also create a single rectangular direct Spot light that uses the new black-and-white image as a Projector image. The light passes through the white-map areas and is blocked by the black-map areas. Line up the projected map with the light fixtures in the scene with relative ease with careful attention to a few sizes throughout the process. This creates the illusion of pools of light with no intensity variations in the overlapping areas. The alignment fine-tunes with the Cropping feature in the Material Editor. Now only this light needs to cast shadows for all the trees.

For the visible-light beams, reveal cones in the scene assigned light yellow material. A Gradient Opacity map produces a more obvious light beam near the light and much less so near the ground. The whole effect is extremely efficient and a complete fake, which makes it artistic.

Tip
This projector-light method works extremely well for interior scenes as well. Use this same method to simulate multiple ceiling fixtures in a room or spotlights in a sports facility, for example.

Exercise 13.1 Creating Exterior Night Lighting

1. Open the file called 13max01.MAX. It's an outdoor scene with a building and two pathways. Several trees and light fixtures line the pathways. Light the scene to highlight the fixture's effect as efficiently as possible while the trees cast shadows. Save the file as Ch13_night_01.MAX.

2. First, create 2D circles to represent the pools of light cast by the light fixtures on the landscape. Copies of these circles then change to flat planes with an assigned bright white material. Right-click the Top viewport, and type W to maximize it. Type H, and select the LIGHT_POLES from the list (as shown in Figure 13.1.) Click the Select button. Click the Zoom Extents Selected button to fill the Top viewport with the five light poles. In the Display panel's Hide rollout, click the Hide Unselected button to hide everything except the light poles.

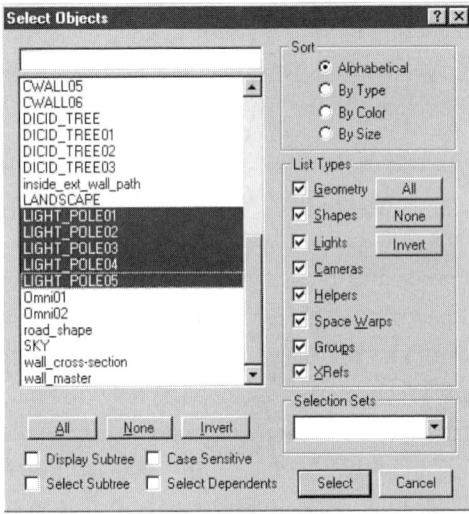

Figure 13.1 LIGHT_POLES selected in hit list.

3. In the Create panel, click the Shapes button. Click the Circle button. In the Top viewport, click and drag a circle of any size. In the Parameters rollout, enter 30'0" in the Radius field. Name this object light_pool01. Click the Align button, and select the light poles in the Top viewport's lower left. In the Align Selection dialog box, check X Position and Y Position. Click OK to align the 2D circle's center with the light pole's center (represented as a light green circle in the Top viewport). The viewport looks like Figure 13.2.

4. In the Edit pull-down menu, select Clone. Check Instance in the Clone Options dialog box, and click OK. This makes an Instance clone in place.

5. Select the Align button, and choose the next light pole. Check X Position and Y Position, then click OK. Repeat Step 4 until you have circles at each of the five light poles. The scene looks like Figure 13.3.

Chapter 13: Using MAX 3 as a 2D Paint Tool   509

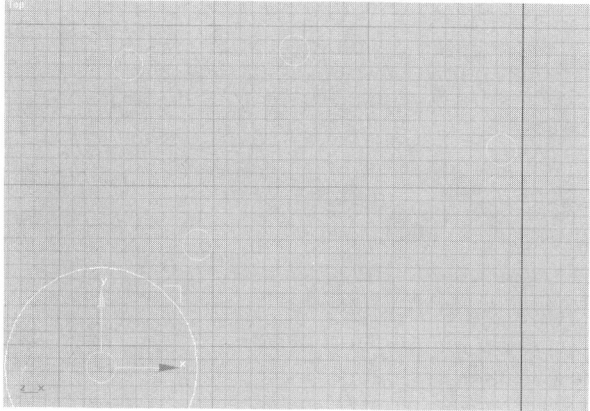

Figure 13.2 Light_pole01 2D circle aligned with LIGHT_POLE01 object center-to-center.

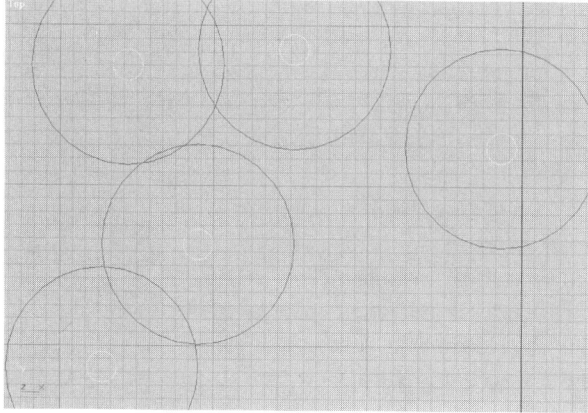

Figure 13.3 Circles at each light pole.

Tip

If you want a different light-pool pattern, use a four-sided Star shape with radiused points. This gives the illusion of four bulbs in the light pole.

6. Type H. Highlight all light_pole shapes, and click OK. In the Edit pull-down menu, select Clone. Leave Copy checked in the Clone Options dialog, and click OK. These shapes are the light beams later in the exercise. Type H, and highlight the five LIGHT_POLE objects. In the Display panel, choose Hide Selected to hide the five new circles and the light poles.

7. Now turn the five original circles into mesh objects. Type H, and highlight the five remaining light_pool shapes. In the Modify panel, click Mesh Select. This turns the 2D shapes into 3D-mesh objects with no thickness.

510   Part II   Materials

> **Note**
> Right-click on one of the shapes and choose Convert to Editable Mesh, which turns the circles into mesh objects. However, doing so makes it more difficult to change the circles' size (if the need arises). Now select any circle, and drop to the Circle level in the Modify Stack. Change the radius, and return to the top of the Stack.

8. Open the Material Editor. Locate the material named BRIGHT_WHITE, and select the sample sphere. If you don't see BRIGHT_WHITE, change the Material Editor display to 6 × 4. Click the Assign Material to Selection. This assigns a fully self-illuminated white material to the mesh circles. Close the Material Editor.

9. Now render the white circles in the Top viewport to create a bitmap for use in a light-projector slot. When it comes time to fit the projected image to the light-pole positions, it helps if you have an idea of how much area is covered by the simulated pools of light. With the circles selected, click the Utilities panel. In the Utilities rollout, select Measure. Measure reports that the circles cover an area about 185 feet by 155 feet. Make note of these dimensions. See Figure 13.4.

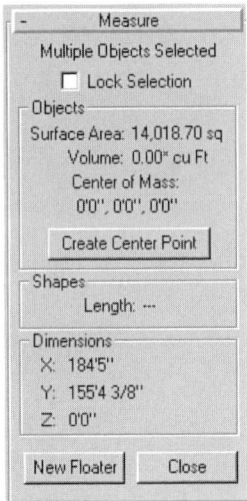

Figure 13.4 The Measure panel, with circle dimensions about 185 feet by 155 feet.

10. Now specify render settings, using the circle area as a basis to determine output resolution. Again, this helps when later aligning the projected image. Click Render Scene. In the Render Scene dialog's Output Size area, enter 1850 in the Width field and 1550 in the Height field. This is the size (in feet times 10) to hold the aspect ratio. Click Close to close the dialog box.

11. In the Top viewport, right-click the Top label, and select Show Safe Frame. This clips the Top viewport display to the aspect of the output resolution's aspect. Select Zoom. Now zoom until no circle is closer to the display's outside than halfway between the yellow and green rectangles. This ensures that all the circles are in the rendered image. The display looks similar to Figure 13.5.

12. Click Render Scene, and select Files. Name the file LIGHTS.PNG. Click Save File, and wait until the Render Output File dialog box appears. Choose Setup. Select RGB 24 bit (16.7 Million), and make sure Alpha is checked. Click OK in the PNG Configuration dialog box. Select Render in the Render Scene dialog box. The rendered image looks similar to Figure 13.6. Close the VFB window and the Render Scene dialog box. You have just created a black-and-white image to use in a spotlight's Projector Map slot. White light passes through the image while remaining black where there is no image.

Chapter 13: Using MAX 3 as a 2D Paint Tool   511

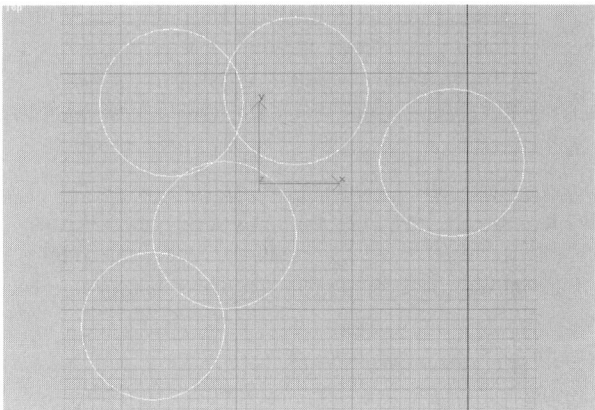

Figure 13.5   Circles almost to edge of outer safe-frame display.

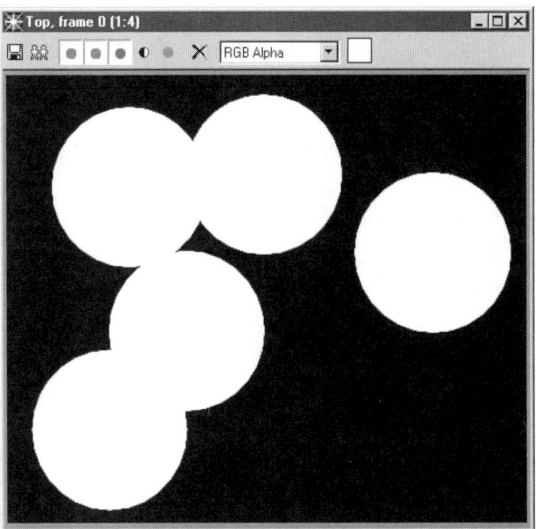

Figure 13.6   Rendered white circles saved as LIGHTS.PNG.

13. Now, place the direct Spot light in the middle of the display. Adjust it as a rectangular light with the same aspect as the display. This makes it easier to line up the image with objects in the scene. In the Create panel, select Lights, then Free Direct. Choose the middle of the Top viewport display to place the light. In the Modify panel's General Parameters rollout, select Cast Shadows. Click Exclude. Highlight the five LIGHT_POLE objects in the left panel, and move them to the right panel. This prevents them from appearing lit and casting shadows by the Free Direct light. The shadows appear unrealistic when coming from above because the light bulbs are actually below the lamps.

14. In the Directional Parameters rollout, click and adjust the Hotspot spinners until the light-blue Hotspot lines touch the yellow lines of Safe Frame on the left and right sides. Move the light in the Top viewport to better center it (if necessary). In the Directional Parameters rollout, choose Rectangle to change the spotlight from a circle to a rectangle.

15. In the Directional Parameters rollout, select None in the Projector map area. Double-click Bitmap in the list, then double-click LIGHTS in the Select Bitmap Image File dialog box. In the Directional Parameters rollout, select Bitmap Fit. Locate the LIGHTS.PNG file that was saved in Step 11. This adjusts the Aspect Ratio to the bitmap's aspect.

16. Open the Material Editor, and select an unused sample sphere. Drag and drop Projector Map onto the sample sphere. Choose Instance in the Copy dialog box, and click OK. Name this level LIGHTS_PROJ. Using the Instance option allows you to adjust the map so that it affects the projected map (if necessary). Close the Material Editor.

Note

The Projector map is not a material, and it can not be assigned to any mesh objects in the scene.

17. Click the Select button or type H, and choose the five light_pool objects. In the Display panel, Hide rollout. Choose Unhide All. Type H again. While pressing the CTRL key, select the five remaining light_pool objects. Now choose Hide Selected. Type W (to maximize all viewports). In the Front viewport, select the Fdirect01 Spot light. Move it up the Y-axis until it is level with the top of the building.

18. Right-click the Camera01 viewport to activate it, and select Render Scene. In the Output Size area, choose 640×480. In the Render Output area, clear the Save File option. Now select Render. The scene looks like Figure 13.7. Pools of light are below each light pole, and the trees cast shadows. The pools overlap cleanly, and only one light calculates the shadow map. The problem with the images is the light pools' hard edge.

19. Open the Material Editor. In the LIGHTS_PROJ Coordinates rollout, enter 0.05 in the Blur Offset field to blur the edges of the map's white areas. Render the Camera01 viewport again, and the pools of light have a softer look.

20. Close all dialog boxes, and save the file. It's already labeled ch13_night_01.MAX.

Figure 13.7 Light pools from fixtures with tree shadows.

Showing Beams of Light

In the real world, you rarely get everything right the first time. For example, when you show off your night-lighting scene, your client announces that the light pools look great but something is missing. You suggest adding a hint of a light-beam effect. Your customer agrees, but time is of the essence so extra render time must be minimal. What do you do?

Adding Volume Light Atmospheric Effects looks nice but adds noticeably to render time. In this next exercise, you use the same copies of the circles as for the light pools image. These circles now create tapered cones under each light fixture. You also assign a light-yellow material with a gradient opacity map. These new objects make convincing light beams without the heavy render times of Volume Lights. Study the material for application to the cones. It's the Gradient Opacity map and the Outward Falloff that make them convincing.

Exercise 13.2   Creating Beams of Light

1. Open the file ch13_night_01.MAX from the previous exercise or from the CD-ROM. It is the night scene with the simulated pools of light. Save the file as ch13_night_02.MAX. Right-click the Top viewport to activate it, and type W to maximize it.

2. In the Display panel, select Hide. Choose Unhide by Name. In the Unhide Objects dialog box, ten light_pool objects are in the list. In the List Types area,

clear Geometry. The first five objects disappear because they contain a Mesh Select modifier and are 3D-mesh objects. The remaining objects are 2D. Select All, and click OK. The circles appear in the Top viewport.

3. Choose Select, and type H. Select the five light_pool objects in the list. Choose Select to close the dialog box, and select the circles. In the Modify panel, select Extrude. Enter 38'0" in the Amount field. Clear Cap Start and Cap End to reduce the number of faces in the objects.

4. Type H, and double-click light_pool06. In the Modify panel, select Taper. Enter –0.83 in the list. This tapers the top of the extruded circle to the size of the fixture. Repeat Step 4 for light_pool07 through light_pool10. Type W to return to four viewports. The Camera01 viewport looks similar to Figure 13.8.

Figure 13.8 Extruded and tapered circles.

 Tip
You can also use the Copy and Paste functions under Edit Stack to copy the Taper modifier to each extruded circle. With this method, you paste the Taper modifier as an Instance. You can also use the new Schematic View to copy and paste the Taper modifier from one circle to the rest.

5. Click the Select button, and type H. Highlight light_pool06 through light_pool10, and choose Select in the dialog box. Open the Material Editor, and click a material sample sphere called LIGHT_CONE. The sample sphere appears as a light-yellow area on the checkered background. In the Material Editor,

choose the Assign Material to Selected button. The cones in the Camera01 viewport appear screened to indicate transparency.

6. In the Top viewport, select the Fdirect01 light. In the Modify panel, General Parameters rollout, select Exclude. In the left panel, highlight light_pool06 through light_pool10. Now click the right arrow to send them to the right panel. You don't want these cones lit by the light or to cast shadows.

7. Render the Camera01 viewport. You now have the illusion of visible dust or moisture particles in the light beams, which are denser near the top and disappear close to the ground. It looks similar to Figure 13.9.

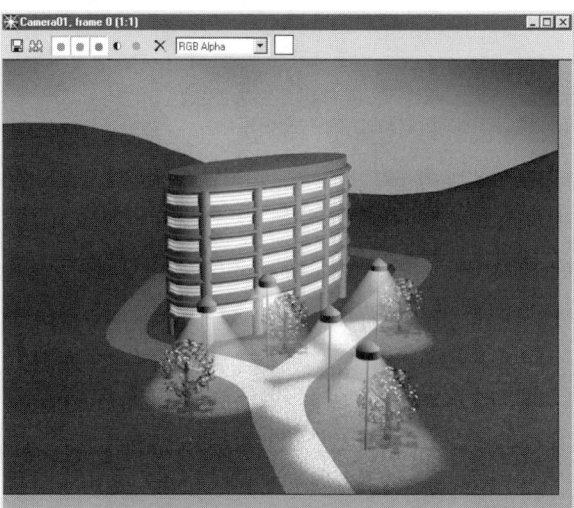

Figure 13.9 Rendered scene with beams of light.

8. Save the file. It's already labeled ch13_night_02.MAX.

Valley Landscape

For Exercise 13.3, think of MAX R3 as a 2D tool to design a bitmap. Once placed in the Displacement map slot of a material, a winding valley is created in a flat plain landscape. The material also contains a bump component that adds small hills and valleys across the landscape. Use the mask bitmap to change the color in the valley's base.

Exercise 13.3   Creating a Winding Valley

1. Open the file called 13imx02.MAX from the CD-ROM. It's a sky dome with a flat plane, camera, and lights. There are also two 2D lines: A curved line that runs across the plane, and a short straight line off to one side. The flat plane has an assigned material called CANYON. Save the file as ch13_valley_01.MAX.

2. Create the flat 2D geometry that is rendered to a file, which makes the valley appear in the flat plane. In the Top viewport, choose Select, and type H. Double-click canyon_path. This is a curving line across the Plane. In the Create Geometry panel, select Standard Primitives, and choose Compound Objects. In the Object Type rollout, click Loft. In the Creation Method rollout, select Get Shape, and type H. Double-click canyon_shape. This lofts a straight line along a curved line to create a curved flat mesh. Name this object CANYON.

Note
You won't see the mesh in any display because the face normals are pointing away from the viewer. To rectify this, assign a 2-sided material.

3. Open the Material Editor, and make sure the second sample sphere is selected. It's called BRIGHT_WHITE and is a white material with full self-illumination. Select Assign Material to Selection, and the curved plane appears in the shaded viewport.

4. Select Render Scene. In the Output Size area, enter 1600 in both the Width and Height fields. This renders to a square image (the same aspect as LANDSCAPE), which makes it easier to fit the map to the LANDSCAPE. Click Close in the Render Scene dialog box.

5. In the Top viewport, pan and zoom the viewport until the blue LANDSCAPE mesh fills the viewport's Safe Frame yellow rectangle on all sides. It looks similar to Figure 13.10.

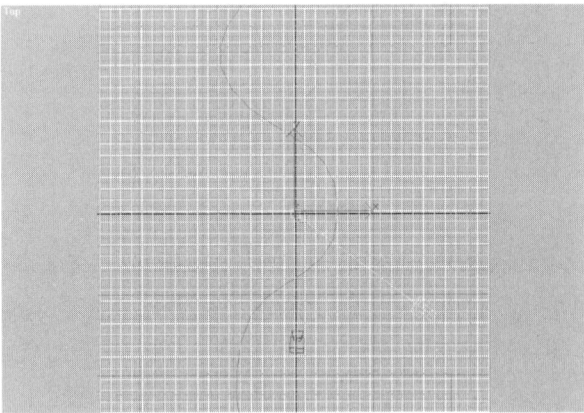

Figure 13.10 Top viewport, zoomed and panned to center LANDSCAPE in Safe Frame.

6. Click the Select button, and type H. Double-click CANYON. In the Display panel's Hide rollout, click Hide Unselected.

Chapter 13: Using MAX 3 as a 2D Paint Tool   517

7. Select Render Scene. Under Render Output, choose Files. Name the file CANYON.PNG, and choose 24 bit (16.7 Million) in the PNG Configuration dialog box. Click OK. Then in the Render Scene dialog box, select Render. The VFB looks like Figure 13.11. Close all dialog boxes. In the Display panel's Hide rollout, click Unhide All, then choose Hide Selected. This reveals everything except the curved plane.

Figure 13.11 Rendered flat curved plane against a black background.

8. Type W to maximize to four viewports, and open the Material Editor. Click the third sample sphere, and name the material CANYON. In the Maps rollout, enter 20 in the Displacement map Amount field, and click None (to the right). Double-click Bitmap, then double-click CANYON in the Select Bitmap Image File list. Name this level *bitmap displ*. A slight bit of deformation is on the sample sphere's surface, but you don't see it in the display. Click Show Map in Viewport, and view the white curve on a black mesh.

Note

The sample sphere's material is already assigned to the LANDSCAPE object.

Caution

Applying displacement mapping creates dense mesh objects. If you use a slow machine, try the Displacement Approx. modifier instead of Displace Mesh. You view the displacement only at render time, but the display isn't quite so slow.

9. You want to see what is happening in your viewports before applying a Displacement Approx. modifier to LANDSCAPE (to view the displacement result at render time). With LANDSCAPE selected, select More in the Modify panel. Double-click Displace Mesh in the World Space modifier list. Notice some displacement of the mesh in the viewport. In the Displacement Approx. rollout, select Custom Settings, then choose Low in Subdivision Presets. The mesh is displaced but as a berm, not a valley.

10. In the Material Editor's Output rollout, choose Invert. This changes the black values of the bitmap to white, and the white values to black. Select Modify, then choose Displacement Approx. Now click Update Mesh. The valley appears in the mesh. However, the sides are too steep.

11. In the Material Editor's Coordinates rollout, enter 0.03 in the Blur Offset field. Select Modify, then Displacement Approx. Choose Update Mesh. This blurs the edges of the black-and-white image, giving smoother sloping sides. Now apply some color and bumps to the landscape. Under Material Editor, select Material/Map Navigator. Now click the top level.

12. Select Shader Basic Parameters, and change the Diffuse color swatch to light blue gray (R110, G145, B180). Click the Map shortcut button to the right of the diffuse swatch. Double-click Noise in the list. Name this level *noise diff*. In the Noise Parameters rollout, enter 0.75 in the High Threshold field and 0.35 in the Low field. Enter 200 in the Size field. Change Color #1 to light green (R85, G125, B60), and change Color #2 to brown (R125, G110, B60).

13. Click the Go to Parent button, then choose None for the Bump map. Double-click Cellular, and name this level *cellular bump*. In the Cellular Parameters rollout, enter 25.0 in the Size field. Render the Camera01 viewport. Now you have a displaced valley with a greenish bubbled surface similar to Figure 13.12.

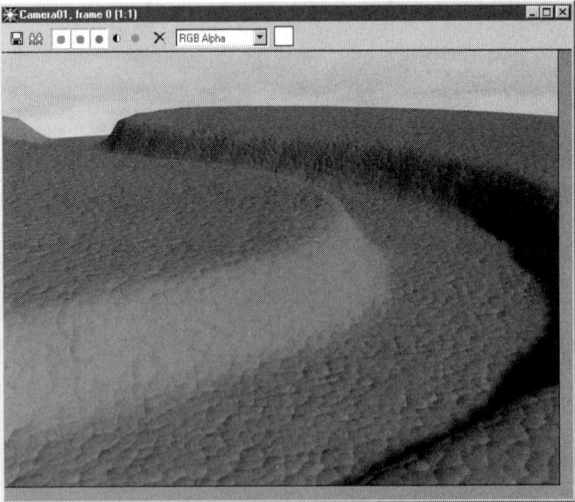

Figure 13.12 Displaced valley with rough greenish surface.

14. The valley floor appears bluish, as though water runs through it. You do this with a mask in the Diffuse slot, using CANYON.PNG as the mask. In the Material/Map Navigator, click the *noise diff* level. In the Material Editor, click the Noise button, and double-click Mask in the list. Select Keep Old Map as Submap, and click OK. In the Navigator, drag and drop the bitmap displ onto the Mask None button in the Mask Parameters rollout. Select Copy, and click OK in the dialog box. Render the Camera01 viewport, and the valley's base is blue.

15. In the Navigator, click the *cellular bump* level. In the Material Editor, click the Cellular button, and double-click Mask. Keep the old map, and check OK. From the Navigator, drag and drop bitmap displ onto the Mask None button, check Copy, and click OK. Render the scene, and now you have a smooth blue valley floor that looks similar to Figure 13.13.

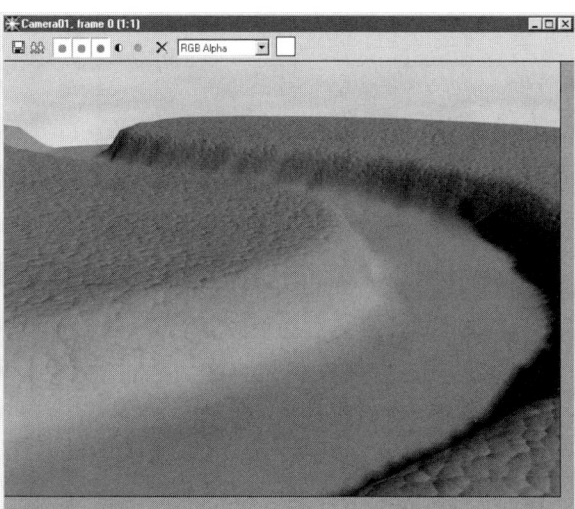

Figure 13.13 Smooth blue valley through landscape.

 Tip

With more than 41,000 faces, Exercise 13.3's mesh slows the display and increases render times. In a production situation, when you have a landscape the way you want it, use Save Selected to save the displaced mesh to disk. Then use Snapshot to make a mesh snapshot, apply an Optimize modifier to simplify the mesh, and collapse the Displacement mapping. Doing this reduces the mesh to under 4,000 faces and produces incredible speed for display and rendering.

16. Save the file. It's already labeled ch13_valley_01.MAX.

Animated Maps and Masks

You often need to have quick-and-dirty 2D animations for use in masks and maps, either in the Material Editor or as a Video Post queue layer. The cost of purchasing and learning 2D-animation software is high. Producing 2D animations one frame at a time in a paint package or with the limited animation capabilities of some paint packages is often time consuming and not very cost effective. 3D Studio MAX R3 is an effective tool in creating several types of 2D animations, including:

- Animating object transforms
- Sub-object level animated transforms
- 2D-object Morphing

Tip

Open the file on the CD-ROM called PAINT_DRIP.MAX. For an example of morphing used on 2D shapes to create an animated series of images, use the new MAX R3 RAM Player to load PAINT_DRIP.ifl. The images are then used as a mask material to reveal one color beneath another. They are also used as a Bump map to create the illusion of thickness in the new paint.

Burning Fuse

Exercise 13.4 is a bomb—literally. The scene contains a bomb and a fuse, with a sparkle made from an animated Particle System along the fuse path. When the sparkle reaches the bottom of the fuse, the bomb explodes in a ball of fire. Your task, if you choose to accept it, is to create a material for the fuse that causes it to disappear above the burn point and to cue a bright, hot glow at the burn line. This requires an animated mask that hides a portion of the fuse material and a coordinated mask that cues the glow. Because the task needs two mask operations, use a Blend material within a Blend material. Each Blend material has its own Mask level. The fuse itself is a lofted mesh, which allows you to take advantage of the lofted mapping coordinates to keep the mask oriented with the fuse (no matter how it twist and turns).

Exercise 13.4 Animated Burning Fuse

1. Open the file called 13max04.MAX from the CD-ROM. It contains the bomb with an animated sparkle along the fuse. Video Post is already set up to cue the sparkle's glow and the burning fuse material's glow that you create in this exercise. Video Post is also configured to render an 'avi' file to the Temp subdirectory of your hard drive. Save the file as ch13_fuse_01.MAX.

2. Open the Material Editor, and notice that the second material sample sphere is active. It is a Standard material with a Speckle diffuse map. Use two levels of

Blend material to complete the whole effect. First, set up the material. Then, in another file, create the animated masks. Finally, come back to the first file to plug the animated masks into your material. In the Material Editor, click the Standard button and double-click Blend in the list. Choose Keep Old Material as Sub-material in the Replace Material dialog box, and click OK. Change the name of the material to BURNING_FUSE. Click the Material/Map Navigator button.

Tip

The BURNING_FUSE material gets complex. The Material/Map Navigator is extremely helpful in finding your way through the hierarchy of material and map levels.

3. In the Material Editor, click the Material #2 button. Select Standard for Material #2, and double-click Blend. Choose Keep Old Material as Sub-material in the Replace Material dialog box, and click OK. Name this material BURNT_FUSE. The Material/Map Navigator looks similar to Figure 13.14.

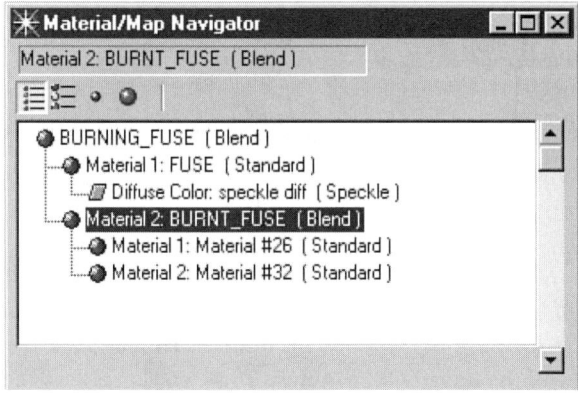

Figure 13.14 Blend material within a Blend material in Navigator.

4. The first level of BURNT_FUSE Blend material is completely invisible. Use an animated mask to reveal the invisible material along the FUSE material, making it seem to disappear over time. Select the Material #1 level of BURNT_FUSE. Name this level INVISIBLE. In the Blinn Basic Parameters rollout, enter 0 in the Specular Level field, the Glossiness field, and the Opacity field.

Tip

It is necessary to set only the Opacity amount to 0 to make a material invisible. If the Specular Level or Glossiness have a setting greater than 0, the invisible portion of the mesh may have specular highlights, ruining the effect.

5. In the Material/Map Navigator, click the Material #2 level of BURNT_FUSE.

Name this level GLOW_CUE. This material needs no special parameters that will be seen in the rendered image. This material's only function is to cue the glow event in Video Post that gives the fuse a bright glowing ring, separating the visible from the invisible portion. The glow event uses a Material Effects channel from which to cue. In the Material Editor, click and hold the Material Effects Channel button, and select 1 in the drop-down list.

Note

There is another material in the scene called SPARK that uses Material Effects Channel 3 to cue another glow effect in Video Post. This glow effect gives the SuperSpray Particle System a glow off each particle. It is possible to have 15 different Material Effects Channels, with Channel 0 at *off*.

6. Save the file. It's already labeled ch13_fuse_01.MAX. In the File pull-down menu, click Reset. Choose Yes when asked if you really want to Reset. This clears everything in the display and resets to all default settings, or the settings saved in MAXSTART.MAX (if you have created one).

Note

When you load 3D Studio MAX R3, there is no MAXSTART.MAX file. If you find yourself with custom settings for units, grids, and so on, set them in an empty file. Then select Save As, with the name MAXSTART.MAX. Every time you Reset or start a new MAX R3 session, all the presets in this file are loaded. Search on *startup* in the Online Help, and look in the section called Startup Files for more information.

7. Now create two masks. One is an animated mask, which starts as a black full-screen image and changes (over 30 frames) to a white full-screen image. This animation reveals INVISIBLE material under FUSE material. The other is a thin white line that animates the screen from the top to the bottom. This cues the Glow effect at the very edge of the reveal. At the bottom of the display, click Time Configuration, and enter 30 in the End Time field. Click OK. This sets the animation to 30 frames, the same time it takes the animate spark to travel from the top of the fuse to the bottom.

Tip

The animated Particle System has a Path Controller with a turned-on Constant Velocity option. This is important in syncing the travel of the animated masks with the moving spark. Without Constant Velocity turned on, the spark slows down on the corners and speeds up on the straightaways. This makes syncing difficult.

8. Right-click the Top viewport to activate it. In the Create panel, select Plane. In the Top viewport, choose one corner of the display, and drag the cursor to the opposite diagonal corner. Name this object FUSE_MASK. The size of the object is not important. What is important is that the object fills the viewport. Click again at the lower left of the Top viewport, and drag over to the lower right side

of the display. Enter 2 in the Length field of the Parameters rollout. This creates a thin strip that animates from top to bottom of the rendered image. Name this object GLOW_MASK.

9. Click the Align button, and choose the FUSE_MASK plane in the Top viewport. Check X Position in the Align dialog box. Set both Current Object and Target Object to Center. Select Apply. This horizontally aligns the two planes. Check the Y Position. Choose Minimum (in both Current and Target columns) to align the bottom edges of both planes. Click OK. Select GLOW_MASK. Click the Select and Link button, type H, and choose FUSE_MASK. This links GLOW_MASK as a child of FUSE_MASK, so you have to animate only FUSE_MASK for them both to be animated.

10. In the Top viewport, zoom in until the display is completely filled with FUSE_MASK, then just a bit more. You want to make sure that when you animate the mask, no black edges are on the sides. Select FUSE_MASK (if it is not already selected). Press the Space bar, or click the Lock Selection Set button. This allows you to move objects off the screen without actually individually selecting them.

Caution
You don't want to zoom in too far or the thin GLOW_MASK is too large in the rendered image.

11. In the Top viewport, click the Select and Move button. Then select Restrict to Y-axis. Move the two objects upward until they are just off the display. Click Animate to turn it on, and go to frame 30. In the Top viewport, move the objects downward until the display is completely filled. Click Animate to turn it off. If you drag the Animation Slider back and forth, or click the Play Animation button, you notice that the objects move down across the viewport, like a curtain dropping.

12. Select both objects in the display, and open the Material Editor. Create a pure white material for application to the objects. This renders pure white against a pure-black background. Name the first sample sphere BRIGHT_WHITE. In the Blinn Basic Shaders rollout, set the Specular color swatch to pure white. Drag and drop the Specular swatch onto the Diffuse, the Ambient, and the Self-Illumination color swatches (check Copy in the Copy or Swap Colors dialog box each time). Choose Assign Material to Selection, and close all dialog boxes.

13. Select Render Scene. In the Render Scene dialog, choose Active Time Segment. Now select 320 × 240 under Output Size. Click the Files button. In the Render Output File dialog box, name the file FUSE_MASK.avi. Choose AVI File in the Save As Type field, and click the Save button. Select Compressor, then choose Cinepak Codec by Radius. Make sure the Compression Quality slider is set at 100, and clear the Key Frame Every option (if it is checked). Click OK. In the Render Scene dialog box, select Render.

Note

If the VFB is not completely black on the first frame and completely white on the last frame, adjust the position of the animated masks or zoom in slightly in the Top viewport. Render the scene again.

14. In the Display panel, click the Hide by Name button, and double-click FUSE_GLOW in the list. Render the scene again to an AVI file named GLOW_MASK. It's an animated horizontal white stripe moving from top to bottom over 30 frames. To turn it off, press the Space bar or choose Lock Selection Set. Save the scene to make sure all changes are saved to FUSE_MASKS.MAX.

15. Open the file called ch13_fuse_01.MAX (that was saved earlier in the exercise). Open the Material Editor, and make sure the BURNING_FUSE sample sphere is active. Open the Material/Map Navigator, and make sure you are at the top level. In the Blend Basic Parameters rollout, click the None button for the Mask, and double-click Bitmap in the list. Locate the file FUSE_MASK.avi, and double-click it in the Select Bitmap Image File dialog box. Name this level *fuse mask*. In the Coordinates rollout, right-click Spinners for Blur, and set it to 0.01. This gives the map a sharp delineation between black and white. Select Show Map in Viewport, and the fuse in the Camera01 viewport turns black.

16. At the bottom of the display, drag the Frame Slider from frame 0 to frame 25. Notice the fuse turning white, moving up from the bottom. Where the fuse is white, you see the INVISIBLE material; where it's black, you see FUSE. You don't want the fuse to disappear from the bottom up, however. In the Coordinates rollout, enter 180 in the W angle field to change the direction of the bitmap. Now it turns white from the top of the fuse down.

Tip

You also reverse the apparent direction of the map by going to the Output rollout and selecting the Invert option to turn black for white.

17. In the Material/Map Navigator, select Material 2:BURNT_FUSE (Blend). Click the None button for the Mask, and double-click Bitmap in the list. Double-click GLOW_MASK.avi in the Select Bitmap Image File dialog box. Name this level *glow mask*. In the Coordinates rollout, enter 180 in the W angle field. Set the Blur amount to 0.01. Click the Show Map in Viewport button, and as you drag the Frame Slider, notice a ring of white animated along with the Particle System from bottom to top. The Material/Map Navigator looks like Figure 13.15.

Chapter 13: Using MAX 3 as a 2D Paint Tool   525

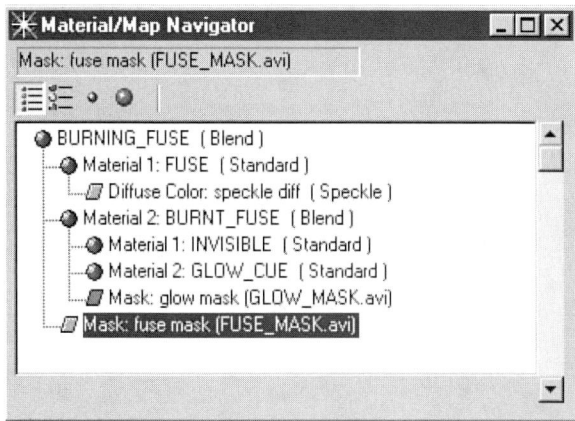

Figure 13.15   Material/Map Navigator for BURNING_FUSE material.

18. In the Rendering pull-down menu, select Video Post. There is already a Video Post queue that looks like Figure 13.16. In the Video Post dialog box, choose Execute Sequence. Check the Range option in the Execute Video Post dialog box, and click the Render button. The frames render in three passes, one for the Camera01 view and two for the glow effects.

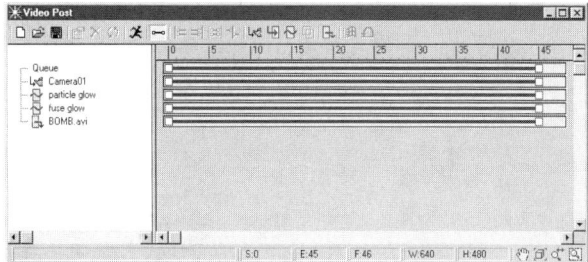

Figure 13.16   Video Post queue, with two glow effects and an Image Output event.

19. When the file is finished rendering, save it. It's already labeled ch13_fuse_01.MAX. In the Rendering pull-down menu, click RAM Player and load the file you just rendered (called BOMB.avi). Play it back, and you see the results of the exercise. Figure 13.17 shows a sample frame.

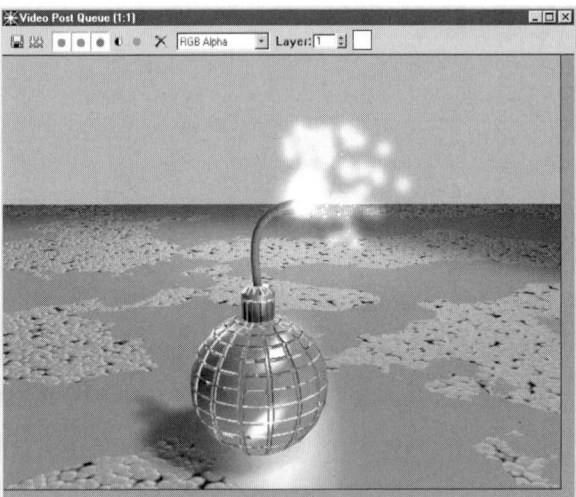

Figure 13.17 Rendered Video Post frame.

Digging a Trench

Sometimes a client likes your still image so much that you're asked to animate it. For example, your client wants you to dig up your winding valley (Exercise 13.3) in an animation—as if the valley is on an alien planet. Although you're short on backhoes in your model library, you do have a space-digging machine. To illustrate the machine moving along as it digs up the valley, just animate the bitmap that was used in the Displacement map slot in Exercise 13.3.

You can load the CANYON.png image into your favorite paint software, copy it 100 times, then laboriously and individually alter each of the animation's 100 frames. Instead, use the existing geometry in MAX R3 to quickly animate the curved plane and render to a new series of images. These new images replace the still-image Displacement map in the CANYON material.

Note

This is also a good application for Discreet Paint*, in which you animate a paint stroke along a vector.

Caution

The next exercise generates large files and uses considerable system resources. If you have a slow computer or limited RAM and hard drive space, create your own smaller files. Use this exercise as a guide.

Exercise 13.5 Digging a Valley

1. Open the file called 13max05.MAX from the CD-ROM. It is the finished file from Exercise 13.3. The Top viewport is maximized, with the CANYON object selected. Save the file as ch13_ani_valley_01.MAX. Use the Scale Deformations of loft objects to animate the lofted mesh growing over time. Then render the results to a series of image files. Substitute the Displacement bitmap in the CANYON material with the new sequence of images. You reveal all the other objects in the scene and render the sequence for playback in the RAM Player. It appears as if the digging machine is cutting the valley from the landscape.

Tip

The animated loft occurs at a constant speed over the 100-frame duration. It's therefore important to note that an animated Dummy object resides along the path. It controls the cutting machine's motion and turns on the Constant Velocity option. Otherwise, synchronizing the two is difficult.

2. In the Modify panel, select Deformations. Choose Scale. This opens the Scale Deformations dialog box, as seen in Figure 13.18. The red horizontal line represents the scaling of the straight-line shape that is lofted along the curved path. The lofted object is a constant width over the entire length.

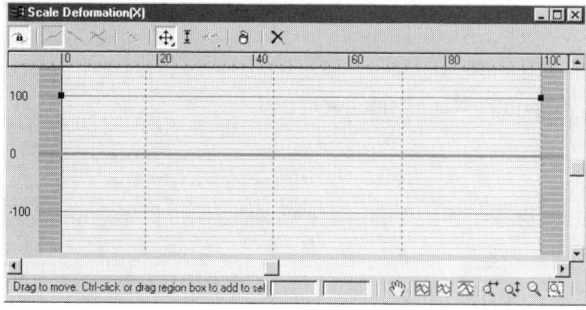

Figure 13.18 Scale Deformations dialog box.

3. In the Scale Deformations dialog box, select Insert Corner Point. Click twice (at a slight distance apart) on the red line to insert two new control points. Select Move Control Point. The dialog box looks similar to Figure 13.19.

4. The rightmost of the two new control points is selected (if not, select it). In the Position field (on the left) at the dialog box's base, enter 70. This is the distance percentage along the loft. In the Amount field (on the right), enter 0.01. This is the scaling percentage along the loft. The Scale Deformation dialog box and the lofted object look similar to Figure 13.20.

528   Part II   Materials

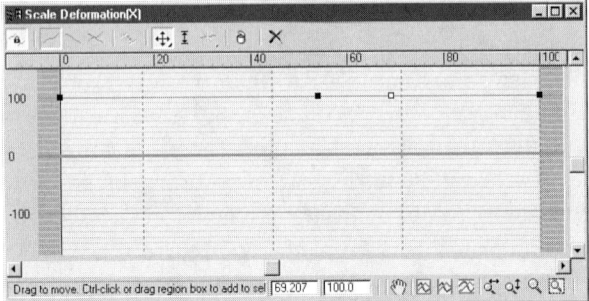

Figure 13.19   Two new control points added to red Scale line.

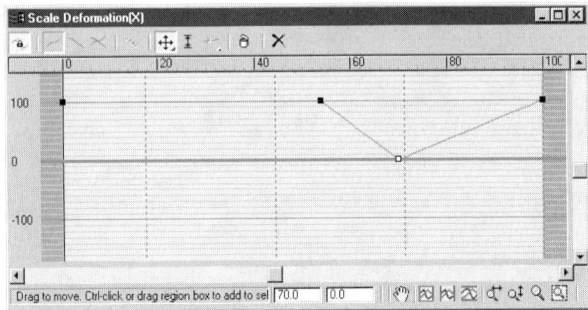

Figure 13.20   Control points set to Position of 70 and Amount of 0.01.

 Caution

Setting the scale Amount to 0 causes occasional problems. Always use a scale Amount of 0.01 to stay on the safe side.

  5. Select the far-right control point. In the rightmost field at the dialog box's base, enter 0.01. Select the second-from-the-left control point. In the leftmost field, enter 69.99. The dialog box looks like Figure 13.21. Now animate the two new control points, moving from left to right. This makes the loft grow over 100 frames from the path's beginning to its end.

Chapter 13: Using MAX 3 as a 2D Paint Tool   529

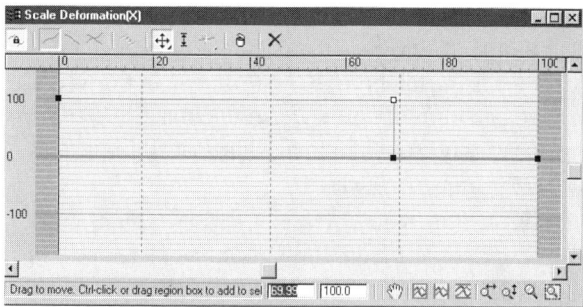

Figure 13.21 Scale Deformation line of a blunt end on the loft object.

6. Drag a selection window around the two center control points to select both of them. Click and hold the Move Control Point button, and choose the horizontal arrow flyout button. Move the two selected control points all the way to the dialog box's left side.

7. Click the Animate button to turn it on. Drag the Frame Slider to frame 100 to make it the current frame. In the Scale Deformation dialog box, drag the two control points all the way to the right of the dialog box. Click the Animate button to turn it off. Close the Scale Deformation dialog box. Drag the Frame Slider back and forth, and you see the loft object grow over the 100 frames.

8. Click the Render Scene button. In the Render Scene dialog box, the Active Time Segment is checked—1600 is both the Height and Width of the Output Size fields. Click the Files button, and save this file to disk as ANICAN.png. In the Render Output File dialog box, choose Setup. Set the PNG Configuration to 24 bit, and check the Alpha Channel option to turn it on. Click OK in the PNG Configuration dialog box. Now select Save (in the Render Output File dialog box), and select Render (in the Render Scene dialog box). MAX renders 100 incremental frames to your hard drive, each at an average size of about 30K. Depending on your machine, this process takes a while. The sequence of images is also available to you on the CD-ROM.

 Note
As a point of reference, an Intergraph TDZ 2000 GL2 with dual P III 500s and 256 megs of RAM took less than fifteen minutes. My dual P II 200 is usually about four times longer at rendering.

 Note
The first few frames are black because the loft object is scaled to 0. Do not stop the rendering.

9. Open the Material Editor, and select CANYON sample sphere (if it isn't already selected). Click the Material/Map Navigator button. Notice there are three places where CANYON.png has been used. You must substitute the sequence that was

just rendered in each case. In the Navigator, select the first Mask CANYON.png. In the Material Editor, select Bitmap Parameters, then Choose Bitmap. In the Select Bitmap Image File dialog box, highlight ANICAN0000.png in the list, check Sequence, and click the Open button. Check OK in the Image File List Control dialog box. This automatically creates an Image File List (IFL) file that loads each image (in order) as the frames render.

10. In the Material/Map Navigator, select the next CANYON.png level. Drag and drop ANICAN0000.IFL from the Navigator onto Bitmap (in the Material Editor). This substitutes CANYON.png with ANICAN0000.IFL. Repeat Step 10 for the last CANYON.png in the Navigator. The Material/Map Navigator looks similar to Figure 13.22. Close the Material Editor and Navigator. Type W to minimize the viewport.

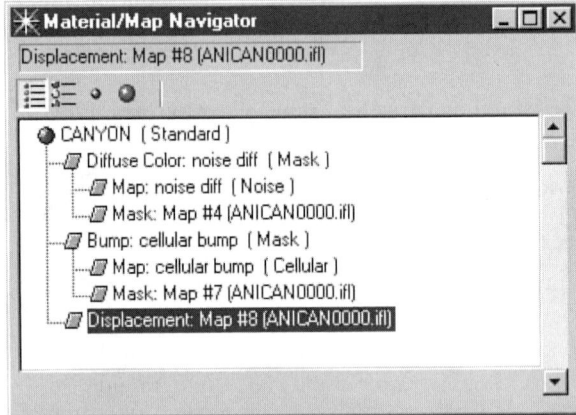

Figure 13.22 Material/Map Navigator with IFL files.

11. Right-click the Camera01 viewport to activate it. In the Display panel, select Unhide All, and the Hide Selected button. This reveals the digging machine, the landscape, and the sky.

 Note
If you drag the Frame Slider back and forth, the digging machine moves forward and backward, but the landscape doesn't change. Update the Displace Mesh modifier to view a displacement map's changes in the viewport. However, the scene renders correctly.

12. Save the file. Click the Render Scene button, and check Active Time Segment. Select 640 × 480, and choose Files. Save the animation to digger.avi. Click OK. Select Render in the Render Scene dialog box. Use the Cinepak Codec by Radius. When the file is rendered, view it with the RAM Player. The rendered AVI file is also on the CD-ROM.

In Practice: Using MAX 3 as a 2D Paint Tool

- **Exterior night scene.** In this exercise, you create a series of 2D circles, turn them into mesh planes, assign a self-illuminated material, and render the image to a bitmap. The bitmap then becomes a Projector Map in a rectangular Direct light (to simulate pools of light on the ground and to cast tree shadows in the scene). A transparent material is assigned to 3D cones in scenes (to simulate beams of light coming from lamps through a damp or dusty atmosphere). These methods are much more efficient than individual lights casting shadows and Volume Light effects on each light. The overall effect is still convincing.

- **Valley landscape.** For the valley, you create a 2D, self-illuminated plane and render it to a bitmap. The bitmap is used in a Displacement map material to physically push the valley into a mesh plane. The depth of the valley is adjusted by the Displacement map Amount. The slope of the valley walls is adjusted by the Blur Amount.

- **Burning fuse.** Here you use two animated maps created in MAX R3. One is a black screen turning completely white. It reveals an invisible material under a visible material (in a Blend material). A second Blend level uses a thin white stripe, animated across a black background to cue a glow effect in Video Post. The illusion is an animated burning fuse, mostly created with materials.

- **Animated valley landscape.** This exercise starts with the valley scene from the previous exercise and animates the bitmap with Scale Deformation. The resulting rendered series of images gives the illusion that a machine traveling across the landscape is digging up the valley. The effect is also used for tires in the sand or a snowmobile breaking through the snow.

Rendering Effects

14   **Cameras, Camera Effects, and Lighting**

15   **Glows and Lens Flares**

16   **Highlights**

17   **Focal Effects**

Chapter 14

Cameras, Camera Effects, and Lighting

Perhaps one of the most challenging aspects of 3D rendering is the proper use of lighting and cameras. All too often, renderings or animations remind you that many people simply don't grasp the key concepts of showcasing the virtual world. Sometimes they blame the software they use. For example, MAX had an earlier reputation of producing renderings that looked too "plastic-like." Perhaps, but the fact still remains that as a computer artist, you are able to stretch the imaginary bounds of the software to obtain the desired effects.

MAX's virtual cameras and lights present you with a host of possibilities for stretching your virtual world's needs. You need only tap into the potential of the camera and light objects to really achieve great renderings and animations.

If you are familiar with real-world lights and cameras, however, you've got your work cut out for you. Nearly all of MAX's settings and properties for lights and cameras relate to the 3D environment on your monitor, not outside your window. For instance, there is no concept of an f-stop in MAX. However, you easily duplicate the effect of stopping down a camera through the Depth of Field module in Render Effects.

Note

Depth of Field, as a Rendering Effect, is part of the Bonus Tool installation in MAX R3. If you wish to use the new Depth of Field feature in Rendering Effects, you'll need to install MAX with the Bonus tool option selected.

To help you make the transition, this chapter seeks to clarify many of the issues and techniques associated with MAX cameras and lights, as they relate to their real-world counterparts. It also explores the many possibilities that exist when you fully exploit the potential of these features. The chapter first looks at real-world camera terminology, and how, or if, the features are duplicated within the virtual world of MAX.

Specifically, you learn the following techniques:

- Real-world camera terminology and how to translate it to MAX
- Setting up lights in MAX, based on traditional techniques
- Specific techniques for simulating certain camera effects

Real-World Cameras

If you look at any camera books, whether on shooting weddings or snapping shots of nature, you find certain common concepts and terms. This section explains what they are and tries to closely map this real-world terminology with features in MAX cameras. Some are easily duplicated, others are not as straightforward, and still others can't be duplicated without the help of a plug-in. If you've never taken a photography class, this section is still relevant. It's not uncommon to discover great techniques in the digital realm while studying real life.

Film-Based Cameras

Film-based cameras record imagery, dependent on a film's exposure to light. The exposed film is then developed and processed. Film-based cameras rely more heavily on light for proper exposure than a video camera. Several factors play into the best-captured imagery taken with a film-based camera, many that are explored later in this book. For now, consider the two predominant types of film-based camera used today: still-image cameras and motion-picture cameras.

Still-Image Cameras

Perhaps the most common form of camera is a still image, or still frame, camera—from disposable cameras that you pick up from the drug store to professional-grade 35mm cameras. The way they work is simple. You first load film that reacts to light. To take a picture, you press a button on the camera. The button opens a shutter, exposing the film to a certain amount of light for a certain amount of time. We all know what happens when you reach the end of the film. You either bring the film in to your local developer to get processed onto paper or—if you're a savvy photographer—you do it yourself. Whatever the case, the end result is a piece of paper with an image on it.

Duplicating a still camera in MAX is, by far, the easiest thing to do. Simulating such effects as film-grain and overexposure, however, is really controlled through effects in Render Effects. In addition, using effects in Video Post, you duplicate many of the special post-processing techniques associated with still-life imagery from a camera. For instance, Adobe Photoshop filters work for many of the effects. The key is knowing where to find everything.

Motion Picture Cameras

Along the same principles of a still-image camera, motion-picture cameras capture action through a series of still images called *frames*. Frames in motion pictures are the exact equivalent to frames in MAX.

For the most part, motion picture films are shot using a wider image aspect ratio than that of video. For instance, your television has an aspect ratio of 4:3 (or 1.33 to 1). This means that it's not totally square, but very close to it. However, most films are shot at an aspect ratio of 1.85:1, or 2.35:1. This produces an image much wider than it is tall. In

MAX, the aspect ratio is achieved through the Rendering Settings dialog box (more on this later). Although custom Image Aspect Ratios (IAR) are configurable, there are several pre-configured preferences that allow you to quickly set up your rendering output, so it matches film aspect ratios.

Other common motion picture effects, such as anamorphic flare effects and distortions, are also achieved through Rendering effects.

Video-Based Cameras

Video cameras work from the same principle as film cameras, with respect to capturing a series of frames through a lens. However, the way the image itself is processed is quite different. The image is converted to an electronic signal after it passes through the lens. It's then processed internally, either to a magnetic source (such as a tape) or to a digital storage device (such as a small hard drive).

Video cameras are the easiest to simulate in MAX because there's little difference in the recorded video versus what you see on the television monitor. Granted, the quality of the videotape itself plays a factor, but by and large the image looks similar. MAX is fairly fine-tuned for output to video. In the Rendering Preferences tab, you set up your video color checking (a process for finding colors unsuitable for television), as well as field order (how the television updates the screen line-by-line). Even the safe frames were originally designed for video—even though they're just as useful, if not more so, for film.

A Note about Aspect Ratios

Notice that when you use the Render Scene dialog box, there are options for rendering to fields. More importantly, however, are the Rendering Resolution and Pixel Aspect Ratio settings. Typically, video rendering output resolution hovers right at about 720×480. This varies, depending on the type of device to which you output, but they're all pretty close. With the Pixel Aspect Ratio setting, you control the square of the pixels.

For a simple test, render out an image at 720×486, using the Preset button and the default image aspect ratio. Clone that Virtual Frame Buffer (VFB). Next, render out to the same resolution, but this time change the Pixel Aspect Ratio to 1.0. See how the original image appears squashed, whereas the more recent rendering looks fine. That's because at a ratio of 1.0, the rendered pixel is exactly square—just like your monitor. If you output the first image to a television monitor, it looks fine because television "dots" are higher than they are wide. Therefore, your television takes a squashed image from a computer and expands it somewhat vertically. Figure 14.1 demonstrates two different versions of pixel aspect ratios.

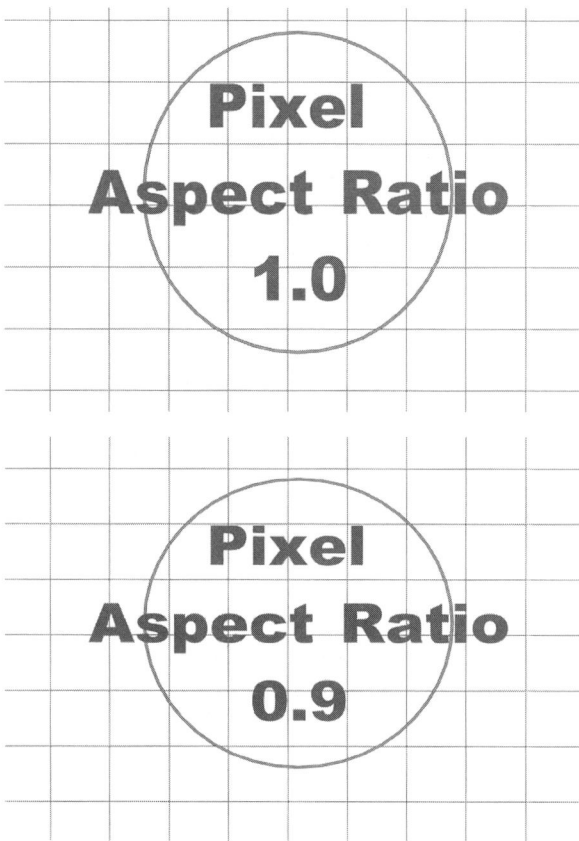

Figure 14.1 & Figure 14.2 The same scene rendered at different pixel aspect ratios. Figure 14.1 represents what a rendering looks like at a typical aspect ratio, used for non-video output. Figure 14.2 is the same scene with a 0.9 aspect ratio, more common for video output. The shortening along the Y-axis is necessary because video monitor pixels are not square.

Film Versus Video-Playback Speeds

NTSC-standard video images are captured at 30 frames-per-second (fps), whereas film is recorded and played back at the slower rate of 24fps. The 30fps rate typically results in video images with crisp and lively characteristics. This is not to say that film imagery does not contain those characteristics; it's just easy to discern the difference between the two.

Try a little test. Watch a TV sitcom, which was more than likely filmed using a video camera. Next, go down to your video store and pick up the latest movie (or have a little fun and actually go to a cinema). Watch the difference. You have to watch closely, but the differences are there. Perhaps the most obvious is the film grain, but even the motion appears to be a little less "hectic" in a film versus a videotaped image. This motion-related difference is a direct result of recording and playback speeds. Even a 6-frame-per-second difference adds up to 360 frames in just one minute—12 seconds of imagery that's either there or not there, depending on the format you're watching. In other words, video at 30fps offers an additional 25 percent more data during the same time. At 60 fields per second, video offers 150 percent more data. This means that field-rendered video has a fluid movement, whereas film has a slight strobe or flickering effect.

Fortunately, in MAX, duplicating this effect of film or video playback is easy to set up, with the Time Configuration dialog. The default playback rate is 30fps, but you can switch at any time between the different rates. Don't worry; the total animation length may change, but that's normal. MAX is simply adjusting itself to the necessary number of frames, to play your file's animation at the specified frame rate. To test this, try this simple example: With NTSC selected, type in 1800 for Length. Then click Film for playback rate. Notice that the playback length jumps down to 1440 frames.

Lens Types

Photographers have all sorts of options when it comes to lens varieties. From a normal lens to a fisheye, the type of subject and the desired effect usually dictates the lens choice. A camera lens is constructed of several "elements" (concave or convex pieces of glass) within the lens's encasement. The placement and arrangement of the elements, along with the length of the lens piece, produce the different photographic effects.

Normal Lens

A *normal* lens provides photographers with the most flexibility, photographically speaking. The lens is capable of focusing to many different lengths and is usually comprised of six elements; some have eight.

All of MAX's cameras use normal lenses. Therefore, assume that your rendered image closely matches what a camera with a normal lens views in real life. However, MAX cameras don't automatically focus to a specific focal length. This is controlled with the Depth of Field module. Along those lines are also the amounts of lens reflections that you see with a normal lens. As mentioned before, a normal lens contains six or eight elements. Therefore, you need to have the same number of lens reflections in your scene in case you encounter any flares.

All other discussed lens types are modifications of the normal MAX lens, through proper post-processing effects (using Flare and Focus). Figure 14.3 shows a rendered image from a normal camera lens, applied with a slight amount of depth-of-field blur.

Figure 14.3 A rendering that shows what it looks like to shoot a scene through a normal lens.

Wide-Angle Lens

A *wide-angle* lens allows the camera to fit more in a frame than a normal lens. However, this usually comes at a price of focal length. To simulate a wide-angle lens, simply adjust the MAX camera so that it views more of the scene: Adjust the field of view, and then use the Depth of Field module in Render Effects to shorten the focal distance of the rendered image. Wide-angle lenses vary in the number of elements, but most use about nine. A rendered example of a wide-angle lens is shown in Figure 14.4.

Figure 14.4 A wide-angle lens was used to shoot the same scene as in Figure 14.3 from the same position. Notice the amount of blurring now occurring, both in the foreground and behind the subject. Simulate the effect of a wide-angle lens focal length by using the Depth of Field module in Render Effects.

Telephoto

A telephoto lens allows the camera to get closer to a subject through a longer lens encasement and with the use of special elements. Essentially, you get closer to a subject with the same focal length. This effect typically makes the subject appear completely in focus (and everything else rapidly out of focus) as they exit the lens's maximum focal range.

To simulate a telephoto lens in MAX, use the Depth of Field module with a shorter focal range. That way, objects rapidly blur as they get outside of that range. Telephoto lenses usually have about five elements. Figure 14.5 was rendered with a MAX "telephoto lens." Note the scene's blur behind the teapot's spout. In this case, the FOV (field of view) used is 15 degrees.

 Note

Focal Range is the area in which subjects appear in focus, as measured in distance from the subject.

Figure 14.5 A rendered image through a telephoto lens. The Depth of Field module created the blur in the background.

Fisheye Lens

A *fisheye* lens doesn't work the same way as other wide angle lenses. It doesn't correct the horizontal lines of an image at extreme angles. As a result, lines are more curved as they reach the outer edges of the frame.

MAX (as it ships) doesn't simulate a fisheye lens with Render Effects. You can, however, render your scene through a convex glass object (such as a hemisphere) that uses a ray-traced map or material.

This does produce some rather lengthy rendering times and is certainly not the ideal solution. However, it is currently the only way to render a scene with the appearance of a fisheye lens attached to the camera.

F-Stops

An *f-stop* is a calibrated number that refers to a small device called the *aperture*, which performs the same function for the lens as your iris does for your eye. By altering the diameter of the aperture, you control both the amount of light and the depth of field of your photographed image. The effect of reducing the aperture's opening is commonly called "stopping down" the lens.

Typically, use the f-stop for situations where you had either too much light or not enough light and corrected it by increasing or decreasing the f-stop. However, since MAX is capable of adjusting its light sources individually or globally, there's no need to simulate this effect through an f-stop parameter. In MAX, you account for light by manipulating the light sources rather than an f-stop.

On the other hand, altering depth of field is definitely within the realm of MAX's capabilities. This is easily simulated through the Depth of Field effect (located in Render Effects). While there is no direct correlation to the camera's f-stop and depth of field value within MAX, the parameters adjusting both Focal Range and Focal Limit alter within the Depth of Field effect, itself. See Chapter 17, "Focal Effects," for more information on how to set up depth of field. Figure 14.6 demonstrates the effect of changing focal settings to simulate stopping down a lens.

Note
Depth of field is how animators refer to the closest and farthest area, where objects in your scene are rendered "in focus".

Figure 14.6 These three images represent the effect of stopping down a lens. The upper-left image simulates a wide aperture setting. Both the upper- and lower-right images use smaller and smaller settings, respectively, to increase the depth of field.

Film Speed

Film speeds designate a particular film's sensitivity to light. The faster the film speed, the more sensitive the film is to light. In most parts of the world, the ISO (International Standard Organization) number designates film speed; however, the DIN and GOST systems are still used in some parts of the world. When you go to the store, for instance, you typically find film speeds ranging from ISO100 to ISO400 (for most consumer-grade film). However, some film can go as low as 25 or as high as 6400.

Slower film speeds are normally best for still-life images or images for which there is enough light. Faster film speeds are typically used for darker scenes, or where fast action must be captured.

As with f-stops, MAX has no direct correlation to film speed. When matching or simulating film speeds within MAX, consider these two things:

- Higher film speeds tend to be less "contrasty" than slower film speeds.
- Higher film speeds are typically more grainy—especially when image size is increased.

Fortunately, MAX is capable of reproducing both of these effects quite easily through Render Effects. Render Effects Brightness and Contrast alters both the contrast and brightness of the image or the animation. Increase the contrast for images taken with a slower film speed. You may also need to slightly decrease the brightness. The reverse is true for simulating higher film speeds.

To add film grain, you need a 2D-image effect plug-in that simulates this. MAX R3 implants its own film-grain effect in Render Effects, thus eliminating a third-party one. In Render Effects, add the Film Grain effect into the queue to get the desired effect. Figure 14.7 demonstrates the usage of both contrast and Film Grain plug-in to simulate film speeds.

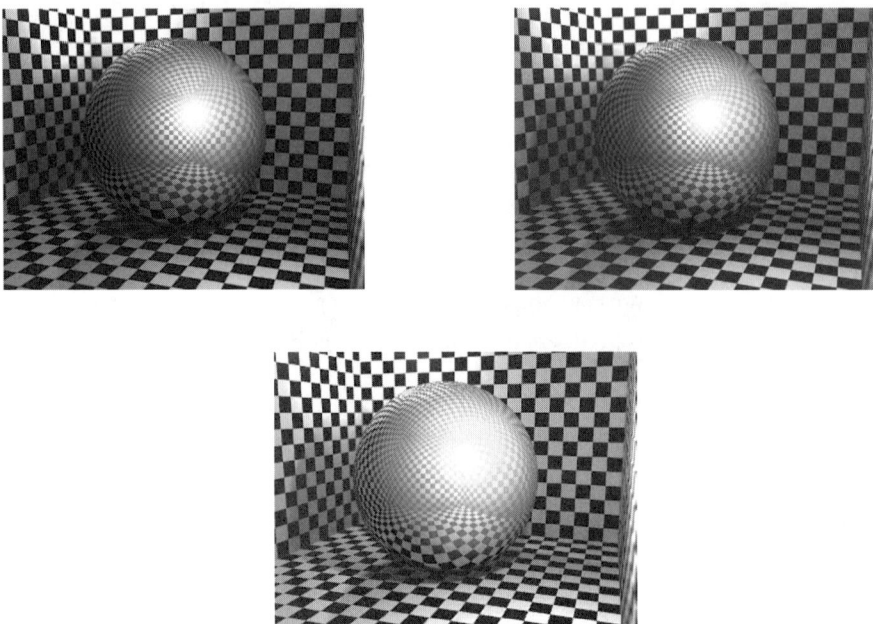

Figure 14.7 Using Focus, Brightness and Contrast, and Film Grain effects, you can simulate different film speeds. This is the same scene with different settings. The top-left image is a representation of a "low film speed," such as ISO100. The top-right image simulates a speed around ISO400 while the lower image simulates a speed of 1000.

Lens Attachments

Lens attachments in real life add effects to the photographed image that are normally not there. For instance, a photographer adds a soft-focus attachment to diffuse a photographed image's light. This softens the image's lines. The easiest way to mimic this with MAX is to use the Render Effects features. Unlike a real camera, however, MAX doesn't constrain you by what you can physically clip onto it. This makes just about anything possible. Reproducing two common-lens attachments' effects is discussed in the Lens Hoods and Soft-Focus Aperture Disk sections.

Lens Hoods

Photographers typically use lens hoods to shield the lens from intensely bright light sources (such as the sun or bright studio lights). With MAX, you basically have a lens hood on your camera at all times. Lens reflections, glows, or flares are added through the

Lens Effects options in Render Effects. In Chapter 15, "Glows and Lens Flares," you learn how to add these effects—essentially removing the lens hood.

Soft-Focus Aperture Disk

The soft-focus aperture-disk lens attachment gives halos to intensely bright areas of an image. Using it in conjunction with a soft-focus attachment, you softly defocus your image and have halos surrounding the bright areas for dramatic effects. MAX provides for this via the Glow and Focus effects.

Composition

Computer animators who don't come from an art background are often never taught the proper way to compose a scene. Scene composition is, perhaps, the most critical aspect of computer imagery—much like in real-life photography. There are several factors to consider. Lighting, camera angle, and FOV all play a role in your composition. If your shot involves motion, you must consider other factors. For instance, your composition may look good at frame 0, but be completely off by the end of the sequence. Fortunately, MAX allows you to adjust all the variables that you need for composition.

A Starting Point

In the virtual world, however, you are not constrained by real life. This means that rather than working with your environment to get the best composition, you make your environment work for you. While this sounds like a bit of a power trip, it can mean more work for you. In the real world, there are constants; concrete factors that we simply can't change. For instance, an oak desk will always be an oak desk and to bring out the characteristics of an oak desk, you probably need to change the room's lighting. In a way, this makes setting up a shot somewhat less of a challenge. Because you can change less, there are fewer variables to be tweaked to get the best shot.

In MAX, everything is a variable; you can alter every aspect of your scene. Take the oak desk. If you don't like the color or the grain of the oak, make changes to the material and leave the lighting alone. In this case, you alter the object's material to suit the lighting—not necessarily a real-world adjustment.

Many novice animators get into tweaking everything over and over again, thinking that it's the only way to get the best rendered image. If you're just starting out with MAX, stick to what you know (at first). If you're experienced with setting up studio lights, set up lights in MAX as in real life. Tweak the lights just like you want them, and *then* start working with the rest of your scene. Once you are a seasoned MAX user, you feel more comfortable with adjusting several parameters at the same time. (Although it's not uncommon for veteran users to stick to adjusting just a few items at a time.) If you have little or no experience, start first with an area of MAX with which you feel comfortable. For instance, most beginners tend to pick up camera placement first, mainly because it's something that you can see without having to render. Lighting is, by far, the most difficult concept to grasp and master in MAX, so it's not advisable to begin with learning lights.

Proper POV

POV, or *point of view*, is the point from which the camera views a scene. Camera placement, whether it's real or virtual, produces radically different results. When establishing POV, you must think about several things:

- What's the intended subject?
- Are there any items in the scene that can enhance the subject?
- Are there any items in the camera frame that "steal" from the intended subject?
- If outdoors, from where is the light coming? If indoors, is the lighting good enough, or can the position or intensity of lights be altered? (For MAX, the latter is true in both cases because you can actually move the sun, if needed!)

Ask yourself all these questions prior to determining your POV. Establishing a POV when working in virtual space is far easier because you can move or alter anything. This is obviously not the case in the real world. However, you can learn a great deal from traditional photography. For instance, sometimes it's useful to try different POVs; not alter the geometry, but use focal effects to accentuate the subject.

Remember: in MAX, POV enhances or ruins your imagery. Thankfully, the camera effects available in MAX make it extremely easy to set up proper POV. Figure 14.8 demonstrates a good POV, to capture the size of the cathedral.

Chapter 14: Cameras, Camera Effects, and Lighting   549

Figure 14.8   Using a flare and dramatic camera angle for a proper POV with the cathedral.

A Feel for FOV

While POV determines the perspective from which you view your subject, *FOV* determines how much you actually see of your subject and what's around it. Much like POV, FOV enhances or ruins your scene if too much or too little is captured in the frame.

Test to see whether your FOV is too narrow or too wide by asking someone to view your image or animation. Ask them what they saw. If they didn't notice your intended subject first, then you need to alter your FOV (and possibly your POV).

When using a perspective viewport with MAX, control the FOV through a camera's FOV spinner or with the FOV button. You can animate FOV through a camera view, just by changing the degrees over time. However, many novices think that altering the FOV means that you alter the camera's location. This is not the case; you're actually altering the viewing area of the camera itself. Altering FOV in MAX also alters the focal length of the lens. That's because in MAX both the focal length and the viewing area alter the same value. If you want to keep the focal length the same but have the camera closer to the subject, use the Dolly button. Keep in mind that the results are very different. Figure 14.9 shows how two different FOV settings produce completely different results from the same camera position.

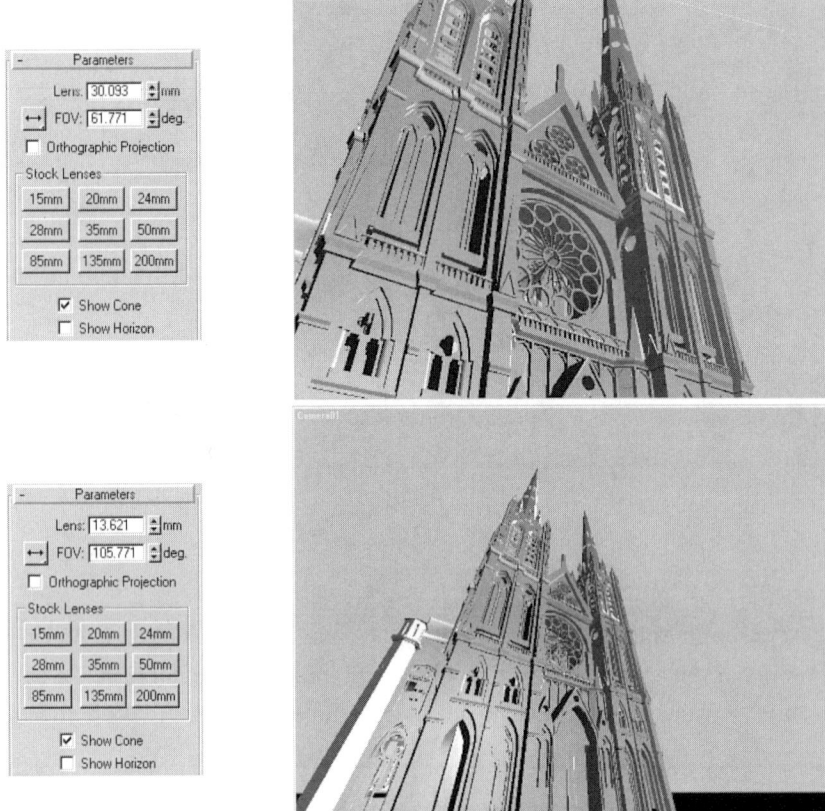

Figure 14.9 Using two different camera FOV settings on the same scene and from the same camera position.

MAX Cameras

So far, this chapter has investigated what real cameras are all about. But the question that most often comes up is, "How well can real-world properties be matched up to cameras within MAX?" Fortunately, most effects are reproducible. Some are easy; some not so easy. It's time to explore some of the necessary key elements for setting up and adjusting your cameras within MAX.

Using the Right Camera

MAX has two built-in camera types: *Free* and *Target*. The cameras work nearly identically; there's no fundamental difference in how they view your scene. Both have the exact controllable settings and both behave the same when their properties are adjusted over time. The difference lies in how they animate.

Target Cameras

A Target camera is a nontraditional, real-world camera, but very traditional in the computer world. A Target camera uses a camera object and a target object to determine its POV. The camera moves independently of the target, and vice versa. Target cameras are great for imagery that involves one or more of the following:

- A fly-around, fly-by, or fly-over
- A tracking shot
- A still

Target cameras have their problems, though. The most common is the *gimbal lock* or *flip-around* scenario. Because the camera always maintains its Z-up-axis relative to its target, certain problems occur when passing close to or directly above the target. Most animators call it the whip-lash problem, and it's the tell-tale sign of a novice animator. Essentially, what happens is that the camera whips around the target object as it passes close by—sometimes in only one to two frames. This situation is completely distracting and unprofessional. While you can't eliminate the problem of gimbal lock, you can minimize the chances of encountering it.

If your shot involves a fly-by, maintain a safe distance from the target (especially if the camera is above or below the target). Try to continue on the same horizontal plane when the camera's near the target. That way the camera rotates on just one axis as it passes by the target, instead of several axes.

If you absolutely need the shot from above or below the target, keep your camera slightly left or right of the course. This way it doesn't pass directly over the target. Otherwise, your camera rotates 180 degrees in one or two frames. Figure 14.10 shows two different possible fly-by paths. The left path causes a 180-degree rotation in less than two frames. The right path produces a smoother fly-by because, as it gets closer, the path's trajectory arcs away from the camera's target.

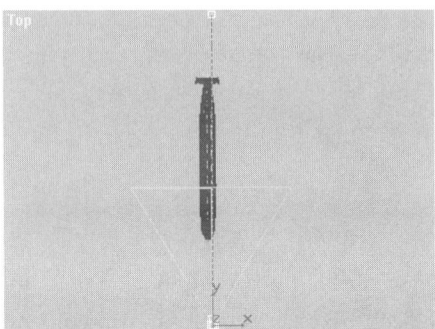 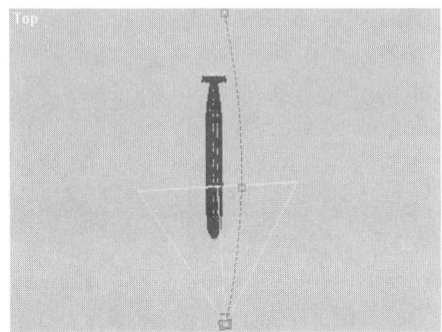

Figure 14.10 Using two possible animation paths for a camera. The right-hand trajectory is more desirable.

When you truck a target camera, you have to move both the camera and its target. While this is not a hassle if you're moving in one direction, it's quite a pain when you try to follow a winding path—say, moving along a winding road that's hugging the cliffs. While many seasoned animators deal with this nuisance, MAX incorporates another type of camera that eliminates the target: a Free camera.

Free Cameras

Free cameras more closely represent a real-world camera. With Free cameras, you basically point a camera object at the subject. Rather than moving a target to an object, use the Move and Rotate transforms to point the camera where you want to look. For many new users, this seems to be the more natural approach to setting up a camera. Free cameras work well for:

- Walkthroughs
- Panning shots
- Path-based animation

The advantage of the Free camera is that it's not constrained by the target's location or the gimbal lock problem. However, this freedom comes at a price. Free cameras actually take more time to set up. MAX does have a feature, however, that allows you to align cameras to an object's normals. This is really the only way to quickly align a Free camera. From there, any fine-tuning is done through Move and Rotate. Understanding transform type-ins is handy when making Free camera adjustments.

Here are some steps for aligning your camera to an object's normals. First, make sure that the face to receive the aligned normals is visible in at least one of the viewports:

1. Select the Free Camera.
2. In the Main toolbar, select Tab Panel. Click and hold the Align button, and wait for the flyout to appear.
3. Choose the Align Camera flyout (it looks like a camera with a grid).
4. Click and hold the object (and face) to which you want to align. Much like the Align Normals tool, Align Camera allows you to choose the specific face that receives the aligned normals by interactively dragging around the selected object.

A Free camera behaves like a Target camera by assigning a Look At controller to the Free camera's Transform track. By doing so, you obtain a tangible target object with which to work. The trouble is, though, that you have the same problems as a Target camera; mainly, the gimbal-lock problem.

Matching a Real-World Camera

MAX's cameras are modified now to mimic their real-world counterparts, with respect to camera-lens focal length. This means that a shot taken with a 35mm camera matches up when you composite the live imagery with the virtual scene, using a 35mm camera lens. Live-action shots using camera-tracking equipment match up properly as well.

If you don't have a camera-tracking system at your disposal, use MAX's Camera Match or Camera Tracker to match your virtual camera to a photograph or an animation. Remember that the Camera Match feature requires you to know the subject's proportions in the photograph to properly match a virtual camera to the scene. This means that you must know size and location of the real-world scene. If you don't have this information, Camera Match probably produces the wrong result. Camera Tracker, introduced in MAX R2.5, only requires distinguishable points within the image to track. Then it tracks those points so the camera movement in your 3D scene matches that of the video. For more information on Camera Tracker, refer to the MAX documentation or *Inside 3D Studio MAX R3 Animation* by New Riders Publishing.

Simulating Real-World Effects

Many effects traditionally created by using lens attachments or through lens manipulation are reproducible in MAX, through the Render Effects processes. Unlike real-world cameras (where image distortion takes place as the light passes through the lens) MAX first photographs the image, and then distorts it through Render Effects.

Using Depth of Field

NEW TO R3   To simulate anything that incorporates a focal effect, use MAX's Depth of Field effect (converted from the Lens Effects Focus module), located within Render Effects. All renderings in MAX are focused to infinity. Lens Effects Focus allows you to add real-life focal effects to your rendered image. Create a general scene blur, a radial blur, or a blur based on a focal node (an object on which you're focusing). As a general rule, almost every scene has some blur in it because every photographic work contains some focal blur. Using it in MAX means that your scenes present an extra sense of photographic realism. However, you need a plug-in for this effect. For more information on using Depth of Field, see Chapter 17, "Focal Effects."

Using Photoshop Plug-Ins

Using Photoshop plug-ins within Video Post allows you to add custom 2D effects. Previously, you did them within Photoshop after you rendered the still image or animation. While Photoshop is a great image-enhancing tool, the application of 2D effects is accomplished more easily through Video Post while you're actually rendering the animation. For still-life imagery, Photoshop effects look great.

However, a serious drawback of using Photoshop effects is that they're evaluated every frame. This produces animations where the effects are inconsistently applied over the course of the sequence. For animated sequences, consider using Adobe Premiere filters. Premiere effects are designed for animation and produce much better results over a sequence of frames. Figure 14.11 shows a rendered image post-processed in Render Effects, with the Photoshop Effect module. Depending on your plug-ins, the effects (especially when combined) greatly expand your output options.

Note

Not all Adobe filters for Photoshop or Premiere can be used in MAX. Filters designed by third parties (such as MetaTools) can be used without any problem. The primary reason for this is that Adobe restricts their internal filters to use in their own software. Third-party developers (such as Black Box or MetaCreations) create generic plug-ins. These plug-ins not only meet the Adobe specifications, they also run on any other software—including MAX—that supports the Adobe Photoshop or Premiere plug-in architecture.

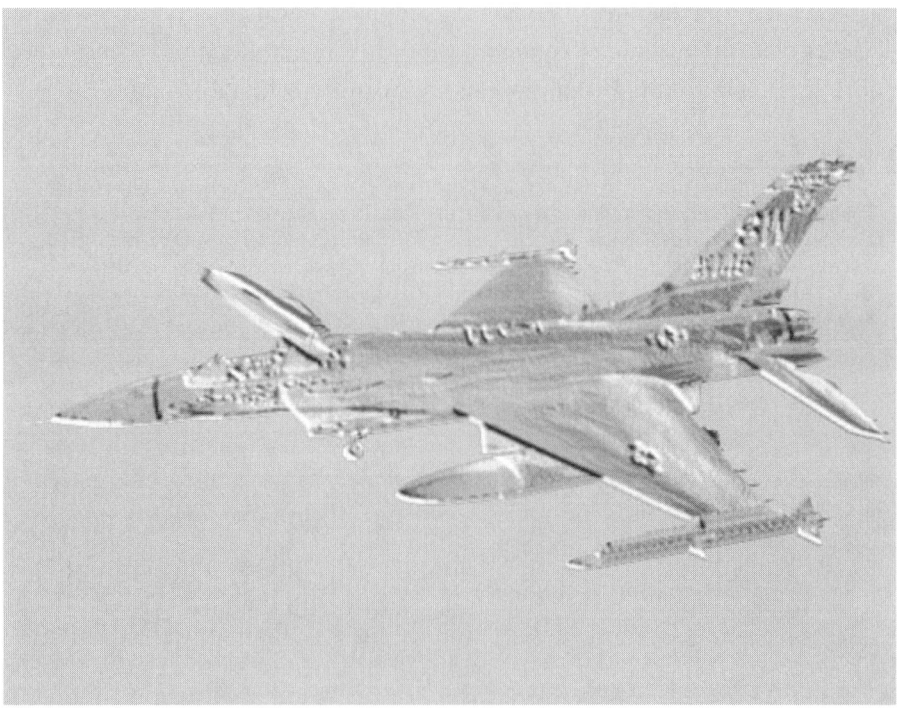

Figure 14.11 A Photoshop effect applied to a rendered image in Render Effects. This particular filter, Emboss, works best for still imagery because it was designed for still effects in Photoshop. For best results with 2D filters in animation, use Premiere filters instead.

As mentioned earlier in this section, one of the easiest techniques to first learn in MAX is setting up a camera. However, many animators simply don't follow any one technique consistently enough to document. There are several guidelines to follow when setting up a camera. By following some sort of guideline, you develop or fine-tune your technique until you're satisfied with one that consistently works for you.

Framing

Framing is how you position and aim your camera so that your subject is within your camera's *viewing plane* or *frame*. When directors want something to be in-frame, they are indicating that they want the object to be within the area viewed by the camera.

MAX offers some useful tools for determining what's in-frame and what's not. With MAX's *safe frames*, you size all the safe-frame regions to their own independent values.

Plus you mask out the area outside the outer-most safe frame, called Live Area. Figure 14.12 shows safe frames, combined with safe-frame masking, at a 70mm aspect ratio. The result is that the Titanic model is framed properly for the "float-by."

Note
If you're not familiar with the term "safe frame," it's a fairly easy concept to understand. Broadcast images are viewed on all sorts of televisions and monitors. Depending on the manufacturer and quality of the viewing device, the viewable area can differ. Most consumer-grade televisions tend to crop as much as an inch of the outer portion of the outer image because of the way they are designed. To prevent you, as an animator, from designing your scene in this non-safe area, use the Safe Frames feature in MAX.

Figure 14.12 Using safe frames and safe-frame masking for a wide aspect-ratio shot. Notice that the scene isn't visible outside of the "Rendered Frame," (outer) safe-frame region. The outer frame represents the live area, the middle is Title Safe, and the inner is Action Safe. Note that you can also specify an additional User Safe area.

Basic Framing

Simple framing involves properly positioning and aiming your camera so that your subject is in-frame, or at least poised to come in-frame during the animation. When framing your scene in MAX, always use safe frames if you intend to go to video. If you're not going to video, you can still use safe frames as a guide to make sure the action or subject is in a consistent location for an animation.

For veteran computer animators, it's second nature to use Transform gizmos to position a camera and its target. However, MAX incorporates buttons in the interface's lower right corner, providing the necessary commands for controlling a camera. Note that a camera viewport must be active for these buttons to appear. If you're familiar with these buttons, then this is a good time to explore by using the new Expert mode for your camera viewport. With this mode, you can manipulate your camera or target through keyboard shortcuts as well as the Transform type-in dialog box.

Compositing-Based Framing

Composite framing is similar to simple framing. The difference is that you frame your virtual scene based on matchable live footage. The footage (moving or not) is sensitive to the camera's position in relation to the background image. The camera's position must be similar to the real camera that photographed the real scene. As mentioned earlier, use Camera Matching for this particular operation, particularly where precision is necessary. Just remember that you need the proportions of the real photographed scene to match up your virtual scene. Figure 14.13 shows Camera Matching against a background to produce the illusion of new office buildings in an empty lot.

Figure 14.13 Camera matching 3D buildings against an image of a site. Using points measured from the actual site in the photograph, Camera Matching computes the original camera perspective. It then applies that setting to your scene's camera for accurate compositing.

Shot Angles

Shot angles, much like focal effects, dramatically change the way the audience perceives your scene. Shot angles are usually set up so that the intended subject (or point of interest) is obvious. With animation, you have the flexibility of moving your camera into position over a series of frames. As a result, the subject gradually comes into frame—not only making the audience aware of what they should see, but also building anticipation of what they're about to see.

Traditional Angles

Traditional shot angles include the obvious. Place the camera head-on with the subject (or slightly off) to exaggerate the subject's size or location in relation to the surroundings. A typical camera angle is shown in Figure 14.14. It's an aircraft carrier's flight deck, taken from the ship's bow.

Figure 14.14 A "typical camera" angle of an aircraft carrier's flight deck. The bridge is the intended subject, with the cannon on the right in the frame simply for dramatic effect.

Unusual Angles

Sometimes there's a need to grossly exaggerate your subjects through intense camera angles and focal-length effects. Perhaps you want to make a baby appear as a giant or a short underpass as a tunnel to infinity. Rather than modeling a scene to mimic these effects, use unusual camera angles instead. Figure 14.15 demonstrates what an unusual camera angle does to a close-up of the ship's bridge.

Figure 14.15 An unusual camera angle makes the ship's bridge appear more dramatic. Using steep camera angles produces an exaggerated effect.

Real-World Scene Lighting

In the real world, lighting takes on many different forms from many different sources. Photographers have numerous options for lighting their scene. Probably one of the most interesting things about photographic lighting is that it rarely involves the available light. This is not just because the film cannot properly expose without a certain amount of light. Photographers often need to change both the location and the color of their light to properly illuminate the subject.

With MAX, there is no film, so you aren't constrained by the limitations of exposure or color reproduction. However, proper lighting placement and color certainly make a difference in the final rendered image. Animators rarely rely on just the default pure-white Omni light to illuminate their scene. They usually employ a mixture of varying intensities and colors, rather than one or two lights of the same intensity and color.

In this section, you get a chance to see real-world light examples and how to best duplicate them within MAX. While there is not always a direct one-to-one correlation, you can usually get strikingly similar results.

Studio Lights

Studio lights are standard lights, such as floodlights and Spot lights. Depending on the subject, combinations of lights are used in various locations and with varied brightness. Note that you can duplicate most studio-style lighting effects within MAX.

Direct Lighting

Direct lighting involves aiming one light (usually a Spot light) from the side of the scene. Direct light often produces dramatic shadows that actually become an essential component of the scene itself.

With MAX, direct lighting is duplicated using a Free or a Target Spot light. Most users prefer target spots because they're much easier to aim. Use shadow maps with them, because raytraced shadows are just too harsh. For a more diffused effect, increase the sample range of the Spot light. This produces softer-edged shadows.

> **Tip**
> It's important to remember that shadow maps use RAM and need an adequate amount allocated to get the best shadows. Start with a value that matches your horizontal rendering resolution. If you need more space, add 100-value increments until the shadow renders to your satisfaction. Avoid going over 1000, unless you have ample RAM.

NEW TO R3
With MAX, all lights are capable of *Inverse Square Decay* or *natural light falloff*. Lights in your scene that use this feature look more natural. However, Inverse Square Decay is a constant equation that's based on the light's intensity, rather than computer-generated attenuation ranges. This means that the light falls off more rapidly than you may expect. If you turn on Inverse Square attenuation and your scene turns excessively dark,

gradually increase the multiplier on your light sources until the light is at a suitable level. MAX R3 allows you to specify the exact point to start the falloff calculation. The parameter, labeled "Start," is located in the Falloff Type pull-down menu in the Attenuation Parameters section of any standard MAX light. Figure 14.16 shows one spotlight used to illuminate the subject.

Figure 14.16 Direct lighting being used to illuminate the subject. Notice the harsh dark side of the teapot.

Fill Lights

Fill lights lessen the effect of harsh shadows produced by a direct-light source. In Figure 14.16, the shadows from the spotlight effectively darken one side of the teapot. If you want to simulate light as it's reflected, use an Omni light with shadow casting turned on. Be sure that it contains a high sample range to diffuse the shadows. However, you probably won't want to use the Inverse Square Decay this time because it leads to large multiplier values. These values, in turn, produce unnaturally large specular highlights on reflective surfaces. Figure 14.17 demonstrates what happens when you add a fill light to a setup similar to the one in Figure 14.16. The image's darker areas are now brightened with the harsh shadow areas better illuminated.

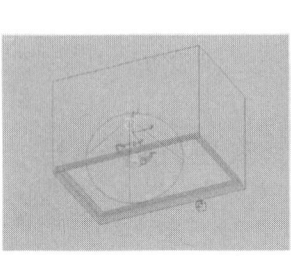

Figure 14.17 Using a fill light to eliminate darker areas of an image.

Lighting Areas Other Than the Subject

Filmmakers and photographers often rely on bounced light to provide certain lighting effects when shooting a scene, especially when trying to simulate natural light.

MAX is incapable of automatically reproducing bounced light, without the addition of specialized radiosity rendering products (such as Lightscape). However, you can simulate bounced light effects. The most common way to bounce light around is not to actually bounce it, but to exclude objects from receiving light from a light source. For instance, to illuminate a back wall with a Spot light without directly affecting the scene's objects, exclude them from receiving light. Then, to make it appear as if bounced light illuminates the back side of the object, use an Omni light that excludes the wall. Figure 14.18 demonstrates this technique.

Note

Lightscape, from Discreet, produces accurate radiosity renderings. If you're striving for accurate lighting based on real-world light information, explore Lightscape. However, if you want simulated radiosity, Luma Object from Cebas (www.cebas.com) does the trick by using standard MAX lights.

Chapter 14: Cameras, Camera Effects, and Lighting 563

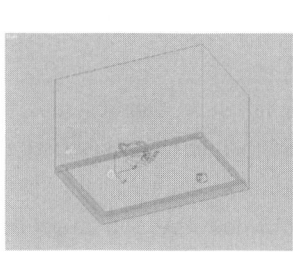

Figure 14.18 Using several lights to simulate bounced light in an indirect-lighting setup.

Flashes

Flashes are typically used to provide instant illumination for scenes in which the lighting is insufficient for the photograph. Because this is primarily the film's limitation, it's not an effect that poses a problem for computer animators. Sometimes, however, you need to simulate a camera flash, strobe light, or lightning bolt. MAX simulates two common types of photography flashes—*direct* and *umbrella*—to produce various effects.

Direct Flashes

A direct flash provides direct illumination from the camera itself. It's an aimed flash that casts enough light in front of the camera to illuminate what is in-frame. Direct flashes produce a bright white or bluish light.

Simulating a flash is fairly straightforward. The most common approach is to use a shadow-casting Omni light. Set the light's color to pure white with a slight blue tint, and the Multiplier to 5 (or more). Slightly reducing the Sample Range also produces more hard-edged shadows, but raytraced shadows are probably too harsh for a flash.

If you have a raytraced, reflective surface, use a Spot light instead of an Omni light. This is because the Raytracer reflects the environment around the object. Using an Omni light, your entire scene is lit by the flash—even behind the camera. The reflective surface reflects the intensely illuminated objects behind the camera, resulting in over-blown specular highlights.

Umbrella Flashes

An umbrella flash produces the same type of flash as a direct flash, but diffuses it so that the end result appears less harsh. Specular highlights are not as blown-out, and the whole scene contains a softer, more general illumination.

Simulating an umbrella flash in MAX is similar to producing bounced-light setups. In the real world, umbrella flashes use bounced light to produce their effect, so you need to do the same through Omni lights. Because each reflection diffuses bounced light, shadows are diffused accordingly. Try sample ranges from 10 to 15, and shadow map sizes of 512 to 1024. Once again, if you have reflective surfaces, you may need to use Spot lights instead of Omni lights to avoid unnecessary intense highlights. Figure 14.19 shows a bright Spot light used head-on to simulate a flash from a camera taking the picture.

Figure 14.19 Simulating a flash-photographed image with an intense Spot light coming from nearly the same location as the camera object.

Other Flashes

For strobe lights or lightning, the process is essentially the same. However, for lighting that involves a direct view of the light sources themselves, use a Render Effects effect (such as Glow or Flare) for the proper effect of a lit light source.

Subject Lighting

Depending on the type of subject you're illuminating, use different variations of light types and styles to get the best results. For instance, lighting a room's interior requires multiple floodlights and (perhaps) a direct light on the subject. For illuminating a character, try using a direct light from one side and a dim fill light on the other side to offset the dark shadows. Whatever the case, first determine where you want the attention focused.

For the most accurate realistic lighting in MAX, two features within the lights must be enabled:

- Shadow casting
- Inverse Square Decay

If you use these two functions, you're almost guaranteed to have proper amounts of light in your scene. Shadow casting is almost a must because all light casts some amount of shadow if it intersects with another object. The thing to remember, however, is restraint. Casting shadows uses RAM, so only cast shadows with lights where absolutely needed.

Positioning

Lighting position helps accentuate your subject. Depending on where you place the light, you can evoke different reactions from your audience. The light's type and quality also plays a role in your final rendering. The images in Figure 14.20 demonstrate the same scene and light, with the light in different positions. Note that in the far right image, where light is shining directly into the camera, the Lens Effect Flare module is used for realism.

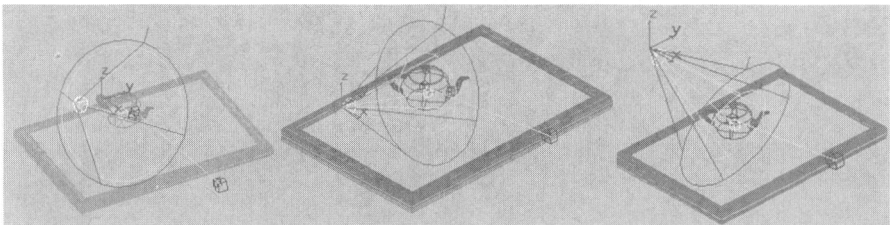

Figure 14.20 Three different light positions enhance different features of the subject. A glow is used on the right-most image to simulate a bright light source.

Dramatic Effects

Dramatic lighting, like unusual camera angles and designed to accentuate certain subject features, is less representative of reality. A common technique is to light a subject from an extreme angle. Rather than the light looking natural, the subject's features (such as edges and contours) are highlighted through intense shadows. If your shadows are too strong or you're losing too much of the frame to darkness, use a nearby fill light that's relatively low in intensity.

Figure 14.21 shows the subject illuminated through dramatic lighting. As you can see, the effects produced by extreme angle lighting makes a difference when you're stressing your subject's topographical features.

Figure 14.21 Dramatic top-down lighting on the subject is used to focus attention on a particular area.

Natural Lighting

Natural lighting is something we encounter every day. Although, as animators, seeing daylight may be infrequent! Light shining through windows and skylights, and direct sunlight are just a sampling of effects that are duplicated in MAX.

Direct Sunlight

Direct sunlight is a challenge to work with, and it's photographed in many different ways. Outdoor photography enjoys the benefit of sunlight as a natural light source, but you frequently have to account for dark, hard-edged shadows with diffusers or fill lights.

When re-creating sunlight, it's best to use a Directional light as your sunlight source because Directional lights cast parallel rays. Although the sun doesn't cast parallel rays, we perceive the rays as parallel. In MAX, *Target Direct* allows you to define a Directional light similar to a Spot light. This takes out most, if not all, of the aiming guesswork.

When creating the light that acts as your sun, remember the time of day in your scene. Some animators like to use the Sunlight system when building the sun itself. With the Sunlight system, you automatically create a sun source, based on the time of day, year, and physical location of your scene. One effect that's not automatically taken into account in MAX is the sun's color (based on the time of day). Actual sunrays pass through varying amounts of atmosphere. The sun is brightest about midday whereas it appears as a deep reddish-orange during dawn and dusk hours. Re-creating this is as simple as changing the sunlight source's color.

You probably need to use fill lights as well. Sunlight is extremely bright. As a result, a great deal of light is reflected off various surfaces. Figure 14.22, demonstrates that although sunlight is the primary light source, reflective surfaces on the Lamborghini are illuminated by reflections of the surrounding scene; most notably the windshield.

Figure 14.22 Simulating direct sunlight against an outdoor image's background.

Moonlight

Fortunately, moonlight isn't all that different from sunlight in its properties. The main difference is the color and intensity of the light itself. You still get much of the same reflection of moonlight on surfaces like you do with sunlight, especially when the moon is very bright.

Much like the sun, moonlight changes color (depending on the moon's location in the sky). However, the moon usually turns from an orange-beige color to a bluish-white color, as it reaches mid-sky. Depending on intensity, shadows exist and can be as intense as sunlight shadows.

MAX Lights

People unfamiliar with a renderer's lighting system may be confused at first. Rather than defining lights through wattage and bulb type, lights are defined by RGB color schemes, as well as a host of other options. If you've worked with 3D programs for some time, however, you're right at home with MAX's lighting system. MAX supports just about every option you want—stopping just short of caustics. With a firm grasp of lighting setups, you're ready to explore by using MAX's lighting system to its fullest potential.

Using the Right Light

With MAX, you have five lights from which to choose. Granted, many of the functions contained within them are similar, but each light contains at least one characteristic that makes it unique. The five light types are:

- Omni
- Free Spot
- Target Spot
- Free Directional
- Target Directional

As previously mentioned, MAX lights incorporate two types of attenuation and two types of decay. Attenuation uses a Near-and-Far value. Near Attenuation is designed to control how far from the light source you begin to see the light. Far Attenuation controls the distance at which the lights effect is completely diminished in relation to the source.

Using the Right Attenuation

NEW TO R3   Attenuation is not the best way to control a light's decay for natural lighting. Instead, use the Inverse or Inverse Squared Decay options. Inverse Decay falls off more slowly than Inverse Squared, but is not as close to real life. Recall that Inverse Squared is natural lighting falloff. Inverse gives you similar results with respect to decay, but tapers off less. Use it if your scene is too dark with Inverse Squared.

MAX R3 no longer uses the attenuation parameters to determine the start point of the decay. Instead, the new Start parameter determines this point.

Contrast and Soften Diffuse Edges

You also control lights' effects on contrast within the area where they shine. The Contrast spinner goes from 0 (normal contrast) to 100 percent. The result at 100 percent is a completely "contrasty" image, in which the image appears to be extremely blown-out. Use this feature to your advantage by exaggerating an image's dominant colors and effectively eliminating its more subtle colors. You control where the contrast is overblown (or not) through the light—mimicking real life, which is the main benefit of using it (versus a Render Effects effect). This is more effective and easier to control than applying an effect to the entire image. Softening the Diffuse Edge through the spinner (of the same name) reduces the sharpness of the region, where diffuse and ambient areas meet. At 0, the light produces a normal transition between the ambient and diffuse properties of a surface. At higher values, it eliminates sharp edges that appear under certain harsh-lighting conditions.

Note that both the Contrast and Soften Diffuse Edge spinners affect light's illumination characteristics. While it doesn't actually brighten or darken a light, it alters the way the light is cast. This is noticeable as brightness changes. A simple test is to render a scene with the Light Multiplier at 5, and then another scene with the Contrast at 100. The light looks brighter in each scene, but the results are fundamentally different. This is demonstrated in Figure 14.23.

Figure 14.23 The effect of using multiplier (left) in lights versus the contrast value (right). Note how "overblown" the left image appears, whereas the right image seems to lose subtle shading differences.

Affecting Ambient, Diffuse, and Specular

NEW TO R3

You control whether or not a light affects the ambient, diffuse, or specular characteristics of a surface. A great use for this feature is when you want to use a fill light on an extremely shiny or reflective surface. If the light is intended to be diffuse, switch off the Affect Specular feature. That way, you get the nice general lighting of a fill light, without the characteristics of reflecting the light source in the surface's specular area.

With MAX R3, the Ambient Only check box determines the affect of a rendered surface's ambient component. This check box turns off the Diffuse and Specular portions, and makes this special light that contributes only to the scene's ambient level.

Omni Lights

Omni lights work well for fill lights. When used with Inverse Square Attenuation and Shadow Casting, the results are quite realistic. One caution about Omni lights—especially when using Multiplier values larger than 1—highly reflective surfaces not only reflect the light, but they also reflect the effect of any nearby surface's light. This nearly doubles the intensity and size of your specular highlight. If you encounter this situation, try using a Spot light with a wide Hotspot/Falloff setting. That way the light is cast in only one direction, effectively eliminating the problem.

Spot Lights

Spot lights, both Target and Free, are useful for directing light and shadows in a specific direction. Spot lights were the original shadow-casting light in the 3D Studio series, so many people are accustomed to using them expressly for that purpose. The effect of shadows is useful, but you now need to determine if the situation requires an Omni light or a Spot light. Spot lights work well as direct lights. Because their area of illumination is constrained within the light's cone, you avoid any messy light spillovers that occur with an Omni light. Spot lights are quite effective when used with Projector maps (more on these later).

Directional Lights

Directional lights, both Target and Free, function similarly to Spot lights in many ways. The primary difference between the two light sources is that Directional lights cast rays in a parallel direction; a Spot light's rays are conical. You typically use Directional lights for outdoor scenes (with objects such as sunlight), where rays and shadows are typically portrayed as parallel. When Directional lights are used with a Projector map, however, a scene is quickly illuminated—as if multiple lights were in the room.

> **Tip**
> Remember that you can animate the attenuation of a Directional light. This means that other effects (such as laser shots) are finished more easily when you combine the light with volumetric atmospheric effects.

Shadow Color and Density

NEW TO R3 Perhaps one of the most significant features to appear in MAX R3 is the ability to control the color and density of shadow maps. Granted, there were ways to do this in the past (through map size settings and raytrace materials), but now you can alter these two properties without having to massage other features of MAX. This also means that you can achieve effects (such as simulated caustics and shadow falloff) by using a map instead of a solid color for the gradient.

Unlike a Shadow map, the Shadow Color and Shadow Color map only affect the appearance of the projected shadow from objects that the light illuminates. When using a Shadow Color map, it's a good idea to have a light source for each object onto which you project the map. The reason is that the map is projected, based on the created shadow and the angle between the light source and the object. This works well if your scene's objects are the same shape and material properties; however, this is rarely the case. In the instance of Figure 14.24, a Radial Gradient map in the Shadow Color map slot creates the caustic effect. If another object (such as a cylinder) is in the scene, add a specific light source with its own Shadow Color map that better displays the cylinder's caustic characteristics.

Figure 14.24 A Shadow Color map creates the caustic highlight on the floor surface. Shadow Color maps allow you to specify colors and shapes to your shadow, independent of light color and characteristics.

Simulating Real-World Lighting Effects

When you mimic the real world, one of the most important aspects to consider is the proper type and amount of lighting. However, this doesn't mean that you must build your lighting model exactly as it occurs in real life. Doing so has the potential to bring even the most tricked-out PC to its knees. As a matter of fact, you can often duplicate real-life lighting with fewer light sources than required in the real world. This is demonstrated by the simple caustic effect in Figure 14.24.

Take an example of an office space that's illuminated by several fluorescent in-ceiling lights. A common technique is to project an image of several lights: Soft-edged rectangles through a Spot or Directional light. The end effect is light that's believable but by no means similar to its real-life counterpart.

Take this scene a step further and use another light from the bottom of the scene to cast a light with similar color to your floor's surface color. This produces an effect similar to radiosity, albeit faked. An example of this is shown in Figure 14.25.

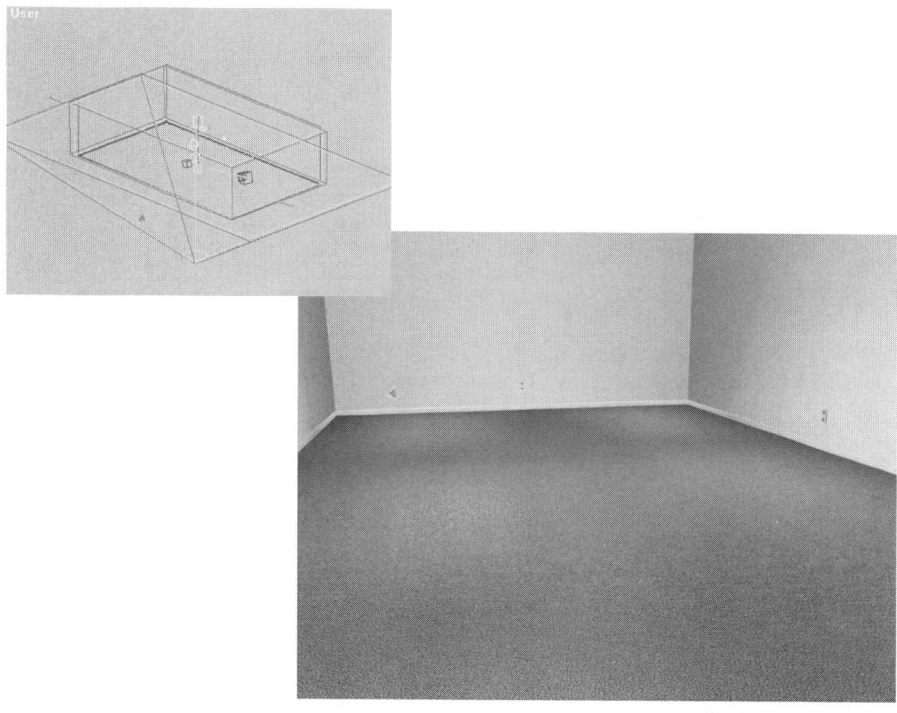

Figure 14.25 A projector-mapped light illuminates a room, as well as another light to produce a reflected light on the walls near the floor.

Lighting Techniques

There are literally hundreds of different techniques for illuminating your scene. A whole book could be devoted to just demonstrating lighting options. While it is not possible to cover all lighting techniques here, there are some hard-and-fast techniques that work well.

Building Up Your Light

A common mistake is to pound all the lights you think you need right into a scene. This might work if you consistently build similar scenes and have discovered a lighting method that consistently works best for you. Since most animators build and work with all sorts of different scenes, there is often little commonality between lighting setups.

Many users start lighting a scene without considering the materials they intend to use. Instead, they rely on MAX's default coloring system for a sense of surface properties. This technique rarely works in the end, though. Your lighting typically changes when you assign the actual material that you intend to use. Usually, it's best to first assign your initial (first draft) materials before you begin with your actual lighting design. Then you can tweak materials in conjunction with the lights, until your scene looks right. Of course, some animators find other methods that work best for them.

When your scene involves multiple light sources, start by introducing one light source at a time. It's usually best to start with lighting the subject by its primary light source. Once you add a light, render the scene. This way, you can check that the light is positioned properly and that its settings (such as color and intensity) are correct. Then add another light source. Each time, you render and check the effect on your scene. Note that you may need to return and adjust some light intensities that you set up earlier. Turn off all other lights if you're trying to compare the effect of two or more lights on an area of your scene. That way, you can properly judge the lights involved and their effect on the scene.

Light Colors

Most of the light that we encounter is tinted with a color. Indoor lighting (especially fluorescent lighting) is usually perceived as white, whereas incandescent lights are perceived as a bright beige color. Note that this is the *perceived* color if you are outside looking in. If you stare into a building at night that is illuminated by fluorescent lights, they appear to be more bluish-green. This is due to the colors your eye perceives, based on the light entering it. Remember: Even at night there is light entering your eye. As a result this affects the color of the lights you see. If your set-up light doesn't look right, observe the same light design in the real world—closely observe it. Your brain knows that the light is white, but what do you actually see?

When setting up lights, color is always a critical factor. White light rarely works for all situations. MAX provides you with a default light of 255 in the R, G, and B channels. This is designed as a quick way to illuminate your scene. However, don't rely on it as your sole color for illuminating your scene. If your scenes look flat, try varying the color and intensity of your lights so that colors you want to accentuate stand out and other colors are muted. A blue surface completely absorbs all red and green light, and reflects the blue to the viewer's eye, in this case, the rendered image. Thus, a light shining on a blue object must contain some blue for the object to appear anything except black.

Lighting Options

When deciding how to illuminate your scene, you must first consider several points. If you know the types of materials that you want to use for a scene, then you're one step closer. If not, determine the types and colors of the materials you intend to use. In an environment where you don't design the materials or you simply can't assign the materials, assign a wireframe color to the object (one that most closely represents what the material looks like). You probably need to tweak the lighting once the actual material is assigned because sometimes you can't account for such effects as reflectivity or bumpiness. At least it's less work than not assigning a similar object color from the color swatch at all.

When your model and your materials (or a close representation of them) is ready, then determine what type of lighting option you want.

Balanced Light

Balanced light is simply a lighting option that involves the usage of multiple light sources to evenly illuminate a scene. Essentially, this option works well for illuminating space (such as a room) that doesn't contain a particular spot where you intend to focus the audience.

Use a combination of fill and direct lights to evenly illuminate your scene. Balanced light typically involves many rendering passes to get it right. For the best effect, make sure there are no "hot-spots" (overly-lit areas) or shadow spots. A nice, even light covers the entire scene evenly.

Large Room Lighting

Because Inverse Squared Decay is the usual method to illuminate a larger room, you may need to illuminate the room in a way that involves more light sources than usual. The previously mentioned technique of using less lights (in favor of more Omni lights) doesn't usually work unless the light is cast in some sort of pattern for easy duplication in a 2D image.

Large room lighting first requires that you set up the room with its normal lighting. This is typically darker than is acceptable. You have two options at this point. You can either:

- Increase the normal lighting of the room via multipliers. Note that you can globally increase the lighting through the Global Lighting setting (located in the Environment dialog box).

- Add lights that emanate from around the camera and point towards the camera's POV. The lights themselves don't need full brightness, just make them bright enough to properly illuminate your subject.

Profile Lighting

Profile lighting is typically used for dramatic effects on profiles of characters. Profile lighting either completely darkens a subject against a very bright or white light or lights a subject through unusual angles (as discussed earlier).

The technique of illuminating a subject from behind and having the profile cast a shadow onto a surface introduces a whole new topic: translucency. Translucency is a function of the Raytrace material (see Note). By applying a translucent material to a thin surface (such as a box with 0 height) you accurately reproduce the effect of a projected shadow profile. Simply aim a shadow-casting light source at your surface and place the profiled object somewhere between the light and the projected surface. Figure 14.26 shows how Raytrace material simulates the effects of translucency, which is needed for realistic profile lighting.

Note

Translucency is the amount of light transmitted through an object. A lit candle illuminates the wax near the flame. As the distance between the candle stem and the flame's location increases, the amount of light transmitted through the wax diminishes. So, the correlation between the thickness of a surface and the amount of translucency determines how much light actually passes through it. Light takes on the tint of a surface as it passes through it.

With Raytrace material, you simulate the effect of translucency through a color or a map. The map color controls the tinted color in a translucent surface.

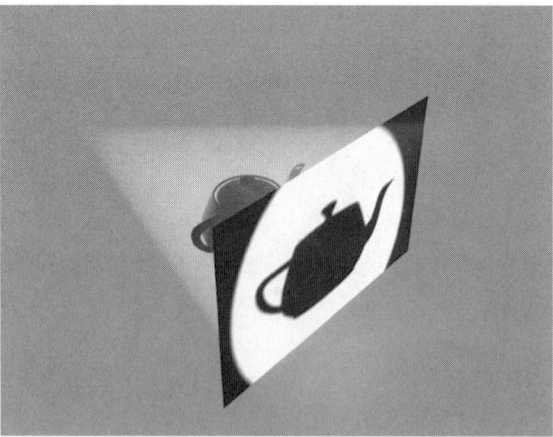

Figure 14.26 Using a translucent Raytrace material to reproduce a profile light setup.

Interior Lighting Simulations

Many times a light source is somewhere in-frame. In such cases, you need to create the proper material and light. You want the proper post-process effect (such as Flare or Glow) to best simulate a light type. This section describes two common lighting simulations: daylight and interior light or light fixtures. It doesn't cover, however, setting up the right material or post effect. For more information on setting up light effects via a material or post process effect, please see Chapter 11, "Designing Fictional and Special Effects Materials" or Chapter 15, "Glows and Lens Flares."

Simulating Daylight

Simulating daylight requires that you know from where the outdoor light is coming. Because this is obviously a fictional outdoor light source, you have three possible situations:

- The point at which the light is entering the room is in-frame.
- The point at which the light is entering the room is out of frame.
- The point at which the light is entering the room is both in-frame and out of frame.

In any of the preceding situations, the perceived light entering the room is often a different color that what is perceived outside, so make appropriate color adjustments. For instance, sunlight entering a room when the point of entry is in-frame is often perceived more brightly or more intensely than it actually is. This is mainly due to the major illumination differences between inside and outside.

If the point of entry is out of frame, you have free reign with the light's intensity. You can also use Projector maps to fake the projection of blinds (or other objects) blocking the daylight's point of entry. Figure 14.27 shows how easy it is to simulate morning light breaking through a kitchen window just by using a projector-mapped Spot light and a fill light to reduce the darker areas.

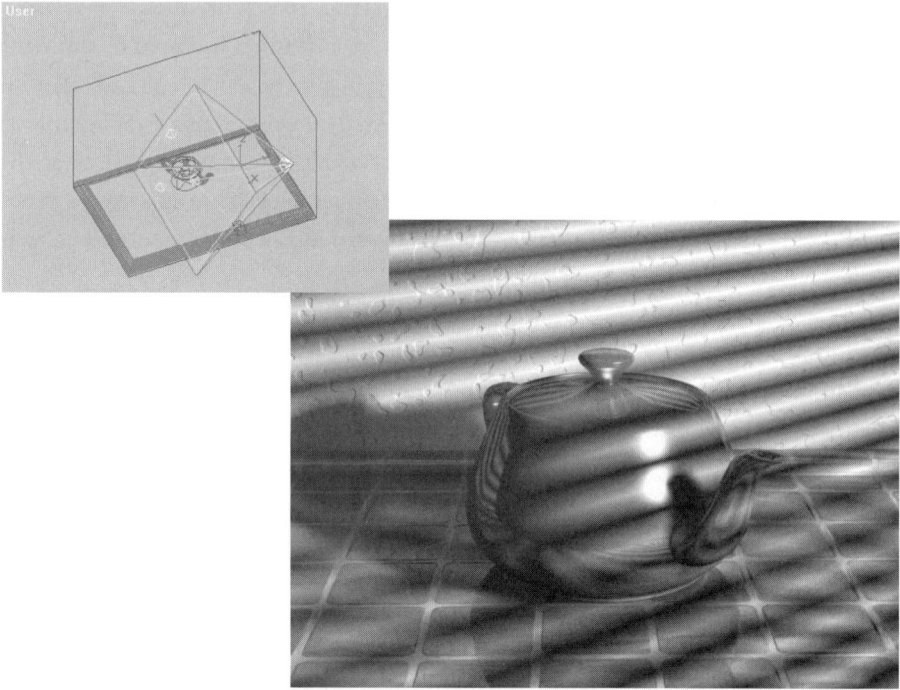

Figure 14.27 Using a projector-mapped Spot light to simulate light coming through the blinds of a kitchen window.

Simulating Light Fixtures

The light casting portion of a light fixture is represented in many ways. For example, examine a lamp with a lampshade. Creating interior lighting is always a challenge. However, with some key features in MAX, this is much easier.

First, the lampshade is open at both ends. Start by placing a shadow-casting Omni light near the intended source. This ensures that the lampshade is properly illuminated. You may get away with two aimed Spot lights here; one aimed up and the other aimed down. If you're cramped for RAM, this may be a better choice. Two Shadow maps calculated at rendering time versus six, from an Omni light, buys some RAM for other things—like maps. This is especially true if you have a number of these situations in your scene. Shadow-casting Omni lights are great, but they do consume a ton of RAM.

With Translucency, a realistically lit lampshade is easily mimicked. Because the light is not actually transmitted (but rather simulated as transmitted) you are still required to add another light source that doesn't cast shadows to illuminate the space. Simply place an Omni light at the same location as the "real" light source, but exclude the lamp and lampshade from illumination and shadow casting. Figure 14.28 demonstrates this functionality.

Figure 14.28 A lampshade, illuminated by using a translucent Raytrace material. The intensity of the light passing through the lampshade is dependent upon the light location, brightness, and density of the object through which it's passing.

All-in-all, interior lighting is fairly easy in MAX. All the controls discussed in this chapter greatly increase the realism of your rendered images and animations.

In Practice: Cameras, Camera Effects, and Lighting

- **Traditional camera types, terminology, and techniques.** Take those traditional concepts and apply them to MAX cameras. Traditional camera methods are easily reproducible and tend to generate the most realistic rendering effects, especially when combined with careful lighting.

- **Special lighting techniques and how to best simulate real-world setups.** With the lighting capabilities of MAX, setting up lights is not all that painful, but it still requires close attention to get it "just right." Focus on using attenuation and proper color to achieve better renderings.

- **Use Render Effects even when it's not obvious to simulate renderings that use a specific f-stop or film speed.** With the right effect, nearly every photographic effect is simulated within MAX.

Chapter 15

Glows and Lens Flares

Simulated lens flares, glows, and highlights have long been a part of computer graphics. In many ways, they help us support the "reality" of the scene by adding effects that our eyes perceive in our daily lives. Oddly enough, some of the effects generated by the Lens Effects module are usually considered undesirable artifacts in traditional filmmaking or photography.

NEW TO R3

With MAX R3, all the lens effects that were featured as independent modules are now consolidated into the new Render Effects feature. This feature is located in the Rendering pull-down menu. This chapter takes you through simulating various effects using the Flares and Glow features of Lens Effects. Covered effects include the following:

- Applying glows to neon signs
- Using glows for backlighting effects
- Using the Raytracer with glows
- Using flare effects for a sunrise effect

In MAX R3, the way you add Lens Effects is different from past versions. You no longer add several entries in Video Post to generate a glow, flare, or highlight. Those elements now exist as a single entry in the Render Effects dialog. Figure 15.1 shows the new interface for Lens Effects in the Render Effects dialog, along with a few added entries. Render Effects are a post-process applied to a rendering. They allow for interactive updates of items such as color balance, brightness and contrast, as well as flares and glows.

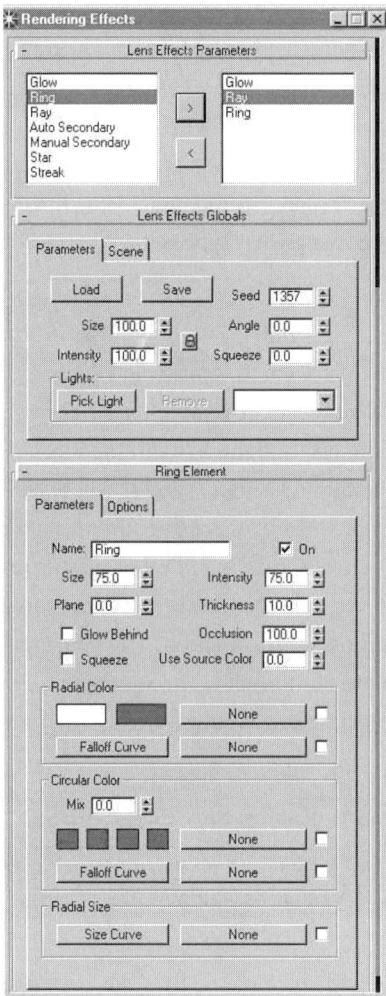

Figure 15.1 The new Lens Effects interface, as part of the Rendering Effects feature in MAX R3. You no longer use Video Post to achieve special lens effects.

Natural Glow and Flare Causes

Glows and camera lens flares are often caused by our perception—that is, the way we view a subject. For instance, if you look at the sun (don't do this, by the way), you perceive to see rays and an intense glow around it. However, if you look at the sun through a camera, you perceive the sun to have sharper rays along with small disc-like halos, called *lens reflections*. In actuality, the sun looks much different up-close-and-personal. It doesn't appear the same when perceived from Earth at all.

Light emanating from a source reflected in the lens elements of a camera causes flares. Flares are actually composed of several elements, one being the lens reflection. The number of reflections is dependent upon the number of elements in the camera lens itself. (Chapter 14 discusses several lens types, as well as the number of elements within each lens.) Other components of a lens flare (such as star, ring, and rays) are dependent on the light source's intensity and its location within the frame of the camera. Lens Effects makes it easy to duplicate flare effects. The trick is knowing what type of flare you want or what camera effect you're trying to simulate.

Bright-light sources illuminating an object's surface creates glows. The glow varies in size and shape depending on the surface type and the light source's intensity. Furthermore, atmospheric conditions affect your perception of a glow. For instance, a car's chrome bumper has an intense glowing halo if illuminated by bright lights. That same bumper appears to be just chrome in normal or dimmer light. Sunlight is an example where perception of glows depends on the atmospheric conditions. For instance, the sun on a hazy day appears with a large glow around it, whereas its glow is tighter and more intense on a clear day. Glows are perceived at the source as well. Lens reflections happen at the camera lens, but a glow occurs at the source object in almost every situation. The Glow feature in Lens Effects accounts for this, but it also allows you to glow the source in a 2D fashion—the glow is not occluded by objects that block the light source's rays.

Note

In MAX R2, there was a separate module called Glow. In MAX R3, Glow is part of the main Lens Effects feature that serves dual purposes: One as a general glow, and the other as a glow for use in a typical lens flare. If you wish to just add a glow to a scene, first add a Lens Effects entry to the Render Effects queue, and then configure the settings as you normally would in MAX R2.

Glows based on reality rely heavily on the intensity and color of the light source itself. For instance, a bright white light, such as a car's headlight, produces a more intense glow than a cool, blue, backlit sign. In either case, to get the proper glow effect you must alter the color, density, size, and softness of the glow. See Figure 15.2.

There are so many aspects that affect how we perceive subjects in real life. In the upcoming sections, you learn how to mimic our real-world perception of glows and flares, using the Lens Effects Glow and Flare elements.

Figure 15.2 Examples of naturally occurring lens flares and glows. The image on the left has a strong but undefined glow, mainly caused by haze in the summer sun. The right-hand image has a crisp, defined glow and flare, caused by better atmospheric conditions. The same camera took both images.

Glow-Keying Elements: Sources

The Glow function of Lens Effects is a great way to glow geometry rather than light sources, which are Flare's specialty. The secret to making a glow look correct, however, is to key off of the right elements. MAX allows you to key your glow off one of several components—or *sources*—within a scene. In this section we explore the common elements from which to key, as well as why to use them. Figure 15.3 shows the Source Select area of the Glow interface.

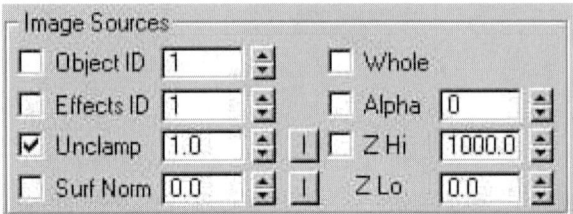

Figure 15.3 The Source Selection area in the Lens Effects Glow function. In MAX R3, this is in the Rendering Effects dialog box (found in the Rendering pull-down menu).

Glowing Objects

Glow allows you to glow objects based on the object (or *G-Buffer*) ID. The main benefit of glowing objects based on their ID is that you can easily select one of several *whole* objects to glow. Pick and choose the exact objects to glow through the G-buffer ID assignment. Through G-buffer ID assignment, glows are occluded by other geometry. For Glow using G-Buffer assignment, the most common problem is that G-Buffer data is not passed behind objects using fully or semi-transparent materials. This means that if your glowing object passes behind a pane of glass, the object renders but the glow disappears. There is a solution for this, however, through the X-ray plug-in from Digimation. X-ray allows G-Buffer data to pass through transparent geometry. An example of X-ray is shown in Figure 15.4.

Glowing specific objects works for most situations. An example of where you use an object as your keying source is a neon sign. The sign itself is a piece of geometry that prevents you from using the Flare element for two reasons:

- Although Flare contains a glow within it, you only glow light sources.
- The glow effect in Flare is circular (except when using Squeeze; then it is oval). This means that you cannot produce a glow that adheres to the contours of the neon sign.

Most neon tubing color is constant. If it isn't, then consider using a glow based on a Material Effects ID (discussed in the next section).

Chapter 15: Glows and Lens Flares 589

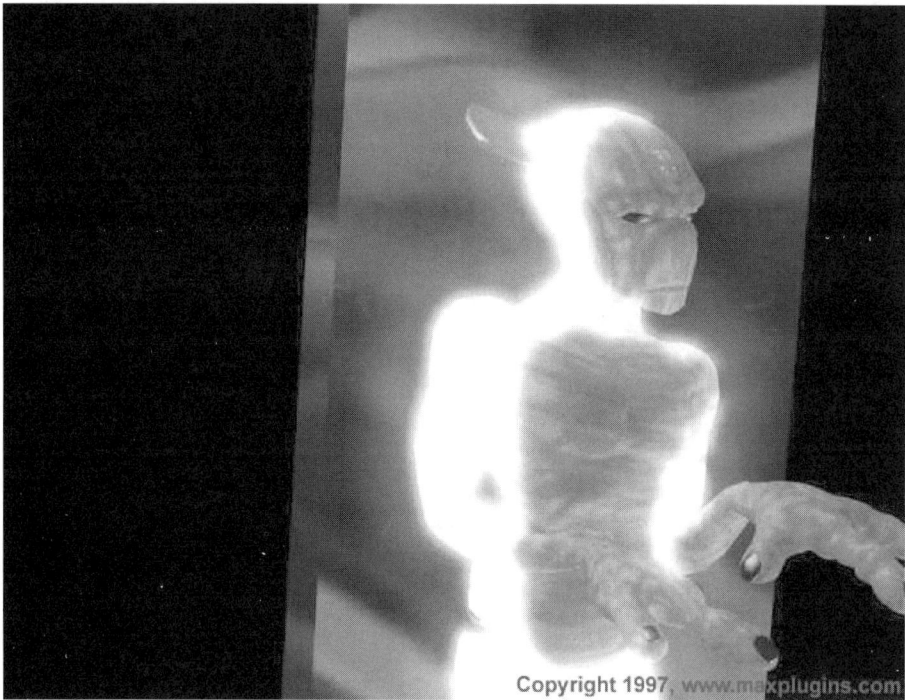

Figure 15.4 An example of Glow with X-ray. Since the G-Buffer data doesn't pass through transparent objects, the X-ray plug-in is employed (to use Object IDs as sources).

Exercise 15.1 Glowing Neon on a Diner Sign

1. Load 15max01.max.
2. Render the Perspective viewport.
3. Notice how the neon tube around the sign is assigned a self-illuminated material. A pink Omni light is also used, creating the appearance of the neon tube emitting light on the sign's post. To glow the neon tube, change its Object G-buffer ID. First select the Pink spline that runs around the edges of the sign.
4. Select the spline, then right-click it. Choose Properties.
5. In the G-Buffer Object Channel field, enter 1. Click OK.
6. Choose Rendering/Effects, then click the Add button. Select Lens Effects, and check Interactive. The scene automatically updates.

7. Double-click the Glow element on the left to add a glow to the scene. Then click the Lens Effects Globals title bar to collapse it (you don't need to alter those parameters for this exercise).

8. Click the Options tab of the Glow element, and set the Object ID to 1. Notice that the Glow is too soft and not the proper color.

9. Click the Parameters tab. Set the Size to 1.5 and Intensity to 30. Every time you type in a value, the rendering changes.

10. Try typing in different values for Size and Intensity until you find one you like. Size 0.4 and Intensity 200 produces an image similar to Figure 15.5.

11. Set the Use Source Color to 100, and notice the rendering.

The end result is a neon tube with a nice subtle glow on it. In succeeding exercises, you learn how to make the sides of the reflective sign glow as well. The final rendering from this exercise is shown in Figure 15.5.

Note
Lens Effects sizes are based on the rendered pixel size. The specified values in the exercise may not work for the same scene rendered at a larger resolution. Often you need to adjust the size parameter (at least) if you render to a different resolution. Figure 15.5, for instance, has the Glow size reduced to 1.0 in order to produce the same look (at 640 × 480 as 320 × 240).

Figure 15.5 The final rendering from Exercise 15.1. Notice that the glow is not lavishly intense—just enough to indicate that the neon tubing is illuminated.

Glowing Material Effects Channels

Glow also allows you to glow objects via the Material Effects channel. In the Material Editor, you assign a material or Sub-Object material a specific channel, from 0 to 15. The Material Effects Channel Assigment area is shown in Figure 15.6.

The main benefit of glowing materials over objects is that you don't necessarily glow the entire object. Many advanced materials contain several material definitions through, say, a Multi/Sub-Object material. With a glow based on a Material Effects channel, you choose the elements to have the added effect.

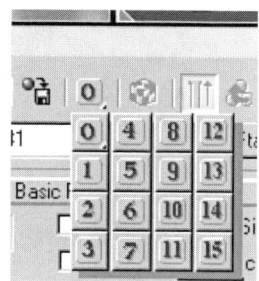

Figure 15.6 The Material Effects Channel Assignment area of the Material Editor. Use it to assign Material Effects channels to any material in your scene. Note that you can use up to 16 Material Effects channels in one scene.

A more subtle benefit of glowing through a Material Effects channel is that you also glow reflections of materials, using the Raytrace material/map. The Raytrace map is capable of transmitting Effects channels in reflections or refractions. As a result, the glow now occurs in areas of your rendering that were previously impossible.

In the next exercise, you learn how to glow the neon tube in Exercise 15.1's diner sign and the sign's chrome frame.

Exercise 15.2 Using Material Effects Channels with Glow

1. Load 15max02.max.
2. Click the Material Editor button or press M on the keyboard.
3. Click the first (upper-left) sample slot with the Pink Neon material in it.
4. Click the Material Effects Channel button, and set the Channel Number ID to 1.
5. Now that the Neon material is defined with a channel of 1, you set that as your source within the Glow element. Select Rendering/Effects.
6. Click the Lens Effects entry, and check Interactive.
7. Click the Glow element within Lens Effects. Select the Options tab.
8. Clear the Object ID checkbox, and check Effects ID. Notice the updated rendering window.

Your neon tubing is still glowing, but so is its reflection in the frame of the sign! That's because the Raytrace material, discussed in Chapter 8, reflects a material's Effects ID. Try experimenting with different size and color settings. Notice that using different colors produces different glows *in* the reflection. When you're done, render out the sequence to .AVI or to a real-time playback device to see the results. Figure 15.7 shows the completed result.

Figure 15.7 The final rendering from Exercise 15.2. Although it is similar to the final output of Exercise 15.1, you now see the glow occurring on the reflection of the neon tube. This is due to using Material Effects IDs instead of Object IDs for sources.

Glowing Unclamped Colors

Unclamped colors represent the pixels in your rendered image that are brighter than pure white. MAX always renders images at 64-bits, but displays them at 24-bits. Other information: Unclamped color values, Object ID, Material Effects ID, Z-buffer, and more may be stored within the image, but MAX does not display it unless told to do so. Unclamped color values are used more within MAX, thanks to the higher maximum values of the Standard or Raytrace material. The Raytrace material benefits most from the fact that MAX's Glossiness and Specular Level settings are unclamped to values of 200 and unlimited, respectively. Metals and glass are more realistic as a result. And, as of R3, MAX's Standard material has Specular Level values up to 999. This allows materials not based on the Raytrace material to also glow (based on unclamped values).

NEW TO R3 In MAX R1.x, an intense light would create an intense specular highlight and usually caused a small glow on an object's surface. Using the Unclamped color region in MAX R3, you easily glow these specular areas and other areas that are brighter than pure white.

In the following exercise, you add a subtle-glow effect to the specular highlights of a Martini glass and cocktail shaker. The intense specular highlights are a result of using the Raytrace material.

Exercise 15.3   Glowing Chrome and Glass

1. Load 15max03.max.
2. Choose Rendering/Effects. Click the Lens Effect/Glow element in the Rendering Effects dialog box.
3. Select the Interactive checkbox to render the scene. Apply the glow to the scene.
4. In the Glow element's Options tab, set the Source to Unclamped and the Amount to 1.5.
5. Click the Parameters tab, and set the Effect Size to 1.
6. Change the Intensity from 100 to 66.
7. Click OK to exit the Glow dialog box.
8. Click the Material Editor button in the main toolbar.
9. Click the lower-left material sample, named Glass.
10. Scroll down to the Raytracer Controls section, and click the Options button.
11. Enable the Global Enable Raytrace checkbox.
12. Click the Render Scene button in the main toolbar or click Update Scene in the Render Effects dialog box to see the rendering with both raytrace reflections and refractions with glow.

Exercise 15.3 gives you a chance to see how the Unclamped color region for glows enhances renderings with intense specular highlights. It also shows why the Raytrace material is ideal for creating these intense highlights. Figure 15.8 shows the final rendering from the exercise.

Tip

When using Raytrace materials with glows, turn off the Global Raytrace option before previewing your rendering. This speeds rendering time without eliminating the specular highlights. However, if you need to analyze the effects of raytracing and glows at the same time, turn off global antialiasing in the Raytrace material (as an alternative).

Additional Glowing Source Options

The remaining keys (Alpha, Z Hi/Low, and Surface Normals) make it painless to add glow effects to other areas of your scene or geometry. They complement the more significant glowing source options (G-Buffer ID, Material Effects ID, and Unclamped colors). In this section, you work with some brief examples for using these other keying methods.

Figure 15.8 The final rendering from Exercise 15.3. The specular highlights contain Unclamped colors, for use as sources for glows. This technique gives metals and glass a more natural look under bright-light conditions.

Alpha

The Alpha parameter allows you to glow the image, based on the alpha channel information present in the image. In other words, as the alpha channel approaches 255—fully opaque—the glow has more of an effect. At a setting of 255, the Alpha source glows with full intensity. Lower values result in less intense glows of the alpha channel.

Z Hi/Low

Z Hi/Low allows you to glow a rendered scene, based on Z-depth. Two values, Hi and Low, work together. The difference between them is the area of your rendered scene that is glowed. Z Hi is the maximum distance from the camera, and Z Low is the distance closest to the camera.

Using this option produces a great "scanner" effect. A beam of light appears to pass through a room, illuminating the objects' edges as it crosses over them.

Surface Normals

The Surface Normals option allows you to glow faces of an object in your scene whose normals are within a certain threshold. These normals are determined by the spinner value. Any faces where normal is between the spinner value and 90 degrees is glowed.

This source option works quite effectively on flat surfaces, such as a cut diamond. As the diamond rotates and the flat surfaces are more perpendicular to the camera, they glow more.

Note

This section primarily treats the sources you can glow as exclusive. However, with MAX R3 you can combine any number of these sources to produce more complex glows simply by checking them.

Glow Effect Restrictions and Controls

Using Glow in a scene allows you to communicate brightness. Crucial elements are controlling the amount of glow and where it occurs in the scene. The Glow feature in MAX allows you to constrict the effect of the glow to specific areas of the keyed source. While it isn't essential to constrain the glow, you enhance the realism of your scene by using the glow effect in moderation. In this section, you see how the Glow element allows you to limit the effect and how the limits work. Figure 15.9 shows the Glow function's Filter Options section. (Note that not all options are discussed.)

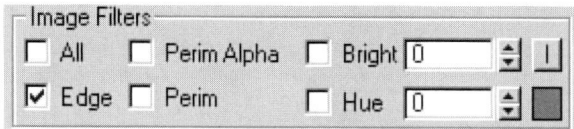

Figure 15.9 The Filter Options section in Glow. Using these settings, you specify where the glow effect occurs on your source.

Glowing the Whole Source: The All Filter

When you use its All filter, the Glow element places the glow effect on the entire source—from the source's center outward. As a result, the effect's size relates to the glow's start at the object's center. This is different from the way other filters work (such as Perimeter).

In Exercise 15.4, you use Glow's All filter and some fine-tuning to better simulate the appearance of fluorescent-light tubes in an office or lab environment.

Exercise 15.4 A Glowing Fluorescent Light Fixture

1. Load 15max04.max.
2. Select Rendering/Effects with Interactive checked. Click the Lens Effects, then Glow.
3. In the Options tab, set the source to Effects ID 1.
4. Make sure All is selected as the filter. At this point, the glow looks too soft. The intensity, color, and size of the glow are wrong. In the next few steps, you change the settings to make the tubes appear to be glowing.
5. Click the Parameters tab.
6. Set the Size of the effect to 1 and Intensity to 100.
7. Click the white color swatch in the Radial Color section, and set it to a deep blue.

At this point the glow looks much better. For further control of the effect, alter the radial color and the falloff. Figure 15.10 shows the completed rendering.

Figure 15.10 The completed light fixture, with a glow added. Not only is Material Effects ID used as a source, but also the Distance Fade options are set so that the glow subsided as the light's tube moves farther from the camera.

Glowing the Perimeter

Glowing the perimeter, either with Perimeter or Perimeter Alpha, gives your keyed source a backlit appearance. This is because the glow effect does not appear on the object, itself, but rather along the edges.

When using either Perimeter or Perimeter Alpha, the Glow element analyzes the specified source and glows just around its edges. Using the Perimeter filter is great for producing backlit signs. It is also used to create halos around geometry or materials. Be aware of a few pitfalls, however, when using the Perimeter options. The first pitfall frequently occurs on scenes without alpha channel information. Alpha channel information is the area of your rendered image that involves transparency.

Perimeter Versus Perimeter Alpha

The difference between the two perimeter options is how they determine where the glow starts. Basically the Perimeter Alpha option uses the alpha channel to determine where the glow starts. Since the alpha channel contains antialiasing information, the glow is also antialiased around your source's edges. The rendered result looks great. However, there are times when your image doesn't contain alpha information or your image is completely opaque (meaning a pure-white alpha channel). Therefore, Glow can't determine where the edges of your source start. This results in an inaccurate or heavily aliased glow.

The Perimeter option is the answer to such problems. While not as precise as Perimeter Alpha, Perimeter provides similar results without relying on alpha information. The main drawback is that the resultant glow is often not the intended effect. So, what to do in this situation?

There is no perfect way around this problem. You can minimize it, however, by tweaking different variables within Glow, to reduce the amount of aliasing around an edge. For instance you can soften the glow effect. If you are using the Gradient color option, reduce the radial transparency near the glow's center by changing the first flag to a dark gray. Then place another, lighter flag somewhere to the left of the first flag. This "Band-Aid" solution works well for animations because still images are often subject to close scrutiny. Just remember that it isn't the perfect solution for all situations.

Working with Backlit Signs

When using either of the Perimeter options for a backlit sign, take care if you plan to view the sign from different angles. This is especially true in an animation. The primary reason is that the glow effect doesn't actually back-light the sign. It simply places a glow around its perimeter. While this works well for most viewing angles, you notice the problem when the view changes to the sign's side. The glow effect appears to glow the entire sign from the side.

Exercise 15.5 shows this problem in a situation where it is more acceptable. You use the same diner sign as before, but glow the "MAX's" portion of the sign, using the Perimeter function.

Exercise 15.5 Glowing the Perimeter of the Logo

1. Load 15max05.max.
2. Choose Rendering/Effects. Click the Logo Glow entry in the effects list, then check Interactive.
3. Click the Glow. In the Glow Element rollout, click the Options tab. Select the Effects ID as the source, and set the Value to 2.
4. Set the Image Filter to Perimeter (Perim).
5. In the Parameters tab, set the Size to 3 and the Intensity to 150.
6. Copy the red (right) color swatch of the radial color section to the white (left) swatch, and notice the rendering.
7. By changing the left color swatch to a value of R255, G10, and B10, you get a better looking glow. The final result is shown in Figure 15.11.

Figure 15.11 Example of the Perimeter filter on a logo. The Perimeter option gives the logo the appearance of illumination from within.

Exercise 15.5 demonstrates an excellent opportunity for using Perimeter. At times, using either Perimeter or Perimeter Alpha backfires, particularly in certain backlit-sign situations. This is especially true when the sign is mounted against a surface. In that case, there is a great deal of aliasing with Perimeter Alpha or inaccurate glows from Perimeter. Figures 15.12 and 15.13 show such a scenario.

Pay close attention to the logo's interior where the letters are cut. To counter this, make a copy of the object that you are glowing with the Perimeter option. Minimize the copy along the object's depth, so that it isn't as deep as the sign itself. Next, place the copy immediately behind the sign. (Make sure that it isn't encased within the original object.) Now set your source as the copy's Object or Material ID. The result is convincing and is easy to animate. The Exercise 15.6 series shows you how to use the object-copy technique.

Figure 15.12 and Figure 15.13 A case where neither Perimeter nor Perimeter Alpha works well. In the image on the top, Perimeter Alpha produces aliased edges. The image on the bottom, which uses Perimeter, produces a softer but less accurate tracing of the logo's perimeter.

Exercise 15.6.1 Creating a Backlit Sign Without Using Perimeter

1. Load 15max06.max.
2. In the Top viewport, select the logo object.

3. In the toolbar, click the Move button.
4. While holding down the Shift key, click and drag the MAX logo object to the Top viewport. Place it along the Y-axis, so that it is above the original logo object.
5. In the Clone Options dialog, select Copy.
6. Open the Modify panel, and click the More button.
7. Choose Xform.
8. Click and hold the Scale button in the toolbar.
9. Choose the Non-Uniform Scale flyout.
10. In the Top viewport, scale down the logo on the Y-axis, until it appears about 1/8 the size of the original logo.
11. In the Modify panel, click the Sub-Object button off.
12. Use the Move command to move the thin logo directly on top of the original logo in the Top viewport. At this point, you have a scaled copy of the original logo sitting directly behind it on the wall. Use the thin copy to key off the glow effect.
13. From the Edit pull-down menu, choose Properties. Set the new logo's G-Buffer ID to 1.
14. Choose Rendering/Effects, then select Interactive. Notice the rendering. (If you want to see the glow settings, select the Lens Effects entry in the effects list.)

This takes time to render on slower computers because quite a bit of raytracing is used in the scene. At first glance, there are numerous adjustments to make. First, the glow effect is not reflected on the wall. This problem is easily corrected by altering the Material Effects channel of the object and using it as the source.

Exercise 15.6.2   Switching the Glow Source

1. In the toolbar, click the Material Editor Button.
2. Assign the "Light" material (upper-left sample slot) to the cloned logo.
3. In the Render Effects dialog box, click the Update Scene button to re-render the scene. (This allows glow to obtain all new-scene settings, such as Material Effects Channel assignments.)
4. In the Options tab of Glow, set the source to Effects ID 1. Clear the Object ID checkbox.
5. Click the Parameters tab. Set the Size to 1 and the Intensity to 150.

The glow's color behind the sign looks fine; however, the glow's reflection is a dull white. This is because Glow is currently glowing a color based on the pixel colors. Set the exact color (or range of colors) that you want for the glow, using the two color swatches—regardless of the color of the pixels generating the glow.

Exercise 15.6.3 Adjusting the Glow's Color

1. Load 15imx06-3.
2. Open the Rendering Effects dialog box.
3. Select the left color swatch for radial color, and set its values to R0, G235, B235.
4. Select the right color swatch for radial color, and set its values to R0, G0, B255.

By making a slight change to the gradient color, the back-light effect is more believable. The Exercise 15.6 series demonstrates two key concepts:

- Instead of using Perimeter or Perimeter Alpha for backlight effects, create a copy of the object and glow the copy.
- When using Material Effects IDs for Glow, use a specific color or gradient to better control the glows' color in reflections or refractions.

The final rendering is shown in Figure 15.14.

Figure 15.14 Glow achieves a backlight effect by using a smaller copy of the original object as the source instead of the Perimeter filter.

 Note

As with a Glow's sources, Glow filters also combine to constrain the effect (based on more than one property in MAX R3). You no longer need to select just one filter for the effect and hope that it filters the right elements in the rendering.

Using Maps and Gradients in Glow

Glow control through maps is, by far, the most powerful aspect of the Glow feature. As a matter of fact, it's what makes the entire Lens Effects feature so useful. With gradients, you design the most intricate glow effects for use in still images or animations. However, it takes a bit of practice.

Note
As of MAX R3, gradients and maps are used to affect only lighting through the Glow feature of Lens Effects in the Render Effects dialog. To achieve the same effect on glowing objects, you still need to use the Video Post-based Lens Effects Glow element.

Controlling colors and transparency (or falloff) with MAX R3 is now enhanced to use any map type supported in MAX. This means that you can use anything from the standard Gradient map to Noise. However, use these maps to control the glow effect only on a light, not objects. For glowing light sources, try the new Glow feature in Render Effects instead of Glow in Video Post.

Radial Color and Falloff

In previous exercises you worked with the color swatches of radial color to achieve glows. However, that technique only allows you to use two different colors for your glow. If you want more explicit control over the glow's color, you need to use a map. Drag a map that MAX supports into the slot for the button labeled None, located next to the right color swatch. The glow uses that map's color information instead of the two color swatches. Figures 15.15 and 15.16 show the same light source, using the standard color swatches on the left and a Gradient Ramp on the right.

To properly control how the glow effect tapers, use a standard linear graph (the Falloff Curve) or a map. The Falloff Curve, as seen in Figure 15.17, is similar to the deformation curves of a Loft compound object. By moving the two points on either side of the graph, you decide how the Radial color falls off—if at all. Figures 15.15 and 15.16 use the graph depicted in Figure 15.17.

Add as many points as you want to control the effect. You also control their tangency, much like the splines that you draw in the interface.

Chapter 15: Glows and Lens Flares 603

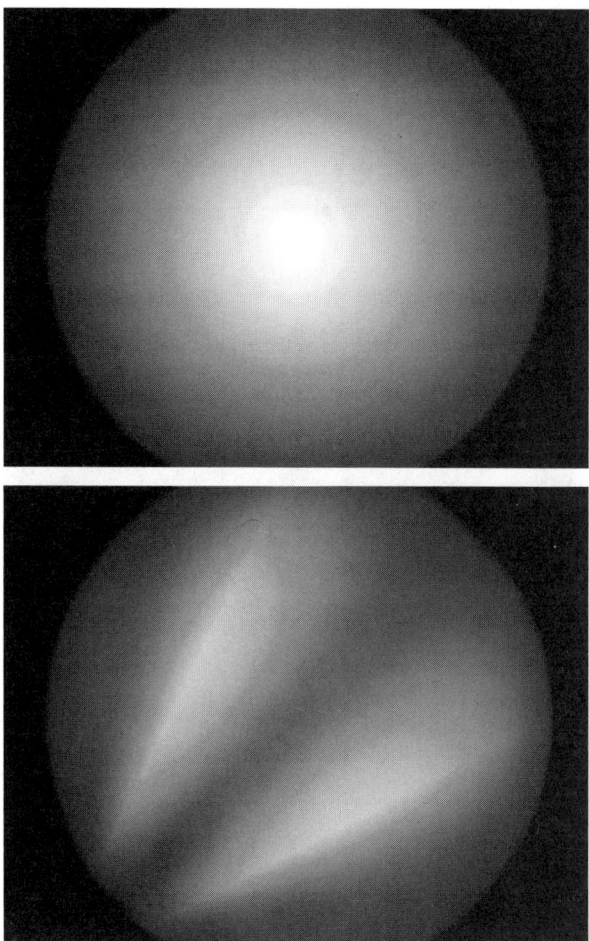

Figure 15.15 and Figure 15.16 These two figures show the same light source applied with the same glow effect. The difference is that the top figure uses the standard two colors for the Radial color, whereas the bottom uses a Gradient Ramp.

A map uses the grayscale values of the image to control the falloff. While you can use almost any map to control the falloff, you probably want to stick with a radial gradient as much as possible. The Radial Gradient map is how light transmits in MAX and how the glow effect is applied to a light source. Using other map types as your primary falloff map causes unpredictable results. Figures 15.18 and 15.19 show a glow's complexity, using a Radial Gradient map as your falloff map.

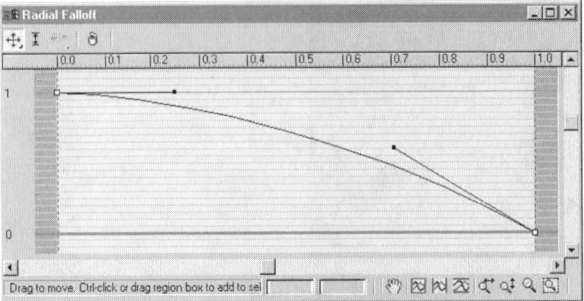

Figure 15.17 The Falloff Curve of the Radial color in a glow effect. This control is similar to the Loft object deformation features. It is also found in other Falloff controls throughout the MAX interface, including other Lens Effects components.

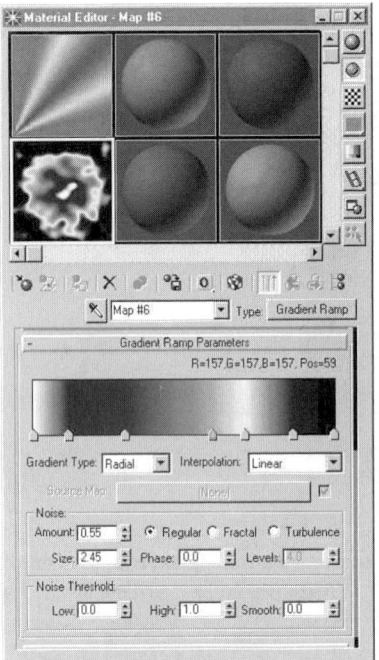
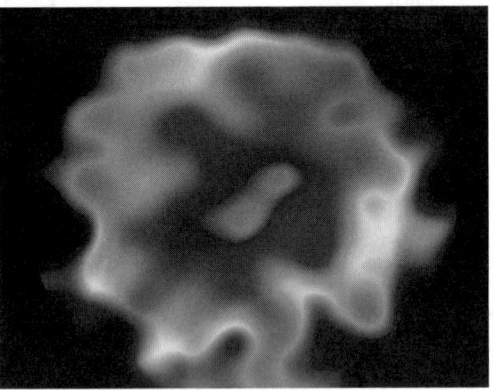

Figure 15.18 and Figure 15.19 A complex glow, using two radial gradients (seen in the left image). The upper gradient controls the color, and the lower gradient controls the falloff.

Circular Color and Falloff

Circular color works much like the circular gradient (discussed in the next section). However, the Circular color in Lens Effects of the Render Effects dialog box works only on lights. Much like Radial color, Circular color is controlled by static colors or by maps.

Its Falloff Curve setup is identical. The primary difference is that the Circular color works by traversing the glow's edge in a clockwise direction. The four color swatches represent the 12-, 3-, 6-, and 9-o'clock positions, respectively, on a glow. The Mix parameter allows you to blend the colors defined in the Radial Color section with the Circular color. At 50, there's an even mix. At 100, the Circular color completely obscures the Radial color.

By using a map, you radically vary the color distribution in the glow. In this case, the Circular color is produced by vertically analyzing the map color. The 12 o'clock color is defined by the first row of pixels, the 3 o'clock is defined by the row of pixels 25 percent down from the top, and so on. Results with maps aren't as predictable, but produce nice halo-type effects. Figure 15.20 shows an effect generated with circular color, using a Gradient Ramp that is using a radial gradient type.

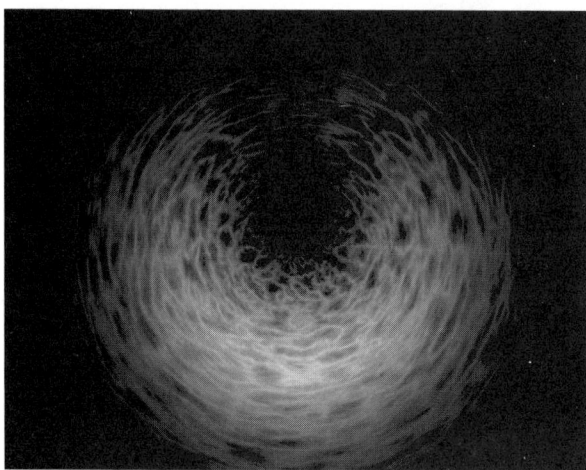

Figure 15.20 A glow effect, using a radial Ramp Gradient map to define the color. While difficult to see the blending of the colors in black and white, notice that the glow's intensity is radically affected with just the two colors.

Using Gradient in the Glow Module of Video Post

Even with the new features of Lens Effects Glow in Render Effects, use the older Glow module in Video Post to more completely fine-tune your objects' glow. There you control colors, using gradients or maps similar to the new Glow of Render Effects.

The next few sections take a look at what the different Glow gradient maps do in Video Post. If you've never set up a glow in Video Post before, following are three simple steps to do this:

Part III Rendering Effects

1. Open Video Post and add a Scene Event, using the Camera view. (Always use a camera when working with Lens Effects in Video Post.)
2. Add an Image Filter Event, using the Lens Effects Glow as the filter.
3. Click the Setup button in the Filter setup dialog box. Then click the Gradients tab.

Radial Versus Circular Uses in Glow

Glow incorporates two types of gradient definitions: Radial and Circular. Use them for both color and transparency. Radial and circular can be used independently, or in conjunction with each other, to produce different styles of glows.

Radial gradient definition is determined in an outward direction from the glowed source's center point. The left side of the gradient is the glowed source's center. The right side is the gradient's outermost extents (determined by the glow's size—both by gradient and by numeral). Figure 15.21 shows the glow effect with different radial transparencies.

Note
You must use the Gradient Color option—defined in the Preferences tab of Glow—to see the results of changing any gradient in Video Post.

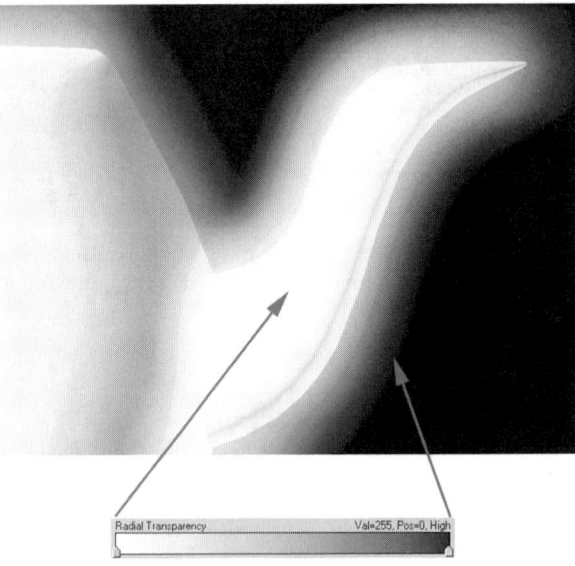

Figure 15.21 How a Radial gradient works. The left-most part of the gradient is the center of the radial cross-section. The right-most part of the gradient represents the effect at its extents.

Circular gradient definition works by controlling the glow as it travels along the perimeter of the object. Alter where the glow takes, as well as its color around the object, by varying grayscale intensities or adding colors to circular gradients.

The trick for circular gradients is that they work based on the direction of an object's edges. This means that if an object has several faces that point in the same direction along its edges, they all have the same glow effect if they fall within the correct threshold. Figure 15.22 shows how the circular gradient works.

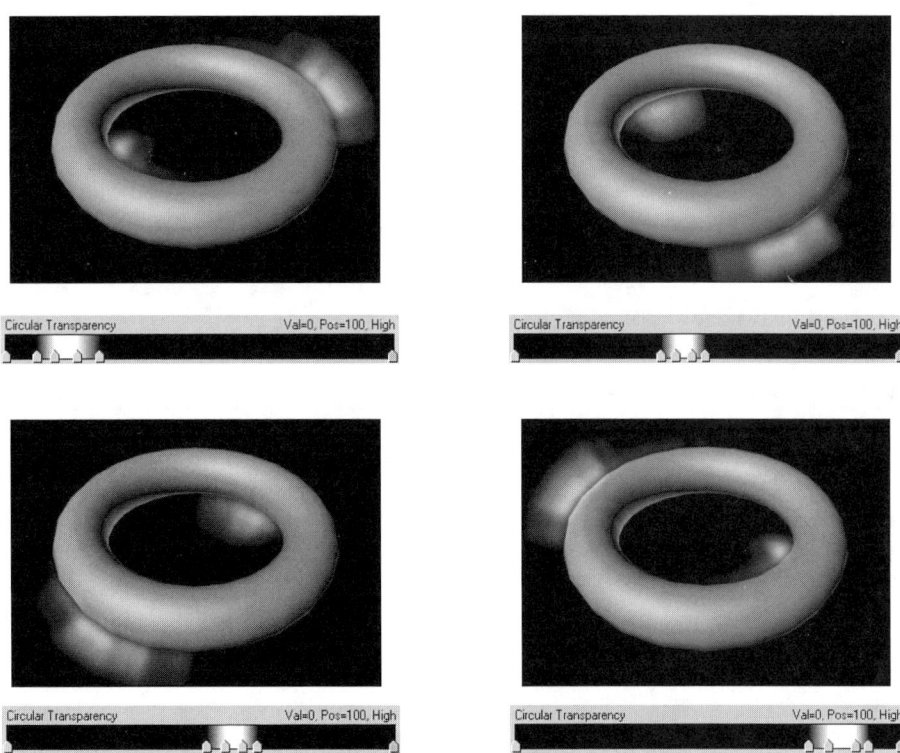

Figure 15.22 How a circular gradient works. The left side of the gradient represents the 0° mark. As you progress from left to right, the gradient's effect travels clockwise around the source object.

Gradient Composition Techniques

Circular and radial gradients in Video Post combine to add, average, or subtract their values and result in a hybrid gradient. Color gradients pair with each other, as well as Transparency gradients.

To control how gradients combine, just right-click over a gradient itself. Toward the bottom of the pop-up menu are several options for combining glows. Depending on which gradient you select, you also define how its corresponding gradient (for example, circular color or circular transparency) is defined.

There are five combination methods for gradients, as follows:

- **High Value.** Compares the values of the two gradients and selects the higher RGB value to determine the glow.
- **Average.** Averages the two RGB values of the gradients—basically (RGB1+RGB2)/2. The resultant value determines the color of the glow.
- **Low Value.** Similar to High Value, but with the opposite effect. Instead of using the high RGB value, MAX uses the low value to create the glow.
- **Additive.** Adds the RBG values of the gradients—RGB1+RGB2=Glow. Exercise caution here, as adding some values together results in pure white.
- **Subtractive.** The opposite of using Additive. The lower value is subtracted from the higher value, resulting in more dull glows.

Note
Nearly every module of Lens Effects uses gradients. All gradients use the same definition and combination methods. Refer back to this section when using gradients in other modules.

Building a Glow

Designing consistently convincing glows takes practice. Don't expect your first few attempts to be completely successful. One of the greatest things about the Lens Effects functions is that they are flexible. One of the worst things about the effects is that you spend a lot of time tweaking your settings until you get the "perfect" glow or flare. Fortunately, there are steps that act as a foundation for most of your glows. You build on that foundation to produce a customized look.

In the end what counts is that the glow looks good. The following sections seek to help those with little experience in using Glow.

Determining the Source

The first item that you must consider is the source of your glow. What type of object is it, and from what sort of material is it made? A common misconception for novices is to glow every light source (or self-illuminating object) in their scene. This doesn't happen in real life.

As stated earlier in this chapter, most glows happen as a result of atmospheric conditions. If it's hazy or smoky, then glows are more prevalent. If it's clear, then only the brightest objects glow.

If it's possible to observe a real-life counterpart of your source, then take advantage of it. Better yet—take a picture and tape it to your monitor. That way, the glow in your scene more accurately resembles the real source. (Remember to use high-speed film if you take a picture of a source at night!)

Most animators often ignore the more subtle glows. However, these glows make a world of difference in a scene's realism. For instance, a polished-brass drawer handle in direct light gives a subtle glow in the bright specular highlights. For effects such as this, it's best to use Unclamped as your source. Set the size of the glow small enough so it's noticeable, but not overpowering, for the scene.

Determining the Color

The color of a glow depends, again, on the atmosphere around your source, as well as the source itself. If the sun rises over a foggy city, the color of the fog is part of the glow's color (along with the bright yellow color of the sun). Unfortunately MAX doesn't automatically do this. A script, however, automates some of this process.

Determining the Intensity

The source's intensity usually creates a glow's intensity level, although atmospherics do play a role. A simple example is a light bulb. If the light bulb is illuminated in a clear room, the glow's intensity is relatively low. However, if that same room is full of smoke and the light bulb is lit at the same intensity, the glow's intensity increases because the smoke particles are also illuminated. If you increase the level of smoke to the point where it's difficult to even see in the room, the glow is again diminished. It has a similar halo around it as in the mildly smoky room—just not as intense.

Building a Flare

Creating a Lens Effects-based lens flare for the first time feels a bit daunting. However, the MAX R3 interface is designed to make it easier for you to build your flares. Furthermore, there's no longer a separate module for Flare, such as in Video Post. Now you can build your flares in Lens Effects, the same area where you built your glow.

Much like building a glow, building a lens flare takes practice. There are several ready-made lens flares that ship with MAX. A good practice is to try building your own lens flare from these. At least that way, your starting point is easier to find. (They're also useful if you need a quick lens flare, and you don't have time to build one.)

The final exercise in this chapter uses some of Flare's commands to produce a sun-generated lens flare at dawn. Use a combination of Flare's effects to produce the overall lens flare. After the exercise, notice what other options refine the lens flare.

Exercise 15.7   Creating a Better Flare

1. Open 15max07.max.
2. Choose Rendering/Effects. Click Update Scene to view a rendering with the flare in its current state.
3. Click Lens Effects entry in the Effect list. Don't turn on Interactive because it takes a while to render.
4. In the Lens Effects Globals section dialog box, click Pick Light. Choose the Omni light named Sun.
5. Click the Glow entry on the right list. Set the Use Source Color to 85 to give the glow an orangish look. Then set the Size to 100, and clear the Glow Behind checkbox.
6. Click the Star right-hand entry. Set Size to 200, Angle to 20, and Qty. to 4. Set the Taper parameter to 0.1 and the Width to 2.0. Make sure to clear the Glow Behind checkbox.
7. The Auto Secondaries need some work. Click the Auto Secondary entry in the right-hand list. Set the Minimum to 0.5, the Maximum to 5.0, and the Intensity to 80. Click Update Scene to view your work.
8. Click the right-hand Ring entry. Set the Size to 5.0, the Intensity to 30, the Thickness to 3, and Use Source Color to 80. Select Update Scene to view your newest changes. There are too many rays. In the right list, select Ray. In Ray Element, select Parameters. Set the number to 40.
9. Click the Update Effect button to view the new settings. Figure 15.23 shows the final rendering.

At this point, your rendering has a nice sun flare. As an added effect, use the Falloff Curve of the Circular color in the Auto Secondary to fade the flares on one side. This produces a more realistic flare in the end because most lens elements are either concave or convex. The resulting flare on the element is not even across the lens; instead it is more prominent on one side or the other.

Chapter 15: Glows and Lens Flares   611

Figure 15.23 This shows the use of several Flare settings, to create a more realistic flare—even from the default flare.

 Tip
For quick, sure-fire flare fade, set the left-most point on the Circular Color Falloff Curve to 0.0. Figure 15.24 shows an example, using the Falloff Curve of Axial Transparency.

Figure 15.24 Use the Falloff Curve for Circular color on the secondary flares. For this to work, you must set the left-most point on the Falloff Curve to 0.0.

If you like building from scratch, though, follow these quick tips for building a flare that saves time:

- **Turn off the elements that you don't need.** For example, if you're building the glow portion of a flare, turn off the secondary lens flares. You don't need them, and they force the glow into the upper-left corner of the Lens Flare interface. When you're ready to move to other elements of your flare, either leave your current element on or shut it off.

- **Copy and Paste!** Every flag in a gradient can be copied and pasted somewhere else. At least a few elements of your lens flare often share the same color. It's a pain to redefine unusual colors all the time. Copying and pasting helps alleviate this hassle. Obviously this isn't much of a problem if you use pure reds, blues, or greens.

- **Use the hue of your source.** It makes defining a lens flare's color much easier. Apply Hue Globally uses the hue of the light source and applies it to every color definition of your lens flare's elements. This avoids having to build a lens flare's color based on your arbitrary gradient settings. For more control over the mixture of your light source's hue and the hue of your flare's elements, use the Hue spinner for each element.

- **Use Multiple Sources.** In Flare, you choose to flare as many light sources as you want. Just use the normal multiple selection commands (Shift or Ctrl). Flare will then flare all the sources with the same settings. This works well for arrays of lights that have the same properties, such as runways or lights on a spaceship.

Take some time to study these guidelines when building flares. You will save yourself a great deal of prep-work that eats up costly production time.

Determine the Source

Determining the flare's source is easy—it's a light. Unlike the Glow module that glows objects, materials, and a host of other items, Flare is designed to glow and flare just lights. This makes it easier for you to determine what your flare looks like.

The trick is to make the lens flare look good for the light source. Sometimes it is simple, such as a dimly lit light bulb. In other cases it may be dramatic, such as an alien sun breaking from around a planet.

Because lens flares incorporate so many elements, they tend to be more artistic than glows or highlights. If you're just starting out building your own lens flares, it's best to observe flares you see—whether in real life or through various media. Science fiction movies and television programs are often great sources for ideas. Also take a camera outside on a nice day and point it towards the sun—just be careful not to look right into the sun! You can observe not only the effect the sun's light has on a camera, but also how the flare moves when you move the camera.

Account for the Environment

Much like a glow on an object, the characteristics of a flare depend a great deal on the kind on environment in which the flare is occurring. For instance, in space a flare may be perfectly crisp because there is no real atmosphere with which to interact. If you try to simulate looking at the sun from the Earth's surface, the atmosphere determines your flare's "crispness." By adding a small Blur effect, you adjust the flare's crispness. A note about using Blur, though: Using it too much actually makes the whole rendering look blurred, as if you're looking through a lens with some residue on it. Typically, increase Blur and the size of the glow to simulate flares in hazy conditions. Figure 15.25 demonstrates a softer flare with a larger glow.

Figure 15.25 A more diffused lens flare, using the Blur Effect. Use this to simulate a flare on a hazy day or through a dirty lens.

Account for the Camera Type

One other element that most people don't think of is the type of camera that you use (or, more appropriately, simulate). For instance, cameras have several types of lenses. Different lenses have different numbers of elements in them. As a result, the number of secondary flares changes. Granted, this can be considered to be nit-picky, but too many secondary flares are distracting and too few go unnoticed. Refer to Chapter 14 for more information on lens types and numbers of elements.

Lastly, if you are going to film or simulate film output, use the Squeeze parameter. If you change the rendering aspect ratio of your scene to a film aspect ratio, the flare does not automatically alter itself. To squeeze the flare into a more "anamorphic" look, use the

Squeeze spinner (along with the checkbox for the corresponding flare element that you want to squeeze).

Figure 15.26 An anamorphic flare, using the Squeeze parameter. Use this parameter for output to film or simulating output to film.

In Practice: Glows and Lens Flares

- **Know glow and flare causes.** In an effort to produce the best computer-generated flares and glows, it helps to understand that their real-life counterparts are caused by atmospheric effects.
- **Assign the glow source.** The Glow element gives you many options for choosing sources. Your choice is often dictated by the type of scene and objects with which you're working. Object ID is ideal for light bulb objects or neon tubing. Material ID is ideal when raytrace reflections or refractions are present in the rendered image.
- **Filter glows.** At times you need to control where the glow effect happens on the object. Through options like Perimeter, Perimeter Alpha, and All, you define where a glow occurs on your selected source.
- **Study sources for glows.** Glows occur from many situations, and are usually the result of various atmospheric conditions. When you're concerned with how a glow should appear, just observe a real-life situation in which the glow occurs. If you're not simulating real-life, use artistic license (coupled with real-life knowledge).

- **Determine sources and camera types for flares.** Because the atmosphere and the type of camera lens you look through cause flares, you need to use the more advanced features of Flare. Hue values take on the color of the flare source. Soften, when used with Effect Size, is best for simulating hazy conditions. Squeeze is used primarily for film output or simulating the "anamorphic" squeeze effect associated with outputting to film.

Chapter 16

Highlights

Whether watching a city street at night or glancing toward a pond at sunset, chances are you've seen a highlight. Highlights, sometimes called sparkles, are multi-pointed streaks that emanate from an intense light source (or reflection of a light source) on a shiny surface.

In 3D Studio MAX R3, you easily simulate this effect by using the Lens Effects Highlight or Lens Effects Flare module (located in Video Post). Similar to the Glow module, Highlight and Flare allow you to add effects to numerous components in your scene. This chapter shows you how to navigate both the Highlight and Flare interfaces, quickly adding highlights to either objects or lights. Following are some of the topics covered in this chapter:

- Controlling the location of the highlight effect
- When to use Highlight versus Flare
- How to use color with Highlight
- The advantage of combining Highlight with Glow
- Techniques to simulate candlelight

Highlight effects in MAX are 2D. Their distance from the camera controls their size and intensity. This is because highlights actually occur in the human eye. Think about it: The highlight is not generated on the object. Candlelight is a good example. We know the flame doesn't produce a cross-like highlight. Your eye, however, sees the candlelight differently, for various reasons (such as eye moisture). The moisture causes the light to be refracted; therefore your brain perceives the candlelight reflecting highlights. You need to remember this later on, when you design your scene for highlight effects.

Highlights present a dramatic effect when used in moderation. On the other hand, they're quite distracting when used in excess. The key here is to determine which objects or light sources you want to accentuate with highlight effects. This is not typically something that you do *while* building a scene, but as an afterthought during the rendering phase of your project. Save yourself some time, though, with early consideration about where you might add effects. This is especially true with shiny surfaces. Since material design can and does occur at many stages throughout an animation's production, keep in mind that some materials produce too many or too few highlights for your scene.

Note
You don't use the Highlight module for light objects; instead, use the Flare module for these objects. Highlight is only intended to work with geometry.

Working with Highlight

Highlight doesn't work like Lens Effects in Render Effects—in the sense that the module is not set up the same way, and you must use Video Post. Highlights are, by far, the most difficult to control of any Lens Effects module effects in Video Post. This is because you have to set up your scene for highlights, rather than setting up highlights for your scene. Every other module of Lens Effects works this way, too. If you want highlights in your scene, you adjust lighting and materials so that your highlights show up in the right place. The Place Highlight command, when used with lights, works well for determining where the Highlight module places the highlight.

Note
Unlike the other major modules of Lens Effects that moved to Render Effects in MAX R3, Highlight remains in Video Post. While you *may* be able to fake highlights with the Star entry in Lens Effects, it's not all that easy. Instead, continue to rely on Video Post and Highlight—they still work fine!

With that thought in mind, there are some things to do ahead of time and even after you start working with Highlight. The following steps ensure that your highlights end up where you want them:

- **Use shiny surfaces.** Highlight is designed to make shiny surfaces appear extremely shiny under bright conditions. The shaders introduced in MAX R3 make it easy to create intense specular highlights because their Glossiness and Specular levels far exceed MAX R2 values.

- **Use bright lights.** Bright light sources bring out the specular highlights of your materials. The brighter the light, the more intense the specular highlight; consequently, your highlights focus more on surface areas.

- **Use Place Highlight.** Place Highlight allows you to pinpoint where the brightest light hits on the geometry. With this command, the highlight's location is precisely assigned.

Highlight uses the same type of source components and filters as Glow does—whether it's the effect in Render Effects or the filter in Video Post. Highlight's Geometry tab, however, contains some specific commands that differ from Glow—namely, in its Effect and Vary sections (Figure 16.1).

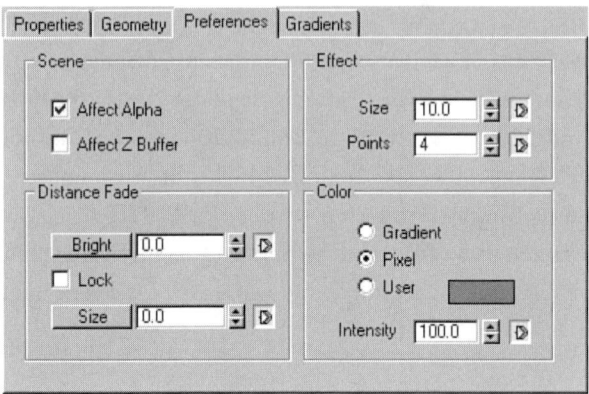

Figure 16.1 The Effect, Distance Fade, and Color sections of the Highlight module Preferences tab.

Using Highlight's Effect Section

The Effect section (located in the Geometry tab) contains three commands: Angle, Clamp, and Alternate Rays. Angle is fairly self-explanatory. How do you determine the highlights' angles? Typically, highlights' angles depend on the angle from which the highlighted source is viewed. This is purely subjective, as the angle differs between looking at the source with the naked eye versus a camera. It is safe to say that if you're viewing a source containing several highlights, all of them must be at the same angle. Otherwise, the effect is distracting.

Clamp enables you to control how many highlights show up on a source. Think of it as a threshold value. You're controlling how many pixels Highlight is skipping over before it adds another highlight to the source. The higher the value, the fewer highlights appear. This number is *very* important when you're highlighting an entire object and want only a few highlights on it (instead of everywhere).

Alternate Rays (or Alt Rays) alternates the size of every other ray in a highlight. The spinner value represents a percentage difference from the maximum Size value of the highlight. Because this effect is repetitive and not random, limit your usage of it. It looks totally computer generated when excessively used. The effect works best when used with Point values of eight and higher, which are set in the Preferences tab.

Using Highlight's Vary Section

The commands available in the Vary section of Highlight attempt to randomize the size, angle, or both, through a random-seed value. The default just varies the size. If you turn on Angle's vary option, you see why it defaults to off. When you randomize the angle, especially on scenes with only a few highlights, it looks quite strange. Use this option only if a scene already contains a ton of randomness (such as a rendering of a table covered with diamonds).

Color Usage with Highlight

Highlight uses the same color options as Glow. However, your highlights may do just fine using Pixel color's default. This is because Highlight works off of a surface's color intensity. Typically, the highlight's color is the surface's color.

Gradient (defined in the Gradients tab) produces nice feathered tips that are a different color from the highlight's center. You may also want to add numerous colors around the highlight. For instance, let's say you're rendering the surface of a CD. Typically, the highlights are rainbow colored, either from the center out or around the highlight itself.

To add colors to the gradient, simply click anywhere on the gradient. Highlight places a small marker, called a *flag*, at the point where you clicked. If you then double-click on the flag, its color changes. Highlight allows for up to 100 flags on a gradient. If you want to delete a flag, just click the flag, and drag it beyond the gradient's extreme left or right sides.

Note
In order for Highlight to use a gradient that you build, you must first switch the Color parameter in the Preferences tab to Gradient. Otherwise, Highlight continues to use the Pixel default as its color.

Using Flare Versus Highlight

Although this chapter focuses on creating highlights, you need not use just the Highlight module to produce them. As a matter of fact, the only way to get highlights on light sources is to use the Flare module. The examples you explore in this chapter demonstrate both modules' capabilities to produce the most desirable effect. However, there are two rules to follow when creating highlights:

- Use the Highlight module for creating highlights on objects.
- Use the Flare module when creating highlights on light objects.

In this chapter, you get a chance to explore three different scenarios where highlights are used.

Combining Highlight with Glow

When using the Highlight module—such as highlighting objects—you often find that combining it with the Lens Effects Glow effect works well. For instance, when shiny metals are under an intense light, there is often a soft, diffused glow around the specular highlights. If you place a small, controlled glow around the Unclamped color region, the metal's shininess looks a bit more dramatic. The highlight enhances the shininess even further. For more information on using the Glow module, refer to Chapter 15, or the MAX documentation. Figures 16.2, 16.3, and 16.4 show that adding a glow to just the specular highlights of shiny metals is a great setup for placing highlights on top. This example file is used in a later exercise, so you can see how it's set up.

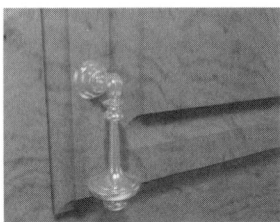  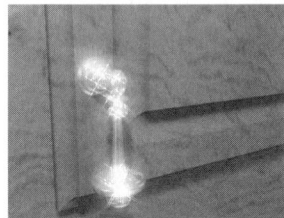

Figure 16.2, Figure 16.3, and Figure 16.4 Three examples of the same shiny-surfaced scene. Figure 16.2 is the rendering, without any effects added. In Figure 16.3, just Glow is used. In Figure 16.4, both Glow and Highlight are used.

Shiny Surfaces

Shiny surfaces (such as metals or glass) are usually part of most renderings. When designing a shiny material, you often find yourself struggling to render the shininess just right. You can frequently make a surface look shinier just by adding a subtle glow and highlight. Even the addition of one highlight makes a surface shinier—without changing the material. Sometimes, the material is shiny and you may need to alter the material's shininess or shininess strength properties. For more information on designing materials, both shiny and dull, refer to Part II, "Materials."

In Exercise 16.1, you use the combination of Glow and Highlight to create the same rendering as shown in Figure 16.2: a brass door handle. First, start by preparing the glow, then add the highlight. The scene uses the Raytrace material for adding the brass handle's intense specular highlights. Figure 16.5 depicts the final result from Exercise 16.1.

Exercise 16.1   Adding Highlights to Shiny Metals

1. Load 16max01.max. Select Render Scene, and view the scene without any highlights.

2. Choose Rendering/Render Effects. Choose the single Lens Effects entry, then check the Interactive check box. This renders the scene.
3. Select Glow (in the right-hand effect list window), and scroll down to the Glow Element rollout. Click the Options tab.
4. Set the source to Unclamped and the value to 1.0.
5. Click on the Parameters tab. For Size, enter 0.2; for Intensity, enter 100.0. This produces a soft glow on the handle's specular highlights.
6. Close the Render Effects dialog box, and choose Render/Video Post.
7. Double-click Lens Effects Highlight, and select Setup.
8. Click Preview, then VP Queue.
9. Set the source to Unclamped and the value to 2.0. Set the filter to All.
10. Click the Geometry tab.
11. Set the Clamp to 20.
12. Click OK (to exit the Highlight dialog box).
13. Render the scene from Video Post at 640×480.
14. Save your completed scene to a new filename.

Figure 16.5 The completed rendering from Exercise 16.1. For shiny surfaces, it's often a good idea to use both Glow and Highlight (to properly accentuate the specular highlights on a surface).

At this point, you have a brightly lit brass door handle, with a soft glow and highlights applied to it. Add or remove highlights by altering the Clamp setting in the Highlight Geometry tab.

Notice that your 640×480 rendering doesn't look the same as the Highlight module's preview. While this isn't the result of a bug, the difference does point out a limitation of using the Preview function. Highlight is based on pixels. Therefore, fewer pixels results in fewer overall highlights. The same rendering at 320×240, by the way, looks identical to Highlight's preview. There's no logical way around this limitation other than rendering out your scene at full resolution to test your Highlight settings.

Candlelight Highlights with Flare

Candlelight, like other light sources, looks different when viewed with the naked eye versus through a camera lens. When you view it with the naked eye, you typically see the flame and perhaps a very subtle glow or highlight right around the flame. Looking through a camera lens presents more of a challenge, though. The glow is usually accentuated, a streak runs through the center of the flame, and you may even have lens element flares.

Adding highlights to a lit candle doesn't generally involve using the Highlight module. You can use Highlight to add a surface effect illuminated by the candle, but not on the candlelight itself. Instead, you use the Flare module. The trick of using Flare is not to go overboard. By default, Flare adds rays, all kinds of secondary flare, and all are usually wrong for candlelight. You need to do a good deal of tweaking to get the highlight just right. One of the best ways to simulate candlelight is to look at a lit candle through a camera, then with the naked eye. Study the candle from different angles and in different ambient-light situations. The highlighting results differ significantly.

If you don't have a candle or a camera, don't worry. Exercise 16.2 takes you through the steps of building one possible situation with a lit candle. Before you start the exercise, take some time to study how the scene is set up. Here are some key items:

- **The Omni light is used.** The light used is a shadow-casting light that is tinted an orange-yellow shade. It's also set to Inverse-squared decay. The result is that the emitted light looks more natural.

- **The candle-wax material.** The candle wax is a Raytrace material, used with the Extra Lighting feature. While Translucency may work here, Extra Lighting (with a gradient intensity map) works better.

- **The Combustion setting.** To produce some sort of flame, you must use Combustion. Although video-captured flames may work, Combustion already comes with MAX. In just a short time, you can easily animate combustion.

In this next exercise, you use what is essentially the *only* method for adding a highlight to a light object—Flare. To properly highlight light sources, you must use Lens Effects in Render Effects. The effect works, but you should only use a few components of Flare. Overuse of Flare is extremely distracting.

Exercise 16.2   Highlighting a Candle

1. Load 16max02.max. Render the scene.
2. From the Rendering menu, choose Effects. Select Lens Effects, and check the Interactive check box. MAX renders the scene and applies the Lens Flare (in its current state).
3. Select Manual Secondary 1 (in the right-side pane). In the Tab Panel pull-down menu, select Main Toolbar, then Material Editor.
4. Click the second row, left-most sample. Then in the Gradient Ramp Parameters window, right-click the gradient. Choose Load Gradient, and load Msec1.dgr. At this point, you've defined the colors for the manual secondary lens flare with a pre-defined gradient.
5. The gradient changes, and the rendering updates. Set the Gradient Type to Radial.
6. In the Rendering Effects dialog box, Manual Secondary Element rollout, set the size of the Manual Secondary 1 to 50, the Plane to 50, Use Source Color to 80, and Intensity to 100.
7. In the Lens Effects Parameters rollout's right-side pane, select Manual Secondary 2.
8. Return to the Material Editor. Click the second row, middle sample. In the Gradient Ramp Parameters rollout, right-click the gradient. Choose Load Gradient, and load Msec2.dgr. Set the Gradient Type to Radial.
9. Return to the Rendering Effects dialog box. Make the second flare smaller than the first by setting the Size of the secondary flare to 3, the Plane value for the secondary flare to 20, Use Source Color to 80, and Intensity to 100.
10. In the Lens Effects Parameters rollout's right-side pane, select Streak. In the Streak Element rollout, set the size to 200, the Angle to 0.0, the width to 3, and the Intensity to 100.
11. Click the Render Scene dialog box to view the full image.

This exercise focuses on the use of Flare to produce a highlight-like effect. To produce this exercise, the author spent time analyzing a real candle through both the naked eye and a camera's lens. The results of Exercise 16.2 are based upon his observations. While nearly every highlight or flare effect is subjective, this exercise gives you an excellent idea of what it takes to produce an accurate, realistic highlight effect. The results from the exercise are displayed in Figure 16.6.

Figure 16.6 The final result of Exercise 16.2. When using Flare to create highlights on light sources, you only need a few components to make the effect look convincing.

Using Highlight on an Entire Object

There are times where you want to add highlights to the entire surface of an object—not just in the bright areas. For instance, you may want to scatter highlights across a surface made out of glitter or sequins. There are occasions where using Unclamped is unsuitable. This is because other shiny or bright surfaces may exist in the rendering—surfaces to which you don't want to add highlights. An example of this is where a character wears a sequined gown, and a band's brass section is behind the character. You want to add highlights to just the gown and not the shiny brass horns. The best option is to highlight by Object ID, and use both the Brightness filter and Clamp threshold to control the amount of added highlights. The final exercise of this chapter explores adding highlights to a morning sunrise over the water. You use the techniques described in this section, adding highlights across the water's surface. As with previous exercises, study the way the scene is set up—primarily, the light source's location and the material used for the water.

Exercise 16.3 Sunrise on Golden Pond

1. Load 16max03.max. Render the Environment viewport.
2. Choose Rendering/Video Post.
3. Double-click the Lens Effects Highlight entry, and select Setup.
4. In the Properties tab, set the Source to Object ID 2.
5. To create highlights based on the brightness of the sun's reflections, choose the Bright filter. Set the value to 200.

6. Open Geometry, and set the Clamp value to 60.
7. Click the Preferences tab.
8. In the Distance Fade section, turn on both Size and Bright. Click the Lock check box, turning it on.
9. To reduce the brightness of the highlights that are far from the camera, set either the Bright or Size value in the Distance Fade section to 1000.
10. Click OK (to exit the Highlight dialog box).
11. Render the scene.

After the scene renders, notice the highlights' nice placement on the water's surface. Once again, try experimenting with highlight settings to see how well (or poorly) the effect adjusts. For an added treat, go to the Render menu, and select Environment. Activate the Clouds environmental effect (that is currently disabled). The rendering time is longer—but well worth it! Figure 16.7 shows the end result with Clouds turned on.

Figure 16.7 The final result from Exercise 16.3, plus Clouds. Notice how the highlights are evenly distributed across the illuminated areas of the water's surface. This is due to using the Clamp feature within Highlight.

In Practice: Highlights

- **Highlight works differently than most of the Lens Effects modules.** Instead of designing a scene's highlight, the reverse is usually the case. More often than not, you find yourself figuring out ways to build a scene while taking advantage of the Highlight module.

- **Highlight is for Geometry; Flare is for light sources.** Remember, when you plan on highlighting a light source, you should use the Flare module. Highlight is only intended to work with geometry and materials.
- **Use Glow and Highlight together.** When highlighting shiny surfaces, it's a good idea to enhance a highlight's effect by also adding a glow (on Unclamped color regions).
- **Use only portions of flare for highlighting lights.** Flare contains components. To use Flare as a highlight-type effect, use only Glow, Secondary Flares, and Streak.

Chapter 17

Focal Effects

If you've ever worked with a real camera, you know about focus. Even if the only camera you use has auto-focus, you at least know that someone or some*thing* focuses in order for the photograph to turn out clear and crisp. When you pick up your pictures from the developer, you see the effects of focus. Some of your pictures are clear and in-focus, some are completely out-of-focus, and others are only partly in focus.

In other software tools, and even in very early versions of MAX, focal effects were impossible without a plug-in. Most of the resulting images looked computer-generated for one reason: no focal effects. If you do a close-up shot of something using MAX, everything is in focus. While this is nice, it doesn't accurately represent what you see in real-life or what a real camera sees.

Note

The Depth of Field effect is a Bonus Tool inside 3D Studio MAX R3. To install Depth of Field as a Render Effect, do a Custom Install and select the Bonus Tools option.

The Depth of Field effect within Render Effects makes it easier for you to simulate camera focal effects. This is done by blurring the scene, based on scene elements (such as focal points, or distance, from the center of the frame out). In any case, Depth of Field helps add more realism to your rendered scenes. The Depth of Field interface is shown in Figure 17.1. To get a better idea of how focus works in MAX R3, we explore:

- Focal terminology
- The three types of focal blurs
- Adjusting and controlling the focus ranges

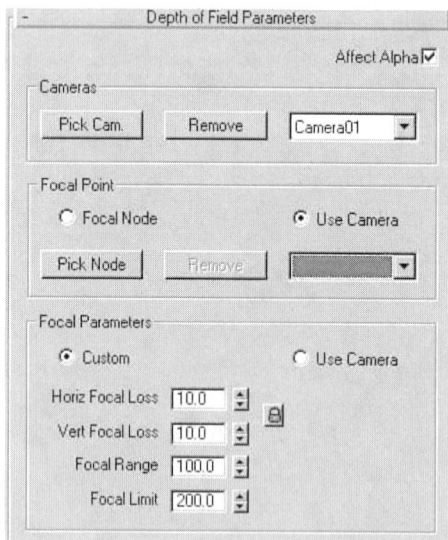

Figure 17.1 The Depth of Field effect's interface. Most of your work is in the Focal Parameters section.

Depth of Field Terminology

Several terms describe how a camera focuses and what the resultant effects are. However, traditional labels don't always match with what programmers call "items" in their interfaces. In Depth of Field, there are three main terms (with concepts) that you must first understand before diving into the effect. They are focal loss, focal range, and focal limit.

The next three sections take you through those three elements. Where possible, parallels are drawn to real-world terminology for those of you with some photography experience. Note that there are many things you can do with the Depth of Field effect to simulate focal effects. It doesn't, however, have any equivalents to such items as f-stops or focal length (with respect to focal properties).

Focal Loss

The Depth of Field effect's Focal Loss settings provide the amount of blur in the scene. The higher the focal loss, the more blur contained in your scene. The Horiz Focal Loss (horizontal blur) and Vert Focal Loss (vertical blur) settings enable you to blur more on one axis than the other. This capability is useful if you're simulating, for example, looking through a pair of glasses, and then taking them off. Several animators complain that it's difficult to look at the Depth of Field effect's preview window when there is more blurring on the horizontal axis than the vertical. It looks too much like they're not wearing their corrective lenses!

The key thing to remember about focal loss is to use it in moderation. The default setting of 10 is usually a good starting point, but you don't want to go much higher. Lower settings—those under 10—produce better depth-of-field effects. The term, Depth of Field, refers to two things. One is where the camera's focal point is (referred to as a *focal node* in the interface). The other deals with how much/how little areas in front of/behind the point are out of focus. For more information on Depth of Field, refer to Chapter 14, "Cameras, Camera Effects, and Lighting." Figures 17.2 and 17.3 show appropriate and inappropriate settings for Horiz and Vert Focal Loss when using a focal point.

Figure 17.2 The proper amount of focal loss for a scene when using a focal point.

Figure 17.3 The same scene, with Focal Loss settings that are too high. Notice an obvious jump from in-focus to out-of-focus, especially along the right side of the teapot (just beyond the spout).

Focal Range

Focal range is the distance outward from the point of interest before focal loss begins to take place. It's best thought of as the "hot spot" area for Depth of Field. The closer the Focal Range value is to 0, the less distance there is before Depth of Field begins to blur the scene. It is calculated on the viewing plane of the camera (the Z-axis, or Z-Buffer, of the rendered scene), rather than the distance that projects spherically outward from the focal point. The viewing plane is the plane that is perpendicular to the viewing axis of the camera. Figure 17.4 shows what a viewing plane looks like.

Why does the effect use the camera's viewing plane? Depth of Field is a post-processed effect; it is applied after the scene is rendered. Depth of Field relies on the Z-Buffer in order to perform its operation. The Z-Buffer is an invisible layer of data that accompanies the rendered image to represent a distance from the viewing plane for each point in the image. In other words, how far away a rendered portion of the scene is from the camera. Because Depth of Field is acting only on a rendered image and has no interaction with your scene's 3D objects, it relies on this Z-Buffer to determine how much to blur any portion of your rendering. The Z-Buffer gives Depth of Field the ability to quickly blur a scene. However, it also means that blur is calculated planar to the camera, which is a problem when focal loss is set high. At higher focal losses, you see a noticeable "blurred wall," which is actually your Focal Limit plane. (See Figure 17.4.) This is an undesirable effect in most cases. If you get a blurred wall, reduce the amount of focal loss. At the very least, it makes the wall less noticeable.

Tip

If you see the focal planes in your rendering, reduce both Focal Loss settings in Depth of Field. While it does not eliminate the focal-plane problem, it minimizes it. Figure 17.3 is a good example of too much focal loss.

Focal Limit

The Focal Limit setting, similar to Focal Range, represents the distance between the maximum Focal Range value and the point where the blur reaches its maximum strength. Again, the best way to think of this is as a falloff value of the blur in relation to the hotspot. (Although the blur is actually getting stronger, not falling off.) You can't set Focal Limit to be less-than-or-equal-to Focal Range. Figure 17.4 shows where the various focal areas exist in a sample image.

Also much like the Focal Range setting, Focal Limit is dependent upon the Z-Buffer data of the rendered image. This means that it's subject to the same limitations as having a "planar" look when focusing on a point. Focal Limit is always a number higher than the Focal Range because a quick ramping of no-blur-to-maximum-blur is noticeable and distracting.

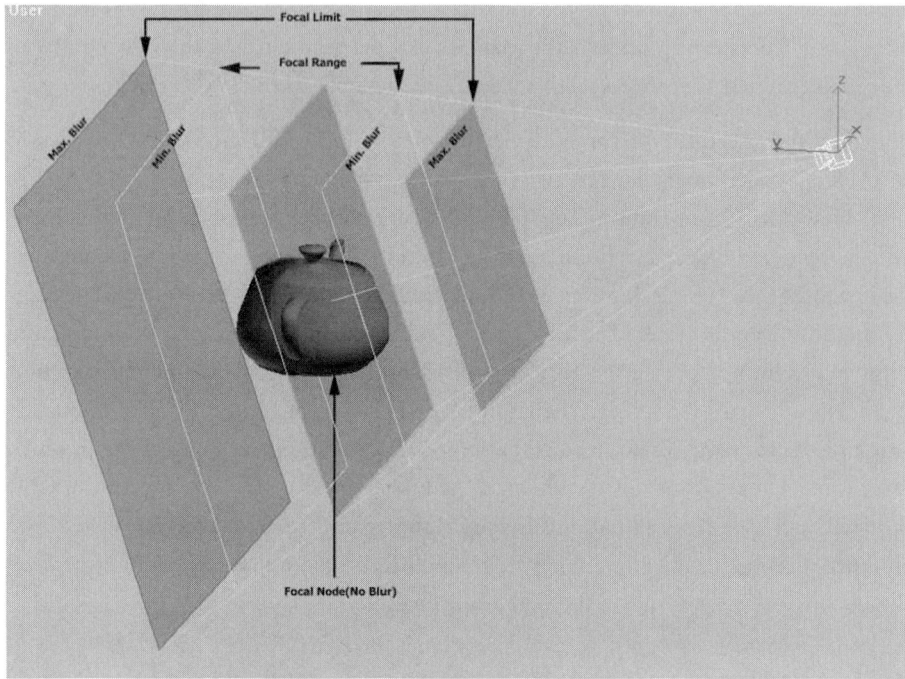

Figure 17.4 A visual representation of the focal areas in the Depth of Field effect. The distance between the focal node and the Focal Range plane contains no blur. The distance between the Focal Range planes and Focal Limit planes is where the blurring occurs. As you reach the Focal Limit planes, the image is blurred at the maximum amount.

General Focal Effects

Two settings provide a nice scene blur when using Depth of Field: Scene Blur and Radial Blur. Each blurs the scene but in different ways. Although these two methods of blur are used less frequently than the Focal Node option (more on that coming up), they are used for a number of situations. In MAX R3, however, you must use the older Focus module of Lens Effects because neither Scene nor Radial Blur is updated in the Depth of Field effect for R3. Figure 17.5 shows the interface for Lens Effects Focus. To get to these parameters, follow these steps:

1. From the Rendering pull-down menu, select Video Post.
2. Add a scene event to the Video Post queue, if you don't have one (such as Camera view).
3. Click the Add Filter button, and select Lens Effects Focus. Then click Setup.

Chapter 17: Focal Effects   637

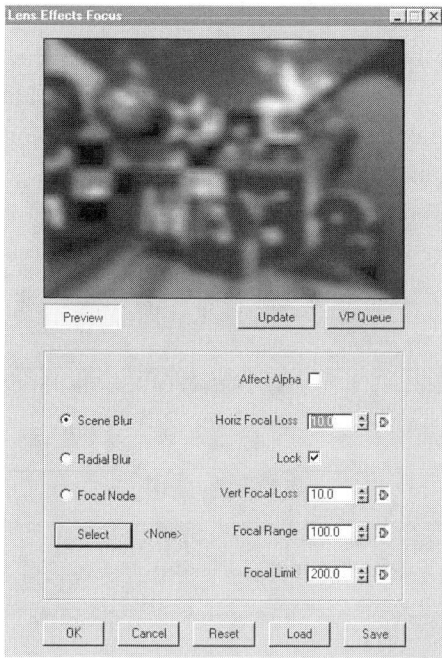

Figure 17.5   The Lens Effects Focus module interface differs slightly from the Depth of Field rendering effect. In order to use a general Scene Blur or Radial Blur, use this module (as opposed to Depth of Field).

Scene Blur

Scene Blur applies a general blur to the entire rendered image, unless it is used with a mask. A mask allows you to specify where the rendered image will be blurred by using an image's grayscale values. Darker areas are treated as transparent; lighter areas are opaque. When using Scene Blur, the only settings that work in the Depth of Field interface are the Focal Loss settings, as well as the Lock and Affect Alpha checkboxes.

Scene Blur, like any other blurring method, offsets all the rendered image's pixels the distance specified in the Focal Loss settings. This is a useful and quick option for those times when you want a blurred background and a focused foreground.

> **Note**
>
> MAX R3 contains a Blur rendering effect to use in place of the Scene Blur (found in Lens Effects Focus). The new Blur, however, has a more typical application for animated scenes. Lens Effects Focus is better suited for depth-of-field effects and blur on static imagery.

NEW TO R3

Radial Blur

Radial Blur creates a blur outward from the image's center. See Figure 17.6. This is where the hotspot/falloff thinking pays off. With Radial Blur, use both the Focal Range and Focal Limit settings. With only a little difference between Focal Range and Focal Limit, you see a noticeable "edge" between focused and blurred. For best results, use a larger difference. Set the Focal Range to 10 and the Focal Limit from 100 to 130. This produces a nice "soft-corner" blur that is good for dream sequences or *Abyss*-like effects. Animating these two values is an eye-focusing experience.

Warning
It's important to point out that both Focal Range and Focal Limit behave differently when used in the Radial Blur method of Lens Effects Focus.

Note
Both Radial and Scene Blur happen in 2D space. They don't rely on the Z-Buffer for results. This means that Focal Range and Focal Limit are 2D parameters. They are 3D parameters when used with the Focal Node setting.

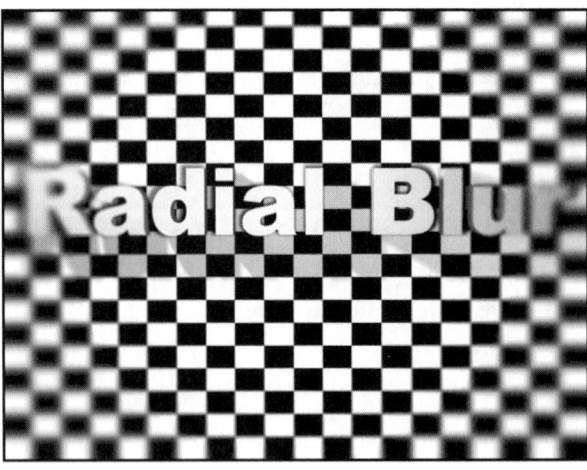

Figure 17.6 A rendering that uses Radial Blur. Notice how the blur emanates outward from the scene's center.

Determining the Focal Point

You probably focus on one or more subjects in your scene, especially during an animation. This is when you start to use the Depth of Field effect's Focal Node parameters.

Before setting the Focal Node in Depth of Field, however, you must select a *focal point*. A focal point is anything—a person, an object, the corner of a building—on which you want your viewers to concentrate. After determining what you want to focus on, you need to determine if you're going to animate that focus item over time. If so, there are a few options to consider:

- **You can animate the camera's target location.** If that is the point you focus on, then your camera will always be focused on its target.

- **You can create a dummy and animate it.** If you're simulating a focal shift for dramatic effects, this is often done without moving the camera or its target. By focusing on the dummy, you don't worry about the camera's target; just where the dummy exists.

- **You can animate the Focal Range and Focal Limit values.** This is perhaps the most tedious way to animate focus. While feasible, it's not practical. It's difficult to keyframe, and there's no visual reference of the focal node's location in the viewports.

Once you determine how your focal point is going to behave, then you use the Focal Node Blur parameters.

In MAX R3, Depth of Field allows you to easily switch between the camera's target and any other object using the Focal Node or Use Camera radio buttons. Normally you just set the Use Camera Radio button and are done with it. There are times, however, where you find yourself wanting to focus on other objects in the scene—or at least use those as a reference point for your focal parameters. To use an object as your focal node, just click the Focal Node radio button. Then click the Pick Node button, and select an object in your scene. You can select anything except cameras. You can, however, select other camera's targets. Figure 17.7 shows the Focal Point section of Depth of Field, along with objects selected in the Focal Node section.

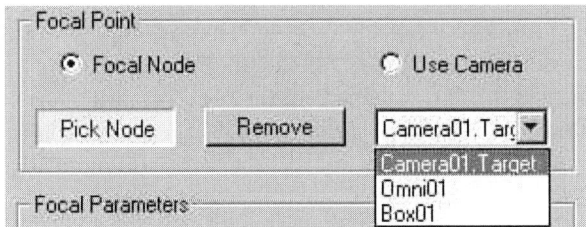

Figure 17.7 The Focal Point settings of the Depth of Field render effect. Here you select whether you want to use the camera's target or another object in the scene as your focal point.

Depth of Field Shift

Enough theory; you're now ready to try some focal effects of your own. Exercise 17.1 uses the Depth of Field effect in Render Effects to replicate a film camera move that draws the viewer's attention from one specific item to another. The method you use shifts the focus from a distant object to a foreground object, forcing the viewer to see something that is lost in a busy scene. Depth of Field changes are an important part of cinematic storytelling. They are equally important in computer animation. Pay close attention to focus the next time you go to the movies or rent a video.

A Cityscape in Depth of Field

Exercise 17.1 is a nighttime street scene in a cityscape. First you direct the viewer's attention to the car by setting the background and foreground out of focus. Next you animate the camera to move a small amount up and to the right, which signals a change. An animated Field of View change fills the display with the new foreground object while keeping the out-of-focus background object large and in the viewer's consciousness. An animated dummy object is the focus node.

Exercise 17.1   Combining Depth of Field Shift with a Camera Move

1. Open 17imx01.max. In the Rendering pull-down menu, click Make Preview. In the Make Preview—Camera02 dialog, select Create to accept the default setting. This renders a thumbnail of the Camera02 viewport.

Note

You can also render the Camera02 viewport to an AVI file for more detailed materials and atmospherics. For this exercise, however, we use the effect of the full screen in focus.

2. In the Rendering pull-down menu, select Render Effects.
3. Click the Add button, and choose Depth of Field from the list. See Figure 17.8. Then check the Interactive checkbox. Make sure the Frame Slider is set to frame 0.
4. Select the Focal Node radio button, and click the Pick Node button. Press the H key on your keyboard, and select BlurDummy01. All blurring during this exercise is determined from the center of the dummy object. In the Focal Parameters section, turn off the Lock button (if it's on). Enter 6.0 in Horiz Focal Loss, 3.0 in Vert Focal Loss, 35.0 in Focal Range, and 600 in Focal Limit. The BlurDummy01 focal node is in the middle of the car and with a Range of 35, the entire car is in focus. The 600 value in Focal Limit softens the edge between in-focus and out-of-focus. The Lens Effect Depth of Field dialog box looks similar to Figure 17.9.

Tip
The blurring effect looks more realistic if you unlock Horiz and Vert Focal Loss, and adjust the entries closer to the aspect ratio of the rendered image size. Rounding off to a Width:Height ratio of 2:1 is a good starting point.

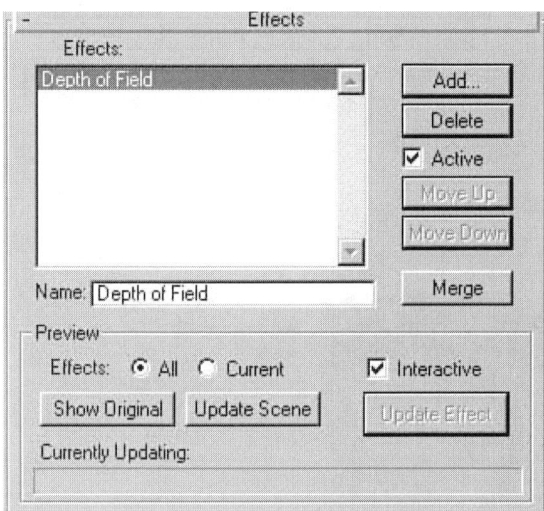

Figure 17.8 The Depth of Field effect in the Render Effects queue. For this exercise, the Interactive checkbox is turned on.

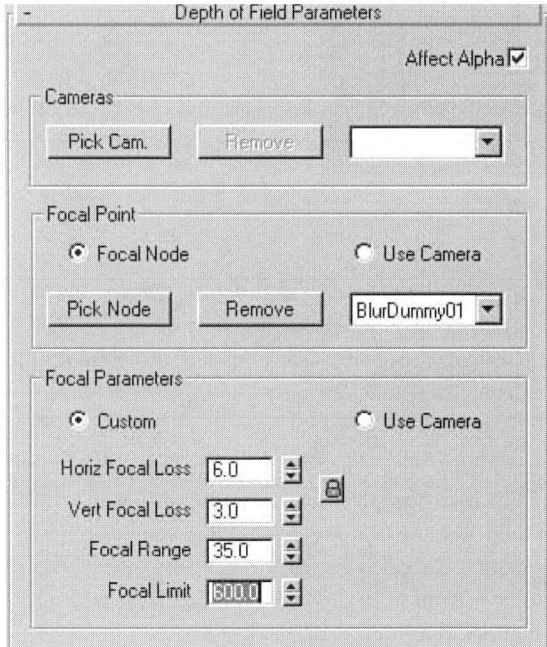

Figure 17.9 Lens Effect Depth of Field Dialog Box and Preview Pane.

5. Click the Animate button to turn it on. Enter 50 in the Frame field, or drag the Frame Slider to frame 50. Click the Update Scene button in the Effects queue section of the Rendering Effects dialog box.

6. Enter 10.0 in Horiz Focal Loss, 6.0 in Vert Focal Loss, 150.0 in the Focal Range field, and 175 in the Focal Limit field. Click the Animate button to turn it off. These settings bring the sign into focus, put the car out of focus, and slightly increase the blurring. Click the OK button in Lens Effect Depth of Field dialog box to close it. See the images rendered in the Effects Preview Pane in Figure 7.10.

Figure 17.10 The Effects Preview Pane.

7. Render the animation by opening the Render Scene dialog box. Change the Time Output to Active Time Segment. In Render Output, turn on Save File. Save your animation to DepthCity.avi. Make sure that your rendering resolution is set, so the scene quickly renders. On a Dual PentiumII 450Mhz, this scene renders one frame in 11 seconds at 320×240 resolution.

8. After the scene is rendered, select Files/View File. Play back the animation. Notice that the animated focus draws your attention from one object to another. In the Preview from Step 1, you had no idea what you were viewing in the animation. Now it's obvious that the car is important at the start, and the sign is important at the end of the animation. Close the Media Player after playing the animation, and close Render Effects.

Chapter 17: Focal Effects   643

9. In the Rendering pull-down menu, click Environment. Click each entry in the Effects list. Then check its Active checkbox to turn it on. Close the Environment dialog box. This activates fog in the scene and volume effects on the streetlights and car headlights.

10. In the Rendering pull-down menu, choose Render. Re-render the scene to a differently named file. Then view it, or view 17imx01Env.avi from the CD.

Tip

Use Depth of Field in MAX to add impact to the storytelling of your animation, but use it only on short sequences. Carefully study the test renders to avoid unwanted artifacts, especially when using Depth of Field in conjunction with atmospheric effects. Try moving the scene's focal node, changing the Focal Range, or increase the Focal Loss settings to correct these anomalies. Be aware, however, that it's difficult to make Lens Effect Depth of Field work with atmospheric effects.

In Exercise 17.1 you set up a Render Effects queue, using Lens Effect Depth of Field to animate a scene's focal blurring. The Horiz and Vert Focal Loss amounts are set to something more in line with the rendered output aspect ratio. This prevents the effect from appearing blurrier at the top and bottom than at the sides.

Depth of Field is a powerful tool in drawing the viewer's attention to specific objects. This action enhances a point in the story, but watch out for artifacts created by the blur.

In Practice: Focal Effects

- **Depth of Field adds focal effects through blur.** The Focal Loss parameter allows you to add more/less blur to the scene. By unlocking Horiz and Vert Focal Loss, you blur the rendered image more/less along a specific axis.

- **Use the Video Post general blur settings for non-focal point effects.** Use Scene Blur and Radial Blur in the Focus module of Video Post to blur a scene without depending on the Z-Buffer. Scene Blur blurs the entire rendered image, and Radial Blur blurs the scene outward from the rendered object's center.

- **Depth of Field is based on depth information from the Z-Buffer.** Because of this feature, focus begins and ends in focal effects. This is based on a planar range rather than a spherical one. At higher Focal Loss settings, this becomes more noticeable.

- **Use dummy objects when simulating focal shifts.** Rather than using the target of the camera, create a dummy object for your focal node. This allows you to create focal shifts without moving the camera or its target.

Part IV

Appendixes

A   AutoCAD and 3D Studio MAX: Sharing Files

B   Designing with Plug-Ins

Appendix A

AutoCAD and 3D Studio MAX: Sharing Files

Many 3D Studio MAX R3 users are also AutoCAD users or work with companies or individuals that create 2D and 3D drawings in AutoCAD. Alas, the process of transferring models between 3D Studio MAX R3 and AutoCAD is not always as seamless as one likes. This appendix covers:

- Options available for importing AutoCAD drawing files into 3D Studio MAX R3, and how those options affect the way you work.
- Type of objects in which 3D Studio MAX R3 translates AutoCAD entities, and tips for making the process more flexible.
- Other import/export file types and their uses for users with older versions of AutoCAD and also for users with other CAD or modeling software.

Why Doesn't 3D Studio MAX R3 Do…?

A common question that long-time AutoCAD users ask is, "Why doesn't 3D Studio MAX do this or that the same way as AutoCAD?" They quickly follow up with the statement, "I've invested a lot of time learning AutoCAD, and I don't want to have to learn new software."

Well—3D Studio MAX *is* new software! Historically both programs developed from totally different sources that had little to do with each other. AutoCAD is an engineering tool, by engineers for engineers, intended to create working-dimensioned drawings and models for manufacturing objects. 3D Studio MAX is a presentation tool, by artists for artists, intended to create realistic renderings and animations to tell a story or present an idea. In the past few years, Autodesk, Discreet/Kinetix, and the Yost Group have put a lot of effort into making the two programs pass data in a predictable and efficient manner. Tools included in MAX R3 (such as Snaps, the Sun Locator, and parametric doors and windows) were developed from discussions with architects and engineers. The trend probably continues in upcoming revisions. In the meantime, analyze your office-work methods and use the available talent to make the process as smooth as possible. There are no hard and fast rules. Start the process with simple files and work your way into more complex projects. Remember that AutoCAD is a drafting/engineering tool, and MAX is a presentation tool.

Note

For those of you relying on AutoCAD as a primary design tool, investigate 3D Studio VIZ. 3DS VIZ has the ability to retain a down-stream link from AutoCAD through its DWG Link feature. Changes made in AutoCAD are (automatically or manually) updated in the VIZ scene, and the AutoCAD layer information remains intact.

The File Import Options

3D Studio MAX R3 offers several options for importing files from other 2D and 3D sources. The current file types that import into MAX R3 are:

- 3D Studio Mesh (.3DS, .PRJ)
- AutoCAD (.DWG)
- AutoCAD (.DXF)
- 3D Studio Shape (.SHP)
- Stereolithography (.STL)
- Adobe Illustrator (.AI)
- IGES (.IGE, .IGS, .IGES)
- VRML (.WRL, .WRZ)

This appendix focuses on importing AutoCAD drawing files (.DWG) because they are the options frequently used for AutoCAD/MAX users. The DWG file import process has the most intelligence in the translation process, resulting in more logical and editable objects in MAX R3.

Note
Visit *www.ktx.com* for any information on updated DWG import files.

When you choose Import/AutoCAD (.DWG) from the Files pull-down menu, two dialog boxes appear: DWG Import and Import AutoCAD DWG File.

AutoCAD DWG Import Dialog Box

The following options are available in the DWG Import dialog box:

- **Merge objects with current scene.** Use this option to keep the existing MAX R3 scene intact, and merge the new AutoCAD models into it. The new objects use the AutoCAD coordinate system for positioning.
- **Completely replace current scene.** This option deletes all objects currently in the MAX R3 scene and imports the AutoCAD objects into the empty scene. This also uses the AutoCAD coordinate system for positioning.

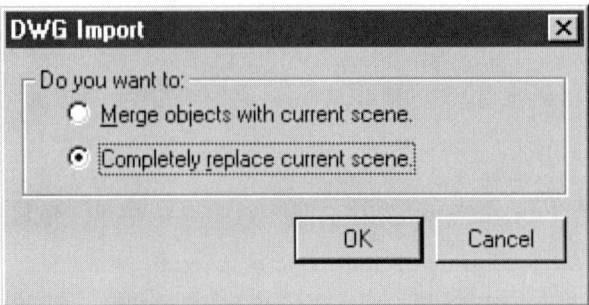

Figure A.1 DWG Import dialog box.

Tip
Your objects may be hundreds of thousands of units from the 0,0,0 MAX R3 coordinate if you import from an AutoCAD drawing that uses Civil Engineering units from State Plane, and so on. Move all objects in AutoCAD to be near 0,0,0 before importing.

Import AutoCAD DWG File Dialog Box

The Import AutoCAD DWG File dialog box (see Figure A.2) is divided into four main areas:

- Derive Object By
- General Options
- Geometry Option
- ACIS Options

The following sections study the options in each of these areas.

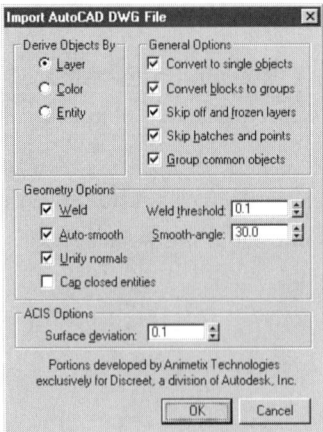

Figure A.2 Import AutoCAD DWG File dialog box.

Derive Object By

One important aspect of importing information from outside sources is how the imported objects are recognized during the import process. The three options for the DWG import method are: Layer, Color, and Entity. Layer uses the AutoCAD layer-naming scheme, Color uses the AutoCAD ACI color assigned to layers or objects in AutoCAD, and Entity uses the AutoCAD entity name to derive Max R3 object names.

- **Layer.** Object names are derived from the AutoCAD layer name. For example, objects on an AutoCAD layer named Floor are named Floor.01, Floor.02, (and so on) in MAX R3. Layer is the most common method of importing from AutoCAD because it offers the most control.

Tip

Importing 2D AutoCAD entities and turning them into 3D objects in MAX R3 is an efficient method of combining the accuracy of AutoCAD and the flexibility of MAX R3. Because of AutoCAD layer names, MAX R3 shapes often need editing (to detach portions of the new object into logical compound shapes). Familiarize yourself with MAX R3 Sub-Object editing methods, such as those found in Chapter 2, "Architectural Modeling." Particularly focus on how to attach and detach 2D Splines to create compound shapes in MAX R3.

- **Color.** Object names derived from the AutoCAD system color number. A red AutoCAD object comes into MAX R3 named Color001.01. This makes it difficult to tell the objects apart because names are not associated with the object.
- **Entity.** This import method is rarely used. The objects have names such as Arc.01, 3Dface.01, and so on. To add to the confusion, names are not only disassociated with the object, but simply assigning names often results in myriad individual objects.

General Options

The General Options area of the dialog box is a catchall for commands that fine-tune various parts of the importing processing.

- **Convert to single objects.** This feature works in conjunction with the Derive From options to make similar AutoCAD objects into one MAX R3 object. For example, all circles with the same thickness on a layer named TANK are combined as a number of circles with one Extrude modifier in MAX R3.
- **Convert blocks to groups.** Block objects in AutoCAD are converted to a MAX R3 group with the same name as the block. Multiple block inserts in AutoCAD change to instance objects in MAX R3.

- **Skip off and frozen layers.** AutoCAD objects on frozen or off layers are ignored in the import process. Common freezable AutoCAD layers are text and dimension layers.

- **Skip hatches and points.** Imported AutoCAD hatch patterns and point entities overwhelms a MAX R3 scene with unusable data. Always check on this.

Tip
Create useful 2D-polyline information in AutoCAD by using the BHATCH command. Under advanced options, select Retain Boundaries. This creates a solid polyline of the area, defined by the hatch pattern. Then import the boundary into MAX R3 as a Spline.

- **Group common objects.** This option imports all AutoCAD objects that are on the same layer, the same entity type, or have the same color into a MAX R3 Group.

Geometry Options

The Geometry Options area of the dialog box allows you to choose various options to modify the geometry as it imports.

The most important option is the welding of vertices. AutoCAD uses internal double-precision math (or 64 decimal places) to calculate points in 3D space. To free computer resources for rendering, MAX R3 uses only single-precision math (or 32 decimal places). The result is potential math-rounding errors, causing vertices to detach. This manifests itself in the MAX R3 file as faces that are slightly out of plane or 2D shapes that are not closed polylines.

Smoothing is a visual effect that makes 3D-mesh surfaces appear smooth or faceted.

Unifying face normals forces the face's normals to point toward (or away from) the mass's center of the 3D-mesh object.

- **Weld.** Globally welds adjacent vertices of AutoCAD objects into a single MAX R3 vertex, based on the Weld Threshold distance. This works only when objects are imported with the Convert to Single Objects option mentioned above.

Tip
Global welding may be problematic. Clear Weld for all ACIS solid models from AutoCAD and from surface models if you are having any problems. You get more predictable results from manually welding objects after they're imported into MAX R3. However, global welding with a Weld Threshold set too high in mesh objects causes smaller details to collapse.

- **Weld Threshold.** Two or more vertices weld into one vertex if their distance is less than or equal to the setting. The range (in system units) is 1 to 999999.

Caution
If an element (such as window trim) projects 2 inches from the façade and the Weld Threshold is set to 2 inches, the trim may suddenly collapse during welding.

- **Auto-smooth.** Auto-smooth assigns smoothing group numbers to faces, based on the angle they meet at a shared edge. If adjacent faces share a common smoothing group number, the edge appears smoothed. If faces don't share a common group, the edge appears sharp.

Tip
Smoothing problems appear in imported DWG files, along with welding problems. They manifest themselves as faces that are darker or lighter than their neighbors. Make sure a MAX R3 object is properly welded; then remove all smoothing group numbers. Manually apply Auto-smooth or specific smoothing group number assignments.

- **Smooth Angle.** Smooth Angle determines the angle faces' intersect for a common smoothing group number. The range is 0 to 90.
- **Unify Normals.** With Unify Normals selected, the import process tries to make all face normals point in the same direction—relative to the object's center. Flipped face normals appear as "holes" in the MAX R3 mesh object. ACIS solid models are already unified and should clear Unify Normals.

Tip
Flipped faces are a fairly common problem with AutoCAD objects. Improperly welded faces can cause flipped faces. First, weld the mesh. Then render the object with a two-sided material applied, or by checking the 2-sided option in Views/Viewport Configuration. This allows you to determine if faces are flipped or missing completely. If faces are flipped, use the Normal modifier or edit the mesh at the Sub-Object/Face level. Proceed to individually flip them.

- **Cap Closed Entities.** This applies a MAX R3 Extrude modifier to all closed AutoCAD entities, and then puts capping faces at each end. Closed AutoCAD entities with no thickness contain an Extrude modifier with a height of 0. They appear as flat faces. When the Cap Closed Entities is cleared, entities with thickness are still extruded. However, no end caps are applied. Entities with no thickness are imported as MAX R3 2D shapes.

ACIS Options

The ACIS Options area affects only mesh objects created using AutoCAD or Mechanical Desktop solid objects. For example, a solid sphere in AutoCAD is a mathematically correct sphere. When it imports into MAX R3, however, it must translate into a set of flat triangular-sided faces. This dialog area allows you to adjust the accuracy of the faces to the true sphere.

- **Surface Deviation.** The Surface Deviation setting is the maximum distance in system units from the surface of an AutoCAD ACIS solid model and the mesh object in MAX R3. The range is 0.001 to 999999. Smaller numbers make a tighter fit, or a more accurate mesh object.

Caution

Small Surface Deviation settings create extremely complex mesh objects in MAX R3. Large settings cause lost detail in a model.

AutoCAD DWG and 3D Studio MAX R3 Entities Translation

The process of translating entities and objects from AutoCAD to MAX R3 (and back again) requires that each software package translate from one object type to another. The following two tables list the entity or object from one program in the first column and its corresponding object type after translation.

Table A.1 AutoCAD DWG to MAX R3 Objects

AutoCAD Entity	3D Studio MAX R3 Object
Point	Point Helper
Line	Spline Shape
Arc	Arc Shape
Circle	Circle Shape
Ellipse	Ellipse Shape
Solid	Closed Spline Shape
Trace	Closed Spline Shape
2D Polyline	Spline Shape
3D Polyline	Spline Shape
Polyline Donut	Donut Shape
Spline	Spline Shape
MLine	Spline Shape
Text (using TTF or PFB)	Text Shape
3D Face	Mesh Object

AutoCAD Entity	3D Studio MAX R3 Object
Polyline Mesh	Mesh Object
Polyface Mesh	Mesh Object
ACIS Object	Mesh Object
Region	Editable Mesh with 0 thickness
Blocks	Objects or Group by option
UCS Definition	Grid Helper
DView (perspective)	Target Camera
Point Light	Omni Light
Spotlight	Target Spot
Distance Light	Directional Light
Thickness Property	Extrude Modifier
Polyline Width	Spline Outline
Color	Object Color by option

Table A.2   MAX R3 Objects to AutoCAD DWG Entities

3D Studio MAX R3 Object	AutoCAD Entity
Circle Shape	Circle
Donut Shape	Donut Polyline
Ellipse Shape	Ellipse
Text Shape	Text (using Standard style)
Spline Shape (1 straight segment)	Line
Spline Shape (coplanar linear segments)	2D Polyline
Spline Shape (non-linear or 3D)	Spline
3D Surfaces	PolyFace Mesh
Cameras	Named DView
Omni Light	Point Light
Spotlights	Spotlight
Directional Light	Distant Light
Grid Helper	Named UCS
Point Helper	Point

Exporting from MAX R3 to AutoCAD is not as common as importing objects from AutoCAD. However, it is easier to create some objects (such as convincing screw threads) in MAX R3 than in AutoCAD.

Tip

An excellent tool included in MAX R3 is the Section option found in the Create/Shape panel. It cuts a 2D-section shape through 3D objects on any plane and converts the section to a 2D Shape (that exports to AutoCAD for dimensioning or creates AutoCAD solid objects).

Other Import/Export Format Options

For users without access to AutoCAD Release 14 drawings or who are experiencing problems with the DWG import process, MAX imports several other file types.

3D Studio 3DS, PRJ

MAX imports files that were created in 3D Studio DOS Release 4 (or earlier) and saved with the endings .3DS or .PRJ (Project files). AutoCAD Releases 13 and 14 have a 3DSOUT command that writes the .3DS format. The .3DS and .PRJ formats are only for 3D objects.

Adobe Illustrator AI

You can import Adobe Illustrator (AI88) files into 3D Studio MAX. This allows you to use 2D-vector objects created in Adobe Illustrator, Corel Draw, or any other software that uses the AI88 format.

Tip
Corel Draw has a Trace feature that traces 2D bitmaps with vectors that are saved in .AI format. This method automatically traces logos or unusual fonts.

When importing AI88 files, 3D Studio MAX converts polygons to Shape objects.

Caution
AI files created with Corel Trace contain large numbers of vertices and may need optimizing in Corel or (manually) in MAX R3.

AI Import Options

Choose an option in the Shape Import dialog box to set the way shape objects are created from imported AI files:

- **Single Object.** All polygons in the AI file are converted to Bézier Splines and placed inside a single composite shape object.
- **Multiple Objects.** Each polygon in the AI file is converted to a Bézier Spline and placed inside an independent shape object.

AutoCAD DXF

DXF files import and export objects to and from AutoCAD (and other programs that support this file format). See Figure A.3 for the Import DXF File dialog box.

Appendix A: AutoCAD and 3D Studio MAX: Sharing Files 657

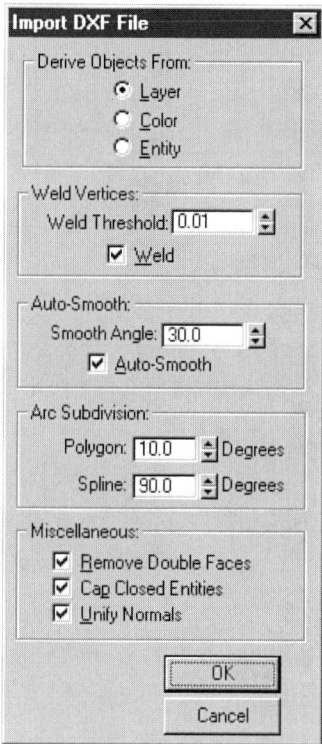

Figure A.3 Import DXF File dialog box.

Tip

Keep the following guidelines in mind when you create your DXF geometry and decide whether to convert by layer, color, or entity:

If you are using the AutoCAD Advanced Modeling Extension (AME) with AutoCAD Release 12, use the SOLMESH command on your AME models prior to saving the DXF file.

With AutoCAD Release 13 or later, use the 3DSOUT command to convert an AutoCAD drawing to mesh objects. This command creates a 3D Studio Release 4 file that imports into 3D Studio MAX.

After importing a DXF file, you may want to divide the resulting 3D Studio MAX objects into smaller objects. Do this by editing at the Sub-Object/Face level and detaching sets of faces into new objects.

Note

Layers are ignored that are frozen or turned off in AutoCAD before saving the DXF file.

The following sections help explain some of the options presented in the Import DXF dialog box.

Derive Objects From Options

MAX R3 objects derive from DXF information in one of three ways. As in the DWG import method, deriving MAX R3 objects based on AutoCAD layers usually makes the most sense. You already assigned layer names in AutoCAD that make sense for your discipline. Retaining the same names for objects in MAX R3 helps increase productivity. Importing by AutoCAD color names and entity names results in named objects in MAX R3 that have little meaning in the context of the scene.

- **Layer.** Each layer with a unique name is converted into a separate object.
- **Color.** All entities of the same color are converted into a single entity.
- **Entity.** Each entity is converted into a separate object.

Weld Vertices

This option welds coincident vertices in the DXF file into single vertices in the 3D Studio MAX mesh. This corrects problems resulting from rounding errors between the two programs. The two options in the Import DXF File dialog box are:

- **Weld Threshold.** Determines the size of the area that vertices must occupy to be welded.
- **Weld.** Turns on the Weld Vertices function. In most cases, you should leave this box selected because unwelded objects cannot be correctly unified or smoothed.

Auto-Smooth

Applies smoothing groups to the geometry, based on the smoothing angle set by the smooth angle spinner. Edges between faces appear faceted in the rendered image when an angle between them is greater than the specified smoothing angle. Edges between faces that are below the specified angle are smoothed.

- **Smooth Angle.** Sets the angle where smoothing occurs.
- **Smooth.** Turns on smoothing.

Arc Subdivision

This area of the Import DXF File dialog box deals with imported objects created through 2D AutoCAD arc entities or the 2D arcs themselves. It explains how the mathematically correct arcs are translated into segmented splines in MAX R3.

- **Polygon Degrees.** Specifies the number of degrees between each vertex in any imported curvature that's converted to a mesh object in 3D Studio MAX. An example might be an extruded spline.

- **Spline Degrees.** Specifies the number of degrees between vertices in an imported curvature that's converted to a Bézier Spline (a shape) in 3D Studio MAX. This may be an arc or a non-extruded spline, for example. Unlike mesh objects, Bézier Splines contain their own curvatures, so you don't need as many vertices. The default setting of 90 degrees is usually adequate.

Miscellaneous

The following three options are located in the Miscellaneous area of the Import DXF File dialog box. Following the bulleted list of options (and their use) is a section describing some of the issues related to the Unify Normals option.

- **Remove Double Faces.** Removes one face wherever two faces occupy the same location. Double Faces gives a flashing effect when rendered to an animation. It is also difficult to apply materials to it, and it causes 3D Boolean operations to fail.

- **Fill Polylines.** Converts closed 2D polylines into mesh objects. Closed, planar, 3D polylines are capped. If the 2D polyline is open, it imports as a spline shape.

- **Unify Normals.** Forces the normals of all faces on each object to face the same way (usually out). If the face normals point in the wrong direction when you render your 3D Studio MAX scene, use the Normal modifier to flip them. For best results, leave this box selected.

The Normal Issue

The successful unification of face normals depends on the welding of coincident vertices. Depending upon the model's precision as AutoCAD created it, the vertices may not be close enough to be considered "coincident." They are not welded, and the faces are not properly unified. In this case, increase the Weld Threshold value in the Import DXF File dialog box.

Converting by layer results in objects consisting of many elements. In certain cases, all the face normals are flipped the wrong way in some of these elements. You can detect this in 3D Studio MAX by clearing Backface Cull in the Display panel or by rendering the objects. Use the Normal modifier to correct this.

If you do not want to flip normals, you can either use 2-sided materials or turn on the Force 2-Sided option in the Render Scene dialog box.

If you load a large scene containing thousands of entities (such as 3D faces) and choose to load an object by entity, the conversion takes a long time. It also produces a huge number of objects to handle in 3D Studio MAX. Avoid this by organizing your DXF file so that these kinds of entities are grouped by layer. Then make the conversion by layer, rather than by entity.

3D Studio SHP

Import 3D Studio R2-R4 2D Shape files with the Import (SHP) option. They import as MAX R3 2D shapes.

3DSIN and 3DSOUT

3DS is the 3D Studio Release 4 mesh file format. You can import and export 3DS files from 3D Studio MAX. PRJ is the 3D Studio Release 4 project file format.

When you import a 3DS or PRJ file, merge the imported objects with the current scene or replace the current scene completely. If you choose to merge the objects with the current scene, you are asked whether you want to reset the length of the scene's animation to the length of the imported file (if the imported file contains animation).

When you import a 3DS file, the following information is important:

- Backgrounds (solid, gradient, and bitmap).
- Fog, Layered Fog, and Distance Cue.
- Ambient light level.
- Subtractive transparency is converted to 3D Studio MAX "Filter" transparency. The filter color is set equal to the Diffuse color.
- Transparency falloff settings.
- All enabled Map channels. Map channels that are turned off in the 3DS file do not import into 3D Studio MAX.
- All Map parameters, including UV transforms, Negative, Mirror, and Rotation. Some Map parameters (such as Blur, Luma, RGB, and Alpha) work differently in 3D Studio MAX. These values convert to new values that produce a similar effect.
- Mask bitmaps import as a 3D Studio MAX mask texture.

Appendix A: AutoCAD and 3D Studio MAX: Sharing Files 661

- When materials with both Texture 1 and Texture 2 are imported, a composite texture is created and added to the Standard material's Diffuse channel.
- Reflection maps, auto-cubics, and mirrors.
- Automatic Reflection Map Nth frame, and Map Size settings.
- SXP translation for Marble and Noise materials.
- 3DS/DOS IK Joint parameters.
- 3D Surfer Patch data.

When you import a 3DS file, the following information is not imported:

- Morph keys.
- Keyframer instances.
- Map channels that are turned off.
- Custom .cub-format cubic maps.
- Decal transparency, using the RGB color of the upper-left pixel of the map.
- When you import a PRJ file, all the above items are imported, plus Shapes.

When you export a 3DS file, the following information is exported:

- Position, Rotation, and Scale animation. If the controller is a TCB controller, the TCB, Ease In, and Ease Out values are also saved. If the controller is any other type of key controller, the keys are saved. However, the tangent information is lost. If the controller is not a key controller, only the object's transformation at frame 0 is saved.
- Basic material color/parameters from the Standard material.
- Single maps with their amount, offsets, scales, and so on.
- Auto-cubics and Mirrors.
- Target cameras, target spotlights, and Omni lights.
- Most "static" parameters for cameras and lights, and animation tracks for Roll, Falloff, Hotspot, and FOV.

When you export a 3DS file, the following information is not exported:

- Composite and procedural maps.
- UV mapping coordinates.

- Grouped object transformations. There is no concept of group hierarchy in the 3D Editor. Groups export to the Keyframer because the Keyframer understands hierarchies.
- Global shadow parameters.

When you export a 3DS file, the following occurs:

- All non-mesh geometry (such as procedural primitives and patches) collapse to meshes before export.
- Objects are exported as they exist on the frame 3D Studio MAX displays at export time. To output morph targets, go to each frame. Export the target to a different filename.
- Meshes save with edge display information and smoothing groups.
- 3D Studio MAX instances save as Keyframer instances.
- Modifier and morph animation is frozen at the current frame, collapsed, and exported as a simple mesh.

Stereolithography STL

An import/export file type in MAX R3 is through the stereolithography file format with the .stl file ending. In order for a mesh object to be used as a stereolithography object, it must have a high surface integrity. Models often import via STL from high-end CAD packages.

Stereolithography files are intended for use with software that slices mesh objects into thin layers of descriptive information, and then translates into a 3D model by "plotting" the layer in a vat polymer with a laser.

While designed primarily for the industrial design and mechanical market, STL file transfer often works well in architecture. STL files imported from FormZ for architecture fit quite nicely in to MAX, with fewer face and normal problems than DXF or DWG.

Tip
MAX R3 has a modifier called STL-Check. It highlights any potential invalid STL features in a MAX R3 mesh object prior to exporting. If you have trouble with imported objects from any source, STL-Check highlights an offending open edge or coincident faces, so you can identify and possibly correct the problem.

The Import STL File Dialog Box Options

The following options are found in the Import STL File dialog box. The options perform the same function as found in other file import methods.

- **Name.** Enter a name for the 3D Studio object created from the STL file. The default is the filename (without an extension) or the name saved internally in the STL file.
- **Weld Vertices.** Welds coincident vertices in the STL file into single vertices in the 3D Studio mesh.
- **Weld Threshold.** Determines the size of the area that welded vertices must occupy. Vertices with distances equal to or less than this value weld into a single vertex.
- **Weld.** Turns on the Weld Vertices function. In most cases, leave this box selected because unwelded objects can't be unified or smoothed.
- **Use Threshold.** If activated, STL import uses the standard 3D Studio welding method. This is a very slow process.
- **Quick Weld.** If activated, STL import uses a welding algorithm optimized for the STL format. This is up to 30 times faster than standard 3D Studio welding and is highly recommended.
- **Auto-Smooth.** Applies smoothing groups to the geometry, based on the smoothing angle set by the smooth angle spinner. Edges between faces with an angle between them that is greater than the specified smoothing angle appear faceted in the rendered image. Edges between faces that are below the specified angle appear smoothed.
- **Remove Double Faces.** Removes one face wherever two faces occupy the same location. This step is recommended.
- **Unify Normals.** Forces the normals of all faces on each object to face the same way (usually out). If the face normals are pointing in the wrong direction when you render your 3D Studio scene, use the Normal modifier to flip them. For best results, leave this box selected.

IGES Files

NEW TO R3 3D Studio MAX R3 now offers the option to import IGES (.IGE, .IGS, IGES) file format. Its primary function imports native NURBS surface information from other high-end CAD and modeling programs that support the same file type.

Note

MAX R3 converts the NURBS surfaces to rigid surfaces. To edit the CVs of imported objects, select the object. Go to the Modify panel, and then click the Make Independent option in Surface Common rollout.

Table A.3 IGES Entities to MAX R3 Objects

IGES Entity Name	3D Studio MAX R3 Object
Circular Arc	Arc Shape
Composite Curve	Spline Shape
Conic Arc	Spline Shape
Copious Data	Single Spline
Plane	NURBS Surface
Line	Spline Shape
Parametric Spline Curve	NURBS Curve
Parametric Spline Surface	NURBS Surface
Point	Point Helper
Ruled Surface	NURBS Surface
Surface of Revolution	NURBS Surface
Tabulated Surface	NURBS Surface
Rational B-Spline Curve	NURBS Curve
Rational B-Spline Surface	NURBS Surface
Offset Curve	NURBS Curve
Offset Surface	NURBS Surface
Boundary Curve	NURBS Surface
Curve on Parametric Surface	NURBS Surface
Trimmed Parametric Surface	NURBS Surface
Bounded Surface	NURBS Surface
Solid	NURBS Surface
Subfigure Definition	Instance
Group	NURBS Object

IGES translation also creates a log file, saved in the form filename.xli. The file contains information about processing the imported model, including error messages that occur during translation. This information is useful for troubleshooting problems that occur during import.

Note

Not all IGES file types or entity types are translated. See the MAX R3 Online Help files for more information.

VRML Files

You can import objects in the form of VRML files into MAX R3. The file types .WRL and .WRZ are recognized from VRML 1.0 VRBL and VRML 2.0/VRML 97. Geometry, materials, lights, perspective cameras and viewpoints, and grouping nodes are imported in the process. Simple animated transformations are also imported. Three options are available in the Import VRML File dialog box:

- **Reset Scene.** Deletes any existing scene when you import a new scene. If unchecked, the new scene is merged into an existing scene.
- **Turn to 3DS Coordinates.** Converts the coordinate system from the Y-axis being up in VRML to the Z-axis being up in MAX R3.
- **Create Primitives.** Converts VRML Box, Cone, Cylinder, and Sphere nodes into corresponding MAX R3 primitives, where possible.

In Practice: AutoCAD and 3D Studio MAX: Sharing Files

- **Make sure your AutoCAD operators are well trained in correct AutoCAD procedures.** To make your AutoCAD-to-MAX-R3 file translation as smooth as possible, make sure your AutoCAD users are adept at layer management, proper use of osnaps, thickness and elevation usage, and choosing ACIS solids versus surface models, and so on.
- **Understanding MAX R3 vertex welding and smoothing group controls is essential to fine-tuning the models imported into MAX R3.** Be aware that global welding upon import collapses small details if the Weld Threshold is set too high for the objects' size.
- **The 3DS file format is the only format that carries material and mapping information back and forth from MAX R3 to AutoCAD.** You must use the 3DSOUT option to preserve material and mapping when you assign materials and mapping coordinates to surfaces in AutoCAD for importing to MAX R3.
- **AutoCAD's 3DSOUT export option transfers atmosphere-enhancing information.** The 3DSOUT export option transfers background, fogging, transparency, ambient lighting, reflection maps, and mask maps information from AutoCAD to MAX R3.
- **Translating 2D shapes and splines is an efficient method of exchanging data between AutoCAD and MAX R3.** AutoCAD is unrivaled in its ability to produce accurate drawings and models. It is often more efficient to create accurate 2D

polylines in AutoCAD, and export them to MAX R3 for modification into 3D objects. The imported 2D data is precise in memory requirements, and you can take advantage of MAX R3's flexible editing to create low face/vertex models that retain the AutoCAD accuracy.

- **The STL import/export option is a reliable method of transferring 3D data to and from AutoCAD.** It also works well for other CAD programs and for MAX R3.

- **IGES import is the only way to import NURBS data from other software programs.** In previous versions of 3D Studio MAX, it was difficult to use NURBS data created in other software packages. MAX R3 now uses the industry-standard IGES file type to import NURBS models and splines. However, not all IGES data types are supported. Go to the online help in MAX R3 for more information.

- **VRML translation is the currently accepted method of working with scenes and animations that are viewable on Internet.** Exporting and importing the VRML file format allows you to generate scenes for viewing on Internet. The viewer moves around in space or manipulates simple objects in the scene. The MAX R3 scenes must contain a very low polygon count with simple textures and lighting, or they overwhelm any system or technology used by the viewer.

Appendix B

Designing with Plug-Ins

MAX offers you a great advantage over other 3D-software users—the ability to expand. Through the use of the plug-in technology built into MAX, you can extend, enhance, or add features to the base product. While MAX is capable of doing many things, there are some areas of the software that are enhanced or replaced by a good plug-in.

Believe it or not, MAX is actually composed of plug-ins. There is a central program called the *core* and everything else is plug-ins. When you start MAX, you see plug-ins initializing in the startup, or *splash,* screen. Along the bottom of the splash screen reads "Initializing..." As plug-ins are initialized, their names appear. This process is fast. MAX is looking for plug-ins, but *not* necessarily loading them into RAM. MAX wants to know what's available, so it can present them to you (the user) when the main interface appears. Only when you use a plug-in does MAX fully load it into memory. The end result is memory usage only when MAX needs it.

Tip

Change MAX's startup screen by renaming any *BMP* file *splash.bmp* and placing it in the root MAX directory. Just make sure it's small enough for you to see the rest of the Windows interface!

Plug-In Names

MAX's plug-ins appear as DLL files within your plug-ins directory, as well as anywhere else you place them on your hard drive. (DLL stands for Dynamic Load Library.) Depending on their type, plug-ins have (at the least) a different last letter in the extension. Table B.1 lists the extension changes.

Table B.1   Plug-In Extensions Defined

Extension	Meaning
.dlo	Objects found in the Create Panel
.dlm	Modifiers
.dlt	Materials found in the Material Editor
.dlc	Animation controller plug-ins
.dlr	Rendering plug-ins
.dle	Plug-ins located in the File/Export command
.dli	Plug-ins located in the File/Import command
.dlu	Other plug-ins found in the Utility Panel
.dlf	Font plug-ins
.dlv	Render Effects/Atmospheric Effects
.dlh	Plug-in SuperSamplers for materials
.dlb	Plug-in shaders for the material editor
.flt	Filters for Video Post
.bmf	Antialiasing filters for Rendering
.bms	Storage plug-ins for raster files (bitmap)
.bmi	Raster file (bitmap) plug-ins

Appendix B: Designing with Plug-Ins

There are other plug-in types, but Table B.1 shows the major ones. The reason for this list is twofold: To illustrate how many types there are, and to show you where to find a plug-in once you install it. Users commonly download plug-ins from a developer or from a Web site, then can't figure out where the plug-in is located or what it does.

Note
Although scripts are plug-ins, they have a .ms, .mcr, or .mse extension and must be loaded via the MAXScript plug-in or through the Windows NT command line.

Plug-In Sources

This Appendix doesn't focus on specific plug-ins or developers. Instead it is designed to give you an idea of how various plug-in types work, and how they might assist you in your day-to-day production life within MAX. It also focuses on plug-ins directly related to the subjects discussed in this book. Therefore, you find information on modeling, material, and rendering plug-ins. For the most up-to-date information, refer to two places on the Internet:

- **The Discreet Web site.** Go to *www.ktx.com* for the latest information on MAX from Discreet. There is also other information on other Discreet products, such as 3D Studio VIZ and Character Studio.

- **The Discreet support forum.** Just enter *support.ktx.com* into the address field of your Web browser. (Note: There's no need for a *www.* at the beginning.)

Plug-ins are frequently updated, so check at least once a month on your favorite sites.

To Pay or Not to Pay?

A frequent issue with users is whether to pay a developer for a plug-in or to just use an available free one (or shareware) on the Internet. When you pay for a plug-in, you usually get your money's worth. However, a number of independent developers post some of their work as a showcase and an experiment of their capabilities.

Pay

Most reputable developers of commercially developed plug-ins provide technical support. If you run into a problem, they can usually get you out of it. They also maintain dedicated testing environments. While some developers test more thoroughly, most spend considerable time developing and testing a plug-in before releasing it for the general market. As a result, MAX runs more smoothly because poorly developed or unstable plug-ins wreak havoc on MAX's overall stability. (See the section "Unplugging Plug-Ins" for remedies.) Developers operate as a business. That means they have dedicated resources (money and people) to develop quality plug-ins. As new versions of MAX emerge, commercial developers are in contact with Discreet to make sure their plug-ins work with the new release. Commercial developers are obligated (just by the nature of the industry) to provide documentation. Free plug-in documentation is sparse, at best. Remember—figuring out a plug-in without adequate reference material and tutorials is both time consuming and frustrating.

Don't Pay

On the other hand, free plug-ins offer a major benefit over commercial plug-ins: They're *free*. That's the best price for a plug-in. Free plug-ins are usually developed by hobbyists who love MAX and love to program. This, however, is *not* indicative of their programming skills. Many free plug-ins provide excellent and useful features for MAX. They're often full-featured and completely stable. However, don't expect this to be the case for everything. There is the occasional rogue plug-in that completely destabilizes MAX.

Whether you choose to go with commercial, free, or both types of plug-ins, remember—that's the power of MAX. You can add to it whenever you need to increase the features or functionality of the base package.

Objects and Modifier Plug-Ins

When you download a plug-in that contains a .dlo or .dlm extension, it's going to show up in your Create or Modify panel. These plug-ins allow you to create new objects or edit objects in a new way.

If an object plug-in is designed correctly, it appears in its own category within one of the seven types of creation categories. Where it appears and what name it displays depends on what the developer wants. Object plug-ins significantly decrease development time of certain geometry types. For instance, if you find yourself frequently making trees by hand, try a plug-in that automatically creates foliage. A design visualization product from Discreet, 3D Studio VIZ, proves the usefulness of new object types with Door and Window objects for architects. Many other object plug-ins extend the Create panel, including objects such as lights and helpers. Figure B.1 shows the MAX interface with a few objects created with object plug-ins.

Figure B.1 Objects created with object plug-ins, available for MAX.

Modifier plug-ins work along the same lines as object plug-ins, but they work by application to various types of objects. Modifiers not only alter the shape of the geometry, but also edit the geometry at the root level. For instance, the Physique plug-in that is part of the Character Studio package from Discreet allows you to edit an object at the vertex level. Figure B.2 shows the MAX interface with a key modified with modifier plug-ins.

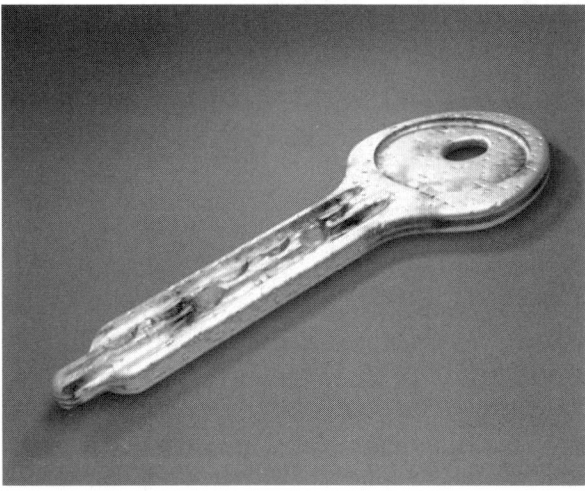

Figure B.2 A key rendered with the Quick Dirt modifier plug-in from Cuney Tozdas, rendered by Osman Safi (osafi@garanti.net.tr). Distributed by Digimation (www.digimation.com).

Material Editor Plug-Ins

When it comes to extending the Material Editor via plug-ins, there are two options: As a complete material or via a map type. Complete materials function much like Standard material. They are often specialized, to enhance existing features or to extend MAX's material and rendering capabilities. Many times new material plug-ins require a new or enhanced rendering engine. The Raytrace material is an example of how a plug-in material type might work. (Rendering engines are discussed in the next section.) If the plug-in is designed to add a map type, then it will appear in the listing of maps available when you click a map slot within the Material Editor. Considering the Raytrace material again, notice that it's also plugged in to MAX as a map as well. Most plug-in renderers work this way because they need special materials to work inside the plug-in rendering engine. Figure B.3 shows a rendering made with both material and map plug-ins available for MAX.

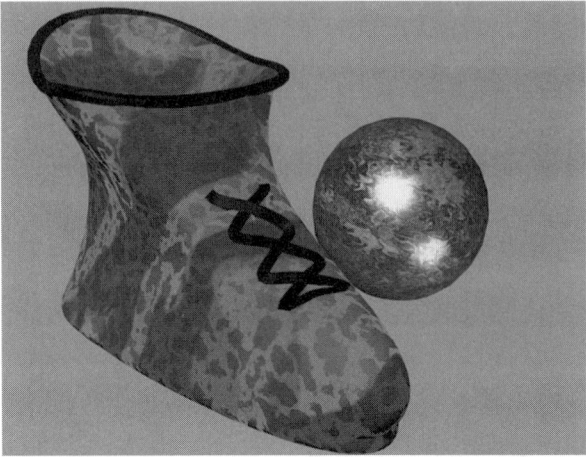

Figure B.3 Material plug-ins are used to render this image.

Rendering and Special Effects Plug-Ins

Many developers contributed to these categories of MAX features. Since MAX R1, several plug-ins have been released that enhance or replace the default Scanline Renderer built into MAX. While this was almost a necessity for MAX R1, the need is less apparent with raytrace added in the MAX renderer—however, developers work to improve upon it as well. Special effects plug-ins include everything from combustible particle systems to special compositing filters. Again MAX ships with Lens Effects, but other lens flare plug-ins contain new or improved features over the standard MAX Lens Effects. Figure B.4 shows an illustration created using a specialized rendering engine.

Figure B.4 A rendering of a MAX scene, using a specialized cartoon rendering engine.

Other Plug-Ins

There are several other plug-in types available for MAX. As a user, it's up to you to find what works best for your needs. This means that you spend time studying and experimenting with all types of plug-ins. Plug-ins range from the more common types mentioned in this appendix to the more unusual ones. (See Figure B.5 for an example of an environmental plug-in.) One plug-in is designed to allow you to print from the Rendering dialog box. Many discussion forums often review plug-ins as they become available. Just check the Discreet support forum to discover the latest in plug-in technology. Take advantage of this resource, as it's not uncommon for several hundred plug-ins to be available for MAX at one time!

Figure B.5 An environmental plug-in is used to create this sunset image, including the land and water.

Unplugging Plug-Ins

Eventually, you are bound to run into poorly developed plug-ins, plug-ins in beta, or rushed-to-market plug-ins that should still be in beta. These plug-ins destabilize MAX. Before you go pointing the finger at MAX for unstableness, check the plug-ins you loaded. Sometimes a plug-in causes unstableness in MAX even if the plug-in is not in use.

If you frequently download from the Internet, the threat of a destabilizing plug-in is always present. So you want to take preventative measures to easily "unplug" a plug-in. You do this by removing it from MAX's plug-in paths. The best rule-of-thumb is to organize your plug-ins into major sub-directories. Then create even more sub-directories for each plug-in. Figure B.6 shows an example of a directory structure for plug-ins. Notice how beta plug-ins are organized in their own separate directory. Figure B.7 shows how the resulting plugin.ini file looks. Plugin.ini is a simple text file that you can edit if you want. Within it are the direct paths to plug-ins and a description of them. There are also entries for the on-line help system. These appear in the Help/Additional Help pull-down menu in MAX.

Appendix B: Designing with Plug-Ins   677

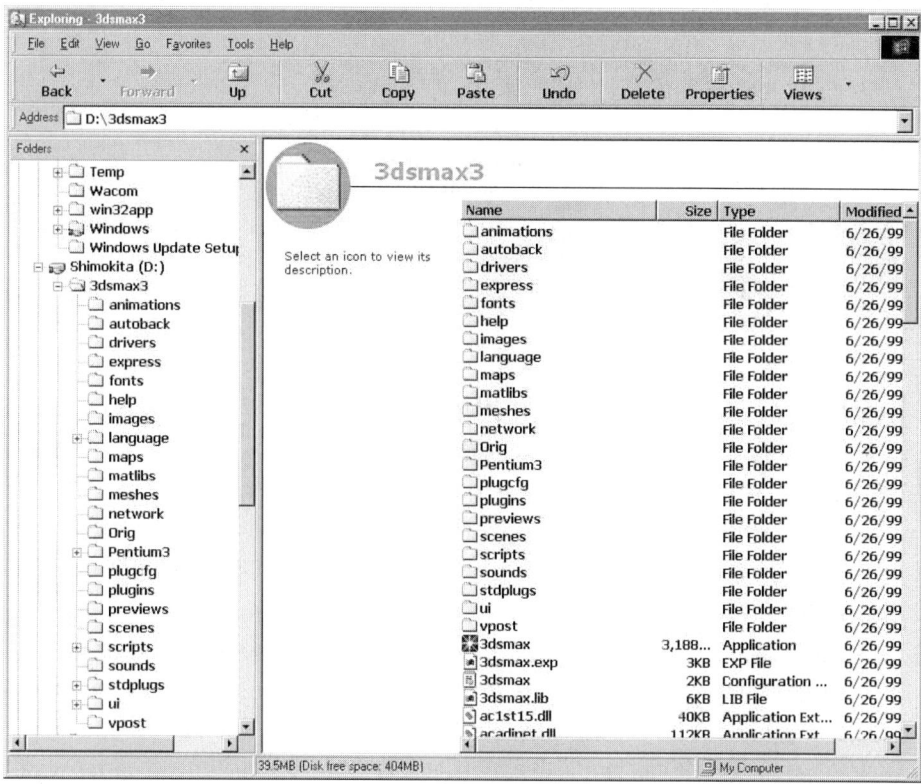

Figure B.6 A directory structure that allows you to pull certain plug-ins out of MAX if they cause trouble or are simply not needed.

MAX maintains the ability to load using an alternative plug.ini file as well. Specify which plug-ins to load. Here are the steps for doing this:

1. Copy plugin.ini to a file (such as allplugs.ini).
2. Create a copy of your 3DSMAX shortcut, and edit its properties.
3. Change the command to 3DSMAX.EXE –p allplugs.ini.
4. Configure this one file to have *all* your plug-ins, and leave the original plugin.ini alone.

```
[Directories]
Standard MAX plug-ins=D:\3dsmax3\StdPlugs
Additional MAX plug-ins=D:\3dsmax3\PlugIns
Plug-ins in Developmen=D:\3dsmax3\BetaSoftware
Plug-ins download from the Web=D:\3dsmax3\Wed Plug-ins
[Help]
MAXScript Reference=D:\3dsmax3\Help\maxscrpt.hlp
Product Support Help=D:\3dsmax3\Help\max_ps.hlp
```

Figure B.7 The plug.ini file, located in the root 3DSMAX directory. This text file is editable by you in Notepad. You can also access its entries through the Configure Paths option in the Customize pull-down menu.

In Practice: Designing with Plug-Ins

- **Take note of a plug-in's file extension.** Plug-ins appear in various places in the MAX interface. MAX is designed so that plug-ins don't "stand out" from the rest of the product. This helps from a usability standpoint, but it's a hassle searching for a newly installed plug-in. Use the chart in this Appendix for help to search for a plug-in's location.

- **The decision to pay is yours.** Plug-ins are sent from many sources throughout the world. Some are commercial; some are freeware. If you buy a plug-in, remember that it's usually a safe bet. It's even better if you can first try it out in a demo version. If you go the free route, just be careful. Sometimes plug-ins wreak havoc on MAX if they're not designed properly.

- **Take out plug-ins when MAX appears to be unstable.** If MAX keeps crashing, you probably have a faulty plug-in. Set up MAX so that it doesn't load third-party plug-ins. Then add them back one at a time. Eventually you locate the offending plug-in.

Index

Numbers

.3DS, importing files, 656
.PRJ, importing files, 656
2D animated graphics versus real-time 3D graphics, 191-192
2D animation, 505, 520
2D floor plan extruded for height
    architectural modeling, 58
    floor plans, extruding, 59-62
2D shapes, cross-sectional modeling, 164
2D sub-object level, editing, 74-76
2D wall elevation extruded for thickness, 69
3D acceleration, 237-238
3D boxes, creating for Boolean operations, 63-65
3D game accelerator cards, 192
3D Studio MAX R3. *See* MAX R3
3D Studio R2-R4 2D Shape files, importing, 660
3D Studio VIZ, 46, 648
3D-Boolean operations, 66
3DS files
    exporting, 661-662
    importing, 660-661

A

Accuracy Explorer, 52
ACIS Options, 654
Active/Inactive in Viewport toggle, 247
Active/Inactive modifier toggle, 247
Adaptive Halton, SuperSampling, 345
adaptive SuperSampling, 345
Adaptive Uniform, SuperSampling, 345
adding
    detail to torsos with MeshSmooth, 306-307
    finishing touches to Macro buttons, 229
    gable ends, 74

    gable windows, 76
    highlights
        to candles, 625
        to entire objects, 626-627
        to shiny surfaces, 622-623
Additive transparency, 342
adjusting colors (glow), 601
Adobe Illustrator AI, 656
Advanced Transparency, extended parameters, 353-354
advantages
    of 2D floor plan extruded for height, 58
    of 2D wall elevations extruded for thickness, 69
    of lofting cross-sections on a path, 79
Affect Ambient, 570
algorithms, SuperSampling, 345-346
aliasing, 362
alien planet surfaces, creating with procedural maps, 472-473
alien skin, creating with procedural maps, 475
aligning
    Free cameras, 552
    Transforms, 195-197
    walls, 69
All Filter, controlling Glow (Render Effects), 595-596
Alpha, Glow sources (Render Effects), 594
Alternate Rays, Highlight, 620
Ambient
    MAX lights, 570
    Raytrace material, basic parameters, 348
amplitude, Water map, 468
Angle, Highlight, 620
animated cropping, 492-493
    bitmaps, 491-493
animated masks
    burning fuses, 520-525
    valleys, 526-527, 529-530

animated materials
   fictional animated materials, 500
      creating plasma engines, 500-501
   man-made animated materials.
     See man-made animated materials
   natural animated materials.
     See natural animated materials

animated valley landscapes, 506

animating water with Noise maps, 489-490

Animating Phase, Water map, 468

animation
   antialiasing, 364
   optimizing, 270
      camera angle, 272
      determining animated entities, 271
      removing nonessential components, 272
   texture maps, optimizing, 272
   tools
      Flex, 258
      flowers, creating, 259-260
      models, creating, 258-260
      Snapshot tool, 258

Animations Slider, 420

anisotropic, 429

Anisotropic shader, 331

anisotropy, specular highlights, 339

antialiasing, 344, 362-363
   animations, 364
   Attenuation, 371-372
   Blurs, 371-372
   Defocusing, 371-372
   detailed geometry, 364
   Fast Adaptive antialiaser, 369-370
   Global Ray antialiaser, 368
   Multiresolution Adaptive antialiaser, 370-371
   raytracing, 363
   rendering problems, 373
   speed, 373
   still-life imagery, 364
   SuperSampling, 344

aperatures, f-stops, 543

APIs (application programming interfaces), calls, 193

Apply to Whole Mesh option, MeshSmooth, 254

applying
   materials to models, 42
   MeshSmooth to models, 253
   Object Space PatchDeform modifier, 134-138
   Skin modifier, 315-316
   Terrain compound object to shapes, 128-130

arc subdivision, DXF files, 658

architectural framework, 111

architectural modeling
   3D Studio VIZ, 46
   beginning, 48
      display units, 48-49
      Home Grid Spacing, 49-50
   combining roofs with Boolean operations, 96-99
   details, 53
      complexity, 55-56
      planning, 54-55
      size of models, 56
      walkthroughs, 56-57
   display units, 48-49
      versus system units, 51
   doors, 100
      bevel profile doors, 104
      beveled doors, 102
      extruded doors, 100
   Home Grid Spacing, 49-50
   MAX R3 versus AutoCAD, 46-47
   objects, naming, 52-53
   Pantone color charts, 55
   Polygonal modeling, 16
   prototype scenes, 52
   roof systems, 89
      gable roofs, 89, 92, 95
      intersecting gables with valleys, 92-94
      L-shaped gable roofs, 89-92
   space frames, 107
      architectural framework, 111
      expansion joints, 111

Lattice modifier, 108-111
wire baskets, 107
storyboards, 54-55
wall systems, 57-58
   2D floor plan extruded for height, 58
   2D wall elevation extruded for thickness, 69
   curtain wall systems, 79
windows, 100
   bevel profile windows, 105-106
   beveled windows, 103-104
   extruded windows, 101-102

arms
   creating with cross sections, 286-287
   shaping with FFD modifiers, 311-313

aspect ratios, Pixel Aspect Ratios, 538

Assign Vertex Color utility, 204

assigning Material IDs, 85-87

attaching shapes to create new openings, 76-78

Attenuation
   antialiasing, 371-372
   Exponential, 372
   MAX lights, 569

Auto-smooth, 653
   DXF files, 658
   Import STL File dialog, 663

AutoCAD
   DWG Import dialog, 649
   files, options for importing, 649
   flipped faces, 653
   Import AutoCAD DWG File dialog
      ACIS Options, 654
      deriving objects, 651
      General Options, 651-652
      Geometry Options, 652-653
   importing survey data, 120-121
   MAX R3, transfers, 47
   translating entities, DWG to MAX R3, 654-655
   versus MAX R3, 46-47, 648

AutoCAD DXF, importing files, 656-657, 659-660

B

B-Spline curves, 21

Background Image, tracing contourlines, 122-125

backlighting, 441

backlit signs, creating without Perimeter, 599-600

backwards raytracing, 359

balanced light, 575

ballpark signs, 494-496, 498

base points, modeling, 41

basic parameters, 337-338.
See also **parameters**
   Raytrace material, 347
      Ambient, 348
      Bump Map, 350
      Diffuse, 348
      Environment map, 350
      Luminosity, 349
      reflection, 349
      shading, 348
      Specular Highlights, 350
      transparency, 349
   Standard material
      color swatches, 337
      Diffuse Level, 338
      opacity, 340
      Roughness, 338
      Self-Illumination, 339-340
      specular highlights, 338-339

beachfront surf, 413-415

beams of light, 513-515

Bevel modifier, 103

bevel profile doors, 104

Bevel Profile modifier, 104

bevel profile windows, 105-106

beveled doors, 102

beveled windows, 103-104

Bezier tangent handles, patches, 22

Bezier technology, patch modeling, 21

binary separation planes. *See* **BSPs**

bitmaps, 327, 491
    animated cropping, 491-493
    cropping, 491
    scaling, 491
black plastic, 451-452
Blend materials, 355
    burning fuses, 520
    lawns, 392
    skies, 401-404
    wildflowers, 387
Blend surfaces
    character modeling, 290, 292-293
    elbows, 291-292
Blinn shader, 332
Blur, 637
Blur Offset, 451
blurring, Depth of Field, 636
    Radial Blur, 638
    Scene Blur, 637
Blurs, antialiasing, 371-372
bolts (threaded), creating with cross-sectional modeling, 164-169
bombs, burning fuses, 498-500
Bonus tool option, Depth of Field, 536
Boolean operations
    3D boxes, 63-65
    3D-Boolean operations, 66
    roofs, combining, 96-99
    rough openings, subtracting, 66-67
bounding boxes, transforms, 195
box primitives, 249
Box Select, 425
boxes, primitives (polygonal modeling), 7
BSPs (binary separation planes), 209
    Z-buffering, 199
building. *See also* creating
    characters with Surface Tools, 298
    colums with lofts, 262-263
    cross sections, 286
    flares, 609, 611-612
        camera types, 613-614
        determining environments, 613
        determining sources, 612
    glows, 608-609
    libraries, 374-376
    models, 248
        with box primitives, 249
        with Loft Objects, 250
        with non-box primitives, 249
        with primitives, 249
    sections, patches, 296
Bump Map, Raytrace material (basic parameters), 350
bump mapping, simulating geometry, 159-161
Bump maps
    Imitating, 216
    mesh distortions, 431
burning fuses, 506
    Blend materials, 520
    creating, 520-525
bushes, 138. *See also* trees

C

calls, APIs, 193
camera angle, optimizing animation, 272
Camera Match utility, 438
cameras. *See also* MAX cameras
    angles, optimizing animation, 272
    building flares, 613-614
    Depth of Field, cityscapes, 640-643
    f-stops, 543-544
    film speeds, 545
    film-based cameras, 537
    lens attachments, 546-547
    lenses, 540
        fisheye lens, 543
        normal lens, 540-541
        telephoto lens, 542
        wide-angle lens, 541
    scene composition, 547
        FOV, 549-550
        POV, 548
        starting points, 547-548
    video-based cameras, 538
candlelight, adding highlights with Flare, 624-625

candles, 478-480
    highlights, adding, 625
Cap Closed Entities, 653
capes, creating with NURBS modeling, 33-35
cardboard, creating, 433-438
caustics, light, 356
Cellular map, 462
    Diffuse maps, 462
    natural animated materials, 486-487
    rendering speed, 463
Chamfer tool, 14
changing Depth of Field, 640
    cityscape, 640, 642-643
channels, map channels, 326
character modeling, 275-276
    Blend surfaces, 290, 292-293
    Editable Mesh, 304-305
    lofts, 285
    MeshSmooth, 305
    with NURBS, 284
    patches, primitives, 293
    polygonal modeling, 303-304
    ruled surfaces, 288
    starting points, 279-281
    with Surface Tools, 298
    types of characters, 277
characters, 282
    Cross Section modifier, creating, 303
    guidelines for designing, 278-279
    Surface modifier, creating, 299-302
    types of, 277
    typical characters, 282
    unusual characters, 282
        staplers, 283
check boxes, SuperSampling, 344
choosing
    a modeling method, 39-40
    patches
        Quad, 295
        Tri, 296
chrome
    creating, 447-450
    glowing, 592-593

cinematics, NURBS, 269
Circular color, glows, 604-605
circular gradient versus radial gradient, Glow (Video Post), 606-607
Clamp, Highlight, 620
cloning, 261
    Instances, 261
    Reference clones, 62
        extruding, 69, 71-73
        positioning, 69, 71-73
cloud mapping, skies, 396-399
clouds, simulating shadows, 404-405
Color Clipboard palettes, 435
color depth, real-time engines, 205
Color Map, 404
color swatches, Standard material (basic parameters), 337
colors
    glows
        adjusting, 601
        building, 609
    Highlight, 621
    Import AutoCAD DWG File dialog, 651
    lights, 574
    limitations of texture maps, 214-215
    Pantone color charts, 55
columns, creating with lofts, 262-263
combining
    Highlight with Glow, 622
    roofs with Boolean operations, 96-99
command line, MAX R3, 37-38
commands
    Place Highlight, 441, 619
    XRef objects, 181
    XRef Scenes, 181
complexity of details, architectural modeling, 55-56
Composite material, 355
composite-based framing, 557
Constant Velocity option, 527
contourlines
    Background Image, tracing, 122, 124-125
    elevations, setting, 125-126

Contrast spinners, MAX lights, 569
control points, 252
   lattice, 310
control vertices (CVs), 31-32
controlling
   Glow (Render Effects), 595
      All Filter, 595-596
      perimeters, 596-598, 600-601
   sections with MeshSmooth, 255-256
converting primitives into Editable Patch objects, 293
convex objects, real-time modeling, 208-209
convex-only polygons, MeshSmooth, 252
Corel Draw, Adobe Illustrator AI, 656
cost of plug-ins, 671-672
CPUs, upgrading, 237
Create Primitives, Import VRML File dialog, 665
creating. *See also* building
   3D boxes for Boolean operations, 63-65
   alien planet surfaces with procedural maps, 472-473
   alien skin with procedural maps, 475
   arms
      with cross sections, 286-287
      shaping with FFD modifiers, 311-313
   backlit signs without Perimeter, 599-600
   ballpark signs, 494-496, 498
   beams of light, 513-515
   bolts (threaded), 164-169
   burning fuses, 520-525
      for bombs, 498-500
   cannons with Editable Mesh, 10-11, 13
   capes with NURBS modeling, 33-35
   characters
      with Cross Section modifier, 303
      with Surface modifier, 299-302
   cloud shadows, 404-405
   custom buttons, 228
   display groups, 241-242
   elbows with Blend surfaces, 291-292
   expansion joint systems, 112-113, 115-116
   exterior night lighting, 507-510, 512
   flares, 610

flowers with animation tools, 259-260
fluorescent light fixtures, 596
fog with procedural maps, 473-474
fuel tanks (motorcycles) with cross-sectional modeling, 174-178
glowing chrome, 592-593
glowing neon, 588-591
glowing perimeters, 597-598
ground cover, 384-386
   lawns, 392-395
   wildflowers, 387-391
hands with patch modeling, 27-28
hoods with NURBS modeling, 33-35
icons for Macro buttons, 226-227
imperfections in materials, 430
intersecting gables with valleys, 92-94
jets from primitives, 211-213
keyboard alternates for editing, 240-241
L-shaped gable roofs, 89-92
leaves, 144-147
   from a leaf cluster, 147, 149-150
levels of curtain wall systems, 80, 82-83
macro buttons, 224-225
macroscripts for libraries, 378-379
man-made materials, 432
   black plastic, 451-452
   cardboard, 433-438
   chrome, 447-450
   glass, 441
   glass vases, 442-446
   metals, 446-447
   paint, 439-441
   paper, 433-438
material imperfections
   with material corruption, 432
   with mesh distortions, 430-431
mesh frames, 112-113, 115-116
models with animation tools, 258-260
multiple levels of curtain wall systems, 87-88
named selection sets with FFD modifiers, 311
Object Xrefs, 266
patch landscapes, 131-133
patch surfaces, 169-171, 173-174
pens (patch ballpoint pens), 169-171, 173-174

radiosity effects with Extra Lighting, 351-352
ruled surfaces, 289
sickles with polygonal modeling, 16-19
skies
   Blend materials, 401-404
   cloud mapping method, 396-399
   Gradient Ramp map, 399-401
space fighters with MeshSmoth Apply to Whole Mesh option, 254-255
sunrises
   on golden ponds, 626-627
   with Reflection Dimming, 343
torsos with Editable Mesh, 304-305
trees, 416-418
valleys, 526-527, 529-530
vegetation
   grass, 418-421
   leaves, 421-424
water
   beachfront surf, 413-415
   pond water, 406-408
   rough water, 409-413
winding valleys, 515-519
windows
   bevel profile windows, 105-106
   beveled windows, 103-104
   extruded windows, 101-102
wing tips with MeshSelect and MeshSmooth, 257-258

cropping Bitmaps, 491

Cross Section modifier, 169-171
   characters, creating, 303
   MAX R3, 30

cross sections
   arms, creating, 286-287
   building, 286

cross-sectional modeling, 164
   cut-away views, 179
      Slice modifier, 179-181
   fuel tanks (motorcycles), 174, 176-178
   generating cross-sections from free-form mesh objects, 174
   patch surfaces, 169-171, 173-174
   threaded bolts, 164-169

curtain wall systems
   architectural modeling, 79
   levels
      creating, 80, 82-83
      lofting, 79
   Material IDs, assigning, 85-87
   multiple levels, creating, 87-88

curved surfaces, imitating, 217

curves, NURBS modeling, 31

custom buttons, 228

custom toolbars, 229-230

cut-away view, cross-sectional modeling, 179

CVs (control vertices), NURBS modeling, 31-32

CWALL objects, optimizing, 84-85

D

daylight, simulating, 577

deactivating, 245

default materials, 325

Defocusing, antialiasing, 371-372

DeleteMesh modifier, 431

Dent map, SuperSampling, 471

Depth of Field, 536, 544, 632-633
   blurring, 636
      Radial Blur, 638
      Scene Blur, 637
   changing, 640, 642-643
   Focal Limit, 635
   Focal Loss, 633
   Focal Range, 634-635
   MAX cameras, simulating real-world effects, 554

designing characters, guidelines for, 278-279

detailed geometry, antialiasing, 364

details
   architectural modeling, 53
      complexity, 55-56
      planning, 54-55
      size of models, 56
      walkthroughs, 56-57

limitations of texture maps, 216
real-time modeling, 206-207
Diffuse
  MAX lights, 570
  Raytrace material, basic parameters, 348
Diffuse color
  paper, creating, 434
  transparency, 341
Diffuse Level, Standard material (basic parameters), 338
Diffuse maps, Cellular, 462
Digimation, X-ray, 588
direct flashes, 563
direct lighting, 560-561
Direct3D, 238
Directional lights, 571
  sunlight, 567
Disable Textures, disabling maps, 245
disadvantages
  of 2D floor plan extruded for height, 58
  of 2D wall elevations extruded for thickness, 69
Discreet
  Lightscape, 562
  plug-ins, 671
  Web site, 671
Displace Mesh modifier, 530
Displacement Approx. modifier, valleys, 517
displacement mapping, 432
  geometry, simulating, 162-164
displays, upgrading, 237-238
Display floater, 239-240
display groups, 241-242
Display Maps, texture, 244-245
display units
  architectural modeling, 48-49
  versus system units, 51
distorting geometry, tools for, 431
divisions, 462
DLLs (Dynamic Load Library)
  MAX file format, 194
  plug-ins, 670

doors, 100
  bevel profile doors, 104
  beveled doors, 102
  extruded doors, 100
Double Sided material, 355
dramatic lighting, 566
dual-pipe versus single pipe, Manual Acceleration, 366-367
duplicating. *See* cloning
DWG file import process, 649
DWG Import dialog, 649
DXF files, importing, 656-657, 659-660
Dynamic Load Library. *See* DLLs

E

edges
  patches, 21-22
  polygonal modeling, 7
Edit Patch, 293
Edit Spline modifier, 20
Editable Mesh
  cannons, 10-13
  Chamfer tool, 14
  character modeling, 304-305
  polygonal modeling, 7, 10
  Sub-Object modes, 8
  torsos, creating, 304-305
Editable Patch, MAX R3, 26-27
Editable Spline Create Line feature, 302
editing
  at 2D sub-object level, 74-76
  Display floater, 239-240
  display groups, 241-242
  hiding geometry, 239
  keyboard alternates, 240-241
  Object Xrefs, 243
Effect section, Highlight, 620
elbows, creating with Blend surfaces, 291-292
elevations, contourlines, 125-126
entities, translating
  AutoCAD DWG to MAX R3 objects, 654-655
  MAX R3 objects to AutoCAD DWG, 655

Entity, Import AutoCAD DWG File dialog, 651
envelopes, Skin modifier, 314-315
Environment map, Raytrace material (basic parameters), 350
environments, building flares, 613
expansion joints, 111-113, 115-116
Explicit mode, Macro Recorder, 224
Exponential, Attenuation, 372
Export Selected, 178
exporting
    files, 3DS files, 661-662
    models into game engines, 194
extended parameters, 341
    Raytrace material, 350
        Advanced Transparency, 353-354
        Extra Lighting, 351-352
        Fluorescence, 353
        Raytracer Controls, 354
        reflections, 354
        translucency, 353
    Standard material, Advanced Transparency, 341
    transparency
        Falloff, 341
        Filter color, 341-342
        Index of Refraction value, 342
        Reflection Dimming, 342
        wire, 342
extended parameters, 341. *See also* parameters
extensions, plug-ins, 670-671
exterior night lighting, 506
    creating, 507-510, 512
external references. *See* Xrefs
Extra Lighting, 351-352
Extrude modifier, 100
extruded doors, 100
extruded windows, 101-102
extruding
    floor plans, 59-62
    Reference clones, 69, 71-73
    walls, 69

F

f-stops, 543-544
faces, polygonal modeling, 6-7
faking. *See* imitating
Falloff, transparency, 341
Falloff Curve, glows, 602-603
far clipping plane, Z-buffering, 199
Fast Adaptive Aliaser, 354
Fast Adaptive Antialiaser, Global Ray Antialiaser, 369-370
FFD modifiers, 310-311, 314
    arms, shaping, 311, 313
    named selection sets, 311
fictional animated materials, 500-501
fictional materials, 456-457. *See also* procedural maps
    ideas for, 456-457
    Noise map, 458
    procedural maps, 457
field of view. *See* FOV
files
    exporting .3DS files, 661-662
    importing, 656
        .3DS, 656
        .PRJ, 656
        3D Studio R2-R4 2D Shape files, 660
        3DS files, 660-661
        Adobe Illustrator AI, 656
        AutoCAD DXF, 656-657, 659-660
        DWG Import dialog, 649
        IGES files, 663-664
        Import AutoCAD DWG File dialog, 650
        stereolithography files, 662
        VRML files, 665
fill lights, 561
Fill Polylines, Import DXF File dialog, 659
film grain, 545
Film Grain effect, 545
film speeds, 545
film versus video-playback speeds, 539-540
film-based cameras, 537

Filter color, 341
Filter transparency, 342
filters, Glow (Render Effects), 601
fisheye lenses, 543
Flare
    candlelight, adding highlights, 624-625
    versus Highlight, 621
flares, 586
    building, 609-612
        camera types, 613-614
        determining environments, 613
        determining sources, 612
    Lens Effects, 586
flashes, 563-564
    direct flashes, 563
    umbrella flashes, 564
Flex modifier, 258
Flex tool, 258
flip-around scenario, 551
flipped faces, 653
floor plans, extruding, 59-62
flowers, creating with animation tools, 259-260
Fluorescence, extended parameters (Raytrace material), 353
fluorescent light fixtures, 596
Focal Limit, 544
    Depth of Field, 635
Focal Loss, Depth of Field, 633
focal points, 638-639
Focal Range, 542-544
    Depth of Field, 634-635
fog, creating with procedural maps, 473-474
FOV (field of view), scene composition, 549-550
Fractal Noise parameters, 460
framing
    basic framing, 556-557
    composite-based framing, 557
    MAX cameras, 555
Free cameras, 552-553
Free Spot light, 560
free-form mesh objects, generating cross-sections, 174
fuel tanks (motorcycles), cross-sectional modeling, 174, 176-178
fuses, burning, 506
    Blend materials, 520
    creating, 520-525

G

G-buffer ID, glowing objects, 588
gable ends, adding, 74
gable roofs, architectural modeling, 89, 92, 95
gable windows, adding, 76
game engines, 194
gel, 341
geometry
    hiding while editing, 239
    real-time 3D graphics, 193
    simulating, 158-159
        bump mapping, 159-161
        displacement mapping, 162-164
        opacity mapping, 161-162
    tools for distorting, 431
Geometry Options, 652-653
gimbal lock scenarios
    Free cameras, 552-553
    Target cameras, 551
glass, 441
    masks, 442
    Specular Level, 444
glass vases, 442-446
Global Exclude, raytracing, 368
Global Ray Antialiaser, 368
global welding, 652
Glossiness, 332
    specular highlights, 338-339
Glow (Render Effects), 586
    controlling, 595
        All Filter, 595-596
        perimeters, 596-598, 600-601
    filters, 601
    gradients, 602

Highlight, combining, 622
maps, 602
objects, Material Effects channel, 591
sources, 587, 593
   Alpha, 594
   objects, 588
   Surface Normals, 595
   switching, 600
   Z Hi/Low, 594

Glow (Video Post), 605
gradient composition, 607-608
radial gradient versus circular gradient, 606-607

glowing unclamped colors, 592-593
glowing chrome, 592-593
glowing fluorescent light fixtures, 596
glowing neon, 588-591
glowing perimeters, 597-598
glows, 586
building, 608-609
colors, adjusting, 601
maps
   Circular color, 604-605
   falloff, 602-603
   radial color, 602
raytrace materials, 593
shiny surfaces, 622-624

Gradient ramp, 605
Gradient Ramp map, 392
skies, 399-401

gradients
composition, Glow (Video Post), 607-608
Glow (Render Effects), 602
Highlight, 621

grass, 418-421
lawns, 392-395

Grid Spacing, 145
ground cover, 383
creating, 384-386

guidelines
for animating Cellular maps, 487
for animating Noise, 486
for designing characters, 278-279

H

Hammersley, SuperSampling algorithms, 345
hands, creating with patch modeling, 27-28
hardware limitations
CPU, 237
display, 237-238
high-resolution modeling, 235
RAM, 236

HDI. *See* Heidi
Heidi, 237
versus OpenGL, 238

hiding geometry while editing, 239
high-resolution,
limitations, 234-235
for low resolution modeling, 210

Highlight, 619
colors, 621
considerations when using, 619
Effect section, 620
Glow, combining, 622
Vary section, 620
versus Flare, 621

highlights, 617-618
adding
   to candles, 625
   to entire objects, 626-627
   to shiny surfaces, 622-623
candlelight, adding with Flare, 624-625
considerations when using, 619
shiny surfaces, 622-624

Home Grid Spacing, architectural modeling, 49-50
hoods, creating with NURBS modeling, 33-35
Horiz Focal Loss, 633
hybrid raytracer, 362

I

IAR (Image Aspect Ratios), 538
icon maker, 228

icons
creating for Macro buttons, 226-227
Place Highlight, 339
ideas for fictional materials, 456-457
IGES
importing files, 663-664
translating to MAX R3 objects, 664
illumination
candles, 478-480
light bulbs, 477
Image Aspect Ratios (IAR), 538
imitating
bump maps, 216
curved surfaces, 217
lighting, 217
imperfections, materials, 430
material corruption, 432
mesh distortions, 430-431
Import AutoCAD DWG File dialog, 650
options
ACIS Options, 654
derviving objects, 651
General Options, 651-652
Geometry Options, 652-653
Import DFX File dialog, 659
Import DXF File dialog, 658-659
Import STL File dialog, 663
Import VRML File dialog, 665
importing
AutoCAD files, options for, 649
DXF files, 658-659
files, 656
.3DS, 656, 660-661
.PRJ, 656
3D Studio R2-R4 2D Shape files, 660
Adobe Illustrator AI, 656
AutoCAD DXF, 656-657, 659-660
DWG file import process, 649
DWG Import dialog, 649
IGES files, 663-664
Import AutoCAD DWG File dialog, 650
stereolithography files, 662
VRML files, 665
survey data from AutoCAD, 120-121

Inactive in Viewport toggle, modifiers, 246-248
Include/Exclude tool, 360
index of refraction, 357-359
Index of Refraction value, transparency, 342
Instances, 261
intensity, building glows, 609
interior lighting simulations, 577
daylight, 577
light fixtures, 578-579
intersecting gables with valleys, 92-94
Inverse Square Decay, 560, 569
large room lighting, 575

J-K

jets, creating with primitives, 211-213
joints, expansion joints, 111

keyboard alternates, 240-241

L

L-shaped gable roofs, 89-92
landscapes, 120
AutoCAD, importing survey data, 120-121
NURBS surfaces, 130
patch grids, 131
patch landscapes, 131-133
Terrain compound object, 121
valleys, 515
large room lighting, 575
Lathe modifier, 262
lattice
control points, 310
patch technology, 21
Lattice modifier, space frames, 108-111
lawns, 392-395
Layer, Import AutoCAD DWG File dialog, 651

leaves, 382, 421-424
   creating, 144-147
   Scatter, canopies, 147-150
lens attachments, 546
   lens hoods, 546
   soft-focus aperture-disk, 547
Lens Effects, 584
   flares. *See* flares
   glows. *See* glows
Lens Effects Flare module. *See* Flare
Lens Effects Highlight. *See* Highlight
lens hoods, 546
lens reflections, 585
lenses, 540
   fisheye lens, 543
   normal lens, 540-541
   telephoto lens, 542
   wide-angle lens, 541
Level of Detail utility, 246
levels, curtain wall systems
   multiple levels, 87-88
   single levels, 80, 82-83
levels of detail. *See* LODs
libraries
   building, 374, 376
   macroscripts, 378-379
light
   beams of, 513-515
   caustics, 356
   raytracing, 356
light bulbs, 477
light colors, 574
light fixtures, simulating, 578-579
lighting, 559. *See also* MAX lights
   exterior night lighting, 506-507
      creating, 507-510, 512
   flashes, 563-564
      direct flashes, 563
      umbrella flashes, 564
   imitating, 217
   natural lighting, 566
      moonlight, 568
      sunlight, 567
   raytracing, 360
   studio lights, 560
      direct lighting, 560-561
      fill lights, 561
      lighting areas other than the subject, 562
   subject lighting, 564-565
      dramatic lighting, 566
      positioning, 565
lighting areas other than the subject, 562
lighting techniques, 573
   building up lights, 573-574
      colors, 574
   interior lighting simulations, 577
      daylight, 577
      light fixtures, 578-579
   lighting options, 575-576
Lightscape, Discreet, 562
limitations
   of CPU, 237
   of display, 237-238
   of high-resolution modeling, 234
      hardware, 235
   of RAM, 236
   texture maps
      colors, 214-215
      details, 216
      map size, 215
Live Area, 555
loading plug-ins, 677
Local Exclude, raytracing, 368
LOD Tester, 199
LOD utility, 200, 202-203
LODs (levels of detail), 199
   real-time games versus prerendered 3D graphics, 199-201
Loft Objects, 250
   transforms, 196
lofted CWALL objects, optimizing, 84-85
lofting, 262
   curtain wall levels, 79
lofts
   columns, building, 262-263
   NURBS, 285

U-Lofts, 269
UV-Lofts, 269

low-resolution models, modifying primitives, 211

Luminosity, Raytrace material (basic parameters), 349

M

macro buttons
    Creating, 224-225
    finishing touches, adding, 229
    icons, 226-227

Macro Recorder, 224-225

macroscripts, 378-379

man-made animated materials, 491

man-made materials
    ballpark sign, 494-496, 498
    black plastic, 451-452
    burning fuses, 498-500
    cardboard, 433-438
    chrome, 447-450
    glass, 441
    glass vases, 442-446
    metals, 446-447
    paint, 439-441
    paper, 433-438
    maps, 491
        Bitmaps, 491
        Marbles, 493-494

managing display groups, 241-242

Manual Acceleration, single pipe versus dual-pipe, 366-367

map channels, 326-327, 425
    procedural maps, 327

map size
    limitations of texture maps, 215
    real-time engines, 205

map types, 326-327

mapped trees, 416-418

mapping
    bump mapping, 159-161
    cloud mapping skies, 396-399
    displacement mapping, 162-164, 432
    Gradient Ramp map, skies, 399-401
    opacity mapping, 161-162

maps. *See also* procedural maps
    Bump maps, mesh distortions, 431
    disabling, 245
        Disable Textures, 245
    Glow (Render Effects), 602
        Circular color, 604-605
        falloff, 602-603
        radial color, 602
    man-made materials, 491
        Bitmaps, 491
        Marble maps, 493-494
    Mix map, 449
    natural animated materials, 485-486
        Cellular map, 486-487
        Noise map, 486
        Planet map, 487-488
        Smoke map, 488-489
        Splat map, 488
    Opacity
        beams of light, 513
        exterior night lighting, 507
    Phase values, 484
    procedural maps, 327-328
        material corruption, 432
    Radial Gradient map, 603
    Standard material, 346
    still images, 506
    texture, 244

Marble maps, 493-494
    Perlin Marble, 493

masks, 442, 506
    animated masks
        burning fuses, 520-525
        valleys, 526-527, 529-530

material corruption, material imperfections, 432

Material Editor
    bitmaps, 327
    plug-ins, 674

Material Editor Basic Parameters rollout, Soften field, 332

Material Effects channel, glowing objects, 591

Material IDs, assigning, 85-87

Material Preview function, 484
materials, 355
    animated materials. *See* animated materials
    applying to models, 42
    bitmaps, 327
    Cellular maps, rendering, 464
    default materials, 325
    fictional materials. *See* fictional materials
    imperfections, 430-432
    libraries, organizing, 374, 376
    man-made materials. *See* man-made materials
    map channels, 326-327
    map types, 326-327
    naming, 376, 378
    organizing, 374
        by naming, 376-378
    Raytrace material. *See* Raytrace material
    rendering materials, 325
    root materials, 325
    shaders. *See* shaders
    Standard material. *See* Standard material

matrix, TM, 195
Matte/Shadow material, 355
MAX cameras, 550. *See also* cameras
    framing, 555-557
        composite-based framing, 557
    Free cameras, 552-553
    normal lens, 540
    shot angles, 558-559
    simulating real-world effects, 553
        Depth of Field, 554
        Photoshop plug-ins, 554-555
    Target cameras, 551-552
    versus real-world cameras, 553

MAX file format, 194
MAX lights, 568. *See also* lighting
    ambient, 570
    attenuations, 569
    Contrast spinners, 569
    diffuse, 570
    Directional lights, 571
    Omni lights, 570
    Shadow Color map, 571
    simulating real-world lighting, 572
    Soften Diffuse Edge spinners, 569
    specular, 570
    Spot lights, 570

MAX R3
    AutoCAD, transfers, 47
    file import options (AutoCAD), 649
    new features, 14
        Animations slider, 420
        anisotropic, 429
        assigning Material IDs to segments of splines, 79
        Box Select, 425
        changing Material IDs, 85
        Color Map, 404
        command line, 37-38
        Cross Section modifier. See Cross Section modifier
        customizing icons in buttons, 229
        Depth of Field, 554
        Editable Patch, 26-27
        Export Selected, 178
        Fast Adaptive Antialiaser, 354, 369-370
        Global Ray Antialiaser, 368
        Gradient Ramp, 399
        Gradient Ramp map, 392
        icon maker, 228
        Include/Exclude tool, 360
        Inverse Square Decay, 560, 569
        Lens Effects, 584
        LOD Tester, 199
        Macro buttons, 226
        Macro Recorder, 224-225
        Map Channels, 425
        MeshSelect button, 136
        Multi-Layer, 406, 429
        Multiresolution Adaptive Antialiaser, 354, 370-371
        natural light falloff, 560
        NURBS Tessellation presets, 36
        NURMS in MeshSmooth, 307
        Object Xrefs, 243
        Oren-Nayer-Blinn, 429, 435
        Path Steps option, 167
        Plane objects, 416
        Render Box Selected, 217
        Render Crop, 216
        right-clicking viewports, 60
        Scatter, 146

Schematic View menu, 68
Select Bitmap Image File dialog box, 129
Selection rollout, 74
Shade Selected Faces, 140
Shaded Lattice, 36
shaders. See shaders
shadow color, 360
Shadow Color map, 571
Skin Modifier, 314, 316
Strauss, 429
Strauss shader, 336
Surface modifier. See Surface modifier
Surface Tools, 26
Swirl map, 464
Terrain compound object, 121
Transform Gizmo, 11
Transform Gizmo tripod, 60
Unclamped Specular Level (Standard Material), 592
Use Shape IDs option, 102
Xrefs, 181, 236
  translating
    entities, MAX R3 to AutoCAD DWG, 655
    to IGES, 664
  updated features
    MeshSmooth. See MeshSmooth
  versus AutoCAD, 46-47, 648

MAXScript, 223, 225

mechanical modeling, 154-155
  modeling tools, 156-157
  output process, 157-158
  presentations, 155-156
  workflow, 157

mesh distortions, material imperfections, 430-431

mesh frames, 112-113, 115-116

MeshSelect, 137
  wing tips, creating, 257-258

MeshSelect button, 136

MeshSelect modifier, 255

MeshSmooth, 14, 251
  adding detail to torsos, 306-307
  Apply to Whole Mesh option, 254-255
  applying to models, 253

character modeling, 305
control points, 252
convex-only polygons, 252
NURMS, 307-310
NURMS-output method, 252
Operate on, 253
Quad Output, 253
sections, controlling, 255-256
Subdivision Amount, 252
wing tips, 257-258

Metal shader, 332, 446

metals, 446-447
  chrome, 447-450

methods, choosing a modeling method, 39-40

Miscellaneous options, DXF files, 659

Mix map, 449

modeled hardwood tree, 139

modeled trees, 139

modeling
  architectural modeling. *See* architectural modeling
  character modeling. *See* character modeling
  choosing a method, 39-40
  cloning, 261-262
  cross-sectional modeling. *See* cross-sectional modeling
  lofting, 262
  materials, applying, 42
  mechanical modeling. *See* mechanical modeling, 154
  NURBS modeling. *See* NURBS modeling, 30
  patch modeling. *See* patch modeling, 20
  polygonal modeling. *See* polygonal modeling, 6
  real-time modeling. *See* real-time modeling, 206
  scripted modeling. *See* scripted modeling, 36
  starting points, 40
    base points, 41
    determining, 38-39
  Sub-Object modes, 8-9
  trees, trunks, 139-143
  Xrefs, 181-182

modeling tools, mechanical modeling, 156-157
models
    animation, optimizing, 270
    creating, 248
        with animation tools, 258-260
        with box primitives, 249
        with Loft Objects, 250
        with non-box primitives, 249
        with primitives, 249
    exporting into game engines, 194
    MeshSmooth, applying, 253
modes of Macro Recorder, 224
modifiers
    Bevel modifier, 103
    Bevel Profile modifier, 104
    Cross Section modifier. *See* Cross Section modifier
    DeleteMesh modifier, 431
    Displace Mesh, 530
    Displacement Approx. modifier, valleys, 517
    Edit Spline modifier, 20
    Extrude, 100
    FFD, 310-311, 314
    Flex, 258
    Inactive in Viewport toggle, 246, 248
    Lathe, 262
    Lattice modifier, 108-111
    MeshSelect, 255
    MeshSmooth modifier. *See* MeshSmooth
    Noise, 458
    Object Space PatchDeform, 134-138
    Optimize, 58, 211
    PathDeform, 134
    plug-ins, 673
    Skin modifier, 314-316
    Slice, 56, 179-181
    STL-Check, 662
    Surface modifier, 30, 169-171
        creating characters, 299-302
    Surface Tools, 25
    Unwrap UVW modifier, 207
    VolumeSelect, 256
modifying primitives for low-resolution models, 211
moonlight, 568

Morpher material, 355
motion-picture cameras, 537
moving objects, TM, 195
Multi-Layer shader, 333, 406, 429
Multi/Sub-Object material, 355
multiple levels, curtain wall systems, 87-88
Multiresolution Adaptive Aliaser, 354
Multiresolution Adaptive Antialiaser, Global Ray Antialiaser, 370-371
myths, scripted modeling, 37

N

Name, Import STL File dialog, 663
named selection sets, creating with FFD modifiers, 311
naming
    materials, 376-378
    objects, architectural modeling, 52-53
natural animated materials
    maps, 485-486
        Cellular, 486-487
        Noise, 486
        Planet, 487-488
        Smoke, 488-489
        Splat, 488
    procedural maps, 484
    water, 489-490
natural light falloff, 560
natural lighting, 566
    moonlight, 568
    sunlight, 567
nature, techniques for simulating, 382-383
neon, creating, 588-591
new features of MAX R3
    Affect Ambient, 570
    Animations slider, 420
    anisotropic, 429
    assigning Material IDs to segments of splines, 79
    Box Select, 425
    changing Material IDs, 85
    Color Map, 404
    command line, 37-38

Cross Section modifier. *See* Cross Section modifier
customizing icons in buttons, 229
Depth of Field, 554
Edit Spline modifier, 20
Editable Patch, 26-27
Export Selected, 178
Fast Adaptive Antialiaser, 354, 369-370
Global Ray Antialiaser, 368
Gradient Ramp, 399
Gradient Ramp map, 392
icon maker, 228
Include/Exclude tool, 360
Inverse Square Decay, 560, 569
Lens Effects, 584
LOD Tester, 199
Macro buttons, 226
Macro Recorder, 224-225
Map Channels, 425
MeshSelect button, 136
Multi-Layer, 406, 429
Multiresolution Adaptive Antialiaser, 354, 370-371
natural light falloff, 560
NURBS Tessellation presets, 36
NURMS in MeshSmooth, 307
Object Xrefs, 243
Oren-Nayer-Blinn, 429, 435
Path Steps option, 167
Plane objects, 416
Render Box Selected, 217
Render Crop, 216
right-clicking viewports, 60
Scatter, 146
Schematic View menu, 68
Select Bitmap Image File dialog box, 129
Selection rollout, 74
Shade Selected Faces, 140
Shaded Lattice, 36
shader. *See* shaders
shadow color, 360
Shadow Color map, 571
Skin modifier, 314, 316
Strauss, 429
Strauss shader, 336
Surface modifier. *See* Surface modifier
Surface Tools, 26
Swirl map, 464

Terrain compound object, 121
Transform Gizmo, 11
Transform Gizmo tripod, 60
Unclamped Specular Level (Standard Material), 592
Use Shape IDs option, 102
Xrefs. *See* Xrefs

night lighting, exterior night lighting, 506-507
creating, 507-510, 512

Noise maps, 458-459
natural animated materials, 486
parameters, 459-461
plasma engines, 500-501
water, animating, 489-490

Noise modifier, 458

Noise Threshold, 461

non-box primitives, 249

Non-Uniform Rational B-Spline. *See* NURBS modeling

Non-Uniform Rational Mesh Smooth. *See* NURMS

normal lenses, 540-541

NURBS (Non-Uniform Rational B-Spline) modeling, 16, 30
cinematics, 269
cross sections, 286
Surface Approximation, 23-24
surfaces, landscapes, 130
U-Lofts, 269
UV-Lofts, 269

NURBS lofts, 285

NURBS modeling, 30
capes, 33-35
characters, 284
curves, 31
CVs, 31-32
hoods, 33-35
shortcomings, 36
uses of, 32-33

NURBS Tessellation presets, 36

NURMS (Non-Uniform Rational Mesh Smooth), 307
MeshSmooth, 307-310

NURMS-output method, MeshSmooth, 252

O

object plug-ins, 672
Object Space PatchDeform modifier, applying, 134-138
Object Xrefs, 265-266. *See also* Xrefs
 creating, 266
 editing, 243
 MAX R3, 243
objects
 adding highlights to entire objects, 626-627
 Glow (Render Effects), G-buffer ID, 588
 Material Effects channel, glowing, 591
 moving TM, 195
 naming architectural modeling, 52-53
Octrees, raytracers, 365
Offset values
 Perlin Marble, 494
 Smoke, 489
Omni lights, 570
opacity, Standard material (basic parameters), 340
Opacity map
 beams of light, 513
 exterior night lighting, 507
 trees, 138
opacity mapping, 221
 geometry, simulating, 161-162
OpenGL versus Heidi, 238
openings
 creating by attaching shapes, 76-78
 sizing, 68
Operate On, MeshSmooth, 253
Optimize modifier, 58, 211
optimizing
 animation, 270
  camera angle, 272
  determining anmated entitites, 271
  removing nonessential components, 272
  texture maps, 272
 lofted CWALL objects, 84-85
 raytracing, 365

options
 DWG Import dialog, 649
 Import AutoCAD DWG File dialog, 650
  ACIS Options, 654
  deriving objects, 651
  General Options, 651-652
  Geometry Options, 652-653
 for importing AutoCAD files, 649
 for lighting, 575-576
 Tessellation, patches, 24-25
Oren-Nayer-Blinn, 429, 435
Oren-Nayar-Blinn shader, 334
organic shapes, polygonal modeling, 15-16
organizing
 materials, 374
  naming, 376-378
  with libraries, 374-376
orientation, specular highlights, 339
output, mechanical modeling, 157-158
Outward Falloff, beams of light, 513

P

paint, 439-441
Pantone color charts, 55
paper, 433-438
parameters. *See also* basic parameters; extended parameters
 Dent map, 471
 Noise maps, 459-461
 Smoke map, 470
 Splat map, 466-467
 Swirl map, 464-465
 Water map, 467-468
 Wood map, 469
parametric doors, 100
parametric objects versus Editable Mesh, 7
parametric windows, 100
Particle System, 522
patch grids, landscapes, 131
patch modeling, 20
 Bezier technology, 21
 Editable Patch, 26-27
 hands, 27-28

shortcomings, 30
Surface Tools, 26
uses for, 25
patch surfaces, cross-sectional modeling, 169-171, 173-174
Patch surface tools, 169
patch technology, lattice, 21
patches, 21
building in sections, 296
character modeling, primitives, 293
edges, 21-22
Quad
choosing, 295
versus Tri, 294-296
Quad patches, 22
stitching, 297-298
with Weld operation, 296
Tessellation, 23-24
options, 24-25
Tri, 296
triangular patches, 22
vertices, 21-22
Path Controller, 522
Path Steps option, 167
PathDeform modifier, 134
paying for plug-ins, 671
pens, patch ballpoint pens, 169-171, 173-174
Perimeter
Glow (Render Effects), controlling, 596-598, 600-601
versus Perimeter Alpha, 597
Perimeter Alpha
Glow (Render Effects), controlling, 596-598, 600-601
versus Perimeter, 597
perimeters
Glow (Render Effects), 596-598, 600-601
glowing, 597-598
Perlin Marble, 493
Phase values, maps, 484
Phong shader, 335
Photoshop, 158
Photoshop Effect module, 554

Photoshop plug-ins, MAX cameras (simulating real-world effects), 554-555
pivot points, 197
Pixel Aspect Ratio setting, 538
Place Highlight command, 441, 619
Place Highlight icon, 339
Planet map, natural animated materials, 487-488
planning details of architectural modeling, 54-55
plug-ins, 670, 675
cost of, 672
DLL, 670
extensions, 670-671
loading, 677
Material Editor, 674
MAX cameras, simulating real-world effects, 554-555
modifiers, 673
objects, 672
paying for, 671
real-time 3D graphics, 193
rendering, 674
special effects, 674
third-party parametric tree plug-ins, 138
unplugging, 676-677
Web sites, 671
X-ray, 588
point of view (POV), 548
points, NURBS modeling, 31
Polygon Degrees, Import DXF File dialog, 659
polygonal modeling, 6, 9
architecture, 16
characters, 303-304
edges, 7
Editable Mesh, 7, 10
creating cannons, 10-11, 13
faces, 6-7
primitives, boxes, 7
shortcomings, organic shapes, 15-16
sickles, 16-19
vertices, 6-7
polygonal objects, FFD modifiers, 310-311, 314
polygons, real-time engines, 194

pond water, 406-408
positioning
   lighting, 565
   Reference clones, 69, 71-73
POV (point of view), scene composition, 548
prerendered 3D graphics versus real-time games, 198
   LODs, 199-201
   Z-buffering, 199
presentations, mechanical modeling, 155-156
primitives, 249
   box primitives, 249
   jets, 211-213
   Loft Objects, 250
   modifying for low-resolution models, 211
   non-box primitives, 249
   patches, character modeling, 293
   polygonal modeling, 7
   transforms, 195
procedural maps, 327-328. *See also* maps
   alien planet surfaces, 472-473
   alien skin, 475
   Cellular, 462-463
   Dent map, 471
   fictional materials, 457
   fog, 473-474
   material corruption, 432
   natural animated materials, 484
   Noise map, 458-459
      parameters, 459-461
   Smoke map, 469
      parameters, 470
   Splat map, 465
      parameters, 466-467
   Swirl map, parameters, 464-465
   Water map, parameters, 467-468
   Wood map, 468
      parameters, 469
profile lighting, 576
prototype scenes, architectural modeling, 52
proxies, Xrefs, 267-268

Q

Quad Output, MeshSmooth, 253
Quad patches
   choosing, 295
   versus Tri, 294-296
Quadrilateral patches, 22
Quick Weld, Import STL File dialog, 663

R

Radial Blur, Depth of Field, 638
radial color, glows, 602
radial gradient versus circular gradient, Glow (Video Post), 606-607
Radial Gradient map, 603
radiosity, 351-352
RAM, upgrading, 236
Raytrace material, 328, 347, 447
   basic parameters, 347
      Ambient, 348
      Bump Map, 350
      Diffuse, 348
      Environment map, 350
      Glows, 593
      Luminosity, 349
      reflection, 349
      shading, 348
      Specular Highlights, 350
      transparency, 349
   extended parameters, 350
      Advanced Transparency, 353-354
      Extra Lighting, 351-352
      Fluorescence, 353
      Raytracer Controls, 354
      reflections, 354
      translucency, 353
   plasma engines, 500-501
raytrace rendering engine versus scanline rendering, 361-362
Raytracer Controls, extended parameters (Raytrace material), 354

raytracers
  hybrid raytracer, 362
  Octrees, 365
  voxels, 365-366
raytracing, 355, 359
  antialiasing, 363
  backwards raytracing, 359
  Global Exclude, 368
  Global Ray Antialiaser, 368
    Fast Adaptive antialiaser, 369-370
    Multiresolution Adaptive antialiaser, 370-371
  light rays, 356
  lighting, 360
  Local Exclude, 368
  Manual Accleration, single versus dual-pipe, 366-367
  optimizing, 365
  Recursive Raytracing, 359-360
  voxel trees, 365
real-time 3D APIs, 193
real-time 3D games, 190
real-time 3D graphics, 193
  versus 2D animated graphics, 191-192
real-time engines
  color depth, 205
  map size, 205
  polygons, 194
  shading modes, 206
  shadows, 203
    vertex coloring and shading, 204-205
  surface properties, 198
  TM, 195
  transforms, 195-196
real-time games
  shading modes, 206
  shadows, 203
  versus prerendered 3D graphics, 198
    LODs, 199-201
    Z-buffering, 199
real-time modeling
  BSPs, 209
  build only necessary objects, 208
  convex objects, 208-209
  details, 206-207

  high-resolution for low-resolution modeling, 210
  opacity maps, 221
  techniques, 211-213, 221-222
  texture maps, 206-207
real-time texture mapping, 218-220
recursion, 359
Recursive Raytracing, 359-360
Reference clones, 62
  extruding, 69, 71-73
  positioning, 69, 71-73
Reference copy, 261
Reflection, Raytrace material (basic parameters), 349
Reflection Dimming
  sunrises, 343
  transparency, 342
Reflection maps, light bulbs, 477
reflections, 356
  extended parameters, Raytrace material, 354
reflective surfaces, 356
refraction, opacity, 340
refractive surfaces, 356
Regular Noise parameters, 460
Relative mode, Macro Recorder, 224
Remove Double Faces
  Import DXF File dialog, 659
  Import STL File dialog, 663
removing rough openings with Booleans, 66-67
Render Box Selected, 217
Render Crop, 216
Render Effects
  Depth of Field. *See* Depth of Field
  Film Grain effect, 545
  Glow. *See* Glow (Render Effects)
  Photoshop Effect module, 554
render resolution, architectural modeling, 55

rendering
  antialiasing, speed, 373
  plug-ins, 674
  problems with antialiasing, 373
  SuperSampling, 373-374
rendering materials, 325
rendering speed, Cellular map, 463
Reset Scene, Import VRML File dialog, 665
resetting transforms, 197
resizing openings, 68
right-clicking viewports, 60
ripples, Water maps, 467
roof systems
  architectural modeling, 89
    gable roofs, 89, 92, 95
  combining roofs with Boolean operations, 96-99
  intersecting gables with valleys, 92-94
  L-shaped gable roofs, 89-92
roofs, combining with Boolean operations, 96-99
root materials, 325
rough openings, subtracting Booleans, 66-67
rough water, 409-413
Roughness, Standard material (basic parameters), 338
ruled surfaces, 288-289

S

safe frames, 555
Scale Deformation dialog box, 423, 527
scaling Bitmaps, 491
scanline rendering engine versus raytrace rendering engine, 361-362
Scatter, 146
  leaves on a canopy, 147, 149-150
Scatter compound object, 271
Scene Blur, Depth of Field, 637

scene composition, 547
  FOV, 549-550
  POV, 548
  starting points, 547-548
Scene Xrefs, 264
Schematic View menu, 68
scripted modeling, 36
  myths, 37
scripting MAXScript, 223-225
Section option, 655
sections, controlling MeshSmooth, 255-256
Select Bitmap Image File dialog box, 129
Self-Illumination, Standard material (basic parameters), 339-340
Shade Selected Faces, 140
Shaded Lattice, 36
shaders, 324, 329, 331. *See also* materials
  Anisotropic, 331, 429
  Blinn, 332
  Metal, 332, 446
  Multi-Layer, 333, 406, 429
  Oren-Nayer-Blinn, 334, 429, 435
  Phong shader, 335
  Raytrace material. *See* Raytrace material
  Standard material
    color swatches, 337
    Diffuse Level parameter, 338
    maps, 346
    opacity, 340
    roughness, 338
    Self-Illumination, 339-340
    specular highlights, 338-339
    SuperSampling. See SuperSampling
  Strauss, 336, 429
shading modes, real-time engines, 206
shadow color, 360
Shadow Color map, 571
shadows
  real-time games, 203
  vertex coloring and shading, 204-205
ShapeMerge, 137

shapes
    attaching to create new openings, 76-78
    Terrain compound object, applying, 128-130
shaping arms with FFD modifiers, 311-313
shellac, 439
Shellac effect, paint, 440
Shellac material, 355
Shininess, 332
Shininess Strength, 332
shiny surfaces, 622-624
shortcomings
    of NURBS modeling, 36
    of patch modeling, 30
    of polygonal modeling, organic shapes, 15-16
shot angles, 558-559
sickles, creating with polygonal modeling, 16-19
simulating
    cloud shadows, 404-405
    geometry, 158-159
        bump mapping, 159-161
        displacement mapping, 162-164
        opacity mapping, 161-162
    nature, techniques for, 382-383
    real-world effects, MAX cameras, 553-555
    real-world lighting, MAX lights, 572
single pipe versus dual-pipe, Manual Acceleration, 366-367
size of models, architectural modeling, 56
sizing openings, 68
skies, 395-396
    Blend materials, 401-404
    cloud mapping, 396-399
    cloud shadows, simulating, 404-405
    Gradient Ramp map, 399-401
Skin modifier
    applying to objects, 315-316
    envelopes, 314-315
Slice modifier, 56
    cut-away views, 179-181

Smoke map, 469
    natural animated materials, 488-489
    parameters, 470
Smooth Angle, 653
Snapshot tool, 258
soft-focus aperture-disk, 547
Soften Diffuse Edge spinners, MAX lights, 569
Soften field, Material Editor Basic Parameters rollout, 332
sources
    flares, 612
    Glow (Render Effects), 587, 593
        Alpha, 594
        objects, 588
        Surface Normals, 595
        switching, 600
        Z Hi/Low, 594
    glows, 608-609
space fighters, creating with MeshSmooth, 254-255
space frames, 107
    architectural framework, 111
    expansion joints, 111
    Lattice Modifer, 108-111
    wire baskets, 107
sparkles. See highlights
special effects, plug-ins, 674
specular, MAX lights, 570
specular highlights, 429
    metals, 446
Specular Highlights
    Raytrace material, basic parameters, 350
    Standard material, basic parameters, 338-339
Specular Level, 332, 338-339, 592
    glass, 444
speed
    2D animated graphics, 191
    antialiasing, 373
    of film, 545
    film versus video playback, 539-540
    real-time 3D graphics, 193

spinners, 569
Splat map, 465
    natural animated materials, 488
    parameters, 466-467
Spline Degrees, Import DXF File dialog, 659
Spot lights, 560, 570
Standard material, 328-329
    basic parameters, 337
        color swatches, 337
        Diffuse Level, 338
        opacity, 340
        Roughness, 338
        Self-Illumination, 339-340
        specular highlights, 338-339
    extended parameters, Advanced Transparency, 341
    maps, 346
    shaders, 329-331
        Anisotropic, 331
        Blinn, 332
        Metal, 332
        Multi-Layer, 333
        Oren-Nayar-Blinn, 334
        Phong, 335
        Strauss, 336
    SuperSampling. *See* SuperSampling
Standard Material, Specular Level, 592
staplers as characters, 283
starting points
    character modeling, 279-281
    modeling, 38-40
        base points, 41
    scene composition, 547-548
stereolithography files
    Import STL File dialog, 663
    importing, 662
still-image cameras, 537
still-image maps, 506
still-life imagery, antialiasing, 364
stitching patches, 297-298
    with Weld operation, 296
STL-Check modifier, 662

storyboards, architectural modeling, 54-55
Strauss shader, 336, 429
studio lights, 560
    direct lighting, 560-561
    fill lights, 561
    lighting areas other than the subject, 562
Sub-Object modes, 8-9
    Editable Mesh, 8
Subdivision Amount, MeshSmooth, 252
subdivision surface. *See* MeshSmooth
subject lighting, 564-565
    dramatic lighting, 566
    positioning, 565
Subtractive transparency, 342
sunlight, direct sunlight, 567
sunrises, creating, 626-627
    with Reflection Dimming, 343
SuperSampling
    Adaptive Halton, 345
    Adaptive Uniform, 345
    Dent map, 471
    Hammersley, 345
    rendering, 373-374
    Standard material, 344
        adaptive SuperSampling, 345
        algorithms, 345-346
        check boxes, 344
SuperSpray Particle System, 522
surf, 413-415
Surface Approximation, NURBS, 23-24
Surface Approximation values, 269
Surface Deviation, 654
Surface modifier, 169, 171
    characters, 299-302
Surface Normals, Glow sources (Render Effects), 595
surface properties, real-time engines, 198
Surface tools, 26
    characters, creating, 298
    Patch surface tools, 169
Swirl map, 464
    parameters, 464-465

switching sources, Glow (Render Effects), 600
System Unit Scale, 51-52
system units versus display units, 51

T

Target cameras, 551-552
Target Direct, 567
Target Spot light, 560
techniques
    for nature, 382-383
    for real-time modeling, 211-213, 221-222
techniques for lighting, 573
    building up lights, 573-574
    interior lighting simulations, 577
        daylight, 577
        light fixtures, 578-579
    lighting options, 575-576
telephoto lenses, 542
Terrain compound object, 121
    applying to shapes, 128-130
Tessellation, patches, 23-24
    options, 24-25
texture
    Display Maps, 244-245
    maps, 244
texture maps, 205
    animation, optimizing, 272
    limitations
        colors, 214-215
        details, 216
        map size, 215
    real-time modeling, 206-207, 218-220
texture memory, 245
third-party parametric tree plug-ins, 138
TM (transform matrix), 195
toolbars, customized toolbars, 229-230
tools
    animation tools, 258
    Chamfer tool, 14

    for distorting geometry, 431
    Include/Exclude tool, 360
Top/Bottom material, 355
torsos
    adding detail with MeshSmooth, 306-307
    creating with Editable Mesh, 304-305
tracing contourlines from Background Image, 122, 124-125
traditional angles, 558
transfers, MAX R3/AutoCAD, 47
Transform Degrade, 36
Transform Gizmos, 11, 14
Transform Gizmo tripod, 60
transform matrix (TM), 195
transforms
    alignment of, 195-197
    bounding boxes, 195
    loft objects, 196
    primitives, 195
    resetting, 197
translating
    entities
        AutoCAD DWG to MAX R3 objects, 654-655
        MAX R3 objects to AutoCAD DWG entities, 655
        IGES entities to MAX R3 objects, 664
translucency, 576, 578
    extended parameters, Raytrace material, 353
translucent materials, 478-480
transparency, 356
    Additive transparency, 342
    Diffuse color, 341
    Falloff, 341
    Filter color, 341
    Filter transparency, 342
    Index of Refraction value, 342
    Raytrace material, basic parameters, 349
    Reflection Dimming, 342
    Subtractive transparency, 342
    wire, 342

trees, 138, 383, 415
    leaves, 382
        creating, 144-147
        Scatter, 147, 149-150
    mapped trees on a plane, 416-418
    modeled hardwood tree, 139
    modeled trees, 139
    opacity mapped trees, 138
    third-party parametric tree plug-ins, 138
    trunks, modeling, 139-143

Tri patches
    choosing, 296
    versus Quad, 294-296

triangular patches, 22
trunks, modeling trees, 139-143
Turbulence Noise parameters, 460
Turn to 3DS Coordinates, Import VRML File dialog, 665
types
    of cameras, building flares, 613-614
    of characters, 277

typical characters, 282

U

U-Lofts, 269
    NURBS, 285
umbrella flashes, 564
unclamped colors, glowing, 592-593
Unclamped Specular Level, Standard Material, 592
Unify Normals, 653
    Import DXF File dialog, 659
    Import STL File dialog, 663
unplugging plug-ins, 676-677
unusual angles, 559
unusual characters, 282
    staplers, 283
Unwrap UVW modifier, 207
updated features, MeshSmooth. *See* MeshSmooth
upgrading
    CPU, 237
    display, 237-238
    RAM, 236

Use Selected Faces Only, 421
Use Shape IDs option, 102
Use Threshold, Import STL File dialog, 663
utilities
    Assign Vertex Color, 204
    Camera Match, 438
    Level of Detail, 246
    LOD, 200, 202-203
    Vertex Color Assignment, 204-205

UV-Lofts, 269
UVW method, 485

V

V Tiling, 400-401
valley landscapes, 506, 515
    animated, 506
valleys
    creating, 526-527, 529-530
    creating winding valleys, 515-519
Vary section, Highlight, 620
vegetation, 383, 418
    grass, 418-421
    ground cover, 383-386
    lawns, 392-395
    leaves, 421-424
    trees. *See* trees
    wildflowers, 387-391
Vert Focal Loss, 633
Vertex Color Assignment utility, 204-205
vertices
    patches, 21-22
    polygonal modeling, 6-7
    Surface modifier, 301
video verus film-playback speeds, 539-540
video cameras, 538
Video Post
    Flare verus Highlight, 621
    Glow, 605
        gradient composition, 607-608
        radial gradient versus circular gradient, 606-607
    Highlight, 619
        colors, 621
        Effect section, 620

Vary section, 620
    versus Flare, 621

viewing distance, architectural modeling, 55

viewports
    Display Maps, 244-245
    Inactive in Viewport toggle, 246, 248
    Level of Detail utility, 246
    maps, disabling, 245-246
    modifiers, 247
    texture mapping, 244
    U-Lofts, 269
    UV-Lofts, 269

Volume Light Atmospheric effect, 507

volumen area. *See* voxels

VolumeSelect, 255

voxel trees, raytracing, 365

voxels, 365-366

VRML files, importing, 665

W

walkthroughs, details of architectural modeling, 56-57

wall systems, architectural modeling, 57-58
    2D floor plan extruded for height, 58
    2D wall elevation extruded for thickness, 69
    curtain wall systems, 79

walls, 69

water, 406
    animating with Noise maps, 489-490
    beachfront surf, 413-415
    natural animated materials, 489-490
    pond water, 406-408
    rough water, 409-413

Water map, 467
    amplitude, 468
    Animating Phases, 468
    parameters, 467-468
    Wave Radius, 468

Water maps, ripples, 467

Wave Radius, Water maps, 468

wave-length fields, Water maps, 468

Web sites for plug-ins, 671

Weld, 652
    Import STL File dialog, 663

Weld operation, stitching patches, 296

Weld Threshold, Import STL File dialog, 653

Weld Vertices, Import STL File dialog, 663

welding. *See* stitching patches

Welds, vertices (DXF files), 658

wide-angle lenses, 541

wildflowers, 387-391

windows, 100
    bevel profile windows, 105-106
    beveled windows, 103-104
    extruded windows, 101-102

wing tips, creating with MeshSelect and MeshSmooth, 257-258

wires, transparency, 342

wire baskets, 107

Wood map, 468
    parameters, 469

workflow, mechanical modeling, 157

X-Z

X-ray, Digimation, 588

Xref Objects, 157, 181-185

Xref Scenes, 157, 181-185

Xrefs, 181-182, 243, 264, 268
    MAX R3, 236
    Object Xrefs, 265-266
    proxies, 267-268
    Scene Xrefs, 264

XYZ method, 485

Z Hi/Low, Glow sources (Render Effects), 594

Z-buffering, real-time games versus prerendered 3D graphics, 199

Learn MAX with a VENGEANCE!!

- **On-Line Training**
- **Plug-in Tutorials**

Superior, high quality lessons and exercises are only a click away.
Visit the leading edge, and secure your place at the top.

- Keyframe and Character Animation.
- Organic Modeling - NURBS and Splines.
- Lights for Mood and Atmosphere.
- Camera Walkthroughs and Fly-by's.
- Creative use of Materials & Mapping.

www.applied-ideas.com

Phone: (858) 695-8001
Fax: (858) 695-1081
E-mail: sales@applied-ideas.com